Harold L. Vogel

Financial Market Bubbles and Crashes, Second Edition

Features, Causes, and Effects

palgrave
macmillan

Harold L. Vogel
New York, NY, USA

ISBN 978-3-319-71527-8   ISBN 978-3-319-71528-5   (eBook)
https://doi.org/10.1007/978-3-319-71528-5

Library of Congress Control Number: 2018935300

Cover image © Anna Nikonorova / Alamy Stock Photo
Cover design by Jenny Vong

Printed on acid-free paper

This Palgrave Macmillan imprint is published by the registered company Springer International Publishing AG part of Springer Nature.
The registered company address is: Gewerbestrasse 11, 6330 Cham, Switzerland

To my dear parents, who would have greatly enjoyed seeing this.

Reprinted with permission from Kevin KAL Kallaugher, www.Kaltoons.com

Prologue

Bubbles are wonders to behold. They take your breath away and make your pulse race. They make fortunes and—just as fast or faster, in the inevitable stomach-churning crash aftermath—destroy them too. But more broadly, bubbles create important distortions in the wealth (e.g., pensions), psychology, aspirations, policies, and strategies of the society as a whole. Bubbles, in other words, have significant social effects and aftereffects.

One would think, given the importance of the subject, that economists would by now have already developed a solid grip on how bubbles form and how to measure and compare them. No way! Despite the thousands of articles in the professional literature and the millions of times that the word "bubble" has been used in the business press, there still does not appear to be a cohesive theory or persuasive empirical approach with which to study bubble and crash conditions.

This book, adapted from my Ph.D. dissertation at the University of London, presents what is meant to be a plausible and accessible descriptive theory and empirical approach to the analysis of such financial market conditions. It surely will not be the last word on the subject of bubble characteristics and theory, but it is offered as an early step forward in a new direction.

Development in this new direction requires an approach that appreciates the thinking behind the standard efficient-market, random-walk, and capital asset pricing models, but that also recognizes the total uselessness of these concepts when describing the extreme behavior seen in the events that are loosely referred to as bubbles or crashes. What is known as behavioral finance, extended here via the notion of a behavioral risk premium, ends up being much more pragmatic.

Yet none of this gets to the heart of the matter: when it comes to asset price bubbles and crashes, the most visibly striking and mathematically important feature is their exponentiality—a term that describes the idea that starting even at relatively slow rates of growth, price changes in each period must soon, by dint of the underlying arithmetic, become astonishingly large. Exponentials appear when the rate at which a quantity changes is proportional to the size of the quantity itself.

Although exponentiality is the essence of any and all bubbles, it is merely a manifestation of short-rationed quantities (not to be confused with the practice of short-selling). In plain English, this means that people make trading decisions based mainly on the amount that, for whatever reasons—fundamental, psychological, or emotional—they need to buy or sell *now*. Considerations of current prices thus begin to take a backseat to considerations of quantities; in bubbles you can never own enough of the relevant asset classes. And in crashes you cannot own too little of them.

The problem, though, is that this rubs against the neoclassical economist's empirically unproven approach in which the participant is presumed to be "rational" calculating automatons tuned into a world with perfect, market to quickly arrive at "equilibrium." However, this will never happen because, if it did, the market would cease to exist; it would disappear as there would be no further need for it.

In extreme market events, as ever more investors stop denying and fighting the tide and join the herd, the rising urgency to adjust quantities is reflected by visible acceleration of trading volume and price changes noticeably biased, to one side or the other. And this is where the magical constant e, which approximately equals 2.718, enters as a way to describe the exponential price-change trajectory that is so distinguishable of bubbles (and crashes).

What a number this e is. It suggests steady growth upon growth, which leads to acceleration. Keep the pedal to the metal in your car or rocket ship and you go faster and faster with each additional moment of elapsed time. It is the mechanism of compound interest. In calculus, it is its own derivative—no other function has this characteristic. Best of all, even a non-mathematician such as I can figure it out using only basic arithmetic.

A brief example suffices to demonstrate the power of compounding (i.e., geometric progression). I sometimes ask MBA students in finance whom I occasionally have the privilege of addressing: "Quick, if I give you one penny today and steadily double the resulting amount every day for the next 30 days after, what will the total then be?" Remember, we're talking here about only one single penny, one measly little hundredth of a dollar and only a month's time. Most guesses of even these bright students are, as most of ours would be, far off the mark. The answer is $10,737,418. That's—starting from a penny— nearly $11 million in a month! It is the ultimate bubble.

More specifically, though, all such compounding begins unimpressively with a largely unremarkable buildup so that on the 8th day of doubling the total is only $2.56, a sum barely sufficient to buy a decent cup of coffee. Yet flash forward to the 29th next-to-last day and the total has reached $5.369 million, which means that valuation rises by $5.369 million in the *single* last day. Given that bubbles and crashes exemplify such exponential-like price-change patterns (e.g., see Figs. 8.6 to 8.8), it should thus not be surprising that the largest magnitude changes per unit time—market "melt-ups" and "crash-downs"— typically occur in the crescendo of buying in approach to the top and the capitulative selling in approach to the bottom. Short-rationing behavior is most evident and intense during such times.

This work should first of all be of interest to financial economists of all stripes and to general readers interested in markets and finance. Yet the potential audience ought to extend also to MBA- and Ph.D.-level students, central bank policy makers and researchers, commercial and investment bankers, investors and speculators, and technical and fundamental market analysts. In this pursuit I have aimed for comprehensibility and comprehensiveness to appeal to and accommodate both generalist and academic readers. To this end, the text is structured so that the first four chapters at most require for assimilation only a background that might include college-level finance and economics courses. A brief glossary of terms and acronyms has also been appended as a convenience for general readers.

Meanwhile, the deeper academic material that might be primarily of interest to serious researchers and financial specialists appears in Part II, where the goal is not to provide extensive coverage of theories that have been around a long time but to instead provide contextual and historical perspectives in support of the new approach that is presented in Part III. This structure allows modules to be readily tailored to different audiences.

This second edition, shaped by the bubble and crash events of the eight intervening years since the first edition, has been enlarged, updated, and reorganized. There are new sections on the global central bank-induced yield-chasing bubble that occurred between 2009 and 2017, on the important relationship between trust and credit, on quantitative easing and other unconventional central bank policies that have been experimentally implemented, on the development of volatility metrics and crash intensity measures, and on the more recent math-imbued stochastic dynamic approaches to modeling bubbles and crashes.

This project would have never been completed without the many great works that came before and the many kind people who provided encouragement, help, and good cheer during its production. The following stand out for particular relevancy, clarity of exposition, and stimulative effects: *Asset Pricing*, rev. ed., by John H. Cochrane; *Quantitative Financial Economics*, 2nd ed., by Keith Cuthbertson and Dirk Nitzsche; *Applied Econometric Time Series*, 2nd ed., by Walter Enders; *Options, Futures, and Other Derivatives*, 5th ed., by John C. Hull; *Thinking, Fast and Slow* by Daniel Kahneman; *Behavioural Finance: Insights into Irrational Minds and Markets* by James Montier; *An Introduction to the Mathematics of Financial Derivatives*, 2nd ed., by Salih Neftci; Robert Prechter's *The Socionomic Theory of Finance*; Richard Thaler's extensive works on behavioral economics; and *Chaos Theory Tamed* by Garnett Williams.

I am fortunate to have met at Birkbeck, University of London, Professor Zacharias Psaradakis, who encouraged my enrollment; Professor John Driffill, who supervised my academic endeavor there; Mr. Nigel Foster, who provided timely clues in programming; and Professor Jerry Coakley, of the University of Essex, for review of an early draft. It was also my pleasure and great fortune to meet Professor Richard A. Werner of Southampton University, whose work significantly influenced this project. He and Dr. Luca Deidda, Associate Professor in Economics at Università di Sassari (and also with SOAS, University of London) interrupted their busy schedules to serve as examiners.

At Palgrave Macmillan, thanks also to senior editor for finance, Tula Weis, and assistant editor for economics, Allison Neuburger, who steadily guided its progress into print. I'm further indebted to the anonymous readers who vetted the text and provided numerous suggestions that have made it far better than it would have otherwise been. Appreciation too for Karen Maloney and Scott Parris of Cambridge University Press who had been supportive through the processing of several editions of my earlier books (*Entertainment Industry Economics* and *Travel Industry Economics*) and for this one's first edition. For any errors and deficiencies that may inadvertently remain, the responsibility is, of course, mine alone.

Bubbles and crashes have long been of immense interest not only to economists but also to the investing public at large. The many illustrious tales of sometimes massive wins and losses incurred within such episodes indeed still fascinate us all. It is my hope and expectation that by the end of this book readers will have a much deeper understanding of such dramatic events and will see them from an entirely new perspective.

New York City   Harold L. Vogel
March 2018

PREFACE

Jonathan Swift, the Irish-born English author of *Gulliver's Travels*, wrote a poem in December 1720 that probably made the first reference to a "bubble" as being a stock price that far exceeded its economic value.[1] Since then asset price bubbles have been extensively reported and studied, with many detailed accounts already extant on the presumed causes, settings, and general characteristics of bubbles.[2]

A review of the literature nevertheless suggests that, although economists constantly talk about bubbles and have conducted numerous studies of them, there has thus far been little progress toward a commonly accepted (or standardized) mathematical and statistical definition or method of categorization and measurement that comes close to describing how investors actually behave in the midst of such extreme episodes.

Most studies outside of the behavioral finance literature take rationality as a starting point and a given even though this axiomatic assumption—itself an outgrowth of neoclassical economics—remains unproven and debatable.[3] It is the intent of this study to conduct an exploration and analysis that might eventually lead to a robust, unified general theory applicable to all types and sizes of financial market asset price bubbles (and also crashes). At a minimum, a comprehensive theory of asset price bubbles would require that the descriptive elements be consistent with the ways in which people actually behave.[4]

An understanding of bubbles is also enhanced through introduction of fractal and exponential features—with fractal being a term connoting fractured and fractional that was coined by Benoit Mandelbrot in 1975. Many natural phenomena such as galactic spirals of stars, mountain ranges and coastlines, clouds, and tree and blood vessel branches are fractal; they are self-similar across different times or distance scales. Compare a tree's branches, for instance, to its twigs and the pattern of the smaller limb is seen to be repeated in the larger one. In addition, the patterns are all intrinsically governed by power-law (i.e., exponential) distributions that also appear in the markets for securities.[5]

These features were introduced into the stock market literature by Mandelbrot (1964) and are discussed in greater detail in Chapter 6 (e.g., Fig. 6.3).[6] Mandelbrot showed that stochastic processes describing financial time series are much better modeled by what's known as stable Paretian (also called L-stable, Lévy, or Lévy-Mandelbrot) distributions than by the normal (i.e., bell-shaped or Gaussian) probability distributions that had been used previously to describe asset price return probabilities. Such probability distributions are of a discontinuous nature, contain a large number of abrupt changes, and in the words of Fama (1965, p. 94) suggest "that such a market is inherently more risky than a Gaussian market…and the probability of large losses is greater."

Aside from their discontinuous nature, the most striking feature of all stable distributions is infinite price-change variance, which contrasts with the finite variance of the normal. Although infinite variance does not even in physics plausibly describe what happens in the real world, this infinite-variance aspect of stable distributions is the one that at least in theory provides a better model with which to capture what happens to returns in the extreme events that are informally known as bubbles and crashes.

Such so-called fat-tailed (leptokurtic) distribution events empirically reflect the seemingly improbable once-in-a-hundred-year flood-type of occurrences that seem to afflict many financial markets every few years. But stability—meaning form invariance under addition—is also important because it makes the distribution self-similar (i.e., fractal) and it links to what are known as power (scaling) laws.[7] This fat-tailed feature is illustrated in Fig. P1.

This all further leads readily to the idea that the theories of nonlinear dynamics (chaos) might be applicable to the study of bubbles and crashes. In nonlinear dynamics, a variable appears to be attracted to a time path or trajectory that

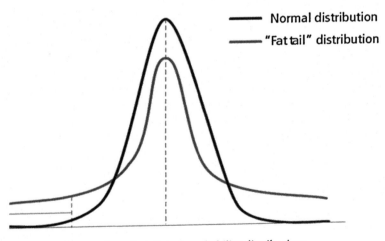

Fig. P1   Normal versus fat-tailed (Lévy) probability distributions

may often look like random behavior but that is instead described by a deterministic equation such as $y = a + bx^2$. These types of equations show how complex chaotic behavior can arise from the simplest of models and that there can be order behind apparent disorder.

Still, of "all the possible paths to disorder, nature favors just a few."[8] From visual inspection alone it would appear that all bubbles (and crashes) are attracted to an exponential-like price-change trajectory.[9] If such an attractor is indeed describable by a power-law distribution, then the need to look to chaos-theoretical approaches in analyzing bubbles is inescapable. Even though it hasn't yet been established that chaos theory has contributed much to understanding of how markets work, an important aspect of this theory is the occurrence of extreme events—i.e., of events being both unexpectedly fast and large, which is surely an apt description of crashes.[10]

But chaos theory is also important for another reason: The basic marker of nonlinear dynamic systems is what is known as sensitive dependence on initial conditions (SDIC). The implication of SDIC is that it becomes impossible to make long-range predictions. This notion, however, conflicts with the extensive studies that followed the Poterba and Summers (1988) article suggesting that although prices are nonstationary (with no constant mean and variance), returns *are* stationary and have a tendency to revert to the mean. This then leads to the notion that markets *are* somewhat predictable over the long run.[11]

Elasticity is an economist's basic arithmetical measure of how much in percentage terms one thing changes when another thing changes. By illustration, if you lower the price of an item by 1%, by what percentage will unit demand for the item increase? If the increase is more than 1%, the demand is said to be elastic. Inelasticity is revealed if a price is raised by 1% and demand remains about the same. As an example, demand for tickets to the Super Bowl or a major film release tends to be inelastic.

As shown in Part III, this notion of elasticity can be extended to describing bubbles and crashes and tied to the aforementioned ideas about fat-tailed distributions, chaos, and stationarity. It turns out that it is *elasticity*—not the price-change (or returns) sequence itself—that most matters.

The innovation here is that in bubbles and crashes, the price-change variance with respect to a variety of risk measures tends to become infinite (just as it is in a stable distribution). Such risk measures might be credit spreads as seen in bond markets, capitalization rates as seen in real estate, or what's known as the equity risk premium (ERP), which in the stock market is the extra expected return above a risk-free rate that is supposed to be earned as compensation for bearing the extra risk of owning equities. Credit spreads in bonds and cap rates in real estate may be substituted for the ERP in stocks because the directional moves of all three measures are the same in all bubble and crash events.

Although the elasticity of variance (EOV) is the main focus, it is supplemented (in Chap. 10) by the different perspectives offered through analysis of runs sequences of positive price changes in bubbles and negative changes in crashes. For instance, in extreme market events high autoregressiveness—gains begetting more gains—leads to the *number* of runs in a predetermined sample period to tend toward one and for the *variance* of the *length* of a run to tend toward zero.

Runs analysis provides a potentially useful description of bubble and crash statistical characteristics and it is a topic worthy of at least some exploration. But this approach is highly arbitrary when it comes to deciding the lengths of sample periods and the number of runs that would be needed to define the occurrence of an extreme event. Runs analysis therefore ultimately leads to a dead end; though descriptive it doesn't explain the underlying trading behavior that generates long-run sequences.

The factors that motivate investor and speculator activities are also explored with reference to theories of behavioral and emotional finance, socionomics (Prechter 2016), and of money and credit. Behavioral finance was developed early on by Kahneman and Tversky (1979, 2000) and then extended by Camerer (1989), De Bondt (2003), and Thaler (1992, 2005). Based on these, a new concept of a "behavioral risk premium" is introduced (Chap. 9). This behavioral risk premium is closely related to emotional finance, a framework later initiated by Tuckett (2011).

Changes in credit availability and interest rates might be expected, a priori, to play a role in the development of bubbles and crashes. And the theory posited here is that extension of credit facilities beyond what can be absorbed readily by the real economy tends to spill over into asset price speculations that, if not early contained, restricted, or withdrawn, will inevitably evolve or metastasize into full-blown "bubbles."[12] Yet this large topic is fraught with difficulties, beginning with frequent imprecision in usage of the term money—an accepted medium of exchange (based on faith) and unit of account—and the term credit, which is a transferable *right* to access money.[13]

Stiglitz and Greenwald (2003, pp. 26–7) say, for example, that "[C]redit can be created with almost no input of conventional factors, and can just as easily be destroyed. There is no easy way to represent the supply function for credit...The reason for this is simple: credit is based on *information*." And because information is asymmetrically derived, imperfect, and costly to gather, "[I]nterest rates are not like conventional prices and the capital market is not like an auction market." Hence, transactions-demand monetary theory (p. 12) is "badly flawed."[14]

All of this unsurprisingly suggests that creation or destruction of credit respectively drives the formation of bubble and crash processes and events. And it furthermore suggests that markets exist only because the prevalent real-world state is one of asymmetric and imperfect contextual and subjective information in which arbitrage is often difficult and costly to implement.

This theoretical line, relating first to studies by Malinvaud (1985) and Bénassy (1986), in effect proposes that considerations of current prices might often take a backseat to those of *desired quantities*—an aspect of trading that appears to be particularly and acutely evident in bubbles and crashes. As one portfolio manager illustratively relates about Citibank's investments in the "Nifty Fifty" stocks (IBM, Merck, Coke, etc.) of the late 1960s and early 1970s, "Once analysts ascertained that the growth prospects were bright, the stocks were bought without regard to valuation...paying P.E. ratios in the 80s and 90s." The greatest perceived risk here was not in overpaying, but in *not owning* them.[15]

Although the present study contains both deductive and inductive elements, wherever possible, the inductive approach is given preference. This contrasts with the primarily deductivist neoclassical methods.[16] Indeed, the previously cited works by Mandelbrot, Fama, and many others on the stable Paretian (and fractal) nature of the fat-tailed returns distributions of stocks—and thus of the direct mathematical ties to power laws and exponentiality—provide not only the inspiration but also an inductive, empirically determined starting point.[17]

In financial economics, however, it is notable that the widely accepted random-walk, efficient-market hypothesis (EMH), and capital asset pricing models (CAPM) all follow only from the presumption (or axiom) that people behave rationally when it comes to money and investments and that their (vague) utility functions are *independent* of each others'. In the wake of an important early Blanchard and Watson (1982) article, the resulting standard approach has been to model bubbles as though they all intrinsically contained at their core a rational valuation component, above which all else is bubble froth.

The trouble is, though, that with asymmetric, imperfect information being an essential operating feature of all market exchanges it is difficult to know even what such a rational valuation component is worth at any point in time. Notable too is that with EMH/CAPM models, informationally efficient markets will almost immediately or instantaneously assimilate news and information and provide at each time the best estimates of "intrinsic" value. Yes, markets usually can and mostly do assimilate information quickly. But estimates of the "correct" price and "value" nevertheless still remain largely unknown and unknowable. The EMH thus misleadingly extends to the assumption that markets will therefore be nearly always at or close to "equilibrium," with the implication that bubbles and crashes are not possible. Crashes, according to the EMH, are all the result only of "exogenous" or "shock" variables.

This project will instead attempt to show that such extreme events are manifestations of collective behaviors that do not at all conform to the neoclassical Walrasian models of equilibrium—that is, models that start by assuming a complete market system and no uncertainty and are "concerned with analyzing a dream world."[18] Especially during extreme events, there is no subtle matching of supply and demand of shares through a considered Walrasian process of *tât-tonnement*.[19] That is because, in approaching the extremes, price changes are often brutally discontinuous and liquidity—which refers to a condition wherein assets are easily convertible into other assets or consumption without loss of value—is at a premium as, in such periods, there is so relatively little of it.[20]

This text provides a clear break with previous methods and models because there is no dependence at all on the key classical financial market assumptions of:

- *independence* of each individual's utility function
- availability of perfect (symmetrical) instantly assimilated information
- rationality or near rationality at almost all times
- mechanistic movement toward price equilibrium with supply and demand functions reconciled in financial markets in the same way as for common utilitarian economic goods and services
- the presence of immediate arbitrage possibilities
- robust and reliable economic laws and constants with gravitas akin to those in physics, biology, and chemistry[21]

The theory is instead inductively based on the empirically demonstrable observation (Fig. P1) that the variance of price changes will tend to rise along with the size of percentage changes in prices themselves. This is a pure function of the rules of arithmetic and of the statistical definition of variance and has nothing to do with the rationality of human behavior, the existence of equilibrium, or any other such idealized notions and constructs. Nothing here is dependent on highly complex models built on the wobbly pillars of assumptions and conditions that are ultimately required to demonstrate that something can or cannot happen.[22]

The idea is simply that via an increasing elasticity of price variance *the market, by its own actions, reveals what it's doing* (i.e., bubbling up or crashing down). A sustained elasticity of greater than 1.0 and tending toward infinity in and of itself provides the definition of and an indication that an extreme event has either probably begun or is already in progress. (Fig. P2).

This relational aspect of variance and returns further guides the idea that bubbles and crashes are formed by a *process* in which time becomes of the essence, urgency becomes the driver, and *quantity* held (instead of price paid or received) becomes the primary concern.[23] The implications of this for attempts at forecasting are severe in that small initial differences can lead to predictions that are far away from what actually ends up happening. That's because bubbles and crashes are by their very nature dynamic (i.e., nonlinear) exponential events that are typically preceded by large-scale systemic financial imbalances.[24]

The goals are to thus establish a viable definition of a financial asset "bubble," to devise a method that allows consistent and convenient comparisons of bubbles in the same or different asset classes (including foreign exchange), to understand why bubbles begin to inflate (and then often later collapse into crashes), and to present and test a theoretical approach that is in harmony with the behavior of investors and with the basic time discounting and risk-adjustment principles of financial economics.

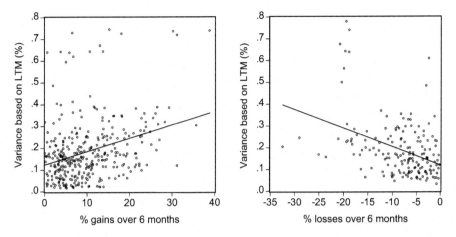

Fig. P2 Variance versus price-change percentages: an example. Gains (left) and losses in percent, S&P 500 Index, 1960:01–2005:12, monthly rolling index percentage change measured over closing prices six months prior, with estimated variance in percent based on rolling last 12 months' data. See also Adrian and Rosenberg (2005, 2008) in which volatility was divided into short-run and long-run components, and it is shown that investors require compensation when holding assets that depreciate as volatility rises. Volatility is not constant over time

In pursuit of these objectives, the new theoretical ideas to be introduced include:

- elasticity-of-variance definitions;
- fractal microbubbles/microcrashes;
- behavioral risk premiums;
- bubble and crash strength indicators;
- volatility metrics that generate an extreme events line (EEL);
- crash intensity categories.

In addition, the underlying financial impetus for why bubbles emerge and crashes occur—respectively, credit creation is in excess of what is needed to finance non-GDP transactions and available cash is insufficient to service debt obligations—is extensively covered.

All of this is developed from a viewpoint that bubbles and crashes are likely to be generated primarily through changes in money and credit conditions. Although the role of money and credit in the fostering and support of bubbles is certainly not a new idea, it is one that is explored in a nontraditional way.

The basis for this approach is that—especially while they are caught up in extreme market events—behavior by both individuals and institutions is often not rational in the usual sense of the word; emotions and mass psychology (i.e., *zeitgeist*) instead become important concomitant factors.[25] As famed investor Warren Buffett has said, "the markets have not gotten more rational over the years...when people panic, when fear takes over, or when greed takes over, people react just as irrationally as they have in the past."[26]

We humans, it seems from recent research in the emerging field of neurofinance, are apparently not wired to do otherwise, that is, to be rational at all times. For one, we tend to have a powerful and difficult-to-overcome urge to join crowds and emulate whatever the crowd is doing.[27] There's a fear of missing out (FOMO). What does the crowd know that we don't? That is always the nagging question.

Importantly related to this, also, is the basic flaw in the underlying and almost universally accepted assumption that supply and demand in the financial markets can be portrayed and modeled in the same way as in the markets for utilitarian goods and services. If, for example, the price of beef or steel or of gasoline or haircuts rises, we consumers tend to seek substitutes and to demand fewer units of such products or services.

But if prices of stocks or commodities or real estate rise just the opposite usually seems to occur as we are drawn to invest in such financial assets and tend to then demand more rather than less of them. For whatever deep-seated reasons, we respond differently to price changes in financial asset markets than to price changes in goods and services markets. If so, and as a result, the traditional financial economics approaches to modeling bubbles and crashes are inevitably destined to fail.

The relevance extends far beyond the usual intramural debates of academia or the direct interests of speculators and investors who would gain advantage if they were somehow able to identify bubbles in their earliest stages—which is just when the risks of missing the impending upswing or of experiencing a crash are the least.

Keynes (1936, [1964], Ch. 12, VI), for example, wrote that:

> [S]peculators may do no harm as bubbles on a steady stream of enterprise. But the position is serious when enterprise becomes the bubble on a whirlpool of speculation. When the capital development of a country becomes a by-product of the activities of a casino, the job is likely to be ill-done.[28]

And Shiller (2000 [2005]) says:

> If we exaggerate the present and future value of the stock market, then as a society we may invest too much in business startups and expansions, and too little in infrastructure, education, and other forms of human capital. If we think the market is worth more than it really is, we may become complacent in funding our pension plans, in maintaining our savings rate...and in providing other forms of social insurance. (p. xii)

> The valuation of the stock market is an important national – indeed international – issue. All of our plans for the future, as individuals and as a society, hinge on our

perceived wealth...The tendency for speculative bubbles to grow and then contract can make for very uneven distribution of wealth. (p. 204)

Still, notwithstanding such views, inflating bubbles are often seen by investors—both individual and institutional—as relatively benign and favorable events. What's not to like? Shares rise easily and participants do not have to be especially skilled and selective when the tide tends to lift almost all boats, often even those of the lowest quality floating on the flimsiest of finances.

Both Wall Street (bankers, lawyers, accountants, analysts, corporate managements, etc.) and Main Street (car dealers, travel agents, brokers, journalists, broadcast/cable networks, airlines, hotels, caterers, restaurants, retailers, limo drivers, dry cleaners, barbers, etc.) are beneficiaries.

And sometimes, as perhaps in the 1990s (but not as for housing in the early 2000s) the bubble makes it much cheaper and easier for new companies developing and promoting important productivity-enhancing technologies to grow and prosper. For the numerous constituencies served well by a bubble's inflation—for instance, investment bankers and tech entrepreneurs in the 1990s and homebuilders, construction workers, mortgage servicers and packagers, and property owners in the early 2000s—the attitude will always be (and has always been), dance while the music plays.[29] "Laissez les bon temps rouler!" ("Let the good times roll!").[30]

Moreover, how can anyone in the government agencies and branches strenuously object? Unless the bubble is immediately accompanied by high price inflation on goods and services, which typically happens only in the later phases, central banks do not have to worry much about uncomfortable issues such as unemployment, weakening exchange rates, capital account deficits, and market freeze-ups and bailouts for failing firms. Treasury coffers are filled from higher capital gains tax realizations and employee payroll tax collections, while budget deficits, including those of states and municipalities, shrink. Politicians everywhere will always welcome having more income to spend and having a richer platform on which to run for re-election.

It is therefore likely that, at least in the beginning and into the middle phases, there is usually a broad coalition in the body politic that has nothing particularly against—or that might even conceivably be tacitly in favor of—the formation of bubbles. It is only in the destructive aftermath that fingers are pointed, blame is affixed, retributions are sought, government institutions flail and bail, and nastiness and distrust pervade.

In sum, a financial asset bubble is perhaps best informally described as a market condition in which the prices of asset classes irresistibly increase to what—especially in retrospect—are seen as ridiculous or unsustainable levels that no longer reflect purchasing power or utility of usage.[31]

It is hoped that the present project, based as it is on readily available data, will prove practical in development of a more statistically rigorous approach to describing bubbles and the crashes that typically ensue.

Harold L. Vogel

Notes

1. The poem, about the South Sea Bubble of 1720, is quoted in Krueger (2005). Its last stanza reads,

> The Nation too too late will find,
> Computing all their Cost and Trouble,
> Directors Promises but Wind,
> South-Sea at best a mighty Bubble.

   Balen (2003, p. 91) says that reference to bubbles "was effectively the creation of the South Sea period, although in fact it had been used earlier. Shakespeare, for example, describes a 'bubble reputation,' and in Thomas Shadwell's *The Volunteers*, written in 1692, men cheated or 'bubbled' each other for profit. Certainly, the use of the word became commonplace in 1720 and contemporary illustrations suggest that it was understood literally: like their counterparts in soap and air...financial bubbles were perfectly formed and floated free of gravitational market forces. But the underlying insinuation was that there would be a day of reckoning, a time when they would grow too large to hold their shape, leaving them to implode with spectacular, and messy, consequences."

   "Let them be bubbl'd by them that know no better" appeared in the 1701 Daniel Defoe pamphlet, *The Free-Holders Plea against Stock-Jobbing Elections of Parliament Men*. Zweig (2015) notes that "bubble" was also a synonym for someone who had been robbed or defrauded and that as such it appeared in a 1676 George Etherege comedy (*The Man of Mode*).

   B. Zimmer in the *Wall Street Journal* of August 24, 2013, indicates that complaints in London journals about bubbles appeared a year prior to Swift's verse. On the 1720 crash era see also Goetzmann et al. (2013).

2. Well-known incidents include the tulip and South Sea bubbles in the 1600s and 1700s, respectively, and the "roaring" 1920s experience. The Japanese stock market/real estate episode that ended in 1989 and the global technology/Internet stock mania of the late 1990s were notable for their persistence and strength. Price movements in housing (2005–2006) and oil (2008) have also been referred to as "bubbles." But for many complex reasons, they aren't entirely comparable to those that occur in securities markets.

3. An axiom is an assumption that no reasonable person could reject as its truth is so self-evident that no one could doubt it.

4. Descriptive is how the world is, as opposed to normative, how it ought to be.

5. An early example of this was shown in the early 1900s by the Italian economist Vilfredo Pareto (1982), who found that in certain societies the number of individuals with an income larger than some value x_0 scaled as $x_0^{-\alpha}$ lustrates how the Gaussian is not self-similar. The Cauchy distribution is the most extreme example of Paretian small-parameter distributions and suggests that losses could be infinite as the center peak is noticeably lower than the Gaussian and with weight shifted to the tails. See also Gabaix (2009), Falconer (2013), and especially Jovanovic and Schinckus (2017) on Gaussian assumptions being historically used for mathematical convenience.

6. See Mantegna and Stanley (2000), Voit (2003, pp. 95–115), Mandelbrot and Hudson (2004), and Vaga (1994, pp. 16–22), who emphasize that it is during bubbles and crashes that the departure from a normal to a Paretian distribution occurs.

7. Officer (1972) was one of the first to study stock return distributions in detail, and Jovanovic and Schinckus (2017) discuss the history and advantages and disadvantages of using stable distributions. Campbell et al. (1997, pp. 19–21) show evidence of "extremely high sample excess leptokurtosis... a clear sign of fat tails." To fit the financial data better, the distributions are usually modified (e.g., truncated) because, in the extreme tails, financial asset returns decay faster than suggested by the unmodified Paretian. See also a related article on catastrophe insurance risk pricing by Lewis (2007) and Weatherall (2013, pp. 65–74) in which fat-tailed distributions such as the Cauchy are explained. A distribution with alpha=2 is normal, alpha=1 is Cauchy. In explaining the Brownian motion and Ito calculus that lies behind the Black-Scholes option-pricing model and other stochastic differential equations, Merton (1992, p. 62) seemingly rejects the Paretian distribution characteristics of infinite variance. Goetzmann (2016b, p. 284) observes that the Black-Scholes option-pricing model was comparable to the heat equation model in thermodynamics.

8. From James Gleick article in Kolata (2013, p. 208).

9. Baumol and Benhabib (1989) describe an attractor as "a set of points toward which complicated paths starting off in its neighborhood are attracted."

10. Scheinkman and LeBaron (1989) found evidence of nonlinear dependence on weekly returns for the value-weighted index of the Center for Research in Security Prices (CRSP). However, for Brooks (2002 [2008]) and Alexander (2001) the issue is far from resolved. See also Vaga (1994, pp. 2–3) and Laing (1991).

11. A proposed resolution of these two opposing aspects, presented in Chap. 10, is that in bubbles (and crashes too) there is an exponential attractor and that SDIC is operative: In such extreme episodes, it is proposed that there is no long-term predictability. But in normal-trending markets the nonlinear dynamic aspects may be either faint or nonexistent, so that mean-reversion and long-run predictability are both then possible. Brock (1991, p. 248) also writes that "[M]ean reversion evidence is controversial. It is sensitive to the Great Depression years..."

12. The word "bubble" thus describes as much a process as a thing.

13. Hartcher (2006, p. vii) wrote, "It is no coincidence that the word 'credit' stems from the Latin *credere* – to believe." A further important distinction is that self-liquidating credit, with loans repaid from sales of produced goods and services, adds value to an economy, whereas non-self-liquidating credit used for non-GDP transactions such as financial asset speculations generally does not.

14. As per the post-1992 experience of Japan, Werner (2005, p. 62) writes, "high powered money, M1 + M2 +CD growth increased sharply. These increases in the money supply failed to be associated with commensurate increases in economic activity." Nor it seems did this increase in money lead to anything resembling a bubble. It was quite the contrary. Between September 1992 and

December 1994, the Nikkei 225 Index essentially traded sideways, in a range from approximately 17,000 to 21,000, but by June of 1995 it had fallen to just above 14,000, close to where it had been three years earlier. The two most recent lows were 7607.88 on April 28, 2003, and 7,162.90 on October 27, 2008.

15. Howard Marks, quoted in Lattman (2011). "Risk in not owning" appears in Bernstein (1996, p. 108). Comparably, in 2017 the NASDAQ's five largest companies—Facebook, Apple, Amazon, Netflix, and Alphabet (Google)—ended up collectively accounting for more market value than all but the five largest equity markets and were known as the Fortunate Five (the FAANG group). Microsoft is sometimes included too.

16. Werner (2005, p. 17) writes, "the neoclassical school of thought is based on the deductive approach. This methodology argues that knowledge is brought about by starting with axioms that are not derived from empirical evidence, to which theoretical assumptions are added." The inductive approach "examines reality, identifies important facts and patterns, and then attempts to explain them, using logic, in the form of theories. These theories are then tested and modified as needed, in order to be most consistent with the facts of reality." Taleb (2005, 2007) provides coverage of problems of induction. Tuckett (2011, pp. 174–7) explains that standard economic theories ignore uncertainty and leave out important aspects including memory, experienced time, and anxiety and excitement that are central to the emotional finance approach. "Consequently, standard theory has little place as a useful tool to explain what happens in financial markets." See also Bezemer (2009, pp. 29–30).

17. West (2017, p. 131) writes: "...power law scaling is the mathematical expression of self-similarity and fractality." The philosophical differences between the deductivist and inductivist approaches to economics are discussed in Keuzenkamp (2000, Chap. 1). George (2007) observes that "Orthodox economics is increasingly dominated by sterile formalism, which refers only to itself."

18. From Evans et al. (2007). As Kamarck (2001, pp. 5–7) has noted: "Walras, in trying to construct an economic theory on the analogy of Newtonian physics, confronted the problem of how there could be any regularity when manias have the richness of emotions, motives, expectations and uncertainties which affect all of us. Walras solved his problem by limiting human beings to a single drive, infinite selfishness...A remarkable aspect of the fundamental assumption is that it lacks substantiation. There is no a priori guarantee that this assumption is true....The rationality-optimization assumption depends on the belief that the individual's choices are his own: that preferences are not influenced by what others do. If people change their choices following on others' actions the demand curves dance around and become indeterminate. Beliefs and emotions drive actions as much as self-interest."

McFarland (2016, p. 68) writes that the "notion of rationality arises in a variety of disciplines...Economists regard behaviour as rational when it maximizes a quantity...Biologists are interested in principles of maximization that relate to fitness."

19. Although securities markets are never in equilibrium in the classical sense, it is possible (in Chap. 8) to devise a practical statistical description of such an idyllic (absolute or perfect, as it is later called) equilibrium, were it ever to be attained. McCauley (2004, p. xi) explains: "There is no empirical evidence for stable

equilibrium…Standard economic theory and standard finance theory have entirely different origins and show very little, if any, theoretical overlap. The former, with no empirical basis for its postulates, is based on the idea of equilibrium…"

20. Liquidity is generally prevalent and available when it is least needed and not when it is most needed. Allen and Gale (2007, p. 52) define liquidity as a condition wherein assets "can be easily converted into consumption without loss of value." Smick (2008, p. 22) writes, "[i]t may be that liquidity, when all is said and done, is not much more than confidence." Hodrick and Moulton (2009) write of earlier papers describing "liquidity as the trade-off between sacrificing on price and timing, assuming that a trader always trades her desired quantity." Keynes defined liquidity in his *Treatise on Money* of 1930 by describing one asset as being more liquid than another "if it is more certainly realisable at short notice without loss." Pension funds and the insurance industry are especially affected by liquidity risk.

Nesvetailova (2010, pp. 6–7) provides a more complex description, explaining that it is a quality of assets, portfolios, markets, and institutions and the probability that a transaction can be completed without major disruption to markets. This includes the depth and speed of a market. Liquidity "…in good economic times is not the same as liquidity in bad times…liquidity to sell is not always the same as liquidity to buy…liquidity can literally vanish overnight…the global meltdown centred on, or at least started as, liquidity drainage from the markets." When risk appetite is large, there is more liquidity and vice versa (p. 125). See also Warburton (2000) and Allen et al. (2011) and Lhabitant and Gregoriou (2008).

Amihud (2002) found that "expected market illiquidity positively affects ex ante stock excess return, suggesting that expected stock excess return partly represents an *illiquidity premium* … expected stock returns are an increasing function of expected illiquidity." His illiquidity measure is the average across stocks of absolute return to dollar volume. The approach, followed also in Amihud et al. (2005), is entirely compatible with the current presentation.

In Russolillo (2016) former Fed Chairman Greenspan shows the share of liquid cash flow that companies are converting into illiquid assets which is computed by taking private domestic nonresidential fixed investment divided by gross domestic business saving. The highest post-WWII ratio was at the end of the 1990s.

21. See Vogel (2017).

22. Barlevy (2012, p. 42) writes that "many of the models…turn out to be highly stylized, relying on a contrived or special set of assumptions, and whose main purpose is to demonstrate that bubbles are possible rather than to capture the main elements of historical episodes." For example, the Allen and Gorton (1993) model on churning bubbles "stipulates 29 assumptions before showing that a bubble is possible in the framework it studies." Another model (Allen, Morris, and Postlewaite 1993) requires "no less than 11 distinct states of the world."

23. "In all investment," as Mehrling (2005, p. 290) writes, "the biggest source of risk is time." In bubbles you don't want to delay lest you miss some of the anticipated gains (and thereby perhaps fail to match your peer group's performance),

and in crashes" you don't want to be the last to hold onto a rapidly vanishing asset. Ludwig von Mises also viewed the market as being a process. Tuckett (2011, p. 122) comments that "Time creates impatience and anxiety."

24. Hunter et al. (2003 [2005], p. xiii) refer to bubbles as "costly, destabilizing episodes." De Bondt (2003, p. 207) observes that "Financial earthquakes undermine the public's trust in the integrity of the market system." Voth (2000) believes that "Higher volatility in asset prices can...lead to instability in the rest of the economy." Cecchetti (2008) says that bubbles contort "economic activity...– not to mention the balance sheets of commercial banks." Werner (2005, p. 229) adds, "Instances of asset inflation are not welfare optimal."

25. Furnham and Argyle (1998, p. 5) write, "the psychological literature again and again shows people to act in ways quite different from the dispassionate, logical, utility and profit-maximisation model so long held by economists."

26. Burnham (2008) provides a popular treatment of the "new science" of irrationality and writes (p. 47) that "our lizard brains tend to make us greedy when we ought to be fearful, and fearful when we ought to be greedy." Burnham's behavioralist approach (p. 33) is that "irrationality is a fundamental part of human nature." The Buffett quote appears in Varchaver (2008).

27. An early classic study was by French psychologist Gustave Le Bon (1895) who wrote: "In crowds it is stupidity and not mother-wit that is accumulated." The book highlighted the characteristics of crowd psychology, which included impulsiveness, incapacity to reason, absence of judgment, exaggeration of sentiments, and irritability.

28. A similar view encompassing both the tech and housing bubbles appears in Laperriere (2008).

29. This paraphrases the now-famous words of Chuck Prince, former CEO of Citigroup, who said (in the *Financial Times*, July 9, 2007) with regard to sub-prime lending and the private equity buyout boom, "[W]hen the music stops, in terms of liquidity, things will be complicated. But as long as the music is playing, you've got to get up and dance. We're still dancing."

30. The expression was a New Orleans slogan that prevailed prior to the devastation of Hurricane Katrina in 2005.Notes

31. Janszen (2008, note 1) writes that the familiar term "bubble" "confuses cause with effect. A better, if ungainly, descriptor would be 'asset-price hyperinflation' – the huge spike in asset prices that results from a perverse self-reinforcing belief system, a fog that clouds the judgment of all but the most aware participants in the market." He asserts that "A financial bubble is a market aberration manufactured by government, finance, and industry, a shared speculative hallucination and then a crash, followed by depression."

Outside of economics and finance, the notion of utility of usage is now being applied to social psychology and behavioral science, information theory, mathematics, and computer science (in "Bubble Studies"). The extension to nonfinancial bubbles across disciplines is covered by Hendricks (2015). Hendricks and Rendsvig (2016) view bubbles as information control problems.

REFERENCES

Adrian, T., & Rosenberg, J. (2005, 2008). Stock Returns and Volatility: Pricing the Long-Run and Short-Run Components of Market Risk. *Federal Reserve Bank of New York and Journal of Finance, 63*(6), 2997–3030.

Alexander, C. (2001). *Market Models: A Guide to Financial Data Analysis.* Chichester: Wiley.

Ali, M. F. (2003). *Stock Market Bubbles, Time-Varying Risk Premia, and Monetary Policy.* Unpublished Ph.D. Dissertation, George Mason University.

Allen, F., & Gale, D. (2007). *Understanding Financial Crises.* New York: Oxford University Press.

Allen, F., & Gorton, G. (1993). Churning Bubbles. *Review of Economic Studies, 60*(4), 813–836.

Allen, F., Morris, S., & Postlewaite, A. (1993). Finite Bubbles with Short Sale Constraints and Asymmetric Information. *Journal of Economic Theory, 61,* 206–229.

Allen, F., Carletti, E., Krahnen, J. P., & Tyrell, M. (2011). *Liquidity and Crises.* New York: Oxford University Press.

Amihud, Y. (2002). Illiquidity and Stock Returns: Cross-Section and Time-Series Effects. *Journal of Financial Markets, 5,* 31–56.

Amihud, Y., Mendelson, H., & Pedersen, L. H. (2005). Liquidity and Asset Prices. *Foundations and Trends in Finance, 1*(4), 269–364.

Balen, M. (2003). *The Secret History of the South Sea Bubble: The World's First Great Financial Scandal.* New York: HarperCollins (Fourth Estate). Also under the title, *The King, the Crook, & the Gambler.*

Barlevy, G. (2012). Rethinking Theoretical Models of Bubbles. In Evanoff et al. (Ed.).

Baumol, W. J., & Benhabib, J. (1989). Chaos: Significance, Mechanism, and Economic Applications. *Journal of Economic Perspectives, 3*(1), 77–105.

Bénassy, J.-P. (1986). *Macroeconomics: An Introduction to the Non-Walrasian Approach.* Orlando: Academic Press.

Bernstein, P. L. (1996). *Against the Gods: The Remarkable Story of Risk.* New York: Wiley.

Bezemer, D. J. (2009). 'No One Saw This Coming': Understanding Financial Crisis Through Accounting Models. MRA Paper No. 15892. http://mpra.ub.uni-muenchen.de/15892/

Blanchard, O. J., & Watson, M. W. (1982). Bubbles, Rational Expectations, and Financial Markets. In P. Wachtel (Ed.), *Crises in the Economic and Financial Structure.* Lexington: Lexington Books.

Brock, W. A. (1991). Causality, Chaos, Explanation, and Prediction in Economics and Finance. In J. Casti & A. Karlqvist (Eds.), *Beyond Belief: Randomness, Prediction, and Explanation in Science.* Boca Raton: CRC Press.

Brooks, C. (2002 [2008]). *Introductory Econometrics for Finance* (2nd ed.). Cambridge: Cambridge University Press.

Burnham, T. C. (2008). *Mean Markets and Lizard Brains: How to Profit from the New Science of Irrationality* (Rev. ed). Hoboken: Wiley.

Campbell, J. Y., Lo, A. W., & MacKinlay, A. C. (1997). *The Econometrics of Financial Markets.* Princeton: Princeton University Press.

Camerer, C. F. (1989). An Experimental Test of Several Generalized Utility Theories. *Journal of Risk and Uncertainty, 2,* 61–104.

Cecchetti, S. G. (2008). Asset Bubbles and the Fed. *Milken Institute Review*, Second Quarter.

De Bondt, W. (2003). Bubble Psychology. In Hunter et al. (2003 [2005]).

Evanoff, D. D., Kaufman, G. G., & Malliaris, A. G., (Eds.). (2012). *New Perspectives on Asset Price Bubbles: Theory, Evidence, and Policy*. New York: Oxford University Press.

Evans, T., Heine, M, & Herr, H. (2007). *Elements of a Monetary Theory of Production*, in Heim and Truger, eds. (2007).

Falconer, K. (2013). *Fractals: A Very Short Introduction*. Oxford, UK: Oxford University Press.

Fama, E. F. (1965). The Behavior of Stock-Market Prices. *The Journal of Business*, *38*(1), 34–105.

Furnham, A., & Argyle, M. (1998). *The Psychology of Money*. New York: Routledge.

Gabaix, X. (2009). Power Laws in Economics and Finance. *Annual Review of Economics*, *1*, 255–293.

George, D. A. R. (2007). Consolations for the Economist: The Future of Economic Orthodoxy. *Journal of Economic Surveys*, *21*(3), 417–425.

Goetzmann, W. N. (2016b). *Money Changes Everything: How Finance Made Civilization Possible*. Princeton: Princeton University Press.

Goetzmann, W. N., Labio, C., Rouwenhorst, K. G., & Young, T. G. (Eds.). (2013). *The Great Mirror of Folly*. New Haven, CT: Yale University Press.

Hartcher, P. (2006). *Bubble Man*. New York: W. W. Norton.

Heim, E., & Truger, A., (Eds.). (2007). *Money, Distribution and Economic Policy: Alternatives to Orthodox Macroeconomics*. Cheltenham: Edward Elgar.

Hendricks, V. F. (2015, September). *Bubble Studies: The Brass Tacks*. London: Bloomsbury. *Leading Frontier Research in the Humanities*.

Hendricks, V. F., & Rendsvig, R. K. (2016). The Philosophy of Distributed Information. In L. Floridi (Ed.), *The Routledge Handbook of Philosophy of Information*. New York: Routledge.

Hodrick, L. S., & Moulton, P. C. (2009). Liquidity: Considerations of a Portfolio Manager. *Financial Management*, *38*(1), 59–74.

Hunter, W. C., Kaufman, G. G., & Pomerleano, M., (Eds.). (2003). *Asset Price Bubbles: The Implications for Monetary, Regulatory, and International Policies*. Cambridge, MA: MIT Press (Paperback, 2005).

Janszen, E. (2008, February). The Next Bubble: Priming the Markets for Tomorrow's Big Crash. *Harper's Magazine*.

Jovanovic, F., & Schinckus, C. (2017). *Econophysics and Financial Economics: An Emerging Dialog*. New York. Oxford University Press.

Kahneman, D., & Tversky, A. (2000). *Choices, Values and Frames*. Cambridge, UK: Cambridge University Press.

Kamarck, A. M. (2001). *Economics for the Twenty-First Century*. Aldershot: Ashgate.

Keuzenkamp, H. A. (2000). *Probability, Econometrics and Truth: The Methodology of Econometrics*. New York/Cambridge, UK: Cambridge University Press.

Keynes, J. M. (1936). *The General Theory of Employment, Interest, and Money*. London/San Diego: Macmillan/Harcourt Brace (1964 reprint).

Kolata, G., (Ed.). (2013). *The New York Times Book of Mathematics*. New York: Sterling.

Krueger, A. B. (2005, April 28). Economists Try to Explain Why Bubbles Happen. *New York Times*.

Laing, J. R. (1991, July 29). Efficient Chaos or, Things They Never Taught in Business School. *Barron's*.

Laperriere, A. (2008, April 3). Questions for the Fed. *Wall Street Journal*.

Lattman, P. (2011, May 12). Howard Marks's Missives, Now for the Masses. *New York Times.*

Lattman, P., Smith, R., & Strasburg, J. (2008, March 14). Carlyle Fund in Free Fall as Its Banks Get Nervous. *Wall Street Journal.*

Le Bon (1895). *The Crowd: A Study of the Popular Mind.* digireads.com, 2009 ed.

Lewis, M. (2007, August 26). In Nature's Casino. *New York Times.*

Lhabitant, F.-S., & Gregoriou, G. N., (Eds.). (2008). *Stock Market Liquidity: Implications for Market Microstructure and Asset Pricing.* Hoboken: Wiley.

Malinvaud, E. (1985). *The Theory of Unemployment Reconsidered* (2nd ed). New York/London: Blackwell.

Mandelbrot, B. (1964). The Variation of Certain Speculative Prices. In P. Cootner (Ed.), *The Random Character of Stock Prices.* Cambridge, MA: MIT Press.

Mandelbrot, B., & Hudson, R. L. (2004). *The (Mis)Behavior of Markets: A Fractal View of Risk, Ruin, and Reward.* New York: Basic Books.

Mantegna, R. N., & Stanley, H. E. (2000). *An Introduction to Econophysics: Correlations and Complexity in Finance.* Cambridge, UK: Cambridge University Press.

McCauley, J. L. (2004). *Dynamics of Markets: Econophysics and Finance.* Cambridge, UK: Cambridge University Press.

McFarland, D. (2016). *The Biological Bases of Economic Behaviour: A Concise Introduction.* New York: Palgrave Macmillan.

Mehrling, P. (2005). *Fischer Black and the Revolutionary Idea of Finance.* Hoboken: Wiley.

Merton, R. C. (1992). *Continuous-Time Finance* (Rev. ed). Oxford: Blackwell.

Nesvetailova, A. (2010). *Financial Alchemy in Crisis: The Great Liquidity Illusion.* London: Pluto Press.

Officer, R. R. (1972). The Distribution of Stock Returns. *Journal of the American Statistical Association, 67*(340), 807–812.

Pareto, V. (1982). *Cours d'Économie Politique.* Oeuvres Complètes. Geneva: Droz.

Poterba, J., & Summers, L. H. (1988). Mean Reversion in Stock Returns: Evidence and Implications. *Journal of Financial Economics, 22,* 27–59.

Prechter, R. R, Jr. (2016). *The Socionomic Theory of Finance.* Gainesville: Socionomics Institute Press.

Russollio, S. (2016, December 6). Greenspan's New Worrisome Gauge. *Wall Street Journal.*

Scheinkman, J. A., & LeBaron, B. (1989). Nonlinear Dynamics and Stock Returns. *Journal of Business, 62,* 311–337.

Shiller, R. J. (2000, 2005, 2015). *Irrational Exuberance.* Princeton: Princeton University Press 3rd ed., 2015.

Smick, D. M. (2008). *The World Is Curved: Hidden Dangers to the Global Economy.* New York: Penguin Portfolio.

Stiglitz, J. E., & Greenwald, B. (2003). *Towards a New Paradigm in Monetary Economics.* New York: Cambridge University Press.

Taleb, N. N. (2005). *Fooled by Randomness.* New York: Random House (2nd paperback ed).

Taleb, N. N. (2007). *The Black Swan.* New York: Random House.

Thaler, R. H., (Ed.). (1992). *The Winner's Curse: Paradoxes and Anomalies of Economic Life.* Princeton: Princeton University Press.

Thaler, R. H., (Ed.). (2005). *Advances in Behavioral Finance* (Vol. II). Princeton: Princeton University Press.

Tuckett, D. (2011). *Minding the Markets: An Emotional Finance View of Financial Instability*. London: Palgrave/Macmillan.

Vaga, T. (1994). *Profiting From Chaos: Using Chaos Theory for Market Timing, Stock Selection, and Option Valuation*. New York: McGraw-Hill.

Varchaver, N. (2008, April 28).What Warren Thinks... *Fortune, 157*(8).

Vogel, H. L. (2017). Are There Any Laws and Constants in Economics? A Brief Comparison to the Sciences. *Journal of Contemporary Management, 6*(1), 73–88.

Voit, J. (2003). *The Statistical Mechanics of Financial Markets* (3rd ed.). Berlin-Heidelberg: Springer-Verlag.

Voth, H.-J. (2003). With a Bang, Not a Whimper: Pricking Germany's 'Stock Market Bubble' in 1927 and the Slide into Depression. *Journal of Economic History, 63*(1), 65–99.

Warburton, P. (2000). *Debt and Delusion: Central Bank Follies That Threaten Economic Disaster*. London: Penguin.

Weatherall, J. O. (2013). *The Physics of Wall Street: A Brief History of Predicting the Unpredictable*. Boston: Houghton Mifflin Harcourt.

Werner, R. A. (2005). *New Paradigm in Macroeconomics: Solving the Riddle of Japanese Macroeconomic Performance*. Houndmills: Palgrave Macmillan.

West, G. (2017). *Scale: The Universal Laws of Growth, Innovation, and Sustainability*. New York: Penguin/Random House.

Zweig, J. (2015, November 14). Deciphering the Dialect: A Wall Street Glossary. *Wall Street Journal*.

CONTENTS

LIST OF FIGURES

LIST OF TABLES

PART I

Background

CHAPTER 1

Introduction

1.1 OVERVIEW

"Every age has its peculiar folly; some scheme, project, or fantasy into which it plunges, spurred on either by the love of gain, the necessity of excitement, or the mere force of imitation," wrote Mackay (1841, p. 354), who early on recognized the main features in humanity's long history of financial speculation.[1]

Circumstantial and anecdotal evidence of speculation can be traced as far back as ancient Rome and Greece and Babylon (Mesopotamia). A Mesopotamian crash of sorts was experienced in 1788 BCE when all debts were eliminated by royal decree. Also, lengthy records of barley prices (as related to a consistent measure of silver) showed large-scale annual fluctuations.[2]

It is important to recognize, however, that as the term is today loosely understood, a "bubble" cannot occur without speculation, but there can be speculation without a "bubble."[3] The presence of mere speculation alone, which was clearly an aspect of trade in the ancient world, is not sufficient to make an asset price "bubble."

Bubbles are instead characterized by a *frenzy* of speculation that, fueled by a ready availability of money and credit, collectively invites, stimulates, and enables broad and extreme participation by the public at large. The major bubbles of the last 400 years—Dutch tulip bulbs in the 1600s and the South Sea and Mississippi Bubbles in the 1700s, the 1929 US stock market, Japanese real estate and equities in the 1980s, the Internet stock boom of the 1990s, and real estate circa 2005—all had these features in common.

In classical Athens of the years 479–323 BCE, for instance, the earliest banks, known as *trapeza* because of the trapezoidal shapes of their dealing tables, were active retail financiers and suppliers of consumer credit and other banking services. According to Cohen (1992, p. 15), *trapeza* were involved with the perfume business, a major Athens obsession heavily dependent on the

© The Author(s) 2018
H. L. Vogel, *Financial Market Bubbles and Crashes, Second Edition*,
https://doi.org/10.1007/978-3-319-71528-5_1

availability of credit. Elementary functions including recordkeeping and credit extension—and thus in all likelihood speculative trading—were evidently already known in those times.[4]

In the days of the Roman Empire, a period roughly covering the years 27 BCE to 476 CE, a review by Garnsey and Saller (1987, p. 47) notes that "individual aristocrats (and emperors) were proprietors of large warehouses, brickyards and pottery works, or the source of loan capital invested by third parties in, among other things, shipping." Real estate and moneylending were also important, as were taxes collected by the Roman authorities. Here too, as Rostovtzeff (1941) makes clear, speculation on price movements and asset valuation undoubtedly occurred:

> The evil effects of the existence of various types of coins were lessened by the establishment of definite rates of exchange. Gold and silver coinage, on the other hand, was monopolized by the state. Though the amount of currency was not sufficient even in these metals, the evils were lessened by the activities of the banks. As agents or concessionaires of the cities, the banks also took an active part in the issue and distribution of local currency, which often led to speculation and profiteering and provoked acute crises. (p. 171)

> The depreciation of money was closely connected with the rise in the prices of products of prime necessity…It is not surprising that under such conditions speculation of the wildest kind was one of the marked features of economic life, especially speculation connected with exchange. (pp. 419–20)

Roman bankers, called *argentarii*, were private businessmen, and as the famed historian Durant (1944, p. 331) recounts, "[T]hey served as money-changers, accepted checking accounts and interest bearing deposits…managed, bought and sold realty (land and buildings), placed investments and collected debts, and lent money to individuals and partnerships." Within this environment, episodes of money scarcity and credit contractions—that is, deflationary crashes—are also known to have occurred. The Panic of 33 AD, for example, involved the first known instance of intervention by a lender of last resort.[5]

As for early bubbles, according to swarup (2014, pp. 83–6), Romans in midfirst-century AD, developed a craze for dining on quite ordinary little fish (red mullets), with competitive bidding sending "prices soaring to stratospheric levels…Tiberius complained bitterly that three mullets had been sold for 30,000 sestertii – enough to pay the annual wages for thirty-three soldiers."

Bubble-like economic activity, as noted by Hughes (2011, p. 134), was also seen in the later days of the Roman Empire:

> Another outlet for Roman wealth and decadence during this time was art…[the] prices of fashionable 'fine' art were fundamentally inflated. Corinthian bronzes were so prized for their workmanship that they cost whole family fortunes. Pliny reported that one ivory table changed hands at 1.3 million sesterces – the price of a large estate…The finest Chinese silk traded…a pound of silk for a pound of gold.

For both Greece and Rome, an inherent and inevitable component of the speculations that occurred was a subtext of familiarity with, and a penchant for, gambling; the nexus between gambling and speculation is strong. Games using *astragali*—small stones (or bones and early versions of dice)—were played by Greek children and adults, and other wagers on the outcomes of events were also common. All of these elements were expanded upon by the Romans. As Schwartz (2006, p. 25) writes, "[f]atalistic Romans gambled incessantly. Gambling was more than a pastime for the Romans—it was a metaphor for life itself."

If so, then the presence of such environmental features raises the question: How could there *not* have been any bubbles?

Although experts on the history of these eras have not been able to specifically identify bubbles per se, that may be because monetary systems were not yet sufficiently developed and/or because price records of transactions never existed, were not comprehensive, or were never found.[6] However, given that banking-type money-creating merchants and goldsmiths are known to also have operated in Babylon, Egypt, tenth-century China (the Song Dynasty from 960 to 1279), and the Mongol Empire of Genghis Khan (1206–1368), it would seem likely that speculation and perhaps "bubble-like" conditions might have sometimes also appeared in those societies too. After all, the ancients' version of what's today known as "quantitative easing" was in those eras simple enough for kings, emperors, dictators, and dynasties to do; they merely lowered the gold and silver content of coins through mixing with baser metals.

Intense mercantile activity throughout these times further involved trade in spices such as cinnamon, cardamom, ginger, pepper, and turmeric that originated on the Indian subcontinent. Such trading in spices and aromatics—and eventually also in silk, ebony, and fine textiles—first extended to the Middle East, especially Egypt (and generally, the Levant), and then later to Europe. For the early Greeks and Romans, speculation must have been a common feature, as spice traders were secretive about their sources.[7] Significant price inflation in third and fourth-century Rome and in fourth-century Egypt was also evident.[8]

China's Song (sometimes spelled Sung) Dynasty, in particular, was known for the development of trade, maritime commerce, paper money, and a unified tax system. Seen as a period of Chinese Renaissance, it was a time when music, painting, architecture, calligraphy, performers, and literacy flourished. With these features in place, some sort of understanding of the implications of credit creation and speculative activity would also have been probable. For example, Gascoigne (2003, p. 124) describes the passion for art and observes with respect to such items that "even if their extreme age was not fully appreciated they stimulated a craze for collection and study of antiquities."

Gernet (1982, pp. 323–5) also writes that "principal wealth in the Sung age...came from commerce and craftsmanship. Ceramics, silks, iron and other metals, salt, tea, alcohol, and printed books were the objects of intense commercial activity...One of the prerequisites for the economic upsurge of the eleventh to thirteenth centuries was a very considerable increase in the means of payment and the spread of the monetary economy...The certificates of deposit issued in favour of merchants in the ninth century...were the precursors of banknotes...This institution....gave powerful assistance to expansion of both the private and state economy during the Sung period."

Kruger (2003, p. 249) notes that "[S]ilver coins as well as iron and copper were in circulation, and variations in rates between them gave rise to much speculation which was fuelled by the state's issue of deposit certificates, opening the way to the use of paper money, first printed in 1024. Commerce also brought in negotiable instruments in the form of cheques, promissory notes, and bills of exchange...China's economy had become a monetary one and the circulation of so much money resulted in inflation."

Speculation was, as Parks (2005, p. 39) explains, also present in Italy's Medici era of the fifteenth century: "Like all major banks at the time, the Medici were merchants as well as bankers. They would procure goods abroad for rich clients: tapestries...chandeliers, manuscript books, silverware, jewels, slaves. They would speculate...There was risk involved...Demand and prices swung alarmingly, depending on how many merchants had sensed a particular gap in the market."

By the 1600s, though, money and credit-extension mechanisms had evolved considerably further and the Netherlands had by then already become sophisticated in applying them. As recalled by Davies (2002, pp. 550–1), "the Amsterdam stock exchange quoted a list of prices as early as 1585...the Dutch East India Company of 1602 and the West India Company of 1621, provided the financial backing for Dutch political and economic competition with England....the public Bank of Amsterdam (Wisselbank) was established in 1609."

About half a century later, the next important innovation—that of lending in excess of metallic reserves in the fashion of a fractional reserve system—was first seen in Stockholm. And with founding of the Bank of England in 1694, many more of the modern banking and currency features such as joint stock ownership and monopoly-issued banknotes began to emerge as it gradually became evident that money was not about metal but instead about credit.[9]

This rapid pace of financial innovation provided the banking and transactions processing structure that was essential to the development of the first documentable bubble episodes—tulips, the Mississippi Company, and the South Sea Company—which ensued (and are detailed in Chap. 2).

Yet although the bursting of all such bubbles was undoubtedly a distinctly unpleasant experience for the speculators directly involved, the historical record suggests that not all bubble endings were necessarily followed by periods of severely depressed economic conditions. Neither the tulip mania nor the South Sea episodes resulted in extended disruption of overall economic growth, whereas the major Japanese bubble of the 1980s ended differently, with decades-long deflation.[10]

Despite the widespread attention that financial bubbles attract, their behavioral characteristics have not been well described or understood from an operational and statistical standpoint. How is a bubble formally defined? What properties do bubbles all have in common? Does the rate of advance have any relationship to the rate of decline? Are there any constants or consistent relationships? Is the behavior fractal—that is, do big (macro) and small (micro) episodes, like a coastline, have jaggedness and self-similarity on all orders of magnitude? Relatively little work has been done on answering such questions.[11]

Such an understanding ought to be of great importance in real-world applications. Central bankers, for instance, might be able to improve economic policy implementation and performance if they could know whether and when their actions were likely to be creating a bubble (or crash). And both investors and speculators could benefit by being able to better position themselves if it were early on possible to determine the potential strength and the approximate stage of a bubble's development.

1.2   On the Nature of Humans and Bubbles

Macro Aspects

No two bubbles or manias follow a path that is exactly the same, but as is later illustrated in Figs. 2.5 and 5.5, all bubbles exhibit a similarity of features that are readily identifiable by visual inspection. Bubbles and their always compelling underlying narratives have, moreover, appeared in politics and opinions, fashion, art, and even science.[12] And all bubbles after bursting leave behind a residue of some financing, production, and service capacities that will no longer ever be needed. Contraction and consolidation then follow naturally, as formerly misallocated capital flows are redirected.

Whether of a political, technological, or monetary nature, announcements and developments that are interpreted as being favorable typically provide the fertile soil in which bubbles are able to sprout and grow large. But this soil alone doesn't necessarily assure a bubble's presence. Additional ingredients are required. And news itself is not one of them as it is often only a coincidental trigger.[13] What happens in markets depends instead on how traders *react* to specific news events.[14]

Those long-lived bubbles that do form will often, however, lead to macro-scale, productivity-enhancing innovations, with some of the historically most important ones being the introduction of canals, railways, automobiles, radios, airplanes, computers, and the Internet.

The manic market reaction to technological innovation in the 1990s was thus not unique and as unprecedented as many of the most fervid participants then believed. Something of the same sort, writes Sylla (2001), had already happened 150 years before: "Britain in the 1840s was in much the position of the United States today...It also had several years of irrational exuberance related to a new network technology, in this case, the railways."[15]

That bubbles and crashes related to such innovations have regularly appeared in the last 200 years in both the United States and the United Kingdom is shown in Table 1.1. A visual overview of real US asset class returns for 1900–2016 appears in Fig. 1.1.

Table 1.1 Stock market crashes, booms, and recessions: United Kingdom and United States, 1800–1940 and 2002

Crashes			Major causes	Recessions	Preceding booms		
Peak	Trough	Real stock price changes (percent)		GDP contraction (percent)	Stock price changes (percent)	Banking panic	Other severe financial distress
United Kingdom							
1808	1812	−54.5	War	−	−	1810	−
1824	1826	−33.6	Latin America mania	−	78.4	1825	−
1829	1831	−27.0	Political agitation	−	−	−	−
1835	1839	−39.1	American boom	−0.6	−	1837	1839
1844	1847	−30.5	Railroad boom	−2.5	51.9	1847	1847–48
1865	1867	−24.5	Overend Gurney crisis	−	48.4	1866	1866
1874	1878	−19.7	European financial crisis	−2.0	−	−	−
1909	1920	−80.5	World War I	−23.6	−	1921	−
1928	1931	−55.4	Great Depression	−5.6	−	−	−
1936	1940	−59.9	Housing boom, war scare	−	−	−	−
Memorandum							
2000	2002	−26.7	Information technology boom	−	78.4	−	−
United States							
1809	1814	−37.8	War	−1.6	−	1804	−
1835	1842	−46.6	Bank war	−9.4	57.2	1837	1837
1853	1859	−53.4	Railroad boom	−8.6	−	1857	1857
1863	1865	−22.5	Civil war	−6.2	20.5	−	−
1875	1877	−26.8	Railroad boom	−	50.5	1873	1873–76
1881	1885	−22.2	Railroad boom	−	51.3	1884	−
1892	1894	−16.4	Silver agitation	−3.0	−	1893	1893–94
1902	1904	−19.4	Rich man's panic	−	29.9	−	−
1906	1907	−22.3	World financial crisis	−6.9	−	1907	−
1916	1918	−42.5	War	−	−	−	−
1919	1921	−24.5	Disinflation, disarmament	−8.3	−	−	−
1929	1932	−66.5	Roaring Twenties and policies	−29.7	201.8	1930–33	1931–32
1936	1938	−27.0	Tight monetary policy	−4.5	−	−	−
Memorandum							
2000	2002	−30.8	Information technology boom	−	165.2	−	−

Source: Bordo (2003) and International Monetary Fund [IMF, (2003, Chap. 2)]. See also Chambers and Dimson (2016, p. 175)

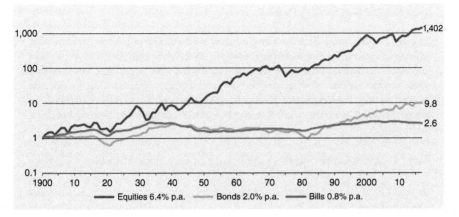

Fig. 1.1 Cumulative returns on US asset classes in real terms, 1900–2016. (Source: Elroy Dimson, Paul Marsh, and Mike Staunton, *Credit Suisse Global Investment Returns Yearbook* (2017, p. 12) and *Triumph of the Optimists: 101 Years of Global Investment Returns*, Princeton, NJ: Princeton University Press (2002). Copyright ©2017 Elroy Dimson, Paul Marsh, and Mike Staunton; used with permission)

Schumpeter (1939, pp. 689–91) also wrote extensively on the role in the business cycle played by innovation and described the linkages between speculation, credit, and central banking. As for stock market speculation, he first notes (p. 683) that it is "availability rather than cost of credit that we should look to." He then observes (pp. 689–91) that "…speculation in stocks does not, or not to a significant extent, 'absorb credit'…the stock exchange is not a sponge but a channel…Since stock speculation does not absorb funds, it must be extremely difficult to stop or to restrain by any of the ordinary tools of central banking."[16]

However, once a bubble has burst, scapegoats are sought and legislative and political inquiries and policy initiatives are typically begun with a widespread sense of outrage and a desire that perpetrators—including also those imagined or fabricated—be punished. The larger the bubble, of course, the more intense is the urge for retribution. "The consequence of a bubble for markets is to reward winners and punish losers with a savage intensity."[17]

This ought not to be surprising in that over the centuries human nature does not appear to have changed much if at all and that episodes of speculative euphoria are always led and fed by, among other things, avarice, envy, emulation of neighbors, and crowd psychology.[18] In fact, many of the investment concepts and vehicles for speculation were devised or invented long ago. Osaka's Dojima Rice Exchange established in 1697, for instance, offered forward contracts as early as the eighteenth century.[19] And behavioral/emotional finance perspectives can be respectively traced back to Dutch merchant Joseph de la Vega in 1688 and to Japanese rice merchant Munehisa Homma, who in 1755 described the role of emotions in affecting rice prices.[20]

Says Chancellor (1999, p. 57):

...there is really very little in our financial understanding that is actually new. Already in the seventeenth century, both in Amsterdam and in London, we find financial derivatives being used for both risk control and speculation. We also find sophisticated notions of value, together with the idea of discounted cash flows and present values. Wagering and probability theory provided contemporaries with an understanding that the risk-reward ratio could, in certain circumstances, be calculated.

Lord Keynes also recognized the nature of speculative bubbles:

It might have been supposed that competition between expert professionals, possessing judgment and knowledge beyond that of the average private investor, would correct the vagaries of the ignorant individual left to himself. – Keynes (1936, [1964], p. 154)

And even former Fed Chairman Alan Greenspan recognized that bubbles are nothing new:

Whether tulip bulbs or Russian equities the market price patterns remain much the same. – Greenspan (1999) and in Haacke (2004, p. 3)

The random-walk and affiliated efficient-market hypothesis (EMH) approaches that emerged from academia in the 1960s (e.g., Samuelson 1965) did provide fresh insights that ultimately led to a deeper understanding of stock price behavior and portfolio risks and rewards. These approaches posited that stock movements are unpredictable (a random walk) because the most recent share prices already presumably reflected all information related to their value and that markets are efficient because they are able to assimilate and react to the randomly timed arrival of new information rather rapidly.

No doubt, the rational-model EMH material provided a starting point and benchmark against which the subsequently discovered behavioral anomalies and psychological quirks of financial market pricing could be tested and compared. Better still, the financial mathematics is neat.

Yet under the EMH's restrictive conditions—in which the real world is a bothersome special case—no bubbles and crashes can or will occur. Such extreme events *do* occur because the theoretical conditions are not ever even closely approximated. History suggests that many events of this kind have occurred.

Utility and Independence

The random-walk/EMH framework has been studied and debated to exhaustion by academics and practitioners. In the early years the random walkers appeared to marshal virtually incontrovertible statistical evidence for the reliability and viability of their models. Yet despite many spirited defenses (e.g., in Malkiel 1999, 2003, 2007), other academic studies [e.g., Lo and MacKinlay (1999) and Poterba and Summers (1988)] gave weight to alternative arguments and interpretations.

The Long-Term Capital Management (LTCM) debacle of 1998—the single-day loss was $553 million on August 21 (*CFA Magazine*, March–April 2006)—had, for instance, cast doubt on the practical usefulness of the EMH theories and models.[21]

More specifically, for many neoclassical economists the key underlying assumption is that investors are at all times rational in *independently* ordering their preferences and in maximizing expected utility, which is vague jargon for the amount of psychological or physiological pleasure—perhaps monetary gain—that is expected to be derived from the outcome of events or from doing something (e.g., buying, selling, owning).[22] The standard presentation of such risk-averse rationality, which results in a concave and increasing utility function, is seen in the left hand panel of Fig. 1.2.

With a utility function of this type, equal movements to either side from the average level of wealth, V_0, will result in unequal changes in utility.[24] According to conventional explanations and models, this is considered the normal state of affairs.[25]

In many spheres of life, though, it in fact appears from research into human behavior, that people are influenced by economically irrelevant factors and will often make decisions in contextual relation to what others are doing and to a personal reference point (as in prospect theory, section 7.1).[26] Nowhere in economic relationships is this seen more prominently than under extreme market conditions.

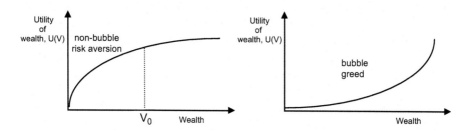

Fig. 1.2 Idealized collective market utility functions, non-bubble risk-averse, left, and nonrational bubble greed, right. The right panel conceptually illustrates the attitudinal conversion (or flip) of market participants from risk aversion to the obliviousness to risk that characterizes bubbles. It essentially portrays an accelerating attitude of "the richer I become, the more I want," monetarily, emotionally, and psychologically[23]

Investors, it seems, rarely make decisions in isolation. Neither do they follow the traditional economic theories, which deal with absolute states of wealth. Instead, behavioral and emotional economics has demonstrated that "losses sting more than gains feel good."[27]

It may be readily inferred from the brief history review of the next chapters that the very formation of a bubble requires the utility functions of investors to become ever less independent (i.e., investors join herds) and that the collective emphasis contagiously shifts progressively from risk aversion to reward seeking and from fear to greed.[28] If so, then there is a broader concept of social rationality that describes what is seen to occur in speculative frenzies. Economic behavior is thereby society-dependent and related to the *zeitgeist* (which is itself also a variable).[29]

In the midst of a bubble, and perhaps even in its absence, there is the possibility that investors may (and usually would) in addition react to actual changes in share prices, thereby creating the potential for chaotic feedback loops.[30] Such feedback is an often-observed feature of speculative bubbles (and crashes) and indicates that chaos theory might be applied to the study of such events even though applications of nonlinear methods have thus far not yielded clear-cut results (Chap. 10).

Psychology, Money, and Trust

One objective is to develop methods that will make it possible to assess financial bubble characteristics across all orders of economic magnitude, moving down from GDP to particular equity (or real estate) markets, to industry sectors, and even then perhaps to individual company share prices.[31] The primary challenge is in finding explanations that are not arbitrary and model-specific and that—in addition to money and credit aspects—are also able to incorporate psychological and emotional elements which may include (sometimes simultaneously) greed, fear, apathy, envy, aggressiveness, remorse, regret, disgust, confusion, and anger. It is therefore important to have some insight into not only the sequential linkage between psychology and money but also into the many nonlinear and asymmetric relationships that have been revealed by studies in behavioral finance.

Psychologists have found that possession of money confers and implies social power and becomes an index of social adequacy.[32] Feelings of empowerment and worthiness are, it appears, principal components of the social atmosphere in which bubbles will sprout and grow. To carry the matter to its extremes, all bubbles rely on a positive psychology, a certain "madness of crowds," and, using a Keynesian figure of speech, lots of high "animal spirits." The general level of optimism or pessimism in a society is then reflected in the correlated and emotionally driven financial decisions of economic participants.[33] By this approach, perceptions of the potential proximity and imminence of new income-generating opportunities thus sequentially arrives prior to the shift to an overall more positive psychological framework. Once started, there is obviously also an ongoing feedback interplay of one on the other.[34]

A positive and relatively trustful psychological mood-influenced environment—generated by and for any number of possible underlying socioeconomic reasons—must therefore be presumed to exist as a precondition for the formation of an asset price bubble. That's because the psychological environment of empowerment that leads to speculation would not or could not ignite and then evolve in the absence of underlying positive money, credit, and opportunistic conditions. There is in history no factual or anecdotal evidence for believing otherwise.

Behavioral studies of how people respond to money and prices have further suggested that anchoring to price levels is important, that relative rather than absolute prices and price changes are what stimulate emotions and motivate actions, that money illusion related to inflation is a common feature, and that the psychology toward potential risk is usually different than that toward potential rewards. All of these aspects, it appears, are what allow bubbles and crashes to occur.

But there is also a deeper relationship between money and psychology that is always operative: It is the aspect of trust and of attempts to banish uncertainty. Booms depend both on a "semblance of certainty" about economic and financial prospects and also on trust that the credit-related products, offered by banks and other providers, will be readily and properly serviced when they come due. If and when such fragile trust is diminished, impaired, or betrayed, the stage is then set for financial crises and crashes to fester and follow. Feedback from the ensuing tide of anger, resentment, and disillusionment will then further weaken or break the bonds of societal trust and turn the financial environment toxic.

At such junctures, price changes will not so much reflect fundamental financial asset characteristics but rather instead the fortunes of potential buyers and how intensely they respond psychologically and emotionally to the disruptive events. "Trust is the ingredient that makes a market economy work.[35]

Martin (2015, pp. 27–9) writes:

Whilst all money is credit, not all credit is money: and it is the possibility of transfer that makes the difference. An IOU which remains for ever a contract between just two parties is nothing more than a loan. It is credit, but it is not money. It is when that IOU can be passed on to a third party....that credit comes to life and starts to serve as money. Money...is not just credit – but transferable credit...What matters is only that there are issuers whom the public considers trustworthy, and a wide enough belief that their obligations will be accepted by third parties.

In effect:

- *"[M]oney is a social relationship of credit and debt."*[36]
- *"[M]oney is equivalent to information... is a relation of trust...we put our trust in trust...Money creation is special...It is created from debt relations...Money is a promise...Trust is only a calculation about risk."*[37]
- *Money "...is not a real thing at all but a social technology...the operating system on which we run our societies and economies."*[38]
- *"When trust is lost a nation's ability to transact business is palpably undermined."*[39]
- *Money and finance together function as time-travel mechanisms because finance (e.g., mortgages and bonds) reallocates value, risk, and capital through time.*[40]

In fact, despite the many centuries-old cultural and social disparagements, grudges, and hostilities often expressed by debtors toward creditors and their usually opaque money and financial dealings, "the ascent of money has been essential to the ascent of man...financial innovation has been an indispensable factor in man's advance from wretched subsistence...money... is trust inscribed."[41]

As in all aspects of life, but especially in finance, trust is thus linchpin and lubricant. It cannot be bought; only earned. Trust is everywhere the bedrock currency for all markets and transactions.

1.3   CENTRAL FEATURES

Although its characteristics have not as yet been precisely described, a market bubble is something that *can* be sensed by many participants while it is occurring. In the late 1980s, for example, popular television shows such as *Wall Street Week with Louis Rukeyser* actively discussed the existence of a Japanese bubble well before the peak at year-end 1989.[42]

Many magazines such as *The Economist* (Sept. 23, 1999) discussed the existence of an Internet stock bubble well ahead of the NASDAQ Index peak above 5000 (5132.52 intraday) on March 10, 2000. An article in *Fortune* published around the time of the peak (Rynecki 2000) concerned itself with "market madness."[43] Rynecki illustrated that in 1999, companies with the steepest income losses gave shareholders the highest gains. And in a *Barron's* Big Money Poll reported in the issue of May 3, 1999, of nearly 200 respondents, 72% saw "signs of a speculative bubble in the market, particularly in certain highflying Internet stocks and some of the so-called Nifty Fifty growth stocks like Microsoft and Intel..."

Warnings in books were, furthermore, widely available. Two such examples were Shiller's *Irrational Exuberance*, a play on then-Fed Chairman Greenspan's famous (but too early) warning phrase in a speech given in December 1996, and *The Internet Bubble* by *Red Herring* magazine publishers Perkins and Perkins (1999).[44] Smithers and Wright (2000), employing Tobin's famous Q ratio (market value of a firm's or economy's assets divided by replacement value of those same assets), also warned at the end of 1999 of the historically extreme valuations seen in the market at that time.[45]

For the most part, though, after a lengthy period of gains, investors and economists have often appeared to be blind to the rising risks of investing and speculation. Even as late as October 16, 1929, renowned Yale economics Professor Irving Fisher authoritatively and famously (or perhaps infamously) proclaimed (on October 15) two weeks before the crash that "stock prices have reached what looks like a permanently high plateau."[46] The following was as likely to have been written in late 1999 as it had been 70 years earlier:

> *For the last five years we have been in a new industrial era in this country. We are making progress industrially and economically not even by leaps and bounds, but on a perfectly heroic scale.*[47] (Forbes, June 1929)

And only a few days prior to the 1989 all-time peak of Japan's Nikkei, there was delusional bliss.[48]

> *Tokyo's stock market is still a ripsnorter as it heads into the 1990s. With the Japanese economy going gangbusters and the ruling Liberal Democratic Party shaking off the influence-peddling scandals that dogged it and the market earlier in 1989, investors are rushing back into stocks. The influx of fresh cash has pushed the Nikkei stock average up 7% since early November, to a record high. And leading market-watchers now say the wild ride could continue into spring. "There may be some volatility," predicts Nomura Securities Co. President Yoshihisa Tabuchi, "but prices will keep climbing.* (BusinessWeek, 25 December 1989)

Ten years later, in the TMT (technology, media, and telecom) bubble of the late 1990s, attitudes hadn't much changed. At that top, many blindly optimistic chief financial officers thought their shares were "undervalued."[49] Federal Reserve Bank officials in late 1999, just prior to the peak, made speeches suggesting that although the rise in equity prices averaging 25–30% over the previous four years was unprecedented, changes in the structure of the economy might provide justification for such moves.[50] One Fed *Quarterly Review* study even argued that the market was then "correctly valued."[51] And in late 1999 only 1% of analysts' recommendations on around 6000 companies were rated as "sell."[52]

At the Bank of England, Governor Eddie George said in December 1999, "…particular strengths of high-technology stocks in equity markets provided a better underpinning of equity values than perhaps had been appreciated." Spain's Economics Minister also said in February 2000: "The stock market is one of the new opportunities where…everyone wins."

Comparable sentiments were, almost as if on cue, also expressed just at the cusp of the housing and credit bubble collapse that began in 2007.[53] Similar optimism was also expressed in 2012 by IMF economists and various government officials even as the Spanish banking and Eurozone crisis was imminent.[54]

The Shanghai/Shenzhen 2015–2017 market bubble and crash also traced what is by now a familiar pattern marked by frenzied small, new, and unsophisticated investors leveraging their life savings into highly speculative shares valued without any connection to economic fundamentals and at an average price-to-earnings ratio that had climbed to 140. So convinced were the fortune-hunters of the authoritarian government's power to control the market and make it levitate at will, that some had even presumed that gains would be forthcoming in celebration of President Xi Jinping's birthday![55] After all, as late as April 2015, the state-controlled media (*The People's Daily*) had editorialized that the bull market was just getting started and still had a long upward run ahead.

Yet prices plunged. And this was despite the government's suspensions of new stock listings, severe restrictions on short-selling, trading halts, encouragement of brokerage firms to set up a $19 billion stabilization fund to prop up shares, interest-rate cuts implemented by China's Central Bank (PBoC), and bans, respectively, on IPOs and insider selling (for investors with stakes exceeding 5% and company executives and directors). In just a few weeks, the market had vaporized $3 trillion of value (from the peak of $10 trillion).[56]

This exponential (or parabolic) rise followed by steep decline (crash), illustrated in Fig. 1.3, characterizes the intensity of an episode that exhibits cyclical and nonlinear features commonly seen in all other bubble and crash episodes in recorded history. It occurred at a time when China's 2016 total debt as a percentage of GDP exceeded 250% as compared to around 150% ten years earlier.[57]

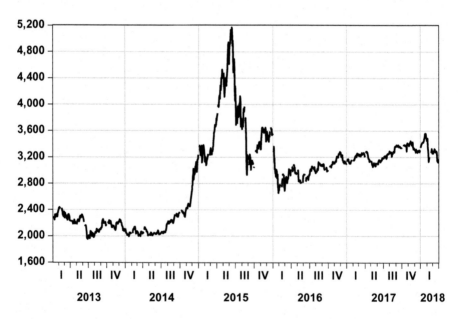

Fig. 1.3 Shanghai Stock Exchange Composite Index, 2013:01–2018:03. (See also Fig. 8.8)

1.4   ON DEFINING BUBBLES

In the physical world it is easy enough to visualize a bubble. We see many examples: a gas expanding in a container, soap or chewing-gum bubbles being blown, or even bubbles containing a liquid surrounded by another liquid of different viscosity—oil and water, for instance. Of course, in all such situations, the gas or fluid within the bubble is surrounded by some surface that gives rise to the pressure or tension that forms a container.

In financial markets—in which participants are both the observers and the observed—it is difficult to visualize the equivalent of such physical containments.[58] Pressure of rising prices and trading volumes pushes against what? Sellers? What is the container that would allow us to think of financial bubbles as being analogous to what is seen in the physical world? If such a container could be defined or readily assumed, then the financial equivalents of the Laws of Thermodynamics and Boyle's Law might be discovered and provide new ways to analyze financial asset price bubbles.[59]

So, are economic or market bubbles, as they have often so loosely been labeled, actually analogous, to one degree or another, to the bubbles commonly seen in the physical world? Is an economic or market bubble analyzable in the same way as a bubble formed by filling a balloon with helium or even one made by blowing chewing gum or by passing a wand through soapy water in a dish? If so, then a significant literature containing methods of potentially great applicability is already available.

It's impossible to go far in this direction, however, before recognizing countless complications in translating designs from the physical world to the world of markets, where demand and supply schedules are at the core determined by the psychological attitudes of participants. In markets, expectations and utility functions shift over time, often dramatically over brief periods. And today's rush to buy can quickly turn into tomorrow's panic to sell.

Generally, a bubble is considered to have developed when assets trade at prices that are far in excess of an estimate of the fundamental value of the asset as determined from discounting of future cash flows using current interest rates and typical long-run risk premiums associated with the asset class. In brief, a bubble may be most simply described as a *large and long-lasting* upward deviation of an asset's price from its "fundamental" value.[60] Under such circumstances speculators are much more interested in profiting from trading in the asset than in its practicality of use, earnings growth potential, or true value.[61]

Yet even recently, the sense among some economists is not only that we do not know that we are in a bubble while it is happening but also that we may not even know if there was a bubble long after it has ended.[62] The following from Bernanke and Gertler (1999, pp. 18–19) illustrates:

> *...ultimately asset prices are endogenous variables, (but) there are periods when asset values seem all but disconnected from the current state of the economy...Advocates of bubbles would probably be forced to admit that it is difficult or impossible to identify any particular episode conclusively as a bubble, even after the fact.*

Voth (2000) writes:

> *There is no commonly accepted definition of a bubble...The New Palgrave describes them as periods of price increases, followed by a sudden and sharp reversal. There is also no widely accepted test that would confirm or refute the existence of a bubble in a particular case.*[63]

Financial economists have (Chap. 6) stretched to make bubble definitions fit the axiomatic standard framework of rationality that has long dominated neo-classical thinking.[64] The traditional economist's mind-set is that if only the right model could be concocted, bubbles (if they indeed do exist) could then be properly explained. Flood and Hodrick (1991, p. 141) make this point in writing that a bubble is "what is left over after market fundamentals have been removed from the price. Since neither bubbles nor market fundamentals are directly observable," they write, "one can never be sure that market fundamentals have been specified appropriately."

Economists have instead tried to find, fit, and test a wide array of fundamental features; perhaps dividends ought to be discounted differently or various measures of earnings or operating revenues of some sorts might provide better proxies in modeling for bubble behavior. To this end, a whole zoology of bubbles has been proposed: rational, near-rational intermittent, intrinsic, collapsing, and so on. Even with all of this, however, financial economists have not arrived at a point where bubbles can be described with much statistical confidence, consistency, or clarity.

In other words, bubbles are difficult to identify because they "are model specific and generally defined from a rather restrictive framework."[65] And "model specific" is an ideal way to summarize the conventional literature. In effect, definitions vary, tests have low power, evidence for bubbles seems to be largely based on market fundamentals that are unobserved, and expected returns are not necessarily or dependably extrapolated from the past.

The traditional approach has for several basic reasons not worked well, if at all. First, the presumption of rationality is not empirically (inductively) demonstrated, so that the entire exercise in reasoning begins from the wrong place. It may also be not only that the utility functions of individuals shift and become more interdependent but that nonmonetary (psychological) payoffs also become relatively more important than purely financial payoffs. The shift, as shall be later more fully described, is from intertemporal considerations of the marginal utility of consumption (and thus of wealth) to the marginal utilities of *other* things—indirect and emotionally weighted wealth proxies such as loss of credibility, holding onto a job, or prestige among peers—that will then begin to take higher priority.

If so, this means that models based only on discounted expected monetary (economic) returns will never be able to tell the whole story: Such models are already from the start greatly misspecified. And this implies that when the market's trains are leaving the stations and the rocket ships are blasting off, time does not stand still; survival depends on—indeed commands—immediate actions, not carefully considered, timed, and measured "rational" weightings and calculations.[66]

In spite of this, it is nevertheless possible to begin by moving backward from the extremes. The largest financial bubbles, in terms of pure breathtaking scale of magnitude and percentage of total population involved, are those that permeate every possible sector of a nation's economy. The Japanese real estate and equities bubble of the late 1980s (Fig. 2.5) and the Internet/technology worldwide bubble concentrated in the United States in the late 1990s (Fig. 2.7) stand out as recent examples.

More directly, a rough measure of how extreme is "extreme" on a macro scale is provided by a comparison of the market capitalization (shares outstanding times share price) of the equity market against a nation's GDP, or output of goods and services (in current dollars). The total US market capitalization as measured by the Wilshire 5000 Index as a percent of GDP is shown in Fig. 1.4, left. Since 1970 the ratio has risen to more than one standard deviation above the mean during what have retrospectively been widely considered to be peaks of bubble episodes (TMT in the late 1990s, housing in 2005, and yield-chasing ending in 2017).[67]

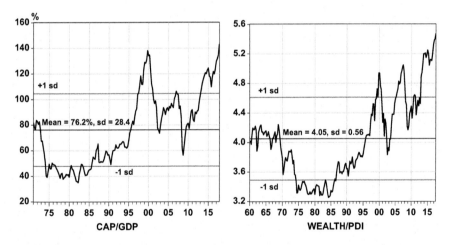

Fig. 1.4 Wilshire 5000 total US market capitalization to US GDP, quarterly, 1970–2017:Q4, left, and a ratio of US total household and nonprofit organizations, total financial assets (wealth) to personal disposable income, quarterly, 1960:01 to 2017:Q3. (Source data: Wilshire Associates, www.wilshire.com/indexes/ and https://fred.stlouisfed.org/series/TFAABSHNO. The market cap data can also be found at http://research.stlouisfed.org/fred2/series/NCBEILQ027S, which measures market value of equities outstanding and is Line 41 in the B.103 balance sheet. See also https://www.advisorperspectives.com/dshort/updates/2017/05/02/market-cap-to-gdp-an-updated-look-at-the-buffett-valuation-indicator)

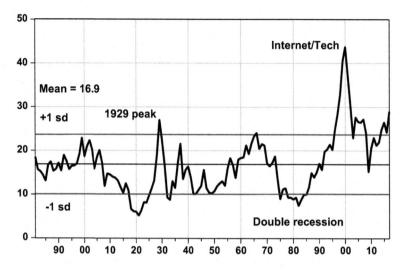

Fig. 1.5 Yale professor Robert Shiller's cyclically adjusted P/E ratios (CAPEs), annually, 1891–2017. Yield-chasing in 2017 led to peak in excess of 1929s. CAPE is based on average inflation-adjusted S&P 500 earnings from the previous ten years that smooths the effect of shorter-term earnings fluctuations. Although the ratio appears to be high for 2017, it will likely fall below +1.0 standard deviation as the low earnings of the Great Recession of 2008–2009 fall out of the calculation and are replaced by the higher earnings of subsequent years. Dividend and earnings data before 1926 are from Cowles and associates, *Common Stock Indexes*, 2nd ed., Bloomington, Ind. For more detail, see www.econ.yale.edu/~shiller/data.htm

A similar ratio taking household and nonprofit organization assets (wealth, including real estate) as a multiple of personal disposable income (Fig. 1.4, right) is also helpful in visualizing bubble zones as being at least one standard deviation above the mean. Figure 1.5 then displays Shiller's cyclically adjusted price-earnings ratio. Here again, any historically derived readings one standard deviation above or below the mean suggest extremes. But, particularly for bubbles, such metrics are often of limited help in timing as the ratios can remain in these "turn-warning" zones over many months and quarters. For most market participants, the longer a bubble persists, the less bubble-like it seems to be.[68]

In the decades since the 1830s, returns on stocks in the 1990s were one of the best and in the 2000s one of the worst (Table 1.2).

1.5   Credit, Debt, and Commonalities

Credits and Debts

It is conventional to think of changes in real interest rates, credit availability, and total debt (including government, corporate, and consumer) as a

Table 1.2 Annual returns in percent, US stocks broadly measured, by decade, 1830s–2000s

1830s	2.8	1920s	13.3
1840s	12.8	1930s	−0.2
1850s	6.6	1940s	9.6
1860s	12.5	1950s	18.2
1870s	7.5	1960s	8.3
1880s	6.0	1970s	6.6
1890s	5.5	1980s	16.6
1900s	10.9	1990s	17.6
1910s	2.2	2000s	−0.5

Source: Yale International Center for Finance databases of the New York Stock Exchange and Ibbotson, *Wall Street Journal*, 21 December 2009

percentage of GDP as—depending on direction of change—being either potential propellants or constraints on the growth and life-cycle characteristics of all macroeconomic expansions, if not also indeed "bubbles." Of these, however, perhaps the most important is credit. As Stiglitz and Greenwald (2003, pp. 199–200) explain,

> *Money is anonymous. Credit is clearly not...the links between money supply and credit or between T-bill rates and lending rates are weak...when the economy is facing a crisis...the usual relationships break down. It is the supply of credit and the terms on which it is available which matter for the level of economic activity.*

It has also not been established as to how high debt as a percent of GDP can go before a bubble becomes unsustainable and bursts. For instance, in the United States, total corporate, household, and government debt grew to 295% of GDP ($31 trillion) in the third quarter of 2002 as compared to 160% at the start of 1980. Yet the US economy continued to grow significantly, at an average annual rate of more than 3%, from 2003 through most of 2007. Only early in the Great Depression of the 1930s was the ratio as high as 264% and it was under 140% in the 1960s and as low as around 110% in the early 1950s.

Still, there must be some point—perhaps it was by early 2008 when the percentage of total debt to GDP was nearly 400% ($53 trillion/$14 trillion)— at which debt loads become so burdensome that an asset price bubble stops expanding and begins to contract (or "burst"). Studies beginning with and after Reinhart and Rogoff's (2009) have suggested that *public* debt-to-GDP levels exceeding 90% for at least five years—that is, "public debt overhangs"— tend to reduce economic growth prospects by roughly one-third as compared to periods when the debt metric was below 90%.[69]

Such conditions would likely begin to appear when income growth and capital gains were no longer sufficient to service the increased costs of new borrowings. Since the crisis of 2008, just US federal debt alone (ex-households, state and local and nonfinancial corporations) has exploded to more than 100% of GDP (Fig. 1.6).

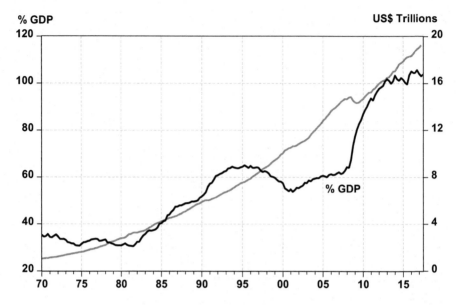

Fig. 1.6 Total US federal debt in $ trillions (right scale) and as a percent of GDP, quarterly, 1970:01 to 2017:03. (Source: fred.stlouisfed.org/series/GFDEBTN and GFDEGDQ)

Although significant price collapses and deflations would more likely begin from such relatively high ratios of debts to equity or GDP, bear markets have obviously occurred and are not necessarily precluded from occurring even at much lower debt/GDP ratios.[70]

Commonalities

While each generation of investors comes to believe that their market experiences are unique, historical records readily demonstrate that bubble and crash patterns resemble those of often never-known or long-forgotten earlier events.

Compare, for instance, the Japanese stock market bubble as measured by the Nikkei 225 index (gray line) that began in 1985 and peaked at 38,916 on 29 December 1989 (intraday high 38,957) and the U.S. Internet/technology episode as measured by the S&P 500 (dark line) that began in 1995 and peaked in early 2000. An overlapping of the two series in Fig. 1.7 reveals remarkable similarities in terms of time for denouement, turning points, and acceleration, all of which can be determined from visual inspection alone. The Japanese and U.S. housing bubbles, occurring about 15 years apart, are equivalently shown in Fig. 1.8.

The similarities are not as unusual as might at first be thought. Roehner (2002, pp. 49–51), for example, shows two overlapping peaks for French

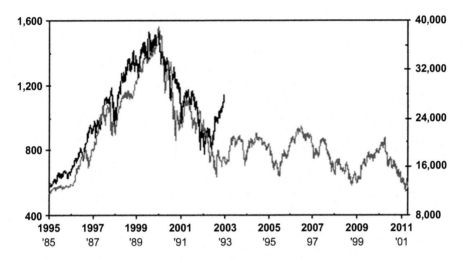

Fig. 1.7 S&P 500 Index, daily closing prices, 1995–2003 (left scale, dark line) versus Nikkei 225 Index, daily closing prices, 1985–2002 (right scale, light line). The low in the Nikkei (not shown) was in April 2003 at 7604

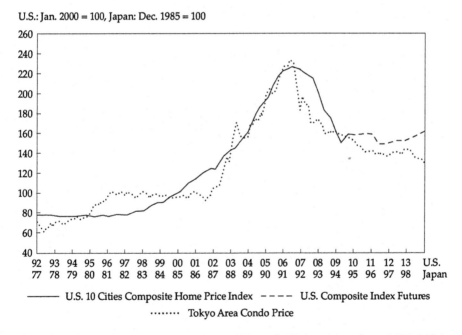

Fig. 1.8 Japan's housing prices, 1977–1999, and US housing prices, 1992–2014. Data as of April 13, 2010, per square meter, and five-month average, projected to 2014. (Sources: Bloomberg, Real Estate Economic Institute Co. (Japan), Standard & Poor's, "Lessons from Japan" by Koo (2010). Copyright (2010), CFA Institute. Reproduced and republished from the *CFA Institute Conference Proceedings Quarterly* with permission from CFA Institute. All rights reserved)

wheat prices during two six-year intervals (Normandy, 1809–1814, and Paris, 1691–1696) that are about *one century apart* and are of the same type as seen in Fig. 1.7. Overlapping price peak comparisons of Tokyo commercial land (1984–1997) with Port Said land near the Suez Canal (1898–1912)—also around 100 years apart (and shown in Roehner)—unmistakably resemble Fig. 1.7 too.

Correspondences even extend to Japan's 1980s real estate bubble and the one in the U.S. some twenty years later (Fig. 1.8) and U.S. housing stocks of 2006 versus information technology stock performance six years earlier (Fig. 2.11). It all goes to show that different bubbles exhibit substantively common features related proportionally to timing of peak-to-trough scaling.[71]

The stages through which all bubbles generally and progressively pass may be thus described as:[72]

- *Stealth*, in which "smart money" quietly and cautiously invests
- *Awareness*, in which price-change momentum builds interest by institutional investors
- *Mania*, during which prices accelerate upward and, accompanied by intense media coverage, the public stampedes into the market's most speculative offerings
- *Euphoria/Blow-off*, with prices briefly spiking to a final frenzied-bidding and short-covering high
- *Crash/Revulsion*, during which the declines from the peak are met initially with disbelief and denials that are later followed by plummeting prices, dismay, despair, and scapegoating

What is known about the general properties of returns, or stylized facts (i.e., well-accepted phenomena), is that for "almost all sets of daily returns obtained from a few years of prices:

- The distribution of returns is not normal[73]
- There is almost no correlation between returns for different days
- The correlations between the magnitudes of returns on nearby days are positive and statistically significant."[74]

These facts are "pervasive across time as well as across markets" and can be seen in studies of a wide variety of markets in different centuries.[75] But as will later be seen, important departures and exceptions from these "facts" occur when markets are bubbling up or crashing down.

NOTES

1. Speculation, Brunnermeier (2001, p. 48) writes, is when "A trader is only willing to buy or hold an asset at a price which is higher than its fundamental value if he thinks that he can resell the asset at an even higher price in a later trading round…A trader speculates if his foremost interest is in cashing in capital gains

rather than enjoying a future dividend stream. Consequently, one might think the fundamental value might be the price which an investor is willing to pay if he is forced to hold the asset forever, that is, if he is not allowed to re-trade." This follows Harrison and Kreps (1978) who in turn follow Keynes (1936 [1964], Ch. 12, VI). And Lefèvre (1923, p. 280) writes, "Speculation in stocks will never disappear. It isn't desirable that it should. It cannot be checked by warnings as to its dangers…The game does not change and neither does human nature" (p. 180). Keynes also said, "It is safer to be a speculator than an investor…a speculator is one who runs risks of which he is aware and an investor is one who runs risks of which he is unaware."

2. In the Babylonian period, some 4000 years ago, Oates (1986, pp. 10–15) explains that "Babylonia, though potentially rich in agricultural products lacked such essential commodities as stone, timber and metal ores…For this reason, trade was of crucial importance…Writing was invented in Mesopotamia as a method of book-keeping." Dunbar (2000, p. 25) notes that in Hammurabi's time, some 3800 years ago, there were crop loans and option-like arrangements and that "recent archaeological research has shown that there was a thriving loan market in ancient Babylon where borrowers could search for the best rate, just as homebuyers do today." See also Samuels et al. (2007), which contains articles about economic circumstances in earlier centuries, and Neal (2015, p. 16) who writes that the first recorded financial crisis occurred in 1788 BC after the king of ancient Uruk in Mesopotamia declared all debts null and void. Goetzmann (2016b, pp. 58–72) also covers this and presents a chart of barley prices.

3. Lei et al. (2001) found in a laboratory experiment that in a "setting in which speculation is not possible, bubbles and crashes are observed." This is nonsensical. McFarland (2016) found that "results obtained in the real world are not the same as those obtained in the laboratory."

4. Even with only a rudimentary coinage system as a basic medium of exchange, it might be inferred, for example, that speculation was a part of every Athenian fishmonger's daily function. As Davidson (1999, p. 8) discusses, "…the undisputed master of the fishmonger's stall was the eel." Eel were regarded as irresistible delicacies (pp. 186–7) and were much sought after and "the price of fresh fish was generally high at Athens." Indeed, as De Soto (2006, p. 51), citing Rostovtzeff (1953, p. 405), writes of the period around 300 BCE, "[T]he Hellenistic period, especially Ptolemaic Egypt, was a turning point in the history of banking because it marked the creation of the first government bank." Rostovtzeff linked this development to "[R]efined accounting, based on a well-defined professional terminology." Also, around 600 BCE, Greek philosopher Thales was said to have cornered the market for olive presses and profited greatly. See Aristotle (1944) *Politics*, section 1259a at www.perseus.tufts.edu

5. *The Annals*, Book VI, pp. 16–17, authored by Tacitus in 109 ACE, describes events circa 33 AD that began when Emperor Tiberius enforced a ceiling on interest rates: "Hence followed a scarcity of money, a great shock being given to all credit…Creditors however, were suing for payment in full…usurers had hoarded up all their money for buying land. The facilities for selling were followed by a fall of prices, and the deeper a man was in debt, the more reluctantly did he part with his property, and many were utterly ruined. The destruction of private wealth precipitated the fall of rank and reputation…" As noted by Calomiris and Meltzer (2016), "Tiberius responded …by making large, interest-free, three-year loans to Roman banks."

6. In response to my email inquiries to Professor Richard Saller of the University of Chicago and Professor Walter Scheidel of Stanford University, both experts on the economic aspects of these eras, neither could readily point to any specific bubble incidents in ancient Greece and Rome. Their writings, however, suggest the presence of significant price variability and cycles of economic activity.

7. Donkin (2003, p. 92) writes that Indian spice exports were mentioned in written works as early as the year 850. See also Keay (2006, p. 46). In an email exchange (June 24, 2008), Keay writes that price speculation can be "taken for granted throughout the history of the spice trade...in the early days of the London and Dutch East India Companies the price of pepper plummeted dramatically every time a fleet returned. Speculators needed to hang on to stocks as long as they could, creating a bubble, but to sell smartly before the bubble burst with reports of returning ships. Intelligence was everything."

8. Benholz (2003).

9. Ferguson (2009, pp. 50–53).

10. On the tulip mania and the South Sea Bubble, Chancellor (1999, pp. 19 and 89) indicates that "the number of mercantile bankruptcies in 1721 did not increase significantly from the previous year and the economy recovered quickly." The economic effects of crashes were also classified by Mishkin and White (2003), who after studying 15 crash episodes of the twentieth century were able to fit them into four categories ranging from no discernable stress on the financial system (e.g., 1940 and 1946), to stress mitigated by Federal Reserve actions (e.g., 1987), to episodes in which minor widening of interest-rate spreads was seen (e.g., 1969–1970, 1990), and to episodes in which large widening of interest-rate spreads was seen (e.g., 1907, 1930–1933). As they note, "one cannot make the case that crashes are always the main cause of financial instability." And market crashes may or may not be accompanied by financial instability. Posen (2003) contains data on the subsequent economic impact after bubbles have burst.

   Detken and Smets (2004) classify "booms" as being either high-cost or low-cost, saying, "Not all booms lead to large output losses...High-cost booms are clearly those in which real estate prices and investment crash in the post-boom periods." Asset price booms are defined "as a positive deviation of an aggregate asset price indicator from its recursively estimated trend by at least 10 percent."

11. The aim is to provide a statistical foundation on which all asset price bubbles (and crashes) can be defined, described, identified, and compared.

12. Hendricks (2015) studies bubbles of all types.

13. Ferreira and Karali (2017) found that "global financial markets are resilient to shocks caused by earthquakes even if these are domestic."

14. Kindleberger (1989, p. 24) has suggested that although no two speculative manias are identical, manias develop along similar lines and have changed little from the distant past to the present. Chamely (2004, p. 359) adds that "examination of famous bubbles in the past shows that they always originated in some genuine good news." 1930s 68 and early 1940s, "Current news and political developments are...soon forgotten; their presumed influence on market trends is not as weighty as is commonly believed." See also Cutler et al. (1989).

15. Chancellor (1999, pp. 125–126) writes that "journals and pamphlets proclaimed the railways as a revolutionary advance unparalleled in the history of the world. They not only focused on the economic benefits of railway transport, but concerned themselves with its more widespread effects on human civilization...

There was no limit to the imagined effects of this revolution...From an investment point of view, it was argued that railway shares would remain 'safe' in midst of panic...The public was gripped by a railway vogue." Nairn (2001) covers technology manias; Oliver (2007) and Kaplan (2011) write that tech stock valuations in 2011 had reached "bubble" dimensions. Pastor and Veronesi (2008) present a general equilibrium model in which stock prices of innovative firms operating in technologically revolutionary sectors exhibit "bubbles."

16. Schumpeter pertains, for instance, to the Japanese experience of the late 1980s, when readily available credit was apparently not fully absorbed by investments in the real economy and instead spilled over into non-GDP transactions. See Noguchi (1994), Werner (2005), and Wood (2005).

17. Greenwald et al. (2001, p. xii).

18. Arnhart (2003) says that "natural selection has shaped human nature to express at least twenty natural desires that are manifested in diverse ways in all human societies throughout history. Human beings generally desire a complete life, parental care, sexual identity, sexual mating, familial bonding, friendship, social ranking, justice as reciprocity, political rule, war, health, beauty, wealth,..." And from Dewey (1922, p. 107): "...human nature remains from age to age the same." However, as noted in http://en.wikipedia.org/wiki/Human_nature, there are many different views and schools of religious, psychological, ethical, economic, political, and philosophic thought on the subject. Of course, human nature of 2000 years ago is documented in the Old and New Testaments. See also Amhart (1998) and Olson (2006) for a review of core personality traits and implications for financial and economic behavior.

19. See Schaede (1989), who writes that "differences to modern futures exchanges can be observed in early mark-to-market procedures and margin requirements." See also West (2000).

20. See Gray and Vogel (2016, pp. 3–5). "De la Vega vividly described excessive trading, overreaction, underreaction, and the disposition effect well before they were documented by modern finance journals... Homma described the role of emotions and how these could affect rice prices...[T]he psychological aspect of the market was critical to ...trading success." Corzo et al. (2014) show Vega's knowledge, 300 years ago, of herding, overconfidence, and regret aversion.

21. The principal trading strategists and/or partners at Long-Term Capital included several well-known economists and Nobel Laureate proponents of EMH-based theories. Capie and Wood (2007, p. xiv) also note that LTCM's solvency was impaired because the derivatives contracts "had clauses that give the counterparties the right to terminate the contract in the event of a default of any kind by a counterparty...counterparties had the right to liquidate any of the defaulting counterparties' assets...*even if the assets are not directly related to the derivatives contracts in question.*" Triana (2009, pp. 253–4) notes that LTCM had been selling volatility so sizeably and aggressively as to have been nicknamed the "Central Bank of Volatility." Each percentage point increase in implied volatility was estimated to have cost LTCM $100 million, and in total, the equity index volatility trades had generated losses of $1.3 billion.

22. In this, transitivity of choice—that is, if A>B and B>C, then A>C—provides the theoretical cornerstone of rationality. A whole school of thought, as described in Werner (2005) and Cassidy (2006), sees the rational expectations hypothesis (REH) as a neoclassical axiom that should not be taken as an established fact and thus not as a given starting point for analysis. Along the same lines, Anand

(1993) goes so far as to say that the normative interpretation of subjective expected utility (SEU), which is equivalent to the REH, is empirically false. He cites studies by Rapoport and Wallsten (1972), Schoemaker (1982), Machina (1987), and Baron (1988). Anand explains that: "It is an essential feature of SEU that it specifies a mathematics of decision, but it is open whether we use it for normative or positive purposes (p. 17)...SEU is false... SEU uses independence in a sense that amounts to requiring that utility is linear with respect to probability...However...agents consistently violate the assumption" (p. 73).

23. Černý (2004, p. 56).

24. Constant absolute risk aversion (CARA) is part of a family of risk aversion utility functions that also includes constant relative risk aversion (CRRA) and hyperbolic absolute risk aversion (HARA). Černý (2004, p. 57) indicates that in evaluating distributions of wealth relative to an initial level of wealth V_0, a proper expression is $U(V)/ U(V_0) = f(V\text{-}V_0)$ for all V and V_0 and the undetermined function, f. The only utility function that meets all the conditional requirements turns out to be exponential.

25. Ariely (2008, p. 240).

26. This effect was first identified by Brickman and Campbell (1971) and in psychology is called the "hedonic treadmill." As such, this utility function representation is probably discontinuous and of the jump variety for individuals but is continuous in the aggregate. It is not the mathematical inverse of the conventional description. From Gao and Schmidt (2005): "...economic agents do not always choose what they really want...[A]lthough such 'irrational' behavior may decrease economic utility, it gives agents psychological satisfaction and subjective comfort, thus increasing their immaterial utility. In this sense, agents remain rational when conducting such behaviors, even though they run directly contrary to neoclassical rationality concepts." See also Taleb (2004).

27. As behavioral economist Kahneman said in a post-Nobel Laureate interview in Schrage (2003): "...the market cannot be completely efficient, because people act irrationally when they are afraid."

28. Tuckett (2011, pp. x–xiii) writes: "traditional economic approaches, including the recent development of behavioural economics, do not capture the essence of what happens in financial markets and why they produce crises...[W]hatever else goes on in an asset boom and bust, it looks primarily like an emotional sequence." See also Poundstone (2010, p. 102).

29. Social rationality and *zeitgeist* are noted by Roehner (2002, p. xvi and p. 40). Along the same lines, Werner (2005, p. 26) notes that "institutions, hierarchies and rankings are important."

30. Cohen (1997, p. xvii) writes that "...many speculative bubbles share a cluster of common features, even when they are separated by centuries and occur on different continents...there is an underlying similarity in the way events unfold that belies the disorderly antics of a frenzied crowd of get-rich-quick speculators." Mantegna and Stanley (2000, p. 5) have noted that "[F]inancial markets exhibit several of the properties that characterize complex systems. They are open systems in which many subunits interact nonlinearly in the presence of feedback." See also Jovanovic and Schinckus (2017).

31. Economists have not generally referred to the notion of a GDP bubble and so there is no specific evidence or literature using this terminology. Such a bubble would, however, be described as an "overheating" economy, which has been

studied at length within the context of business and economic cycles. A GDP bubble could also be defined in terms of overall price changes (inflation/deflation) of goods and services rather than through changes of share prices. Treynor (1998) suggests relating a bubble to its own statistical dynamic features—that is, autocorrelating its features.

32. Furnham and Argyle (1998, p. 102) write that "[M]oney confers social power... [and] can easily be seen as an index of social adequacy or worthiness (or, indeed, its opposite)."

33. Nofsinger (2005) and Angeletos and La'O (2013).

34. If so, this at the least inherently suggests that, loosely speaking, the outer skin (i.e., container) of a financial bubble, its outer limit, is determined or defined in part by both the amount of money and credit available and by the collective psychological state of investors, of speculators, and of the population as a whole. The opposite extreme of such a state of collective euphoria—a crash or a panic—would then be tantamount to being what might be called an "inverse" or negative bubble. Shiller (2000) uses the term "negative bubble" several times beginning at page 62. And Shiller (2002) discusses bubble characteristics of US real estate prices. On social mood influences on financial behavior, see Olson (2006) and especially Prechter (2016). Negative bubbles are also discussed in Allen and Gale (2007, p. 247).

35. King (2016, pp. 18–22).

36. Fragment is from Ryan-Collins et al. (2011, p. 9).

37. Pixley (2012, pp. 3–23 and 193). Trust in the stock market is analyzed in Guiso et al. (2008).

38. Martin (2015, p. 33).

39. Greenspan (2007, p. 256).

40. Goetzmann (2016b, p. 4) and French (2009), especially regarding malinvestment implications.

41. Ferguson (2009, pp. 4 and 30–31).

42. *Wall Street Week with Louis Rukeyser*, December 4, 1987, and December 2, 1988.

43. See *The Economist*, September 5, 1999, and April 18, 1998. Warnings about bubbles also came from famed investors Warren Buffett and John Templeton. On ABC's *Nightline* in 1999 Buffett said, "You know that valuations are high, by historic standards. You know that the level of speculation is high, by any historic standards, and you know that it doesn't go on forever...but you don't know when it ends." And Sir John Templeton told *Nightly Business Report* in December 1999 that "Internet stocks were a bubble" (He was shorting them). Around the same time, economist Henry Kaufman warned, "The bubble is already very, very big... The question is not if the asset bubble will burst, but when."

44. Fed Chairman Greenspan, however, had wavered a bit on the subject of bubble visibility. In a speech in August 2002 he said, "As events evolved, we recognized that, despite our suspicions, it was very difficult to definitively identify a bubble until after the fact – that is, when its bursting confirmed its existence...Human psychology being what it is, bubbles tend to feed on themselves, and booms in later stages are often supported by implausible projections of potential demand." See www.federalreserve.gov and Stout (2002). Greenspan also later suggested, in a December 19, 2002, speech to the Economic Club of New York, that even if a bubble could be reliably identified in advance, bursting it might require raising interest rates so high as to crush the economy, and that bubbles might be an

unavoidable by-product of long economic expansions with low inflation and hence act as "tinder for asset price speculation."

In this speech, Greenspan said,

> *If the bursting of an asset bubble creates economic dislocation, then preventing bubbles might seem an attractive goal. But whether incipient bubbles can be detected in real time and whether, once detected, they can be defused without inadvertently precipitating still greater adverse consequences for the economy remain in doubt... nothing short of a sharp increase in short-term rates that engenders a significant economic retrenchment is sufficient to check a nascent bubble. The notion that a well-timed incremental tightening could have been calibrated to prevent the late 1990s bubble is almost surely illusion.*

O'Driscoll (2007) opines that this speech is the source of "what can be best described as the Greenspan Doctrine." Hayford and Malliaris (2005) argue that "the Fed has paid significant attention to valuation of the stock market...valuation was an important variable in the Fed's decision-making and its conduct of monetary policy." More on Greenspan's strategies of the time appears in Ip (2004) and Mallaby (2016). Rebello (2005) reviews the Fed meeting transcripts of 1999 which show that although "the Fed's staff forecasters regarded U.S. stock prices as irrationally high, they underestimated the size of the bubble." At the peak, tech and telecom issues represented more than 41% of the value of the S&P 500. Public perceptions and attitudes in the Internet bubble are discussed in Browning and Dugan (2002).

See also "The Great Market Bubble Debate," *BusinessWeek*, May 29, 2000, in which Andrew Smithers, co-author of *Valuing Wall Street* (who was bearish), debates bulls, Professor Jeremy J. Siegel and Kevin A. Hassett, co-author of the book *Dow 36,000*. Hassett says, "Nobody has ever made a convincing case that there's been a stock market bubble in the U.S." Smithers says, "The evidence for a bubble is in the economy as well as the stock market. What bubbles do is create unrealistic expectations for future returns from equities and other assets. Therefore, they tend to depress savings...when you get a bubble in the stock market, it produces profound disequilibrium in the economy." Siegel says "I really am concerned with these companies that have P/E ratios of 90, 100, and above. I still think stocks, as a diversified portfolio, are the best long-run investment."

45. Chernow (2009) refers to economist Roger Babson, "whose gloomy forecasts were mocked even as the economy stagnated in the sweltering summer of 1929. On Sept. 5, 1929, Babson reiterated his doomsday cry: 'Sooner or later a crash is coming, and it may be terrific'." Similarly, Akerlof and Shiller (2009, pp. 66–7) recall a quote from *New York Times* reporter Alfred Noyes, who in writing of the speculative mania of 1929 said: "It was not in all respects an agreeable task to point out in the *Times* what seemed to me the very visible signs of danger. Expression of such comment had to meet the denunciatory comment that the writer was trying to discredit or stop American prosperity."

Similar early recognition of the great housing bubble that began to deflate in late 2005 appeared in Shiller (2002), in *Barron's* (Abelson 2005), in the *New York Times* (Rich and Leonhardt 2005), and in Witter (2006) who noted that:

- 32.6% of new mortgages and home-equity loans in 2005 were interest-only, up from 0.6% in 2000.

- 43% of first-time home buyers in 2005 put no money down.
- 15.2% of 2005 buyers owed at least 10% more than their home is worth.
- 10% of all home owners with mortgages had no equity in their homes.
- $2.7 trillion dollars in loans would adjust to higher rates in 2006 and 2007.

The impact of the US housing bubble's collapse on employment is covered in Byun (2010).

46. *New York Times* and *Milwaukee Journal,* October 16, 1929. In the month prior, Fisher foreclosed the possibility of any crash, saying on September 5, 1929, "There may be a recession in stock prices, but not anything in the nature of a crash...the possibility of which I fail to see." Similarly, as told by J.K. Galbraith in *The Great Crash, 1929,* p. 70, around the same time economics writer Joseph Lawrence confidently stated that "stocks are not at present over-valued."

47. From Harman (2000, p. 10).

48. *The Economist* magazine in April 1989 said in regard to the Japanese market that "...The implication is that shares may be underpriced." See also Voth (2000). The delusional bliss was similar with regard to housing and the role of derivative securities circa 2007. *Business Week* (February 19, 2007, p. 34) wrote, "...derivatives let financial institutions and traders manage their risks with mind-blowing precision." Even after two Bear Stearns funds had already collapsed and Countrywide Financial had warned of broader credit problems, *Business Week* (August 6, 2007, pp. 23–4) in its Outlook section wrote: "...a severe financial crunch is unlikely....The extent of the subprime problem remains small...The squeeze in the credit markets as a result of the subprime mess is far from a severe one...the widening of risk spreads has not been great...the yield spread on corporate bonds rated BBB...had increased to 1.5% from 1.25% at the end of June. That's little different from the 1.47% average for all of 2006." However, in fairness to the magazine, the same issue carried an article ("The Subprime Mess: Let the Blame Begin," p. 32) critical of the role played by ratings agencies such as S&P, which was owned by McGraw-Hill, the publisher.

49. Zweig (2008) writes that according to surveys of hundreds of companies conducted by Duke University economist John Graham, "[D]uring the week of March 13, 2000, the absolute peak of the market bubble, 82% of finance chiefs said their shares were cheap, with only 3.4% saying their stock was overvalued".

50. Lee (2004, pp. 20–1).

51. McGrattan and Prescott (2000), using a standard macroeconomic growth model, found that "the market is correctly valued" and, barring any institutional changes, predicted a small future equity premium.

52. According to Zacks Investment Research data. The percentage of "buys" was 69.5%.

53. Hale (2007), in a *Wall Street Journal* op-ed piece entitled "The Best Economy Ever," said that the entrepreneurial energy unleashed in developing countries "set the stage for extraordinary economic growth." In a *Fortune* magazine interview entitled "The Greatest Economic Boom Ever" that was summarized by Kirkland (2007), then-US Treasury Secretary Hank Paulson, albeit in a somewhat hedged and cautious manner, and advising vigilance, said, "This is far and away the strongest global economy I've seen in my business lifetime." Sorkin (2009, p. 49), however, reveals that in a meeting with President Bush,

Paulson actually had expressed concerns about the markets and that "the economy was overdue for a crisis," as early as August 2006.

54. In Thomas (2012), "Spanish financial leaders in influential positions mostly played down concerns that something might go terribly wrong." And, the 2007 IMF Global Financial Stability Report declared that weakness in US housing prices posed no systemic threat.

55. Sharma (2015a). Hong and Xie (2018) write of government surveillance and warnings against aggressive selling.

56. Barboza (2015a, b).

57. Lyons and Hong (2016). French (2009, p. 116) suggests that money spilled into stocks after China's government in 1991 cracked down on a bubble in stamp prices as described in McGregor (1991).

58. In a stock market bubble people act with what might readily be called "infectious" greed, and in a crash with, "infectious" despair in which no such physical containment is possible. Shiller (2006) says, "Bubbles are not purely psychological phenomena. They are an epidemic, and an epidemic requires contagion. An epidemic (bubble) can exist only if conditions favor contagion…One reason financial bubbles are mysterious is that their time pattern depends on the contagion rate of the enthusiasm, the spread of optimism and excitement for the market." The analogy is with biological models as described by Daley and Gani (1999). However, this approach is probably too great a stretch for a financial market theory in which investors and speculators have all types of objectives and time horizons and are of different sizes and levels of sophistication and knowledge. See also Shiller (2000, [2005] p. 257), Bailey (1957), and Kenourgios et al. (2011) on market contagion. On contagiousness see also Gladwell (2002, pp. 9–11), Berger (2016), and Porras (2016).

59. For example, the Perfect Gas Law defines an ideal gas which behaves at all pressures in the same way that real gases behave at low pressures. Isenberg (1992) describes the physics of soap bubbles.

Ultimately the only such possible price/valuation container for share prices is—using the real risk-free rate of interest—the point at which the equity risk premium is zero (see Fig. 8.1) and at which the presumed law of one price (LOOP), *if* it is actually operative, ensures through arbitrage that share prices cannot possibly go any higher for more than a relatively brief time. Noguchi (1994) and Werner (2005) have already shown that credit availability (in the case of the Japanese land and equity inflations of the 1980s) is thus far the closest that an economist can come to capturing, isolating, and measuring the "gas" that collectively fills a bubble's balloon.

60. The large and long-lasting aspects are emphasized by Blinder (2013, p. 29), from where this description appears. Goetzmann (2016a) defines "a bubble as a large price decline after a large price increase (i.e., a crash after a boom)." He finds that the frequency of bubbles is quite small (i.e., bubbles are rare), with the unconditional frequency being 0.3–1.4%. The definition of a market boom is a doubling in a one-to-three-year period. See earlier version at www.nber.org/papers/w21693

61. Shiller (2000 [2005], p. 5) defines a speculative bubble as "an unsustainable increase in prices brought on by investors' buying behavior rather than by genuine, fundamental information about value," with Kindleberger (1987), who sees a bubble as "attracting new buyers – generally speculators – interested in profits from trading in the asset rather than its use or earning capacity," and with

Stiglitz (1990), who says: "if the reason that the price is high today is *only* because investors believe that the selling price will be high tomorrow – when fundamental factors do not seem to justify such a price – then a bubble exists." According to Kindleberger, a typical bubble evolves in five stages: displacement, boom, euphoria, peak, and bust. From Kindleberger (1996 [1989], p. 13) and Kindleberger and Aliber (2011, p. 30), "The word *mania* emphasizes the irrationality; *bubble* foreshadows the bursting." Schwartz (1986, p. 255), however, notes that "the word 'bubble' has supplanted the pejorative 'mania'."

Another practical definition of a bubble also appears in Fleckenstein and Sheehan (2008, p. 189), where Jeremy Grantham, Chairman of Boston money management firm, GMO, says: "bubbles are definable events when the price action is two standard deviations from a long-term trend." Based on this criterion, Grantham's research found that the US stock market (peak in 2000) and real estate bubbles (peak 2005–2006) were the 28th and 29th bubbles, respectively, in financial history beginning with the Dutch tulip craze. Grantham's definition also appears in Grant (2008, p. 385), in which he says that such an event might be expected once in 40 years or so. See also the *GMO Quarterly Letter*, Q1 2014, available at www.gmo.com and Grantham (2014).

In Fleckenstein and Sheehan (p. 94), John Makin, in the American Enterprise Institute's *Outlook* of November 9, 2000, is quoted as saying that "A stock market bubble exists when the value of stocks has more impact on the economy than the economy has on the value of stocks." Martenson (2011, p. 80) writes that "a bubble exists when asset prices rise beyond what incomes can sustain." Roubini and Mihm (2011, p. 17) explain that "asset bubbles develop even before the credit supply booms, because expectations of future price increases are sufficient to foster a self-fulfilling rise in the asset's price."

From Case and Shiller (2004): "A bubble occurs when exaggerated expectations of future price increases generate unusual demand either by people who fear being priced out of a market or by investors hoping to make a lot of money fast. A bubble is a self-fulfilling prophecy for a while, as successive rounds of buyers push prices higher and higher. But…bubbles carry the seeds of their own destruction. Only time is needed for the bubbles to end." Shiller (2002) discusses feedback and bubbles and in Shiller (2015, p. xv) calls bubble episodes as "speculative epidemics." Brunnermeier (2008) provides a formal and detailed modern definition for the *New Palgrave Dictionary of Economics*, in which he refers to bubbles as "asset prices that exceed an asset's fundamental value because current owners believe that they can resell the asset at an even higher price in the future." Brunnermeier's article further observes that:

[T]here are four main strands of models that identify conditions under which bubbles can exist. The first class of models assumes that all investors have rational expectations and identical information. These models generate the testable implication that bubbles have to follow an explosive path. In the second category of models investors are asymmetrically informed and bubbles can emerge under more general conditions because their existence need not be commonly known. A third strand of models focuses on the interaction between rational and behavioral traders. Bubbles can persist in these models since limits to arbitrage prevent rational investors from eradicating the price impact of behavioral traders. In the final class of models, bubbles can emerge if investors hold heterogenous beliefs, potentially due to psychological biases, and they agree to disagree about the fundamental value.

Garber (2000, pp. 4–12) notes further that "bubble" is "a fuzzy word filled with import but lacking a solid operational definition…The definition of *bubble* most often used in economic research is that part of asset price movement that is unexplainable based on what we call fundamentals. Fundamentals are a collection of variables that we believe should drive asset prices…we truly cannot know if the speculation was unsound until after the fact."

In the 1992 version of the *New Palgrave Dictionary of Money and Finance* (edited by Newman et al.), Kindleberger says,

> *The theoretical literature uses the assumption of the market having one mind and one purpose, whereas it is observed historically that market participants are often moved by different purposes, operate with different wealth and information and calculate within different time horizons…the theoretical literature has yet to converge on an agreed definition of bubbles, and on whether they are possible.*

Hassett (2002, p. 21), for instance, says "a *financial bubble* is a period when the price of an asset (stocks, real estate, tulips, etc.) suddenly soars for irrational reasons and then collapses." But then, "what are irrational reasons?" In a *Barron's* interview of September 1, 2011, Jim Grant said: "A bubble is a bull market in which the user of the word, 'bubble' has not fully participated." See also Brown (2008), Dholakia and Turcan (2014), and Barlevy (2015) who writes on the greater fool theory. It's also been quipped that a bubble is when people are making money that's greatly disproportionate to their knowledge, skills, and work ethics.

62. The following also pertains:

> *…whether with hindsight the run-up in asset prices in the late 1990s was a result of bubble behavior. …this question is quite difficult to answer…The inability to identify asset price bubbles ex ante should be sufficient reason for policymakers to be cautious about taking pre-emptive actions…The inability to identify asset price bubbles ex post…should cause policymakers to take pause…* Kroszner (2003, p. 7)

But McGrattan and Prescott (2003, p. 274) wrote that there was no asset bubble in 1929: "…the reason for the 1929 crash was not that the stock market was overvalued relative to fundamentals…"

Bierman (1991, pp. 5–7) even suggested some 60 years after the event that the stock market was not obviously too high in 1929 and that it perhaps wasn't too high at the 1987 peak either. "[T]here will always be a reasonable scenario that will justify the level of prices. Prices go up because many people are betting that the expected value, based on some scenario, justifies the current price."

63. The quotation continues "…Diba and Grossman (1988) suggest that, in the case of a rational bubble, the first-order difference of stock prices will be nonstationary. Campbell and Shiller (1987) argue that, if dividends and stock prices fail to co-integrate, there is evidence of a bubble; a unit root in the price-dividend ratio implies 'irrational exuberance' (Craine 1993)."

64. Articles in Colander (2006) show that there is a growing body of what is called post-Walrasian analysis in which information is the source of differences between the older and newer approaches. For post-Walrasians, as Mathews writes in the Colander volume (p. 80), "rationality, equilibrium, and greed are replaced with purposeful behavior, sustainability, and enlightened self-interest." See also Lansing (2010).

65. Sornette (2003, p. 285).

66. Keuzenkamp (2000, p. 116) writes: "All models are wrong: Kepler's, Tinbergen's, Friedman's, and 'even' those of contemporary econometricians. Some, however, are useful. Kepler's clearly were, as were Tinbergen's and Friedman's. They shared a common respect for simplicity." Usefulness is the aim of the current project. Einstein's maxim, as recalled in Medio (1992, p. 3), was that "things must be made as simple as possible, but not simpler." A sign in Einstein's office at Princeton also said: "Not everything that counts can be counted, and not everything that can be counted counts."

67. Total market cap-to-GDP, according to a *Fortune* magazine interview in 2001, is Warren Buffett's favorite long-term predictive indicator. As seen in Fig. 1.4, once it sustainably rises above one standard deviation it suggests that a peak is near. However, Lleo and Ziemba (2015) suggested that this MV/GNP ratio is of limited usefulness as a crash forecasting tool. An almost identical line is traced by taking Wilshire 5000 total market cap as a multiple of US domestic final sales for the entire US economy (not shown). Final sales is one of the cleanest (i.e., least adjusted and manipulated) series from which to form ratios.

68. Surowiecki (2004, p. 250).

69. Subsequent articles include Reinhart et al. (2012) and Pattillo et al. (2011).

70. Empirical studies are from Allen and Gale (2000), Stiglitz and Greenwald (2003), and Werner (2005). Werner (2005, pp. 181–245) demonstrates that if monetary policy is correctly measured as it is applied to the credit creation mechanism of a nation's banking system, it explains speculative capital flows into stocks, real estate, and the nonfinancial sectors of the economy.

71. Roehner (2002, pp. 167–72) uses price multipliers and dispersion criteria.

72. The summary partially follows the phases described in a chart by Hofstra University Professor Jean-Paul Rodrigue available at http://en.wikipedia.org/wiki/File:Stages_of_a_bubble.png

73. Lognormal is used instead of normal because, in the random-walk approach, adding or subtracting a random change might result in a stock price eventually and impossibly wandering below zero. As noted in Poundstone (2005, p. 122), Samuelson found a simple fix to the problem in Bachelier's original thesis of 1900. The idea was to multiply by a random percentage change instead of adding or subtracting a random amount. This works because a stock within this framework might over a certain time be as likely to double as to halve. The lognormal is thus a geometric random walk.

74. Taylor (2005, p. 51).

75. Booth and Gurun (2004) studied daily returns at the Florentine currency market of 1389–1432, Harrison (1998) investigated London stock trading of 1724–1740, and Mitchell et al. (2002) analyzed the London fixed income market of 1821–1860.

References

Abelson, A. (2005, January 31). Unhappy Ending? *Barron's.*

Akerlof, G. A., & Shiller, R. J. (2009). *Animal Spirits.* Princeton: Princeton University Press.

Allen, F., & Gale, D. (2000). Bubbles and Crises. *Economic Journal, 110*(January).

Allen, F., & Gale, D. (2007). *Understanding Financial Crises.* New York: Oxford University Press.

Allen, F., & Gorton, G. (1993). Churning Bubbles. *Review of Economic Studies, 60*(4), 813–836.

Allen, F., Morris, S., & Postlewaite, A. (1993). Finite Bubbles with Short Sale Constraints and Asymmetric Information. *Journal of Economic Theory, 61.*

Amihud, Y. (2002). Illiquidity and Stock Returns: Cross-Section and Time-Series Effects. *Journal of Financial Markets, 5.*

Amihud, Y., Mendelson, H., & Pedersen, L. H. (2005). Liquidity and Asset Prices. *Foundations and Trends in Finance, 1*(4).

Anand, P. (1993). *Foundations of Rational Choice Under Risk.* Oxford: Oxford University Press.

Angeletos, G.-M., & La'O, J. (2013). Sentiments. *Econometrica, 81*(2).

Appley, M. H. (Ed.). (1971). *Adaptation-Level Theory.* New York: Academic Press.

Ariely, D. (2008). *Predictably Irrational: The Hidden Forces that Shape Our Decisions.* New York: HarperCollins.

Arnhart, L. (2003). Human Nature is Here to Stay. *The New Atlantis, 2*(Summer), 65–78.

Bailey, N. T. (1957). *The Mathematical Theory of Epidemics.* London: C. Griffin.

Balen, M. (2003). *The Secret History of the South Sea Bubble: The World's First Great Financial Scandal.* New York: HarperCollins (Fourth Estate). Also under the title, *The King, the Crook, & the Gambler.*

Barboza, D. (2015a, July 13). China's Incendiary Market Is Fanned by Borrowers and Manipulation. *New York Times.*

Barboza, D. (2015b, July 7). Chinese Investors Who Borrowed are Hit Hard by Market Turn. *New York Times.*

Barlevy, G. (2012). Rethinking Theoretical Models of Bubbles, in Evanoff et al. (2012).

Barlevy, G. (2015). Bubbles and Fools. *Economic Perspectives*, Q2. Chicago: Federal Reserve Bank of Chicago.

Baron, J. (1988). *Thinking and Deciding.* Cambridge, UK: Cambridge University Press.

Baumol, W. J., & Benhabib, J. (1989). Chaos: Significance, Mechanism, and Economic Applications. *Journal of Economic Perspectives, 3*(1), 77–105.

Berger, J. (2016). *Contagious: Why Things Catch On.* New York: Simon & Schuster (Paperback edition).

Bernanke, B. S., & Gertler, M. (1999, 2000). *Monetary Policy and Asset Price Volatility.* Federal Reserve Bank of Kansas City, presented at Jackson Hole, Wyoming conference, August. www.kc.frb.org and 2000, NBER Working Paper No. 7559.

Bernholz, P. (2003). *Monetary Regimes and Inflation.* Cheltenham, UK: Edward Elgar.

Bezemer, D. J. (2009). 'No One Saw This Coming': Understanding Financial Crisis Through Accounting Models. MRA Paper No. 15892. http://mpra.ub.uni-muenchen.de/15892/

Bierman, H., Jr. (1991). *The Great Myths of 1929 and the Lessons to be Learned.* Westport: Greenwood Press.

Blinder, A. S. (2013). *After the Music Stopped: The Financial Crisis, The Response, and the Work Ahead.* New York: Penguin Press.

Booth, G. G., & Gurun, U. G. (2004). *Financial Archaeology: Capitalism, Financial Markets, and Price Volatility.* Working paper. East Lansing: Michigan State University.

Bordo, M. (2003). *Stock Market Crashes, Productivity Boom and Bush, and Recessions: Some Historical Evidence* (Unpublished). Washington, DC: International Monetary Fund, *World Economic Outlook*, Ch. 2.

Brickman, P., & Campbell, D. T. (1971). Hedonic Relativism and Planning the Good Society. In M. H. Appley (Ed.), *Adaptation-Level Theory*. New York: Academic Press.

Brown, B. (2008). *Bubbles in Credit and Currency: How Hot Markets Cool Down*. New York: Palgrave Macmillan.

Browning, E. S., & Dugan, I. J. (2002, December 16). Aftermath of a Market Mania. *Wall Street Journal*.

Brunnermeier, M. K. (2001). *Asset Pricing Under Asymmetric Information: Bubbles, Crashes, Technical Analysis, and Herding*. New York: Oxford University Press.

Brunnermeier, M. K. (2008). Bubbles. In S. N. Durlauf & L. E. Bluem (Eds.), *New Palgrave Dictionary of Economics* (2nd ed.). London: Macmillan.

Burnham, T. C. (2008). *Mean Markets and Lizard Brains: How to Profit from the New Science of Irrationality* (Revised ed.). Hoboken: Wiley.

Byun, K. J. (2010). The U.S. Housing Bubble and Bust: Impacts on Employment. *Monthly Labor Review, 133*, 3–17.

Calomiris, C. W., & Meltzer, A. (2016). Rules for the Lender of Last Resort: Introduction. *Journal of Financial Intermediation, 28*(October), 1–3.

Camerer, C. F. (1989). An Experimental Test of Several Generalized Utility Theories. *Journal of Risk and Uncertainty, 2*, 61–104.

Campbell, J. Y., & Shiller, R. J. (1987). Cointegration and Tests of Present Value Models. *Journal of Political Economy, 95*(5), 1062–1088.

Capie, F. H., & Wood, G. E. (2007). *The Lender of Last Resort*. London/New York: Routledge.

Case, K. E., & Shiller, R. J. (2004, August 24). Mi Casa Es Su Housing Bubble. *Wall Street Journal*.

Cassidy, J. (2006, September 18). Mind Games: What Neuroeconomics Tells Us about Money and the Brain. *The New Yorker*.

Cecchetti, S. G. (2008). Asset Bubbles and the Fed. *Milken Institute Review*, Second Quarter *10*(2), 44–53.

Černý, A. (2004). *Mathematical Techniques in Finance: Tools for Incomplete Markets*. Princeton: Princeton University Press.

Chambers, D., & Dimson, E. (Eds.). (2016). *Financial Market History: Reflections on the Past for Investors Today*. Charlottesville: CFA Institute Research Foundation. http://www.cfapubs.org/doi/pdf/10.2470/rf.v2016.n3.1.

Chamley, C. P. (2004). *Rational Herds: Economic Models of Social Learning*. New York: Cambridge University Press.

Chancellor, E. (1999). *Devil Take the Hindmost: A History of Financial Speculation*. New York: Farrar, Straus, Giroux.

Chernow, R. (2009, October 23). Everyman's Financial Meltdown. *New York Times*.

Cohen, E. E. (1992). *Athenian Economy and Society: A Banking Perspective*. Princeton: Princeton University Press.

Cohen, B. (1997). *The Edge of Chaos: Financial Booms, Bubbles, Crashes and Chaos*. Chichester: Wiley.

Colander, D. (Ed.). (2006). *Post Walrasian Macroeconomics: Beyond the Dynamic Stochastic General Equilibrium Model*. New York: Cambridge University Press.

Corzo, T., Prat, M., & Vaquero, E. (2014). Behavioral Finance In Joseph de la Vega's Confusion de Confusiones. *Journal of Behavioral Finance, 15*(4), 341–350.

Craine, R. (1993). Rational Bubbles: A Test. *Journal of Economic Dynamics and Control, 17*, 829–846.

Cutler, D. M., Poterba, J. M., & Summers, L. H. (1989). What Moves Stock Prices? *Journal of Portfolio Management, 15*(3), 4–12.

Daley, D. J., & Gani, J. (1999). *Epidemic Modelling*. Cambridge, UK: Cambridge University Press.

Davidson, J. N. (1999). *Courtesans & Fishcakes: The Consuming Passions of Classical Athens*. New York: Harper Perennial.

Davies, G. (2002). *A History of Money: From Ancient Times to the Present Day* (3rd ed.). Cardiff: University of Wales Press.

De Bondt, W. (2003). Bubble Psychology. in Hunter et al. (2003 [2005]).

De Soto, J. H. (2006). *Money, Bank Credit, and Economic Cycles* (trans: Stroup, M. A.). Auburn: Ludwig von Mises Institute.

Detken, C., & Smets, F. (2004). *Asset Price Booms and Monetary Policy*. Working Paper Series No. 364 (May). Frankfurt: European Central Bank. www.ecb.int

Dewey, J. (1922). *Human Nature and Conduct: An Introduction to Social Psychology*. New York: Modern Library.

Dholakia, N., & Turcan, R. V. (2014). *Toward a Metatheory of Economic Bubbles: Socio-Political and Cultural Perspectives*. New York: Palgrave Macmillan.

Diba, B. T., & Grossman, H. I. (1988). The Theory of Rational Bubbles in Stock Prices. *Economic Journal, 98*(392), 746–754.

Donkin, R. A. (2003). *Between East and West: The Moluccas and the Traffic in Spices Up to the Arrival of Europeans*. Darby: Diane Publishing Company and American Philosophical Society.

Dunbar, N. (2000). *Inventing Money: The Story of Long-Term Capital Management and the Legends Behind It*. Chichester: Wiley.

Durant, W. (1944). *Caesar and Christ: A History of Roman Civilization and of Christianity from Their Beginnings to A.D. 325*. New York: Simon & Schuster.

Evanoff, D. D., Kaufman, G. G., & Malliaris, A. G. (Eds.). (2012). *New Perspectives on Asset Price Bubbles: Theory, Evidence, and Policy*. New York: Oxford University Press.

Falconer, K. (2013). *Fractals: A Very Short Introduction*. Oxford, UK: Oxford University Press.

Fama, E. F. (1965). The Behavior of Stock-Market Prices. *The Journal of Business, 38*(1), 34–105.

Ferguson, N. (2009, May 17). Diminished Returns. *New York Times*.

Ferreira, S., & Karali, B. (2017). Do Earthquakes Shake Stock Markets? *PLoS One, 10*(7), e0133319. https://doi.org/10.1371/journal.pone.0133319.

Fleckenstein, W. A., & Sheehan, F. (2008). *Greenspan's Bubbles: The Age of Ignorance at the Federal Reserve*. New York: McGraw-Hill.

Flood, R. P., & Garber, P. M. (Eds.). (1994). *Speculative Bubbles, Speculative Attacks and Policy Switching*. Cambridge, MA: MIT Press.

Flood, R. P., & Hodrick, R. J. (1991). Asset Price Volatility, Bubbles, and Process Switching. In Flood, R. P., & Garber, P. M. 1994).

Flood, R., Hodrick, R., & Kaplan, P. (1986). *An Evaluation of Recent Evidence on Stock Market Bubbles*. NBER Working Paper #1971 in Flood and Garber (1994), *Speculative Bubbles, Attacks and Policy Switching*. Cambridge, MA: MIT Press.

French, D. E. (2009). *Early speculative Bubbles and Increases in the Supply of Money* (2nd ed.). Auburn: Ludwig von Mises Institute.

Furnham, A., & Argyle, M. (1998). *The Psychology of Money*. New York: Routledge.

Gabaix, X. (2009). Power Laws in Economics and Finance. *Annual Review of Economics, 1*, 255–293.

Galbraith, J. K. (1988). *The Great Crash, 1929* (2nd ed.). Boston: Houghton-Mifflin.

Gao, L., & Schmidt, U. (2005). Self is Never Neutral: Why Economic Agents Behave Irrationally. *Journal of Behavioral Finance, 6*(1), 27–37.

Garber, P. M. (2000). *Famous First Bubbles: The Fundamentals of Early Manias.* Cambridge, MA: MIT Press.

Garnsey, P., & Saller, R. (1987). *The Roman Empire: Economy, Society and Culture.* Berkeley: University of California Press.

Gascoigne, B. (2003). *The Dynasties of China: A History.* New York: Carroll and Graf.

George, D. A. R. (2007). Consolations for the Economist: The Future of Economic Orthodoxy. *Journal of Economic Surveys, 21*(3), 417–425.

Gernet, J. (1982). *A History of Chinese Civilization* (trans: Foster, J. R.). Cambridge, UK: Cambridge University Press.

Gladwell, M. (2002). *The Tipping Point: How Little Things Can Make a Big Difference.* New York: Little Brown.

Goetzmann, W. N. (2016a). Bubble Investing: Learning from History. In D. Chambers, & E. Dimson (Eds.). *Financial Market History.* Charlottesville, VA: CFA Research Foundation.

Goetzmann, W. N. (2016b). *Money Changes Everything: How Finance Made Civilization Possible.* Princeton: Princeton University Press.

Grant, J. (2008). *Mr. Market Miscalculates: The Bubble Years and Beyond.* Mount Jackson: Axios Press.

Grantham, J. (2014, May 5). Jeremy Grantham Remains Bullish on Stocks. *Barron's.*

Gray, W. R., & Vogel, J. R. (2016). *Quantitative Momentum.* Hoboken: Wiley.

Greenspan, A. (1999, August 27). *New Challenges for Monetary Policy.* Presented at the FRB Kansas, *Jackson Hole Symposium.*

Greenspan, A. (2007). *The Age of Turbulence: Adventures in a New World.* New York: Penguin.

Greenwald, B. C. N., Kahn, J., Sonkin, P. D., & van Biema, M. (2001). *Value Investing: From Graham to Buffett and Beyond.* New York: Wiley (Paperback edition).

Guiso, L., Sapienza, P., & Zingales, L. (2008). Trusting the Stock Market. *Journal of Finance, 63*(6), 2557–2600.

Haacke, C. (2004). *Frenzy: Bubbles, Busts and How to Come Out Ahead.* New York: Palgrave Macmillan.

Hale, D. (2007, July 31). The Best Economy Ever. *Wall Street Journal.*

Harman, Y. S. (2000). *Bubbles, Fads, and the Psychology of Investors.* Unpublished PhD dissertation, Florida State University.

Harrison, P. (1998). Similarities in the Distribution of Stock Market Price Changes Between the Eighteenth and Twentieth Centuries. *Journal of Business, 71*(1), 55–79.

Harrison, M. J., & Kreps, D. (1978). Speculative Investor Behavior in a Stock Market with Heterogeneous Expectations. *Quarterly Journal of Economics, 89*, 519–542.

Hartcher, P. (2006). *Bubble Man.* New York: W. W. Norton.

Hassett, K. A. (2002). *Bubbleology: The New Science of Stock Market Winners and Losers.* New York: Crown.

Hayford, M. D., & Malliaris, A. G. (2005). Is the Federal Reserve Stock Market Bubble-Neutral? In A. G. Malliaris (Ed.). *Economic Uncertainty, Instability and Asset Bubbles: Selected Essays.* Hackensack: World Scientific.

Heim, E., & Truger, A. (Eds.). (2007). *Money, Distribution and Economic Policy: Alternatives to Orthodox Macroeconomics.* Cheltenham: Edward Elgar.

Hendricks, V. F. (2015). *Bubble Studies: The Brass Tacks*. London: Bloomsbury. *Leading Frontier Research in the Humanities*, (September).

Hendricks, V. F., & Rendsvig, R. K. (2016). The Philosophy of Distributed Information. In L. Floridi (Ed.), *The Routledge Handbook of Philosophy of Information*. New York: Routledge.

Hodrick, L. S., & Moulton, P. C. (2009). Liquidity: Considerations of a Portfolio Manager. *Financial Management, 38*(1), 59–74.

Hughes, R. (2011). *Rome: A Cultural and Personal History*. New York: Random House/Vintage.

Hunter, W. C., Kaufman, G. G., & Pomerleano, M., eds. (2003). *Asset Price Bubbles: The Implications for Monetary, Regulatory, and International Policies*. Cambridge, MA: MIT Press (Paperback, 2005).

International Monetary Fund [IMF]. (2003). When Bubbles Burst. *World Economic Report*. Washington, DC: IMF.

Ip, G. (2004, November 18). Fed Chief's Style: Devour the Data, Beware of Dogma. *Wall Street Journal*.

Isenberg, C. (1992). *The Science of Soap Films and Soap Bubbles*. New York: Dover.

Janszen, E. (2008, February). The Next Bubble: Priming the Markets for Tomorrow's Big Crash. *Harper's Magazine*.

Jovanovic, F., & Schinckus, C. (2017). *Econophysics and Financial Economics: An Emerging Dialog*. New York: Oxford University Press.

Kahneman, D., & Tversky, A. (2000). *Choices, Values and Frames*. Cambridge, UK: Cambridge University Press.

Kamarck, A. M. (2001). *Economics for the Twenty-First Century*. Aldershot: Ashgate.

Kaplan, D. A. (2011, July 25). Don't Call It The Next Tech Bubble – Yet. *Fortune, 164*(2), 48–56.

Keay, J. (2006). *The Spice Route: A History*. Berkeley: University of California Press.

Kenourgios, D., Samitas, A., & Paltalidis, N. (2011). Financial Crises and Stock Market Contagion in a Multivariate Time-Varying Asymmetric Framework. *Journal of International Financial Markets, Institutions & Money, 21*, 92–106.

Keuzenkamp, H. A. (2000). *Probability, Econometrics and Truth: The Methodology of Econometrics*. New York/Cambridge, UK: Cambridge University Press.

Keynes, J. M. (1936). *The General Theory of Employment, Interest, and Money*. London/San Diego: Macmillan/Harcourt Brace (1964 reprint).

Kindleberger, C. (1987). Bubbles. In J. Eatwell, M. Milgate, & P. Newman (Eds.), *The New Palgrave: A Dictionary of Economics*. London: Macmillan.

Kindleberger, C. (1996 [1989]). *Manias, Panics, and Crashes: A History of Financial Crises* (3rd ed.). New York: Wiley (2nd ed., 1989).

Kindleberger, C., & Aliber, R. Z. (2011). *Manias, Panics, and Crashes: A History of Financial Crises* (6th ed.). Houndmills: Palgrave Macmillan.

King, M. (2016). *The End of Alchemy: Money, Banking and the Future of the Global Economy*. New York: W. W. Norton.

Kirkland, R. (2007, July 12). The Greatest Economic Boom Ever. *Fortune*.

Kolata, G. (Ed.). (2013). *The New York Times Book of Mathematics*. New York: Sterling.

Koo, R. C. (2010). Lessons from Japan: Fighting a Balance Sheet Recession. *CFA Institute Conference Proceedings Quarterly, 27*(4), 28–39.

Kroszner, R. S. (2003 [2005]). Asset Price Bubbles, Information, and Public Policy. In Hunter et al. (2003).

Kruger, R. (2003). *All Under Heaven: A Complete History of China*. Chichester: Wiley.

Laing, J. R. (1991, July 29). Efficient Chaos or, Things They Never Taught in Business School. *Barron's.*

Lansing, K. J. (2010). Rational and Near-Rational Bubbles Without Drift. *Economic Journal, 120*(549), 1149–1174.

Laperriere, A. (2008, April 3). Questions for the Fed. *Wall Street Journal.*

Lattman, P., Smith, R., & Strasburg, J. (2008, March 14). Carlyle Fund in Free Fall as Its Banks Get Nervous. *Wall Street Journal.*

Le Bon. (1895). *The Crowd: A Study of the Popular Mind.* digireads.com. 2009 ed.

Lee, T. (2004). *Why the Markets Went Crazy.* New York: Palgrave Macmillan.

Lefèvre, E. (1923). *Reminiscences of a Stock Operator.* New York: George H. Doran. Reprinted 1980 by Fraser Publishing, Burlington VT.

Lei, V., Noussair, C. N., & Plott, C. R. (2001). Nonspeculative Bubbles in Experimental Asset Markets: Lack of Common Knowledge of Rationality vs. Actual Irrationality. *Econometrica, 69*(4).

Lewis, M. (2007, August 26). In Nature's Casino. *New York Times.*

Lhabitant, F.-S., & Gregoriou, G. N. (Eds.). (2008). *Stock Market Liquidity: Implications for Market Microstructure and Asset Pricing.* Hoboken: Wiley.

Lleo, S., & Ziemba, W. T. (2015). *Can Warren Buffett Also Predict Equity Market Downturns?* https://ssrn.com/abstract=2630068, https://doi.org/10.2139/ssrn.2630068

Lo, A. W., & MacKinlay, A. C. (1999). *A Non-Random Walk Down Wall Street.* Princeton: Princeton University Press.

Lyons, J., & Hong, S. (2016, November 1). Series of Bubbles Rattles China. *Wall Street Journal.*

Machina, M. J. (1987). Choice Under Uncertainty. *Journal of Economic Perspectives, 1,* 121–154.

Mackay, C. (1841). *Extraordinary Popular Delusions and the Madness of Crowds* (1995th ed.). New York: Wiley.

Malkiel, B. G. (1999). *A Random Walk Down Wall Street,* 7th ed., 8th ed. (2003), 9th ed. (2007), 11th ed. (2015). New York: W. W. Norton.

Malkiel, B. G. (2003). The Efficient Market Hypothesis and Its Critics. *Journal of Economic Perspectives, 17*(1), 59–82.

Mallaby, S. (2016). *The Man Who Knew: the Life and Times of Alan Greenspan.* New York: Penguin/Random House.

Mandelbrot, B. (1964). The Variation of Certain Speculative Prices. In P. Cootner (Ed.), *The Random Character of Stock Prices.* Cambridge, MA: MIT Press.

Mandelbrot, B., & Hudson, R. L. (2004). *The (Mis)Behavior of Markets: A Fractal View of Risk, Ruin, and Reward.* New York: Basic Books.

Mantegna, R. N., & Stanley, H. E. (2000). *An Introduction to Econophysics: Correlations and Complexity in Finance.* Cambridge, UK: Cambridge University Press.

Martenson, C. (2011). *The Crash Course: The Unsustainable Future of Our Economy, Energy, and Environment.* Hoboken: Wiley.

Martin, F. (2015). *Money: The Unauthorized Biography – From Coinage to Cryptocurrencies.* New York: Random House/Vintage (Paperback edition).

McCauley, J. L. (2004). *Dynamics of Markets: Econophysics and Finance.* Cambridge, UK: Cambridge University Press.

McFarland, D. (2016). *The Biological Bases of Economic Behaviour: A Concise Introduction.* New York: Palgrave Macmillan.

McGrattan, E. R., & Prescott, E. C. (2000). Is the Stock Market Overvalued? *Federal Reserve Bank of Minneapolis Quarterly Review, 24*(4), 20–40.

McGrattan, E. R., & Prescott, E. C. (2003). Testing for Stock Market Overvaluation/ Undervaluation. In Hunter et al. (2003 [2005]).

McGregor, J. (1991, December 19). China Cancels Its Red-Hot Stamp Market, But Traders Hope Crackdown Will Pass. *Wall Street Journal*.

Medio, A. (1992). *Chaotic Dynamics: Theory and Applications to Economics*. Cambridge, UK: Cambridge University Press.

Mehrling, P. (2005). *Fischer Black and the Revolutionary Idea of Finance*. Hoboken: Wiley.

Merton, R. C. (1992). *Continuous-Time Finance* (Revised ed.). Oxford, UK: Blackwell.

Mishkin, F. S., & White, E. N. (2003). Stock Market Bubbles: When Does Intervention Work? *Milken Institute Review* (Second Quarter), 5(2), 44–52.

Mitchell, H., Brown, R. L., & Easton, S. A. (2002). Old Volatility – ARCH effects in 19th Century Consol Data. *Applied Financial Economics, 12*(4), 301–307.

Nairn, A. (2001). *Engines that Move Markets: Technology Investing from Railroads to the Internet and Beyond*. Hoboken: Wiley.

Neal, L. D. (2015). *A Concise History of International Finance from Babylon to Bernanke*. Cambridge, UK: Cambridge University Press.

Nesvetailova, A. (2010). *Financial Alchemy in Crisis: The Great Liquidity Illusion*. London: Pluto Press.

Nofsinger, J. R. (2005). Social Mood and Financial Economics. *Journal of Behavioral Finance, 6*(3), 144–160.

Noguchi, Y. (1994). The 'Bubble' and Economic Policies in the 1980s. *Journal of Japanese Studies, 20*(2), 291–329.

Oates, J. (1986). *Babylon* (rev ed.). New York: Thames and Hudson.

O'Driscoll, G. P., Jr. (2007, August 10). Our Subprime Fed. *Wall Street Journal*.

Officer, R. R. (1972). The Distribution of Stock Returns. *Journal of the American Statistical Association, 67*(340), 807–812.

Oliver, M. J. (2007). Financial Crises. In M. J. Oliver & D. H. Aldcroft (Eds.), *Economic Disasters of the Twentieth Century*. Cheltenham: Elgar.

Oliver, M. J., & Aldcroft, D. H. (Eds.). (2007). *Economic Disasters of the Twentieth Century*. Cheltenham: Elgar.

Olson, K. R. (2006). A Literature Review of Social Mood. *Journal of Behavioral Finance, 7*(4).

Parks, T. (2005). *Medici Money: Banking, Metaphysics, and Art in Fifteenth Century Florence*. New York: W. W. Norton.

Pastor, L., & Veronesi, P. (2008). *Technological Revolutions and Stock Prices*. NBER Working Paper No. 11876.

Pattillo, C., Poirson, H., & Ricci, L. A. (2011). External Debt and Growth. *Review of Economics and Institutions, 2*(3), 1–30.

Perkins, A. B., & Perkins, M. C. (1999). *The Internet Bubble: Inside the Overvalued World of High-Tech Stocks – And What You Need to Know to Avoid the Coming Shakeout*. New York: Harper Business.

Pixley, J. (2012). *Emotions in Finance: Booms, Busts and Uncertainty* (2nd ed.). Cambridge, UK: Cambridge University Press.

Porras, E. R. (2016). *Bubbles and Contagion in Financial Markets, Vol 1: An Integrative View*. New York: Palgrave Macmillan.

Posen, A. S. (2003). *It Takes More than a Bubble to Be Japan*. WP 03-9, Institute for International Economics. http://www.petersoninstitute.org/publications/wp/03-9.pdf

Poterba, J., & Summers, L. H. (1988). Mean Reversion in Stock Returns: Evidence and Implications. *Journal of Financial Economics, 22.*

Poundstone, W. (2005). *Fortune's Formula: The Untold Story of the Scientific Betting System That Beat the Casinos and Wall Street.* New York: Hill and Wang/Farrar, Straus and Giroux.

Poundstone, W. (2010). *Priceless: The Myth of Fair Value.* New York: Hill and Wang (Farrar, Straus and Giroux).

Prechter, R. R., Jr. (2016). *The Socionomic Theory of Finance.* Gainesville: Socionomics Institute Press.

Rapoport, A., & Wallsten, T. S. (1972). Individual Decision Behaviour. *Annual Review of Psychology, 21.*

Rebello, J. (2005, March 7). Fed Officials Worried in 1999 About Managing Stock "Bubble'. *Wall Street Journal.*

Reinhart, C. M., & Rogoff, K. S. (2009). *This Time Is Different: Eight Centuries of Financial Folly.* Princeton: Princeton University Press.

Reinhart, C. M., Reinhart, V. R., & Rogoff, K. S. (2012). Public Debt Overhangs: Advanced-Economy Episodes since 1800. *Journal of Economic Perspectives, 26*(3), 69–86.

Rich, M., & Leonhardt, D. (2005, March 25). Trading Places: Real Estate Instead of Dot-coms. *New York Times.*

Roehner, B. M. (2002). *Patterns of Speculation: A Study in Observational Econophysics.* Cambridge, UK: Cambridge University Press.

Rostovtzeff, M. (1941). *The Social and Economic History of the Roman Empire.* Oxford: Clarendon.

Rostovtzeff, M. (1953). *The Social and Economic History of the Hellenistic World* (Vol. 1). Oxford: Oxford University Press.

Roubini, N., & Mihm, S. (2011). *Crisis Economics: A Crash Course in the Future of Finance.* New York: Penguin.

Russollio, S. (2016, December 6). Greenspan's New Worrisome Gauge. *Wall Street Journal.*

Ryan-Collins, J., Greenham, T., Werner, R., & Jackson, A. (2011). *Where Does Money Come From?: A Guide to the UK Monetary and Banking System.* London: New Economics Foundation.

Rynecki, D. (2000, April 3). Market Madness: What the Hell is Going On? *Fortune, 141*(7).

Samuels, W. J., Biddle, J. F., & Davis, J. B. (Eds.). (2007). *A Companion to the History of Economic Thought.* Oxford, UK: Blackwell.

Samuelson, P. A. (1965). Proof that Properly Anticipated Prices Fluctuate Randomly. *Industrial Management Review, 6.*

Schaede, U. (1989). Forwards and Futures in Tokugawa-period Japan: A New Perspective on the Dojima Rice Market. *Journal of Banking and Finance, 13,* 487–513.

Scheinkman, J. A., & LeBaron, B. (1989). Nonlinear Dynamics and Stock Returns. *Journal of Business, 62,* 311–337.

Schoemaker, P. J. H. (1982). The Expected Utility Model. *Journal of Economic Literature, 20,* 529–563.

Schrage, M. (2003). *Daniel Kahneman: The Thought Leader Interview. Business+Strategy.* Booz, Allen, & Hamilton and. http://ebusiness.mit.edu/schrage/Articles/DanielKahnemanInterview.pdf

Schumpeter, J. A. (1939). *Business Cycles: A Theoretical, Historical, and Statistical Analysis of the Capitalist Process.* New York: McGraw-Hill.

Schwartz, A. J. (1986). Real and Pseudo-Financial Crises. In F. H. Capie & G. E. Wood (Eds.), *The Lender of Last Resort.* London: Routledge.

Schwartz, D. G. (2006). *Roll the Bones: The History of Gambling.* New York: Gotham Books (Penguin Group).

Sharma, R. (2015a, July 7). China's Stock Plunge Is Scarier Than Greek Debt Crisis. *Wall Street Journal.*

Shiller, R. J. (2000, 2005, 2015). *Irrational Exuberance* (3nd ed.). Princeton: Princeton University Press.

Shiller, R. J. (2002, December 17). Safe as Houses? *Wall Street Journal.*

Shiller, R. J. (2006). Irrational Exuberance Revisited. In R. N. Sullivan & J. J. Diermeier (Eds.), *Global Perspectives on Investment Management.* Charlottesville: CFA Institute.

Smick, D. M. (2008). *The World Is Curved: Hidden Dangers to the Global Economy.* New York: Penguin Portfolio.

Smithers, A., & Wright, S. (2000). *Valuing Wall Street: Protecting Wealth in Turbulent Markets.* New York: McGraw-Hill.

Sorkin, A. R. (2009). *Too Big To Fail: The Inside Story of How Wall Street and Washington Fought to Save the Financial System – and Themselves.* New York: Viking.

Sornette, D. (2003). *Why Stock Markets Crash: Critical Events in Complex Financial Systems.* Princeton: Princeton University Press.

Stiglitz, J. E. (1990). Symposium on Bubbles. *Journal of Economic Perspectives, 4*(2), 13–18.

Stiglitz, J. E., & Greenwald, B. (2003). *Towards a New Paradigm in Monetary Economics.* New York: Cambridge University Press.

Stout, D. (2002, August 30). Greenspan Says Fed Could Not Prevent Market Bubble. *New York Times.*

Sullivan, R. N., & Diermeier, J. J. (Eds.). (2006). *Global Perspectives on Investment Management.* Charlottesville: CFA Institute.

Surowiecki, J. (2004). *The Wisdom of Crowds.* New York: Doubleday.

Swarup, B. (2014). *Money Mania: Booms, Panics and Busts from Ancient Rome to the Great Meltdown.* New York: Bloomsbury Press.

Sylla, R. (2001). The New Media Boom in Historical Perspective. *Prometheus, 19*(1), 17–26.

Taleb, N. N. (2004). Bleed or Blowup? Why Do We Prefer Asymmetric Payoffs? *Journal of Behavioral Finance, 5*(1).

Taleb, N. N. (2005). *Fooled by Randomness.* New York: Random House (2nd paperback edition).

Taleb, N. N. (2007). *The Black Swan.* New York: Random House.

Taylor, S. (2005). *Asset Price Dynamics, Volatility, and Prediction.* Princeton: Princeton University Press.

Thaler, R. H. (Ed.). (1992). *The Winner's Curse: Paradoxes and Anomalies of Economic Life.* Princeton: Princeton University Press.

Thaler, R. H. (Ed.). (2005). *Advances in Behavioral Finance* (Vol. II). Princeton: Princeton University Press.

Thomas, L., Jr. (2012, June 27). Spain Officials Hailed Banks as Crisis Built. *New York Times.*

Treynor, J. L. (1998). Bulls, Bears, and Market Bubbles. *Financial Analysts Journal, 54*(2), 69–74.

Triana, P. (2009). *Lecturing Birds on Flying: Can Mathematical Theories Destroy the Financial Markets?* Hoboken: Wiley.

Tuckett, D. (2011). *Minding the Markets: An Emotional Finance View of Financial Instability.* London: Palgrave Macmillan.

Vaga, T. (1994). *Profiting From Chaos: Using Chaos Theory for Market Timing, Stock Selection, and Option Valuation.* New York: McGraw-Hill.

Varchaver, N. (2008, April 28). What Warren Thinks... *Fortune, 157*(8).

Vogel, H. L. (2017). Are There Any Laws and Constants in Economics? A Brief Comparison to the Sciences. *Journal of Contemporary Management, 6*(1), 73–88.

Voth, H.-J. (2000). *A Tale of Five Bubbles – Asset Price Inflation and Central Bank Policy in Historical Perspective.* Discussion Paper 416. Canberra: Australian National University. http://econrsss.anu.edu.au

Voth, H.-J. (2003). With a Bang, Not a Whimper: Pricking Germany's 'Stock Market Bubble' in 1927 and the Slide into Depression. *Journal of Economic History, 63*(1), 65–99.

Warburton, P. (2000). *Debt and Delusion: Central Bank Follies That Threaten Economic Disaster.* London: Penguin.

Weatherall, J. O. (2013). *The Physics of Wall Street: A Brief History of Predicting the Unpredictable.* Boston: Houghton Mifflin Harcourt.

Werner, R. A. (2005). *New Paradigm in Macroeconomics: Solving the Riddle of Japanese Macroeconomic Performance.* Houndmills: Palgrave Macmillan.

West, M. D. (2000). Private Ordering at the World's First Futures Exchange. *Michigan Law Review, 98*(8), 2574–2615.

Witter, L. (2006, August 21). The No-Money-Down Disaster. *Barron's.*

Wood, C. (2005). *The Bubble Economy: Japan's Extraordinary Speculative Boom of the '80s and the Dramatic Bust of the '90s.* San Luis Obispo: Solstice/London: Sidgwick & Jackson, 1992, and New York: Atlantic Monthly Press.

Zweig, J. (2008, August 30). With Buybacks, Look Before You Leap. *Barron's.*

Zweig, J. (2015, November 14). Deciphering the Dialect: A Wall Street Glossary. *Wall Street Journal.*

CHAPTER 2

Bubble Stories

2.1 TULIPS

The relatively new and sophisticated financial structure that had evolved in the Netherlands circa 1600 enabled tulip bulbs to become the object of frenzied and rapid bidding by a *wide* range of public participants whose leveraged activities were accelerated by the introduction of forward contracts. Just prior to the mania, bulbs were not priced much above other rare plants. But then, in the 1630s, a lull in the Thirty Years' War (started 1618, ended 1648) released war-created money and credit to fuel other speculative activities. Once wealthy families began to use ownership of bulbs as a means of conveying their social status, prices of rare specimens—whose unusual flames of different petal colors were caused by a nonfatal "mosaic" virus—began to quickly rise.[1] Earlier eras might have contained bubble-like incidents or precursors, but with the appearance of notarized written contracts, fully documentable price records relating to broad public participation became available.[2]

The economic consequences of the rising interest in tulip cultivation were initially benign; growers of the 1620s had to develop new commercial and industrial skills that involved harvesting, picking, packaging, storage and security, and shipping to handle the rapidly expanding tulip trade. Prices for houses, land, horses, and other luxuries of every sort rose in value (Mackay 1841). And Amsterdam of the early seventeenth century, being the Wall Street of that time, witnessed rapid and substantive organization of banking, investment, and other related functions—none of which would have been possible without the increasing availability and use of credit bolstered by massive capital inflows from trade and commerce and seizures of Spanish vessels (probably filled with gold).[3]

Beckman (1988, p. 4) writes:

It is difficult to determine at precisely what point the desire to acquire tulips as a collector's item or status symbol was overshadowed by the greed associated with rampant speculation. What is known is that, in the time-tried fashion, greed suppressed

© The Author(s) 2018
H. L. Vogel, *Financial Market Bubbles and Crashes, Second Edition,*
https://doi.org/10.1007/978-3-319-71528-5_2

reason and the desire for amassing wealth in the tulip market of the Netherlands became the primary purpose of tulip trading....In the hands of the profiteers and promoters the tulip became a speculative vehicle...Speculation in tulips became the preoccupation of the day.

The reasons that bulbs and not some other asset class captivated the imaginations of the population are not specifically known, but it's probable that bulbs were preferred because they were more easily transferable, transportable, and financeable than other asset classes of the time.[4] The activity ultimately attracted the participation of average citizens, from farmers, seamen, and mechanics to chimney sweeps—the 1630s equivalent of the legendary shoeshine-boy tipsters on the Wall Street of the late 1920s.

After converting their properties, including real estate and jewelry to cash, people of all classes bought tulips and planted all available land with bulbs in the hope of cultivating a rare-colored specimen, perhaps a red with black dots around the center, which, according to a grading system that had developed, could then be sold for enormous premiums. The first futures and options markets were then formed as traders on the Tulip Exchanges began to recognize that they never actually had to physically acquire bulbs, but only to track the price movements of contracts that they hoped to later resell to higher bidders.

Not surprisingly, the action and the grading systems generated a need for analysts, whose function it was to estimate future values of the various tulip species. In a forerunner of the modern division between technical and fundamentalist approaches, some of the analysts (technicians) argued that the value was going to be wherever the market was trending, whereas others (fundamentalists) carefully studied petal formations, angles and lengths of stems, density of color, and so forth to make a forecast of prices.

Never, though, did it become widely conceivable during the giddy price rise and buildup of massive public demand—that is, during the tulip mania—that the long-term trend could be anything but up. By 1637, the highest price for a bulb, *Semper Augustus,* had reached 5200 guilders and compared to 120 guilders for a thousand pounds of cheese, 300 guilders for a small town house, and an average annual wage of somewhere between 200 and 400 guilders.[5]

With all of this loose, easy money sloshing around in the Dutch economy scams and frauds inevitably abounded. A big problem on farms, for example, was that of cows eating the bulbs. Hence, some brilliant promoters attempted to create a speculative market in tulip-cow milk! Manipulators would train animals such as dogs or cats to dig up tulip fields in an attempt to create scarcity, speculator pools would be formed to make it appear that a particular species was suddenly in demand, and to drive prices higher rumors of all kinds were regularly propagated. Thus the mania for bulbs became among the first and most famous—or perhaps more properly, infamous—bubble episodes ever recorded.[6]

Of course, supply eventually overwhelmed demand and prices then rapidly collapsed. And defaults by buyers unable or unwilling to pay for contracts made earlier were common, with many banks failing and many citizens left holding a few bulbs and bereft of their life savings. Although this happened nearly 400 years ago, the sequence of events readily describes the development and deflation/decay of more recent bubbles.

2.2   ENGLAND AND FRANCE, 1700S

The tulip affair, lasting only from around 1634 to a peak by early 1637, was followed some 85 years later by the equally notorious (John Law's) Mississippi Company Bubble in France—which involved conversion of French national debt into company shares—and by the adjacent South Sea Bubble in England.

South Sea Bubble

The South Sea Bubble of the early 1700s was as sophisticated as anything later seen in that it involved the shares of one of only three publicly listed companies on the early equivalent of the London Stock Exchange. The South Sea Company (SSC) was ostensibly formed around 1711 to exploit a monopoly of trade in South America, the West Coast of North America, and points westward. But it was actually a privatization designed to finance England's debts in a time of heavy government spending and already high taxes. Holders of British government securities were forced to exchange their low-risk bonds for shares in the new company, which was promoted with tales of great silver and gold mine assets in South America.

The SSC shares did not perform especially well during the first years after their introduction. But Parliament's passage of the South Sea Act in 1717 enabled the company to raise capital, and soon thereafter interest in the shares was stirred and boosted in part because there were few other convenient ways for relatively prosperous people to invest. The plan was for the Company to pay off the entire national debt, earning the spread between the previously issued high-coupon government debt that was purchased and the lower-coupon securities offered to the government in return.

By 1720 the company was authorized to issue one monetary unit of new stock for every monetary unit of national debt that it assumed, thereby positioning the inside directors of the company to profit handsomely from any further rises in share prices. These new shares were then promoted and distributed to a wider public, which, as Gleeson (1999, p. 16) explains, ultimately involved "over half a million people, equivalent to two-thirds of the entire population of the city of London at the time."

Leaks and rumors concerning South American silver mine discoveries and "informed speculation" related to easing in Spain's trade policies attracted additional share buyers, who assumed that England's cotton, woolen, and industrial goods would be profitably traded for Mexican silver and gold (even though the company actually "had barely traded in its life" and had owned barely a ship).[7] Though a few cautionary voices in Parliament spoke against the

Company, the bubble was by then inflating rapidly—in the first half of 1720 the share price had risen by more than 700%—and flotations of newly issued shares were oversubscribed.

To keep the price up, SSC directors even declared an unexpectedly large dividend before opening another subscription round. And to take advantage of the buying frenzy, several companies with similar structures were soon established. Most of the new companies formed had no substance and existed only to enrich the promoters.[8] One share prospectus was for a company that would carry on an undertaking of great advantage, but nobody would know what that was, whereas another raised one million in capital for a "wheel of perpetual motion."[9]

These fly-by-night enterprises were starting to divert capital from the SSC shares. To remedy the situation, the well-connected directors with friends in high places saw to it in 1720 that Parliament passed a Bubble Act that made it illegal for companies without a royal charter to operate and thus exist. SSC shares, which had been trading the previous year at 130, had by early July reached 1000 before quickly plummeting to 640.[10] Yet even that was merely a resting point as by autumn 1720, all attempts at propping up the stock price had failed. In a typical end-of-bubble swirl of retributions, recriminations, "cooked books" fraud, and controversy, the shares had fallen to 400, a loss of 60% in two months.[11] At the end, England's credit system and credibility were left in tatters.

This bubble's history is traced in Fig. 2.1 and is quite typical in terms of trough-to-peak price gain proportions and evolution over time as compared to other bubble episodes that are illustrated in Figs. 5.4 and 7.8 (and similarly measured in Roehner 2002, Chap. 7). Nevertheless, an important distinction between the South Sea and the Mississippi Bubbles is made by Cowles (2002, p. v), who explains that "The South Sea Company…did not have the power to increase the money supply, in order to push up its share price."

Mississippi Bubble

France too had a bubble at around the same time, with the English and French versions loosely connected by a Scottish gambler named John Law.[12] The difference was that the English version was a plain swindle, whereas the French one was on a larger scale and more politically convoluted.[13]

Law started well, introducing paper currency into the French economy. Later, despite vociferous opposition, the accomplished banker was able to persuade the French political powers to give him control over exploitation of the Louisiana Territory and the Mississippi Delta Region, where French pioneers had settled in 1699 and where large gold deposits were presumed to lie. Yet what made Law—a shrewd gambler skilled in numbers and keenly intuitive about economics—so effective and also so dangerous was that he well understood credit and banking.[14]

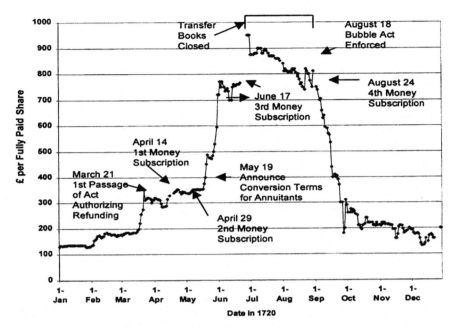

Fig. 2.1 South Sea Bubble share prices, 1720. Data compiled by Neal (1990), *The Rise of Financial Capitalism*. Reproduced with permission. See also White (1990), in which the Neal article appears. Global Financial Data, Yale School of Management Historical Financial Research Data, and Frehen et al. (2013)

As directed by Law, in 1718 the newly nationalized bank (Banque Royale) ended convertibility of paper notes to gold. As a result, the bank was limitlessly able to increase (i.e., "print") the supply of paper notes as demanded by the public's seemingly insatiable appetite for purchase of shares in the Mississippi Company (*Compagnie des Indes*). Share prices of the company doubled several times (in 1719 from 500 to 10,000 livres) as reports of huge gold deposits and potential for increased fur and tobacco trade were widely circulated. The more shares rose, the more shares were issued as publication and distribution of promotional engravings of Louisiana gold, silver, and emeralds attracted the eager participation of ordinary citizens.

> *...throughout the summer of 1719, Paris was engulfed in unprecedented speculative madness. By mid-August the shares that three months earlier had languished at 490 livres were being snapped up at 3,500. A carnival atmosphere descended on the city... Money was easy to borrow, and since you only needed put down a 10 percent deposit to play the market, people from all walks of life rushed to sell their châteaux, their diamonds, their cows, and other crops to join in...By October the share price was 6,500 livres.*[15]

On the basis of a declared dividend of 40%, hype and false promises, and a vastly expanded money supply, the share price had by 1720 climbed 40-fold from the level of three years earlier.

Still, to some of the more astute observers, it soon became evident that earnings could not possibly be large enough to sustain a dividend of such size, especially in the face of sporadic reports and rumors that the Mississippi enterprise was experiencing operating difficulties and incurring heavy losses. These concerns were then amplified by the frauds and misallocations usually seen in a bubble's aftermath. It turned out that the French government had siphoned off much of the company's capital to support itself and had actually invested little in Mississippi. Many of the shares had been purchased not with full payments of cash but with 10% down.

In an effort to stave off the impending collapse, Law printed more currency and placed restrictions on the amounts of gold and silver that citizens could legally possess. But rising demand for precious metals (i.e., hard money) continued unabated and was accompanied by emergence of a thriving black market and smuggling operations; the price of the shares tumbled from a high of 20,000 *livres* in January 1720 to 5000 *livres* five months later. The crowds of speculators who had so recently lauded John Law now hated him with a vengeance, subjecting him to insult, ridicule, and life-threatening attack, but of course never blaming themselves. By the end of that year not only the Mississippi Company but also the whole French economy had essentially collapsed.

In effect, both the South Sea and Mississippi episodes were driven by attempts in Britain and France to consolidate the huge national debts that had accumulated during the War of the Spanish Succession. The intent was to convert short-term, high-interest government debts into low-interest, long-term securities.[16] But as Neal (1990, p. 34) explains:

> It is not clear, however, that swindling and bribery were the primary elements in the bubble...a good deal of the traditional evidence on the South Sea Bubble takes on a different meaning. It appears to be less a tale about the perpetual folly of mankind and more about financial markets' difficulties in adjusting to an array of innovations.

Although France had in the end become economically much more enduringly and deeply scarred and stressed than England, for both countries, Faber's introduction to Cowles (1990, p. vii) appears to best capture the importance of these episodes:

> The saga of the Mississippi and South Sea Company is historically relevant because it contains all the major features of subsequent manias. Shady characters, corruption, fraud, dubious practices, the creation of money and the extension of risky loans in order to keep the speculative orgy going...and then the panic during which greed and euphoria is replaced by fear and the speculators' desire to get out at any price.

"What was missing from the Mississippi Bubble, in contrast to the South Sea Bubble," Goetzmann, (2016b, p. 358) says, "was the wellspring of innovation."

2.3   BRITISH RAILWAY MANIA

Travel and shipment by rail is today so common and accepted as a part of the everyday economic landscape that it is difficult to imagine that the shares of railway companies in the United Kingdom of the 1840s were swept up in a development frenzy that was comparable in scope and size to the speculative bubbles that occurred in the 150 years that followed. In the 1840s, the rapid development of rail technology—for example, steam-powered locomotives and iron tracks—was hugely revolutionary and disruptive to the economic system of the time: people and goods could now much more than ever before be easily transported and not be dependent on often-frozen canals and waterways or unpaved and rutted roads.

The stage for the great railway mania of the 1840s—preceded by a similar canal mania extending over the 40 years prior—was however actually set in 1825.[17] In that year, London Stock Exchange prices, supported by a phase of monetary expansion, peaked around when the government repealed the Bubble Act that had been passed just after the South Sea experience of 1720.[18]

This repeal not only allowed the general public to purchase shares of stock but also enabled companies to heavily and shamelessly present themselves as virtually riskless investments in the emerging media channels of the day—the newspapers, which had sprung up to cover this new industry. Promotional stock deals, some allowing investors to purchase shares with merely a 10% deposit, abounded. There was no limit on the number of railroad companies that could be created simply by submitting a Bill to Parliament without any regard for financial viability. Anyone could thus form a railroad company. Many towns—without giving a thought to physical and fiscal feasibility—clamored for their own railroads. And, unsurprisingly, members of Parliament were heavy (and obviously conflicted) early investors.

With the speculative fires lit by ease of entry, ample publicity, and wild dreams and fantasies of limitless wealth creation, middle-class families began to pour their life's savings into rail-company shares. Capital investments in these companies between 1844 and 1846 soared by around ten times before later collapsing once the Bank of England raised interest rates and, thereby, the cost of capital. By 1846, however, it had become increasingly apparent that many railroads were largely void of any assets, profits, 100 or prospects. The ensuing crash from around 1846 to 1850 carried the price index of British railway shares back to where they'd been prior to 1840 and wiped out all of the mania's gains.[19]

As is usual in the wake of a bubble and crash of this magnitude, there were numerous revelations of widespread fraud and mismanagement. But unlike in some previous bubbles, the railway mania was ultimately beneficial, helping to spur early economic growth and development of a large and sophisticated railway transportation infrastructure that was as productively useful as the later telecom bubble of the late 1990s turned out to be: Both bubbles left behind valuable and systemically important networks. And the same can be said for the Chicago land bubble of 1830 to 1841 in which prices soared (by 40,000%). Access to the Great Lakes and the Atlantic Ocean via construction of the Erie Canal system brought low-cost large-volume transportation to the upper Midwest.

2.4   THE ROARING TWENTIES

The Crash of 1929 and the Great Depression that followed were preceded by the exuberant economic expansion period known as the Roaring Twenties, an era that has already been extensively reviewed in many fine books.[20]

The 1920s, like the 1990s, were a period of rapid economic growth and introduction of new technologies. Radio became a major medium for entertainment and communications, commercial air travel began to be extended around the world, and numerous household appliances and gadgets—taking advantage of the new widespread availability of small electric motors and of the emergence of national electrification networks—were being introduced and eagerly bought by consumers earning rising real disposable incomes. Automobiles and roads also developed rapidly during these years, thereby adding many new jobs and payrolls and contributing to a surge in productivity.[21]

Figure 2.2 illustrates just how spectacular the stock market's rise was during the Roaring Twenties: from the start of 1925 to September 1929, a span of less than five years, the market more than tripled, whereas prior to its 1920 close at 72, the Dow had been range-bound for two decades.

In fact, the 1920s began inauspiciously with a sharp, painful economic slump in 1920–1922; steel output dropped by 50% and wholesale prices fell sharply.[22]

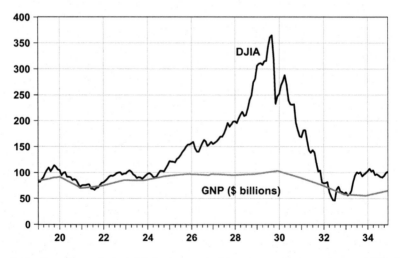

Fig. 2.2 Dow-Jones Industrial Average monthly average closing prices and US GNP in $ billions 1919–1934

A likely significant factor that led up to this was the great global influenza pandemic of 1918–1919, which infected an estimated 28% of Americans and resulted in the deaths of several hundred thousand people. The recovery in the United States, however, was by 1922 becoming forceful. Except for a mid-decade pause when home building peaked, overall growth had by decade's end extended to boom proportions. In that span, the number of automobiles owned had nearly quadrupled to 23 million, and many fortunes were made (but some also lost in the Florida land boom circa 1924).[23]

After two major hurricanes in 1926 had cooled interest in Florida real estate, attention then turned full-bore to the stock market, which came to be seen as a better game for speculators. By early 1927 many of the highly leveraged owners of property who had taken out mortgages for as little as 10% of the prevailing purchase price had—as again later happened in the 2007–2008 housing collapse—been wiped out. In both episodes, a slowing of residential real estate sales accompanied by accumulation of unrepayable debts contributed to the ultimate collapse.[24]

World War I (WWI) ended with most of Europe bankrupt and with Germany—at the time the world's second largest economy after the United States—insolvent as a consequence of the imposed reparations of the Treaty of Versailles. Germany attempted to deal with this dire situation by increasing social spending, running huge budget deficits, and also trying to inflate away its debts. But as default neared, massive amounts of capital flowed out of Europe and into the relatively safe-haven US markets, thereby further stoking the rise in equities and, in effect, importing bubble fuel.

International banking considerations related to the unfulfilled reparations obligations and loans left over from the armistice of WWI and the many confounding and conflicting attempts to maintain the gold standard then led New York Fed governor Benjamin Strong in August of 1927 to cut interest rates by 0.5 to 3.5%. It was a controversial and divisive decision, with, as Ahamed (2009, pp. 298-9) explains, "[F]our reserve banks... insisting that such a move would only fuel stock market speculation." That is indeed what happened (even though rates were raised six months later). By 1927, Ahamed (p. 502) writes, "the Fed was thus torn between two conflicting objectives: To keep propping up Europe or to control speculation on Wall Street. It tried to do both and achieved neither."

For the last third of the 1920s trading in stocks became a national obsession. "By the summer of 1929 the market not only dominated the news. It also dominated the culture," Galbraith (1988, p. 79) wrote in his classic review. And an important book of this age—analogous in timing and theme to *Dow 36,000* by Glassman and Hassett (1999a) in the later Internet episode—was *Common Stocks as Long Term Investments* by Edgar Smith (1924). That ordinary investors threw caution to the winds and faithfully and confidently invested in the "New Era," as President Calvin Coolidge had called it, can be confirmed from data showing that brokers' aggressive margin loan extensions for stock purchases rose from approximately $2.5 billion in 1926 to a peak of around

$8.5 billion in 1929. And the sky was the limit for the tech darlings of the day. The price-to-earnings (P/E) ratio for Columbia Gramophone reached 165 and for Radio Corporation of America, 73.

Just before the Great Crash began, few bearish words were heard, even though the stock market's advancing-to-declining issues ratio had begun to descend in 1928, industrial activity had already largely peaked by June of 1929, broker loan call rates had soared—the New York Fed had raised interest rates by 1% to a relatively high 6% in August—and the London market had already on September 20 begun to collapse.[25]

As in other boom periods, though, stock promoters and swindlers offering get-rich-quick schemes proliferated and frauds of all types were perpetrated. Although major banks and utility holding companies and leveraged trusts were among the participants and the ultimate casualties, it was the public that lost the most as unemployment subsequently soared and personal assets were eviscerated.

At the end, the Great Depression that began on Wall Street had been spread around the world, with bankruptcies, bank closings, and business foreclosures a common economic feature in many countries. To the people who lost their life savings and suicidally jumped from buildings, to the brokerage firms that tried to have their margin calls covered to avoid bankruptcy, and to the more than 20% of the American people unemployed in the Great Depression that followed, the losses and threats of loss were painfully real.

A variety of interpretations of causes of the Crash of 1929 have since emerged, with some even controvertibly finding that the market might not actually have been overvalued prior to the event.[26] Bernanke (1983), however, provides a plausible overview when he writes of what actually happened in the financial sector after 1929:

> ...because markets for financial claims are incomplete, intermediation between some classes of borrowers and lenders requires nontrivial market-making and information-gathering services. The disruptions of 1930–33...reduced the effectiveness of the financial sector as a whole in performing these services. As the real costs of intermediation increased, some borrowers (especially households, farmers, and small firms) found credit to be expensive and difficult to obtain. The effects of this credit squeeze on aggregate demand helped convert the severe but not unprecedented downturn of 1929–30 into a protracted depression...money was easy for a few safe borrowers, but difficult for everyone else.

2.5   JAPAN 1989

The Japanese economy, in 1989 the second largest in the world, began to overheat in the mid-1980s (Table 2.1) as one export market after another was conquered by sophisticated marketing and production of good-quality, technologically based products that belied the earlier post-WWII image that "made in Japan" meant "cheap and shoddy." With few natural resources of its own and a domestic market that was limited in size, Japan became the chief

Table 2.1   Trends in Japanese GDP and stock and land value assets, 1981–1992

FY	GDP (¥ trillion)	Interest rate[a] (%)	Asset value[b] (¥ trillion)		Ratio to GDP × interest rate	
			Stock	Land	Stock	Land
1981	261	8.34	81	128	2.572	4.089
1982	273	8.24	91	135	2.747	4.082
1983	286	7.71	107	139	2.885	3.760
1984	305	7.17	138	149	3.232	3.494
1985	324	6.09	169	176	3.177	3.308
1986	338	5.14	230	280	3.498	4.260
1987	354	4.90	301	449	4.166	6.217
1988	377	4.96	394	529	5.184	6.961
1989	403	5.63	527	521	7.362	7.272
1990	434	6.91	478	517	7.611	8.235
1991	457	5.49	373	504	4.475	6.058
1992	465	5.54	297	428	3.400	4.900

Notes

[a]Interest rate is yield on long-term national bonds

[b]Stock value is the total market value of stocks listed in the Tokyo Stock Exchange (the first section). Land value is total residential land value in Tokyo (National Account Statistics data)

Source: Originally published in Noguchi (1994, p. 292). Reprinted with permission

consumer products exporter to the world. Its interlocking banks and industrial companies, the *keiretsu*, all owned shares in others' enterprises (Table 2.2) and as a group seemed invincible.

The Japanese, who had also come to control the largest global banks as measured by assets, appeared as though they would soon own the world—gobbling up at high prices famous European works of art (e.g., $90 million for Van Gogh's *Portrait of Dr. Guichet*), American entertainment companies such as Columbia Pictures and CBS Records, swank golf resorts such as Pebble Beach, and trophy office buildings in major cities on every continent.

As shown in Fig. 2.4, Japanese stock market capitalization as a percentage of GDP far outpaced economic growth, soaring from around 40% in 1975 to 150% at the end of the 1980s. In terms of points gained (Fig. 1.7), the Nikkei 225 Index tripled between 1985 and the peak at the end of 1989. And by then, "the Japanese stock market had a value of about $4 trillion, which was about 44 percent of the world's equity market capitalization (compared to 15 percent in 1980). To put that in perspective, the value of the equity on all the stock exchanges in the United States in August 1992 was less than $5 trillion."[27]

Similar inflation was also seen in Japanese and Tokyo real estate prices, where at the height of the frenzy, the few square blocks occupied by the Imperial Palace at the center of Tokyo had an imputed value equivalent to that of all the land in California or all of Canada. It was also estimated that a *square meter* in Tokyo's exclusive Ginza district was valued at $330,000.[28]

Table 2.2 Funds raised and used by nonfinancial corporations, net, billion ¥, 1980–1990

	Funds raised			Use of funds raised	
	Borrowing from banks	Equity and bond issues	Other	Net increase in financial assets	Other
1980	13,602.0	4332.1	7049.5	12,343.6	12,640.0
1981	16,497.9	6210.2	10,106.3	20,966.9	11,847.5
1982	17,380.3	6063.9	8240.2	15,657.9	16,026.5
1983	18,085.0	4750.1	6117.2	16,016.7	12,935.6
1984	20,672.8	7074.3	13,700.6	27,135.2	14,312.5
1985	25,157.7	7787.8	3546.0	23,553.2	12,938.3
1986	26,611.7	9135.9	−6339.9	17,126.1	12,281.6
1987	25,868.2	12,632.8	42,971.0	59,045.8	22,426.2
1988	29,989.2	19,414.7	27,063.4	53,412.0	23,055.3
1989	37,484.5	15,638.8	31,872.5	39,729.5	47,266.3
1990	39,484.5	15,638.8	31,872,3	39,729.5	47,266.3
Total	185,088.6	90,891.9	129,692.5	257,790.7	147,982.3

Source: Originally published in Noguchi (1994, p. 294) and Economic Planning Agency (1992). Reprinted with permission

Actively traded single golf course membership prices – meanwhile reflecting not enthusiastic access to the game but to the amount of land covered by the course – had soared to US$8 million each. And given that land prices across Japan had quadrupled and the home-price-to-income ratio had risen to 18.1 in under ten years, it was possible for some analysts to extrapolate that by 1991 Japan's total real estate was worth nearly $20 trillion – "more than 20 percent of the world's wealth... at about five times that of the United States."[29]

Energized by a peaking of a baby-boom spending cycle (circa 1989) and easy money and credit availability linked to a Bank of Japan export-encouraging strategy, ordinary citizens using margin piled into stocks, giving little consideration to high valuations.[30] Japan's market capitalization as a percent of world market capitalization in 1989 rose to a high of around 45%. Meanwhile, bearish commentary was scarce and the prevailing attitude was that "Western valuation methods did not apply in Tokyo."[31]

Indeed, the world media were filled with stories about how the unique, cohesive nature of Japanese culture and society and rising technical productivity implied that permanently higher valuations were not only justifiable but also ensured. After all, the Japanese automobile industry, renowned for its purposeful attention to detail and organizational structure, had already beaten the lugubrious American car makers to a pulp in terms of both "fit and finish" of their products as well as in the comparative profitability of each unit produced.

It was also widely assumed to be only a matter of time before Japan would— just as they already had earlier done in steel and shipbuilding—completely overtake the United States in chips and microprocessors, supercomputers, and digital televisions. The Japanese, it seemed, were even buying up all of Hawaii,

winning possession of Hawaii's most luxurious resorts and hotels. Their sophisticated electronic exports were in high demand everywhere and their cartels
were able to take advantage of the relatively much more open free trade policies
abroad than at home.[32]

It would thus have been easy to conclude, from watching all of this har-
ried—bordering on hysterical—activity, that Japan's economy was growing by
leaps and bounds. But, in fact, the country's average annual real GDP from
1975 to 1989 actually grew only by around 4% as compared to 9.4% from
1955 to 1973. And even this 4% was undoubtedly enhanced in Japan and elsewhere by the sharp (>50%) decline in the inflation-adjusted price of oil between
1980 and the early 1990s.[33]

Stock and land asset values as related to Japanese GDP are shown in Tables
2.1 and 2.2 and reveal the large step-up in borrowing from banks and in issuance of debt and equity securities by Japanese corporations from 1985 to
1990.[34] As Werner (2003) convincingly demonstrates, this steep, virtually
unrestrained, and premeditated increase in lending by banks for speculative
purchases was amply abetted by secretive Bank of Japan "window guidance"
(i.e., credit creation and allocation) policies that were willfully promulgated by
a small group of individuals at the top.[35]

The merrymaking was soon thereafter ended with a contraction of credit
availability, especially for the aggressive bank real estate lending activities that
had propelled the steep rise of Japanese land prices.[36] Once credit availability
began to shrink—in part related to implementation of the Basel I accord of
1988 which tightened bank capital adequacy ratios—aggressive stock market
speculators who had bought heavily on margin began to experience crushing,
obliterating losses.[37] At the same time, it was also finally recognized that government, corporate, and banking debts were overwhelmingly disproportionate
to earnings potential (although the political will to break up the cozy *keiretsu*
arrangements and to write off the mass of bad loans was still absent).[38]

By the end, the losses incurred were so large in relation to capital that the
banks became wards of the state. The overwhelming motivation to hide toxic
debts then led generally to an environment in which the existence of zombie
banks and companies was tolerated even while otherwise healthy companies
were starved of loans needed for survival.[39]

The relative price performance of the Nikkei 225 versus the S&P 500 and
the Dow-Jones Industrial Average (DJIA) from 1984 to 1990 is depicted in
Fig. 2.3. The Nikkei's huge run-up of the 1980s is clearly visible here. However,
even 13 years after it had topped—after interest rates of near zero for an
extended period, heavy government spending on public construction projects,
and several bouts of recession and weak growth—the Japanese stock market
still traded at only a fraction of where it had peaked: The Nikkei was approximately 8700 in December of 2002 (and at around 8% of total world market
capitalization) as compared to nearly 40,000 in December of 1989.[40] The
1990s came to be known as *ushinawareta junen*—The Lost Decade. The DJIA
and S&P 500 indexes, meanwhile, climbed to new highs.

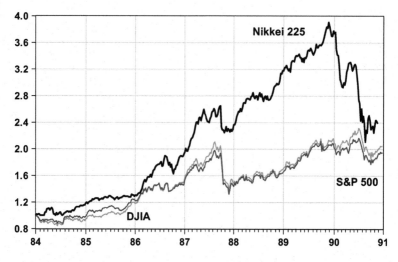

Fig. 2.3 Nikkei 225 versus S&P 500 and Dow-Jones Industrial Average normalized weekly prices, 1984–1990 (see also Ziemba and Schwartz (1991, p. 186) for a similar chart going back further and Loeys and Panigirtzoglou (2006), who illustrate five-year real price returns for Japan's Topix and for the S&P 500. The five-year real price return on the S&P 500 from 1905 to 2006 had never exceeded 30%, whereas the Topix slightly exceeded this return in the late 1980s)

Another perspective consistent with earlier Fig. 1.4, is also provided by market capitalization as a percent of GDP. This ratio is the broadest and among the simplest indicators of valuation exuberance. And it shows that Japan's market cap peaked at nearly 150% of GDP and at that time far above the ratio for the United States at that time (Fig. 2.4).

That the Japanese real estate bubble of the 1980s largely coincided with that of the Tokyo stock market can then be seen in Fig. 2.5. Land prices peaked a year after stocks and subsequently continued to slide for another 15 years or so.

2.6   Tech/Internet Stocks, 1987 and 2000

The time was August 1982 and the stock market indexes as measured by the Dow-Jones Industrials and the S&P 500 were marking new lows at 777 and 102, respectively. A busy day on the NYSE would see 60 million shares traded (versus two billion 20 years later). The back-to-back recessions of the early 1980s were just ending; Fed Chairman Paul Volcker had in the previous two years used double-digit interest rates to wring inflation down from an average annual rate above 13% in 1980 over 1979 to around 3% for 1983 over 1982. The bond market had already bottomed after sliding for more than three decades.

In addition, the personal computer, introduced circa 1975 in the form of a kit (the Altair), had finally been developed to the point where ordinary people,

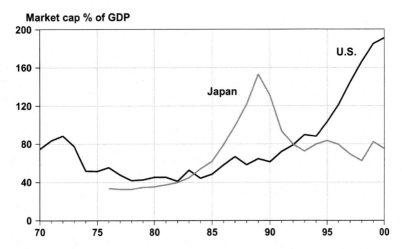

Fig. 2.4 Total stock market value (capitalization) as a percent of respective GDP, United States (NYSE, AMEX, and NASDAQ) and Japan (TSE, all section listings) 1970–2000. (Data sources: US Department of Commerce, *World Stock Exchange Fact Book*, 2004, Bank of Japan, University of Hong Kong. See also Hall (2001). The Wilshire 5000 calculation of Fig. 1.4 shows the same timing and directional progression but a lower peak)

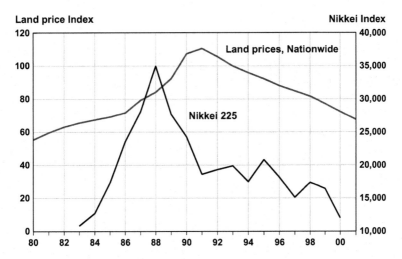

Fig. 2.5 Japanese real estate price indices, 1990 = 100, all national, 1980–2001 and semi-annual average for Nikkei 225 index. Tokyo prices (not shown) roughly tripled between 1985 and 1988 (see also Ziemba and Schwartz (1991, p. 189) for 1955–1990 commercial land price index). (Sources: Siebert (1999, p. 9); also, Japan Real Estate Institute, Bloomberg Index series, JPNLPTALL and JNLPTRES, and Datastream)

not solely hobbyists, began to find uses for it in playing primitive games and adopting the first VisiCalc spreadsheets. Just the year before, in 1981, it had been a major news event when IBM introduced its first personal computer product, effectively endorsing the technology. But although the technical theories and implementations of large-scale communications networks had already been developing for 20 years, nothing resembling the Internet as we know it today was then conceivable.[41]

The earlier mini-boom in tech stocks—ignited by the introduction of personal computer products from IBM and Apple as based on new microprocessor and memory-storage chips developed by Intel—soon fizzled. By 1984—the year of the famous anti-Big Brother (i.e., anti-IBM) television commercial that had been produced by Apple and shown at that year's Super Bowl broadcast—investors and speculators alike had begun to shun tech shares even though unit sales of personal computers had already multiplied by 20-fold in five years to 15 million annually. Overcapacity in chip production had led to severe price cuts and rapidly declining revenues and profits.

However, with the bond market spurting to new highs, interest in stocks had by 1986 generally returned. The US long-bond (8%) futures easily broke through par (100) and reached prices not seen in more than a generation. By 1987 confidence had risen to the point that the S&P 500 had more than tripled from its 1982 closing low of 102.42 to 336.77 (closing on August 25, 1987). The Dow-Jones Industrials had meanwhile topped at 2722.42 (closing price on August 25, 1987) as compared to the 776.92 closing low just five years before on August 12, 1982.

For institutional investors, confidence was further bolstered by the widespread use of what came to be known as "portfolio insurance," peddled by advisory firms as a way to insulate portfolios from serious loss using a strategy of selling (shorting) proportionately more and more futures positions as the markets declined. Individuals too were again being attracted to the technology sector as Microsoft's highly successful launch as a public company just the year before heralded the start of an era in which millions of personal computers would be sold as far into the future as anyone could see.

But for reasons not yet fully understood the market couldn't hold onto its gains. The ensuing crash of 1987 culminated on October 19—on a then all-time record trading volume of 604.3 million shares—with a one-day decline in the Dow-Jones Industrials of 508.32 points (22.6%) that percentagewise was almost twice the 11.7% drop of October 29, 1929. Declines of comparable magnitudes were also seen around the same time in other important stock markets: As measured in local currency units, drops ranged from 11.4% in Austria to 45.8% in Hong Kong, where the market was thereafter shut for a week. The FTSE-100 Index lost 10.8% on that day and another 12.2% the following day.[42]

Jacobs (1999, pp. 183–202) explains the event as follows:

> [S]ynthetic portfolio insurance in 1987 performed a role similar to that played by margin speculation in the crash of 1929. Just as margin buying elevated the bull

*market of the 1920s, portfolio insurance increased demand for stocks in the 1982–7
period. And just as the automatic, trend-following stock sales of portfolio insurers
exacerbated the 1987 crash, so the trend-following stock sales forced by margin calls
accentuated the decline in stock prices in 1929...In the wake of the crash, portfolio
insurance vendors blamed... – everything but the strategy itself...During the crash,
transaction costs skyrocketed. Liquidity dried up...Portfolio insurance failed just
when it was most needed.*

And Henriques (2017, p. 3) characterizes the event as one in which Wall
Street players:

*...became far more homogenized, subscribing confidently to academic theories that
led giant herds of investors to pursue the same strategies at the same time with vast
amounts of money...It is not an overstatement to say that Black Monday was the first
modern crash, the first to spotlight...fundamentally new risks.*

The losses in the Dow-Jones Industrials and the FTSE-100 are illustrated in
Fig. 2.6.

Yet much to the surprise of almost everyone, the market's sudden plunge
did not foreshadow or lead to any serious problems in the real economy: The
DJIA, crash and all, nevertheless actually ended 1987 slightly higher than
where that year had begun (with real GDP gaining 3.4% in 1987 and another
4.1% in 1988).

The market turbulence of 1987 thus only briefly interrupted the rise in tech
sector share prices. With the 1989 fall of the Berlin Wall and the presumed end
of the Cold War in sight, investors began to talk of a "peace dividend" in which
defense spending would significantly decline as a percentage of GDP and
thereby liberate and redirect capital for uses in the civilian sectors.

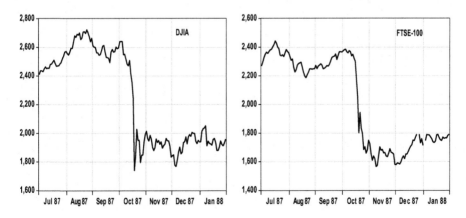

Fig. 2.6 The October 1987 crash illustrated for DJIA (left) and FTSE-100, July 1987
through January 1988, daily

In retrospect, the Gulf War period of 1990–1991 was merely another pause in the climb to higher valuations: The first mid-January 1991 night (January 14) that the United States began to attack Iraqi command and control centers was the first night that a massive rally in stocks and bonds began. By the end of 1991, the DJIA was pushing toward new all-time highs near 3200. Only two years later, it had reached 4000. And, thanks to the invention of browser software, the Internet was starting to become commercially useful and to fire up the imaginations of investors everywhere. The following summarizes key technology events.[43]

1975	First PCs on sale	1993	Mosaic browser released
1978	Apple II introduced	1995	Netscape IPO
1981	IBM unveils its first PC	1997	Amazon.com IPO
1986	Microsoft IPO	1999	Priceline.com IPO
1991	World Wide Web created	2000	NASDAQ tops 5000

Still, there can be no doubt that passage by the US Congress of the Telecom Act of 1996, which was presumed at the time to be highly deregulatory, was important: It unleashed, and seemed to justify, the spending of countless hundreds of billions of dollars on telecom and cable investments, many later seen to be of dubious merit. And it led to unprecedented spending on Internet-related advertising in all media. *The Standard*, now defunct but at the time one of the top magazines of this genre, in the year 2000 sold 7400-plus ad pages, more than any magazine in US history; a typical issue had the heft and size of a small-city phone directory.

Fund management companies meanwhile began to merge into much larger units, each time diminishing the diversity not only of opinion but also of portfolio and fund management structures.[44] Emphasis within brokerages also turned more toward rewarding sales, promotional, marketing, political, conference-organizing, and investment-banking skills than toward provision of insightful, penetrating analysis that might disagree with mainstream views.[45]

Fund managers, moreover, generally failed to recognize that earnings growth projections in support of higher future prices were largely a function of the bubble itself. And analysts would hardly ever look beyond their customary comparisons of stocks and bonds on the basis of relative (e.g., yield spreads) rather than absolute values. A stock would be labeled as "undervalued" if its various metrics fell below those of a similar company; for instance, a price-to-earnings ratio of 50 would appear inexpensive compared to one of 70. Meanwhile, the whole equity market's valuation was itself aligned with and derived from comparisons to a bond market then in the midst of its own liquidity-driven bubble.

In March 1999, AOL "with a stock market capitalization of US$140 billion was worth more than Walt Disney, Viacom and CBS combined, and well over twice as much as General Motors." The ten largest market cap stocks of the S&P 500 were in early 2000 trading at a p/e ratio—more accurately, a price-tofantasy ratio – of 62.6.[46]

Such inflated values relative to historical norms appeared in other major markets too. In London, just around the peak, several high-admission-price conferences and courses promised to instruct investors on how to account for the differences between conventional and new valuation-model results. Terra Networks, a spin-off of Spain's Telefonica, sported a capitalization of €25 billion despite an absence of profits. Share prices would soar by just adding dot-com (or an e or I) to the name of a tired, old company or by reporting financially irrelevant data (e.g., number of web-page views).[47] Hong Kong police were required to control crowds applying for the vastly (many hundreds of times) oversubscribed IPO of an Internet company with almost no revenues, no profits, and a website still under construction.[48]

At the time it was indeed not unusual for companies with virtually no *revenues* to be valued at billions of dollars. Unlike the situation in the classical model of perfect competition in which abnormally high profits attract new entrants, in the TMT (telecom, media, technology) bubble new entrants appeared even though there were no profits to begin with.[49] Here, the catch phrase leading to a successful fund-raising campaign was "burn rate." This supposed indicator of potential future growth suggested the speed at which a new enterprise was burning through its initial capital and depleting cash—the higher the rate, the higher the valuation—rather than as a metric of time-to-bankruptcy, the normal and correct interpretation. Such a flight *from* quality in the bubble phase is, of course, the ironically opposite extreme of the frantic flight *toward* quality (and liquidity) that's always seen in crashes.

By the peak, the bull market in tech stocks had taken the NASDAQ to an unprecedented price-earnings multiple of 245 as compared to a range of 15–30 for most of the NASDAQ's existence since 1971. In the aggregate, Internet shares traded at an average of around 35 times *revenues*.[50] The S&P 500 meanwhile rose above 35 times earnings—more than twice its long-run average.

Yet rather than throttling back the frenzy with tighter credit policy, the Fed – in response to widespread "Y2K" concerns that the nation's older computer system codes would catastrophically malfunction once the calendar turned into the new century year of 2000 – actually moved in the opposite direction. The Fed expanded the monetary base by 8.7% (a 17.4% annual rate) in the half year between the end of June 1999 and the start of January 2000.

All of this allowed telecom companies to raise trillions of dollars, with which they rushed to build expansive and expensive networks composed of millions of miles of fiber-optic cables buried under city streets and seas. The resulting capacity glut, wherein under 3% of the installed fiber was used as of 2002, quickly sent bandwidth prices down by an average of more than 65% and eventually led to the bankruptcies and massive scandals of companies such as WorldCom, Enron, Global Crossing, and Qwest.[51]

The heights achieved by high-tech and telecom stocks as reflected primarily in the NASDAQ 100 Index as compared to the overall NASDAQ Composite Index and the S&P 500 Index are displayed in Fig. 2.7. As the three lines are all indexed (first week of 1995 = 1.0), it can be seen that at the

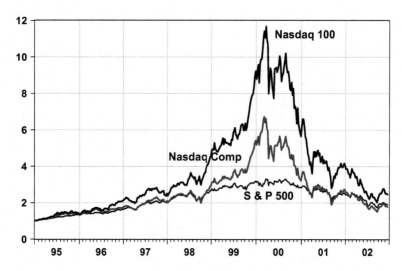

Fig. 2.7 NASDAQ 100, NASDAQ Composite, and S&P 500 indexed weekly (first week of 1995 = 1.0), January 1995 to December 2002. (Source data: Yahoo Finance)

subsequent peak, the NASDAQ 100 rose by nearly twelve times, the NASDAQ Composite by around six times, and the S&P 500 by approximately three times.

This chart also helps to illustrate an intensity measure that broadly enables comparisons of all bubbles and corresponds to the crash intensity metric that is later developed (Sect. 3.3). As shown by Dent and Panchioli (2017, pp. 182-192), the origin of the bubble is the point in time at which a linear upward trend begins to accelerate onto an exponential trajectory, For the NASDAQ 100 that would be mid-1996 when trading around 635 and rising to completion after 3.75 years to a March 2000 peak at 4,398. Here, the peak-to-origin index ratio – i. e., its intensity – was approximately 6.9, which compares to the later housing bubble's ratio of 4.3 as measured from mid-2002 at around 300 to an early 2005 peak at 1,300 (Fig. 2.9) and to a 1920s DJIA ratio of around 4.0. Subsequent crashes then almost always return prices close to the bubble origin's linearlly extrapolated trendline, which is at price levels near to where the bubble began. Although many such events play out over a period of six or seven years, the downside phase will typically last around half the time that was expended in the preceding rise and end in collapse.

The severe pressure for professional investors to participate is reflected in the sector concentration displayed in Fig. 2.8. A comparison of the infotech and later housing bubbles then later appears in Fig. 2.9.

Evidently, the degree of the market portfolio's diversification is not stable over time. And because of this, in a bubble episode, the market portfolio's ability to reduce exposure to firm-specific risk is markedly diminished. "The greatest benefits in risk reduction," as Merton (1992, p. 31) has observed, "come from adding a security to the portfolio whose realized return tends to be higher

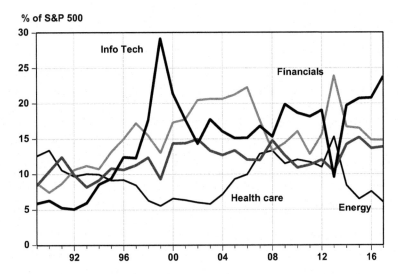

Fig. 2.8 Industry sector concentration (year-end) in the S&P 500, sector percent of total market value of S&P 500, 1989–2017. Note that an 11th sector for real estate was carved out from financials in 2016. (Source data: Standard and Poor's)

when the return on the rest of the portfolio is lower." That does not apparently happen in the real world of a major index like the S&P where—particularly in crashes—directional correlations of index components tend toward 1.0 (Fig. 3.3). Often there is more risk for the same expected return or, equivalently, a lower return for taking the same risk.

As the TMT bubble illustrates, at a top most participants will actively ignore or ridicule "prudent" professionals proffering historical knowledge and wisdom. Cautionary advice is considered to be worthless and detrimental to current-period performance: Naysayers are not at all heeded, let alone tolerated. And in going against the grain of a bubble by moving to cash or short-selling, "[E]arly looks a lot like wrong."[52]

Most participants must thus by necessity either be oblivious to a bubble's existence or be unable to resist participation as bubble-riding comes increasingly to be seen as a viable and rational investing strategy.[53] As a leading technology investor noted at the time, "You either participate in this mania, or you go out of business. It's a matter of self-preservation."[54]

By comparison to the previous periods, 1995–2000 was remarkable in terms of price gains, dividend yield declines, and total returns. Indeed, none of the other listed periods came close to what—even with major financial crises included—occurred in the last six years of the 1990s. Stock market capitalization as a percentage of nominal GDP, as displayed in Fig. 1.4, clearly showed that prior to 1997 (and even going back to 1929), this ratio had not been above 100%.

2.7   HOUSING, CREDIT, AND COMMODITIES, 2002–2008

Housing and Credit

Housing markets are usually analyzed somewhat differently than those for readily tradable shares or bonds. That is because housing transactions involve relatively large individual transactions, low liquidity and/or infrequency of trading, and absence of portability (i.e., immobility) of the underlying assets. However, given that housing is a major asset class in which a worldwide bubble ultimately involved trillions of dollars more than even in preceding the tech stock episode, it is instructive to briefly review its history. (The IMF estimated that in the aftermath global GDP declined 1.5% in 2009.)

The basic underlying forces here (i.e., expansive credit followed by contraction) were the same as always. Only with housing there was a much greater apparent impact on overall consumption patterns and prices: Swarms of unqualified but credit-crazed borrowers ended up buying vastly overvalued homes.[55]

The centrality of real estate-related lending to macroeconomic activity and the inherent systemic fragility that this entails is why, when housing bubbles burst, the ensuing damage is so great. Indeed, mortgage lending against the collateral value of a private home or commercial property is especially attractive to banks and other lenders because the value will normally be much more easily appraised than in most other asset classes (including capital investments for business enterprises).

Moreover, because asset values in economic expansions practically by definition tend to rise, the outstanding mortgage loans usually become much more serviceable and collateralizable and thus of diminishing risk to lenders. In expansions, any defaults on real property debts also will then be much more readily handled via refinancings, foreclosures, and resales.[56]

The starting date for the main upleg of this event was late 2001, just after the tragic terrorist attacks of September 11 of that year. The collapse of the Internet stock bubble and the economic sluggishness that followed led the Federal Reserve Board of Governors under Chairman Greenspan to drop the target Fed funds rate to a low of 1% (June 2003) from a high plateau of 6.5% (May 2000 to January 2001).[57] The banking system responded in turn by aggressively marketing and extending on relatively easy terms loans of all types, including those for automobiles and credit cards.

Some of the greatest efforts were focused on providing mortgages to the previously untapped and far-from-creditworthy borrowers in the subprime market—that is, to those with no income, no jobs, and no assets (which were known as NINA, NINJA, or no-doc loans).[58] Support for this came implicitly from politicians of all types and stripes and also from the *American Dream Downpayment Act* passed by the US Congress in 2003 for the purpose of creating a program that would make it easier for the poor to secure first mortgages. As a result, nearly half of mortgage originations in 2004–06 were of the default-prone adjustable-rate (ARM) type.[59] For at least over the short term, the lending industry found such loans to initially be quite profitable.

At the same time, a host of what become known as structured finance products, including collateralized debt obligations (CDOs), collateralized loan obligations (CLOs), credit default swaps (CDS), constant-proportion debt obligations (CPDOs), asset-backed commercial paper conduits (ABCPs), and other such hybrid and derivative mortgage-backed securities (MBS), began to be widely distributed in markets around the world.[60] Yet hardly a month went by without another new variant being concocted by Wall Street's "quants." Examples included CDO²s and even CDO³s—that is, CDOs composed of other CDOs—all of which, of course, compounded their ultimate toxicity.[61] Highly leveraged banking institutions and major private equity and hedge funds were eager participants, often massively packaging and both buying and selling on a large scale.[62]

The relatively generous yields promised on supposedly highly rated securities (by agencies such as Moody's, Fitch, and S&P) and the fees for distribution and packagings were too great to ignore. Managers took it for granted that their slicing and dicing of these securities into risk tranches—the lowest of which would supposedly be contained or quarantined in case of trouble—would keep them safe and sound., with such issues illogically, irresponsibly, and incongruously actually deemed to be safer than the loans on which they were based. But how could that be? Value-at-Risk (VaR) calculations—largely based on assumptions of a normal return distribution, stable price correlations, constant volatility, and low covariance of the tranches—told the bankers and buyers that it was so.[63]

As the sector's activities expanded—and as banks and brokerages no longer seemed to have had any particular need or obligation to investigate the creditworthiness of housing-related borrowers—the packagers and distributors increasingly functioned more as intermediaries than principals. After all, they were only passing loan repayments through to the ultimate buyers of such collateralized securities (and could stockpile any such as yet unsold assets in off-balance sheet accounts through what are called conduits and structured investment vehicles (SIVs)).[64]

In this feverish environment, professional risk managers who counseled caution lost their jobs because, as in one famous incident, they were not taking *enough* risk.[65] That many of the underlying loans were being made on the basis of highly inflated asset prices to a segment of the population (i.e., subprime) that would have never qualified for such mortgages or conventional loans in the old days was now not a concern; lenders and investors figured that in case of default, the worth of the house would always exceed the worth of the loan.[66] Banks could thus provide all sorts of exotic mortgages with new features and names (e.g., hybrid, no-doc, interest-only, negative amortization, balloon, and option ARMs) without worry about being repaid because they could immediately sell them into the secondary market.[67] The only thing anyone had to "know" was that housing prices would never decline.

As a result, it was not unusual to see crowds and bidding frenzies whenever blocks of new housing units were opened for public sale. Many of these most aggressive buyers never intended to actually reside in the units; they were leveraged speculators taking advantage of easy credit and regulatory conditions and buying only with the intention of quickly flipping them to someone else at a higher price. For a number of years, this was a high-probability bet. Meanwhile, major builders also continued to accumulate large inventories of undeveloped lots, sometimes buying outright or at other times using options.

These bullish elements were directly reflected in homebuilder shares which, as shown in Fig. 2.9, began a parabolic/exponential rise around the same time (2000) that other sectors were correcting excesses of the preceding TMT bubble and were thereby pulling the S&P and NASDAQ averages lower. In the span of six years, this S&P Homebuilders Index rose nearly tenfold, whereas the broader market averages only approximately doubled off of their lows.

The price bubble is also obvious in Fig. 2.10, where the large departure of real US home prices above long-term trends can be readily seen. How people (also in the United Kingdom) binged on debt, buying new homes (and other things) that they could afford less and less relative to their total financial obligations and incomes, then appears in Fig. 2.11.[69] As is evident from visual inspection alone, price changes on the upswing traced an exponential pattern and appeared to be attracted onto a trajectory that was notably different from what had come before.

In some communities it seemed as though every other neighbor had as a sideline become a licensed property sales agent. At the same time, many accounts of how ordinary people were getting rich in real estate appeared in the popular press. Accompanying this was a barrage of ads on radio, television, and

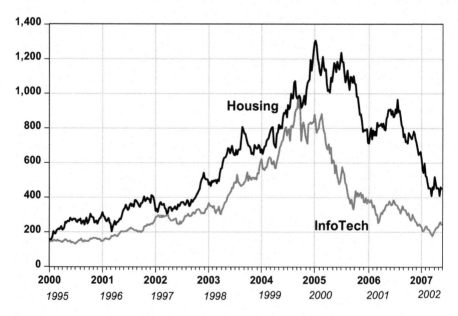

Fig. 2.9 S&P Homebuilder's Index, 2000–2007 versus S&P Information Technology Index 1995–2002, weekly. (Source: S&P, Bloomberg, S5Home<index> and S5 INFT<index>. Notice the characteristic shape of the bubbles and their subsequent collapse)[68]

the Internet promoting easy-to-get mortgage financings or refinancings, including home equity lines-of-credit (HELOCs).

Refinancing on existing properties rose to such heights that many owners came to use their homes as automatic teller machines, converting their rising net equity into cash for expensive cars, boats, vacations, restaurant meals, and other previously unaffordable luxuries. Few, though, paid any attention to the warning signs, which were already rather well known and disseminated in written commentary by many of the analysts and academics who regularly study pricing in this sector.[70] Participants were more likely to appreciate the views of those who were skeptical of or denied that a housing bubble even existed."[71]

The expansionary phase then extended generally through late 2006, with the great lending excesses of the previous years and the ensuing credit contractions becoming by Q3 2007 painfully apparent in all the related markets (though market analysts had, as usual, been optimistic only a few weeks earlier).[72] Credit spreads (above Treasury securities) widened dramatically and several CDO-laden hedge funds required massive infusions of life-supporting cash or were altogether collapsed and shuttered. Risk was everywhere being rapidly repriced. And as the extent of the overvaluations was being recognized, credit markets around the world began to seize up and become dangerously dysfunctional. The most exotic and untradeable securities were, as a result, marked to "make-believe."[73]

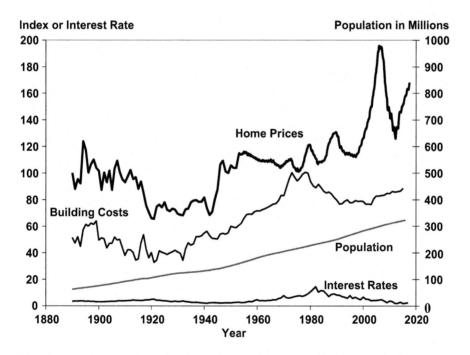

Fig. 2.10 Long-term trends of population, long rates, building costs, and home prices, annual, 1890–2016. (Source data: Shiller's website, available at www.irrationalexcuberance.com. [Similar chart also appears in Shiller's *Irrational Exuberance*, third ed. (2015)])

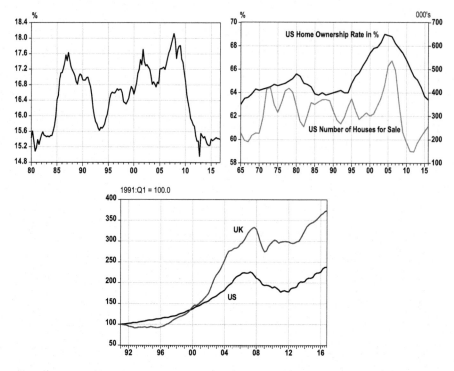

Fig. 2.11 Total household financial obligations as a percentage of disposable personal income, the financial obligations ratio (FOR), quarterly 1980:Q1 to 2016:Q4, left panel; new home sales in 000s and home ownership rates in percent, annual, 1965–2016 (right); US and UK housing price index, quarterly, 1991 = 100, 1991:Q1 to 2016:Q4 (lower). (Sources: Federal Reserve Board, available at https://fred.stlouisfed.org/series/FODSP; US Department of Housing and Urban Development, available at https://www.huduser.gov/portal/ushmc/hs_exh.html, https://www.census.gov/construction/nrs/historical_data/index.html; US Census Bureau, available at www.census.gov/hhes/www/housing/hvs/qtr406/q406tab5.htm, https://www.fhfa.gov/DataTools/Downloads/Pages/House-Price-Index-Datasets.aspx#qpo; and Nationwide Building Society, UK, available at www.nationwide.co.uk/about/house-price-index/download-data#xtab:regional-quarterly-series-all-properties-data-available-from-1973-onwards)

By early 2008, it had become clear that worldwide balance sheet write-offs collectively totaling at least $600 billion in the United States and $1 trillion globally would ultimately need to be taken. Housing foreclosures and payment delinquencies also reached unprecedented levels, stock markets declined significantly, the dollar foreign exchange rate suffered prolonged weakness, and the economy wobbled toward recession—one which turned out to be of greater than average duration (Fig. 2.12 and Table 2.3). Sales of new cars plummeted and consumer credit card debt defaults rose. And yet, even in the face of declining demand, home prices proved to be "sticky" as owners could

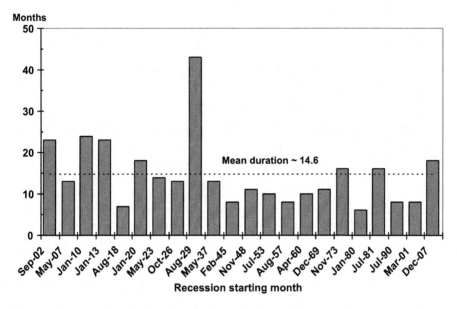

Fig. 2.12 Recession lengths in the United States from monthly starting dates, 1900–2009

Table 2.3 Economic recession dates in the United States, 1969–2009

Start	Sample #	End	Sample #	Length in months
Dec-69	89	Nov-70	100	11
Nov-73	136	Mar-75	152	16
Jan-80	210	Jul-80	216	6
Jul-81	228	Nov-82	244	16
Jul-90	336	Mar-91	344	8
Mar-01	463	Nov-01	471	8
Dec-07	545	Jun-09	563	18

	Contraction	Expansion	Cycle	
	Peak to trough	Previous trough to this peak	Trough from previous trough	Peak from previous peak
1854–2001 (32 cycles)	17	38	55	56[a]
1854–1919 (16 cycles)	22	27	48	49[b]
1919–1945 (6 cycles)	18	35	53	53
1945–2001 (10 cycles)	10	57	67	67

Earlier recession lengths in months beginning: August 1929, 43; May 1937, 13; February 1945, 8; November 1948,11; July 1953, 10; August 1957, 8; April 1960, 10

[a]31 cycles
[b]15 cycles
Source: NBER. http://www.nber.org/cycles.html

not readily adjust to the new environment and bring themselves to sell at a loss: Markets could not clear.[74]

As in all such aftermaths, numerous frauds, swindles, and malfeasances and lapsed or ignored regulation at many institutions, large and small, were exposed through a parade of investigations, recriminations, and calls for the imposition of additional regulatory procedures and banking practice oversights.[75] As shown previously in Figs. 1.7 and 1.8, price progression from bubble to crash phase followed the common and by now familiar pattern that is illustrated for housing and technology in Fig. 2.9.

Commodities

The great expansion of credit availability during this period eventually also spilled over into the prices of virtually all commodities, lifting them to new heights (Fig. 2.13). Feedback effects from demand related to new housing construction (lumber, copper, aluminum, cement, etc.) undoubtedly contributed to the speculative excesses.

However, bubbles in commodities ought to be distinguished from those in other financial market assets because commodities:

- are often perishable (though obviously not oil, gold, or silver);
- incur some cost of physical storage and shipping (whereas securities are stored and shipped as nearly costless electronic bookkeeping entries);

Fig. 2.13 CRB Index (Reuters/Jefferies), monthly 1970:01–2018:03. (Source: https://www.investing.com/indices/thomson-reuters---jefferies-crb-historical-data. Bloomberg index identifier, CRY

- have an available supply that in any year (e.g., wheat, corn, copper, etc.) cannot be rapidly expanded (whereas the supply of securities can be);
- are often consumed rather quickly after being produced (whereas book-keeping entries may last forever and aren't consumed).

These differences are large enough to suggest that commodity bubbles, whose peaks are usually sharper than those of stocks, are a breed apart from those found in other financial markets.[76]

Still, at the height of the expansionary credit boom that began in earnest just after the dot-com collapse, such distinctions scarcely mattered to the many pension, hedge, endowment, and commodity funds that played in this area. Commodities came to be viewed by such funds as an underinvested alternative asset class that appeared to enhance portfolio diversification as well as expected returns. The relatively large amounts of money that consequently bought into a relatively fixed and largely perishable supply then pushed prices above even those seen in the highly inflationary 1970s. But by late 2008 all of this went into reverse as a spreading global recession caused a steep drop in demand and as funds found no haven (or benefits of diversification) in owning them: By early 2009, the CRB Index had fallen back to where it had been in the mid-1970s.

2.8   YIELD-CHASING, 2009–2017

The liquidity crisis and crash that followed in the wake of the scandalous collapse in the value of housing-related paper and the associated failure of several systemically important firms (including Lehman Brothers and AIG in September 2008) prompted the Federal Reserve to undertake unprecedented "emergency" measures intended to spur a new virtuous round of economic growth: first via reduction of short-term (Fed funds) interest rates to near zero (Fig. 2.14) and then more unconventionally via massive long-term bond-purchasing through so-called quantitative easing (QE) programs. At the Fed the main motivation was to reduce unemployment and at the ECB to support the sovereign debt of fiscally impaired countries.

In all, from 2009 through 2013, there were distinctly four such Fed programs implemented, each of which was progressively larger but more dangerously experimental as the annual percent change in current dollar GDP averaged around 2.4% and resulted in slower growth at the end than at the beginning. The Fed ended up buying more than 70% of new Treasury issues and with a $4.0 trillion balance sheet amounting to around 25% of U.S. GDP.[77]

Similar QE programs were further activated (more than 500 times) by the European Central Bank, the Bank of England, the Bank of Japan, and others. This collectively and from a much smaller base prior to 2009 expanded major central bank balance sheets by more than $11 trllion in six years.[78] For its part, the Swiss National Bank – striving to weaken the franc relative to euros and dollars – bought massively into debt and equity securties. It raised its balance sheet to GDP ratio to 125%. And via ownership of major (>$1 billion) stakes

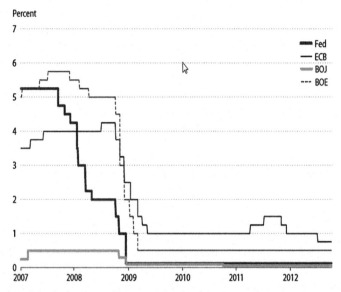

NOTE: The main policy rates for the Fed, ECB, BOJ, and BOE are, respectively, the federal funds target rate, the main refinancing operations fixed/minimum bid rate, the uncollateralized overnight call rate, and the official Bank rate.
SOURCE: Fed, ECB, BOJ, and BOE.

Fig. 2.14 Central Bank (Fed, ECB, BOJ, and BOE) main policy rate timelines, 2007–2013. (Source: Fawley and Neely 2013)

in shares of Apple, Microsoft, Amazon, Facebook, Exxon, and other important stocks, effectively became the world's largest hedge fund! Meanwhile, European "junk" bonds – fully decoupling from reality and of any suggestion of higher than average risk – were traded at greatly inflated prices and yields absurdly close to or even sometimes below those of U.S. Treasuries.

The astonishing and unprecedented enlargement of the Fed's balance sheet (and thus of monetary base) is shown in Fig. 2.15. Studies have indeed suggested that expansion of the US monetary base is reflected in upward movements in major equity markets that may persist for as much as six months.[79]

Even prior to the QE experiment, however, central banks had already adopted a near-zero interest-rate policy (ZIRP) that—in data spanning centuries—hadn't ever before been attempted.[80] The combined effect of a decline of medium- and long-term interest rates was in theory designed to directly boost prices of stocks and bonds and real estate so as to generate a ("trickle-down") wealth effect that would encourage a rise in consumer confidence and spending.[81] If so, it should have ostensibly and rapidly reduced unemployment and underemployment (relative to skills) and also precluded the possibility of a period of dreaded deflation such as had long been experienced in Japan. Nevertheless, economic growth rates in the U.S. and Europe remained stubbornly muted until mid-2017.

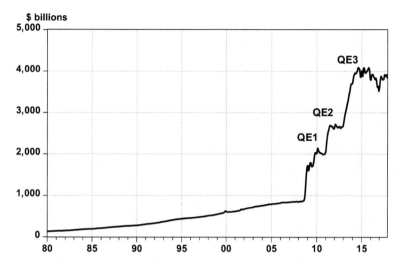

Fig. 2.15 US Adjusted Monetary Base (i.e., reserves), 1980–2017: Q4 in $ billions. (Source: St. Louis Federal Reserve Bank, http://research.stlouisfed.org/fred2/series/ BOGMBASE). On QE, see also Sect. 4.3

The effect of these policies was in fact felt much more in financial markets— particularly at large commercial banks and brokerages—than in the real under- lying economies. Despite the aggressive QE in the United States, the ratio of civilian employment to population fell from a high of just above 63% in 2009 and stayed under 59% from mid-2009 through 2014. The all-time peak of 64.7% was in April 2000. And in Japan, the largest QE program in history— launched in April 2013 and equal to 25% of GDP—led only to sputtering growth: two years later, in 2015, GDP fell at annualized rates of 0.7% in Q2, 0.8% in Q3, and 1.4% in Q4 (with unemployment already low).[82]

Investors around the world, confident of ongoing central bank support, clamored for all sorts of higher-yielding and riskier assets with the view that QE and ZIRP—and later, negative interest rates (NIRPs)—would be extended into the distant future. It was widely assumed, moreover, that money "print- ing" by the central banks was practically infinite (even though the Fed can only create reserves that are not money and become money only when banks make loans from their reserves or purchase assets).[83] Correlation between Fed asset purchases and the S&P 500 was an unusually high 90% during much of this time. And historians noted that negative interest rates—wherein you pay a bank or government entity for the "privilege" of parking money—hadn't ever been sustainably experienced in 5000 years of financial data.[84]

Somewhat counter-intuitively perhaps, but clearly contra to standard financial presumptions in which high growth is inevitably linked to high returns, it seems from Fig. 2.16 that on a country-by-country basis the higher

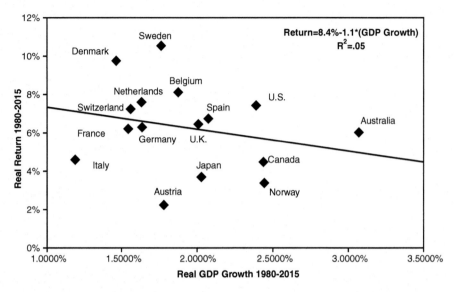

Fig. 2.16 GDP growth and stock market returns for the developed markets, 1980–2015. (Source: copyright GMO Quarterly Letter (Q1, 2016), Datastream, MSCI. Reproduced with permission)

the growth the *lower* the realized return or, equivalently, the lower the growth the higher the return. For at least a few markets in Europe and also the United States, the yield-chasing years provide vivid, prima facie evidence.[85]

It turns out that policies promulgating QE, NIRP, and ZIRP instead rewarded speculation, discouraged savings, undermined longer-term productivity-enhancing capital investments (Fig. 2.17), led to massive amounts of corporate share repurchases, diminished the earnings potential of banks, lowered the banking system's ability and willingness to extend credit, and placed severe pressure on pension and insurance funds as their returns fell woefully below actuarial assumptions. By the fall of 2017, this globally intense yield-seeking episode had lured both individual and institutional investors into buying a broad range of risky assets at high prices.[86]

Near-zero rates also channeled credit to the safest borrowers that included some but far from all governments, corporations (e.g., Apple), and the wealthy at the expense of small savers and businesses.[87] As had similarly happened in the 1920s, and under the notion that "there is no alternative (TINA)," capital again fled from debt-hobbled European countries such as Greece, Spain, and Portugal (and even from slower-growing China) into the apparent relative safety of US and Canadian luxury real estate, equity, and bond markets.

To apply a master concept developed by Taleb (2012), the entire monetary system had, by force of global central bank policies, been made more fragile. The policies had, in the words of Grant (2016), "inflated projected cash flows

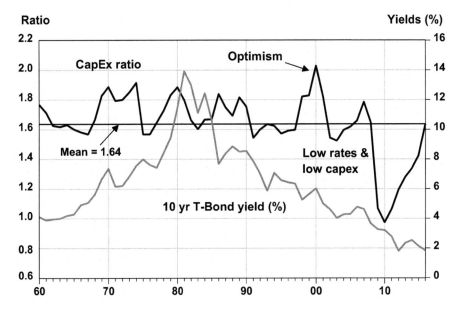

Fig. 2.17 One of Greenspan's favorite ratios (see Mallaby 2016). US business capital expenditures for structures and equipment divided by corporate net cash flow with IVA, 1960–2016. Comparison to ten-year Treasury bond constant maturity series suggests that lower interest rates did not much stimulate investments in long-term assets. Maximum optimism registered in high-inflation late 1970s and TMT bubble era of the late 1990s. Further inclusion of investments in intellectual properties (not shown) does not change the analysis as the resulting ratio line is shifted higher but still largely follows the pattern in tandem. (Sources: BEA.gov and Census.gov. See also Fig. 6.1)

and anesthetized perceptions of risk." By dampening the normally small corrective movements of the markets—the movements that make the system more robust to shocks and therefore *antifragile*—the QE policies will instead likely increase the size and intensity of any subsequent crash. In effect, QE central banks exhaust and/or forfeit any further alternative policy options.[88]

The folly of implementing QE and of chasing yields ultimately leaves central banks with fewer (or no) means to cushion any subsequent crashes; calls into question the authority, political independence, and credibility of central banks; and arguably reduces economic activity far below what it otherwise ought to have been.[89]

Financial history has taught that bubbles tend to form when bank liquidity is high, which then leads banks to underprice risk. The ratio of liquidity relative to asset prices—for whatever many reasons, including political, technological, and psychological—will at crucial junctures always inevitably shrink and cause the bubble to burst. This lesson will again be repeated once experimentation with globally massive QE policies ends.[90] A comparative summary of selected recent bubbles and their subsequent crashes appears in Fig. 2.18. The story it tells is that such events are not as rare nor as confined to a specific time or place or asset class as most of us think.

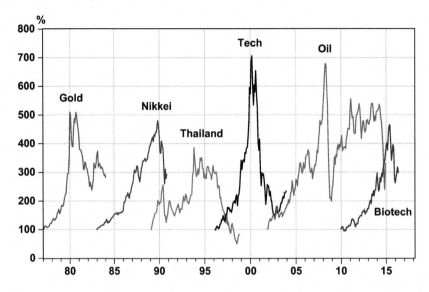

Fig. 2.18 Selected bubbles and crashes since 1975, percent changes from relative lows of monthly series, indexed from lows. A bubble here is defined as a rise in excess of 300% and a crash as a decline from peak to at least half of peak. (Biotech is an arguable exception, falling almost 50% off its peak.) Source data: Yahoo and Google Finance, Investing.com, St. Louis Fed, Thailand (SET index). Indexed Oil series is WTI crude in dollars per barrel, gold in dollars per troy ounce, biotech is S&P Select Industry index

2.9   CONCLUSIONS

All bubbles have many elements in common, with rapidly rising money supply and falling savings rates being primary correlates.[91] But "not all bubbles are alike…what makes some bubbles more dangerous than others is credit."[92]

Attempts have been made to classify bubbles into various types. It is useful, for example, to distinguish bank-centered bubbles such as that in housing from those involving areas (e.g., tech stocks) in which direct bank lending plays a far more limited role.[93] Currency exchange and interest-rate differentials can also contribute to the exportation and/or importation of bubbles.

A further distinction is that some bubbles (e.g., the South Sea Bubble) are based on extensive frauds that don't leave behind in their destructive wakes much foundational capital and knowledge development. Yet others—for example, railroads in the United Kingdom of the 1800s, Florida real estate in the 1920s, and tech/Internet in the 1990s—do leave behind a foundation for further growth.

Major bubbles all tend eventually to retrace the entire gain and return to the trendline base price from which they first began to inflate.[94] This can be seen in price charts of U.S. stocks in 1929 and 2000, Japanese stocks and commercial properties in 1990–91, and U.S. residential assets in 2005. But the same thing happened in smaller bubbles which included frenzied bidding for electronics and "space-age" -related shares in the early 1960s, conglomerates at the end of that decade, the Nifty-Fifty large-cap one-decision shares of the early 1970s, and biotechnology and microelectronics new issues in the1980s.[95]

The historical record suggests that bubbles appear in many forms, with some initiated primarily by and related to technological changes and others primarily to money, banking, and credit policies and conditions. Also, greatly different money and credit conditions in different countries and regions will tend to expedite the import or export of bubbles and the ensuing crashes. In the 1920s, gold and capital were attracted to the United States and away from Europe, thereby providing fuel for the infamous stock market speculation of the late 1920s.[96] In the late 1990s, emerging markets in Asia (e. g., Thailand) were flooded with speculative bubble-creating capital inflows. And post-2009, relatively early and large QE policies contributed to global yield-chasing bubbles in stocks, bonds, and real estate.

When they finally burst, all bubbles are financially devastating for the direct participants; society at large will often be collaterally damaged. However, the bubbles most closely tied to major technological changes will normally contain the seeds for positive long-run contributions to economic growth and prosperity. Few if any such lasting benefits, though, will typically be accrued or discerned from those episodes tied mostly to money, banking, and currency-related flows.

High average returns do not necessarily suggest the presence of bubbles because high and rising returns *alone* do not a bubble make! But what all bubbles seem to have in common is[97]:

- High expectations for continuing rapid price rises;
- Overvaluation compared to historical averages;
- New elements, such as technology for stocks or immigration for housing;
- New investors and entrepreneurs drawn in;
- Considerable popular and media interest;
- Relaxed monetary policy[98];
- Participation using highly leveraged and innovative financial instruments;
- Notable increases in trading volume.[99]
- "Wall Street people learn nothing and forget everything."[100]
- Belief in human perfectibility and ingenuity.[101]
- Growing divergence between the interests of agents and principals, wherein popular (and herding) agents are increasingly oblivious to risk as they fearlessly advise or decide what to do with other people's money.[102]
- More money than ideas, willing suspension of disbelief based on grains of truth, rejection of valuation norms, and a fear of missing out (FOMO).[103] People feel they *must* buy.

Additional anecdotal signs include the introduction of new financial jargon (e.g., "swaptions," "CDOs"), as well as newly contrived financial metrics. Also,

IPOs come to market at an accelerated pace and at an increasingly early stage of a young company's history, "covenant-lite" bond sales proliferate, stock prices tend to rise quickly on announcements of splits and stylistic name changes, and the lead news stories on television are more frequently about investments.

In every episode from tulips onward, there is inevitably throughout the bubble-building process also a steady degradation and disparagement of standards by both institutional and individual investors. This was evident in the notion that a mere tulip bulb might be worth the equivalent of a house. In 1929, levitation was achieved with liberal margin lending for stock purchases. And in 1999, just a wild *rumor* that a company might be adding dot-com to its name was enough to send its stock soaring. Every bubble episode on record furthermore shows that lawyers and journalists (even in 1720) were complicit too and that herding behavior (discussed later) was prevalent and explicit.[104]

In the more recent versions, investment bankers and analysts, in the pursuit of IPO and merger fees and bonuses, readily cloaked themselves in presumptions that—in the new paradigm shift, as it was called—trees could actually grow to the sky (Internet shares), that managements (e.g., Enron, MCI, AOL) spoke only the truth and reported earnings results using conventional accounting methods, that (housing) auditors and ratings agencies were nonconflicted and just following the rules, that portfolio managers could consistently generate market-beating returns (Madoff's $50 billion Ponzi swindle circa 2008), and that central banks would always have your back (yield-chasing).

Yet it was in the housing episode of the early 2000s—a massive worldwide event led by housing but also involving stocks, fine arts and collectibles, and natural resources too—that the ultimate disappearance of any standards whatsoever was perhaps most flagrant and shameful of all. That's because, unlike in earlier times, centuries of accumulated knowledge (wisdom is another story) and experience about the nature of risk were totally ignored and/or disregarded. Flight from quality and toward ever-riskier ventures thus, in a sense, defines a bubble and makes it what it is.

Giant banks and Wall Street firms (e.g., Citigroup, Wachovia, WaMu, UBS, Bear Stearns, Lehman, and Merrill Lynch) that clearly should have known better gorged themselves on paper that was developed and issued on the flimsiest and most questionable of assumptions, all while mortgage brokers and appraisal and debt ratings firms raced competitively to a bottom in which lending criteria no longer existed.[105]

History shows that bubbles and their subsequent collapses typically end in the wreckage of personal and corporate reputations and in a whirlwind of impoverishment, fraud, distrust, recriminations, searches for villains and scapegoats, frustrations, and anger.[106] More regulation piled upon already-existing massive, unwieldly, and unenforceable or unenforced regulation is always, in these situations, the convenient but at best trivially effective post-event solution proposed by politicians. Such regulations do not prevent recurrences and, arguably, may even slow or impede an eventual economic recovery.[107]

Notes

1. As told by Beckman (1988, p. 2), initially, "the price of a tulip bulb was only marginally higher than that of other rare plants." But tulips took on the aura of a status symbol for families of means. And after a while, "it was the rare specimens that attracted the most attention and commanded the highest prices." Knight (2014, Chap. 1) also covers tulip cultivation and the market's frenzy and writes, "…anyone with money but without tulips was judged simply to have bad taste." Tulips were originally from Turkey and brought to Leyden in 1593 by a Viennese botany professor. As described by Bissonnette (2015), a somewhat comparable but of course much less economically significant mentality in the late 1990s involved Beanie Baby toys.

2. See Garber (1990, pp. 22–7, 2000, p. 44), who makes the point about "written contracts entered into before a notary."

3. Buchan (1997, p. 101) observes that "the Dutch appeared to have uncovered some magic of credit." French (2006) presents documentary evidence of the expansion of such credit.

4. As Davidson and Rees-Mogg (1992, p. 147) suggest, tulips became "a preferred rarity for speculative trade" because "the bulbs were smaller and more easily transported than porcelain or painting…they could be traded almost like coins or tokens in a futures market." As Mackay (1841, [1995], p. 90) writes, "…the rage among the Dutch to possess them was so great that the ordinary industry of the country was neglected, and the population, even to its lowest dregs, embarked in the tulip trade."

5. From data in MacKay (1841 [1995], p. 91), Chancellor (1999, p. 18), Garber (2000, p. 82). Garber questions some of these value comparisons, yet also notes (pp. 37–43) that demand for bulbs in France apparently drove some of the speculation. The history of this time is also covered in Dash (1999) and in Goldgar (2007), who suggest that tulip prices listed in the classic articles on the subject (e.g., Posthumus) ought not be trusted. Thompson (2007) writes that the collapse of prices was tied to the defeat of the German princes—the main sources of demand. The term "speculation" is defined by Harrison and Kreps (1978), who follow Keynes (1936 [1964], Chap. 12, VI). See also Brunnermeier (2001, p. 48) and Scheinkman and Xiong (2003) and a popular review of the tulip bubble in Mansharamani (2011).

6. Posthumus (1929, p. 449) writes, "The tulip offered a timely outlet for the general financial euphoria, in which from 1634 onwards the ordinary person could add his demand…Even the poor could join the tulip craze." Davies (2002, p. 553) adds that "[I]f this was not 'mania', there never has been any… The modern world's first financial mania, based on a sound and growing industry, and liberally supplied with plentiful and new kinds of credit, thus subsided with surprisingly little economic damage. It had encouraged participation by a larger portion of the ordinary population of a nation than any other mania up to the Wall Street boom of 1929." Neal (2015, p. 66), however, questions the historical emphasis on the tulip mania prices, writing that Dutch pamphleteers might have mistaken inflated option strike prices for fixed option fees on forward contracts.

7. From Balen (2003, p. 76), who further explains (p. 88) that the South Sea Company "had no business plan and no market for its goods; indeed, it had no financial prospects whatsoever other than the self-fulfilling nature of its enter-

prise. It attracted investors because investors were attracted to it." Behavioral similarities to the Internet craze of almost 300 years later are striking.

8. This rings familiar in modern times; witness the Florida real estate swindles of the 1920s or the many now-defunct Internet/telecom companies of the late 1990s. Also, as Dale (2004, pp. 7–8) explains: "In the absence of Reuters, Bloomberg, and other screen-based information services, eighteenth century traders and investors had to rely very largely on the coffee house and the press for information...The London coffee houses fulfilled several important functions. First and foremost, they were a source of political, economic, and financial information."

9. Beckman (1988, p. 21) and Dale et al. (2005).

10. Even then a fear of round numbers was evident. Such round number-phobia has been echoed frequently in the market. For instance, the DJIA stalled at around 1000 in 1972, and more recently the market stalled at just above 10,000. According to Balen (2003, p. 61), prices actually began to rise from levels well below 1000 *livres*: "Those who had bought at the bottom of the market, for a few hundred *livres*, could not believe their luck; those who pocketed the profit went on spending sprees which forced up the price of land and houses. They bought horses too, and furniture, books, works of art and jewelry...The term 'millionaire' was coined during these heady times." But as described in Krueger (2005) and in Temin and Voth (2004), even then, the conservative Hoare's Bank made a conscious decision to "ride" the bubble by investing its own funds while knowing that South Sea shares were overpriced. Early use of the term "millionaire" is also described in Gleeson (1999, p. 157). See also Scheinkman (2014, pp. 12–15).

11. By the end of 1720, after more severe public losses, Parliament also passed a bill (*The South Sea Sufferers Act*) to confiscate the profits of the South Sea Company directors. In post-"bubble" aftermaths, it is typical for scapegoats to be sought and for legislative and political inquiries and policy initiatives to be pursued. In the United States, Sarbanes-Oxley legislation is a recent similar response to conditions after 2000. See also Frehen et al. (2013) and Goetzmann (2016, pp. 333–44) on legal and economic background on the ten years leading up to 1720.

12. Law's adventurous life is recounted in Gleeson (1999). See also Ferguson (2008, pp. 138–56) and Knight (2014, Chap. 2).

13. Buchan (1997, pp. 142–3) writes:
    "This astonishing scheme was not simply plucked out of the air. The principle...was the principle of the English South Sea company of 1711–12: capital is subscribed in government obligations, the interest on which provides the working capital for the company's operations. Law went a stage further. In refunding the debts of the state, he clearly intended to make good the public creditors not from arbitrary and unpopular taxes but from commercial profits. That was bold in the extreme..." Buchan then (p. 144) concludes: "I do not think Law's System was a fantasy or fraud...the scheme was...doable."

14. Balen (2003, p. 50) notes, "He knew that a bank did not have to be the passive recipient of other people's money. It could be instead a driving force of the economy, a motor which could create wealth by granting credit." Gleeson (1999, p. 44) writes of Law that "study of probability reawakened his natural mathematical talent, and the urge to use it drew him to one of the new obsessions of the age: the science of economics." Gleeson (p. 80) then writes: "He saw money as a scientist might an array of laboratory equipment and chemicals,

as substance for experiment and a subject for theory." Pribram (1983, pp. 74–5) observes that Law "deserves a special place in the history of economic reasoning because he was the first to examine the national and international significance of the economic effects caused by the issuance of paper money...he felt free to recommend the use of a currency which had no original use value at all. With this transformation of the role of money, he anticipated the idea of a 'managed currency.'"

15. Gleeson (1999, pp. 138–45).

16. Garber (2000) and Bierman (1991), for example, do not necessarily view these events as bubbles. Bierman suggests that the South Sea situation was a combination of a failed economic venture and a scam. Garber argues that speculators made decisions based on the best economic analysis available. And Schacter et al. (1985) characterize the South Sea speculation as not a random event, but instead a period of hysterical, irrational behavior by investors. In addition, Frehen et al. (2009) examined a broad cross section of newly available stock price data for British and Dutch firms in 1720 and found evidence of speculation about Atlantic trade and insurance company innovations. Neal (2015, pp. 72–99) and Knight (2014, Chap. 3) also review these events.

17. From around 1800 to 1840, canals had themselves been the basic transportation efficiency improvement of the day, and shares of canal companies (primarily Grand Junction Canal in the United Kingdom) had been at the center of several stock price bubbles.

18. See Neal (2015, pp. 160–166).

19. See also Camplin and Beighton (2010) and Odlyzko (2010).

20. See Frederick Lewis Allen's 1931 classic book, *Only Yesterday,* Sobel (1968), Brooks (1969), Galbraith (1988), Klingaman (1989), Klein (2001), and Morris (2017).

21. More detail in Allen (1931) and Napier (2007, pp. 77–82). Development of air travel is covered in Vogel (2016).

22. As is usual, the imminent deflation was not seen by the experts. From Grant (1996, p. 138): "True to form, economists and intellectuals were taken aback by the change. A poll of economists, bankers, and government officials in the *New York Evening Post* at year-end 1919 had found deep-rooted optimism." Napier (2007, pp. 12–16) tells the story of the decade preceding the 1921 low. See also Grant (2014).

23. See Crossen (2005) and Shiller (2013). Schwartz (1986, p. 255) observes that the Florida land boom should not be linked to a pattern of monetary growth. The boom was centered in Miami and boosted by a 1924 Florida constitutional amendment prohibiting income and inheritance taxes and extensive Chamber of Commerce advertising. The Great Miami Hurricane of September 1926 soon "dampened" enthusiasm. Morris (2017, pp. 106–09) provides more background.

24. Gjerstad and Smith (2014, p. 89) write that the effects of monetary contraction that appeared late in 1930 were preceded by a 40% decline in residential construction from 1925 to 1929.

25. In using broker margin loan data, Rappoport and White (1993) found that "rates paid on those loans contained information about lenders' perception of a possible bubble in the market." During the period of the presumed bubble, "the call rate and the time rate for brokers' loans rose well above other rates, suggest-

ing that lenders no longer regarded brokers' loans as very safe…We view the premia on brokers' loans as reflecting fears of a crash." As told by Voth (2003), similar concerns, as expressed by rising margin requirements, were also seen prior to the 1927 collapse of prices on the Berlin Stock Exchange. See also Geisst (2004, p. 186) and Chari et al. (2003) in which it says that no consensus has formed on the main forces behind the Great Depression.

26. Bierman (1991) argues that the largest declines in the market actually occurred in the two years following October 1929 and that several "myths" have been perpetuated. Among the most important were that the stock market in 1929 was clearly overvalued and that its fall was inevitable. Bierman instead maintains that in reality it was the statements and actions of US government officials that led to the market's decline.

    Mishkin and White (2003, p. 62) say more precisely that the Fed increased its policy of "direct pressure" by instructing member banks to limit "speculative loans" to brokers in February 1929 and that the Fed then raised the discount rate in August 1929. None of this apparently suppressed the demand for credit to buy stocks. Upon the market's collapse in October 1929, "the Federal Reserve Bank of New York engaged in a classic lender-of-last-resort operation… member banks could borrow freely….the crisis was contained, and there were no panic increases in money market rates…the premium on brokers' loans collapsed…Unfortunately, the Federal Reserve Board did not approve of the New York Fed's intervention. It censured the New York bank, and in spite of the recession…the Federal Reserve Board maintained its tight monetary policy." Ip (2005) recounts additional details, as does Napier (2007, p. 131), who writes that the Federal Reserve Bank of New York bought $160 million of government securities in October 1929 even though it had been authorized by the Federal Reserve Board to buy only up to $25 million. The FRB not only strongly disapproved of this action but also ignored later pleas for such larger purchases. Garside (2007, p. 67) observes that "[S]tabilization by monetary expansion…was ruled out by the policy-makers' fervent belief that already nervous markets would react adversely to signs of fiscal impropriety." See also Ahamed (2009, pp. 320–24) and Johnson (1991, pp. 236–45), who write that whenever there were signs of faltering growth, the Fed's basic policy after 1927 had been to administer increasing doses of credit, which fueled speculation but did little to help the "real" economy.

    De Long and Shleifer (1991), meanwhile, maintain that one-fifth of the increase in stock prices from 1927 to 1929 and about one-half of the collapse in prices from 1929 to 1931 were caused by shifts in irrational investor sentiment rather than revisions of estimates of fundamental values. They contend that the decline after 1929 was excessive and not based on rational revisions of stock valuations.

    Cole and Ohanian (1999) discuss the Great Depression from a neoclassical perspective and find that the theory provides an incomplete description. Presscott (1999) looks at the Great Depression in terms of the labor market.

    Klein (2001, p. xiii) writes that the crash "ranks high on the list of unsolved puzzles for scholars, who have yet to come up with convincing answers to the two crucial questions of what caused the crash and what role, if any, it played in bringing on the grinding depression that followed."

27. Stone and Ziemba (1993).

28. *Wall Street Journal*, 10 November 2003. See also Stone and Ziemba (1993).
29. Stone and Ziemba (1993). Figures in Wood (2005, 1992, p. 8) are slightly different. Sheng (2009, p. 55) notes that Japan sits on less than 3% of the world's surface area. Golf data appear in Ziemba et al. (2018, p. 226).
30. For example, see Asako (1991, p. 169) and Voth (2000, p. 10), who explain that the central bank kept the interest rate low in 1987 despite the Japanese economy operating near full capacity. This strategy was initiated in September of 1985 by the so-called Plaza Accord of the G-5 countries. Mora (2008) found that banks increased real estate lending when, due to deregulation, *keiretsu* could obtain public financing and thus reduce dependence on banks. He found that "a 0.01 increase in a prefecture's real estate loans as a share of total loans causes 14–20% higher land inflation compared with other prefectures over the 1981–91 period." French and Poterba (1991) found that around half of the discrepancy between P/E ratios in the US and Japanese stock markets during this period was due to differences in accounting practices of the two countries, but even so, they were unable to completely explain the movements of Japanese share prices.

   Grant (1996, pp. 152–9) provides a concise review, noting that in 1987, large Japanese companies "could borrow at 1 or 2 percent and invest the proceeds in government bonds at 6 percent...The most expansive element of the bull-market system was that banks were able to count a percentage of their stocks as a contribution to their own capital. Thus, as the stock market rose, so did the banks' capital and so did their lending capacity." The easy money was the Bank of Japan's response to help Japanese exporters whose profits were being squeezed by the rising exchange value of the yen caused by the Plaza Accord.
31. *The Economist*, 17 March 2012, "Shares and Shibboleths." See also Swarup (2014, Chap. 4).
32. Werner (2003, p. 3) writes that "open doors and free markets meant that Japan's growth machines wreaked havoc." The purposeful industrial growth structure—with its emphasis on market share and interlocking corporate ownership and de-emphasis of shareholder rights and profits—was first established just prior to the 1940s and then expanded and extended well into the 1980s. This was much different than in the Japanese economy of the 1920s.
33. Yergin (2009, p. 778).
34. Noguchi (1994, pp. 293–5) writes that "the funds that were raised were not all channeled into plant and equipment investment; quite a large portion was used for what was called 'zai-tech,' or financial engineering, including deposits in banks and trust accounts and the purchase of other financial assets offering high yields...The unprecedented land speculation of the latter part of the 1980s was thus supported by an enormous volume of lending by financial institutions to the real estate industry." Ito and Iwaisako (1996) agree, but also say that the asset price increases of the late 1980s were "not explained by any asset pricing model based on fundamentals or rational bubbles."
35. Werner (2003, pp. 140–78) shows that a small clique of BOJ Governors, especially Yasushi Mieno in the late 1980s and later Toshihiko Fukui, were instrumental. Mieno, furtively operating in the background during the 1980s, condoned the almost limitless high-quota lending practices, letting others later take the blame for creating the bubble. Then, after becoming governor in late 1989, Mieno totally reversed course through severe restraint of bank lending, thereby initiating the subsequent collapse. This was done within the framework

of a political power play against the rival Ministry of Finance and ostensibly advanced for the purpose of restructuring the economy so that it would conform to a presumed path of long-term sustainable growth—a strategy pursued even at the expense of a subsequent prolonged, high-unemployment recession. Hilsenrath and Fujikawa (2011) update the story from the Bank of Japan's perspective. Also surely a factor was the practice of *amakudari*, in which ex-officials from the Ministry of Finance and central bank were hired upon retirement to be senior executives by the large private banks. Their former junior subordinates, then promoted into regulatory positions of power, found it difficult to confront their previous bosses, even as the banks were on the edge of collapse. Rajan (2010, p. 63) notes that as Japanese exports came under pressure, the BOJ purposely intended to boost stock and property markets so that there would be a turn toward more robust domestic consumption via a wealth effect.

36. See Werner (2005, pp. 232–6), where it is explained that aggressive lending practices were the "main determinant of Japanese land prices in the 1980s" and that this "bubble" was "due to excessive credit creation for non-GDP transactions." Such credit availability issues and the important role of agency relationships in the banking are further explored in Allen and Gale (2000), who support the view that "Financial fragility occurs when positive credit expansion is insufficient" and that bubbles are a result of the "inability of lenders to observe how risky borrowers' investments are." Deidda and Fattouh (2005) write about bank monitoring of loans, "[M]onitoring is costly, nonverifiable and nonobservable." Cooper (2008, p. 124) also writes with regard to identification of bubbles that "if credit creation is running substantially ahead of growth then that growth is likely itself to be supported by the credit creation, and will not be sustained once credit expansion ends."

37. Ayers (2014, p. 142) writes that "Basel I was especially hard on Japanese banks, which had most of their assets in the riskiest category, resulting in much higher leverage than Basel I allowed."

38. Additional factors also included an adverse shift in foreign exchange rates, a spike in imported oil prices related to the Gulf War of 1991, and the gradual realization that Japan was a gerontocracy, with potentially large domestic needs to support a relatively large aging population. Murase (2012) provides an alternative view using an overlapping generation model (OLG).

39. See Kindleberger and Aliber (2011, p. 3) and Onaran (2012, p. 18), who write: "the finance ministry was directing the banks to hide their toxic waste so they would look healthier…This evergreening of nonperforming loans was widespread during the 1990s in Japan. So the zombie banks created zombie companies, whose death was postponed because the banks didn't want to recognize their losses…As the day of reckoning was delayed, it had multiple negative consequences…Lending to healthy firms declined while loans to zombie companies were rolled over." Also, as the comprehensive Hoshi and Kashyap (1999) study has summarized, Japanese banking deregulation in the 1980s initiated a shift from bank financing to capital market funding, but did relatively little for savers.

40. Fackler (2008) quotes economists and former BOJ officials saying that "the biggest lesson they learned was that cutting rates alone has almost no effect

when the financial system has fallen into a crisis as deep as the one Japan faced in the 1990s." The article notes that the money created just continued to pile up in commercial banks, which didn't lend because of fears of counterparty defaults. Paralysis only began to dissipate when lenders became convinced that there would be no further sudden large defaults, and that took a long time. Werner (2003) provides a detailed historical treatment. See also Koo (2010).

41. Segaller (1999).
42. Rappoport and White (1993, 1994) find similarities between the experiences of 1929 and 1987. But Bates (1991) finds that attempts to explain the causes of the 1987 crash have not been successful given the scarcity of major adverse economic developments occurring at that time. Siegel (1992) "confirms that changes in consensus corporate profit forecasts and interest rates were completely unable to explain the rise and subsequent collapse of stock prices in 1987." Among the crash causes that are nonetheless frequently cited, according to a University of Melbourne review (available at www.arts.unimelb.edu), were (a) computer trading and derivative securities, illiquidity; (b) trade and budget deficits; (c) overvaluation.

   In Lucchetti (2007), former NYSE chief economist William Freund is quoted as saying in regard to October 19, 1987, "There's no question...the order systems failed, and that added to the panic." And Das (2006, p. 203) writes that "The markets had gapped hugely. Trading was not continuous. Markets, it seemed, hadn't read the efficient market theorem."

   The event has been analyzed in works by Abken (1988), Leland and Rubinstein (1988), White (1990), Malliaris and Urrutia (1992), Toporowski (1995), and Benzoni et al. (2010) and reported by Norris (1987). Regarding the 1987 crash, Brock (1991) also wrote, "In my opinion, no satisfactory explanation has been found." The Brady Commission (Presidential task force) study, however, probably comes closest to identifying the major problem. The Commission concluded that "portfolio insurance," involving the sale of S&P 500 futures, was an important cause of the decline. See also Dunbar (2000, pp. 93–5), Jacobs (1999), and Henriques (2017). The fatal flaw was that investors who were supposed to buy stocks from portfolio insurers on the way down had neither the obligation nor the now-diminished collateral with which to buy.

   Bernstein (2005b, p. 285) goes directly to the heart of the matter. He writes: "A conventional put option *commits* the seller of the put to buy the underlying shares at a specified price; the contract to do so is secured by cash collateral. The arrangements as to price and purchase are set in advance and are secured by an agreement enforceable in a court of law...The investors without portfolio insurance flatly refused to play the part of the seller of the put. They had made no advance commitment whatsoever to oblige the investors with portfolio insurance by taking stock off their hands at the current price, and they had no intention of putting up the cash to do so." Pepper and Oliver (2006, p. 114) also show that percentage growth of the MZM measure of money supply in real terms declined sharply beginning in January 1987 and thereby portended a crash. See also Black (1988), Bose (1988), Malliaris and Urrutia (1992), Caplin and Leahy (1994), Vandewalle et al. (1998a, b), Feigenbaum (2001), and Benzoni et al. (2010).

43. See Thurm and Brown (2002).
44. Lee (2004, pp. 117–22).
45. See, for example, Knee (2006) and Reingold and Reingold (2006).
46. Lee (2004, pp. 11–16) and Sommer (2014).
47. This was also seen in 1962, when speculators were fascinated with electronics and just the addition of "tronics" or "data" to somewhere in the name of a company immediately raised the P/E multiple.
48. In Britain, as *The Guardian* of December 11, 1999, wrote, "...financial markets are in the grip of an unprecedented stock-buying fever as punters rush to buy almost any share with a whiff of the internet about it....people report spending up to a day waiting for a free line to some stockbrokers and then having to wait up to an hour more before it is answered." This is also quoted in Balen (2003, p. 46). A well-known example of the mania's intensity was the November 13, 1998, IPO of TheGlobe.com Inc., which went from $9 to a high of $97 on the first day. Another example: The shares of Priceline, an eight-month old company that had already burned through $100 million and had no notable assets quadrupled in value to $10 billion on its first day of trading, March 30, 1999. See also Coakley et al. (2007) on the tendency of post-IPO profitability performance to decline in this bubble. A spate of social-media offerings in 2011 also initially traded at high valuations: Zynga at 33 times previous year's revenue, LinkedIn at 36 times, for examples. And in early 2017, the IPO of Snap, a company built on self-erasing text and photos, had an initial valuation of $24 billion, though it was annually showing losses of hundreds of millions of dollars.
49. Near the end, around 80% of the IPOs were for profitless companies. In reviewing this period, Gasparino (2005, p. 39) writes, "...stocks during the Net bubble were driven by something that couldn't be measured by conventional analysis. The driving force was emotion. People wanted to believe that the Internet could make them rich." See also Bernanke et al. (1996).
50. As Dreazen (2002) describes, the bull market in tech stocks was based largely on widely held myths: "dot-coms made good investments, the New Economy would never experience a recession (the last one had been ten years prior), small telecom companies could beat the mighty Bells," and most damaging, "the fallacy that Internet traffic was doubling every three months." As reported by Vincent (2010), however, the dot-com mania was "a straightforward product of the developed world's baby-boomer generation reaching their age of peak equity accumulation...Had the Internet not existed, another vehicle for speculative fervor would undoubtedly have been discovered." See also Ofek and Richardson (2001).
51. A brief but comprehensive comparison between the recent fiber-optic bubble and those that occurred in previous network industry booms such as telegraphs (1847–1865), railroads (1873–1994), and the telephone (1894–1913) is presented in Gross (2002). A similar brief review, "The Beauty of Bubbles," appears in *The Economist*, December 18, 2008. As for the telecom stock inflation aspects, see Blumenstein (2001) and Lowenstein (2004).
52. Quote from Yale's CIO, David Swensen in Mansharamani (2011, p. xv).
53. Biggs (2006, pp. 178–80) was Morgan Stanley's widely followed equity strategist at the time and recounts the surrounding euphoria and the disdain that greeted his relatively early turn toward tech stock bearishness. "In December

1999 I went to a 15% weighting in technology, which was less than half of its weight in the S & P 500...It was a very painful spring...Some of my clients became upset as their portfolios lagged, and I was subjected to considerable abuse....The young, swaggering tech types in the office rolled their eyes...I said tech and the Internet stocks were in a mania like tulips...The crowd thought I was either crazy or senile."

See also Sato (2016) and Brunnermeier and Nagel (2004) who found that at the market's peak in March 2000, hedge funds held 31% of their portfolios in stocks with the highest price-to-sales ratios and did not exert a moderating influence on stock prices. Another example is from Galbraith (1944) who writes that renowned banker Paul Warburg was accused of "sandbagging American prosperity" when he warned of a possible collapse in 1929.

54. Quote from Roger McNamee in Nocera (1999). It is similar to one from Keynes who famously said, "The market can stay irrational longer than you can stay solvent." Similarly, Mauboussin (2006, p. 88) summarizes, "...if no one else is rational, it doesn't pay for you to be." Bitmead et al. (2004) wrote that "under certain conditions, people may succumb to systematic behavioral biases...and...are generally overconfident in their own abilities." In his November 2013 newsletter, John P. Hussman writes, "The problem with bubbles is that they force one to decide whether to look like an idiot before the peak, or an idiot after the peak." And Anderson (1949, p. 196) wrote: "...the wilder the craze the higher the type of intellect that succumbs to it."

55. Cecchetti (2008) reports on research indicating that "a 10 percent increase in housing wealth raises consumption by between 1.1 and 1.7 percent, whereas the same change in stock-market wealth only increases consumption by something like 0.2 percent." See also the IMF's *World Economic Outlook*, April 2008, available at www.imf.org/external/pubs/ft/weo/2008/01/c3/Box3_1_1.pdf. It shows what are called house-price gaps—price increases not accounted for by fundamental drivers of house prices—for 1997–2007, with the price increases in the United States, Italy, and Japan at around 11%, as compared to Ireland, the Netherlands, and Britain at around 30%, France at more than 20%, Spain at about 17%, and Germany at only 2%. In Carney (2013) it is noted that the housing boom in Spain and Ireland was three to four times as intense as the peak of the US boom if scaling for relative population sizes are included. Barboza (2010) writes of a 2010 housing bubble in China and Laing (2013) and Fong and Wei (2016) update. Davis (2011a, b) explains that real estate had been the foundation for China's tremendous growth since 1990 and that by 2011, real estate prices had begun to notably decline. See also "China Real Estate Bubble," *60 Minutes*, March 30, 2014. See also Justiniano et al. (2015) on the effects of credit supply increases and looser lending constraints on the housing market.

56. This may largely explain why mortgage loans as a percent of bank lending portfolios have roughly doubled over the past century from about 30% in 1900 to about 60% today. See Jordá et al. (2014).

57. Nonsensical encouragement—to replace a bubble with another—also came from economist Paul Krugman, who wrote in an August 2, 2002, *New York*

Times editorial: "To fight this recession...Alan Greenspan needs to create a housing bubble to replace the Nasdaq bubble."

58. There was even what came to be known as the Alt-A (alternative) category for borrowers with good credit scores but without documentation (i.e., with credit quality between prime and subprime, and with income unverified). As described in Schwartz (2008), the Alt-A "liar's loans" market ultimately grew to $500 billion to $1 trillion and presented its own unique set of problems for companies such as Thornburg Mortgage. See also Doherty (2008) on the problems in auction-rate securities, which are long-term debts with short-term features, as their interest rates are meant to be reset in weekly or monthly Wall Street brokers' auctions. Insufficient bids in February 2008 caused firms to stop supporting the market and caused a freeze-up.

59. Calomiris and Haber (2014, p. 254).

60. Most such CDOs ended up owning pieces of perhaps hundreds of bonds, each of which contained possibly thousands of individual mortgages. This diversification was presumed to make investors less vulnerable to any potential problems of a single borrower or security. Mollenkamp and Ng (2007) provide an overview of a CDO's mechanics, while Milne (2009) provides a more detailed explanation. CPDOs, as explained in Mollenkamp and Whitehouse (2008), "provide income to investors by selling insurance against a default to other buyers. However....they can suffer losses when insurance costs rise." Mollenkamp et al. (2008) discuss how AIG's forecasting for credit default swaps went awry. See also Nocera (2009a), Tett (2009), and O'Harrow and Dennis (2008a, b, c), in which historical background is provided. Milne (2009, pp. 195–257) provides timeline details. Ng and Pleven (2009) describe AIG's securities lending practices. Taibbi (2009) describes *synthetic* CDOs that were "backed not by actual monthly mortgage payments made by real human beings, but by the wild promises of other irresponsible lenders." These were "derivative contracts filled with derivative contracts." See also Morgenson and Story (2009) and Gorton (2010), who provide the detailed mechanics of such structured products. Story (2010a) explains derivatives clearinghouse trading rules and the influence of banks.

Gorton (2008) explains how repurchase (repo) agreement market ("shadow banking system") haircuts and the fears of default were central to the crisis. This shadow banking system, based on complex derivatives and off-balance sheet vehicles, evolved over the 25 years leading up to the crisis. Gorton (2010, p. 58) writes that the shadow banking system is, in fact, banking and that banking "is about the creation of information-insensitive debt." Due to evaporation of collateral values, debt in the crisis instead became information-sensitive; "the panic happened in the shadow banking system, not the regulated system."

Lohr (2008, 2009) provides a more general overview of how the human factor was left out of models. Nocera (2009b) discusses the weaknesses of Value-at-Risk models. Dash and Creswell (2008) describe how CDOs and the absence of adequate risk controls contributed to the massive problems at Citigroup. Crovitz (2009) writes, "It's now clear that the data that banks used were distorted by years of government initiatives to promote homeownership. Government-mandated loans led house prices ever higher and house-price volatility ever lower. When VaR models looked back, they wrongly modeled a low risk of default." Triana (2009, 2012) provides a critical review of underlying financial models and theories. Dowd and Hutchinson (2010, Chap. 5) do the same, finding flaws that include assumptions of Gaussianity, of stable underlying laws, of relatively unchanging parameters involving correlations and volatilities, and of behavioral and institutional obstacles. Derman (2011, p. 4) provides a more detailed analysis, writing, "[T]he great financial crisis has been marked by the failure of models both qualitative and quantitative." More on Fed models is in Hilsenrath (2012). Weatherall (2013), however, shows the importance of models and how they are being improved. See also Buiter (2009), Cassidy (2009), Gray and Vogel (2016), and Jovanovic and Schinckus (2017).

61. Lowenstein (2008b) explains how CDOs were assembled and rated. Morris (2008, p. 79) writes that "you collect the risky tranches of a number of CDOs, which can sometimes be the hardest to place, and use them to support a new CDO, with a range of high-to-low risk-rated tranches. Highly rated bonds magically materialize out of a witches' soup of very smoky stuff." Nocera (2010) explains that "normal" CDOs contained actual bonds, whereas the synthetic versions contained cred-default swaps that "referenced" specific groups of mortgage bonds and that no longer required a constant stream of subprime loans. Using synthetics, the supply of CDOs could then go to infinity. Bernstein and Eisinger (2010) discuss the self-dealing and fake demand for CDOs that investment banks crafted in order to sustain short-term earnings performance and executive bonuses.

Gasparino (2009) writes that the Federal Reserve's "Basel" capital standards provided banks owning mortgage-backed securities relatively more credit than for holdings of other types of assets and that, by 2004, the SEC had also allowed such standards to be applied to investment bank holdings.

Triana (2009, pp. 99–121) provides an accessible review of Gaussian copula methods which model the probabilistic behavior of multiple random variables and as are also described in Wilmott and Orrell (2017, pp. 101–103). The early copula article by Li (2000) is also discussed in Salmon (2009), who writes that a single correlation number is dangerously misleading because correlations are actually highly unstable over time. From an operational perspective, Patterson (2010, p. 195) writes, "The Gaussian copula was, in hindsight, a disaster."

62. Gross leverage ratios are a gauge of funds borrowed against equity and had been commonly scaled up by a factor of 20 or 30. In the last weeks of Bear Stearns' independence, the ratio was 33, and Carlyle Capital was at 24 just before it was liquidated. See Boyd (2008), Kelly (2008a, b, c, 2009a, b), Kelly et al. (2008), Lattman et al. (2008), and Cohan (2012).

63. Wilmott and Orrell (2017, p. 56) provide criticisms of the VaR method of risk measurement. Along with the erroneous assumption that share price returns are normally distributed, VaR also doesn't indicate how much might be lost on days when the VaR number is exceeded.

64. Wessel (2008) writes that the paper was being increasingly dispersed to ever weaker hands that, when conditions deteriorated, couldn't hold on and ultimately contributed to the volatility by dumping. See also Reilly and Mollenkamp (2007), Lowenstein (2008a), and Nocera (2009a, b).

65. This important example was the firing of the chief risk manager at Merrill Lynch by then-CEO E. Stanley O'Neal. The manager had reportedly strongly objected to the purchase of mortgage originator First Franklin for $1.3 billion

in December 2006, at the very top of the housing bubble, from Cleveland's National City Corp. By early 2008, after taking losses of at least $11.5 billion in write-downs, Merrill closed the unit entirely. See the many newspaper accounts of this throughout the summer and fall of 2007, Cassidy (2008), Pulliam et al. (2008), Gasparino (2009, pp. 164–177), and Morgenson (2008b), who discuss the synthetic derivatives (combinations of CDOs and credit default swaps) that impaired Merrill Lynch. Cohan (2010) later writes of O'Neal's belated recognition of the problem's enormity and attempt to sell the firm in 2007. Story (2010b) describes how massive amounts of toxic paper were hidden in Merrill's structured entities. See also McLean and Nocera (2010) and Dunbar (2011).

As told by Sender et al. (2008), prior to bankruptcy Lehman too forced out anyone who opposed taking on more risk. According to McDonald and Robinson (2009, pp. 268–9), CEO Richard Fuld, Jr. first began excluding the company's bearish risk expert from important meetings and then demoted her. It was also later revealed that a Lehman whistle-blower was fired just after raising concerns about the firm's accounting. See Corkery (2010). Nesvetailova (2010, p. 92) writes also that at HBOS, one of Britain's largest mortgage lenders, the chief executive fired "an internal risk compliance manager who had warned management about the excessive risks in its loan portfolios."

According to the *Financial Crisis Inquiry Commission Report* released in 2011 and discussed in Craig and Protess (2011), Morgan Stanley and Citi were much closer to total failure than had been thought. See also Lybeck (2011) and Turner (2016).

66. Local banks and savings and loan organizations had been familiar with their local communities of borrowers and with local real estate values. Importantly, they held the loans on their balance sheets. They personally knew their borrowers and could quickly work to resolve any payment problems that might arise. In the new scheme of things, loans from a small town in the middle of the United States might end up in a package bought by a fund in Australia, Japan, or London, for example. Such packaging of mortgages and ostensible transfer of risk and responsibility meant that buyers of the structured products—being created in ever larger amounts by brokers and bankers who each earned handsome fees along the way—ended up with little knowledge of what the underlying assets were truly worth. Central to the whole problem was that mortgages in the United States were nonrecourse, meaning that banks could only repossess the house itself from people unable to pay off their loan commitments and could not attach other assets as collateral. Securitization of mortgage-backed securities was initially allowed by the Reagan administration in 1984. By 2004, one-third of subprime mortgages were being extended without any serious assessments of a borrower's ability to pay. Der Hovanesian (2008) and Laing (2008) provide more on the sleazy underbelly of the mortgage boom.

Stein (2008) suggests that the floodgates for such seemingly reckless activity were opened by new Securities and Exchange Commission rules in 2004 known as "Alternative Net Capital Requirements for Broker-Dealers That Are Part of Consolidated Supervised Entities." These rules allowed banks to count "hybrid capital instruments," subordinated debt, deferred returns of taxes, and even securities "for which there is no ready market" as a part of capital. The rules reduced the overall amount of capital needed to trade in risky assets.

The CBS network's *60 Minutes* program, "The Bet That Blew Up Wall Street," that was broadcast October 26, 2008, further suggested that the Commodity Futures Modernization Act of 2000 passed by the US Congress removed any restrictions on regulations of credit default swaps and was thereby an important cause of the credit market turmoil of 2008 that resulted in the demise of Bear Stearns and Lehman. See also Carney (2008) and Hilsenrath et al. (2008). This Act made it impossible to regulate swaps as either gambling bets or as securities issues.

Duhigg (2008) recounts how Congress (particularly Democrats) and also hedge fund managers had pressured Fannie Mae—a government-sponsored mortgage insurance company—into making more home loans available to low-income borrowers. "Whenever competitors asked Congress to rein in the company, lawmakers were besieged with letters and phone calls from angry constituents, some orchestrated by Fannie itself." As early as 2000, it had announced the intention to buy $2 trillion in loans from low-income, minority, and risky borrowers by 2010. Regulators soon increased the company's affordable-housing goals, with the Department of Housing and Urban Development requiring that 22% of loans in 2005 should be to low-income borrowers. See also Holmes (1999), who wrote that Fannie Mae "has been under increasing pressure from the Clinton Administration to expand mortgage loans among low and moderate income people…banks, thrift institutions and mortgage companies have been pressing Fannie Mae to help them make more loans to so-called subprime borrowers." Congress also enabled mortgage securitization through the Secondary Mortgage Market Enhancement Act of 1984 and the Tax Reform Act of 1986, which created the Real Estate Mortgage Investment Conduit (REMIC). Adding to this, the Boston Fed in 2003 issued a paper entitled "Closing the Gap: A Guide to Equal Opportunity Lending" which said that "Lack of credit history should not be seen as a negative factor in obtaining a mortgage." The tax advantages from REMIC significantly increased the attractiveness of mortgage-backed securities. Rajan (2010, pp. 21–45) views growing income and educational inequality as the politically motivating factor behind such credit extensions and provides a brief history of such motivations as applied to housing.

Ferguson (2008) provides a history of Fannie Mae and Morgenson and Rosner (2011) relate Fannie Mae to the major political pressures to encourage home ownership. Along the same lines, Gasparino (2009, p. 111) writes that secretary of housing, Henry Cisneros, in 1995 directed Fannie Mae and Freddie Mac to buy and guarantee mortgages of relatively low-income borrowers amounting to 42% of their annual business volume. This was central to the Cisneros-directed National Homeownership Strategy that was purposefully aimed at increasing home ownership rates by lower-income minority households. Successor Andrew Cuomo (later to be Governor of New York State) then moved the number up to 50% and directed the companies to buy mortgages of borrowers with "very low income."

For more historical details, see also Halbfinger and Powell (2010), Allison (2012), and Calomiris and Haber (2014, p. 19) who explain that once the Clinton administration pressured Fannie and Freddie to lower their underwriting standards, these "progressively weaker standards applied to *everyone*…a 2006 survey by the National Association of Realtors found that 46 percent of first-time homebuyers made no down payment at all." Gramm and Solon (2013) trace the problems to the first Clinton presidential campaign of 1992 and explain that Cisneros assured that "pension investments in affordable housing are as safe as pension investments in stocks and bonds." This resulted in bank regulators pressuring banks to make subprime loans, with each bank assigned a letter grade on how many such loans were made.

The American Dream Downpayment Act signed by President George W. Bush in 2003 was another step in the same direction. Norberg (2009) provides a detailed history and Cassidy (2009, p. 252) traces the birth of the modern subprime industry to the Depository Institutions Deregulation and Monetary Control Act of 1980, which lifted the cap on allowable bank and thrift interest-rate charges. However, legislation in 1984 and 1986 was relatively more important than that of 2003.

Securitizations of residential mortgages, called participation certificates, were initiated in the 1920s and helped boost the real estate market. And Ginnie Mae issued its first mortgage-backed security in 1970. But by 1992, as told by Roberts (2008), Congressional pressure for more loans to low- and moderate-income borrowers had intensified. The Community Reinvestment Act (CRA), first passed in 1977, was "strengthened" in 1995. The earlier Equal Credit Opportunity Act of 1974 was also similarly motivated. Arguably, all of this was also an outgrowth of the late 1980s savings and loan scandal, which resulted in bans against the banking practice of "red-lining" poor neighborhoods. Bajaj and Leonhardt (2008) also indicate that the Clinton administration's Taxpayer Relief Act of 1997, which exempted most home sales from capital gains taxes, widely incentivized people to view home investments as a tradeable asset class. Also involved was the Federal Housing Administration (FHA), which did nothing to restrain home appraisers from making the unrealistically high home-value estimates that were used to support extension of mortgages to people without sufficient income to carry them. Only after the first major wave of defaults and foreclosures did the FHA issue in 2009 a Home Valuation Code of Conduct.

Garrison (2001, p. 111) had earlier written that the Depository Institutions Deregulation and Monetary Control Act (DIDMCA) of 1980 "...drove commercial banks to alter their lending policy so to accept greater risks in order to achieve higher yields." On the same subject, former Fed Chairman Greenspan says in a CNBC documentary ("House of Cards") of February 12, 2009, that "If we tried to suppress the expansion of the subprime market, do you think that would have gone over very well with the Congress?" He also argued in a don't-blame-me article (Greenspan 2009a) that "home mortgage rates had become gradually decoupled from monetary policy" and that the high correlation between home prices and mortgage rates was "a far better indicator of rising home prices than the fed-funds rate...No one...employs overnight interest rates – such as the fed-funds rate – to determine the capitalization rate of real estate." A further defense appears in Colvin (2010). Chan (2011) summarizes the report of the Financial Crisis Inquiry Commission that "casts a wide net of blame, faulting two administrations, the Federal Reserve and other regulators."

In a later speech, "The Crisis," presented to the Brookings Institution and summarized in Chan (2010), Greenspan "acknowledged that the central bank failed to grasp the magnitude of the housing bubble but argued, as he had before, that its policy of low interest rates was not to blame...He stood by his conviction that little could be done to identify a bubble before it burst, much less to pop it...I fear that preventing bubbles will in the end turn out to be infeasible"; Mallaby (2016, pp. 208–27) shows that Greenspan early understood linkages between interest rates and housing prices.

In a speech at the American Economic Association annual conference, January 3, 2010, Fed chairman Bernanke said that regulatory failure, not low interest, rates were responsible for the housing bubble and the financial crisis that followed. "It is difficult to ascribe the house price bubble either to monetary policy or to the broader macroeconomic environment," said Bernanke. Available at http://www.federalreserve.gov/newsevents/speech/2010speech. htm. Counterpoints are provided by Taylor (2010), Jaroncinski and Smets (2008), Wessel (2010), and O'Driscoll (2008). Roll (2011) suggests that the entire crisis was misdiagnosed. Dunbar (2011) writes of important identifiable regulatory lapses at the Fed.

Gjerstad and Smith (2009), however, write, "The hypothesis we propose is that a financial crisis that originates in consumer debt, especially consumer debt concentrated at the low end of the wealth and income distribution, can be transmitted quickly and forcefully into the financial system." The 1997 elimination of taxes on residential capital gains of up to $500,000 contributed to the subsequent housing bubble. And, they added, as housing expenditures in the United States and elsewhere have historically absorbed about 30% of personal income, a doubling of prices without commensurate increases in income made a crash inevitable. Changes to CPI calculations for housing also led to important underestimation of inflation rates. See also Wallison (2014) on the possibility of a new housing bubble beginning to form in 2013 because the FHA is requiring down payments of just 3.5% and Fannie Mae, 5%, as compared to once-traditional 10–20% prior to 1992. See also Gjerstad and Smith 2014).

67. In option adjustable-rate mortgages (ARMs), borrowers were allowed to decide how much they wanted to pay each month.

68. Additional comparisons of this kind, that is, indexed durations of major bubbles, appear in *The Economist*, 21 June 2007. Virtually all such events tend to play out over a period of six or seven years, with the last third of the period containing the collapse.

69. Morgenson (2008a) provides an example of how consumers binged on borrowing and observes that loan repayment is now much less important to lenders than the fees and charges that the loans generate. And from Cecchetti (2008): "[H]ouse prices have typically been something like 14 times their annual rental rate. By mid-2006, prices had risen to more than 18 times rent." Himmelberg et al. (2005), however, attempt to "correct four common fallacies about the costliness of the housing market." They explain, for instance, that "the price of a house is not the same as the annual cost of owning...high price growth is not evidence per se that housing is overvalued....so accelerating house price growth and outsized price increases in certain markets are not intrinsically signs of a bubble...conventional metrics for assessing pricing in the housing market such as price-to-rent ratios or price-to-income ratios generally fail to reflect accurately the state of housing costs." Their main conclusion, however, is that "[A]s of the end of 2004, our analysis reveals little evidence of a housing bubble." See also Muelbauer et al. (2011) and note 70.

70. Ed Hyman at ISI Group, Yale's Robert Shiller, and David Rosenberg, formerly at Merrill Lynch (see Abelson 2006). Cassidy (2002) and Case and Shiller (2003, 2004) were prescient. Despite the early and persistent warnings published by their *own* research arm, however, top management at Merrill, obviously paying no heed, nonetheless ended up investing (note 65) most heavily in housing-related securities and operations at the very peak. It is yet another typical instance of the delusive unwillingness to listen to naysayers that appears at the tops of all bubbles.

71. McCarthy and Peach (2004), in December 2004, wrote, "As for the likelihood of a severe drop in home prices, our examination of historical national home prices finds no basis for concern...home prices have risen in line with increases in personal income and declines in nominal interest rates. Moreover, expectations of rapid price appreciation do not appear to be a major factor behind the strong housing market." From Krainer (2003): "...the house price/rental value ratio does not indicate that house prices are drastically out of line with their historical relationship with rental values." Leonhardt (2010) recounts that the Fed entirely misinterpreted conditions of the time, with Chairman Greenspan saying in 2004 that the rise in home values was "not enough in our judgment to raise major concerns," and with successor Bernanke saying in 2005 that a housing bubble was "a pretty unlikely possibility." As late as May 2007, Bernanke held that Fed officials "do not expect significant spillovers from the subprime market to the rest of the economy." Fed successor Janet Yellen on January 22, 2007, was similarly optimistic that fears of a collapse have been largely allayed. See Booth (2017, p. 75) who also later wrote that the Fed is not so mysterious as it is myopic Appelbaum (2012, 2013), Blinder (2013), a *Washington Post* October 27, 2005, article by Nell Henderson about Greenspan's "no national bubble, just local 'froth'", Bernanke's "no housing bubble to burst", and Mayer and Sinai (2005) for optimistic views on housing industry prospects. Countering the then-prevailing optimism was a perceptive Dallas Fed article by DiMartino and Duca (2007).

    It should not have been surprising that the chief economist for the National Association of Realtors, David Lereah, in his February 2006 book (*Why the Real Estate Boom Will Not Bust*) was saying that it was still a good time to buy. *Time* magazine's cover story of June 13, 2005, was "Home $weet Home."

    Gallin (2004) relates housing purchase prices to rents, however, and comes closer to calling the bubble. This paper is cited in Shiller (2008), which discusses why so few professional economists had been able to recognize the housing bubble until it had burst. Yet Zhou and Sornette (2006, 2007) early identified this bubble and its turning point. Bezemer (2009) lists those who correctly predicted. Barth (2009) provides a detailed history. Barlevy and Fisher (2010) design a rational expectations model in which speculative housing price bubbles can emerge. Gouldey and Thies (2012) explain the deadweight loss to society when the market cannot quickly clear. By 2006, the household debt-to-income ratio had risen to almost 120% in the United States and 140% in the United Kingdom versus 70% and 90%, respectively, in 1986.

72. Silber (2012, p. 10) writes that former Fed Chairman Paul Volcker was in 2005 the exceptional early skeptic and critic of the growing housing bubble. Much more typical was a Browning (2007b) article near the end of May 2007, at the cusp of the huge economic downturn, which quotes a small group of

seasoned investors who "believe the U.S. market is in the midst of another long period of gains...This group of extreme optimists believes that global economic strength will keep shares rising for much longer than has been common in previous eras." Reinhart and Rogoff (2009, p. 214) noted that as late as April 2007, the IMF concluded in its *World Economic Outlook* "that risks to the global economy had become extremely low." Adebambo et al. (2015), however, showed that institutional investors and financial analysts were somewhat aware of the impending crisis as seen in their preference for investments in nonfinancial stocks. See also "Houses Built on Sand," *The Economist*, September 13, 2007.

73. In the valuing of securities on bank and brokerage balance sheets, the most liquid securities are marked to the prices of similarly traded items. Other securities without actively traded counterparts then need to be "marked-to-model," which requires making important assumptions about the probability that the paper will pay off on schedule. However, the most exotic and toxic securities in this crisis were "marked to make-believe," which suggested that no one truly knew what their value was and that accountants were simply using their best judgment. This all follows the Financial Accounting Standards Board rules (FAS 157) on how public companies must value their assets when reporting earnings. Level 1 is mark-to-market value, based on price quotes in public markets. Level 2, which includes many CDOs, permits use of "observable inputs" to value assets when market prices aren't readily available. As for Level 3, for which inputs are unobservable? Guess. See, for example, Weil (2007), in which accounting expert Jack Ciesielski of the *Analyst's Accounting Observer* remarked in regard to Level 3, "It's akin to voodoo." See also Schwartz and Creswell (2008), SFAS 157, and "Level 3: An Investors' Guide," *Wall Street Journal*, June 2, 2008. In response to intense Congressional pressure from the House Committee on Financial Services, the FASB abandoned SFAS 157 on March 16, 2009. This abandonment of mark-to-market accounting removed the threat of widespread insolvency and gutting of bank capital through markdowns. It thereby cleared the way for the giant market rally to begin. Adrian and Shin (2010) show "that marked-to-market leverage is strongly pro-cyclical."

74. See Leamer (2007).

75. There was plenty of blame and ignorance to go round. See Ip et al. (2008) and Friedman and Kraus (2011). On increasing regulation, see Weisman (2008) and Williamson (2008). On the bailout of Fannie Mae and Freddie Mac, see Hagerty et al. (2008). The Treasury's performance during the crisis is reviewed by Nocera and Andrews (2008). Ferguson (2009), however, writes "that crises are more often caused by *bad* regulation than by *deregulation*." Deregulation was not the problem and, in fact, contributed to the development of many beneficial financial innovations.

76. The EOV approach toward crashes and bubbles that is later developed transcends the differences between financial market and commodity assets.

77. Fed Chairman Bernanke admitted in November 2010 that QE was designed to raise stock prices that "will boost consumer wealth and help increase confidence, which can also spur spending." But after a year (2013) in which $800 billion of bonds were purchased, the 10-year treasury's yield actually rose by almost 100 basis points. The QE4 implementation called for monthly Fed purchases of $85 billion of bonds per month ($40 billion of mortgage-backed securities and $45 billion of Treasuries) amounting to a $1 trillion per year rise

in the Fed's balance sheet holdings on top of the $2 trillion it had already accumulated from the earlier rounds. Details of Fed decisions in 2009 appear in transcripts released in 2015 and in reviews of them by Appelbaum (2015) and Morgenson (2015).

78. A paper presented at the August 2013 Jackson Hole conference by Krishnamurthy and Vissing-Jorgensen (2013) also suggested that QE or large-scale asset purchases, first used by the Bank of Japan in 2001, are not well understood and are less potent than the Fed and other central banks have assumed. See Bernasek (2013), Bhidé and Phelps (2013), McKinnon (2013), Malpass (2015), and Acharya and Naqvi (2016).

79. Adrangi et al. (2016).

80. Data collected by Sharma (2015).

81. Ewing (2014) writes that the ECB's negative deposit rate in 2014 might have helped some borrowers, the easy money did not reach struggling European businesses.

82. See Lyons and Inada (2017).

83. The term "money printing" is widely used but is greatly misleading. In the QE programs, money can be "pumped" into reserves but is not "printed" until commercial banks extend credit to consumers and businesses. Thus, instead of being "printed," central bank policies actually resulted in massive accumulation of commercial bank "excess reserves" which don't quickly translate into economic growth. "Helicopter" money, referring to a phrase coined by Milton Friedman and linked also to former Fed chairman Bernanke, is an extreme version of money stimulus. The Fed's Board of Governors website explains that the Fed has no legal authority to print money and is not involved in "printing" it. Reserves are not included in M1 or M2 money supply data but are a part of the monetary base.

84. Post the Brexit vote in June 2016, Dutch 10-year sovereigns reached their lowest yields in 500 years. The Bank of England's benchmark rate was at its lowest in 322 years. See Freeman (2016).

85. This outcome would not surprise proponents of the socionomic theory of finance as per Prechter (2016).

86. Irwin (2014) relays how the bubbling spread to assets of all kinds. As discussed in Giles (2014), the BOE tried to restrain a new UK housing bubble by employing controversial "macroprudential" tools that included the potential to change home loan-to-income ratios, stress tests, and bank capital requirements even while not overtly affecting forward guidance and interest-rate decisions.

87. Zero rates were actually counterproductive in that they reduced bank collateral, a lubricant of the important repo market said Columbia Prof. Charles Calomiris on a Bloomberg Radio interview, September 23, 2016.

88. See Poole (2013). Fed chair Janet Yellen, confident of Fed policies and models, said in a June 27, 2017, meeting at the British Academy in London that "she does not believe there will be another financial crisis in our lifetimes, thanks largely to reforms of the banking system since the 2007–09 crash." In later testimony to Congress (July 12), she walked back the comments saying that "I believe we have done a great deal since the financial crisis to strengthen the system and to make it more resilient…we can never be confident that there won't be another financial crisis." Prins (2018), however, labels central bankers "illusionists" and conjurers. See also Chap. 1, note 43.

89. Huszar (2013) writes of how ineffectual and disruptive QE policies had become. See also Poole (2013) about prospects for unwinding QE and Chen et al. (2011) about the tepid growth response from such Large-Scale Asset Purchase Programs (LSAPs). Hilsenrath (2013) wrote that as estimated by San Francisco Fed President John Williams, the 2010 QE program brought the jobless rate down 0.25% from what it would otherwise have been, or about 0.04 point for every $100 billion created to buy bonds! See also Hamilton and Wu (2012), Gagnon et al. (2011), and Gilchrist et al. (2015).

    In a March 2015 speech concerning policy normalization, Fed Vice Chairman Stanley Fischer said, "we have developed and tested new operational tools to control the federal funds rate…we will use the rate of interest paid on excess reserves as our primary tool to move the Fed funds rate…[W]e also plan to use an overnight reverse repurchase agreement facility, as needed" (www. federalreserve.gov/newsevents/speech/fischer20150323a.htm).

90. Acharya and Naqvi (2012).

91. From Voth (2003), "[T]he majority of bubbles have been associated with unusually high growth, unusually low inflation, a deteriorating current account, a rapid rise in the money supply as well as falling savings rates." And in viewing the wreckage from the housing bubble, Frank (2008) writes that "market failure occurs when two conditions are met. First, people confront a gamble that offers a highly probable small gain with only a very small chance of a significant loss. Second, the rewards received by market participants depend strongly on relative performance."

92. From Jordá et al. (2015) who studied bubbles in housing and equity markets in 17 countries over the past 140 years. See also Hilsenrath (2017).

93. Dent (2006, p. 80) classifies bubbles into asset, structural instability, and technology types, saying that "[T]echnology bubbles are very different in that they create residual new infrastructures that would not be created by normal economic incentives." Blinder (2008) distinguishes between bank-centered bubbles such as in housing and other asset bubbles such as in tech stocks, where bank lending "plays a minor role, or none at all." Housel (2010) distinguishes between valuation bubbles, such as in the dot-com episode, when investors paid incredibly high prices for companies with no revenues, and income bubbles in which banks like Citigroup or homebuilding stocks appeared to have reasonable valuations of earnings until it was later understood that those earnings were greatly inflated by unsustainable subprime lending and flimsy derivatives transactions. Jenkins (2010) writes that "[B]ubbles, after all, are essentially products of environments that leave companies confused or misled about where their long-term interests really lie."

    Another useful distinction is that although credit bubbles (e.g., 2003–2007) contain the same psychological ingredients and motivations as do equity bubbles, credit bubbles have been found by Hong and Sraer (2012) to be quieter than typically loud high-transaction-rate equity bubbles because the upside payoff on debt is bounded and the volume of trading is inherently limited by time to redemption and high prices.

94. Major bubbles are by Boston-based money management firm Grantham, Mayo, and Van Otterloo (GMO) as rising by at least two standard deviations above trendline.

95. Malkiel (2015, pp. 56–78) provides a succinct review of these smaller bubbles.
96. Ahamed (2009).
97. Listed in Calverley (2004, p. 13) and similarly in the *GMO Quarterly Letter*, Q! 2014. Chambers and Dimson (2016, p. 174) also compiled a similar list of seven common features of bubbles. Edward Chancellor also writes (following Schularick and Taylor 2009) in the March 2010 *GMO White Paper* entitled China's Red Flags that rapid credit growth is the most important leading indicator of financial instability. The presence of an asset price bubble is the second most reliable crisis indicator. Low interest rates and strong money growth are also good warning signs."
98. French (2009, p. 115) concludes that the common factor to all bubbles "has been a monetary intervention or tremendous increase in the supply of money, ultimately leading to ...malinvestments."
99. See Sect. 8.4, Hong and Stein (2007), and Scheinkman (2014, p. 15).
100. Quotation from legendary security analyst and investor Benjamin Graham.
101. Paraphrase from Paumgarten (2009).
102. Authers (2010, p. 5).
103. "There They Go Again...Again" Howard Marks, Oaktree Capital Management Letter, July 2017.
104. The young armies of brokerage and hedge fund rocket scientists hired to model and measure risk were ineffectual and arguably also contributed to the mess.
105. See Goodman and Morgenson (2008).
106. Berman et al. (2002) recount the recent end-of-bubble bogus telecom swaps, whereas Schlesinger and Gruley (2002) trace the personal experiences of small investors and their brokers and advisors. Stiglitz (2003) interprets the broad political environment in which the tech bubble was formed and sustained. And Roehner (2002, p. 139) relates how as is typical the market collapse in Japan in the early 1990s also exposed scandals and led to numerous official inquiries. The $50 billion Madoff fraud that came to light in December 2008 was one of the most prominent to come out of the credit-bubble collapse. See also Henriques and Kouwe (2008) and Gerding (2013) on regulation and law aspects.
107. Case in point is the 2500-page Dodd-Frank legislation of 2010, for which interpretation and implementation were still being decided several years later and during which time many financial industry firms were hamstrung by heightened operational uncertainty.

References

Abelson, A. (2006, January 30). Fun and Games. *Barron's*.
Abken, P. A. (1988). Stock Market Activity in October 1987: The Brady, CFTC & SEC Reports. *Economic Review. LXXIII*(3). FRB of Atlanta.
Acharya, V. V., & Naqvi, H. (2012). Bank Liquidity and Bubbles: Why Central Banks Should Lean Against Liquidity, in Evanoff et al. (2012).

Acharya, V., & Naqvi, H. (2016). On Reaching for Yield and the Coexistence of Bubbles and Negative Bubbles. Available at SSRN: https://ssrn.com/abstract=2618973 or https://doi.org/10.2139/ssrn.2618973

Adebambo, B., Brockman, P., & Yan, X. (2015, August). Anticipating the 2007–2008 Financial Crisis: Who Knew What and When Did They Know It? *Journal of Financial and Quantitative Analysis, 60*(4).

Adrangi, B., Chatrath, A., Macri, J., & Raffiee, K. (2016). The US Monetary Base and Major World Equity Markets: An Empirical Investigation. *Review of Economics and Finance, 6*, 49–64.

Adrian, T., & Shin, H. S. (2010). Liquidity and Leverage. *Journal of Financial Intermediation, 19*(3), 418–437, and Federal Reserve Bank of New York.

Ahamed, L. (2009). *Lords of Finance: The Bankers Who Broke the World*. New York: Penguin.

Allen, F. L. (1931). *Only Yesterday: An Informal History of the 1920s*. New York: Harper Perennial.

Allen, F., & Gale, D. (2000). Bubbles and Crises. *Economic Journal, 110*, 236–255.

Allison, J. A. (2012). The Fed's Fatal Conceit. *Cato Journal, 32*(2), 265–278.

Anderson, B. M. (1949). *Economics and the Public Welfare: Financial and Economic History of the United States, 1914–1946*. Princeton: D. Van Nostrand.

Anderson, J. (2008, February 19). Wall Street Banks Confront a String of Write-downs. *New York Times*.

Appelbaum, B. (2012, January 13). Inside the Fed in '06: Coming Crisis and Banter. *New York Times*.

Appelbaum, B. (2013, January 18). Days Before 2007 Crisis, Fed Officials Doubted Need to Act. *New York Times*.

Appelbaum, B. (2015, March 5). In Eye of Economic Storm, the Fed Blinked. *New York Times*.

Asako, K. (1991). The Land Price Bubble in Japan. *Ricerche Economiche, XLV*(2–3), 451–468.

Authers, J. (2010). *The Fearful Rise of Markets: Global Bubbles, Synchronized Meltdowns, and How to Prevent Them in the Fugure*. Saddle Brook, NJ: FT Press.

Ayres, R. U. (2014). *The Bubble Economy: Is Sustainable Growth Possible?* Cambridge, MA: MIT Press.

Bajaj, V., & Leonhardt, D. (2008, December 18). Tax Break May Have Helped Cause Housing Bubble. *New York Times*.

Balen, M. (2003). *The Secret History of the South Sea Bubble: The World's First Great Financial Scandal*. New York: HarperCollins (Fourth Estate). Also under the title, *The King, the Crook, & the Gambler*.

Barboza, D. (2010, March 5). Market Defies Fear of Real Estate Bubble in China. *New York Times*.

Barlevy, G., & Fisher, J. D. M. (2010). *Mortgage Choices and Housing Speculation*. Chicago: Federal Reserve Bank of Chicago.

Barth, J. R. (2009). *The Rise and Fall of the U. S. Mortgage and Credit Markets*. Hoboken: Wiley (with Milken Institute).

Bates, D. S. (1991). The Crash of '87: Was It Expected? The Evidence from Options Markets. *Journal of Finance, 46*(3), 1009–1044.

Beckman, R. (1988). *Crashes: Why They Happen – What to Do*. London: Sidgwick & Jackson.

Benzoni, L., Collin-Dufresne, P., & Goldstein, R. S. (2010). *Explaining Asset Pricing Puzzles Associated with the 1987 Market Crash*. Working Paper 2010–10, Federal Reserve Bank of Chicago.

Berman, D. K., Angwin, J., & Cummins, C. (2002, December 23). As Market Bubble Neared End, Bogus Swaps Provided a Lift. *Wall Street Journal*.

Bernanke, B. S. (1983). Nonmonetary Effects of the Financial Crisis in the Propagation of the Great Depression. *American Economic Review, 73*(3), 257–276.

Bernanke, B. S., Gertler, M., & Gilchrist, S. (1996). The Financial Accelerator and the Flight to Quality. *Review of Economics and Statistics, 78*(1), 1–15.

Bernasek, A. (2013, August 4). What the Nation Got for $800 Billion. *New York Times*.

Bernstein, P. L. (2005b). *Capital Ideas: The Improbable Origins of Modern Wall Street*. Hoboken: Wiley (Paperback edition).

Bernstein, J., & Eisinger, J. (2010, August 26). Banks' Self-Dealing Super-Charged Financial Crisis. Available at www.propublica.org/article/banks-self-dealing-super-charged-financial-crisis

Bezemer, D. J. (2009). 'No One Saw This Coming': Understanding Financial Crisis Through Accounting Models. MRA Paper No. 15892. Available at http://mpra.ub.uni-muenchen.de/15892/

Bhidé, A., & Phelps, E. (2013, July 16). Central Banking Needs Rethinking. *Wall Street Journal*.

Bierman, H., Jr. (1991). *The Great Myths of 1929 and the Lessons to be Learned*. Westport: Greenwood Press.

Biggs, B. (2006). *HedgeHogging*. Hoboken: Wiley.

Bissonnette, Z. (2015). *The Great Beanie Baby Bubble: Mass Delusion and the Dark Side of Cute*. New York: Portfolio/Penguin.

Bitmead, A., Durand, R. B., & Ng, H. G. (2004). Bubblelepsy: The Behavioral Wellspring of the Internet Stock Phenomenon. *Journal of Behavioral Finance, 5*(3), 154.

Black, F. (1988). An Equilibrium Model of the Crash. *NBER Macroeconomics Annual, 3*. Cambridge, MA: MIT Press.

Blinder, A. S. (2008, June 15). Two Bubbles, Two Paths. *New York Times*.

Blinder, A. S. (2013). *After the Music Stopped: The Financial Crisis, The Response, and the Work Ahead*. New York: Penguin Press.

Blumenstein, R. (2001, June 18). Web Overbuilt: How the Fiber Barons Plunged The Nation into a Telecom Glut. *Wall Street Journal*.

Booth, D. D. (2017). *Fed Up: An Insider's Take on Why the Federal Reserve Is Bad for America*. New York: Portfolio (Penguin).

Bose, M. (1988). *The Crash*. London: Bloomsbury Publishing.

Boyd, R. (2008). The Last Days of Bear Stearns. *Fortune, 157*(7), 40–43.

Brock, W. A. (1991). Causality, Chaos, Explanation, and Prediction in Economics and Finance. In J. Casti & A. Karlqvist (Eds.), *Beyond Belief: Randomness, Prediction, and Explanation in Science*. Boca Raton: CRC Press.

Brooks, J. (1969). *Once in Golconda: A True Drama of Wall Street, 1920–1938*. New York: Wiley (Paperback edition, 1999).

Browning, E. S. (2007, May 23). Why Market Optimists Say This Bull Has Legs. *Wall Street Journal*.

Browning, E. S. (2007b, May 23). Why Market Optimists Say This Bull Has Legs. *Wall Street Journal*.

Bruner, R. F., & Carr, S. D. (2007). *The Panic of 1907: Lessons Learned from the Market's Perfect Storm*. Hoboken: Wiley.

Brunnermeier, M. K. (2001). *Asset Pricing Under Asymmetric Information: Bubbles, Crashes, Technical Analysis, and Herding*. New York: Oxford University Press.

Brunnermeier, M. K., & Nagel, S. (2004, October). Hedge Funds and the Technology Bubble. *Journal of Finance, LIX*(6) and AFA 2004 San Diego Meetings; EFA 2003 Annual Conference Paper No. 446. Available at http://ssrn.com/abstract=423940

Buchan, J. (1997). *Frozen Desire: The Meaning of Money*. New York: Farrar Straus Giroux.

Buiter, W. H. (2009, March 3). The Unfortunate Uselessness of Most 'State of the Art' Academic Monetary Economics," *Financial Times*, March 3.

Calomiris, C. W., & Haber, S. H. (2014). *Fragile by Design: The Political Origins of Banking Crises and Scarce Credit*. Princeton: Princeton University Press.

Calverley, J. P. (2004). *Bubbles and How to Survive Them*. London: Nicholas Brealey.

Camplin, B., & Beighton, J. (2010). *Railway Mania*. Middlesbrough: Middlesbrough Institute of Modern Art.

Capie, F. H., & Wood, G. E. (Eds.). (2007). *The Lender of Last Resort*. London/New York: Routledge.

Caplin, A., & Leahy, J. (1994, June). Business as Usual, Market Crashes, and Wisdom After the Fact. *American Economic Review, 80*(3).

Carney, B. M. (2008, July 5). The Credit Crisis Is Going to Get Worse. *Wall Street Journal*.

Carney, B. M. (2013, February 23). Why the Euro Crisis Isn't Over. *Wall Street Journal*.

Case, K. E., & Shiller, R. J. (2003, September). Is There a Bubble in the Housing Market? *Brookings Papers on Economic Activity*, 2.

Case, K. E., & Shiller, R. J. (2004, August 24). Mi Casa Es Su Housing Bubble. *Wall Street Journal*.

Cassidy, J. (2002, November 11). The Next Crash. *The New Yorker*.

Cassidy, J. (2008, March 31). Subprime Suspect. *The New Yorker*.

Cassidy, J. (2009, October 5). Rational Irrationality. *The New Yorker*.

Casti, J., & Karlqvist, A. (Eds.). (1991). *Beyond Belief: Randomness, Prediction, and Explanation in Science*. Boca Raton: CRC Press.

Cecchetti, S. G. (2008). Asset Bubbles and the Fed. *Milken Institute Review*, Second Quarter.

Chambers, D., & Dimson, E., eds. (2016). *Financial Market History: Reflections on the Past for Investors Today*. Charlottesville: CFA Institute Research Foundation. Available at http://www.cfapubs.org/doi/pdf/10.2470/rf.v2016.n3.1

Chan, S. (2010, March 19). Greenspan Concedes That the Fed Failed to Gauge the Bubble. *New York Times*.

Chan, S. (2011, January 26). Financial Crisis Was Avoidable, Inquiry Finds. *New York Times*.

Chancellor, E. (1999). *Devil Take the Hindmost: A History of Financial Speculation*. New York: Farrar.

Chari, V. V., & Kehoe, P. J. (2003) *Financial Crises as Herds: Overturning the Critiques*. Staff Report 316, Federal Reserve Bank of Minneapolis.

Chari, V. V., Kehoe, P. J., & McGrattan, E. R. (2003). Accounting for the Great Depression. *Federal Reserve Bank of Minneapolis Quarterly Review, 27*(2), 22–27.

Chen, H., Cúrdia, V., & Ferrero, A. (2011, December). The Macroeconomic Effects of Large-Scale Asset Purchase Programs. *Federal Reserve Bank of New York Staff Report* No. 527.

Coakley, J., Hadass, L., & Wood, A. (2007). Post-IPO Operating Performance, Venture Capital and the Bubble Years. *Journal of Business Finance and Accounting, 34*(9–10), 1423–1446.

Cohan, W. D. (2010, May 3). Merrill Lynch's $50 Billion Feud. *Fortune, 161*(6).

Cohan, W. D. (2012, April). How We Got the Crash Wrong. *Atlantic Monthly*.

Cole, H. L., & Ohanian, L. E. (1999). The Great Depression in the United States from a Neoclassical Perspective. *Federal Reserve Bank of Minneapolis Quarterly Review, 23*(1), 2–24.

Colvin, G. (2010). Alan Greenspan Fights Back. *Fortune, 161*(3), 60–64. Straus, Giroux.

Cooper, G. (2008). *The Origin of Financial Crises: Central Banks, Credit Bubbles, and the Efficient Market Fallacy.* New York/Petersfield: Vintage (Paperback)/Harriman House.

Corkery, M. (2010, March 16). Lehman Whistle-Blower's Fate: Fired. *Wall Street Journal.*

Cowles, V. (2002). *The Great Swindle: The Story of the South Sea Bubble.* Hong Kong: Hindsight Books. [Copyright H. Crowley 1960].

Craig, S., & Protess, B. (2011, February 10). Morgan Stanley and Citi Were Closer to Brink Than Thought. *New York Times.*

Crossen, C. (2005, August 3). Land in 1920s Florida Was So Hot, People Sold Underwater Lots. *Wall Street Journal.*

Crovitz, L. G. (2009, January 26). Bad News Is Better Than No News. *Wall Street Journal.*

Dale, R. (2004, 2012). *The First Crash: Lessons from the South Sea Bubble.* Princeton: Princeton University Press.

Dale, R. S., Johnson, J. E. V., & Tang, L. (2005). Financial Markets Can Go Mad: Evidence of Irrational Behaviour During the South Sea Bubble. *Economic History Review, LVIII*(2), 233–271.

Das, S. (2006). *Traders Guns & Money.* Harlow: Prentice-Hall/Pearson.

Dash, M. (1999). *Tulipomania: The Story of the World's Most Coveted Flower and the Extraordinary Passions It Aroused.* New York: Crown Publishing.

Dash, E., & Creswell, J. (2008, November 23). Citigroup Pays for a Rush to Risk. *New York Times.*

Davidson, J. D., & Rees-Mogg, W. (1992). *The Great Reckoning.* London: Sidgwick & Jackson.

Davies, G. (2002). *A History of Money: From Ancient Times to the Present Day* (3rd ed.). Cardiff: University of Wales Press.

Davis, B. (2011a, June 27). China Risks Being Next Property-Bubble Blow Up. *Wall Street Journal.*

Davis, B. (2011b, June 9). The Great Property Bubble of China May Be Popping. *Wall Street Journal.*

De Long, J. B., & Shleifer, A. (1991). The Stock Market Bubble of 1929: Evidence from Closed-end Mutual Funds. *Journal of Economic History, 51,* 675–700.

Deidda, L. G., & Fattouh, B. (2005). *Banks, Financial Markets and Growth.* Working Paper 2005/11. London: SOAS, University of London and CRENoS. Available at www.crenos.it/working/pdf/05-11.pdf

Dent, H. S., Jr., & Pancholi, A. (2017). *Zero Hour.* New York: Portfolio/Penguin.

Dent, H. S., Jr. (2006). *The Next Great Bubble Boom: How to Profit from the Greatest Boom in History, 2006–2010.* New York: Simon & Schuster (Free Press).

Der Hovanesian, M. (2008, November 24). Sex, Lies, and Mortgage Deals. *BusinessWeek.*

Derman, E. (2011). *Models Behaving Badly: Why Confusing Illusion with Reality Can Lead to Disaster, on Wall Street and in Life.* New York: Free Press.

DiMartino, D., & Duca, J. V. (2007). The Rise and Fall of Subprime Mortgages. *Federal Reserve Bank of Dallas Economic Letter, 2*(11), 1–8.

Doherty, J. (2008, May 26). The Sad Story of Auction-Rate Securities. *Barron's.*

Dowd, K., & Hutchinson, M. (2010). *Alchemists of Loss: How Modern Finance and Government Intervention Crashed the Financial System.* Chichester: Wiley.

Dreazen, Y. J. (2002, September 26). Wildly Optimistic Data Drove Telecoms to Build Fiber Glut. *Wall Street Journal*.

Duhigg, C. (2008, October 4). Pressured to Take More Risk, Fannie Reached a Tipping Point. *New York Times*.

Dunbar, N. (2000). *Inventing Money: The Story of Long-Term Capital Management and the Legends Behind It*. Chichester: Wiley.

Dunbar, N. (2011). *The Devil's Derivatives: The Untold Story of the Slick Traders and Hapless Regulators Who Almost Blew Up Wall Street*. Boston: Harvard Business School Publishing.

Economic Planning Agency. (1992). *Kokumin keizai keisan nenpo* [National Account Statistics]. Economic Planning Agency.

Evanoff, D. D., Kaufman, G. G., & Malliaris, A. G. (Eds.). (2012). *New Perspectives on Asset Price Bubbles: Theory, Evidence, and Policy*. New York: Oxford University Press.

Ewing, J. (2014, September 3). Europe Crisis Is Resistant to Medicine of Low Rates. *New York Times*.

Fackler, M. (2008, December 19). Japan Offers a Possible Road Map for U.S. Economy. *New York Times*.

Fawley, B. W., & Neely, C. J. (2013). Four Stories of Quantitative Easing. *Federal Reserve Bank of St. Louis Review, 95*(1), 51–88.

Feigenbaum, J. A. (2001). A Statistical Analysis of Log-Periodic Precursors to Financial Crashes. *Quantitative Finance, 1*(3), 346–360.

Ferguson, N. (2008, December). Wall Street Lays Another Egg. *Vanity Fair*.

Ferguson, N. (2009, May 17). Diminished Returns. *New York Times*.

Fong, D., & Wei, L. (2016, October 8). Fears Rise of China Housing Bubble. *Wall Street Journal*.

Frank, R. H. (2008, October 4). Pursuit of an Edge, in Steroids or Stocks. *New York Times*.

Freeman, J. (2016, September 1). The 5,000-Year Government Debt Bubble. *Wall Street Journal*.

Frehen, R. G. P., Goeztmann, W. N., and Rowenhorst, K. (2013). "New Evidence on the First Financial Bubble," *Journal pf Financial Economics*, 108(3) and Yale ICF Working Paper No. 09-04. Available at SSRN: http://ssrn.com/abstract=1371007

French, D. E. (2006). The Dutch Monetary Environment During Tulipmania. *Quarterly Journal of Austrian Economics, 9*(1), 3–14.

French, D. E. (2009). *Early Speculative Bubbles and Increases in the Supply of Money* (2nd ed.). Auburn: Ludwig von Mises Institute.

French, K. R., & Poterba, J. M. (1991). Were Japanese Stock Prices Too High? *Journal of Financial Economics, 29*, 337.

Friedman, J., & Kraus, W. (2011). *Engineering the Financial Crisis: Systemic Risk and the Failure of Regulation*. Philadelphia: University of Pennsylvania Press.

Gagnon, J., Raskin, M., Remache, J., & Sack, B. (2011). "Large-Scale Asset Purchases by the Federal Reserve: Did They Work?" Federal Reserve Bank of New York, *Economic Policy Review*, 17. Available at www.newyorkfed.org/research/staff_reports/sr441.html

Galbraith, J. K. (1944). *A Short History of Financial Euphoria*. New York: Penguin (Paper 1993).

Galbraith, J. K. (1988). *The Great Crash, 1929* (2nd ed.). Boston: Houghton-Mifflin.

Gallin, J. (2004). *The Long-Run Relationship Between House Prices and Rents*. Working Paper 2004–50. Washington, DC: Federal Reserve Board.

Garber, P. M. (1990). Who Put the Mania in Tulipmania?, in White, ed. (1990).

Garber, P. M. (2000). *Famous First Bubbles: The Fundamentals of Early Manias.* Cambridge, MA: MIT Press.

Garrison, R. W. (2001). *Time and Money: The Macroeconomics of Capital Structure.* London/New York: Routledge.

Garside, W. R. (2007). The Great Depression, 1929–33. In M. J. Oliver & D. H. Aldcroft (Eds.), *Economic Disasters of the Twentieth Century.* Cheltenham: Edward Elgar.

Gasparino, C. (2005). *Blood on the Street.* New York: Free Press.

Gasparino, C. (2009). *The Sellout: How Three Decades of Wall Street Greed and Government Mismanagement Destroyed the Global Financial System.* New York: Harper Business.

Geisst, C. R. (2004). *Wall Street: A History from Its Beginnings to the Fall of Enron.* Oxford: Oxford University Press.

Gerding, E. F. (2013). *Law, Bubbles, and Financial Regulation.* New York: Routledge.

Gilchrist, S., López-Salido, D., & Zakrajšek, E. (2015). Monetary Policy and Real Borrowing Costs at the Zero Lower Bound. *American Economic Journal: Macroeconomics, 7*(1), 77–109.

Giles, C. (2014, June 25). Crashing the Party: The Central Bank Has New Tools to Stop Bubbles. *Financial Times.*

Gjerstad, S. D., & Smith, V. L. (2009, April 6). From Bubble to Depression? *Wall Street Journal.*

Gjerstad, S. D., & Smith, V. L. (2014). *Rethinking Housing Bubbles.* New York: Cambridge University Press.

Glassman, J. K., & Hassett, K. A. (1999a). *Dow 36,000: The New Strategy for Profiting from the Coming Rise in the Stock Market.* New York: Times Books.

Gleeson, J. (1999). *Millionaire: The Philanderer, Gambler, and Duelist Who Invented Modern Finance.* New York: Simon & Schuster/Touchstone.

Goetzmann, W. N. (2016b). *Money Changes Everything: How Finance Made Civilization Possible.* Princeton: Princeton University Press.

Goldgar, A. (2007). *Tulipmania: Money, Honor, and Knowledge in the Dutch Golden Age.* Chicago: University of Chicago Press.

Goodman, P. S., & Morgenson, G. (2008, December 27). Saying Yes, WaMu Built Empire on Shaky Loans. *New York Times.*

Gorton, G. B. (2008). Information, Liquidity, and the (Ongoing) Panic of 2007. *American Economic Review, Papers and Proceedings, 99*(2), 567–572.

Gorton, G. B. (2010). *Slapped by the Invisible Hand: The Panic of 2007.* New York: Oxford University Press.

Gouldey, B. K., & Thies, C. F. (2012). Asset Bubbles and Supply Failures: Where Are the Qualified Sellers? *Cato Journal, 32*(3), 513–538.

Gramm, P., & Solon, M. (2013, August 12). The Clinton-Era Roots of the Financial Crisis. *Wall Street Journal.*

Grant, J. (1996). *The Trouble with Prosperity: The Loss of Fear, the Rise of Speculation, and the Risk.* New York: Times Books (Random House).

Grant, J. (2014). *The Forgotten Depression –1921: The Crash That Cured Itself.* New York: Simon & Schuster.

Grant, J. (2016, September 10). Hostage to a Bull Market. *Wall Street Journal.*

Gray, W. R., & Vogel, J. R. (2016). *Quantitative Momentum.* Hoboken: Wiley.

Greenspan, A. (2009a, March 11). The Fed Didn't Cause the Housing Bubble. *Wall Street Journal.*

Gross, D. (2002). The Fiber-Optic Network Bubble: Back to the Future. *Milken Institute Review* (First Quarter).

Hagerty, J. R., Simon, R., & Paletta, D. (2008, September 8). U.S. Seizes Mortgage Giants. *Wall Street Journal.*

Halbfinger, D. M., & Powell, M. (2010, August 24). As HUD Chief, Cuomo Earns A Mixed Score. *New York Times.*

Hall, R. E. (2001). Struggling to Understand the Stock Market. *American Economic Review, 91*(2), 1–11.

Hamilton, J. D., & Wu, J. C. (2012). The Effectiveness of Alternative Monetary Policy Tools in a Zero Lower Bound Environment. *Journal of Money, Credit and Banking, 44,* 3–46.

Harrison, M. J., & Kreps, D. (1978). Speculative Investor Behavior in a Stock Market with Heterogeneous Expectations. *Quarterly Journal of Economics, 89,* 519–542.

Henriques, D. B. (2017). *Anatomy of a Crash: A First-Class Catastrophe.* New York: Holt.

Henriques, D. B., & Kouwe, Z. (2008, December 11). Prominent Trader Accused of Defrauding Clients. *New York Times.*

Hilsenrath, J. E. (2012, December 31). Fed's Computer Models Pose Problems. *Wall Street Journal.*

Hilsenrath, J. E. (2013, December 17). Meltdown Averted, Bernanke Struggled to Stoke Growth. *Wall Street Journal.*

Hilsenrath, J. E. (2017, September 23). What We Know About Financial Bubbles: Bubbles Aren't Necessarily Bad Things. *Wall Street Journal.*

Hilsenrath, J. E., & Fujikawa, M. (2011, March 1). Japan's Bernanke Hits Out At His Critics in the West. *Wall Street Journal.*

Hilsenrath, J. E., Solomon, D., & Paletta, D. (2008, November 10). Paulson, Bernanke Strained for Consensus in Bailout. *Wall Street Journal.*

Himmelberg, C., Mayer, C., & Sinai, T. (2005). Assessing High House Prices: Bubbles, Fundamentals and Misperceptions. *Journal of Economic Perspectives, 19*(4), 67–92.

Holmes, S. A. (1999, September 30). Fannie Mae Eases Credit to Aid Mortgage Lending. *New York Times.*

Hong, H., & Sraer, D. (2012). *Quiet Bubbles,* NBER Working Paper 18547. Available at www.nber.org/papers/w18547

Hong, H., & Stein, J. C. (2007). Disagreement and the Stock Market. *Journal of Economic Perspectives, 21*(2), 109–128.

Hoshi, T., & Kashyap, A. (1999). The Japanese Banking Crisis: Where Did It Come From and How Will It End? *NBER Macroeconomics Annual.* Cambridge, MA: MIT Press and in Evanoff et al. (2012).

Housel, M. (2010, September 28). A Tale of Two Bubbles. Available at www.fool.com/investing/general.

Huszar, A. (2013, November 12). Confessions of a Quantitative Easer. *Wall Street Journal.*

Ip, G. (2005, December 7). Long Study of Great Depression Has Shaped Bernanke's Views. *Wall Street Journal.*

Ip, G., Hagerty, J. R., & Karp, J. (2008, March 19). Housing Bust Fuels Blame Game. *Wall Street Journal.*

Irwin, N. (2014, July 8). From Stocks to Farmland, All's Booming or Bubbling. *New York Times.*

Ito, T., & Iwaisako, T. (1996). Explaining Asset Bubbles in Japan. Bank of Japan, *Monetary and Economic Studies, 14,* 143–193, and Working Paper No. 5358. NBER.org.

Jacobs, B. I. (1999). *Capital Ideas and Market Realities: Option Replication, Investor Behavior, and Stock Market Crashes*. Oxford, UK: Blackwell.

Jaroncinski, M., & Smets, F. R. (2008, July/August). House Prices and the Stance of Monetary Policy. *Review*, Federal Reserve Bank of St. Louis.

Jenkins, H. W., Jr. (2010, December 22). Next, an Aircraft Bubble? *Wall Street Journal*.

Johnson, P. (1991). *Modern Times: The World From the Twenties to the Nineties* (rev ed.). New York: Perennial Classics/HarperCollins.

Jordá, Ò., Schularick, M., & Taylor, A. M. (2014). *The Great Mortgaging: Housing Finance, Crises, and Business Cycles*. Federal Reserve Bank of San Francisco, Working Paper 2014–23. Available at http://www.frbsf.org/economic-research/publications/working-papers/wp2014-23.pdf

Jordá, Ò., Schularick, M., & Taylor, A. M. (2015). Leveraged Bubbles. *Journal of Monetary Economics, 76*(Supplement), S1–S20.

Jovanovic, F., & Schinckus, C. (2017). *Econophysics and Financial Economics: An Emerging Dialog*. New York: Oxford University Press.

Justiniano, A., Primiceri, G. F., & Tambalotti, A. (2015, February). Credit Supply and the Housing Boom. *Federal Reserve Bank of New York Staff Reports*, no. 709.

Kelly, K. (2008a, May 29). Bear Stearns Neared Collapse Twice in Frenzied Final Week. *Wall Street Journal*.

Kelly, K. (2008b, May 28). Fear, Rumors Touched Off Fatal Run on Bear Stearns. *Wall Street Journal*.

Kelly, K. (2008c, May 27). Lost Opportunities Haunt Final Days of Bear Stearns. *Wall Street Journal*.

Kelly, K. (2009a, May 9). Inside the Fall of Bear Stearns. *Wall Street Journal*.

Kelly, K. (2009b). *Street Fighters: The last 72 Hours of Bear Stearns, the Toughest Firm on Wall Street*. New York: Portfolio (Penguin Group).

Kelly, K., Ng, S., & Strasburg, J. (2008, March 13). In Dealing With Bear Stearns, Wall Street Plays Guardedly. *Wall Street Journal*.

Keynes, J. M. (1936). *The General Theory of Employment, Interest, and Money*. London/San Diego: Macmillan/Harcourt Brace. (1964 reprint).

Kindleberger, C. (1996 [1989]). *Manias, Panics, and Crashes: A History of Financial Crises* (3rd ed.). New York: Wiley. (2nd Ed., 1989).

Kindleberger, C., & Aliber, R. Z. (2011). *Manias, Panics, and Crashes: A History of Financial Crises* (6th ed.). Houndmills: Palgrave Macmillan.

Klein, M. (2001). *Rainbow's End: The Crash of 1929*. New York: Oxford University Press.

Klingaman, W. K. (1989). *1929: The Year of the Great Crash*. New York: Harper & Row.

Knee, J. (2006). *The Accidental Investment Banker: Inside the Decade That Transformed Wall Street*. New York: Oxford University Press.

Knight, T. (2014). *Panic, Prosperity, and Progress: Five Centuries of History and the Markets*. Hoboken: Wiley.

Koo, R. C. (2010). Lessons from Japan: Fighting a Balance Sheet Recession. *CFA Institute Conference Proceedings Quarterly, 27*(4), 28–39.

Krainer, J. (2003). House Price Bubbles. *Economic Letter* (#2003–06), Federal Reserve Bank of San Francisco.

Krishnamurthy, A., & Vissing-Jorgensen, A. (2013). The Ins and Outs of LSAPs. http://kansascityfed.org/publicat/sympos/2013/2013Krishnamurthy.pdf

Krueger, A. B. (2005, April 28). Economists Try to Explain Why Bubbles Happen. *New York Times*.

Laing, J. R. (2008, July 14). Bottom's Up: This Real-Estate Rout May Be Short-Lived. *Barron's*.

Laing, J. R. (2013, June 24). Where Will It End? *Barron's*.

Lattman, P., Smith, R., & Strasburg, J. (2008, March 14). Carlyle Fund in Free Fall as Its Banks Get Nervous. *Wall Street Journal*.

Leamer, E. E. (2007). Housing Is the Business Cycle. In *Housing, Housing Finance, and Monetary Policy*. Kansas City: Federal Reserve Bank of Kansas City.

Lee, T. (2004). *Why the Markets Went Crazy*. New York: Palgrave Macmillan.

Leland, H. E., & Rubinstein, M. (1988). Comments on the Market Crash: Six Months After. *Journal of Economic Perspectives, 2*(3), 45–50.

Leonhardt, D. (2010, January 6). If Fed Missed This Bubble, Will It See a New One? *New York Times*.

Li, D. (2000). On Default Correlation: A Copula Function Approach. *Journal of Fixed Income, 9*(4), 43–54.

Loeys, J., & Panigirtzoglou, N. (2006). Are Alternatives the Next Bubble? *Journal of Alternative Investments, 9*(3), 54–76.

Lohr, S. (2008, November 5). In Modeling Risk, the Human Factor Was Left Out. *New York Times*.

Lohr, S. (2009, September 13). Wall Street's Math Wizards Forgot a Few Variables. *New York Times*.

Lowenstein, R. (2004). *Origins of the Crash: The Great Bubble and Its Undoing*. New York: Penguin.

Lowenstein, R. (2008a). Long-Term Capital: It's a Short-Term Memory. *New York Times*.

Lowenstein, R. (2008b, April 27). Triple-A Failure: The Ratings Game. *New York Times*.

Lowenstein, R. (2016). *America's Bank: The Epic Struggle to Create the Federal Reserve*. New York: Penguin (Paperback).

Lucchetti, A. (2007, October 16). After Crash, NYSE Got the Message(s). *Wall Street Journal*.

Lybeck, J. A. (2011). *A Global History of the Financial Crash of 2007–10*. Cambridge, UK: Cambridge University Press.

Lyons, J., & Inada, M. (2017, February 27). The World's Most Radical Experiment in Monetary Policy Isn't Working. *Wall Street Journal*.

Mackay, C. (1841). *Extraordinary Popular Delusions and the Madness of Crowds* (1995 edn). New York: Wiley.

Malkiel, B. G. (7th ed., 8th ed. (2003), 9th ed. (2007), 11th ed. (2015)). *A Random Walk Down Wall Street*. New York: W. W. Norton,

Mallaby, S. (2016). *The Man Who Knew: The Life and Times of Alan Greenspan*. New York: Penguin/Random House.

Malliaris, A. G., & Urrutia, J. L. (1992). The International Crash of October 1987: Causality Tests. *Journal of Financial and Quantitative Analysis, 27*(3), 353.

Malpass, D. (2015, January 22). The World's Monetary Dead End. *Wall Street Journal*.

Mansharamani, V. (2011). *Boombustology: Spotting Financial Bubbles Before They Burst*. Hoboken: Wiley.

Mauboussin, M. J. (2006). *More Than You Know: Finding Financial Wisdom in Unconventional Places*. New York: Columbia University Press.

Mayer, C., & Sinai, T. (2005, September 19). Bubble Trouble? Not Likely. *Wall Street Journal*.

McCarthy, J., & Peach, R. W. (2004, December). Are Home Prices the Next 'Bubble'? Federal Reserve Bank of New York, *Economic Policy Review*.

McDonald, L. G., & Robinson, P. (2009). *A Colossal Failure of Common Sense: The Inside Story of the Collapse of Lehman Brothers*. New York: Crown.

McKinnon, R. I. (2013, July 30). The Near-Zero Interest Rate Trap. *Wall Street Journal*.

McLean, B., & Nocera, J. (2010). *All the Devils Are Here*. New York: Penguin Group (Portfolio).

Merton, R. C. (1992). *Continuous-Time Finance* (rev ed.). Oxford, UK: Blackwell.

Milne, A. (2009). *The Fall of the House of Credit*. Cambridge, UK: Cambridge University Press.

Mishkin, F. S., & White, E. N. (2003). Stock Market Bubbles: When Does Intervention Work? *Milken Institute Review*, Second Quarter.

Mollenkamp, C., & Ng, S. (2007, December 27). Wall Street Wizardry Amplified Credit Crisis. *Wall Street Journal*.

Mollenkamp, C., & Whitehouse, M. (2008, March 17). Banks Fear a Deepening of Turmoil. *Wall Street Journal*.

Mollenkamp, C., Ng, S., Pleven, L., & Smith, R. (2008, November 3). Behind AIG's Fall, Risk Models Failed to Pass Real-World Test. *Wall Street Journal*.

Mora, N. (2008). The Effect of Bank Credit on Asset Prices: Evidence from the Japanese Real Estate Boom During the 1980s. *Journal of Money, Credit and Banking, 40*(1), 57–87.

Morgenson, G. (2008a, November 8). How the Thundering Herd Faltered and Fell. *New York Times*.

Morgenson, G. (2008b, July 20). Given a Shovel, Americans Dig Deeper Into Debt. *New York Times*.

Morgenson, G. (2015, March). At the Fed in 2009, Rolling Dice in a Crisis. *New York Times*.

Morgenson, G., & Rosner, J. (2011). *Reckless Endangerment: How Outsized Ambition, Greed, and Corruption Led to Economic Armageddon*. New York: Times Books (Henry Holt).

Morgenson, G., & Story, L. (2009, December 24). Banks Bundled Bad Debt, Bet Against It and Won. *New York Times*.

Morris, C. R. (2017). *A Rabble of Dead Money: The Great Crash and the Global Depression, 1929–39*. New York: Public Affairs.

Muelbauer, J., Duca, J., & Murphy, A. (2011). Home Prices and Credit Constraints: Making Sense of the U.S. Experience. *Economic Journal, 121*(532), 533–551.

Murase, H. (2012). Macroeconomics of Weak Corporate Governance: An alternative Theory of Japan's Lost Decade. *Japan Society of Monetary Economics*. Available at http://www.jsmeweb.org/kinyu/pdf/journal/full-paper34en-murase.pdf

Napier, R. (2007). *Anatomy of the Bear: Lessons from Wall Street's Four Great Bottoms* (2nd ed.). Hampshire: Harriman House.

Neal, L. D. (1990). How the South Sea Bubble Was Blown Up and Burst: A New Look at Old Data, in White (1990).

Neal, L. D. (1998, May–June). The Financial Crisis of 1825 and the Restructuring of the British Financial System. *FRB St. Louis Review*.

Neal, L. D. (2015). *A Concise History of International Finance from Babylon to Bernanke*. Cambridge, UK: Cambridge University Press.

Nesvetailova, A. (2010). *Financial Alchemy in Crisis: The Great Liquidity Illusion*. London: Pluto Press.

Ng, S., & Pleven, L. (2009, February 5). An AIG Unit's Quest to Juice Profit. *Wall Street Journal*.

Nocera, J. (1999). Do You Believe? How Yahoo! Became a Blue Chip. *Fortune, 139*(11), 76–92.

Nocera, J. (2009a, February 28).Propping Up a House of Cards. *New York Times*.

Nocera, J. (2009b, January 2). Risk Mismanagement. *New York Times*.

Nocera, J. (2010, April 17). A Wall Street Invention That Let the Crisis Mutate. *New York Times*.

Nocera, J., & Andrews, E. L. (2008, October 22). Struggling to Keep Up as the Crisis Raced On. *New York Times*.

Noguchi, Y. (1994). The 'Bubble' and Economic Policies in the 1980s. *Journal of Japanese Studies, 20*(2), 291–329.

Norberg, J. (2009). *Financial Fiasco: How America's Infatuation with Homeownership and Easy Money Created the Economic Crisis*. Washington, DC: Cato Institute.

Norris, F. (1987, October 26). The Crash of 1987. *Barron's*.

O'Driscoll, G. P., Jr. (2008, May 20). Asset Bubbles and Their Consequences. Cato Institute Briefing Paper No. 103.

O'Harrow, R., Jr., & Dennis, B. (2008a, December 30). A Crack in The System. *Washington Post*.

O'Harrow, R., Jr., & Dennis, B. (2008b, December 31). Downgrades and Downfall. *Washington Post*.

O'Harrow, R., Jr., & Dennis, B. (2008c, December 29). The Beautiful Machine: Greed on Wall Street and Blindness in Washington Certainly. *Washington Post*.

Odlyzko, A. (2010). *Collective Hallucinations and Inefficient Markets: The British Railway Mania of the 1840s*. Minneapolis: University of Minnesota.

Ofek, E., & Richardson, M. (2001). DotCom Mania: The Rise and Fall of Internet Stock Prices. Working paper, No. 8630, National Bureau of Economic Research.

Onaran, Y. (2012). *Zombie Banks: How Broken Banks and Debtor Nations Are Crippling the Global Economy*. New York: Bloomberg Press/Wiley.

Patterson, S. (2010). *The Quants: How a New Breed of Math Whizzes Conquered Wall Street and Nearly Destroyed It*. New York: Crown (Random House).

Paumgarten, N. (2009, October 12). The Secret Cycle. *The New Yorker*.

Pepper, G., & Oliver, M. J. (2006). *The Liquidity Theory of Asset Prices*. Chichester: Wiley.

Poole, W. (2013). Prospects for and Ramifications of the Great Central Banking Unwind. *Financial Analysts Journal, 69*(6), 33–39.

Posthumus, N. W. (1929, May). The Tulip Mania in Holland. *Journal of Economic and Business History*.

Prechter, R. R., Jr. (2016). *The Socionomic Theory of Finance*. Gainesville: Socionomics Institute Press.

Presscott, E. C. (1999). Some Observations on the Great Depression. *Federal Reserve Bank of Minneapolis Quarterly Review, 23*(1), 25–31.

Pribram, K. (1983). *A History of Economic Reasoning*. Baltimore: Johns Hopkins University Press.

Prins, N. (2018). *Collusion: How Central Banks Rigged the World*. New York: Perseus.

Pulliam, S., Ng, S., & Smith, R. (2008, April 16). Merrill Upped Ante as Boom as Mortgage Bonds Fizzled. *Wall Street Journal*.

Rajan, R. G. (2010). *Fault Lines: How Hidden Fractures Still Threaten the World Economy*. Princeton: Princeton University Press.

Rappoport, P., & White, E. (1993). Was There a Bubble in the 1929 Stock Market? *Journal of Economic History, 53*, 549–574.

Rappoport, P., & White, E. (1994). Was the Crash of 1929 Expected? *American Economic Review, 84*, 271–281.

Reilly, D., & Mollenkamp, C. (2007, August 30). 'Conduits' in Need of a Fix. *Wall Street Journal*.

Reingold, D., & Reingold, J. (2006). *Confessions of a Wall Street Analyst*. New York: HarperCollins.

Reinhart, C. M., & Rogoff, K. S. (2009). *This Time Is Different: Eight Centuries of Financial Folly*. Princeton: Princeton University Press.

Roberts, R. (2008, October 3). How Government Stoked the Mania. *Wall Street Journal*.

Roehner, B. M. (2002). *Patterns of Speculation: A Study in Observational Econophysics*. Cambridge, UK: Cambridge University Press.

Roll, R. (2011). The Possible Misdiagnosis of a Crisis. *Financial Analysts Journal, 67*(2), 12–17.

Roubini, N., & Mihm, S. (2011). *Crisis Economics: A Crash Course in the Future of Finance*. New York: Penguin.

Salmon, F. (2009, March). Recipe for Disaster: The Formula That Killed Wall Street. *Wired, 17*(3).

Sato, Y. (2016). "Fund Tournaments and Asset Bubbles," *Review of Finance*, 20(4) (July).

Schacter, S., Hood, D., Gerin, W., & Adreassen, P. (1985). Was the South Sea Bubble a Random Walk? *Journal of Economic Behavior and Organization, 6*, 323–329.

Scheinkman, J. A. (2014). *Speculation, Trading, and Bubbles*. New York: Columbia University Press.

Scheinkman, J. A., & Xiong, W. (2003). Overconfidence and Speculative Bubbles. *Journal of Political Economy, 111*(6), 1183.

Schlesinger, J. M., & Gruley, B. (2002, December 27). A Tale of a Broker and His Clients and an Era's End. *Wall Street Journal*.

Schularick, M., & Taylor, A. (2012). Credit Booms Gone Bust: Monetary Policy, Leverage Cycles and Financial Crises, 1870–2008. *American Economic Review, 102*(2), 1029–1061.

Schwartz, A. J. (1986). Real and Pseudo-Financial Crises. In F. H. Capie & G. E. Wood (Eds.), *The Lender of Last Resort*. London: Routledge.

Schwartz, N. D. (2008, March 16). Wait. Weren't These Safer Bets? *New York Times*.

Schwartz, N. D., & Creswell, J. (2008, March 23). What Created this Monster? *New York Times*.

Segaller, S. (1999). *Nerds 2.0.1: A Brief History of the Internet*. New York: TV Books.

Sender, H, Guerrera, F., Larsen, P. T., & Silverman, G. (2008, September 15). Broken Brothers: How Brinkmanship Was Not Enough to Save Lehman. *Financial Times*.

Sharma, R. (2015, May 12). The Federal Reserve Asset Bubble Machine. *Wall Street Journal*.

Sheng, A. (2009). *From Asian to Global Financial Crisis: An Asian Regulator's View of Unfettered Finance in the 1990s and 2000s*. New York: Cambridge University Press.

Shiller, R. J. (2008, November 1). Challenging the Crowd in Whispers, Not Shouts. *New York Times*.

Shiller, R. J. (2013, April 21). Before Housing Bubbles, There Was Land Fever. *New York Times*.

Siebert, H. (1999). Some Lessons from the Japanese Bubble. Kiel Working Paper No. 919, Kiel: Kiel Institute of World Economics. Available at http://opus.zbw-kiel.de/volltexte/2003/27/pdf/268909717.pdf

Siegel, J. J. (1992). Equity Risk Premia, Corporate Profit Forecasts, and Investor Sentiment Around the Stock Crash of October 1987. *Journal of Business, 65*(4), 557.

Silber, W. L. (2012). *Volcker: The Triumph of Persistence.* New York: Bloomsbury Press.

Smith, E. L. (1924). *Common Stocks as Long-Term Investments.* New York: Macmillan.

Sobel, R. (1968). *The Great Bull Market: Wall Street in the 1920s.* New York: Norton.

Sommer, J. (2014, March 30). In Some Ways, It's Looking Like 1999 in the Stock Market. *New York Times.*

Stein, B. (2008, April 27). Wall Street, Run Amok. *New York Times.*

Stiglitz, J. E. (2003). *The Roaring Nineties: A New History of the World's Most Prosperous Decade.* New York: Norton.

Stone, D., & Ziemba, W. T. (1993). Land and Stock Prices in Japan. *Journal of Economic Perspectives, 7*(3), 149–165.

Story, L. (2010a, December 12). A Secretive Banking Elite Rules Trading in Derivatives. *New York Times.*

Story, L. (2010b, August 10). Hidden From the Light: Regulators Unearth Merrill's Dodging of Risk Disclosures. *New York Times.*

Swarup, B. (2014). *Money Mania: Booms, Panics and Busts from Ancient Rome to the Great Meltdown.* New York: Bloomsbury Press.

Taibbi, M. (2009, October 14). Wall Street's Naked Swindle. *Rolling Stone.*

Taleb, N. N. (2012). *Antifragile: Things That Gain from Disorder.* New York: Random House.

Taylor, L. (2010). *Maynard's Revenge: The Collapse of Free Market Macroeconomics.* Cambridge, MA: Harvard University Press.

Temin, P., & Voth, H.-J. (2004). Riding the South Sea Bubble. *American Economic Review, 94*(5), 1654–1668.

Tett, G. (2009). *Fool's Gold.* New York: Free Press.

Thomas, D. L. (1967 [2001]). *The Plungers and the Peacocks: 170 Years of Wall Street.* New York/London: Texere Publishing.

Thompson, E. A. (2007). The Tulipmania: Fact or Artifact? *Public Choice, 130*(1–2), 99–114.

Thurm, S., and Brown, K. (2002, October 18). Tech Will Be Back, Past Slumps Suggest, as Innovators Revive It. *Wall Street Journal.*

Toporowski, J. (1995). *The Economics of Financial Markets and the 1987 Crash.* Aldershot: Elgar Publishing.

Triana, P. (2009). *Lecturing Birds on Flying: Can Mathematical Theories Destroy the Financial Markets?* Hoboken: Wiley.

Triana, P. (2012). *The Number That Killed Us: A Story of Modern Banking, Flawed Mathematics, and a Big Financial Crisis.* Hoboken: Wiley.

Turner, A. L. (2016). *Between Debt and the Devil: Money, Credit, and Fixing Global Finance.* Princeton: Princeton University Press.

Vandewalle, N., Ausloos, M., Boveroux, P., & Minguet, A. (1998a). How the Financial Crash of 1997 Could Have Been Predicted. *European Physical Journal B, 4*(2), 139–141.

Vandewalle, N., Ausloos, M., Boveroux, P., & Minguet, A. (1998b). The Crash of October 1987 Seen as a Phase Transition: Amplitude and Universality. *Physica A, 255*(1), 201–210.

Vandewalle, N., Ausloos, M., Boveroux, P., & Minguet, A. (1999). Visualizing the Log-Periodic Pattern Before Crashes. *European Physical Journal B, 9*(2), 355–359.

Vincent, M. (2010, February 12). Baby-boomers, Bubbles and Emerging Markets. *Financial Times*.

Vogel, H. L. (2016). *Travel Industry Economics: A Guide for Financial Analysis*. New York/Switzerland: Springer.

Voth, H.-J. (2000). *A Tale of Five Bubbles – Asset Price Inflation and Central Bank Policy in Historical Perspective, Discussion Paper 416*. Canberra: Australian National University. http://econrsss.anu.edu.au.

Voth, H.-J. (2003). With a Bang, Not a Whimper: Pricking Germany's 'Stock Market Bubble' in 1927 and the Slide into Depression. *Journal of Economic History, 63*(1), 65–99.

Wallison, P. J. (2014, January 6). The Bubble Is Back. *New York Times*.

Weatherall, J. O. (2013). *The Physics of Wall Street: A Brief History of Predicting the Unpredictable*. Boston: Houghton Mifflin Harcourt.

Weil, J. (2007, August 22). Wells Fargo Gorges on Mark-to-Make-Believe Gains. Bloomberg.com.

Weisman, S. R. (2008, May 28). With Bold Steps, Fed Chief Quiets Some Criticism. *New York Times*.

Werner, R. A. (2003). *Princes of the Yen: Japan's Central Bankers and the Transformation of the Economy*. Armonk/London: M. E. Sharpe (East Gate Books).

Werner, R. A. (2005). *New Paradigm in Macroeconomics: Solving the Riddle of Japanese Macroeconomic Performance*. Houndmills: Palgrave Macmillan.

Wessel, D. (2008). "Lessons from the Housing Bubble," *Wall Street Journal*, May 29.

Wessel, D. (2010, 14 January). Bernanke's Puzzling Bubble Logic. *Wall Street Journal*.

White, E. N. (Ed.). (1990). *Crashes and Panics: The Lessons from History*. Homewood: Dow-Jones-Irwin.

Wigmore, B. A. (1985). *The Crash and Its Aftermath: A History of Securities Markets in the United States, 1929–1933*. Westport: Greenwood Press.

Williamson, E. (2008, March 24). Political Pendulum Swings Toward Stricter Regulation. *Wall Street Journal*.

Wilmott, P., & Orrell, D. (2017). *The Money Formula: Dodgy Finance, Psuedo Science, and How Mathematicians Took Over the Markets*. Hoboken: Wiley.

Wood, C. (2005). *The Bubble Economy: Japan's Extraordinary Speculative Boom of the '80s and the Dramatic Bust of the '90s*. San Luis Obispo/London: Solstice/Sidgwick & Jackson, 1992, and New York: Atlantic Monthly Press.

Yergin, D. (2009). *The Prize: The Epic Quest for Oil, Money & Power* (rev ed.). New York: Free Press (Simon & Schuster).

Zhou, W. X., & Sornette, D. (2006). "Is There a Real-Estate Bubble in the US?," *Physica A 361*.

Zhou, W. X., & Sornette, D. (2007). Analysis of the Real Estate Market in Las Vegas: Bubble, Seasonal Patterns, and Prediction of the CSW Indexes. *Physica A, 387*.

Ziemba, W. T., & Schwartz, S. L. (1991). The Growth in the Japanese Stock Market, 1949–90 and Prospects for the Future. *Managerial and Decision Economics, 12*(2), 183–195.

Ziemba, W. T., Lleo, S., & Zhitlukhin, M. (2018). *Stock Market Crashes: Predictable and Unpredictable and What to Do About Them*. Singapore and Hackensack, NJ: World Scientific.

CHAPTER 3

Crash Stories

The *New Palgrave* entry says a "crash" is "[W]hen a precipitous decline in value occurs for securities or assets that represent a large proportion of wealth."[1] And if there is anything in markets that can top the emotional intensity of bubbles—which always eventually implode because they by definition involve non-sustainable increases of stock prices and indebtedness—it is crashes.[2]

For those caught on the wrong side of them, crashes are sweat-inducing, gut-wrenching events that can shake even the most battle-hardened of market veterans. Crashes are thus relatively quick and deep plunges of asset prices (not necessarily involving banking deposits): They are financial asset pricing quakes that vaporize in the space of hours or days what required many months and often many years to build. A crash is thus always representative of a high-volatility condition. Early identification of crash conditions is also generally much more important than in bubbles because in sideways, upward trending, or bubbly markets, you can stay in the game for a long time without much thought and apprehension about possible loss of assets. A crash, in contrast, requires acute and immediate attention and responsive action.

3.1   CRASHES, PANICS, AND COLLAPSES

Like bubbles, panics and crashes too have a long history. One of the earliest occurred in ancient Rome, which by AD 33 had become an extensively monetized economy.[3] At the time, officials of Emperor Tiberius concluded that a boom in private lending had become excessive. It was then accordingly decided that monetary tightening, along the lines suggested by the edicts of Julius Caesar, was needed. Such tightening was enforced through regulations involving capital adequacy requirements for lenders. Lo and behold, it was soon discovered that most of the senators were in violation of the new regulations! Loans were called in. The property market collapsed. Bankruptcies spread far and wide. And the Emperor finally caved by implementing a massive bailout. This is by now a familiar pattern.

© The Author(s) 2018
H. L. Vogel, *Financial Market Bubbles and Crashes, Second Edition,*
https://doi.org/10.1007/978-3-319-71528-5_3

Still, there are nuances. A popular and common definition of a crash is a 20% or so decline in a few days or at most over only a couple of months.[4] The definition used by Ursua and Barro (2009)—cumulative real returns of minus 25% or worse—is similar.[5]

Such definitions, however, are not particularly useful unless they also specify the amount of time over which the decline occurs. Not only does a price drop of 50% (in an index, stock, or economy) arithmetically require a 100% gain to recoup the loss, it also requires an often lengthy expanse of time during which there is exposure to risks, new and unknown. This time aspect—in which the amount of time exposure to the market may be as critical to performance as is timing the market—is therefore of greater importance in describing crashes than bubbles. Inflation of bubbles can often extend over many months or even years. Crashes happen *fast*.[6]

In most other respects, though, the practical problems in defining and analyzing crashes are in many ways similar to those encountered with bubbles. Everyone, it seems, knows that a crash has occurred after they've experienced one but, as with bubbles, statistical features are often rather arbitrary or absent.[7]

Even so, Wilmott (2001, p. 394) provides an apt and precise description of what is special about a crash—which is when correlations (p. 340) go to one:

> *...Obviously a crash is a sudden fall in market prices, too rapid for the liquidation of a portfolio. But a crash isn't just a rise in volatility. It is characterized by a special relationship between individual assets. During a crash, all assets fall together. There is no such thing as a crash where half the stocks fall and the rest stay put. Technically, this means that all assets become perfectly correlated...A high degree of correlation makes diversification impossible.*[8]

As is illustrated in Fig. 3.1, higher historical volatility is associated with higher returns correlations for both bubbles (left panel) and crashes (right panel).

All of this is just another way of saying that once herding becomes prevalent, diversity of opinion—and also the theoretical notion of complete markets—dissipates (i.e., diversity approaches a limit of zero). In crashes there is—much more so than in bubbles—also a contemporaneous collective reduction in time horizons for expected returns.

Diversity of horizons will normally tend to keep the markets relatively stable. And trading experiences carried over from the preceding bubble may have deeply implanted "invest-for-the-longer-term" and "buy-on-dips" goals and strategies. But as people are forced to abandon these bull-market prescriptions, liquidity disappears and prices gap wide open to the downside.[9] It becomes a time when you are often compelled to sell not what you want to sell but what you still *can* sell.[10]

Although these ideas reflect the essence of crashes (and also apply to panics), the relationship of bubbles to crashes (and vice versa) nonetheless remains rather nebulous. It is not at all clear, for instance, that bubbles must end in

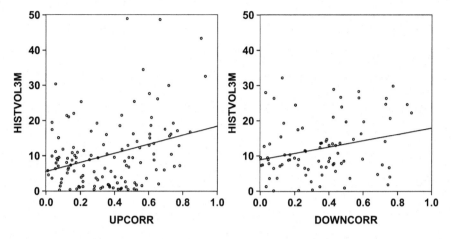

Fig. 3.1   Historical volatility, based on three-month at-the-money call options for the S&P 500 related to positive and negative return correlations within the 500 stocks in the index, 2004:2017:09

crashes or that crashes require bubbles to precede them.[11] Germany in 1927, for example, seems to have experienced a crash without a preceding bubble.[12]

The definitional line between crashes and panics is also a bit blurry as the two terms are often used interchangeably. Nevertheless there is a difference. A panic is a stampede out of a theater on fire. In the case of market crashes, the fire might be the collapse of a major bank, a fund, an insurance company, a brokerage firm, a foreign currency, or of any or all of these combined. In every such situation, mob psychology and flight-for-survival instincts and reflexes govern the action.

Yet each instance differs in its details: The mania and subsequent crash of Japan in the 1990s ensued without a panic because "depositors believed that government would socialize the loan losses."[13] However, the Panic of 1907, also known as the Bankers' Panic, involved numerous runs on national and local banks and ruin for many companies.[14] This panic was of particular importance because of its intensity and speed—NYSE prices fell almost 50% from the peak over a three-week period—and because it eventually led to establishment of the Fed in 1913. But unlike panics of 1873, 1893, 1907, or 1931, the crash of 2008–2009 was for the most part centered not in retail but in wholesale banking that involved commercial paper, "repos", and derivatives in the "shadow banking" system.[15]

It is easy to understand why the term "panic" has been historically applied to sudden fear-driven runs (i.e., withdrawals) on bank deposits that have also often led to system-wide liquidity crises.[16] Such crises can be caused by a wide variety of economic ailments and imbalances that might include hyperinflations, currency debasements, external and domestic debt defaults, politically corrupted and/or otherwise compromised banking systems, and, as in 2008–2009, bank runs on other banks.[17]

But generally, as Redleaf and Vigilante (2010, pp. 4–5) write in reference to the financial stresses of *2008*:

> *Like most grave financial crises, the mortgage crunch and the crash were crises of information. That's what panics are...the real problem was not that some of the banks were broke but at the critical moment none of them could prove they weren't. It became impossible for either executives or regulators to fully understand the financial condition of any great modern bank.*[18]

Certainly, a sense of panic is elemental to a crash as it motivates hurried emotional rather than thought-based tactical selling. And through feedback effects (i.e., autoregressiveness), a crash can fuel further panic—which is symptomatic of a betrayal of trust.[19]

Yet history has shown that a crash may occur without a panic, even though it is conceivable that a crash might cause a panic or a panic might cause a crash. One prominent example of a crash without a panic is the experience of Japan in 1990, a year when market prices halved (from around Nikkei 40,000 to 20,000).[20]

As Roehner (2002, pp. 143–4) explains:

> *A crash is a sudden price fall in a couple of days or weeks, while a collapse refers to a bear market which lasts at least several months and possibly a couple of years. A crash does not necessarily lead to a collapse nor is a collapse necessarily preceded by a spectacular crash...A crash is a microeconomic phenomenon, which results from a panic among investors; on the contrary a collapse is a macroeconomic phenomenon...*

By all such accounts, it thus appears that crashes unfold or crystallize much faster (because of fear) than do bubbles and, as a result, their start and end points ought generally to be much more precisely defined (both visually and statistically) than are those of bubbles.[21] Analysis might thus intuitively begin by first comparing crash severities through measurements of peak-to-trough price percentage declines and number of days expended in moving from high to low (sometimes converted to an average percentage loss per day).[22] That there is substantial variation in peak-to-trough data appears in Table 3.1.

Some ambiguity also inevitably remains as to whether an episode can be classified as a crash—as in the brevity of the 1987 (38 days) episode—or as a Roehner-type collapse, as in the lengthy 1973 to 1974 (436 days) experience. What, for example, was the NASDAQ decline from the 2000 high, which was greatest in terms of total (77.9%) percentage lost? The descent required 647 days for completion, and the average percentage loss per day was actually *less* than the average for the S&P episodes. On this basis it might well be argued that despite the large total percentage lost, the NASDAQ's decline from the 2000 high was not a crash but a collapse.[23]

Yet there is also nothing that precludes a collapse from being punctuated fractal-like by a series of smaller-scale crashes (perhaps as from the alternative

Table 3.1 Crash or collapse? Important peak-to-trough moves (>10%), daily closing prices, S&P 500, 1962–2011, and NASDAQ, 1984–2011

S&P 500	Peak		Trough	Total		# trading days	Avg loss per day	
				Points lost	% lost		Points	%
9-Feb-66	94.10	29-Aug-66	74.53	19.57	20.8	139	0.14	0.15
14-May-69	106.16	26-May-70	69.29	36.87	34.7	260	0.14	0.13
11-Jan-73	120.24	3-Oct-74	62.28	57.96	48.2	436	0.13	0.11
31-Dec-76	107.46	6-Mar-78	86.90	20.56	19.1	296	0.07	0.06
28-Nov-80	140.52	12-Aug-82	102.42	38.10	27.1	430	0.09	0.06
10-Oct-83	172.65	24-Jul-84	147.82	24.83	14.4	199	0.12	0.07
25-Aug-87	336.77	19-Oct-87	224.80	111.97	33.2	38	2.95	0.87
16-Jul-90	368.95	11-Oct-90	295.50	73.45	19.9	62	1.18	0.32
24-Mar-00	1527.46	4-Apr-01[a]	1103.25	424.21	27.8	251	1.69	0.11
9-Oct-07	1565.15	10-Mar-08	1273.37	291.78	18.6	104	2.81	0.18
29-Apr-11	1363.61	3-Oct-11	1099.23	264.38	19.4	108	2.45	0.18
				avg[b]	25.8	211	1.07	0.21
Alternatives:								
24-Mar-00	1527.46	11-Mar-03	800.73	726.73	47.6	741	0.98	0.06
19-May-08	1426.63	20-Nov-08	752.44	674.19	47.3	130	5.19	0.36
19-May-08	1426.63	9-Mar-09	676.53	750.1	52.6	202	3.71	0.26
NASDAQ								
27-Aug-87	455.8	7-Dec-87	293.70	162.10	35.6	70	2.32	0.51
17-Jul-90	469.5	17-Oct-90	325.10	144.40	30.8	65	2.22	0.47
27-Apr-94	800.39	27-Jun-94	694.16	106.23	13.3	69	1.54	0.19
21-Jul-98	2018.46	8-Oct-98	1420.94	597.52	29.6	56	10.67	0.53
10-Mar-00	5048.62	9-Oct-02	1114.11	3934.51	77.9	647	6.08	0.12
31-Oct-07	2859.12	17-Mar-08	2177.01	682.11	23.9	94	7.26	0.25
29-Apr-11	2873.54	3-Oct-11	2335.83	537.71	18.7	108	4.98	0.17
				avg[b]	32.8	158	5.01	0.32
Alternatives:								
5-Jun-08	2549.94	20-Nov-08	1316.12	1233.82	48.4	118	10.46	0.41
5-Jun-08	2549.94	9-Mar-09	1268.64	1281.3	50.2	190	6.74	0.26

[a]The entire decline might also be measured to the post-terrorist attack low of 965.80 on September 21, 2001, which would be 36.8%. Thus the alternative row below
[b]This average excludes the last row alternatives
Source: Author's calculations based on Yahoo.com data

lines of Table 3.1 for May 2008 to November 2008, in which the average losses per day were relatively large). Such definitional difficulties therefore prompt the search for a more objective, formal, and/or robust statistical approach to describing crash characteristics.[24]

Still—for whatever are their immediate causes—panics, crashes, and collapses are universally at their core crises of the dissolution of confidence and trust, in counterparty solvency, in creditors, in governments, and in clients, as much as of in capital.[25] Trust and confidence are always what is then in shortest supply; it is a shortage seen time and again from the study of all such extreme events, no matter when they've occurred. "A company is only as solvent as the perception of its solvency."[26]

Business Cycle Aspects

The downward sides of business cycles are often seen as causes for panics and crashes. But any such cycles are inevitable and unavoidable because that's the nature of nature in life as well as in economies and markets.[27]

During the nineteenth and early twentieth centuries, Gorton (1988) found that banking panics were related to business cycles and were not random or "sunspot" events.[28] In the worst of such crises, it was the dissolution of trust that ultimately made financial institutions reluctant to lend "to each other or to anyone else at *any* price."[29]

In reviewing eight centuries of financial crises initiated by a broad array of problems (high inflation rates, currency debasements, etc.), Reinhart and Rogoff (2008, 2009) also showed that serial defaults have been rather regularly experienced in many countries and at many times and for a variety of reasons, not all cycle-related.[30] Such crises are seen as being "amplification mechanisms," rather than triggers of recessions. A list of declines of 15% or more in real per capita GDP (Table 3.2) indicates that such occurrences were rather frequent and widespread prior and up to WWII.

As for the United States, the relationship between business cycle downturns and changes in stock prices is shown in Table 3.3. As Siegel (2008, p. 211), explains, "...out of the 46 recessions from 1802, 42 of them, or more than 9 out of 10, have been preceded (or accompanied by) declines of 8 percent or more in the total stock returns index." And there have been instances (as in 1957, 1980, or 1990) in which the peak of the business cycle virtually coincided with that of the market.

A summary quoting the IMF (2003, p. 64) further suggests that "[F]our salient patterns emerge from the comparisons made over many crash episodes:

- Stock market crashes in both countries were frequent (10 in the United Kingdom, 13 in the United States).
- More than half of the crashes in each country were associated with recessions...
- Only about one-third of all crashes were associated with a preceding boom...
- Most of the crashes cum recessions were triggered by monetary policy tightening and also involved banking panics."[31]

3.2   NOWHERE TO HIDE

It has also been observed that deflation (i.e., through default or withdrawal) of excess credit is the one factor all major depressions have in common.[32] The process spirals downward and becomes asymmetrical "when the value of asset prices falls to a level at which the value of collateral in general is no longer

Table 3.2 Declines of 15% or more in real per capita GDP for post-Great Depression years (mean for 27 contractions 26.9%)

Event	Country	Years	% fall in real per capita GDP
Great Depression	Argentina	1929–1932	19
	Chile	1929–1932	33
	Mexico	1926–1932	31
	Peru	1929–1932	29
	Uruguay	1930–1933	36
	Venezuela	1929–1932	24
	Malaysia	1929–1932	17
	Sri Lanka	1929–1932	15
WWII	Peru	1941–1943	18
	Venezuela	1939–1942	22
	Indonesia[a]	1941–1949	36
	Malaysia[b]	1942–1947	36
	Philippines[c]	1940–1946	59
	South Korea	1938–1945	59
	Sri Lanka	1943–1946	21
	Taiwan	1942–1945	51
Post-WWII depressions	Argentina	1979–1985	17
	Argentina	1998–2002	21
	Chile	1971–1975	24
	Chile	1981–1983	18
	Peru	1981–1983	17
	Peru	1987–1992	30
	Uruguay	1981–1984	17
	Uruguay	1998–2002	20
	Venezuela	1977–1985	24
	Indonesia	1997–1999	15
	Philippines	1982–1985	18

[a]No data for 1942–1948
[b]No data for 1941–1945
[c]No data for 1943–1946
Source: Barro (2006) as based on data from Maddison (2003)

Table 3.3 Market declines prior to business cycle recession recognition, S&P 500, 1948–2017

Recession	Peak of stock index	Peak of business cycle	Lead time of peak	Decline in stock index (%)
1948–49	May '48	Nov '48	6	−8.9
1953–54	Dec '52	Jul '53	7	−4.3
1957–58	Jul '57	Aug '57	1	−4.9
1960–61	Dec '59	Aug '60	4	−8.7
1970	Nov '68	Dec '69	13	−12.1
1973–75	Dec '72	Nov '73	11	−16.3
1980	Jan '80	Jan '80	0	0.0
1981–82	Nov '80	Jul '81	8	−4.1
1990–91	Jul '90	Jul '90	0	0.0
2001	Aug '00	Mar '01	7	−22.9
2007–09	Oct '07	Dec '07	2	−5.4
		Average	5.4	−8.0.0

Source: Jeremy Siegel (2008, p. 212; 2014, p. 233)

sufficient to cover the bank loans being secured."[33] This is another way of saying that while the rate of growth in credit itself is important, in crashes the ratio of credit to collateral (i.e., leverage ratios) is at least as important too.

As a bubble expands and people eventually use easy credit to bid up stocks as well to buy things that they would otherwise be unable to afford, they inevitably first run out of additional new credit facilities to pay all of the affiliated debt servicing obligations that they have already accumulated. Meanwhile, the assets that had been used as collateral for such loans are at the same time apt to be of diminishing value as compared to assumed valuations during the more buoyant bubble phase. That's how, for example, home and car owners in 2008 found themselves to be, in the jargon of the lending industry, "upside-down"— a condition in which the debt obligation is larger than the current market value (selling price) of the asset and/or the maturity of debt is less than the maturity of assets being funded.[34]

Once credit growth slows or turns negative, the pinch is then felt through a relative shortfall of cash and/or its equivalents.[35] Cash flow disappears, asset prices collapse, balance sheets are pulled underwater, and bankruptcies follow. The panics of the nineteenth and early twentieth centuries in fact typically began with a sudden drain on bank deposits, which then led, in a self-reinforcing constriction on credit extensions, to banks calling in loans so as to be able to service the increased demands for cash and liquidity.[36] When "risk aversion rises sharply, liquidity evaporates."[37]

Other things are also different in crashes than in bubbles, wherein stock loan margin growth does not appear to be nearly as important a variable as is bank credit expansion. In crashes, instead, constriction of stock loan margin availability seems to make a decline more severe. A rise in prices is reversed once potential stock buyers run out of borrowing power and cash and are *forced* to liquidate.[38] When you can't sell what you want to, you end up selling whatever you can.[39]

Some additional perspective is provided by the high-yield spreads depicted in Fig. 3.2. The high-yield spread-to-worst (from Treasuries) calculation shows that not all stock market crashes are accompanied by panicked dumping of risky bonds. The stock market crash of October 1987, for example, did not make a notable impact in these spreads, which actually peaked much later, in December of 1990. The low spread at March 1997, though, is more consistent with an ongoing bubble process.[40] The large spread in October 2002 *did* indeed coincide with an important low in stocks.[41] In effect, all trades are spreads because the trader swaps the return on cash for the hoped for return from whatever financial asset is being bought.[42]

The number of monthly advances as a percentage of the total of 500 stocks in the S&P 500 Index is then shown in Fig. 3.3. At crash lows it would be expected (à la Wilmott) that almost everything is down together; hence the percentage of *advancing* stocks out of 500 should be nearly zero at market index troughs and perhaps pushing toward 100% at peaks.

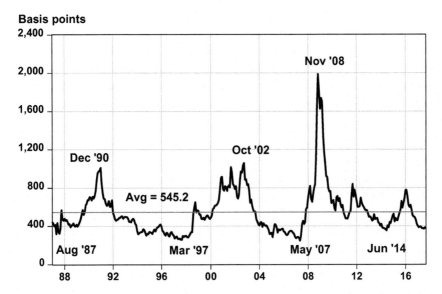

Fig. 3.2 High-yield "junk" (bond) spreads-to-worst from Treasuries (average basis points, solid line), monthly from 1987:01 to 2017:12. (Sources: Bank of America Merrill Lynch data. High Yield Option-Adjusted Spread available at: http://research.stlouisfed. org/fred2/graph/?chart_type=line&s[1][id]=BAMLH0A0HYM2&s[1] [range]=10 yrs. First 20 data based on Smith Barney/Citigroup index)

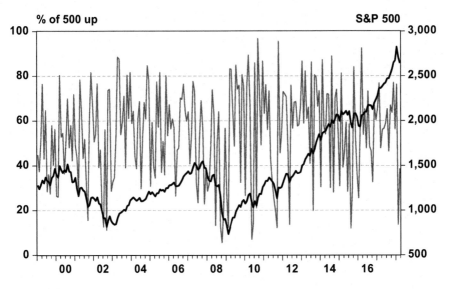

Fig. 3.3 In a bear phase, there's no place to hide: percentage of S&P 500 stocks rising in the month (unsmoothed raw data) and monthly S&P 500 Index (right-hand scale), January 1999 to March 2018. (Source data: Standard & Poor's. See also Campbell et al. (2002))

An important low of 15.6%, with a month-end S&P 500 reading at 1040.94, was registered in September 2001, the month of the terrorist attacks in the United States. But a year later, in September 2002, the percentage of advancing issues was 11.2%—only this time with the index depressed to 815.29. And in October 2008, just after the failure of Lehman Bros., the percentage of advancing issues bottomed at 5.6%. In essence, in a crash there is no place to hide as at intra-month crash lows it isn't unusual for the percentage of up stocks to be nearly (and effectively) zero.

Note too that the early high was 80.2% and coincident with the major index peak in March 2000 (with S&P 500 = 1527.46 on March 24). That a high in the percentage does not necessarily always correspond to a high in prices is, however, seen in April 2003, when the price index was 916.92 and still well below the level of March 2000.

The ratios in Figs. 1.4 to 1.6 indicate when total market capitalization as a percent of GDP, debt as a percent of GDP, and price-to-earnings measures are high relative to their histories. And a similar heuristic indicator using a bond-to-to stock earnings yield differential (BSEYD) model to predict crash thresholds was studied by Lleo and Ziemba (2012, 2015, 2018). The theory behind this hypothesis is that optimal asset allocation between stocks and bonds (and possibly also other asset class securities) is sensitive to *relative* yields; a high bond yields would likely shift investments out of stocks and into bonds and thereby provide—if not an outright crash warning—at least a potential sell signal. Such relatively high yields would also affect the real economy as businesses would under such conditions be unable to afford to take on new loans for future growth and/or rollover existing ones given that current and expected profits would be much diminished.

As with the bubble ratios, the BSEYD approach thus at best provides more a rough rule of thumb than a loud and clear bell that rings when the peak has arrived. With BSEYD there is no way to know when and how deep a possible crash might turn out to be. And because it uses longer term, 10-year treasury yields, it to an extent overrides the socionomic interpretation that markets can and regularly do rise along with short-term interest rates and will often fall along with lower rates (Fig. 4.1).

BSEYD instead likely suggests that markets have broadly entered either buy or sell zones (Fig. 3.4) in which investors ought to be particularly alert to the heightened probability but not certainty that an important turning point and market event might imminent or be already occurring. The zones are defined as being greater than one standard deviation above and below the mean. The similar model used by the Fed, "is a special case of the BSYED model when the difference between the long bond and the earnings yield on equities is zero."[43]

3.3   Storm Cats

Given that crashes are much more distinctive in their intensity, speed, and beginnings and endings than are bubbles makes it possible to introduce an arithmetic crash scale that is somewhat akin to the well-known Saffir-Simpson

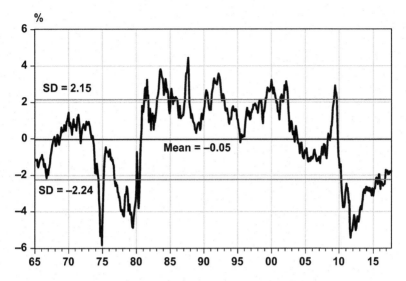

Fig. 3.4 A BSEYD display of US ten-year Treasury bond yields minus S&P 500 earnings yield (inverted P/E ratio) monthly in percent, 1965:M01 to 2017:M10. Similar to Lleo and Ziemba (2015), which instead used 30-year Treasury yields and a model that "has called many but not all crashes. Those called have high interest rate bonds relative to the trailing earnings to price ratio." Crash warnings in the sell zone (i.e., >1 s.d. above the mean) were too early in 1984, roughly correct in 1987 and in early 2000, and late in 2009 probably because the preceding bubble was concentrated more in housing/real estate than equities. Buy signals (i.e., >1 s.d. below the mean) were roughly correct in 1975, 1979, and 2011. Ziemba et al. (2018, pp. 115–6) shows that the empirical distribution of BSEYD models are far from Gaussian but provide a rough approximation for equity risk premiums

hurricane classification system which evaluates storms on a weakest to strongest scale of one to five based on wind speeds, potential property damage, and flooding.

As indicated in Table 3.1, within the last 50 years the most important crash episode of the last 50 years for a broad-based index began at the S&P peak at 336.77 of August 25, 1987, and ended on October 19, 1987—38, trading days later—while generating an average per day loss of 2.95 points and 0.87%. The most dramatic and climactic part of this episode occurred on October 19, 1987, when the S&P 500 fell by a record 22.61% in one day—the largest price change over the briefest time on record.[44] With the subsequent implementation of stock exchange "circuit breaker" rules, the likelihood of this ever happening again is remote.

The very intensity and brevity of this crash, however, allow it to be used as a point of reference against which to arithmetically scale (i.e., benchmark) other crash episodes. Ten crashes in the S&P 500 and six in the NASDAQ are compared in Fig. 3.5 on the basis of average percentage losses per day taken as a percent of the S&P 500 average loss per day (0.87%) seen in 1987.

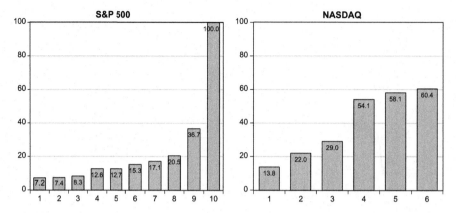

Fig. 3.5 Crash intensity comparisons for the S&P 500 and NASDAQ based on Table 3.1 data. Bars show the relative average daily percent decline in each episode as a percent of the average daily percent decline in the Crash of 1987. Bar number 10 in the S&P (left panel) is the Crash of 1987. For the S&P, bars 1 through 9 began: (1) 28-Nov-80; (2) 31-Dec-76; (3) 10-Oct-83; (4) 11-Jan-73; (5) 24-Mar-00; (6) 14-May-69; (7) 9-Feb-66; (8) 9-Oct-07; (9) 16-Jul-90. For the NASDAQ, bars 1 through 6 began: (1) 10-Mar-00; (2) 27-Apr-94; (3) 31-Oct-07; (4) 17-Jul-90; (5) 27-Aug-87; (6) 21-Jul-98. (Source: Vogel and Werner 2015)

In this visual representation, crashes broadly fall into three categories. Several S&P episodes are below 25% of the intensity of the Crash of 1987 and these might be labeled as category 1 storms. But given that shares of companies in the NASDAQ are generally less seasoned and financially sturdy than those in the S&P, it is not surprising to find several NASDAQ episodes that are above 25% and up to around 60% of the intensity of the 1987 S&P experience. These might be labeled as category 2 events.

Finally, any crashes that are above 60% of the intensity of the Crash of 1987 might be labeled as category 3 events. They are so potentially catastrophic ("cat3cats" or C3Cs) as to be able to not only wreck a market's infrastructure but also a nation's economy.

3.4   Conclusions

The main lesson is that in extreme market events, *diversity* of investors' opinions and of expected-return time horizons go toward zero, while, especially in crashes, *correlations* of directional price movement of all assets in a market go toward 1.0. These features make it somewhat easier to define and identify crashes than bubbles because, with any broad market index, a sample period's percent of price-up issues in a crash period will always be far below 50%. This is in contrast to more tranquil periods in which markets are traded by people with widely different time horizons, attitudes toward risk, investing styles, information, abilities, and luxury of time to interpret the information received.[45]

Crashes also differ from bubbles in that they tend to be faster and more violent and are likely to be started by cash growth insufficiency (as measured perhaps in the near-cash MZM series) and by stock loan borrowing limits and constraints (margin). In this situation, margin speculators are *involuntarily* forced by lenders and regulatory mark-to-market rules to immediately dump (disown) shares into a descending market's liquidity vortex and vacuum.[46] The ending of easy credit conditions strips away the illusion of wealth (and also the belief that the market cannot crash).

A crash always involves a relative scarcity of cash equivalents (with which to service debts) and/or the perception and expectation that other nearby entities (counterparties) will soon encounter such scarcity. That's because risk can be time-shifted and redistributed but never entirely eliminated. In the context of the broader financial market ecosystem someone somewhere will always be left holding the bag (of risk). And in extreme event conditions, this can lead to unknown, unpredictable, and unhedgeable repercussions and consequences for everyone else.

Crashes begin when growth of credit is no longer sufficient to support previously arranged debt repayment obligations.[47] Collateral values underlying credit extensions then begin to sink as the worth of stocks and properties (i.e., collateral) fall and risk is repriced.

Hence, crashes are at their cores liquidity-shortage events, whereas bear markets—which often culminate in a crash or an intermittent series of crashes—are normally more closely related to slowing of earnings growth, inflation or deflation, and a downturn in the (sometimes cyclical) availability of credit. The definitional lines between what is called a "bear market" and a "crash" (or "panic") are often blurred and confused.

Cash thus holds its value but credit loses it. Cash is hoarded and transaction mediums disappear.[48] And this can only be reversed when, after a long period of adjustment, creditors again begin to accept as a basis for new loans the values placed on collateral. Of all assets, cash normally has the greatest optionality.

In crashes and panics, too, there is a flight toward fundamental quality, which is the opposite of what occurs in bubbles, when there is marked disdain for such relatively stodgy investments and for cash. Small company stocks also appear to be harmed more than large ones by credit tightening (and benefit relatively more from the easy credit of bubbles).

There is thus a large kernel of truth in the Wall Street expressions that in bubbles, "cash is trash," but in crashes, "cash is king."[49] For in a crisis—regardless of whether the subject is a large financial institution, a small fund, or an individual speculator—it is not the total amount of capital involved as much as the relative amount of readily available liquidity that matters most. Availability of increasingly scarce liquidity is the ultimate determinant of survival.

In crashes the focus accordingly shifts from the potential growth of earnings and from income statements to the perceived and actual strengths of balance sheets.[50] An easily found joy of investing on the way up then turns viciously challenging and difficult, even nightmarish, on the way down.

Bear markets in stocks are thus bull markets in cash and in overall societal distrust. In such markets, "[F]or many people the 'long run' quickly becomes the 'short run'."[51]

After a collapse of credit has begun and before they are again able and willing to expand lending activities, banks need considerable time (as in 2009) to first repair their own balance sheets by replenishing their own lost or otherwise impaired capital.[52] Although bank capital-to-asset ratios can be raised either through sales of equity or debt securities (difficult and expensive in a crisis), the initial propensity is to shed the riskiest assets. In effect this means that as existing loans are repaid they are not sufficiently replaced in size and quantity by new extensions—especially to those younger and smaller firms which for their survival are at that point most in need of credit.[53]

Even so, however, replenishment of banking system capital cannot alone lead to greater lending activity and eventual resumption of growth. Potential borrowers also need to be able to visualize and expect that loans will likely generate a risk-adjusted return that is in excess of the cost of capital. In deep business cycle downturns, such confidence in the future is never easily or quickly restored and is the opposite of what happens around bubble peaks, which is when confidence in the future is strongest.

An informal listing of conditions that are commonly seen in the progression toward crashes includes the following[54]:

- First concerns about rising price multiples appear.
- News reports begin to cast doubt on the potential for profits growth.
- Corporate failures begin to emerge.
- Numerous frauds, scandals, systems hacks, and scams begin to appear.
- Traders buying on margin begin to feel pressure from lenders.
- Crash-protection hedges and strategies begin to fail.
- Liquidity evaporates and it becomes more likely that there are no prices at which to trade.
- Fear of staying in (FOSI) extends and intensifies. People feel they *must* sell.

Not every steep rise in prices is a bubble and not every rapid decline in prices is a crash. That is the way it should be if the definitions and methods that are later proposed are to play any useful analytical roles. Extreme market events are always tied to money and liquidity conditions—and therefore to banking policies and procedures. The next chapter links bubble and crash stories to their basic economic and financial roots.

NOTES

1. Described by Martin (2015, pp. 83–4) and Swarup (2014, Chap. 2).
2. The term "crash" suggests a frighteningly broad and sudden decline in price. Crash became a familiar financial term around 1817, when poet Samuel Taylor Coleridge described a credit collapse in his *Biographia Literaria* as being "a rapid series of explosions and a consequent precipitation of the general system."

According to Zwieg (2015), "crash" was repeatedly used in William Armstrong's 1848 *Stocks and Stock-Jobbing in Wall Street*.

3. Newman et al. (1992).

4. In October 1987 the Dow-Jones Industrial Average fell 22.6% in one day, and in October 1929, there were two back-to-back days in which this index fell 12.8% and then 11.7%. The informal definition is mentioned in Browning and Lobb (2008). Wood (2007), however, writes, "There is, unsurprisingly, no formal, rigorous definition of what comprises a stock market crash, as opposed to a fall, decline, or to borrow a broker's term, 'correction'."

5. Ursua and Barro (2009) studied 251 such stock market crashes and 97 depressions and found that "in 71 cases the timing of a market crash matched up to a depression." See Barro (2009). Barro and Ursua (2009) define a depression as at least a 10% decline in real per capita GDP.

6. See also note 3, Chap. 9.

7. Mishkin (2003, p. 55) makes the point directly:

> ...*defining a stock market crash or collapse is simple. When you see it you know it. However, attempting a more precise definition and measurement over the course of a century is more difficult. The choice of stock market index, the size of the collapse, and the time frame of the decline are key factors.*

Another workable, but nonetheless also arbitrary definition of a crash appears in Ziemba and Ziemba (2007, p. xvii) in a discussion of a bond-stock crash prediction model that takes the difference between the long bond and the equity earnings yield. The definition of a crash is a "10% or more fall within one year from the current equity price."

8. A vivid example was the September 29, 2008, one-day plunge in the Dow-Jones Industrials of 777.68 (−6.98%) points and in the S&P 500 of 106.59 (−8.79%) points. On that day, all 30 Dow stocks fell, and only one of 500 stocks in the S&P (Campbell Soup) rose (12 cents or 0.3% to $37.75). All 30 Dow stocks also fell in the 678.91-point (−7.33%) plunge on October 9, 2008. That same day, the S&P 500 shed 7.62% (75.02 points) to end at 909.92, with all of its sectors posting large losses. Also, on the May 20, 2010, Dow-Jones Industrials decline of 376.36 points all stocks in this average as well as in the DJ Transports and DJ Utilities closed down, while 497 of 500 names in the S&P 500 closed down. On that day, 98.8% of total volume was to the downside. The plunge of August 8, 2011, 6.6% in the S&P and 5.5% in the Dow-Jones Industrials, also saw all 500 stocks in the S&P and 30 stocks in the DJIA fall. The advance/decline ratio of 0.014 (1/69) for that day was the lowest on record, with 44 stocks up and 3033 down. The second lowest ratio of 0.015 occurred on May 13, 1940, the day after Germany invaded Holland, Belgium, and France. Zweig (2008a) observed that by July 1932, after the Dow had lost 88% in 36 months, "only five of the roughly 800 companies that still survived on the New York Stock Exchange had lost *less* than two-thirds of their value from their peak in 1929." Again, on November 9, 2011, 499 of the S&P 500 stocks (except for Best Buy) closed lower on a day that this index fell to 1229.10, down 46.82 points.

Campbell et al. (2002) also found evidence of increasing correlation for international stock index returns in the tails, which is an indication of spreading contagion between financial markets during extreme market conditions. See also Skypala (2014) and Fabozzi et al. (2014) on asset diversification.

9. Paraphrases Peters (1994, p. 47) who writes,

> *As long as investors with different investment horizons are participating, a panic at one horizon can be absorbed by the other investment horizons as a buying (or selling) opportunity. However, if the entire market has the same investment horizon, then the market becomes unstable. The lack of liquidity turns into panic.... during panics and stampedes, the market often skips over prices.*

Lowenstein (2008) also observes that "...markets aren't so random. In times of stress, the correlations rise. People in a panic sell stocks—all stocks. Lenders who are under pressure tighten credit to all." Formal models of herding and financial crises are discussed in Chari and Kehoe (2000, 2003). And Greenspan (2008) says, "Negative correlations among asset classes, so evident during an expansion, can collapse as all asset prices fall together, undermining the strategy of improving risk/reward trade-offs through diversification." Along the same lines, Alpert (2008) discusses how in the bear market of 2008 many "quant" funds were dismayed to find that the low-covariance investments upon which they had depended quickly became high-covariance as per Wilmott. See also Lauricella (2009). Futia (2009, p. 24) writes that "[C]rowds suppress the dissenting views of nonmembers and amplify the consensus views of their members."

10. In agreement with Prechter (2016), Bookstaber (2017, p. 15) also recognizes that in crashes, "as prices drop you have more *sellers*."

11. In Laise (2010), Professor Didier Sornette is quoted as finding that "only about two-thirds of bubbles end in a crash." And Herrera and Perry (2003, p. 139) have noted that "Most (but not all) bubbles end in crashes, and there are crashes without bubbles." However, Visco (2003, p. 166) confusingly says, "...bubbles are identified from the fact that a crash has occurred, even if not all crashes are the result of the burst of a bubble." See also Wood (2007).

12. Voth (2003) argues that the 11% one-day decline of the German market on May 13, 1927, was not preceded by an ending of a bubble but instead by policy mistakes of the Reichsbank acting on the misguided belief that "[C]redit that could have been used to fund productive investment was being diverted to the stock market..." Werner (2003, pp. 53–4) has further observed that the Reichsbank had enormous power and "had been made independent from the government after the hyperinflation of 1924, it could do as it wished." The bank was seen a Germany's "second government," and its credit and resource allocation methods and policies were later admired and emulated by the Japanese.

13. An example was the run on Northern Rock in the United Kingdom, September 2007. The definition paraphrases Bruner and Carr (2007, p. 190), who also (pp. 153–72) observe that system complexity, buoyant growth, inadequate safety buffers, inadequate leadership, and real economic shocks are factors that have often preceded panics. See also Oliver (2007, pp. 182–187) for further definitional refinements. Schularick and Taylor (2012) define financial crises as "events during which a country's banking sector experiences bank runs, sharp increases in default rates, accompanies by large losses of capital that result in public intervention, bankruptcy, or forced merger of financial institutions."

14. On the Panic of 1907 see Bruner and Carr (2007) and Nations (2017).

15. Kindleberger and Aliber (2011, p. 5).

16. Reinhart and Rogoff (2009) and Schularick and Taylor (2012) provide extensive coverage. Gorton (2010, p. 3) wrote that in the panic that began in 2007,

the bank run was relatively invisible "because it was a run by banks and firms on other banks."

17. Actual retail panic episodes in this time included IndyMac in California and Northern Rock in the United Kingdom.

18. Allen et al. (2009) provide a concise overview of recent studies of financial crises. Gorton (2010, pp. 16–7) further elaborates, saying that panics such as the one starting in August 2007 occur "when information-insensitive debt becomes information sensitive due to a shock, in this case, the shock to subprime mortgage values due to house prices falling." According to Gorton (1988), bank panics occur "when depositors demand such a large-scale transformation of deposits into currency that, at the contracted for exchange rate (of a currency dollar for a deposit dollar), the banking system can only respond by suspending convertibility of deposits into currency." See also Gorton (2009).

19. In reviewing panics of the 1800s in the United States, England, and France, Juglar (1916 [1966], pp. 2–3, 21) and his translator/interpreter (DeC. W. Thom) wrote that:

> *a commercial panic is always a financial panic…A crisis or panic may be defined as a stoppage of the rise of prices…the period when new buyers are not to be found… A panic may be broadly stated as due to overtrading, which causes general business to need more than available capital, thus producing general lack of credit.*

Schumpeter (1934, p. 219) later explained that "…there are also panics without a crises. And further there are crises without real panics. The intensity of the panic does not in any case bear a necessary relation to the importance of the crisis." And philosopher/economist John Stuart Mill, as far back as 1867, wrote (in *Credit Cycles and the Origin of Commercial Panics*) that "Panics do not destroy capital; they merely reveal the extent to which is has been destroyed by its betrayal into hopelessly unproductive works."

An early example of an important crisis is provided by Buchan (1997, p. 208), who writes: "The crash of the City of Glasgow Bank, which closed its doors on October 2, 1878, was the greatest bank failure in the history of the United Kingdom, and destroyed more than a tenth of Scotland's banking capital."

20. Wilson et al. (1990) studied crash, panic, and volatility relationships and found instances such as in October 1929, when the crash was initially unrelated to a banking panic and when preceding volatility for "stock, bond, and commercial paper returns was not unusually high." However, "[B]efore 1914 panics and crashes typically occurred around the same time." Although the line of causation from banking panic to market crash or vice versa is not clear, there appears to be some evidence that volatility after a panic/crash tends to remain high at least for a while. In Kindleberger and Aliber (2011, p. 5), it is noted that Japan was a mania and a crash without a panic "because depositors believed that government would socialize the loan losses."

21. Mallaby (2016, p. 56) writes that Greenspan recognized in the 1950s that "markets could crash instantly…In contrast, bubbles inflated only slowly."

22. On this aspect, Greenspan (2013, p. 10) writes that the severity of a bursting bubble's destruction is determined "by the degree of leverage employed by the holders of those toxic assets." Brooks and Katsaris (2003) point to abnormally high trading volume as a possible crash indicator. Chen et al. (2000) observed that asymmetric volatility is "a tendency for volatility to go up with negative returns." The effect was seen in August 1987 and was also observed by Galbraith

(1988), who reported that, in the months leading up to the 1929 crash, trading reached the then astonishing peaks of four to six million shares. Ofek and Richardson (2001) chronicled the same effect at the end of the dot-com bubble of 2000, as did Garber (1989) for prices of rare tulip bulbs back in 1636. Vandewalle et al. (1999) found a tendency for volatility to cluster around times of a crash as participants become increasingly synchronized in their trading (i.e., through herding and nonindependence of individuals' utility functions). Based on the research of Gehring and Willoughby (2002), Taleb (2005, p. 68) also writes, "the degree of rationality in decisions made subsequent to a gain is extremely different from the one after a loss."

Another technical indicator, named after the Hindenburg zeppelin explosion and crash in 1937, is known as the Hindenburg Omen. It is based largely on watching for an unusual number of NYSE 52-week highs and lows and correctly pointed to a crash in October 2008. The signal requires that in a rising market, the number of stocks reaching new one-year highs must not be more than twice the number of one-year lows and that the proportion of stocks reaching such highs and lows both exceed 2.5% of the total listed on the NYSE. See Russolillo and Kilgore (2010). Silver (2012a, p. 354) shows a crash probability table suggesting that the chance of a market crash, defined as a 20% decline in prices net of dividends and inflation, rises along with the P/E ratio.

23. Allen and Gale (2007, p. 83) suggest that a panic is akin to and suggestive of a crash rather than a collapse, which is macroeconomically induced. Also, in examining data from 1834 through 1987, Schwert (1989) found that "stock volatility increases after stock prices fall, it increases during recessions, and it increases around major financial crises." Hamilton and Lin (1996) concluded that business cycle recessions might be a primary cause for fluctuations in the volatility of stock market returns.

24. See Vogel and Werner (2015).

25. Case studies presented in Ziemba and Ziemba (2007, p. xiii) indicate that hedge fund and other banking system disasters all follow a recipe or pattern in which the deteriorating fund or institution has typically overbet, in the sense of having too many poorly diversified positions relative to underlying capital and to the ultimate availability of liquidity in times of need. The examples of Merrill Lynch, Citicorp, and Bear Stearns in the subprime loans crisis of 2007–2008 and hedge fund Amaranth's demise due to massive losses in natural gas come readily to mind. Tapia (2014) further proposes that the "main feature of a crisis is the temporary interruption of capital accumulation."

Poor diversification occurs, the Ziembas say, because low-probability events are often assigned zero probability and are therefore not included in risk scenarios and/or are misspecified in stress testing. Many such tests might also erroneously assume that bond and equity prices are directionally correlated. In a crash, however, equity prices fall even as bond prices generally rise, "so that the bond/Stock correlation is negative."

26. The quotation is from former Oppenheimer analyst Meredith Whitney in Gongloff (2008) and is analogous to nineteenth-century's British journalist Walter Bagehot's words, quoted in the Anders column of the *Wall Street Journal*, March 19, 2008; "Every banker knows that if he has to prove that he is worthy of credit, however good may be his arguments, in fact his credit is gone." In Carney (2008), Milton Friedman's co-author, then 92-year-old Anna Schwartz expressed the view that Bernanke's Fed is fighting the last war

when it comes to the credit squeeze. In 2008, she said, the problem was not a shortage of liquidity, but a shortage of credibility and trust in counterparty banks. "The Fed," she argued, "has gone about as if the problem is a shortage of liquidity. That is not the basic problem. The basic problem for the markets is that the balance sheets of financial firms are credible... So to assume that the whole problem is inadequate liquidity bypasses the real issue." Also, in a 1986 article ("Real and Pseudo-Financial Crises") reproduced in Capie and Wood (2007, p. 245), she writes: "A financial crisis is fueled by fears that the means of payment will be unobtainable at any price and, in a fractional reserve banking system, leads to a scramble for high-powered money. It is precipitated by actions of the public that suddenly squeeze the reserves of the banking system."

From Lowenstein (2008): "Failing to inspire confidence, banks cannot raise (enough) capital; thus, they do not lend." The September 2008 bankruptcy of the Lehman investment bank was a prime example of this. Also contributing was regulation of things that didn't need to be regulated and the absence of regulation of things requiring it. Short-sellers, for instance, were a convenient political target in the 2008 collapse of share prices, but there were few complaints about them when the tech and housing bubbles were inflating. And once the prices began to fall, if the stocks were such "bargains," where were all the buyers? The answer with regard to the demise of the major Wall Street firms is that the buyers weren't interested because they had no confidence in the opaque accounting that allowed firms to carry on their books as assets pieces of paper that were extremely illiquid and difficult-to-value and to then count these complex "securities" as "capital." The much-vaunted quantitative and VaR models used by all firms were, as noted by Hansell (2008), either circumvented, manipulated, or ignored by management. See also Leonhardt (2008), Triana (2009, 2012), and Craig et al. (2008).

27. Dardik (2017) writes of the nature of nature in which everything moves in waves of waves; everything is fractal, and there are no discrete boundaries.
28. Dent (2016, p. 135) argues otherwise, explaining that sunspot cycles between 8 and 13 years are dependent on the pull of large planet orbits and, most significantly, showed that 88% of crashes and recessions in the past 200 years happened in the downside of this cycle. The presumed reason is that on the cycle's downside the Earth receives less radiational energy and people overall tend to be more depressed (as in winter with SAD) and economic activity thus becomes more sluggish. Dent (p. 104) places great weight on the occurrence of four other cycles: (a) generational spending, 39 years; (b) geopolitical, 34–36 years; (c) boom/bust, 8–13 years; and (d) innovation, 45 years.
29. Tuckett (2011, p. 8).
30. They write, "[G]lobal economic factors, including commodity prices and center country interest rates, play a major role in precipitating sovereign debt crises." Concerning sovereign debt and banking crises (2009, p. xxvi), "[B]oth have histories that span centuries and cut across regions." They also note (pp. 142–172) that price collapses in real estate appear to surround banking crises.
31. Financial crisis history is shown at http://www.stock-market-crash.net/index.htm

See also Evans (2003) and Wood (2007, p. 248), who write, "it would seem reasonable to say...that stock market crashes lead to recessions only if they are allowed to produce monetary contractions..."

32. Paraphrase of a 1957 investment letter written by early Elliott Wave analyst Hamilton Bolton.
33. Pepper and Oliver (2006, p. 55).
34. This was an important factor in the US savings and loan crisis of the 1980s and is what happened in the housing crash when relatively low short-term "teaser" adjustable-rate mortgages (ARMs) were automatically reset to higher long-term rates. See Greenspan (2013, p. 71).
35. Miller (2002, p. 84) in writing about the experimental economics approach, pioneered by Nobel Laureate Vernon Smith, says that "…making more cash available to traders both increases the likelihood and the size of market bubbles." See also Hall (2001, pp. 9–11), who examines liquidity using corporate cash flows, Smith et al. (1988), and Dufwenberg et al. (2005).

It seems likely that an inverted yield curve condition (in which short rates are above long rates) might also be a harbinger of a forthcoming credit contraction and thus of eventual constraints on cash availability given that the price of near-cash under such circumstances is relatively high. On this, see Estrella and Mishkin (1996) and Berge and Jordá (2010), in which the yield curve's relation to the Conference Board's *Leading Economic Index* is discussed.

The point at which cash shortage becomes critical—that is, the point at which over-indebted investors are forced to sell even their most secure and highest-quality positions to pay off loan obligations—has been informally called the "Minsky moment," after economist Hyman Minsky first described the situation with his Financial Instability Hypothesis. See Lahart (2007) and Minsky (1996 [2008]). At a Minsky juncture, severe demand for cash may trigger a downward price spiral that forces central banks to ease.

Wilmott (2001) writes that in a crash, "all assets fall together," with the direction of changes in returns thus tending toward perfect correlation. And this then further suggests that in a large crash there are few if any truly safe harbors. In such circumstances—and contrary to the CAPM's hypothetical notion of reduction of risk through diversification—there is no place to hide. A prime example of this is provided in a *Fortune* magazine interview ("Is Buy-and-Hold Dead and Gone?" October 28, 2008) with Robert Arnott, chairman of Research Affiliates in Pasadena. Of the crash of 2008, "Arnott says that of the 16 different asset classes…every single one except U.S. Treasuries was down in September. That was the first month in three decades that 15 out of 16 categories were down at the same time." Another instance of pressure to raise cash is provided by Patterson (2010, p. 227), who writes of the problems in August 2007 faced by large hedge fund Medallion: "Medallion's models predicted that the positions would move back to equilibrium. But the snapback didn't happen. The positions kept declining. There was no equilibrium." Increasing correlation in S&P 500 component stocks is also discussed in Browning (2010).

Montier (2007, p. 457) describes what he calls a Kindleberger/Minsky model, in which the progression to bubbles and then to crashes follows a typical path from displacement (new technologies and methods are disruptive to existing profit allocations) to credit creation to euphoria to a critical stage of financial distress and then finally to revulsion (capitulation). Kindleberger discusses Minsky's model in his second chapter.

Experimental economists have, furthermore, been able to confirm the importance of liquidity to sustenance and propagation of bubbles. Caginalp et al. (2001), for example, report on laboratory experiments indicating that a bubble can be reduced if there is "less total cash than value of total shares," there are deferred dividends, and there is "a bid-ask book that is open to traders. Conversely, a large bubble arises when the opposite conditions exist."

36. An oft-cited study of the Crash of 1929 by Bernanke and Gertler (1989) essentially agrees, saying that impairment of access to credit for firms and households acts as a financial accelerator that exacerbates declines in consumer spending and production. See Koo (2010) for US parallels to Japan's problems.

37. Greenspan (2013, p. 39).

38. Credit constrictions have been also manifested in a seizing up of commercial paper rollovers (e.g., Penn Central 1970, subprime mortgages 2007, Continental Illinois 1984, and markets for newer instruments such as collateralized debt obligations and loans 2007). This happens when banks, brokerages, and other lenders demand more cash and collateral, thereby reducing the credit that they are willing to extend. Banking analyst Meredith Whitney, quoted in Anderson (2008), for example, wrote with regard to the enormous write-downs of 2007–2008, "As the banks are trying to recover they will not lend. They are all about self-preservation at this time." For a description of the September 2008 commercial paper freeze-up, see Nocera (2008). Former Deutsche Bank analyst Michael Mayo is also known for his massive 1999 report recommending sale of banking stocks. See *Wall Street Journal*, 26 March 2009, November 5, 2011, Ewing (2010), Mayo (2011), and www.fdic.gov/bank/historical/history/ 235_258.pdf

39. "[T]he rush to sell these assets," note Kindleberger and Aliber (2011, p. 13), "becomes self-fulfilling and so precipitous that it resembles a panic." Bookstaber (2017, p. 16) makes the same point: "...the common crowd that shared similar views...scurries in all directions. Some are fighting for their lives in the face of margin calls and redemptions, others stepping onto the sidelines to become observers."

40. March 1997 was just three months after Greenspan's "irrational exuberance" speech, in which he said, "...sustained low inflation implies less uncertainty about the future, and lower risk premiums imply higher prices of stocks and other earning assets. But, how do we know when irrational exuberance has unduly escalated asset values?" Hartcher (2006, pp. 124–5) indicates that "Greenspan was deliberately and conclusively leading an effort to manage the risks inherent in a major bubble." About the subsequent years, Hartcher (2006, p. 132) writes: "The Fed...was feeding cheap money into the bubble. Far from restraining the bubble, the Fed was its most important accomplice." Fleckenstein and Sheehan (2008, p. 20) support this view. But Siegel (2006) says that in hindsight, there was no bubble at the time. Goodman (2008) takes a critical look at Greenspan's legacy with regard to derivative securities.

41. Roehner (2000) shows that in the months following a crash there is a connection between the fall of stock prices and an increase in the range of interest rates (i.e., the spread) for bonds. The negative correlation between stock prices and the spread variable relied on a sample of eight crash episodes from 1857 onward to 1987. The spread concept is also applied in a popular Fed model that is tested

for its ability to predict the stock market's direction and that is discussed in Koivu et al. (2005).

42. "All trades are spreads" appeared in a November 2016 article by H. L. Simmons in *Modern Trader* magazine.

43. Ziemba et al. (2018, p 7).

44. In the Crash of 1929, the Dow-Jones Industrial Average fell 11.73% on October 29 and 12.82% on October 28, which was the largest daily percentage price decline on record for a major index until October 19, 1987.

45. Surowiecki (2004, p. 29).

46. Crashes are by nature relatively rapid affairs, whereas in a "bubble" environment, no one is forced (unless being already short the stock and having to cover) to involuntarily buy a stock. Persuaded, encouraged, egged-on, yes, that may be common, but forced—no.

47. In borrowing from the Austrian School of economics, Grant (1996, p. xiv) wrote, "Booms do not merely precede busts. In some important sense, they cause them...people in markets periodically miscalculate together." Grant (1996, p. 126) further elaborates: "In the Austrians' judgment, there is one principal source of collective error: interest rates. Set them too low and people will overreach. They will borrow to excess and, with every good intention, build the marginal, redundant capital project." Buiter and Sibert (2004) discuss "deflationary bubbles" and show that in a model "where money is the only financial asset... such bubbles are consistent with the household's transversality condition if and only if the nominal money stock is falling." On transversality see note 1 of Chap. 6.

    From von Mises (1996, pp. 554), "The boom can last only as long as the credit expansion progresses at an ever-accelerated pace." Mises (pp. 555–72): "Business booms as long as the banks are expanding credit more and more... The boom ends because the forces which brought it about are no longer in operation. The additional quantity of circulation credit has exhausted its operation upon prices and wage rates...The final outcome of the credit expansion is general impoverishment...There is no means of avoiding the final collapse of a boom brought about by credit expansion."

48. Gorton (2010, p. 37) says that in a panic, "cash is hoarded, and there is a shortage of transactions mediums."

49. This is historically correct, but there are important indications that to prevent or offset any future crashes that might occur as a result of inability to service the already massive amounts of existing government debts and the resulting deflations, central banks will resort to what's coming to be known as a "war on cash." Implementation of this has already been seen in 2016 in India, where large denomination bills have been removed from circulation, in Cyprus circa 2012–2013 where cash deposits (many from troubled Greece) were abruptly and involuntarily converted (after a "haircut") into shares of the bank, and in various subsequent studies and talks suggesting that this is maybe being elsewhere considered. See also Summers (2017, pp. 179–204) and unrelated Summers (2016).

50. Mehrling (2011, p. 16): "Eventually, and long before interest rates reach 15 percent, the effects of higher market interest rates are felt on nonbubble balance sheets throughout the economy, and it is those effects that bring the bubble to an end...debtors hold on for as long as they can, hoping that some other balance sheet will prove to be the weakest link."

51. From von Mises (1979, p. 63).
52. Adrian and Shin (2008) argue that "the growth rate of aggregate balance sheets may be the most fitting measure of liquidity in a market-based financial system" and find that "institutions increase their leverage during booms and reduce it during downturns...financial institution leverage is *pro-cyclical*; the expansion and contraction of balance sheets amplifies, rather than counteracts the credit cycle."
53. Congdon and Hanke (2017).
54. See Vines (2005, p. 14).

REFERENCES

Adrian, T., & Shin, H. S. (2008, January/February). Liquidity, Monetary Policy, and Financial Cycles. *Current Issues in Economics and Finance*, Federal Reserve Bank of New York, *14*(1). Available at: http://www.newyorkfed.org/research/current_issues/ci14-1.pdf

Allen, F., & Gale, D. (2007). *Understanding Financial Crises*. New York: Oxford University Press.

Allen, F., Babus, A., & Carletti, E. (2009). Financial Crises: Theory and Evidence. *Annual Review of Financial Economics, 1*. Palo Alto: Annual Reviews.

Alpert, B. (2008, July 14). The Numbers Speak for Themselves. *Barron's*.

Anderson, J. (2008, February 19). Wall Street Banks Confront a String of Write-downs. *New York Times*.

Barro, R. J. (2006). Rare Disasters and Asset Markets in the Twentieth Century. *Quarterly Journal of Economics, 121*(3), 823–866.

Barro, R. J. (2009, March 4). What Are the Odds of a Depression? *Wall Street Journal*.

Barro, R. J., & Ursua, J. F. (2009, May 5). Pandemics and Depressions. *Wall Street Journal*.

Berge, T. J., & Jordá O. (2010, August 9). Future Recession Risks. San Francisco: *Economic Letter*, Federal Reserve Board of San Francisco.

Bernanke, B. S., & Gertler, M. (1989). Agency Costs, Net Worth, and Business Fluctuations. *American Economic Review, 79*(1), 14–31.

Bookstaber, R. (2017). *The End of Theory: Financial Crises, the Failure of Economics, and the Sweep of Human Interaction*. Princeton: Princeton University Press.

Brooks, C., & Katsaris, A. (2003). *Regime Switching Models of Speculative Bubbles with Volume: An Empirical Investigation of the S&P 500 Composite Index*. Reading: IMSA.

Browning, E. S., & Lobb, A. (2008, October 10). Market's 7-Day Rout Leaves U.S. Reeling. *Wall Street Journal*.

Bruner, R. F., & Carr, S. D. (2007). *The Panic of 1907: Lessons Learned from the Market's Perfect Storm*. Hoboken: Wiley.

Buchan, J. (1997). *Frozen Desire: The Meaning of Money*. New York: Farrar Straus Giroux.

Buiter, W. H., & Sibert, A. (2004). *Deflationary Bubbles*. Working Paper No. W10642, NBER.

Caginalp, G., Porter, D., & Smith, V. L. (2001). Financial Bubbles: Excess Cash, Momentum, and Incomplete Information. *The Journal of Psychology and Financial Markets, 2*(2), 80–99. See also, *Journal of Behavioral Finance*.

Campbell, R., Koedijk, K., & Kofman, P. (2002). Increased Correlation in Bear Markets. *Financial Analysts Journal, 58*(1), 87–94.

Capie, F. H., & Wood, G. E. (Eds.). (2007). *The Lender of Last Resort*. London/New York: Routledge.

Carney, B. M. (2008, October 18). Bernanke Is Fighting the Last War. *Wall Street Journal*.

Chari, V. V., & Kehoe, P. J. (2000). *Financial Crises as Herds*. Working Paper 600, Federal Reserve Bank of Minneapolis.

Chari, V. V., & Kehoe, P. J. (2003). *Financial Crises as Herds: Overturning the Critiques*. Staff Report 316, Federal Reserve Bank of Minneapolis.

Chen, J., Hong, H., & Stein, J. C. (2000). *Forecasting Crashes: Trading Volume, Past Returns and Conditional Skewness in Stock Prices*. NBER Working Paper No. 7687.

Congdon, T., & Hanke, S. H. (2017, March 14). More Bank Capital Could Kill the Economy. *Wall Street Journal*.

Craig, S., McCracken, J., Luccehtti, A., & Kelly, K. (2008, December 29). The Weekend That Wall Street Died. *Wall Street Journal*.

Dardik, I. (2017). *The Nature of Nature: The Discovery of SuperWaves and How It Changes Everything*. New York: Rodale.

Dent, H. S., Jr. (2016). *The Sale of a Lifetime: How the Great Bubble Burst of 2017–2019 Can Make You Rich*. New York: Penguin/Random House.

Dufwenberg, M., Lindqvist, T., & Moore, E. (2005). Bubbles and Experience: An Experiment. *American Economic Review, 95*(5), 1731–1737.

Estrella, A., & Mishkin, F. S. (1996). The Yield Curve as a Predictor of U.S. Recessions. *Current Issues in Finance and Economics*, (2)7. Federal Reserve Bank of New York.

Evans, L. L., Jr. (2003). *Why the Bubble Burst: US Stock Market Performance Since 1982*. Cheltenham: Edward Elgar.

Ewing, J. (2010, July 12). Crisis Awaits World's Banks as Trillions Come Due. *New York Times*.

Fabozzi, F. J., Focardi, S. M., & Jonas, C. (2014). *Investment Management: A Science to Teach or an Art to Learn?* Charlottesville: CFA Institute Research Foundation.

Fleckenstein, W. A., & Sheehan, F. (2008). *Greenspan's Bubbles: The Age of Ignorance at the Federal Reserve*. New York: McGraw-Hill.

Futia, C. (2009). *The Art of Contrarian Trading: How to Profit from Crowd Behavior in the Financial Markets*. Hoboken: Wiley.

Galbraith, J. K. (1988). *The Great Crash, 1929* (2nd ed.). Boston: Houghton-Mifflin.

Garber, P. M. (1989). Tulipmania. *Journal of Political Economy, 97*(3), 535–560.

Gehring, W. J., & Willoughby, A. R. (2002). The Medial Frontal Cortex and the Rapid Processing of Monetary Gains and Losses. *Science, 295*, 2279–2282.

Gongloff, M. (2008, March 17). Crunch Proves a Test of Faith for Street Strong. *Wall Street Journal*.

Goodman, P. S. (2008, October 8). Taking Hard New Look at a Greenspan Legacy. *New York Times*.

Gorton, G. B. (1988). Banking Panics and Business Cycles. *Oxford Economic Papers*, 40.

Gorton, G. B. (2009). Information, Liquidity, and the (Ongoing) Panic of 2007. *American Economic Review, 99*(2), 567–572.

Gorton, G. B. (2010). *Slapped by the Invisible Hand: The Panic of 2007*. New York: Oxford University Press.

Grant, J. (1996). *The Trouble with Prosperity: The Loss of Fear, the Rise of Speculation, and the Risk.* New York: Times Books (Random House).

Greenspan, A. (2008, March 16). We Will Never Have a Perfect Model of Risk. *Financial Times.*

Greenspan, A. (2013). *The Map and the Territory: Risk, Human Nature, and the Future of Forecasting.* New York: Penguin.

Hall, R. E. (2001). Struggling to Understand the Stock Market. *American Economic Review, 91*(2), 1–11.

Hamilton, J. D., & Lin, G. (1996). Stock Market Volatility and the Business Cycle. *Journal of Applied Econometrics, 11*(5), 573–593.

Hansell, S. (2008, September 18). How Wall Street Lied to Its Computers. *New York Times.*

Hartcher, P. (2006). *Bubble Man.* New York: W. W. Norton.

Herrera, S., & Perry, G. E. (2003). Tropical Bubbles: Asset Prices in Latin America, 1980–2001. In Hunter et al. (2003 [2005]).

Hunter, W. C., Kaufman, G. G., & Pomerleano, M. (Eds.). (2003). *Asset Price Bubbles: The Implications for Monetary, Regulatory, and International Policies.* Cambridge, MA: MIT Press (Paperback edition, 2005).

International Monetary Fund [IMF]. (2003). When Bubbles Burst. *World Economic Report.* Washington, DC: IMF.

Juglar, C. (1966). *A Brief History of Panics and Their Periodical Occurrence in the United States* (3rd ed.). New York: A. M. Kelley. Reprint of the 1916 Edition Translated by DeC. W. Thom.

Kindleberger, C., & Aliber, R. Z. (2011). *Manias, Panics, and Crashes: A History of Financial Crises* (6th ed.). Houndmills: Palgrave Macmillan.

Koivu, M., Pennanen, T., & Ziemba, W. T. (2005). Cointegration Analysis of the Fed Model. *Finance Research Letters, 2,* 248–259.

Koo, R. C. (2010). Lessons from Japan: Fighting a Balance Sheet Recession. *CFA Institute Conference Proceedings Quarterly, 27*(4), 28–39.

Lahart, J. (2007, August 18). In Time of Tumult, Obscure Economist Gains Currency. *Wall Street Journal.*

Laise, E. (2010, March 13). The Professor Who Chases Financial Bubbles. *Wall Street Journal.*

Lauricella, T. (2009, July 10). Failure of a Fail-Safe Strategy Sends Investors Scrambling. *Wall Street Journal.*

Leonhardt, D. (2008, September 30). Lessons from a Crisis: When Trust Vanishes, Worry. *New York Times.*

Lleo, S., & Ziemba, W. T. (2012). Stock Market Crashes in 2007–2009: Were We Able to Predict Them? *Quantitative Finance, 12,* 1161–1187.

Lleo, S., & Ziemba, W. T. (2015). Some Historical Perspectives on the Bond-Stock Yield Model for Crash Prediction Around the World. *International Journal of Forecasting, 31.*

Lleo, S., & Ziemba, W. T. (2017). Can Warren Buffett Forecast Equity Market Corrections? Available at https://ssrn.com/abstract=2630068 or https://doi.org/10.2139/ssrn.2630068

Lowenstein, R. (2008, September 6). Long-Term Capital: It's a Short-Term Memory. *New York Times.*

Maddison, A. (2003). *The World Economy: Historical Statistics.* Paris: OECD.

Mallaby, S. (2016). *The Man Who Knew: the Life and Times of Alan Greenspan*. New York: Penguin/Random House.

Martin, F. (2015). *Money: The Unauthorized Biography – From Coinage to Cryptocurrencies*. New York: Random House/Vintage (Paperback edition).

Mayo, M. (2011). *Exile on Wall Street: One Analysts Fight to Save the Big Banks from Themselves*. Hoboken: Wiley.

Mehrling, P. (2011). *The New Lombard Street: How the Fed Became the Dealer of Last Resort*. Princeton: Princeton University Press.

Miller, R. M. (2002). *Experimental Economics: How We Can Build Better Financial Markets*. Hoboken: Wiley.

Minsky, H. P. (2008). *Stabilizing an Unstable Economy*. New York: McGraw-Hill. (1996), New Haven: Yale University Press.

Mishkin, F. S.(2003). U.S. Stock Market Crashes and Their Aftermath: Implications for Monetary Policy. In Hunter et al (2003 [2005]).

Montier, J. (2007). *Behavioural Investing: A Practitioners Guide to Applying Behavioural Finance*. Chichester/Hoboken: Wiley.

Nations, S. (2017). *A History of the United States in Five Crashes: Stock Meltdowns that Defined a Nation*. New York: William Morrow (HarperCollins).

Newman, P., Milgate, M., & Eatwell, J. (Eds.). (1992). *The New Palgrave Dictionary of Money and Finance*. London: Macmillan Press.

Nocera, J. (2008, October 1). As Credit Crisis Spiraled, Alarm Led to Action. *New York Times*.

Ofek, E., & Richardson, M. (2001). *DotCom Mania: The Rise and Fall of Internet Stock Prices*. Working paper, No. 8630, National Bureau of Economic Research.

Oliver, M. J. (2007). Financial Crises. In M. J. Oliver & D. H. Aldcroft (Eds.), *Economic Disasters of the Twentieth Century*. Cheltenham: Elgar.

Oliver, M. J., & Aldcroft, D. H. (Eds.). (2007). *Economic Disasters of the Twentieth Century*. Cheltenham, UK: Elgar.

Patterson, S. (2010). *The Quants: How a New Breed of Math Whizzes Conquered Wall Street and Nearly Destroyed It*. New York: Crown (Random House).

Pepper, G., & Oliver, M. J. (2006). *The Liquidity Theory of Asset Prices*. Chichester/West Sussex: Wiley.

Peters, E. E. (1994). *Fractal Market Analysis: Applying Chaos Theory to Investment and Economics*. New York: Wiley.

Prechter, R. R., Jr. (2016). *The Socionomic Theory of Finance*. Gainesville: Socionomics Institute Press.

Redleaf, A., & Vigilante, R. (2010). *Panic: The Betrayal of Capitalism by Wall Street and Washington*. Minneapolis: Richard Vigilante Books.

Reinhart, C. M., & Rogoff, K. S. (2009). *This Time Is Different: Eight Centuries of Financial Folly*. Princeton: Princeton University Press.

Roehner, B. M. (2000). Identifying the Bottom Line After a Stock Market Crash. *International Journal of Modern Physics, C, 11*(1), 91–100.

Roehner, B. M. (2002). *Patterns of Speculation: A Study in Observational Econophysics*. Cambridge, UK: Cambridge University Press.

Russolillo, S., & Kilgore, T. (2010, August 14). 'Hindenburg Omen' Flashes. *Wall Street Journal*.

Schularick, M., & Taylor, A. (2012). Credit Booms Gone Bust: Monetary Policy, Leverage Cycles and Financial Crises, 1870–2008. *American Economic Review, 102*(2), 1029–1061.

Schumpeter, J. A. (1934). *The Theory of Economic Development: An Inquiry into Profits, Capital, Credit, Interest and the Business Cycle.* Trans. Opie. Cambridge, MA: Harvard University Press edition. 1961.

Schwert, G. W. (1989). *Business Cycles, Financial Crises, and Stock Volatility.* Working Paper No. 2957, NBER (May).

Siegel, J. J. (2006, December 6). Irrational Exuberance, Reconsidered. *Wall Street Journal.*

Siegel, J. J. (2008, 2014). Stocks for the Long Run (4th and 5th eds.). New York: McGraw-Hill.

Silver, N. (2012). *The Signal and the Noise: Why So Many Predictions Fail – But Some Don't.* New York: Penguin.

Skypala, P. (2014, September 1). Ditch the Hokum on Asset Diversification. *Financial Times.*

Smith, V. L., Suchanek, G. L., & Williams, A. W. (1988, September). Bubbles, Crashes, and Endogenous Expectations in Experimental Spot Asset Markets. *Econometrica, 56*(5).

Summers, L. H. (2016, February 16). It's Time to Kill the $100 Bill. *Washington Post.*

Summers, G. (2017). *The Everything Bubble: The Endgame for Central Banking.* North Charleston: CreateSpace Independent Publishing.

Surowiecki, J. (2004). *The Wisdom of Crowds.* New York: Doubleday.

Swarup, B. (2014). *Money Mania: Booms, Panics and Busts from Ancient Rome to the Great Meltdown.* New York: Bloomsbury Press.

Taleb, N. N. (2005). *Fooled by Randomness* (2nd paperback ed.). New York: Random House.

Tapia, J. A. (2014). *From the Oil Crisis to the Great Recession: Five Crises of the World Economy.* Paper presented January 3 at the ASSA annual meeting in Philadelphia.

Triana, P. (2009). *Lecturing Birds on Flying: Can Mathematical Theories Destroy the Financial Markets?* Hoboken: Wiley.

Triana, P. (2012). *The Number that Killed Us: A Story of Modern Banking, Flawed Mathematics, and a Big Financial Crisis.* Hoboken: Wiley.

Tuckett, D. (2011). *Minding the Markets: An Emotional Finance View of Financial Instability.* London: Palgrave Macmillan.

Ursua, J. F., & Barro, R. J. (2009). *Stock-Market Crashes and Depressions.* Working Paper Series, No. w14760. Cambridge, MA: National Bureau of Economic Research.

Vandewalle, N., Ausloos, M., Boveroux, P., & Minguet, A. (1999). Visualizing the Log-Periodic Pattern before Crashes. *European Physical Journal B, 9*(2), 355–359.

Vines, S. (2005). *Market Panic: Wild Gyrations, Risks, and Opportunities in Stock Markets.* Singapore: Wiley (Paperback edition).

Visco, I. (2003). Comments on Recent Experiences with Asset Price Bubbles. In Hunter et al. (2003).

Vogel, H. L., & Werner, R. A. (2015). An Analytical Review of Volatility Metrics for Bubbles and Crashes. *International Review of Financial Analysis, 38,* 15–28.

Von Mises, L. (1979, 2006). *Economic Policy: Thoughts for Today and Tomorrow.* Chicago: Regnery/Gateway. Third ed. 2006. Available at http://books.google.com/books/download

Voth, H.-J. (2003). With a Bang, Not a Whimper: Pricking Germany's 'Stock Market Bubble' in 1927 and the Slide into Depression. *Journal of Economic History, 63*(1), 65–99.

Werner, R. A. 2003). *Princes of the Yen: Japan's Central Bankers and the Transformation of the Economy.* Armonk/New York/London: M. E. Sharpe. (East Gate Books).

White, E. N. (Ed.). (1990). *Crashes and Panics: The Lessons from History.* Homewood: Dow-Jones-Irwin.

Wilmott, P. (2001). *Paul Wilmott Introduces Quantitative Finance.* Chichester: Wiley.

Wilson, J. W., Sylla, R. E., & Jones, C. P. (1990). Financial Market Panics and Volatility in the Long Run, 1830–1988. In E. N. White (Ed.), *Crashes and Panics: The Lessons from History.* Homewood: Dow-Jones-Irwin.

Wood, G. E. (2007). Stock Market Crashes. In M. J. Oliver and D. H. Aldcroft (Eds.), *Economic Disasters of the Twentieth Century.* Cheltenham, UK: Elgar.

Ziemba, R. E. S., & Ziemba, W. T. (2007). *Scenarios for Risk Management and Global Investment Strategies.* Chichester: Wiley.

Ziemba, W. T., Lleo, S., & Zhitlukhin, M. (2018). *Stock Market Crashes: Predictable and Unpredictable and What to Do about Them.* Singapore and Hoboken, NJ: World Scientific.

Zweig, J. (2015, November 14). Deciphering the Dialect: A Wall Street Glossary. *Wall Street Journal.*

CHAPTER 4

Money and Credit Features

William McChesney Martin Jr., Fed Chairman from 1951 to 1970, famously said that "Our purpose is to lean against the winds of deflation or inflation, whichever way they are blowing, but we do not make those winds." The statement is by now a hoary part of central banking's conventional wisdom but it is inaccurate and misleading. As this chapter illustrates, central banks are not inherently independent of politics, they tend to be more reactive than proactive in their policies, they aren't always clear and transparent in signaling intentions, strategies, and goals, and they have a proclivity toward blowing bubbles and a reluctance to restrain them.[1] They don't like to play the villain.[2]

There's no way to understand extreme market events without understanding central bank histories, motivations, and procedures.

4.1   HISTORICAL PERSPECTIVES

Theories

Business cycle theories go back more than 150 years to the days of philosopher-economist John Stuart Mill's *Principles of Political Economy* of 1848. Mill was early to recognize that business cycles are functions of the interplay between credit and debt. When expanding credit spilled over from the financial sector to the rest of the economy, psychologically driven speculative manias and booms were generated. These then ultimately collapsed when credit growth became insufficient to service the debts that had been already incurred. Mill's approach was surprisingly astute and far ahead of its time.

Business cycles were also explored by economist William Stanley Jevons, who in 1884 proposed that fluctuations in agricultural plantings and output were related to changes in activity on the sun's surface. This Sunspot Theory at first seemed plausible, as the length of business cycles was thought to be

© The Author(s) 2018

H. L. Vogel, *Financial Market Bubbles and Crashes, Second Edition*,
https://doi.org/10.1007/978-3-319-71528-5_4

approximately 10.4 years and close to the average sunspot cycle length. But the linkage to economic activity was not later supported. The more important contribution of Jevons turned out to be the idea that future production decisions in business cycles are to a degree self-fulfilling.

Before the Great Depression of the 1930s a mercantilist theory was prevalent. This was based on the idea that the wealth and power of nations depended on the amount of gold held and that trade surpluses would generate inflows of gold and thereby expand the money supply. To mercantilists, growth of gold reserves and of the economy were directly associated. Although simplistic, this theory was a precursor of modern monetarist approaches.

The classical model that then evolved assumed perfect competition and homogeneous preferences of individuals, whose behavior is unaffected by money illusions, which means that changes in money supply do not have any effect on real economic activities and aggregate outputs. In this approach, there are no differences between financial and any other types of transactions and, indeed, there is little or no role for credit policies.[3]

After the Great Depression exposed the explanatory inadequacies of these notions several other ideas were presented. Irving Fisher's 1933 debt-deflation theory looked at excessive indebtedness as an important factor leading to economic downturns. Machlup (1940, p. 55) tied extensive speculation by the public to an increase in the supply of bank money. And, dubious of the practical efficacy of monetary policies, Keynes's famous 1936 *General Theory* instead emphasized the need for fiscal policy interventions to offset significant declines in output.[4]

As such, the Keynesian approach had by the 1950s come to dominate the thinking of government policy strategists and academics. But soon thereafter, the monetarists, led by Milton Friedman, began to make headway. Monetarists based their theories on the belief that perfect information does not exist and that changes in the money supply, through adaptive expectations, drive business cycles. Friedman's main complaint was that imperfectly informed central bankers generated instability in prices and output through their irregular and misguided attempts to manipulate money supply.

Fascination with rational expectations (RE)—an extension of the classical models, but containing probabilistic elements that presumably can be used to forecast future events—then followed in the 1980s. Taken to its logical extreme, however, the neoclassical RE approach inherently implied that all observable monetary and fiscal policies will be irrelevant and ineffective.

In fact, it was not until the mid-1980s that more tractable financial accelerator models first explicitly recognized the imperfectly competitive and informationally asymmetric nature of markets. In these models, the cost and availability of credit are seen to have pivotal effects on macroeconomic and financial market behavior. Still, such models did not provide clear prescriptions for monetary policy strategies, nor were they fully persuasive with regard to what the effectiveness of such policies might be. Increases in money supply might, for example, inflate asset price bubbles without sustainably boosting real economic growth.

Around the same time, however, more complex models of credit rationing that included financial accelerator features were introduced. The credit-rationing approach posits that markets operate with asymmetric information, that borrowers and lenders are not all alike in their preferences, that credit constraints will fluctuate over the business cycle and amplify or dampen swings, and that, because of changing risk perceptions, disequilibrium is probably a permanent feature of markets and the economy.[5]

In contrast to the financial accelerators, in which price rationing of credit is assumed, credit-rationing models instead hypothesize that credit is *quantity*-rationed, that is, lenders will always impose borrowing limits, which will vary according to business cycle conditions. In an economic downturn, for example, borrowers who are financially weakest and most in need of credit extensions are the ones who—regardless of the price they are willing to pay—will encounter the most restrictions and/or denials. An important implication of this is that interest rates are unlikely to reflect the actual (and productive) availability of credit (a view held by the Austrian school of economics, which also posits that the existence of economic equilibrium is "nonsense").[6]

The credit-rationing approach thus aligns with the theories of Malinvaud (1985) and Bénassy (1986) and also with the present empirical work on bubble and crash formations.[7] At cyclical extremes in the economy, just as at financial market extremes, it is credit quantity availability much more than credit's price that governs the action and the outcome—which can be inflation, asset bubbles, economic growth, or a mix of all three.

But when it comes to credit, *only* banks (and their central banks) can create it out of *nothing*.[8] That's because the accounting procedures and conventions of banks differ entirely from those of nonfinancial corporations or non-bank financial institutions (e.g., stockbrokers) who also engage in lending activities.

> *...banks uniquely combine lending and deposit-taking activities under one roof and* they do not have to segregate client accounts...*[T]he main component of the official 'money supply' as announced by central banks (M1, M2,M3, M4)...is created almost entirely through...re-classifying banks' accounts payable as fictitious 'customer deposits.'...neither the borrower nor the bank actually made a deposit at the bank.* (Werner 2014b)

In brief, "[Banks do not loan money. They loan credit. They create this credit and charge interest for the use of it."[9]

Even so, however, it's fundamentally important to understand that a market "doesn't care who you are. You're a trade to the market... a bank is a relationship."[10] As King (2016, Chap. 2) makes clear,

[F]or over two centuries, economists have struggled to provide a rigorous theoretical basis for the role of money, and have largely failed...even the existence of money has proved something of a mystery for economic theorists...governments allowed the creation of money to become the by-product of the process of credit creation.

Realities

Although the notion that interest rates and stock prices always move inversely is conventional wisdom on Wall Street, there is ample evidence that this wisdom is often incorrect, misleading, or inapplicable: A decade of interest rates declining to virtually zero revived neither Japanese share prices nor economic growth in the 1990s.[11]

As for the U.S., Fed funds rates fell from 6.5% in June 2000 to 1.25% by December 2002, yet the market experienced its longest losing streak since the 1930s. And rate cuts beginning in 2007 appeared to provide little or no support for share prices and economic growth. In the space of one year, the Dow-Jones Industrials fell 40.3% from a closing peak of 14,164.53 on October 9, 2007, to a trough of 8451.19 (7882.51 intraday) on October 10, 2008, even while rates dropped from 4.75% to 1.5% and the economy slipped into recession.

The late 1960s and 1970s were also turbulent, but in contrast to the early 2000s, inverse directional movements between rates and stock prices were frequent. In the 1970s, the rise in short-term rates from around 6% to 16% was unusually rapid and unexpected, with significantly higher borrowing costs leading immediately to an erosion of corporate profits and to suppression of share prices through much higher discounting of downward-revised future cash-flow expectations.[12]

Short-term interest-rate histories for the UK and the US vis-à-vis stock market performances are illustrated in Fig. 4.1. It can be seen (note arrows) that in both countries there are periods when interest rates and market indexes move in tandem in the same direction (e.g., late 1987–1990 and 1994–1998 in the United Kingdom) and other periods when they moved inversely (1989–1993).

Another example: from October 2007 to March 2008 the DJIA *fell* 54%, while Fed funds rates declined from around 4.75% to nearly zero. But from March 2003 to October 2007, the DJIA *rose* 88% even as Fed funds rates climbed from 1.25% to 4.75%. Conversely, from July 2012 to December 2013, the DJIA rallied 27% at the same time that the US ten-year Treasury note yield more than halved to 3.05% from 1.38%.

Hence, rising rates didn't necessarily impede a rising market nor did falling rates cushion a falling market, even though real equity returns do tend over the long term to diminish in a period of tightening (i.e., rising rates) and to increase in a period of easing.[13] Still, the magnitude of the positive

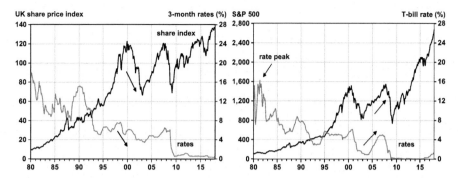

Fig. 4.1 Treasury bill rates (three-month) and stock market indices, FTSE-100 and Bank of England, monthly, 1984:01 2015:12, left (rates down, market down) and S&P 500 and Federal Reserve, right (rates up, market up). (Sources: Bank of England, Federal Reserve data)

returns relative to directional changes of interest rates does not appear to be decisive, predictable, or dependable.[14]

The inconsistent relationship between asset returns and interest rates is also seen in the affects of interest-rate movements on the growth of GDP. Annualized changes in GDP appear to track the effective Fed funds rate reasonably well (Fig. 4.2) at least up until 2005 or so, when a generally rising funds rate prior to 1980 largely coincided with relatively high nominal growth of GDP. But in the years of *near-zero* rates, from 2009 onward, GDP growth was relatively small. Central bank-supported global stock and bond markets instead rose to record-setting heights, with yield-starbed investors acting as willing accomplices. Evidently, the interplay between interest rates and the economic growth is one thing and market asset returns quite another!

Great fault may also be found in the widely accepted view that central banks are in full control of short-term interest rates (via open-market operations and repurchase agreements, i.e., repos). They are not.

Ryan-Collins et al. (2011, p. 71) explains that:

> *The central bank cannot directly determine the market rate of interest in the inter-bank market, but it can affect the market rate of interest by lending or borrowing reserves itself on this market to try and keep this rate close to the policy rate.*

Moreover, rather than central banks determining how much credit banks can issue, "one could argue that it is the banks that determine how much central bank reserves and cash the Bank of England must lend to them. The tail wags the dog."[15]

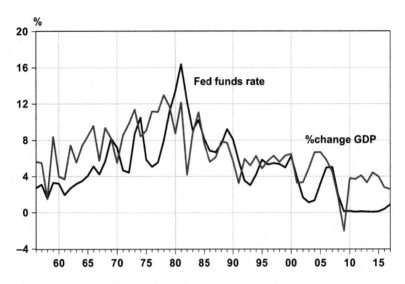

Fig. 4.2 Effective Fed funds rate (in %) versus percent changes in nominal US GDP, annual averages, 1956–2017. (Sources: Federal Reserve Bank of St. Louis and US Bureau of Economic Analysis)

A trace of changes in the Fed funds rate (or almost equivalently, LIBOR) and three-month Treasury bill yields (Fig. 4.3) shows that this central bank (and also others) has rarely (if ever) led Treasury bill rates up or down and usually follows with a lag of several weeks or months. The conventional wisdom thus has it backward: Central banks are largely reactive, not proactive.[16]

4.2   LIQUIDITY ISSUES

Liquidity may mean many things to many people, but at its core it involves "a force which exerts individuals to effect a financial transaction when they would not otherwise do so."[17] This description is entirely consistent with a liquidity theory of asset prices as presented by Bénassy and Malinvaud.[18]

That the linkages between monetary policy and stock market prices are tenuous and that it is inadvisable, even dangerous, for central banks to base policy decisions on stock market prices has been suggested by Mishkin and White (2003, pp. 75–6). "[I]t is very hard," they say, "for monetary authorities to determine if a bubble has actually developed."[19]

Along similar lines, Anna Schwartz (1986, p. 255) wrote, "Bubbles, like bankruptcies would occur even if the money stock were free of destabilizing cyclical swings. The Florida land boom of 1925–6 and the gold price bubble of 1979–80 were created by opportunities those markets appeared to offer rather than the pattern of monetary growth."

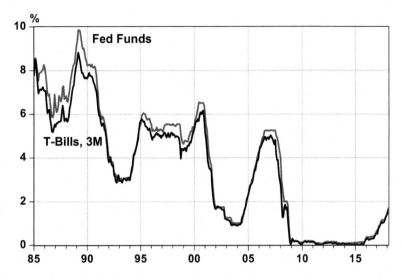

Fig. 4.3 The Fed follows: Three-month market Treasury bill rates (dark line, TB3) versus FOMC Fed funds rates (gray line), January 1985 to March 2018. (Sources: Federal Reserve Open Market Committee, http://www.federalreserve.gov/fomc/fundsrate.htm and https://fred.stlouisfed.org/series/TB3MS and FEDFUNDS)

Increasingly, though, it is being realized that macroeconomic price stability is not necessarily concomitant with financial sector stability. Even if central bankers were to know when and how much to suppress the expansion of asset bubbles—something that is not known—they would probably discover that raising interest rates might not reliably have much effect on impeding a bubble's growth but would instead tend to destabilize the economy.[20] That's because central banks cannot at any time fully assess the inherent and ever-changing risk preferences of the global marketplace. Reliable estimates of the real equilibrium interest rate (r-star) at which policy is neither accommodative nor restrictive have also been elusive. And the effectiveness of monetary policy is continually subject to debate.[21] It isn't even clear whether raising interest rates will at all times and phases of growth, inhibit inflation. High rates sustained over a long enough time will certainly do so eventually. But it is conceivable that there may be times and circumstances in which the effect might for a while be the opposite.[22]

In fact, most of the bubbles of the last 200 years have occurred in relatively low inflationary environments featuring rapid growth of productivity and credit. Other aspects, including liquidity, bank loan-to-collateral ratios, and credit creation in the financial sector, are now—post the 2000 and 2007 experiences—increasingly taken to be at least as important as interest rates when it comes to the creation of bubbles and crashes.[23]

From the Japanese studies reviewed earlier, however, it would seem that the prime suspect behind the formation and support of bubbles involves an excessive (by historical standards and ratios) creation of bank loans that finance non-GDP transactions such as those for speculative securities, real estate, commodities, and massive private equity deals. In brief, it is the increase in bank loans acting in conjunction with money supply (M2) growth—and not just M2 growth alone—that fosters and underwrites such asset price inflations.[24]

The rationale is that such excess liquidity, for whatever reasons (viz., Japan, 1985–1990, or the United States, 2011–2017), sloshes into the financial markets because it cannot be quickly or profitably invested, deployed, or readily absorbed into the real economy. The repetitious lesson from history is that unproductively arranged excessive credit creation always ultimately turns into bad (unrepaid or unrepayable) debts.[25]

Five separate US money-related monthly time series, M1, nonborrowed reserves, business loans, stock margin loans, and MZM—i.e., zero maturity assets redeemable at par on demand and without penalty or risk of loss—were visually compared and also regressed against the S&P 500. Of these, the trajectory of the MZM series as displayed in Fig. 4.4 most closely mirrors that of the S&P 500.[26] But here's the most interesting part: The S&P appears—in defiance of conventional wisdom—to almost always lead (i.e., anticipate) by a month or two the large directional changes in the MZM series![27]

The entire process likely operates primarily through the actions of speculators and investors who—given enough liquidity (i.e., easy access to credit) to ignite speculative fires—begin to regard risk as something that no longer matters or that perhaps may not even exist. The public then on-balance changes its

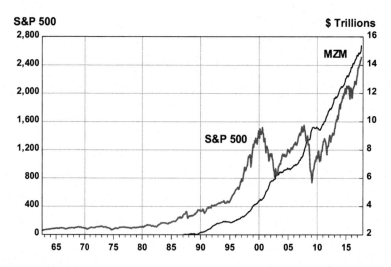

Fig. 4.4 MZM versus the S&P 500 monthly, 1962:08 to 2017:12. The regression equation, log (SPINDX) = 1.98 + 0.971*log (MZM), shows a *p*-value of 0.00, and *R*-squared adjusted of 0.948. The Durbin-Watson stat is 0.024, which suggests that there is autocorrelation

liquidity ("saving-for-a-rainy day") preference. The fractional reserve banking system, in which banks can essentially create (and also withdraw) credit at will, thus makes banks active conduits and collaborators in the bubble formation (and also later deflation) process.[28]

None of this necessarily precludes the possibility of experiencing dual-sector bubbles, such as occurred in the late 1980s in Japan, when both real estate and stocks soared together. When a relatively high percentage of total non-GDP transaction loans is channeled into real estate, for instance, it may be more difficult for a strong stock market bubble to also form at the same time: Investments in real estate may detract from, crowd out, and/or divert some speculative capital away from investments in equities. Still, given a sufficiently large amoun8t of non-GDP transactional lending, feedback effects from gains in one sector would likely spill over in support of asset price gains in other sectors.

4.3   Role of Central Banks

All central banks are, in one way or another, charged with dual operational mandates to preserve both price and systemic financial stability. As such, in times of financial distress they are presumably well-positioned to be the lenders of last resort—taking on the roles of lenders and managers and finding it, as Fischer (1999) notes, "useful to have the power to create money." But it is a power that has often been misapplied and abused.[29] It has been said that when evaluating competing policy prescriptions, the Fed acts more as an adjudicator than a banker.[30] The Fed, in its own words, was designed to "act as a bank *to* the federal government" and is not a bank *of* the government (www.frbservices.org). It acts a "bank for banks."[31] Yet, in a crisis atmosphere such as that which existed in 2008–2009, the private debt of highly leveraged financial institutions is usually converted by the central bank into public debts to be serviced by taxpayers.[32]

The banks have by now strayed far from Bagehot's classic (Bagehot 1873) rule that in a financial panic, lend freely and early at high interest rates but only against good collateral: Banks have, since the crisis of 2008, instead become *investors* of last resort—issuing debt to buy more debt (and in Japan to even buy equities) that is collateral of often indeterminable or questionable quality.[33]

The critical notion is that illiquidity yields readily to insolvency and that *"the line between solvency and liquidity is not determinate during a crisis."*[34] That is because this very indeterminacy always appears in the midst of panic or crash conditions, when major decisions must be made with severe limits on available information and time. In each episode, historically and currently, the basic cost/benefit and moral hazard-related question to be answered by the lender of last resort (LOLR) is then whether a financial institution is too big to fail (and thus ought to be bailed out).[35] The financial crisis of 2007–09 further demonstrated that the traditional lender of last resort has by now evolved into the *dealer* of last resort by providing a kind of tail-risk insurance.[36]

Although the role of central banks in times of bubbles and crashes (including those in foreign exchange markets) has been widely studied, the analyses have tended to be channeled through the neoclassical perspectives of equilibrium and optimization models, business cycles, and the rational expectations hypothesis.[37] Monetary policy as executed through changes in Fed funds rates is typically the main issue of concern, although studies have suggested that the decisive factor in both bubbles and crashes appears to be the degree of credit availability.[38]

Prior to the global problems that appeared in early 2007, most of the literature had advised against monetary policies that reacted directly to changes in asset prices, whether they were parts of bubbles or of crashes.[39] It was a mop up after pop up policy. Indeed, Bernanke and Gertler (1999 [2000]) argued that "[R]ules that directly target asset prices appear to have undesirable side effects." And Hayford and Malliaris (2005) concluded that although "the Fed has paid significant attention to the valuation of the stock market…the Federal funds rate target has…not been *increased solely* to offset a potential stock market bubble."[40] Yet it is amply evident in transcripts of Fed meetings in the 1990s that the central bank has long been actively interested in what the stock market is doing and that especially after 2009 it has been more purposefully involved.[41]

What is written in theoretical journals and what actually occurs in the *realpolitik* of markets are two different things.[42] "[A]cademic finance built a theory of finance without the macroeconomy just as neoclassical macroeconomics had built a theory of the macroeconomy without finance," Martin (2015, p. 217) explains. In the midst of the credit crisis of 2008, for instance, Fed Chairman Bernanke indicated that the central bank *would* in the future consider discarding its aversion to interfering with asset-price bubbles.[43]

Given that central banks are at heart political creations, it is always much easier to prescribe than to actually lean against the wind and tighten.[44] The policy dilemma faced by all central banks is that relative financial stability represented by periods absent of bubbles might sometimes require restraint of credit expansion, whereas prevention or avoidance of economic contraction requires the more politically expedient opposite—a policy of constant promotion of credit expansion.[45] "Liquidity and solvency problems reinforce one another on the way down, just as credit expansion and asset valuations do on the way up."[46]

As former Fed Chairman Greenspan said in 1996, "We have great difficulty in monetary policy when we confront stock market bubbles."[47]

Studies conducted after the financial system's near-collapse in 2008 are nevertheless starting to change the previous thinking, in which credit growth prescriptions and policies and the financial structures of banks and large corporations had often been previously assumed to have little bearing on macroeconomic features. Upon closer inspection, it has been found that money, credit, and output aggregates had been much more closely aligned with each other prior to than after 1945.

Since then, credit aggregates (bank assets to GDP in Fig. 4.5) have expanded much faster than either money or bank loans through implementations of technological and securities market innovations, allowances of higher banking system leverage ratios, and increasing activism by lenders of last resort. This means that in the future, central bankers will no longer be able to as readily ignore or dismiss the potential systemic effects of their credit policy initiatives.[48] The Fed's decision to almost entirely eliminate bank reserve requirements in the early 1990s is a case in poin: Retrospectively, that initiative might arguably be considered to have been the spark that ignited and sustained the easy credit conditions under which the subsequent tech and housing bubbles were formed.

As for crashes—if price declines are rapid enough and appear to threaten overall economic and financial stability—central banks will normally react aggressively by opening credit windows wide to commercial (and even investment) banks, dropping interest rates and margin requirements, and generally providing what had become known in the United States as the Greenspan "put." The market crises of 1987 and of 1998 (Long-Term Capital Management, etc.), as well as the subprime mortgage credit freeze-ups of 2007–2008, are illustrative.[49]

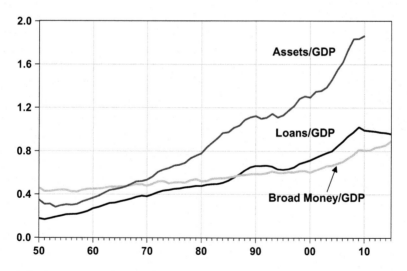

Fig. 4.5 Aggregates relative to GDP (year effects), bank loans/GDP, broad money/ GDP, and bank assets/GDP, 1950–2015. (Sources: NBER, and courtesy of Schularick and Taylor (2012) with updates)[50]

Still, relatively few empirical studies of the *effectiveness* of central bank risk-management policies on asset prices during crash conditions are to be found in the literature.[51] Perhaps this is because of the inherent difficulties in defining crashes and, as has been historically seen, the greatly varied aftereffects that such events have had on economic stability (e.g., contrast macroeconomic conditions after the crashes of 1929 and 1987). Either way, though, should a situation be threatening enough to the stability of the economy or the viability of a large lending organization, the first response with regard to repayment terms will be to amend, extend, and pretend.[52]

Even with easy credit policies in place, the basic banking dilemma in or just after a crash remains: It's that lenders (central and otherwise) can open all the credit windows as wide as they like, but potential borrowers will only commit to bearing the burden of interest cost and principal repayments if faith in the future and belief in opportunity (i.e., positive psychology) begins to outweigh concerns about incurring such obligations.[53]

Although central banks may wish to provide massive amounts of low-cost credit, they generally cannot coerce businesses and consumers to borrow or to *want* to engage in expansive economic activity. It is thus the collective perception of expected potential opportunity or the lack thereof even more than the actual cost or availability of credit itself that likely becomes most important in determining how effective central bank policies will be.[54] Borrowers' sentiment will further depend more on social mood trends and conditions and biased beliefs about probable future cash flows than on discount rates.[55] Clearly, if banks are reluctant to lend and companies and consumers to borrow, GDP growth and money velocity at best remain subdued and stagnant (Fig. 4.2).

Moreover, should prospective borrowers with less than pristine balance sheets and/or credit histories—often young, unseasoned, and relatively small business that have the greatest need to borrow and the greatest potential to grow rapidly—seek loans, they will likely be denied as bank regulators with recent troublesome experiences still fresh in mind will always at such junctures opt for safety and tend to nix extensions of riskier-than-average and more speculative loans. As Neal (2015, p. 167) explains:

> *higher-risk borrowers have to provide collateral for additional loans just as the financial collapse decreases the value of their collateral. The outcome may be either a general wave of bankruptcies, or ... a widening circle of payment stops that discourages normal investment and consumption.*

In other words, no matter how low (or even negative, as in 2014–2016) central banks are able to depress interest rates, for such less seasoned enterprises, the interest rate is effectively infinite. Once the zero lower bound (ZLB) for interest rates and the ability to cut the *price* of credit further is reached through the use of conventional tools, the only alternative next step has been to use unconventional policies that aim to increase *quantities* through implementation of what's come to be known as quantitative easing (QE).

Such QE strategies, initially involving only long-term bond-buying pro-grams, were then however iinevitably lnked to the Fed's interest payments on excess reserves (IOER)—i.e., on reserves that are not money and are not counted as part of the money stock. Although the ostensible goal was to boost growth and employment, the *administrated* IOER basically paid banks *not* to lend (even as massive liquidity was injected into financial markets). IOER—begun with the Emergency Economic Stabilization Act of 2008—meant that the Fed's greatly enlarged balance sheet (Fig. 2.15) was being used as a giant credit allocator, somewhat arbitrarily favoring (post 2008) one sector of the economy (housing) over others.[56]

Between 2009 and 2016, massive American QE "stimulus" (with similar ECB policies for Europe) was applied by the Fed as follows:

QE1: December 2008 to March 2010 (purchases including $1.25 trillion mortgage-backed securities).

QE2: November 2010 to June 2011 (purchases of $600 billion long-matu-rity Treasuries).

Operation Twist: September 2011 to October 2012 (buy long-term Treasuries and sell short-term Treasuries).

QE3: September 2012 to October 2014 ($40 billion and $45 billion per month of mortgage-backed and Treasuries, respectively).[57]

If these policies had been truly medicinal, the economies in Europe and America and Japan too should by 2016 have been flourishing, not floundering: The long-run costs and unintended consequences – including politically desta-bilizing exacerbation of class-income inequalities, annihilation of pension fund returns, interference with market price signals, and malinvestments – of such grand policies are yet to be fully tallied even as their net benefits have been questioned.[58]

As in Japan and Europe, zero or negative interest-rate policies (ZIRPS and NIRPs) had in fact been economically *deflationary*. NIRP guarantees a loss, so investors and savers are scared into the anti-growth behavior of hoarding cash.[59] That there is a limit to such policies is ever more apparent as, for the first time in history, total debt on balance sheets of the top-ten central banks in 2017 amounted to around 30% of world GDP (as compared to around 10% ten years earlier).[60] The potential practical consequences of this are unfathomable and unknown but probably not virtuous.

The weak tractions and inherent lags in applying QE policies are suggested in Fig. 4.6, which shows that in its ongoing efforts to jump-start Japan's econ-omy out of a two-decade long deflationary malaise, Bank of Japan's Governor Haruhiko Kuroda, near the end of 2014, directed the $1.1 trillion Government Pension Investment Fund to increase holdings of stocks from around 24% to 50%. The impression on the stock market and the economy (which again slipped into recession in late 2015) was underwhelming.[61]

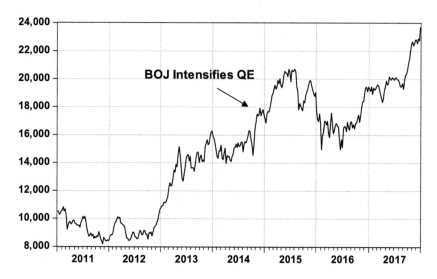

Fig. 4.6   Nikkei 225 Average, weekly, 2011–2017:Q4. BOJ buys stocks

As for the United States, even three years after administering a total $2 trillion of QE, Fed experts still didn't know if it actually worked.[62] And similar ambiguity will probably long surround so-called quantitative tightening (QT) that's intended to slowly shrink the Fed's balance sheet starting 2017:Q4.

That's because central banks inevitably encounter what's known as Goodhart's Law, which is the monetary equivalent of the Heisenberg uncertainty principle of physics. Goodhart's Law says that the more central bankers intervene in markets, the less they will know about real economic conditions and the greater the need for more intervention.[63] "The possibility that monetary authorities become unable to meet lender of last resort duties cannot be ruled out."[64]

4.4   Conclusions

This chapter suggests that money and credit conditions do indeed have a relationship to the creation and sustainability of bubbles.[65] The problem is that the parameters of such relationships (as with much else in economics) are difficult to empirically substantiate. In part, this may be due to the rather imprecise statistical signature of bubbles (and crashes).

The literature relating credit and money measures to such extreme events is thus surprisingly uneven and unsettled. It largely places the most emphasis on interest-rate policy decisions as pertaining to economic growth potential and price stability and not so much directly on the creation and mediation of bubble and crash events themselves.

Tests of money and credit series further advise that interest-rate policy levers such as Fed funds rates can fertilize the soil in which bubbles can grow.

Moreover, it appears that bank credit creation begins with decreases in nonborrowed reserves that then work through to increases in business and/or consumer lending only if borrowers are confident.[66] The resulting rises in the values of loan collateral then feed back to into more credit extensions which in later stages make it difficult for central bank interest-rate policies to act as be impediments: The stronger the boom, the less the interest rate on loans will to the borrower matter.[67]

Yet, already outstanding obligations and the massive addition of new systemic debts (federal state and local, household, and corporate) weigh down everything, including the money multiplier that describes the rate at which reserves are converted into money. It may thus be inferred that relatively weak loan demand rather than restrictive supply might be the root cause of why— when debt loads are high – central banking policies are so much less potent than would otherwise be expected.[68]

Once lending exceeds what can be readily absorbed by or used for GDP transactions, the excess spills over into incremental demand for shares and/or other leverageable financial assets, including real estate and commodities. This is consistent with what happened in the Japanese bubble of the late 1980s and also the subsequent credit and housing bubble of the early 2000s: Central banks sometimes make big policy blunders and mistakes.[69]

A long line of theoretical work relating money, credit, and output aggregates has not sufficiently weighted financial structure and credit growth aspects and the probable relationships these have to the occurrence of extreme market events. Credit, it seems, has not in the literature been given sufficient credit.

Although many studies conclude that it is difficult for central banks to find and then adopt policies that can slow or forestall bubble formations, bankers are nevertheless attentive to stock valuations and directions of movement. Yet interventionistic policy prescriptions (raising or lowering rates, opening or closing windows, etc.) appear to be much more directly, actively, and visibly applied in crash than in bubble conditions.[70] In crashes any remaining pretentions as to the political independence of the central bank disappear. In brief, "[T]he science of 'bubble' management is, so far, imaginary."[71]

What is certain—from even as far back as 1832—is that the demand for money in ordinary times is diametrically different than is the demand for it in periods of panic.[72] Politically influenced central banks currently have asymmetric and predominantly neoclassically based reactions and approaches (e.g., DSGE models). They will never hesitate to quickly lower interest rates and to open borrowing windows wide in the case of a crash, but only with great reluctance will they attempt to restrain the bloating (and blowing) of bubbles.[73] That's because, in essence, the Fed and other central banks were established so that credit could be made easy![74]

For bankers and brokers of all types, and especially for entrepreneurs and speculators, interest rates held artificially low (i.e., cheap credit) have always been hallucinogenic. And because central banks are never fully insulated from populist politics and zeitgeist, they are generally also unable to early adjust policies at the optimal times, that is, ahead of important economic turning points.[75] Central banks have failed before and likely will again.[76]

It thus seems that all important central banking policy errors—in particular the targeting of inflation while not recognizing or adequately responding to asset price bubbles—are related to the use (and misuse) of flawed neoclassical assumptions and the absence of any awareness, thought, or understanding of the socionomic precepts such as:

- Financial asset prices do not at all respond to supply and demand in the same way as do prices of goods and services;
- People do not react independently of each other, they herd;
- The macroeconomy does not behave mechanistically and cannot be controlled as if it did;[77]
- Macroeconomic stability does not guarantee capital market stability.[78]
- It's much easier, relatively, to hedge against interest-rate risk than credit default risk and practically impossible to hedge against liquidity risk—which is largely unknowable in its scale and timing.

"Permit me to issue and control the money of a nation and I care not who makes its law" is of unconfirmed origin but is a quip that's entirely consistent with the themes of monetary history.[79]

Notes

1. See note 38.
2. From Mallaby (2017).
3. See Knoop (2008, p. 71) and also Werner (2003, p. 4), who write that at best, the neoclassical approach "sees no role for credit policy and at worst simply assumes money does not exist."
4. Swedish economist Knut Wicksell was also skeptical of monetary policy maneuvering, but from a perspective different from that of Keynes. According to Wicksell, a central bank's reduction in interest rates interfered with the natural equilibrium between savings by individuals and business investments in capital goods. In this view, lower interest rates could not be sustained by savings. The central bank would eventually face a difficult choice between reducing rates further to allow a potentially inflationary investment boom to continue or to raise interest rates and thereby cause an economic slump that ends up being worse than the one the bank had been earlier trying to prevent. See Wapshott (2011, p. 42).
5. See, for instance, Stiglitz and Weiss (1981) and Stiglitz and Greenwald (2003).
6. Austrians view central bank interest-rate manipulations as being a root cause of bubbles. Onaran (2012, p. 17) writes that "when there are zombie banks in the mix, the money doesn't trickle down to the consumers or the small entrepreneurs. Zombies that borrow from the central bank at zero would rather lend to borrowers who can afford to pay higher rates since the zombie needs to heal its broken balance sheet as quickly as possible through profits." Zombies might

thus end up lending at high rates to risky emerging market borrowers instead of to safer but lower-yielding domestic borrowers. Gjerstad and Smith (2014) further suggest that that the role of household and bank balance sheets has not been adequately represented in the modeling of economic cycles. They view the economic downturn of 2009 as being a balance sheet recession in which "no amount of bond purchases by the Federal Reserve could encourage banks to issue new mortgages."

7. A taxonomy of financing profiles in Minsky (2008, pp. 230–32) explains that in hedge finance, prospective income flows cover interest and principal; in speculative finance, near-term income flows will cover only interest; and in Ponzi finance, near-term receipts are insufficient to cover interest payments, so that debt increases. Koo (2010) notes that once a Ponzi stage is reached, debt-deflation dynamics force companies to focus on deleveraging, not on profit maximization, and this leads to a "balance sheet recession" as in Japan of the 1990s. The result is a lack of demand for credit even at near-zero interest rates.

See also Schularick and Taylor (2012), who summarize the entire theoretical history of money, credit, and macroeconomic thinking into three main viewpoints: (a) The money view, with chief proponents Friedman and Schwartz (1963), which says that narrow and broad money supply strongly influences output over the short term; (b) the Modigliani-Miller approach which theorized that corporate debt-equity structures were irrelevant, that such structure was inconsequential, and that finance was a veil; and (c) the credit view, endorsed by Mishkin, Bernanke, Gertler, and others drawing from Irving Fisher's work in the 1930s and in which the "mechanisms and quantities of bank credit matter, above and beyond the level of bank money." Bank balance sheets may thus have macroeconomic implications. Minsky's view is that "Stability is always destabilizing."

8. As Werner (2003, p. 45) puts it, "Banks don't have money. They simply create it by granting 'credit' to someone. This does not cost them anything, as loans are *created* out of nothing...but an entry into a bank's computer." This follows from the credit creation theory of banking. See also Werner (2014a, b) and Werner (2016).

About banks, Griffin (2002, p. 168) adds that they thus create "money out of *debt*." Pixley (2012, p. 22) explains that money is created by the debtor-creditor contract and the promise of repayment. Calomiris and Haber (2014, pp. 29–35) write, "the major outputs of a bank... are debt contracts primarily in the form of IOUs payable to the bank. The major inputs to the bank...are...contracts... IOUs payable to depositors...Any enterprise whose inputs and outputs consist primarily of promises to repay debts is inherently unstable and risky...The business of banking is the creation and trading of contracts."

In following the works of Austrian economists such as Ludwig von Mises and Friedrich A. Hayek, De Soto (2006, p. xxvi) suggests that the power granted by governments to create money and credit is what causes "boom, crisis, and economic recession." De Soto (pp. 503–4) goes so far as to say that credit expansion is recessive in nature and that "...such cycles perpetually recur due to an institutional cause...the cause lies in the privilege granted to bankers allowing them, in violation of traditional legal principles, to loan out the money placed with them on demand deposit, thus operating with a fractional reserve. Governments have also taken advantage of this privilege in order to obtain easy financing in moments of difficulty, and later, via central banks, to guarantee easy credit terms and inflationary liquidity."

9. Quote from Howe (1915, p. 24f) appears in Werner (2016).

10. Said by JP Morgan Chase CEO Jamie Dimon in Micklethwait (2016), who continues, "I can't desert you and expect to have a strong relationship afterward."

11. See Werner (2003).

12. Ritter and Silber (1974, p. 288) say:

> *The central bank has substantial influence over the supply of credit, but only limited influence over the demand for it, so interest rates may fluctuate for reasons that have nothing to do with the Federal Reserve's actions. Tight money generally means a rise in interest rates (at least for a while), but a rise in interest rates does not necessarily mean tight money…excessively easy money might also produce a rise in interest rates (if, for example, it generates inflationary expectations).*

13. Cutler et al. (1991), however, found that "short term rates are negatively correlated with excess returns on other assets." See also Durham (2001, 2003) and "Rate Cuts, Cheer or Jeer?" *Wall Street Journal*, September 27, 2007. Michaelson (2010) argues that very low rates impair economic growth. A comparison of earnings growth rates to ten-year Treasury bond yields also shows that as long as earnings growth exceeds the bond yields, the market is likely to rise even if yields do too.

14. Extensive studies by professors Elroy Dimson, Paul Marsh, and Mike Staunton have in fact shown that in the United States and United Kingdom real equity returns rose by an average of 6.2% in both countries for all periods (starting from 1913 in the United States and 1930 in the United Kingdom). And real equity and bond returns did indeed perform notably better than the long-term averages after rates had fallen and more poorly after rates had risen. Real returns remained positive in either case.

    After rates fell, real equity and bond returns, respectively, averaged 9.3% and 3.6% in the United States and 8.2% and 2.5% in the United Kingdom. After rate increases, real equity and bond returns, respectively, averaged 2.3% and 0.3% in the United States and 1.7% and 2.5% in the United Kingdom. Presented in the *Credit Suisse Global Investment Returns Sourcebook 2016 and Triumph of the Optimists: 101 Years of Global Investment Returns*, Princeton, NJ: Princeton University Press (2002). © 2016 Elroy Dimson, Paul Marsh, and Mike Staunton; used with permission. Sources also include the Dimson-Marsh-Staunton database; Bank of England, Federal Reserve, Global Financial Data, and Thomson-Reuters Datastream.

15. From Ryan-Collins et al. (2011, p. 104). Monetary policy, as former Fed governor Jeremy Stein has said, "is fundamentally in the business of altering risk premiums such as term premiums and credit spreads. So monetary policymakers cannot wash their hands of what happens when these spreads revert sharply. See Stein's comments on "Market Tantrums and Monetary Policy", US Monetary Policy Forum, February 28, 2014, at: www.federalreserve.gov/newsevents/speech/stein20140228a.htm

16. Former Fed Chairman Alan Greenspan reportedly admitted as much in a television about the housing bubble and keeping interest rates low for too long in 2002–2003: "the market, not the Fed, made the decision on the level and the

time, and the market is never wrong; it is what it is. If investors in trillions of dollars worth of U.S. Treasury debt worldwide had demanded higher interest, they would have gotten it, period." As for long-term rates, Greenspan said: "in 2004, we tried to raise the mortgage rates by moving the ten-year Treasury note up, and we failed. Because – every time we raise short-term rates historically, long-term rates moved with us....We moved up rates. Ten year notes were flat to down. We tried again in 2005. Same thing. Had we done it in 2002, I have no doubt that we would have failed...We had no control, that I could see, which would have made any difference in the extent of the bubble that was emerging."

Similarly, in Greenspan's book of 2007 (p. 377) he says, "[w]e had increased the federal funds rate, and not only had yields on ten-year treasury notes failed to rise, they'd actually declined...Seeing yields decline at the beginning of a tightening cycle is extremely unusual." See also Wessel (2009. p. 58), where Greenspan indicates that "the Fed was impotent: global flows of money were so great they overwhelmed the Fed's ability to make credit scarce or costlier by moving up short-term rates." Steil and Swartz (2010) suggest that in the future the Fed will lose control of the Fed funds rate. LIBOR will be replaced by 2022 with a Secured Overnight Financing Rate (SOFR). See Frost (2017).

17. From the foreword to Pepper and Oliver (2006).
18. It also fits well with the Austrian school's view that injection of money through credit expansions moves the intertemporal structure of production toward disequilibrium. Garrison (2001, p. 84, 108) notes that "[C]heap credit favors a reallocation of resources among the stages of production that is inconsistent with intertemporal preferences of consumers...the artificially low rate of interest causes production plans to become more future-oriented and consumption plans to become less so." Austrian-school economists believe that wants are satisfied by individual choices and values and that the Fed does not determine interest rates, which are determined by markets.
19. Caruana (2003, p. 539) says "the way monetary stability and financial stability interact with each other seems a particularly complex topic...[E]mpirical evidence on the usefulness of asset prices in predicting future price and output developments is not conclusive."
20. See Yellen (2009) about uncertainty of timing and action against bubbles. Pollock (2016) makes a strong case that Fed doesn't know what it's doing as policies are "based on debatable theories and guesses of a committee of economists...in the name of pursuing stability."
21. From Ohanian (2018): "...data provide substantial evidence against the view that monetary policy is an effective stabilization tool...irrespective of the level of r-star."
22. Emergence of cryptocurrencies, of course, only add complications. See also Cochrane (2018).
23. See White (2009) and also Malliaris (2012).
24. The earliest expression of this came from renowned economist Alfred Marshall, for whom the difference between growth in the money supply and nominal GDP (say, using M2+CDs as compared to national income) is sometimes referred to as the Marshallian k. It is, in effect, an inverse of monetary velocity. As based on data from 47 countries from 1960 onward, Vague (2017) in "Rapid Money Supply Growth Does Not Cause Inflation" (http://evonomics.com/

moneysupply) debunked the dominant monetarist notion that rapid money supply growth is the cause of inflation. Data is available at http://www.privat-edebtproject.org/inflation-data.php and http://debt-economics.org/review-data.php. Mallaby (2016, p. 47) writes that Alan Greenspan's early partner, William Townsend, "saw that if banks pumped out a large volume of loans, investors would have more cash to throw around and more of it would push up stock values." As Mallaby (2016) makes clear, Greenspan was extremely aware of stock prices and sensitive to policy impacts on those prices. See also Tully (2007).

25. "The main factor determining 'excessive' lending," Werner (2005, pp. 230–31) explains, is whether credit "is used for 'productive' or 'unproductive' purposes....namely speculative lending for financial transactions." See also Werner (2005, pp. 196–200), Werner (2003, p. 6), Detken and Smets (2004), Garrison (2001, p. 72), and Kiyotaki and Moore (1997). For the Austrian school, however, malabsorption of excessive lending is readily explained by the notion that credit expansions lead to unsustainable booms because intertemporal capital and production structures are distorted by a shift of consumption weighted heavily to the present.

26. Results of significance were generated only when testing the truncated span from 1984:12 to 2005:12 and over the entire data set extending from 1962:08 to 2016:12 taken at once. The probable reason this is seen might be related to the Plaza Accord (foreign exchange) regime shift that began around 1985. Changes in stock margin loans did not contribute importantly. Test results appear in greater detail in the first edition of this book. See also Corsi and Sornette (2014).

27. This is counter to conventional wisdom but is consistent with Elliott Wave and socionomics principles as described in Prechter (2016). Elliott Wave theory also fits with Dardik (2017, p. 135) who writes about nature and that waves are the unique regularities that permeate everything, are nonlinear, and are a commonality that appears on all scales—that is, are fractal. Strogatz (2003) writes that nonlinearity is present in everything and everywhere.

28. See Werner (2005) and Stiglitz and Greenwald (2003). Diamond (1997) provides perspective, writing that "the banking system creates liquidity in two ways. First, banks fill the liquidity gap in markets by diverting demand for liquidity from markets. This improves the market's liquidity, increasing the price of illiquid assets above what it is when all assets are held directly. Second, if investors are sufficiently risk-averse and enough do not participate in markets, bank deposits provide higher short-term returns than the market."

29. Goodhart (2011) explains that although the primary objective of such banks has always been maintenance of price and financial stability, the interpretation of their role varies over time. Three relatively stable epochs of interpretation were the Victorian era, 1840s–1914; government control, 1930s–1960s; and triumph of the markets, 1980s–2007. Bernholz (2003, p. 19) in surveying the long history of inflation writes, "[M]onetary regimes binding the hands of rulers, politicians and governments are a necessary condition for keeping inflation at bay."

30. Conti-Brown (2016, p. 174).

31. Summers (2017, p. 13).

32. Jacobs and King (2016, p. 18) and Blyth (2013).

33. See Mehrling (2011) and Neal (2015, p. 305). Martin (2015, p. viii)) writes, "more debt to solve a debt crisis; more money to solve a monetary crisis." King (2016, Chap. 7) explains that the "essential problem with the traditional LOLR is that, in the presence of alchemy, the only way to provide sufficient liquidity is to lend against bad collateral." See also Acharya and Thakor (2016), Calomiris and Meltzer (2016), and Calomiris et al. (2016).

34. A review of credit and central banking issues appears in Capie and Wood (2007). The quotation is from Fischer (1999), as reproduced in Capie and Wood (2007, pp. 426–7). Fieler and Bell (2011) argue that the Fed has become unaccountable, writing that the "principle check on its power is the self-restraint of its chairman...Had Mr. Bernanke saved Lehman, who would have enforced the statute that he had violated? No one." Singleton (2011) reviews central banking in the twentieth century. King (2016, Chaps. 3, 4) writes, "...it is never easy to distinguish between a liquidity and a solvency problem. In only a matter of days, a shortage of liquidity can turn into a solvency question...the distinction between liquidity and solvency is one that may be observable only after a detailed examination of a bank's balance sheet, difficult for the authorities and impossible for investors...For liquidity to be valuable it must be reliable."

35. Capie (2007) and Goodhart (2007) provide a wide-ranging discussion. Knoop (2008, pp. 165–8) notes that two broad theoretical categories have been used to describe the causes of banking crises. In belief-based models, banking failures are related to changes in expectations of future economic and financial conditions. In fundamentals-based models, adverse business cycle fluctuations in the financial fundamentals of banks can lead to crises. Policy prescriptions are different in each theory. "In belief-based models, bank runs alone are the cause of banking crises, meaning deposit insurance and/or a strong lender of last resort are sufficient to prevent banking crises. However, in fundamentals-based models, deposit insurance and crisis lending might actually increase the probability of banking crises by encouraging moral hazard." Milne (2009, p. 24) explains that a major cause of the 2008 financial crisis was a "maturity mismatch – too much short-term borrowing in order to finance long-term bank loans" and notes (p. 39) that "the banking crisis has triggered the downturn rather than the downturn triggering the banking crisis." Sometimes it's the other way around. He also notes (p. 173) that trading desks generally hedged out interest-rate and credit-related risks, but not liquidity risk. See also Browning (2011) on moral hazard and the Fed.

36. Mehrling (2011, p. 138). See also Carlson and Wheelock (2012).

37. Gilchrist and Leahy (2002) provide a survey. Garrison (2001, p. 10) presents the Austrian school's approach and writes, "...there has been an overemphasis of expectation in modern theory which is ultimately attributable to the corelessness of modern macroeconomics..." Werner (2005, p. 268) suggests that numerous analyses of the effectiveness of standard operational tools such as changes in reserve requirements, in the discount rate, and in the supply of banking system reserves have yielded few new insights. Hilsenrath (2010) writes that "[A]fter studying more than a decade of deflation in Japan, economists have slowly realized they have no idea how it works." Former US Congressman Ron Paul (2009) suggests disbanding the Fed entirely.

38. See Werner (2005) and Posen (2003).

39. Delusion at the Fed is evident when, prior to becoming Chair Janet Yellen said on June 30, 2009, that the "Fed's analytical prowess is top-notch, and our forecasting record is second to none." Booth (2017, p. 164) provides a critique of the Fed's forecasting problems. And Werner (2016) shows that the economic role of banking and credit has been misunderstood and misapplied to policy decisions for more than a century.

40. This is recounted in Mishkin and White (2003), in Mishkin (2003), and in Goodfriend (2003), for instance. Roubini (2006), though, makes the case that "[O]ptimal monetary policy should pre-emptively deal with asset bubbles rather than just mop up the mess that they cause after they burst." Barlevy (2007, 2012) reviews the arguments for and against taking early policy steps to slow or break a bubble. The role of the asymmetric information available to money management agents is central in deciding whether there might be a Pareto optimal outcome for society as a whole to acting early or to mopping up the economic mess after a bubble bursts on its own.

   Blinder (2008) argues that there are two different types of bubbles. In bank-centered bubbles (e.g., housing), where "the central bank is also a bank supervisor and a regulator, it is extraordinarily well placed to observe and understand bank lending practices—much better positioned than almost anyone else. Beyond merely knowing more, part of a bank supervisor's job is to make sure that banks don't engage in unsafe and unsound lending, and to scowl at or discipline them if they do." But in situations such as the tech-stock boom, Blinder argues that the central bank has much less ability to predict or control the outcome, as even relatively large changes in the Fed funds rate appear to have little effect.

41. Examples of how the Fed acted during many crises since the late 1980s are provided in Fleckenstein and Sheehan (2008). Some commentators in the popular press (e.g., *Washington Post*) named the President's Working Group on Financial Markets formed to react to rapidly falling stock prices (created by Executive Order 12631 of March 18, 1988), the "Plunge Protection Team." It was suggested that the US government be secretly allowed to buy stock index futures to save the markets and economy from catastrophe. See Fromson (1997), Crudele (2006), and Paul (2009, p. 95). This thinking extends internationally, as the following clip from Reuters (Brussels, February 11, 2008) demonstrates: "Finance leaders from the Group of Seven industrialized nations discussed collective action to calm markets if price moves become irrational." In fact, the Plunge Protection concept and its very existence was acknowledged by none other than Dr. Bernanke, who wrote, in Bernanke and Reinhart (2004), "Monetary policy works for the most part by influencing the prices and yields of financial assets, which in turn affect economic decisions and thus the evolution of the economy." Fed Chairman Bernanke said in his Jackson Hole speech of August 13, 2012, that large-sized asset purchases "also appear to have boosted stock prices…[T]his effect is potentially important, because stock values affect both consumption and investment decisions." In other words, the Fed is targeting stock prices and taking credit for doing so. International coordination of this type is described in Hilsenrath and Blackstone (2012). For the quantitative easing episodes of 2009–2010 (QE1), 2011 (QE2), and 2012–2013 (QE4), correlations for the DJIA versus the Fed's balance sheet (in dollars) were, respectively, 0.72, 0.76, and 0.94.

In 2005, Jean-Claude Trichet, President of the European Central Bank, asked in Trichet (2005) whether we can be sure that asset price bubbles even exist, saying, "...there is a fundamental difficulty in calling an observed asset price boom a bubble: it must be proved that given the information available at the time of the boom, investors processed this information irrationally." Cooper (2008, p. 112) notes that buried in this statement is the EMH assumption that investors will always have information necessary to make informed judgments.

Guha (2008) discusses the possibility of the Fed "leaning against the wind" and also the perception of asymmetry of policy when asset prices are rising and when they are falling. In the wake of the 2008 credit crises, it seems likely that central bankers of the future will be much less tolerant of asset price bubbles than they have been in the past. Arestis and Karakitsos (2004, pp. 29–33) clearly indicate a preference for intervention based on the idea that "[N]et wealth as a percent of disposable income is mean reverting" and that once this ratio goes above 500%, monetary policy ought to be tightened. Net wealth of the private sector, they maintain, is always a primary transmission mechanism in asset price inflations. As of 2016 the plunge protection concept has been taken to an extreme by the central banks of China and Japan. See Fig. 4.6.

42. Auerbach (2008, pp. 167–70) writes with regard to a March 1994 Fed tightening that:

> [T]ranscripts of FOMC meetings from 1994 released over five years later, revealed that Greenspan was using monetary policy to 'prick the bubble' in the stock market...Greenspan had expected that by raising interest rates the Fed would reduce stock prices.

As to the late 1990s bubble itself, Auerbach says:

> The Greenspan Fed did not initiate the bubble, but it did help finance it in the last half of the 1990s by adding over a trillion dollars to the supply of money from 1996 to 2000...[G]rowth in the money supply during the stock-market bubble was a by-product of the Fed's policy to target interest rates...Not only did the Fed's policy help finance the stock market bubble, Fed policy was also based to a small but significant extent on previous changes in stock prices.

Van Overtveldt (2009, p. 75) also writes, "Thus, evidence is quite strong that Greenspan's Fed followed a Taylor rule for the period leading up to 2001–2."

That the Fed purposely inflated the stock market was revealed by Chairman Bernanke himself in a *Washington Post* op-ed of November 4, 2010, in which he wrote: "...higher stock prices will boost consumer wealth and help increase confidence, which can also spur spending. Increased spending will lead to higher incomes and profits that, in a virtuous circle, will further support economic expansion."

Fed intentions, policies, and strategies have become somewhat less opaque, as the following Greenspan statement circa 2004 that appeared in Appelbaum (2011) suggests. With tongue-in-cheek, Greenspan said: "Since I've become a central banker, I've learned to mumble with great coherence...If I seem unduly clear to you, you must have misunderstood what I said."

43. Clews (2002) indicates that Bank of England staff continually monitor asset market prices and consider them in formulating monetary policy decisions. He notes that "attempts to forecast inflation on the basis of purely statistical rela-

tionships with asset prices have by and large not been successful...If bubbles tend to grow when left unchecked, that may strengthen the case for giving them special attention in the policy process and for using monetary policy to prick them early on." Along the same lines, Greenspan, in Greenspan (2009), writes, "It has rarely been a problem of judging when risk is historically underpriced. Credit spreads are reliable guides. Anticipating the onset of crisis, however, appears out of our forecasting reach....I do not question that central banks can defuse any bubble. But it has been my experience that unless monetary policy crushes economic activity and, for example, breaks the back of rising profits or rents, policy actions to abort bubbles will fail. I know of no instance where incremental monetary policy has defused a bubble."

The failure to predict the financial crisis that began in 2007 through application by the Fed and other central banks of dynamic stochastic general equilibrium (DSGE) models has led to experimentation with new agent-based models (ABMs), which do not assume that the economy necessarily moves toward equilibrium. Such models use a bottom-up approach which assigns behavioral rules to each agent. See "Agents of Change," *The Economist*, July 22, 2010, and Wang and Wen (2009), who use a DSGE model to "characterize conditions for the existence of rational bubbles that grow on goods with fundamental values." Kocherlakota (2009) uses a similar approach, showing that "collateral scarcity can generate a stochastic bubble in the price of collateral." Also of interest is Fed official V.V. Chari, who testified before Congress in July 2010 that DSGE models aren't well suited for analysis of extremely rare events. Ayres (2014, pp. 24–5) writes that such models "generally assume that economic growth occurs in Walsrasian equilibrium," but the models "all have a fundamental weakness, namely the inherent assumption of equilibrium itself. This makes them essentially useless for predicting financial instability (e.g., bubbles)..."

44. In a speech of October 15, 2008, to the Economic Club of New York (http:// www.federalreserve.gov/newsevents/speech/bernanke20081015a.htm) and the subsequent q&a that is covered on the same day by Bloomberg.com, Bernanke said that supervision and interest rate policies can minimize the "dangerous phenomenon" of bubbles. As described by Lahart (2008b), this suggests that the Fed is reconsidering its traditional aversion to interfering with asset price bubbles even though there remain strong arguments against doing so. However, in a January 2013 University of Michigan forum (covered in Bloomberg.com/news/2013-02-22), reversion to the old bubble-bursting aversion was evident when Fed Chairman Bernanke said, "the first line of defense if bubbles emerge needs to be regulatory and supervisory actions rather than changes in monetary policy." White (2011) and Kuttner (2012) review the pros and cons of policies aimed at preventing or dampening bubbles.

A speech by Fed Vice Chairman Donald Kohn of October 9, 2009, available at http://federalreserve.gov/newsevents/speech/kohn20091009a.htm, hinted that the Fed might be rethinking its previous aversion to popping bubbles ahead of time. However, in a later, pre-retirement interview (Hilsenrath 2010), Kohn backpedals: "I have yet to be convinced that we can lean against these bubbles with monetary policy in a predictable and productive way...I think there are a lot of open questions about the extent to which monetary policy contributed to the bubbles and the extent to which modest tightening of monetary policy on the way up or easing on the way down can address the bubbles. The principle way that we have for dealing with these instabilities is through supervision and regulation." See also Wessel and Frangos (2013).

In a speech of October 18, 2011 (available at www.federalreserve.gov/newsevents/speech/bernanke20111018a.htm), Bernanke indicated that the Fed would "'lean against' movements in asset prices or credit aggregates in an effort to promote financial stability" and that central bankers should not ignore possible financial imbalances. The Fed would conduct policy consistent with the Tinbergen rule which states that if the number of policy targets surpasses the number of instruments then some targets may not be met.

After the second "quantitative easing" (QE2) policy began to be implemented by the Fed in late 2010, the Fed, however, began to openly admit to stock market manipulation. In a January 13, 2011, forum (http://www.fdic.gov/news/conferences/SBTranscript.pdf) sponsored by the Federal Deposit Insurance Corp., Fed Chairman Bernanke said, "I do think that our policies have contributed to a stronger stock market, just as they did in March of '09, when we did the last iteration of this. The S&P 500 is up about 20 percent plus." Such market manipulation was officially enabled by the "Working Group on Financial Markets" law (note 41) that was created in response to the crash of 1987. Hilsenrath (2012b) describes how the Fed came to approve the 2012 QE3 program. By June 14, 2017, however, the FOMC meeting minutes revealed some concern about bubbles: "...in the assessment of a few participants, equity prices were high when judged against standard valuation measures."

The Fed's reluctance to at all interfere in what might be a bubble can be traced back to the mid-1920s, when even then it was recognized, according to Ahamed (2009, pp. 276–77), that it was difficult "to distinguish between an advance in stock prices warranted by higher profits and the rise driven purely by market psychology." The Fed's leader at the time was Benjamin Strong, who "was convinced that the Federal Reserve should not try to make itself an arbiter of equity prices."

Barlevy (2008) extends the Allen and Gorton (1993) model and says that "raising interest rates or imposing down payment (or margin) requirements can both be used to prevent bubbles." Hilsenrath (2009) quotes Bernanke as saying that financial booms are "perhaps the most difficult problem for monetary policy this decade." Suhadolnik et al. (2010) suggest that robot traders might eventually be used to dampen or offset bubble dynamics.

In an April 7, 2010, speech to the Economic Club of New York, Federal Reserve Bank of New York president William Dudley said that "a bubble is difficult to discern...rules limiting loan-to-value ratios or leverage, are likely to prove superior to monetary policy...the tools used to respond to each bubble will likely have to be different and tailored to the features of the particular bubble in question...Credit bubbles that burst threaten the stability of the financial system much more directly than equity bubbles....[H]istorical experience does not suggest that bubbles are very sensitive to the level of short-term interest rates." See Dudley (2010) at http://www.newyorkfed.org/newsevents/speeches/2010/dud100407.html and also Mishkin (2008) at http://www.federalreserve.gov/newsevents/speech/mishkin20080515a.htm

Bernanke (2003) had earlier expressed the view that "...monetary policy can lower stock prices only to the extent that it weakens the broader economy, and in particular that it makes households considerably worse off." Moreover, "...

the stock price multiplier of monetary policy is between 3 and 6 – in other words, an unexpected change in the federal funds rate of 25 basis points leads, on average, to a movement of stock prices in the opposite direction of between 3/4 percentage point and 1–1/2 percentage points...the main reason that unanticipated changes in monetary policy affect stock prices is that they affect the risk premium on stocks. In particular, a surprise tightening of policy raises the risk premium, lowering current stock prices, and a surprise easing lowers the risk premium, raising current stock prices." See Bernanke and Kuttner (2005), Van Overtveldt (2009, p. 138), Swanson and Williams (2012), and Taylor (2012, 2013).

45. Meltzer (2009) argued that "the Fed has sacrificed its independence and become the monetary arm of the Treasury: bailing out A.I.G., taking on illiquid securities from Bear Stearns and promising to provide as much as $700 billion of reserves to buy mortgages. Independent central banks don't do what this Fed has done. They leave such fiscal action to the legislative branch...The central bank was made independent expressly so that it could refuse to finance deficits." Meltzer (2012) more generally viewed the Fed's credit policies and bailouts as misguided, adding that "[O]ver-response to short-run events and neglect of longer-term consequences of its actions is one of the main errors that the Federal Reserve makes repeatedly."

See also Kaufman (2009), who suggests that the Fed will likely become even more politicized than it is now, and Wessel (2009, p. 39) who wrote: "Congress had created what would become a fourth branch of government, nearly equal in power in a crisis to the executive, legislative, and judicial branches." Conti-Brown (2016) provides a detailed study of Fed independence as does Binder and Spindel (2017). O'Driscoll (2011) recalls the 1951 Fed and Treasury accord which again gave the Fed the ability to run monetary policy independent of fiscal policy. Malpass (2011) writes with regard to the Fed's 2011 Operation Twist that "[S]ince the financial crisis, the Fed has been transforming itself from a monetary policy agency into a market-intervention shop." At the end of 2012 newly elected Japanese Prime Minister Shinzo Abe openly interfered with the independence of the country's central bank by pressuring the Bank of Japan to "print" money and to weaken the yen. As such it was a blatant move to strip a major central bank of its independence. On doubts as to effectiveness see Dvorak and Warnock (2013a,b). Tognato (2012), Meltzer (2013), Porter (2017), and LeBor (2013) on the BIS, the central bank's central bank. Mallaby (2016, pp. 138–145) writes of how President Nixon was displeased by the Fed's attempts to remain independent. Earlier, Granville (2017) recalls, it had been Lyndon Johnson pressuring Fed Chairman Martin. And similar political demands appeared before and during the H.W. Bush presidency.

46. See Cooper (2008, p. 89) and also Acharya and Naqvi (2012). Notable is the Fed's departure from its founding "real bills" legislation, which as Mayer (2001, pp. 148–9) explains made the only paper eligible for discount at the district Fed banks to be "notes, drafts, and bills of exchange arising out of actual commercial transactions...[with] a maturity at the time of discount of not more than ninety days." Mayer writes that "by limiting the paper 'eligible' for discount and specifically excluding stocks and bonds, real bills theory expressed the strong and continuing fear of politicians and commentators that left to their own devices, the banks would misdirect the credit resources of the nation to speculation in

real estate and on the stock exchange." The Fed's actions in the crisis beginning in 2007 and even in earlier periods suggest that the real bills doctrine has long been ignored and discarded.

Paul (2009, p. 14) writes that "The Fed is in the business of generating inflation...the entire reason for the Fed's existence is to generate more, not less of it."

47. Mehrling (2011, p. 17).

48. Mallaby (2016, p. 498).

49. Greenspan himself said, in Greenspan (2004),

> *The 1998 liquidity crisis and the crises associated with the stock-market crash of 1987 and the terrorism of September 2001 prompted the type of massive ease that has been the historic mandate of a central bank. Such crises are precipitated by the efforts of market participants to convert illiquid assets into cash...at crucial points...simple rules will be inadequate as either descriptions or prescriptions for policy.*

Ahamed (2009, p. 15) writes that in the time of the gold standard, central banks "therefore acquired a second role – that of forestalling bank panics and other financial crises" and Chap. 8 note 36.

50. Schularick and Taylor (2012) conclude that prior to the end of WW II, aggregate money and credit measures were much more closely aligned than in today's "Age of Credit, where financial innovation and regulatory ease has permitted the credit system to increasingly delink from monetary aggregates, setting in train an unprecedented expansion in the role of credit in the macroeconomy." Credit growth, they find, is a "powerful predictor of financial crises," and that such crises are "credit booms gone wrong."

Fairless (2016) shows European Central Bank balance sheet assets as a percentage of GDP rose to around 37% in 2016 from around 15% in 2008. Over the same time, the Fed's ratio rose to 24% from 8%.

51. Werner (2007, p. 204) suggests that "Fiscal policy can only be effective if it is supported by monetary policy...the coordination of fiscal and monetary policy is crucial." After the September 2008 bailouts of AIG, Fannie Mae, etc., new questions have arisen as to the whether the Fed's role has changed and whether its ability to set policy has been compromised. However, Mishkin (2009) argues that aggressive monetary policy is effective during a financial crisis. Milne (2009, p. 257) writes of central banks, that "[T]heir role in a crisis is the reallocation of funds between banks. Funds or guarantees of funding for the entire banking sector have to come from government, not the central bank...the ability of central banks to plug directly the wholesale funding gap faced by commercial banks is limited" (p. 283). Cecchetti et al. (2010) say that failure to solve fiscal problems "ultimately threaten the credibility of present monetary policy arrangements." Woodford (2002) writes about the reduction of reserve requirements and concludes that such reductions are unlikely to "seriously impair the Fed's ability to pursue macroeconomic stabilization policy." The ECB's decision in 2012 to create money in an attempt to save the euro is detailed in Blackstone and Walker (2012). See also Reddy (2008) and Hobusch et al. (2014/15) in which interest rate spreads are shown to trigger financial crises.

Changes over time in theoretical approaches and assumptions complicate comparative studies of policy effectiveness. The Austrian school's view, for instance, is that the very validity of the rational-expectations theory that underlies many central bank policies and strategies ought to be questioned. From Garrison (2001, p. 21): "[E]mbracing the rational-expectations theory had the effects of bringing long-run conclusions into the short run." In economics it is also impossible to contrast and compare outcomes if, say, one specific policy remedy rather than another had been applied. See also Wood (2007).

52. In large commercial real estate lending, banks might pretend that loans will ultimately be repayable at some distant future date. On this see Mollenkamp and Wei (2010). But the same can also be seen in the actions of central banks and governments and in cases such as the Greek debt crisis of 2010. Kiyotaki and Moore (1997) develop a model "in which credit constraints arise naturally because lenders cannot force borrowers to repay their debts unless the debts are secured...[B]orrowers' credit limits are affected by the prices of collateralized assets. And at the same time, these prices are affected by the size of the credit limits." See also Dubecq et al. (2010) and Calomiris and Haber (2014, p. 207), who write that "[I]f a bank makes only solid loans to solid borrowers, there is little chance that its loan portfolio will all of a sudden become nonperforming."

53. This is a version of the old colloquialism, "You can lead a horse to water, but you can't make it drink."

54. Garrison (2001, p. 37) writes that "the demand for loanable funds represents the borrowers' intentions to participate in the economy's production process."

55. On mood, see Prechter (2016). Greenspan (2013, pp. 144–5) recognized this point in writing that companies are uninterested in long-term capital commitments unless they are fairly certain of future returns on investment. Confidence is revealed by total capital expenditures taken as a percentage of cash flow, a ratio that has ranged from 0.67 to 1.39. A ratio greater than 1.0 would suggest an environment of such optimism to borrow and invest.

56. Huang et al. (2015).

57. Plosser (2018) observed that the enlarged balance sheet and IOER positions were coming to be viewed by some economists as presenting an alternative to conventional Fed fund and discount window policy implementation tools.He writes (p. 15), "...how does one conduct monetary policy with two instruments working through perhaps different channels...A large Fed balance sheet that is untethered to the conduct of monetary policy creates the opportunity and incentive for political actors to exploit the Fed..." Taylor (2018, p. 20) says, "[W]ithout IOER, the federal funds rate would drop to zero."

58. At the Jackson Hole Fed meeting of August 31, 2012, James Bullard, president of the Federal Reserve Bank of St. Louis, said, "I'm a little – maybe more than a little bit – worried about the future of central banking." Pixley (2012, p. 151) also writes: "monetary policy of high interest rates had not prevented the speculative boom of the 1920s...low interest rates were totally ineffective in reviving economic activity." See "Global Economy: Not So Different This Time" by Harding and C. Giles, *Financial Times*, September 9, 2012.

   White (2012) evaluates the desirability of ultra-easy monetary policy and concludes that there are limits to what central banks can do. He argues that such policies not only threaten the independence of central banks but also affect the health of financial institutions and the functioning of financial markets. Blackstone and Wessel (2013) write about Swiss intervention. Benmelech and

Bergman (2012) study the limitations of monetary policy in stimulating credit and investment and that small contractions in monetary policy can lead to a collapse in lending. See Sharma (2015c), Malpass (2015) on ineffectiveness of stimulus programs, Davidson and McGrane (2015) on Fed transparency, Eavis (2015) on failure of stimulus policies to channel investment flows toward much-needed infrastructure projects, and Appelbaum (2018) on rethinking policy. Calomiris and Haber (pp. x and 12) write: "banks' strengths and shortcomings are the predictable consequences of political bargains...the fragility of banks and the scarcity of bank credit reflect the structure of a country's fundamental political institutions." Mallaby (2016, p. 5) writes that "...toward the end of Volcker's tenure, Reagan appointees at the Fed staged a revolt against his tight-money policy...."

Vigna (2016) quotes former BOE governor Mervyn King saying, "[t]he banking system has been practicing a kind of alchemy – the idea that through fractional-reserve accounting, banks can turn risk into safety. They can take deposits, use them to leverage risky bets, and have the whole thing pay off in some never-ending virtuous cycle. It's a myth, of course. There's an alchemy in the sense that we pretend that these very safe and liquid deposits can be used to finance highly illiquid and risky investments, and that's simply not true."

Jacobs and King (2016, pp. 2–3) opine that the Fed "is a mutant institution of government...the Fed is an inequality generator."

59. Kantchev et al. (2016) show that consumers save more in countries with low or negative rates and companies hoard cash. Booth (2017) writes of the economic damage that central bank policies since 2009 have inflicted on the middle- and lower-income classes.

60. From Williamson (2017): "With respect to QE, there are good reasons to be skeptical that it works as advertised, and some economists have made a good case that QE is actually detrimental." Williamson (2015a) explains that "[T]he theory behind QE is not well-developed. From Williamson: "[I]n general, one can conclude there should be little confidence in our knowledge of the quantitative effects of QE, let alone the qualitative effects. The existing theories are not well developed and have not been confronted by the empirical evidence in ways that shed light on how and to what extent QE works...There is little solid evidence about the effects of QE on...employment, unemployment, GDP, and inflation." Spence and Warsh (2015) and Wallison (2015) provide additional criticisms. In defense of his record as Fed Chairman, Bernanke (2015a, b) asserts that QE was indeed effective in reducing unemployment. However, Dent (2016, p. 50) writes: "Quantitative easing is the crack cocaine of the financial world...It's also the stupidest thing ever done!" See also Brown (2014, 2015).

61. After 2015, Japan's economy responded sporadically with eight quarters of modest growth at a low unemployment rate (2.5%) but with GDP again dipping by 0.2% in Q1 2018. See Schlesinger and Nakamichi (2014) on the BOJ increase in QE, The BOJ had begun buying exchange-traded funds (ETFs) as early as 2011. By the end of September 2016, around 30% of all the companies in Japan's major equity indexes were owned by the BOJ, which had become one of the top ten shareholders. Six years prior, the percentage was just above zero. See also Chap. 2 and Nakamichi and Ito (2015) and Soble (2016).

62. Williamson (2015b) about interest on excess reserves (IOER) and phases and failures of applied QE after 2009, and Taylor (2016) on a rules-based Fed. Mackintosh (2017) noted that Fed Chair Janet Yellen, after the September 20, 2017, meeting, "came as close as she's ever likely to get to accepting that quantitative easing is still poorly understood even by the experts...Left unsaid: No one's really sure how, or if, QE works." In a September 26, 2017, speech at the National Association for Business Economics in Cleveland Dr. Yellen also came as close as ever to admitting that policy makers were baffled and basically flying blind. She said, "...our framework for understanding inflation dynamics could be misspecified in some fundamental way....job gains continue to run well ahead of the longer-run pace we estimate would be sufficient...there is a risk that the labor market could eventually become overheated..."

The net number of new jobs added in the United States from 2008 to 2016 was 6.735 million, which per dollar of Fed balance sheet debt (~$3.1 trillion) added over the same span was around $450,000 per job. But this figure is controversial for several reasons, especially in that estimates on new jobs are made using birth/death adjustments. Fed critic Todd (2017), who spent 20 years at the Fed banks in New York and Cleveland, wrote: "For all the exotic measures attempted by the Federal Reserve after 2008, none delivered expansion of bank credit, M-1, M-2, or GDP." He further suggests that an important part of the breakdown of the monetary transmission mechanism involved the October 2008 Fed decision to pay interest on bank reserves without making a distinction between required and excess reserves. The interest rate of 0.25% per annum ran from December 2008 to December 2015, after which it was raised to 0.50%. See also Heller (2017) and Thornton (2017).

63. Goodhart's 1975 paper for the Federal Reserve Bank of Australia said that when an indicator becomes the object of policy, it ceases to function as an indicator. This is also mentioned in Rickards (2014, p. 87). Then-Fed Chairman Bernanke at the Jackson Hole, Wyoming annual conference, August 2011 even said: "Most of the economic policies that support robust economic growth in the long run are outside the province of the central bank."

64. Pixley (2012, p. 34).

65. Ferguson (2008, p. 123) writes that "without easy credit creation a true bubble cannot occur. That is why so many bubbles have their origins in the sins of omission or commission of central banks."

66. Kaminska (2012), though, quotes Peter Stella, former head of Central Banking and Monetary and Foreign Exchange Operations at the IMF as saying that "there is absolutely no correlation between bank reserves and lending. And, more fundamentally, that banks do not lend 'reserves.'" That is, borrowers must have sufficient confidence in the future to want to incur loan obligations and banks must be willing and able to extend loans. The reserves by themselves do not translate into growth of money supply until such conditions are met. Japan in 2013 provides a good example, with Dvorak and Warnock (2013a) writing, "Japanese companies and individuals still don't feel confident enough to borrow and invest."

67. As recounted by Norris (2013), Minsky-following Australian economist wrote in Keen (1995) that in a boom lending standards are gradually reduced and asset prices rise along with confidence that the outlook is favorable and that most investments will probably succeed. It then becomes widely accepted that

the income-earning ability of assets is far less important than the expected capital gains. In this stage, buyers pay high prices and finance their purchases with ever-rising amounts of debt. But when something goes wrong, the immediate need for liquidity leads to asset markets flooded by selling as the boom turns into a bust.

68. Brunnermeier and Koby (2017) show that accommodative monetary policy reaches a point at which it is counterproductive. That in part happens when the resulting lower bank margins reduce lending and credit expansion capability and availability.

69. With respect to the 1927 Reichsbank episode, Voth (2000, 2003) states that central banks also sometimes make important policy mistakes. And despite employment of an army of Ph.D. economists (~1000), many more Fed errors and miscues that begin with a structural inability to forecast consistently, accurately, and reliably have since then occurred. See Brown (2014, 2015) on mistakes of the ECB.

70. Greenspan (2013, p. 138 and p. 154) writes: "In my eighteen and a half years as Fed chairman, I received a figurative truckload of requests from Congress urging an easier monetary policy. I don't recall ever receiving a single request urging the Fed to tighten…the political response to policy makers' actions heavily biases …toward catering to short-term benefits, largely disregarding long-term costs."

71. From Cochrane (2013). See also Hilsenrath and Harrison (2015) on Fed uncertainty of how to deflate bubbles. Even more disturbing is the Fed study by Chang and Li (2015), in which it was found that a surprisingly high proportion of published economics research findings are not replicable.

72. As relayed in Martin (2015, p. 208), this first appeared in writings by Thomas Joplin in 1832.

73. Capie and Wood (2007, p. xvi), say that "the record of central banks when tightening money because they are worried about a 'bubble' is not encouraging; on more than one occasion their doing so has produced a sharp downturn in the real economy." See also "Bubble Warning," *The Economist*, 7 January 2010 and Kindleberger and Aliber (2011, p. 64): "The efforts of central bankers to limit and control the growth of money have been offset in part by the development of new and very close substitutes for money."

The propensity of modern central bank interventions in the credit markets are discussed in Lacker (2012). Steiil (2012) concludes that a central bank's "balance sheet is ultimately a dangerous substitute for political will and public accountability." Cochrane (2012) suggests that central banks have increasingly become central planners by unaccountably intervening in a wide variety of markets. Pringle (2012) touches on the same topic. Appelbaum et al. (2013) discuss the ineffectiveness of central bank quantitative easing policies as of 2013. Meltzer (2013) argues that rules-based decisions provide are preferable.

From Kroszner (2016): "Central banks are being asked to move from being 'fire extinguishers' – providing liquidity to douse the flames of a crisis after it has started – to being 'smoke detectors,' finding hot spots and preventing smoke from turning into fire."

Rickards (2011, p. 33) opines: "For the really big messes – those involving crowd unrest, food riots, looting, refugees and general collapse – the Fed has no answer and societies inevitably turn to the military for solutions."

74. This unconventional view is posited by socionomics (www.socionomics.net) and appeared in *The Elliott Wave Theorist*, July 2002.
75. When things do go awry; the default position is to ascribe blame not to policy errors but to ineffective banking supervision and inadequate regulatory codes. See also Binder and Spindel (2017).
76. Examples of failed central banks include the French central bank which failed four years after its founding in 1716, the (First) Bank of the United States formed by Congress in 1791, and the Second Bank of the United States which lasted only 20 years after its creation in 1816. On economic forecasting problems see, for example, Dominguez et al. (1988), Mayer (1999), Potter (2011), Fair (2012), Dovern et al. (2013), and Hendry and Mizon (2013).
77. This is where analogy to sandpiles and avalanches goes wrong. It is also where so-called macroprudential policies, a current topic attracting great interest, will likely founder. See also Siklos (2017).
78. Mallaby (2016) amply discusses these issues, including the Fed's inability to prove that low inflation leads to higher productivity. Indeed, between 2010 and 2017 economists lamented that productivity growth was low and so was the rate of inflation. Mallaby (p. 635) also writes: "Greenspan and his chief lieutenant were not willing to act against potential bubbles unless they had conclusive proof of their existence, which was another way of saying that they would never act against them." The case for inflation targeting taking precedence over responses to asset bubbles began with Bernanke and Gertler propositions at the Jackson Hole meeting in August 1999 (p. 553). The dual mandate of targeting full employment *and* inflation that most central operate under only introduces further complications and virtually guarantees that financial asset price stability will be sacrificed on the altar of the other two objectives and thus not be attained.
79. Sources are not clear on whether or when Mayer Rothschild reportedly said this.

References

Acharya, V., & Naqvi, H. (2012). The Seeds of a Crisis: A Theory of Bank Liquidity and Risk Taking Over the Business Cycles. *Journal of Financial Economics, 106*(2), 349–366.

Acharya, V., & Naqvi, H. (2016, January 13). On Reaching for Yield and the Coexistence of Bubbles and Negative Bubbles, available at SSRN: Acharya, Viral V. and Naqvi, Hassan, On Reaching for Yield and the Coexistence of Bubbles and Negative Bubbles. Available at https://ssrn.com/abstract=2618973 or https://doi.org/10.2139/ssrn.2618973

Acharya, V. V., & Thakor, A. V. (2016). The Dark Side of Liquidity Creation: Leverage and Systemic Risk. *Journal of Financial Intermediation, 28*, 4–21.

Ahamed, L. (2009). *Lords of Finance: The Bankers Who Broke the World*. New York: Penguin.

Allen, F., & Gorton, G. (1993). Churning Bubbles. *Review of Economic Studies, 60*(4), 813–836.

Appelbaum, B. (2011, March 25). Fed to Take a Step Out from Behind the Veil. *New York Times*.

Appelbaum, B. (2018, January 10). Fed Is Urged to Rewrite Its Playbook. *New York Times*.

Appelbaum, B., Ewing, J., Tabuchi, H., & Thomas, L. Jr. (2013, May 29). Central Banks Act with a New Boldness to Revitalize Economies, *New York Times*.

Arestis, P., & Karakitsos, E. (2004). *The Post Bubble US Economy*. Houndmills, Hampshire: Palgrave Macmillan.

Auerbach, R. D. (2008). *Deception and Abuse at the Fed: Henry B. Gonzales Battles Alan Greenspan's Bank*. Austin: University of Texas Press.

Ayres, R. U. (2014). *The Bubble Economy: Is Sustainable Growth Possible?* Cambridge, MA: MIT Press.

Bagehot, W. (1873). *Lombard Street: A Description of the Money Market*. New York: Scribner, Armstrong & Co.

Barlevy, G. (2007). *Economic Theory and Asset Bubbles*. Economic Perspectives, Federal Reserve Bank of Chicago, Third Quarter.

Barlevy, G. (2008). A Leverage-Based Model of Speculative Bubbles, Working Paper 2008–01, Federal Reserve Bank of Chicago.

Barlevy, G. (2012). Rethinking Theoretical Models of Bubbles. In Evanoff et al. (2012).

Bénassy, J.-P. (1986). *Macroeconomics: An Introduction to the Non-Walrasian Approach*. Orlando: Academic.

Benmelech, E., & Bergman, N. K. (2012). Credit Traps. *American Economic Review, 102*(6), 3004–3032.

Bernanke, B. S. (2003, October 9). Monetary Policy and the Stock Market: Some Empirical Results, Banking and Finance Lecture, Widener University, Chester, PA., October 2 and at London School of Economics, London. Available at http://www.federalreserve.gov/boarddocs/speeches/2003/20031002/default.htm

Bernanke, B. S. (2015a). *The Courage to Act: A Memoir of a Crisis and Its Aftermath*. New York: W. W. Norton.

Bernanke, B. S. (2015b, October 5). How the Fed Saved the Economy. *Wall Street Journal*.

Bernanke, B. S., & Gertler, M. (1999, 2000, August). *Monetary Policy and Asset Price Volatility*. Federal Reserve Bank of Kansas City, Presented at Jackson Hole, Wyoming Conference. Available at www.kc.frb.org and 2000, NBER Working Paper No. 7559.

Bernanke, B. S., & Kuttner, K. (2005). What Explains the Stock Market's Reaction to Federal Reserve Policy? *Journal of Finance, 60*(3), 1221–1257.

Bernanke, B. S., & Reinhart, V. R. (2004). Conducting Monetary Policy at Very Low Short-Term Interest Rates. *American Economic Review, 94*(2), 85–90.

Bernholz, P. (2003). *Monetary Regimes and Inflation*. Cheltenham: Edward Elgar.

Binder, S., & Spindel, M. (2017). *The Myth of Independence: How Congress Governs the Federal Reserve*. Princeton: Princeton University Press.

Blackstone, B., & Walker, M. (2012, October 3). How ECB Chief Outflanked German Foe in Fight for Euro. *Wall Street Journal*.

Blackstone, B., & Wessel, D. (2013, January 9). Button-Down Central Bank Bets It All. *Wall Street Journal*.

Blinder, A. S. (2008, June 15). Two Bubbles, Two Paths. *New York Times*.

Blyth, M. (2013). *Austerity: The History of a Dangerous Idea*. New York: Oxford University Press.

Booth, D. D. (2017). *Fed Up: An Insider's Take on Why the Federal Reserve Is Bad for America*. New York: Portfolio (Penguin).

Bordo, M. D., Cochrane, J. H., & Seru, A. (Eds.). (2018). *The Structural Foundations of Monetary Policy*. Stanford: Hoover Institution Press.

Brown, B. (2014). *Euro Crash: How Asset Price Inflation Destroys the Wealth of Nations* (3rd ed.). London: Palgrave Macmillan.

Brown, B. (2015). *A Global Monetary Plague: Asset Price Inflation and Federal Reserve Quantitative Easing*. London: Palgrave Macmillan.

Browning, E. S. (2011, August 29). Fed Faces Old Foe as Hazard Returns. *Wall Street Journal*.

Brunnermeier, M. K., & Koby, Y. (2017). The Reversal Interest Rate: The Effective Lower Bound of Monetary Policy. Available at ir.princeton.edu/markus/publications/reversal-interest-rate-effectove-lower-bound-monetary-policy.

Calomiris, C. W., & Haber, S. H. (2014). *Fragile By Design: The Political Origins of Banking Crises and Scarce Credit*. Princeton: Princeton University Press.

Calomiris, C. W., & Meltzer, A. (2016). Rules for the Lender of Last Resort: Introduction. *Journal of Financial Intermediation, 28*, 1–3.

Calomiris, C. W., Flandreau, M., & Laeven, L. (2016). Political Foundations of the Lender of Last Resort: A Global Historical Narrative. *Journal of Financial Intermediation, 28*, 48–65.

Capie, F. H. (2007). The Emergence of the Bank of England as a Mature Central Bank. In F. H. Capie and G. E. Wood (2007).

Capie, F. H., & Wood, G. E. (Eds.). (2007). *The Lender of Last Resort*. London/New York: Routledge.

Carlson, M. A., & Wheelock, D. C. (2012). *The Lender of Last Resort: Lessons from the Fed's First 100 Years* (Working Paper 1012-056a). Federal Reserve Bank of St. Lois. Available at http://research.stlouisfed.org/wp/2012/2012-056.pdf

Caruana, J. (2003). Banking Provisions and Asset Price Bubbles. In Hunter et al. (2003 [2005]).

Cecchetti, S. G., Mohanty, M. S., & Zampolli, F. (2010, March). The Future of Public Debt: Prospects and Implications. *BIS Working Papers*, No. 300.

Chang, A. C., & Li, P. (2015). Is Economics Research Replicable? Sixty published Papers from Thirteen Journals Say 'Usually Not'. Washington, DC: Board of Governors of the Federal Reserve System, Discussion Series 2015–083. Available at https://doi.org/10.17016/FEDS.2015.083

Clews, R. (2002). Asset Prices and Inflation. *Bank of England Quarterly Bulletin*, (Summer).

Cochrane, J. H. (2012, September 1). The Federal Reserve: From Central Bank to Central Planner. *Wall Street Journal*.

Cochrane, J. H. (2013, August 27). The Danger of an All-Powerful Federal Reserve. *Wall Street Journal*.

Cochrane, J. H. (2018). Lessons from the Quiet Zero Lower Bound. In M. D. Bordo et al. (2018).

Conti-Brown, P. (2016). *The Power and Independence of the Federal Reserve*. Princeton: Princeton University Press.

Cooper, G. (2008). *The Origin of Financial Crises: Central Banks, Credit Bubbles, and the Efficient Market Fallacy*. New York: Harriman House/Vintage (Paperback).

Corsi, F., & Sornette, D. (2014). Follow the Money: The Monetary Roots of Bubbles and Crashes. *International Review of Financial Analysis, 32*, 47–59.

Crudele, J. (2006, June 20). The Day I Met the Plunge Protection Team. *New York Post*.

Cutler, D. M., Poterba, J. M., & Summers, L. H. (1991). Speculative Dynamics. *Review of Economic Studies, 58*, 529–546.

Dardik, I. (2017). *The Nature of Nature: The Discovery of SuperWaves and How It Changes Everything*. New York: Rodale.

Davidson, K., & McGrane, V. (2015, July 14). Janet Yellen's Fed Flounders in Political Arena. *Wall Street Journal*.

De Soto, J. H. (2006), *Money, Bank Credit, and Economic Cycles* (trans: Stroup, M. A). Auburn: Ludwig von Mises Institute.

Dent, H. S., Jr. (2016). *The Sale of a Lifetime: How the Great Bubble Burst of 2017–2019 Can Make You Rich*. New York: Penguin/Random House.

Detken, C., & Smets, F. (2004, May). Asset Price Booms and Monetary Policy. Working Paper Series No. 364.Frankfurt: European Central Bank. Available at www.ecb.int

Diamond, D. W. (1997). Liquidity, Banks, and Markets. *Journal of Political Economy, 105*(5), 928–956.

Dominguez, K. M., Fair, R. C., & Shapiro, M. D. (1988). Forecasting the Depression: Harvard Versus Yale. *American Economic Review, 78*(4), 595–612.

Dovern, J., Fritsche, U., Loungani, P., & Tamirisa, N. (2013). Information Rigidities in Economic Growth Forecasts: Evidence from a Large International Panel. *IMF Working Paper*, WP/13/56. http://www.imf.org/external/pubs/ft/wp/2013/wp1356.pdf

Dubecq, S., Mojon, B., & Ragot, X. (2010). Fuzzy Capital Requirements, Risk-Shifting and the Risk Taking Channel of Monetary Policy. Paper presented at American Economic Association Annual Meeting, Denver, 2011.

Dudley, W. C. (2010). Asset Bubbles and the Implications for Central Bank Policy. Federal Reserve Bank of New York. Available at: http://www.newyorkfed.org/newsevents/speeches/2010/dud100407.html

Durham, J. B. (2001). *The Effect of Monetary Policy on Monthly and Quarterly Stock Market Returns: Cross-Country Evidence and Sensitivity Analyses*. Washington, DC: Federal Reserve, Board of Governors.

Durham, J. B. (2003). *Does Monetary Policy Affect Stock Prices and Treasury Yields? An Error Correction and Simultaneous Equation Approach*. Washington, DC: Federal Reserve, Board of Governors.

Dvorak, P., & Warnock, E. (2013a, November 18). Japan's Banks Find It Hard to Lend Easy Money. *Wall Street Journal*.

Dvorak, P., & Warnock, E. (2013b, March 21). Stagnant Japan Rolls Dice on New Era of Easy Money. *Wall Street Journal*.

Eavis, P. (2015, December 18). A Missed Opportunity of Ultra-Cheap Money. *New York Times*.

Evanoff, D. D., Kaufman, G. G., & Malliaris, A. G. (Eds.). (2012). *New Perspectives on Asset Price Bubbles: Theory, Evidence, and Policy*. New York: Oxford University Press.

Fair, R. C. (2012). Analyzing Macroeconomic Forecastability. *Journal of Forecasting, 31*, 99–108.

Fairless, T. (2016, December 7). Ceiling Closes in on ECBs Bond Buying. *Wall Street Journal*.

Ferguson, N. (2008, 2009). *The Ascent of Money: A Financial History of the World*. New York: Penguin.

Fieler, S., & Bell, J. (2011, April 6). Our Unaccountable Fed. *Wall Street Journal*.

Fischer, S. (1999, January 3). On the Need for an International Lender of Last Resort, Delivered at the American Economic Association and American Finance Association meeting and in F. H. Capie and G. E. Wood (Eds.), *The Lender of Last Resort*. London: Routledge.

Fleckenstein, W. A., & Sheehan, F. (2008). *Greenspan's Bubbles: The Age of Ignorance at the Federal Reserve*. New York: McGraw-Hill.

Friedman, M., & Schwartz, J. (1963). *A Monetary History of the United States: 1867–1960*. Princeton: Princeton University Press.

Fromson, B. D. (1997, February 23). Plunge Protection Team. *Washington Post*.

Frost, J. (2017, November 2). Introducing the Secured Overnight Financing Rate (SOFR). Federal Reserve Bank of New York.

Garrison, R. W. (2001). *Time and Money: The Macroeconomics of Capital Structure*. London/New York: Routledge.

Gilchrist, S., & Leahy, J. V. (2002). Monetary Policy and Asset Prices. *Journal of Monetary Economics, 49*, 75–97.

Gjerstad, S. D., & Smith, V. L. (2014). *Rethinking Housing Bubbles*. New York: Cambridge University Press.

Goodfriend, M. (2003). Interest Rate Policy Should Not React Directly to Asset Prices. In Hunter et.al. (2003).

Goodhart, C. A. E. (2007). Myths About the Lender of Last Resort. In F. H. Capie & G. E. Wood (Eds.), *The Lender of Last Resort*. London: Routledge.

Goodhart, C. A. E. (2011). The Changing Role of Central Banks. *Financial History Review, 18*(2), 135–154.

Granville, K. (2017, June 15). A President at War with the Fed, 5 Decades Back. *New York Times*.

Greenspan, A. (2004). Risk and Uncertainty in Monetary Policy. *American Economic Review, 94*(2), 33–40.

Greenspan, A. (2007). *The Age of Turbulence: Adventures in a New World*. New York: Penguin.

Greenspan, A. (2009, March 27). We Need a Better Cushion Against Risk. *Financial Times*.

Greenspan, A. (2013). *The Map and the Territory: Risk, Human Nature, and the Future of Forecasting*. New York: Penguin.

Griffin, G. E. (2002). *The Creature from Jekyll Island: A Second Look at the Federal Reserve* (4th ed.). Westlake Village: American Media.

Guha, K. (2008, May 16). Troubled by Bubbles. *Financial Times*.

Hayford, M. D., & Malliaris, A. G. (2005). *Is the Federal Reserve Stock Market Bubble-Neutral?*, in Malliaris (2005).

Heim, E., & Truger, A. (Eds.). (2007). *Money, Distribution and Economic Policy: Alternatives to Orthodox Macroeconomics*. Cheltenham: Edward Elgar.

Heller, R. (2017). Monetary Mischief and the Debt Trap. *Cato Journal, 37*(2), 261–247.

Hendry, D., & Mizon, G. E. (2013). Unpredictability in Economic Analysis, Econometric Modeling and Forecasting. Working Paper No. 2013-W04, Oxford.

Hilsenrath, J. E. (2009, December 2). Fed Debates New Role: Bubble Fighter. *Wall Street Journal*.

Hilsenrath, J. E. (2010, June 18). Fed Deputy Says Rules Changed Too Slowly. *Wall Street Journal*.

Hilsenrath, J. E. (2012b, September 28). How Bernanke Pulled the Fed His Way. *Wall Street Journal*.

Hilsenrath, J., & Blackstone, B. (2012, December 11). Inside the Risky Bets of Central Banks. *Wall Street Journal*.

Hilsenrath, J. E., & Harrison, D. (2015, December 12). Fed's Unsolved Puzzle: How to Deflate Bubbles. *Wall Street Journal*.

Hobusch, E., Nikolova, I., Mironenko, A., Edilashvili, T., & Zulfiquar, Maham (2014/15). Interest Rate Policy Changes as a Trigger of a Financial Crisis, WS 2014/15, Rhine-Waal University Faculty of Society and Economics.

Howe, R. H. (1915). *The Evolution of Banking: A Study of the Development of the Credit System*. Chicago: C. H. Kerr & Company.

Huang, D., Jiang, F., Tu, J., & Zhou, G. (2015). Investor Sentiment Aligned: A Powerful Predictor of Stock Returns. *Review of Financial Studies, 28*(3), 791–837.

Hunter, W. C., Kaufman, G. G., & Pomerleano, M. (Eds.). (2003). *Asset Price Bubbles: The Implications for Monetary, Regulatory, and International Policies*. Cambridge, MA: MIT Press (Paperback edition, 2005).

Jacobs, L. R., & King, D. S. (2016). *Fed Power: How Finance Wins*. New York: Oxford University Press.

Kaminska, I. (2012, July 3). The Base Money Confusion. *FTAlphaville*.

Kantchev, G., Whittall, C., & Inada, M. (2016, August 8). Are Negative Rates Backfiring? Here's Some Early Evidence. *Wall Street Journal*.

Kaufman, H. (2009, October 10). The Real Threat to Fed Independence. *Wall Street Journal*.

Keen, S. (1995). Finance and Economic Breakdown: Modelling Minsky's Financial Instability Hypothesis. *Journal of Post Keynesian Economics, 17*(4), 607.

Kindleberger, C., & Aliber, R. Z. (2011). *Manias, Panics, and Crashes: A History of Financial Crises* (6th ed.). Houndmills: Palgrave Macmillan.

King, M. (2016). *The End of Alchemy: Money, Banking and the Future of the Global Economy*. New York: W. W. Norton.

Kiyotaki, N., & Moore, J. (1997). Credit Cycles. *Journal of Political Economy, 105*(2), 211–248.

Knoop, T. A. (2008). *Modern Financial Macroeconomics: Panics, Crashes, and Crises*. Oxford: Blackwell.

Kocherlakota, N. R. (2009, April). *Bursting Bubbles: Consequences and Cures*. Federal Reserve Bank of Minneapolis and IMF Conference, Washington, DC.

Koo, R. C. (2010). Lessons from Japan: Fighting a Balance Sheet Recession. *CFA Institute Conference Proceedings Quarterly, 27*(4), 28–39.

Kroszner, R. S. (2016, October 8). Sebastian Mallaby's Biography Shows That Alan Greenspan Foresaw the Housing Crisis. *Wall Street Journal*.

Kuttner, K. N. (2012). Monetary Policy and Asset Price Volatility. In Evanoff et al. (2012).

Lacker, J. M. (2012). Understanding the Interventionist Impulse of the Modern Central Bank. *Cato Journal, 32*(2), 247–253.

Lahart, J. (2008b, October 17). Fed Rethinks Stance on Popping Bubbles. *Wall Street Journal*.

LeBor, A. (2013). *Tower of Basel: The Shadowy History of the Secret Bank that Runs the World*. New York: PublicAffairs/Perseus.

Machlup, F. (1940). *Stock Market, Credit, and Capital Formation*. London: William Hodge and Company. Available at www.Mises.org

MacKintosh, J. (2017, September 22). $2 Trillion Later, Does the Fed Even Know if Quantitative Easing Worked? *Wall Street Journal*.

Malinvaud, E. (1985). *The Theory of Unemployment Reconsidered* (2nd ed.). New York/London: Blackwell.

Mallaby, S. (2016). *The Man Who Knew: The Life and Times of Alan Greenspan*. New York: Penguin/Random House.

Mallaby, S. (2017, June 24). The Fed Should Surprise Us. *Wall Street Journal*.

Malliaris, A. G. (2012). Asset Price Bubbles and Central Bank Policies. In Evanoff et al. (2012).

Malpass, D. (2011, September 21). The Fed 'Twist' That Won't Dance. *Wall Street Journal.*

Malpass, D. (2015, January 22). The World's Monetary Dead End. *Wall Street Journal.*

Martin, F. (2015). *Money: The Unauthorized Biography – From Coinage to Cryptocurrencies.* New York: Random House/Vintage (Paperback edition).

Mayer, T. (1999). *Monetary Policy and the Great Inflation in the United States: The Federal Reserve and the Failure of Macroeconomic Policy, 1965–1979.* Cheltenham: Edward Elgar.

Mayer, M. (2001). *The Fed: The Inside Story of How the World's Most Powerful Financial Institution Moves the Markets.* New York: Free Press (Simon & Schuster).

Mehrling, P. (2011). *The New Lombard Street: How the Fed Became the Dealer of Last Resort.* Princeton: Princeton University Press.

Meltzer, A. H. (2009, May 4). Inflation Nation, *New York Times.*

Meltzer, A. H. (2012). Federal Reserve Policy in the Great Recession. *Cato Journal, 32*(2), 255–263.

Meltzer, A. H. (2013, January). What's Wrong with the Fed: What Would Restore Independence? American Economic Association Meeting. Available at www.aeaweb.org/aea/2013conference/program/meetingpapers.php and *Cato Journal,* 33(3) (Fall).

Michaelson, J. C. (2010, August 11). The High Costs of Very Low Interest Rates. *Wall Street Journal.*

Micklethwait, J. (2016, March). Jamie Dimon on Finance: 'Who Owns the Future?'. *Bloomberg Markets, 25*(1).

Milne, A. (2009). *The Fall of the House of Credit.* Cambridge, UK: Cambridge University Press.

Minsky, H. P. (2008). *Stabilizing an Unstable Economy.* New York: McGraw-Hill (1996), New Haven: Yale University Press.

Mishkin, F. S. (2003). U.S. Stock Market Crashes and Their Aftermath: Implications for Monetary Policy. In Hunter et al. (2003 [2005]).

Mishkin, F. S. (2008). How Should We Respond to Asset Price Bubbles? Board of Governors of the Federal Reserve System. Available at http://www.federalreserve.gov/newsevents/speech/mishkin20080515a.htm

Mishkin, F. S. (2009). Is Monetary Policy Effective During Financial Crises? Available at www.aeaweb.org/annual_mtg_papers/2009/

Mishkin, F. S., & White, E. N. (2003). Stock Market Bubbles: When Does Intervention Work? *Milken Institute Review* (Second Quarter).

Mollenkamp, C., & Wei, L. (2010, July 8). To Fix Sour Property Deals, Lenders 'Extend and Pretend'. *Wall Street Journal.*

Nakamichi, T., & Ito, T. (2015, March 11). BOJ Helps Tokyo Stocks to Soar. *Wall Street Journal.*

Neal, L. D. (2015). *A Concise History of International Finance from Babylon to Bernanke.* Cambridge: Cambridge University Press.

Norris, F. (2013, July 19). The Time Bernanke Got It Wrong. *New York Times.*

O'Driscoll, G. P., Jr. (2011, July 26). Why the Fed Is Not Independent. *Wall Street Journal.*

Ohanian, L. E. (2018). Should Policy Makers Worry About R-Star? In M. D. Bordo et al. (2018). *The Structural Foundations of Monetary Policy*. Stanford: Hoover Institution.

Oliver, M. J., & Aldcroft, D. H. (Eds.). (2007). *Economic Disasters of the Twentieth Century*. Cheltenham: Elgar.

Onaran, Y. (2012). *Zombie Banks: How Broken Banks and Debtor Nations Are Crippling the Global Economy*. New York: Bloomberg Press/Wiley.

Paul, R. (2009). *End the Fed*. New York: Grand Central Publishing (Hachette).

Pepper, G., & Oliver, M. J. (2006). *The Liquidity Theory of Asset Prices*. Chichester: Wiley.

Pixley, J. (2012). *Emotions in Finance: Booms, Busts and Uncertainty* (2nd ed.). Cambridge University Press: Cambridge, UK.

Plosser, C. I. (2018). The Risks of a Fed Balance Sheet Unconstrained by Monetary Policy. In M. D. Bordo et al. (2018). *The Structural Foundations of Monetary Policy*. Stanford: Hoover Institution Press.

Pollock, A. J. (2016). Does the Federal Reserve Know What It's Doing? *Cato Journal*, 36(2), 385–392.

Porter, E. (2017, March 15). The Fed vs. the Angry Masses. *New York Times*.

Posen, A. S. (2003). It Takes More than a Bubble to Be Japan. WP 03–9, Institute for International Economics. Available at http://www.petersoninstitute.org/publications/wp/03-9.pdf

Potter, S. (2011). The Failure to Forecast the Great Recession. Liberty Street Economics, Federal Reserve Bank of New York. http://libertystreeteconomics.newyorkfed.org/2011/11/the-failure-to-forecast-the-great-recession.html#.U3aW3Kgo-Hs

Prechter, R. R., Jr. (2016). *The Socionomic Theory of Finance*. Gainesville: Socionomics Institute Press.

Pringle, R. (2012). *The Money Trap: Escaping the Grip of Global Finance*. New York: Palgrave Macmillan.

Reddy, S. (2008, September 22). Fed Could Suffer If New Role Clashes with Policy-Setting. *Wall Street Journal*.

Rickards, J. (2011). *Currency Wars: The Making of the Next Global Crisis*. New York: Portfolio/Penguin.

Rickards, J. (2014). *The Death of Money: The Coming Collapse of the Monetary System*. New York: Portfolio/Penguin.

Ritter, L. S., & Silber, W. L. (1974). *Principles of Money, Banking, and Financial Markets*. New York: Basic Books.

Roubini, N. (2006). Why Central Banks Should Burst Bubbles. *International Finance*, 9(1), 87–107.

Ryan-Collins, J., Greenham, T., Werner, R., & Jackson, A. (2011). *Where Does Money Come From?: A Guide to the UK Monetary and Banking System*. London: New Economics Foundation.

Schlesinger, J. M., & Nakamichi, T. (2014, November 10). How BOJ's Kuroda Won the Vote for Stimulus Expansion. *Wall Street Journal*.

Schularick, M., & Taylor, A. (2012). Credit Booms Gone Bust: Monetary Policy, Leverage Cycles and Financial Crises, 1870–2008. *American Economic Review*, 102(2), 1029–1061.

Schwartz, A. J. (1986). Real and Pseudo-Financial Crises. In F. H. Capie & G. E. Wood (Eds.), *The Lender of Last Resort*. London: Routledge.

Sharma, R. (2015c, January 16). How Spending Capped the Global Recovery. *Wall Street Journal*.

Siklos, P. L. (2017). *Central Banks into the Breach: From Triumph to Crisis and the Road Ahead*. Oxford: Oxford University Press.

Singleton, J. (2011). *Central Banking in the Twentieth Century*. Cambridge, UK: Cambridge University Press.

Soble, J. (2016, February 16). Abenomics Hits a Wall. *New York Times*.

Spence, M., & Warsh, K. (2015, October 27). The Fed Has Hurt Business Investment. *Wall Street Journal*.

Steil, B. (2012). What Should a Central Bank (Not) Do? *Cato Journal, 32*(2).

Steil, B., & Swartz, P. (2010, August 19). Bye-Bye to the Fed-Funds Rate. *Wall Street Journal*.

Stiglitz, J. E., & Greenwald, B. (2003). *Towards a New Paradigm in Monetary Economics*. New York: Cambridge University Press.

Stiglitz, J. E., & Weiss, A. (1981). Credit Rationing in Markets with Imperfect Information. *American Economic Review, 71*(3), 393–410.

Strogatz, S. (2003). *Sync: The Emerging Science of Spontaneous Order*. New York: Hyperion.

Suhadolnik, N., Galimberti, J., & Da Silva, S. (2010). Robot Traders Can Prevent Extreme Events in Complex Stock Markets. *Physica A, 389*, 5182–5192.

Summers, G. (2017). *The Everything Bubble: The Endgame for Central Banking*. North Charleston: CreateSpace Independent Publishing.

Swanson, E. T., & Williams, J. C. (2012). Measuring the Effect of the Zero Lower Bound on Medium-and Longer-Term Interest Rates. Federal Reserve Bank of San Francisco, Working Paper 2012–02.

Taylor, J. B. (2012, March 29). The Dangers of an Interventionist Fed. *Wall Street Journal*.

Taylor, J. B. (2013, January 29). Fed Policy Is a Drag on the Economy. *Wall Street Journal*.

Taylor, J. B. (2016, December 21). The Case for a Rules-Based Fed. *Wall Street Journal*.

Taylor, J. B. (2018). Alternatives for Reserve Balances. In M. D. Bordo et al. (2018). *The Structural Foundations of Monetary Policy*. Stanford: Hoover Institution Press.

Thornton, D. L. (2017). Federal Reserve Mischief and the Credit Trap. *Cato Journal, 37*(2), 263–285.

Todd, W. F. (2017). The Fed's Failed Policies. *Cato Journal, 37*(2).

Tognato, C. (2012). *Central Bank Independence: Cultural Codes and Symbolic Performance*. New York: Palgrave Macmillan.

Trichet, J-C. (2005). Asset Price Bubbles and Monetary Policy. Available at http://www.ecb.int/press/key/date/2005/html/sp050608.en.html

Tully, S. (2007). Why the Private Equity Bubble Is Bursting. *Fortune, 156*(4).

Van Overtveldt, J. (2009). *Bernanke's Test: Ben Bernanke, Alan Greenspan, and the Drama of the Central Banker*. Chicago: Agate.

Vigna, P. (2016, March 26). Mervyn King on the Limits of Central Banks. *Wall Street Journal*.

Voth, H.-J. (2000). *A Tale of Five Bubbles – Asset price Inflation and Central Bank Policy in Historical Perspective* (Discussion Paper 416). Canberra: Australian National University. http://econrsss.anu.edu.au

Voth, H.-J. (2003). With a Bang, Not a Whimper: Pricking Germany's 'Stock Market Bubble' in 1927 and the Slide Into Depression. *Journal of Economic History, 63*(1), 65–99.

Wallison, P. J. (2015, November 5). Bernanke and the Slow-Growth Crew. *Wall Street Journal*.

Wang, P., & Wen, Y. (2009). Speculative Bubbles and Financial Crisis. Working Paper 2009-029B, Federal Reserve Bank of St. Louis.

Wapshott, N. (2011). *Keynes Hayek: The Clash that Defined Modern Economics*. New York: W. W. Norton.

Werner, R. A. (2003). *Princes of the Yen: Japan's Central Bankers and the Transformation of the Economy*. Armonk/London: M. E. Sharpe (East Gate Books).

Werner, R. A. (2005). *New Paradigm in Macroeconomics: Solving the Riddle of Japanese Macroeconomic Performance*. Houndmills: Palgrave Macmillan.

Werner, R. A. (2007). The Link Between Fiscal and Monetary Policy – Lessons for Germany from Japan. In E. Heim and A. Truger, eds. (2007).

Werner, R. A. (2014a). Can Banks Individually Create Money Out of Nothing?—The Theories and the Empirical Evidence. *International Review of Financial Analysis, 36*, 1–19.

Werner, R. A. (2014b). How Do Banks Create Money, and Why Can Other Firms Not Do the Same? An Explanation for the Coexistence of Lending and Deposit-Taking. *International Review of Financial Analysis, 36*, 71–77.

Werner, R. A. (2016). A Lost Century In Economics: Three Theories of Banking and the Conclusive Evidence. *International Review of Financial Analysis, 46*, 361–379.

Wessel, D. (2009). *In Fed We Trust: Ben Bernanke's War on the Great Panic*. New York: Crown/Random House.

Wessel, D., & Frangos, A. (2013, July 9). Central Bankers Hone Tools to Pop Bubbles. *Wall Street Journal*.

White, L. J. (2011). Preventing Bubbles: What Role for Financial Regulation? *Cato Journal, 31*(3), 603–619.

White, W. R. (2009). *Should Monetary Policy "Lean or Clean?"* http://dallasfed.org/assets/documents/institute/wpapers/2009/0034

White, W. R. (2012). Ultra Easy Monetary Policy and the Law of Unintended Consequences. Globalization and Monetary Policy Institute, Working Paper No. 126, Federal Reserve Bank of Dallas. www.dallasfed.org/assets/documents/institute/wpapers/2012/0126.pdf

Williamson, S. D. (2015a, July). Current Federal Reserve Policy Under the Lens of Economic History: A Review Essay. Federal Reserve Bank of St. Louis Working paper 2015-015A.

Williamson, S. D. (2015b). Monetary Policy Normalization in the United States. *Federal Reserve Bank of St. Louis Review, Q2, 97*(2), 87–108.

Williamson, S. D. (2017). Quantitative Easing: Does This Tool Work? *The Regional Economist*, Third Quarter. www.stlouisfed.org

Wood, G. E. (2007). Stock Market Crashes. In M. J. Oliver, & D. H. Aldcroft (Eds.), *Economic Disasters of the Twentieth Century*. Cheltenham: Elgar.

Woodford, M. (2002, April 2001). Financial Market Efficiency and the Effectiveness of Monetary Policy, Federal Reserve Bank of New York Symposium.

Yellen, J. (2009, April 16). A Minsky Meltdown: Lessons for Central Bankers. Presented at 18th Annual Hyman Minsky Conference.

Theories Past

Once bubbles turn into crashes, as they all ultimately do, there is an upsurge—a bubble, if you will—in studies and books on the subject that will often refer to or are based on the older theoretical concepts that are reviewed here in Part II.

This theoretical survey section might thus be of limited interest to general readers—many of whom may choose to skip or skim through after reading just the introduction.

But the survey should nevertheless provide a convenient reference for any deep research on bubbles and crashes. The section covers random walks, efficient markets, capital asset pricing models, utility, rationality, and other behavioral aspects. Finance professors and students, CFAs, portfolio managers, and analysts looking for a refresher on the subjects all ought to find this coverage to be efficient and useful.

Most importantly, however, the material here further serves as background, bridge, and setup for the new approach that is developed in Part III.

CHAPTER 5

Random Walks

When it comes to bubbles, economists have spent the last 50 years metaphorically gunning their engines, spinning their wheels and going nowhere. This lack of progress may be attributed to many things but certainly not to absence of applied intellectual or computational horsepower.

The major underlying problem has been that it is impossible to pin down what is known as "fundamental value." This difficulty is then compounded by the rather widespread yet questionable presumption that when people make investment decisions they are by and large economically rational beings and examples of *homo economicus*—that is, unemotional trading automata unaffected by losses or gains from previous trades and investments and hermetically sealed off from the "irrationalities" of other players in the markets.

Socionomics and behavioral finance experiments, however, have shown these notions to be demonstrably false and that the human brain reacts differently when making buy and sell decisions about economic items such as cars, carpets, sofas, soaps, or soups than about financially related items such as stocks, bonds, real estate, gold, oil, or foreign exchange. A consumer's orientation to price differs from that of a speculator's because financial prices are not directly related to effort, utility, or cost (except in a behavioral framework of anchoring).

This chapter reviews and explains why the random-walk and efficient-market hypotheses and capital asset pricing theories that have been developed and vigorously debated over the last fifty years do not accommodate of bubbles and crashes. The objective, however, is not to engage in battle with proponents of these theories, nor is it to debunk, deny, or disrespect the theories themselves, which have contributed to an understanding of the interplay between risks and rewards. It's just that these theories were not originally designed nor specifically intended to explain bubble and crash phenomena. The motivation is instead to suggest that another approach is needed in describing, defining, and measuring such extreme events.

© The Author(s) 2018
H. L. Vogel, *Financial Market Bubbles and Crashes, Second Edition,*
https://doi.org/10.1007/978-3-319-71528-5_5

All of this then sets the stage for the later development of different and broader interpretations of a fictional "equilibrium" concept and of required returns (i.e., including behavioral payoffs) as compared to the long-prevailing approaches.

5.1   THE EFFICIENT-MARKET HYPOTHESIS

An efficient market is generally defined as one that always fully reflects all available information.[1] But whether markets are actually efficient is itself a large topic. For present purposes, it is sufficient to consider the irony that—despite all of the work done in reviewing and analyzing the histories of previous market bubbles—the efficient-market hypothesis (EMH) and the affiliated random-walk concepts actually prompt and promote the idea that, under the presumed theoretical conditions, bubbles (and also crashes) *cannot* occur. This is correct as far as it goes—that is, as a great thought experiment in armchair economics—but it's otherwise totally useless for any practical purposes.

Basic EMH tenets are that investors are rational, that all public information—including fundamental aspects such as company earnings, cash flows, balance sheet ratios, and economic growth projections—is already discounted and that price moves only when and as new information is (randomly) received.

Although there may be some irrational individual participants, the theory posits that too many people trade in the market for it to be wrong. Today's returns are independent of yesterday's and of tomorrow's. And if a large enough sample of such independently and identically distributed (*iid*) data is collected, the resulting probability distribution will have a finite variance and closely approximate a normal (bell-shaped) distribution, with prices following a pattern like that which might be traced by a drunken person stumbling in the dark, that is, a random walk. As Lo and MacKinlay (1999, p. 49) put it, "The essence of the random walk hypothesis is the restriction that the disturbances ε_τ are serially uncorrelated…"

In this stochastic process, the current period's returns, X_t, are usually interpreted as the logarithm of the total payoffs including dividends and expressed as $X_t = \mu + X_{t-1} + \varepsilon_t$, with $E[\varepsilon_t] = 0$ for all t and drift μ an arbitrary parameter. But the crucial random-walk model assumption is that the *conditional* expectation—and not merely the unconditional expectations—is zero. Symbolically, this is expressed as $E[\varepsilon_t| X_{t-1}] = 0$ rather than as $E[\varepsilon_t] = 0$.

Early tests of various versions of the random-walk hypothesis are now of primarily historical interest.[2] But it is relevant to the current study to recognize that some of the earliest work (e.g., by Mood 1940) included runs tests, which are comparisons of the number of sequences and frequency of sequences and reversals of consecutive positive and negative returns for stocks.

A sequence of ten returns, as Campbell et al. (1997, p. 38) show, may be represented by 1001110100. This sequence of six runs contains three runs of 1s (of length 1, 3, and 1, respectively) and three runs of 0s (of length 2, 1, and

2, respectively), whereas the sequence 0000011111 contains the same number of 0s and 1s but only two runs (see also Sects. 5.4 and 10.2).

Still, by the time of the classic Lorie and Hamilton (1973) survey of the field, the EMH was already fracturing into strong, semi-strong, and weak versions. And a more recent review by Beechey et al. (2000) indicated that the EMH, although it is the right place to start when thinking about asset price formation, "cannot explain some important and worrying features of asset market behavior."

That assertion would also be agreeable to Lo and MacKinlay (1999, p. 6) who concluded that "[E]ven after three decades of research and literally thousands of journal articles, economists have not yet reached a consensus about whether markets – particularly financial markets – are efficient or not."[3] And Summers (1986) even earlier thought that the evidence does not establish financial markets as being efficient in the sense of rationally reflecting fundamentals. In part this is because certain types of statistical methods used to test the hypothesis of market efficiency have no power against the alternative that financial market prices deviate widely and frequently from rational valuations.

The strong form of the EMH suggested that fundamental analysis is totally irrelevant and useless because prices would have already fully incorporated all tradable public and private information—that is, all that is knowable.[4] In the semi-strong version, the markets were deemed efficient *because* of the valuation work of large numbers of securities analysts. Price changes behaved randomly because valuations were themselves always being revised in response to new information about companies and to continuous reassessments about growth prospects for the overall economy. In the weak version, which merely asserts that price changes are independent and may be a random walk, the restrictions were relaxed even more.

By the late 1970s, so confident were the proponents that Jensen (1978) wrote: "[T]here is no other proposition in economics which has more solid empirical evidence supporting it than the EMH."

5.2   CAPITAL ASSET PRICING MODELS

At the same time that the EMH was taking shape, modern portfolio theory (MPT) was evolving into what came to be known as the capital asset pricing model (CAPM) that could be used to theoretically determine a required rate of return for an asset. Markowitz (1952), Tobin (1958), Sharpe (1964), Lintner (1965), Treynor (1965), Mossin (1966), and others extended the theory, which assumed that investors (in an environment free of transaction costs and taxes) are rational and would behave in such a way that they would shift assets to an efficiency frontier (Fig. 5.1) that provided the greatest expected (probability-weighted) return for the least risk. That is, if two assets or portfolios had the same expected return, any rational individual would, by definition, prefer the one with less risk: It would be the better investment.

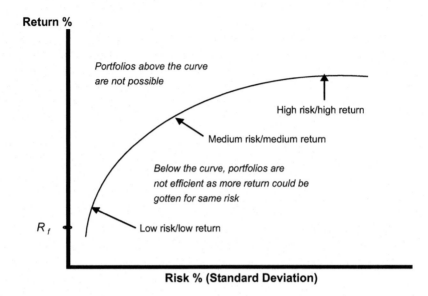

Return %

Portfolios above the curve
are not possible

High risk/high return

Medium risk/medium return

Below the curve, portfolios are
not efficient as more return could be
gotten for same risk

R_f

Low risk/low return

Risk % (Standard Deviation)

Fig. 5.1   Optimal portfolios lie on the efficient frontier. R_f is the risk-free return

Optimal portfolios would also contain combinations of capitalization-weighted risky assets and a "riskless asset" such as US Treasury bills. Levels of risk, according to Tobin's Separation Theorem, could then be adjusted by changing the relative amounts of the riskless asset held or by borrowing at the riskless interest rate to leverage the proportion of risky assets. In the end, the higher the proportion of riskless assets, the lower would be the standard deviation of the portfolio's returns, and vice versa.

Within this framework, different optimal portfolios reflecting an asset manager's risk-preference profile could then be constructed along a straight line, the capital market line (CML). This line would be tangent to the efficiency frontier that is shown in Fig. 5.2. A rational investor would choose a portfolio that provided the highest possible rate of return for any given risk as measured by the standard deviation. The preference is for a portfolio that is tangent to the efficient frontier rather than lower down in the interior of the region. The efficient frontier is where the optimal portfolios lie.

Sharpe himself cautions, though, against using *ex ante* (i.e., conditional expectations) constructs to predict future relationships. In other words, realized average returns are not expected returns.[5] To summarize from a quotation by Sharpe in Burton (1998):

> *The CAPM was and is a theory of equilibrium. Why should anyone expect to earn more by investing in one security as opposed to another? You need to be compensated for doing badly when times are bad…The key insight of the Capital Asset Pricing Model is that higher expected returns go with the greater risk of doing badly in bad times. Beta is a measure of that. Securities or asset classes with high betas tend to do worse in bad times than those with low betas.*

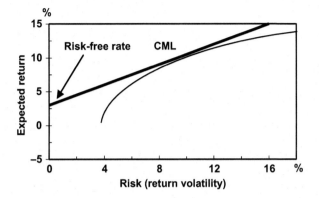

Fig. 5.2   The capital market line is tangent to the efficient frontier that passes through the risk-free rate on the expected-return axis

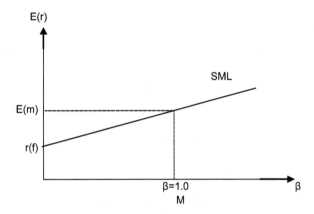

Fig. 5.3   The security market line is the linear relationship between the expected-return prediction and the covariance with the market portfolio. Expected rate of return prediction = $r_f + \beta \, [E \, (r_m) - r_f]$. This β_i differs across all i securities. The slope of the SML, the market risk premium = $E \, (r_m) - r_f$

In the CAPM structure investors are not compensated for assuming non-market risks because the optimal portfolios are all along the CML, the slope of which in Fig. 5.2 is often referred to as the market price of risk. The CAPM thus provides a prediction that determines how much investors will be compensated for taking higher risks. This extra risk is measured relative to the CML and can be depicted by another line (Fig. 5.3) called the security market line (SML), with a slope and y-axis intercept different from that of the CML.[6]

$$\beta_i = \left[\mathrm{cov}\left(r_i, r_m\right) \right] / \sigma_m^2 \text{ and } \sigma_i^2 / \sigma_m^2 = 1,$$

where r_f = risk-free return, r_m = expected return on market portfolio, r_i = return on security i, and σ_m^2 = variance of return on market portfolio, with expected return on security i = risk-free return + (premium per unit of risk).

This SML provides *beta*, a linear measure of the sensitivity of a security's risk to that of the market's (actually the slope of the line). A security that is twice as risky in terms of its variance relative to the market has a *beta* of 2.0, which means that for every 1% change in an overall market index (e. g., the S&P 500), this particular stock or security would be expected to change by 2% in the same direction as that of the index. This line (Fig. 5.3) also intercepts the *y*-axis at a height above zero that is called *alpha*, a measure of the residual returns above (or below) those that are obtained just from market movements.[7] As such, *alpha* (the residual or nonmarket related return, plus or minus) can be known only after the fact.

The combination of EMH and CAPM came generally to be known as modern portfolio theory (MPT).[8] It showed that the return from a security can be broken into two components, "unsystematic" risk, which Modigliani and Pogue (1974) note "can be washed away by mixing the security with other securities in a diversified portfolio," and "systematic" risk, "which cannot be eliminated by diversification." The implication is that a risky (i.e., high variance of returns) asset can reduce overall portfolio risk if it has a negative covariance with assets that are already held in the portfolio.[9] "The only risk that investors should be compensated for bearing is the risk that cannot be diversified away. Only systemic risk will command a risk premium in the market."[10] Critics, however, contend that this is naïve.[11]

5.3   VOLATILITY ASPECTS

This is still an important insights but with little to offer in the way of explaining how economic and financial market bubbles are formed and how they can be characterized. There is an even a more fundamental question as to whether the CAPM measures risk properly. That's because, on a deeper level, risk can be further separated into three kinds that include volatility itself, then volatility of volatility, and then the standard error of volatility of volatility.[12]

In all of this the question of how to best measure risk is central. Many if not most investors—especially those with long-term horizons—for instance, might view riskiness in terms of the probability of permanent loss of capital and thus be much less concerned with the short-run volatility of returns. If so, then the entire CAPM/EMH approach is flawed.[13]

Volatility and Modern Portfolio Theory

The MPT approach has been criticized from many different angles. The stock market crash of October 1987 and the steep decline into March 2009 only raised further questions concerning the vaunted efficiency of the market. But

MPT still has its staunch defenders.[14] The theoretical deficiencies are ironically well explained by Burton Malkiel, one of its pioneers and chief proponents, who wrote:

> *Although the preponderance of statistical evidence supports the view that market efficiency is high, some gremlins are lurking about that harry the efficient-market theory and make it impossible for anyone to state that the theory is conclusively demonstrated...I worry about accepting all the tenets of the efficient-market theory, in part because the theory rests on several fragile assumptions.*[15]

If the market—however it is defined (i.e., it might include the S&P 500, commodities, real estate, and foreign exchange)—rises or falls by 1% and the stock rises or falls 2%, its beta is 2.0. And the higher the beta of any stock or portfolio, the higher should be the expected return.[16] According to MPT, *beta* is the only (systematic) risk that is rewarded and matters even though there are, of course, situations in which lower *beta* stocks will sometimes produce higher comparative returns. But

> *The actual relationship between beta and the rate of return has not corresponded to the relationship predicted in theory...betas for individual stocks are not stable over time.*[17]

The basic problem is that *beta* estimation is backward-looking. Investors want and need to know the *beta* that will prevail over the future holding period of the asset; they would not find much use in knowing the characteristic (and probably greatly varying) *betas* of the past. "It is very difficult (indeed probably impossible) to measure *beta* with any degree of precision," says Malkiel.[18]

Critics of the MPT and EMH approaches would also say that returns are incorrectly described as following a normal or lognormal probability distribution (pdf) with finite mean and variance, that markets are not "efficient" in reflecting all public information almost instantly and in estimating intrinsic value, and that investors are not always rational and risk-averse (with risk measured as the standard deviation of returns).[19] "One cannot conclude from the unpredictability of markets that they are efficient."[20]

Moreover, "[T]he EMH says nothing about liquidity. It says that prices are always fair whether liquidity exists or not or alternatively, that there is always enough liquidity. Thus, the EMH cannot explain crashes and stampedes."[21] The upshot is that "[W]hen markets are considered 'stable' the EMH and CAPM seem to work fine. However, during panics and stampedes, those models break down...A stable market is not the same as an 'efficient' market, as defined by the EMH. A stable market is a liquid market."[22]

So-called postmodern portfolio theory (PMPT) has tried to mitigate these theoretical blemishes.[23] Some of this was done by replacing standard deviation with other measures of downside risk, by permitting non-normal return distributions, and by arguing that efficient markets do not require that all participants be rational, only that some be rational. And there is still no robust theory to as yet explain why size and value considerations (as extended by Fama and French) ought to predict returns.[24]

The LTCM disintegration of 1998 and the market meltdown of 2008 furthermore vividly illustrated that volatility itself does not take account of the risks of leverage and impaired or inadequate liquidity.[25] In a crash, *it is the liquidity imbalance of one leg versus the other* that *causes the hedge to fail:* Hedging a risky or illiquid position with a lower-risk liquid one—which is the usual situation—will thus under tumultuous conditions render the hedge inescapably ineffective. So the hedge that was supposed to reduce exposure to extreme market events actually boomerangs.[26]

Volatility Implications

The one thing for sure is that volatility raises awareness of risk (and quiescence the opposite). "Stock prices appear to be too volatile to be considered in accord with efficient markets," says Shiller (2000, p. 188) in summarizing his earlier work in 1981. "If stock prices are supposed to be an optimal predictor of the dividend present value, then they should not jump around erratically when the true fundamental value is growing along a smooth trend."[27]

Shiller's original study, as based on extension of a standard dividend-discount model, is important because it leads to the unmistakable conclusion that stock market bubbles are likely to exist because stock prices exhibit excess volatility.[28] "[W]e never know how great volatility should be or even could be," Shiller writes.[29] As is readily displayed in Fig. 5.4, over the long run, prices diverge from smooth fundamental earnings (and dividends) trends.[30] The changing volatility of the market is then shown in Fig. 5.5.

Another view of volatility and its fractal features is then provided by Fig. 5.6 from which it can be seen that the frequency of occurrence of small average monthly variances for the S&P 500 is many times that of the fewer and farther-between large variance episodes. This empirical record shows approximately that for every doubling of variance, the likelihood of such an event drops by more than half: the larger the variance, the rarer it is—and with relatively long stretches of tranquility being sporadically interrupted by violent upheavals.[31]

What emerges is that capital market returns are not well explained by the pure random-walk normal or lognormal models. Markets instead appear to adhere more closely to what are known as Pareto-Lévy (also called stable Paretian, L-stable, or Lévy-Mandelbrot) distributions, with tails that are fatter than the normal bell-shaped distribution and with peaks that are higher than that of the normal (Fig. P1). These distributions have infinite variance, are self-similar (or fractal, as Mandelbrot called them in 1975) with respect to time, and are stable under addition (i.e., the sum of stable random variables is also a

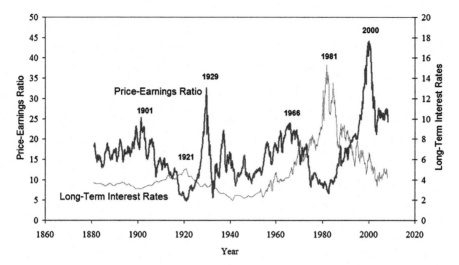

Fig. 5.4   Real S&P P/E ratios and interest rates, 1865 to 2016. (Source: Yale Prof. Robert Shiller's website data at www.irrationalexuberance.com/ie_data.xls. The more volatile series on the average will travel between any two dates selected a longer path over the same time elapsed and therefore must move at a higher average velocity)

stable random variable). "Large events," in the words of Bak (1996, p. 16), "follow the same law as small events." And in the greater scheme of things statistical, the normal is merely a special case of the stable Paretian.[32]

In brief, Mandelbrot-type models of the distribution of returns do not necessarily preclude random movement of prices yet appear to provide better descriptions of what happens in extreme market events. However, even though the fat-tailed feature of market data is accepted, the issue has not been entirely resolved, with Merton (1992, p. 59) writing: "...the infinite variance property of the non-Gaussian stable distributions implies that most of our statistical tools which are based upon finite-moment assumptions...are useless."[33]

In all, there is apparently no single model of stochastic stock price dynamics that is fully accepted by the research community, although several alternative models to geometric Brownian motion have been proposed. "The models differ among themselves not only with respect to the shape and leptokurtosis of the pdf, but also with respect to key properties such as:

- the finiteness or infiniteness of the second and higher moments of the distribution;
- the nature of stationarity present on a short time scale or asymptotically;
- the continuous or discontinuous character of $\Upsilon(t)$ – or ln $\Upsilon(t)$; and
- the scaling behavior of the stochastic process."[34]

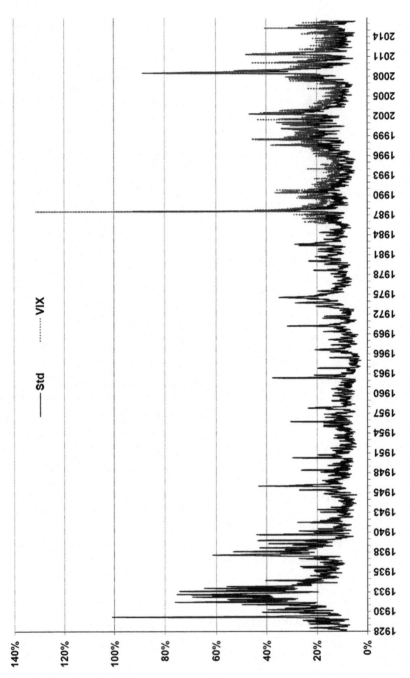

Fig. 5.5 Rolling annualized standard deviation of S&P 500 daily returns, 1928–2016. (Source: [Schwert (2016), available at http://schwert. simon.rochester.edu/spvol.pdf.] © G. William Schwert. VIX is the option volatility index)

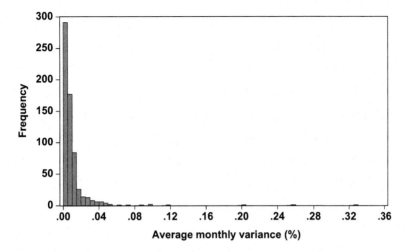

Fig. 5.6 Frequency of occurrence versus average monthly variance in percent, S&P 500, 1960:01 to 2013:04 as calculated using daily returns data. Of the 640 months, around 45% of the estimated variances (290) fall into the smallest category. (Source data: Yahoo Finance)

Some alternatives have included a mixture of Gaussian distributions and stochastic models having time-dependent variance over short time intervals.[35] This means that high-volatility periods are followed by more high-volatility periods and low-volatility periods by low-volatility (i.e., there is clustering) and that volatility evolves continuously over time.[36] It is also possible that risk measures other than volatility are important to investors.[37]

That volatility and the *size* of percentage changes in prices (either positive or negative) are positively related was shown in Fig. P2. But this is different from research in several studies showing that changes in stock return volatility are negatively correlated with *returns* themselves: That is, volatility tends to rise in response to bad news and fall in response to good news.[38] Studies also suggest that prices and volatility measures notably change at approximately the same time.[39]

In addition, what might be called an extreme events line (EEL) can be generated from a scatterplot of implied versus historical volatility as is shown in Fig. 5.7. In bubble and crash episodes the contemporaneous ratio of implied versus historical volatility spikes dramatically above an ordinary least squares (EEL) regression line that has been estimated by inclusion of data points extending over all types of market environments (i.e., extreme and tranquil).

In all, volatility appears to be as difficult to predict as returns on stocks. An important impediment here is that, as James Grant has written, "Vol is not a stock, not a bond. It is motion." The closely watched CBOE Volatility "fear" Index (VIX) does not predict what volatility will be, only what investors think it will be. The link between volatility and expected returns thus seems tenuous, with studies indicating that a consistent relationship between risk and returns

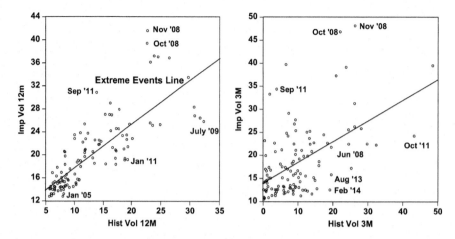

Fig. 5.7 Implied volatility versus past realized historical volatility, 12 months (left) and 3 months, 2004:09 to 2014:06. The tranquility zone is the area below the EEL, which is the boundary between extreme market event volatility and non-extreme market volatility. For the 12 months data, the estimated OLS equation (including 118 observations) is IV = 10.13 + 0.76 HV (and p-values of 0.0), and for 3 months data, it is IV = 14.01 + 0.45 HV (and p-values of 0.0). On the left-hand panel, October and November 2008 and September 2011 are more than two standard errors above the EEL because crashes crystallize faster than bubbles. The s.e. of regression is 3.79 for the left panel and 6.53 for the right (Source: Vogel and Werner (2015))

Table 5.1   S&P 500 volatility regimes and returns

	Returns (%)	Volatility (%)
1930–1945	3.41	28.85
1946–1968	12.92	16.90
1969–1977	2.59	20.31
1978–1999	17.20	12.51
2000–2008	−3.56	20.11
2009–2016	14.27	10.55

Source: Ben Carlson, "The Becalming of Stock Volatility," *BloombergView*, February 8, 2017, available at http://www.bloombergquint.com/markets/2017/02/08/the-becalming-of-stock-volatility

has not reliably been found.[40] Volatility of S&P 500 returns for various periods are provided in Table 5.1.

Still, in the era of central bank quantitative easing, volatility has become a large asset (or motion) class that now functions as a reflexive influence on risk and an input factor for active-portfolio strategists.[41] At least until the next major crash occurs—and esspecially in a low interest rate environment – money managers will continue to view volatility as a dependable potential alternative source of excess returns. Yet the short-vol approach appears to be no more than a version of the market destabilizing "portfolio insurance" strategies used in the Crash of 1987.[42]

5.4   Conclusions

The powerful intuitive appeal and foundation of modern portfolio theory is derived from the idea that investors are paid for accepting risk. This core concept forms the basis for the EMH, CAPM, and assumptions of normal or near-normal distribution of returns and associates the presumed random nature of stock market variations with the notion of economic equilibrium.[43] Such equilibrium, though, is inexorably linked to the assumption of rationality because if prices turned out to be too high or low (as in bubbles and crashes), this would imply that market participants were not making rational decisions.[44]

The theory, moreover, relies on the idea that distributions of asset price movements are predictable, even though such predictability has not been empirically supported (see Sect. 10.4). As told by Skidelsky, the EMH "assumes that financial markets are equivalent to insurance markets." But from the perspective of Keynes, they are not at all equivalent.[45]

This central idea—that risk determines reward—is flawed because markets compensate investors for being right and not for accepting risk but for reducing it.[46] CAPM falls apart because risk isn't simply reflected by the standard deviation of returns. And markets and stocks are not stably correlated. About the EMH, Lo (2012) writes: "...efficient and irrational markets are two extremes, neither of which fully captures the state of the market at any point in time." In bubbles and crashes, the "'madness of mobs' replaces the wisdom of crowds."

What the EMH has however importantly done in positing that markets are efficient and that prices are rationally determined is provided a base case—a null hypothesis, if you will—against which outcomes of alternative and more empirically robust approaches (e.g., behavioral finance and socionomics) can be compared and tested. Yet the theory doesn't mean that the price at which trades occur is right. Prices are never right as no one knows whether they are too high or low. And because of this, the market is tough to beat.[47]

Professional money managers are often constrained by size and other institutional considerations and criteria, all of which lead to market inefficiencies and inconsistencies with respect to CAPM theory predictions. For instance, with open-end fund formats in which investors can withdraw their money quickly, underperforming portfolio managers will always have a great fear of being wrong and alone and will thus rarely stray far from consensus views.[48] Were they to do so, their decisions (and sanity) would normally be severely questioned and fund withdrawals by clients would likely ensue.

As a result, portfolio *alphas* as defined in the CAPM are scarce, herding is prevalent, and pockets of long-term market inefficiency are thus being created rather than—as the EMH would instead suggest—being eliminated.[49] If so, then the old Wall Street quant-department saw—"In a bubble, speculators and investors make the mistake of buying *beta* thinking that it is *alpha*"—is apt.[50]

After the 1987 crash, critics such as Lawrence Summers and Robert Shiller were most direct and concise. In a *Wall Street Journal* interview (Donnelly

1987), Summers said about the event that it's "a little like saying the efficient-market theory didn't hold because the market in reality wasn't efficient." In the same article, Shiller said, "The efficient-market hypothesis is the most remarkable error in the history of economic theory."[51] Fischer Black was quoted as saying, "The [theory] is right. It just doesn't work."[52] And indeed, even Eugene Fama, an early proponent of the EMH, is quoted by Bernstein (2005), as having written that the "CAPM is a theoretical triumph and an empirical disaster."[53]

Mainstream finance theory—dependent as it is on efficient markets, rational expectations, equilibrium economics, and optimization—fails because:[54]

- Discounted present values of infinite streams of future payouts are not observable and the knowledge of economic agents, and thus of equilibrium conditions, is limited, even in a probabilistic sense.[55]
- No aggregate utility functions with characteristics required to justify equilibrium can be obtained.
- Economies and markets can never be in equilibrium and "fundamental values" for financial assets are always slippery conceits.

Whether or not the CAPM (and also EMH) might be an empirical disaster does not depend, however, on the occurrences of bubbles and crashes. The point is that the EMH/CAPM approach cannot be sensibly applied to the study of extreme market events. From a practical standpoint, these are at best shallow theories. And when it come to bubble and crashes the are logically incoherent and hollow.[56]

NOTES

1. According to Fama (1970), "[A] market in which prices always 'fully reflect' available information is called 'efficient'." A key insight by Fama (1991) is that "market efficiency per se is not testable. It must be tested jointly with some model of equilibrium, an asset-pricing model." Without such a model, the degree of the market's efficiency is indeterminate. In Clement (2007) Fama elaborates: "You can't test models of market equilibrium without market efficiency because most models of market equilibrium start with the presumption that markets are efficient....Tests of market efficiency are tests of some model of market equilibrium and vice versa. The two are joined at the hip...prices could be random and still be inefficient...what market efficiency says is that the deviation of the realized price from the equilibrium expected value is unpredictable based on any past information." However, as is expressed throughout the current text, the core problem with this approach is that the nineteenth-century mechanistic notion that markets are ever in "equilibrium," always moving toward "equilibrium," or even that "fundamental value" can be adequately estimated is totally inapplicable to financial markets. See also Radner (1968) and Fama and Litterman (2012).

    Fox (2009, p. 193) quotes Clive Granger and Oskar Morgenstern, writing in their 1970 book, *Predictability of Stock Prices*: "The random walk hypothesis does not say that price changes are unpredictable: it says they are not predictable using (linear) combinations of previous price changes." See also Shleifer (2000) and Lo (2004) for historical perspective.

2. Campbell et al. (1997, p. 34).

3. Lo and MacKinlay (1999, p. 5) suggest that, at least early on, many economists implicitly and erroneously linked the random-walk hypothesis and the EMH. It is easy to see how the two ideas might be confused, even though many researchers "have shown in many ways and in many contexts that the random walk hypothesis is neither a necessary nor a sufficient condition for rationally determined security prices."

4. On the EMH, as Ross (2003, p. 213) explained, "critics of this hypothesis argue that new information is absorbed by different investors at different rates; thus, past price movements are a reflection of information that has not yet been universally recognized but *will* affect future prices." Evidence from statistical analysis of a large base (110,000) of actual discount brokerage trading records by Coval et al. (2002) suggests further that there are some individual investors who are consistently able on a risk-adjusted basis to beat the market—which is a violation of even a weak form of the EMH. It appears that such traders are better able to *exploit* market inefficiencies than are large professional money managers.

In my own experience as a professional fundamental analyst, I can point to several instances in which deep company and industry knowledge and research provided significantly large market-beating results, particularly when going against the grain of normally bullish consensus opinion and taking a longer-term view. However, such opportunities do not arise frequently. I also can point to others such as James Chanos, founder of Kynikos Associates, who, for example, brought early attention to the problems at Enron (which lost all value), or William Ackman, head of Pershing Square Capital Management, who identified important weaknesses at mortgage bond insurer MBIA (which fell from around $70–$10, April 2007 to January 2008). Similarly, see Lewis (2010) *The Big Short*, on Steven Eisman's correct predictions on subprime mortgage defaults.

5. As indicated in Dugan (2005), Sharpe believes that the ratio is misused. "Past average experience may be a terrible predictor of future performance," he says.

6. An offshoot of this approach (known as the Treynor ratio) then for any specified period of time enables the estimation and ranking of the expected excess return for portfolio, p, above the risk-free rate, r_f, per unit of the portfolio's *beta*, b_p, as $E(r_p - r_f)/b_p$. The Treynor Ratio is similar to the Sharpe ratio, which instead measures expected excess return per unit of standard deviation.

7. By the late 1970s, when Wall Street came to embrace the CAPM approach, a new *beta-* and *alpha-* measuring industry had been formed in the brokerage community. Importantly, in applications of the CAPM and decisions concerning asset allocations, Markowitz is quoted in Bernstein (2007, p. 159) as saying, "It isn't the variance you have to worry about, it's the covariance."

8. In a review of the October 2013 Nobel Laureate prize to Robert Shiller, Eugene Fama, and Lars Hansen, Asness and Liew (2014) explain that the joint hypothesis (see note 1) is that the EMH holds and that the capital asset pricing model (CAPM) is how prices are set. "CAPM says the expected return on any security is proportional to the risk of the security as measured by its market *beta*. Nothing else should matter…Say you…find evidence against this pairing (as has been

found). The problem is, you don't know which of the two (or both) ideas you are rejecting. EMH may be true, but CAPM may be a poor model of how investors set prices…You can have an efficient market that is hard to beat because of the limits of arbitrage." See also Montier (2002, pp. 31–6) on instances of failed arbitrage.

9. The inherent contradiction between different approaches is noted by Fox (2009, p. 149), who observes that in the CAPM "of Treynor, Sharpe, Lintner, and Black, risk could be manipulated and controlled and reduced, but never entirely eliminated – not even in theory." But in "the no-arbitrage version pioneered by Merton, the right combination of securities could eliminate risk entirely." The Sharpe ratio's measurement of returns to risk using price variances is also potentially misleading as the calculation includes upside deviation, which many or most investors consider to be favorable. For most people, risk is actually reflected in the downside deviations. The Sortino ratio, developed by Frank A. Sortino, reflects this bias by calculating the denominator only using downside deviations (i.e., those of negative asset returns).

10. Quote from Malkiel (1999, p. 235). Chua et al. (2009) suggest that diversification is a grossly oversimplified concept, showing that "[C]orrelations, as typically measured over the full sample of returns, often belie an asset's diversification properties in market environments when diversification is most needed." This is supported in a *Barron's* interview in Willoughby (2010) with Lou Harvey, founder of Dalbar, an investment ratings firm in Boston. Dalbar's study found "that all of the methods based on modern portfolio theory worked within a certain range. Outside of that range, they all failed."

11. From Fabozzi et al. (2014, p. 34): "…although diversification is considered to be a sound probabilistic concept, the benefits of diversification may change as market states change…as correlations and expected returns change. The naïve belief that by simply diversifying a portfolio the investor is protected against major losses is just that – naïve."

12. This paraphrases the words of stochastic modeling expert Dr. Peter Carr, currently affiliated with New York University, but it is an offshoot of the important Heston (1993) and Bates (1996) model approaches. See also Mandelbrot and Hudson (2004, p. 125).

13. Bailey (2005, p. 160), for example, says, "the CAPM implies that each asset's *beta*-coefficient, β_j is a more appropriate measure of risk than its standard deviation of return, σ_j." Greenwald et al. (2001, p. xvii) say that permanent loss of capital is "the more common-sense understanding of risk." In Baker-Said (2008), Taleb notes that people mistake low volatility for low risk. Hassett (2002, p. 17) also argues that the traditional way of evaluating risk by equating it with volatility is inherently flawed and incomplete as it makes buying a stock like wagering on a coin flip. If a stock fluctuates a lot in price it is regarded as risky. If the price is stable, then it is not. However, this simplistic notion doesn't recognize that the shares of new companies trying something completely new may fundamentally alter the economic landscape. Shares of such companies may thus be less risky despite the volatility that derives from the shares being relatively unseasoned. That's because unlike the coin-flip situation, where there is a 50% probability of heads or tails, "when a firm is trying something completely new…there are no probabilities. Nobody knows for sure what might happen." The inappropriateness of measuring risk via volatility of share prices would therefore, by extension,

be applicable to the market as a whole. In Wallace (2010), behavioral finance authority Meir Statman says, "risk is not what underlies outperformance...[I]t's emotion; it is sentiment." Taylor (2010, p. 3) writes that "Keynes explicitly and emphatically rejected the notion that risk is quantifiable."

Black et al. (1972) provided additional evidence that the specifications of the CAPM are faulty. Using four subperiods of 105 months each, the authors found that the slope of the SML was flat for the third-period sample and negative for the fourth-period sample. These results say that returns in the third period were the same regardless of risk and that in the fourth period *higher risk provided lower returns*, not higher, as the CAPM theory would have predicted (indeed, demanded). With this evidence of instability in the risk/return tradeoff, it becomes more difficult to support the notion that collective investor behavior is always rational (i.e., valuing and pricing securities on the basis of all available information). From the behavioralist's standpoint that is discussed in the next chapter, Statman (1995) adds:

> *The assumptions about human behavior that underlie the CAPM are not simplified versions of observed behavior. Rather, they contradict observed behavior... Standard finance does not do well...as a descriptive theory of finance. Investors regularly overlook arbitrage opportunities, fail to use Markowitz's principles in constructing their portfolios, and fail to drive stock returns to levels commensurate with the CAPM.*

14. Burton Malkiel, a pioneer in the development of the random-walk/EMH approach, has continued in Malkiel (1999 [2003, 2007], pp. 13–15) to endorse the concept that "Investors would be far better off buying and holding an index fund than attempting to buy and sell individual securities or actively managed mutual funds...I conclude that reports of the death of the efficient market theory are vastly exaggerated." In the eighth edition (2003, p. 258), he says, "I believe the stock market is fundamentally logical." However, he then explains that "a number of studies by academics and practitioners, completed during the 1980s and 1990s have cast doubts on the validity of the theory." In the eighth edition (2003) he writes of the weaknesses:

> *The first is that perfect pricing exists...Another fragile assumption is that news travels instantaneously... Finally, there is the enormous difficulty of translating known information about a stock into an estimate of true value. (pp. 194–5)*

> *Although we still have much to learn about the market's evaluation of risk, I believe it is fair to conclude that risk is unlikely to be captured adequately by a single beta statistic (the risk measure of the CAPM). It appears that several other systematic risk measures affect the valuation of securities. Unfortunately, beta also has its warts. The actual relationship between beta and rate of return has not corresponded to the relationships predicted in theory during the last third of the twentieth century. Moreover, betas are not stable from period to period, and they are very sensitive to the particular market proxy against which they are measured. (pp. 237–8)*

See also eleventh edition (2015).

15. In Malkiel (1999, pp. 194–5). Gulko (2005) writes: "Investors do not need to be rational for markets to be efficient...price efficiency and individual irrationality are not necessarily mutually exclusive."

16. Malkiel (1999 [2003, 2007], pp. 235, 244) says: "Markets can be efficient even if many market participants are quite irrational. Markets can be efficient even if stock prices exhibit greater volatility than can apparently be explained by fundamentals such as earnings and dividends."

17. Malkiel (2015, pp. 226–7).

18. A detailed defense of the random walk/EMH against more recent challenges (e.g., indications of the possibility of partial long-term predictability of returns as based on negative serial correlation studies) is offered in Malkiel (2003). Rockel (2010) provides a concise description of the EMH and writes of Markowitz, explaining why MPT is still correct. Kaizoji and Sornette (2008) provide a review of bubbles and crashes as related to the EMH.

19. Bailey (2005, p. 144) further condenses these assumptions into three sets of conditions: (1) asset markets are in equilibrium, (2) all investors behave according to a mean-variance criterion, and (3) investors base their decisions on the same values of means, variances, and covariances. And Montier (2002, p. 86) concisely states the CAPM assumptions, among which are no transaction costs, no taxes, size of trading positions acquired not affecting market prices, and investors sharing a common time horizon. Jovanovic and Schinckus (2017, p. 11) note that use of logarithmic returns of stocks rather than of prices provides assurance that the stochastic process is stationary.

    Peters (1994, pp. 30, 43–4) also writes that "the term structure of volatility shows that the stock market is not a random walk. At best, it is a stochastic 'bounded' set...This means that there are limits to how far the random walker will wander before he or she heads back...This is not unexpected because the EMH and the CAPM are equilibrium models."

    From the perspective of the adaptive market hypothesis of Lo (2017, p. 3), "the EMH isn't wrong, it's just incomplete." Lo's approach is interesting but flawed and unconvincing, for as Prechter (2016, p. 400) writes: "[W]hile nature produces many successful species, no 'species' of speculator learns anything reliable or achieves long-run financial success, so there must be no process of adaptation, natural selection or evolution going on...." This view is supported by the ever-recurring patterns of speculation and bubbles that date back centuries and as discussed in Chaps. 1, 2, and 3. That is, there is absolutely no evidence that via a natural selection process, a new species of asset speculator has evolved. People make the same mistakes and misjudgments again and again.

20. Wilmott and Orrell (2017, p. 25).

21. Peters (1994, p. 42).

22. Peters (1989, 1991, 1996) makes a further case against the EMH through application of what is known as rescaled range analysis, or "range over standard deviation" (R/S), which was originated by H. E. Hurst in the early 1900s. Hurst took the range of the data in a time series, that is, the maximum minus the minimum, and standardized the number by dividing by the standard deviation of the observations, which provides a dimensionless ratio. He found that many natural phenomena, including temperatures, rainfall, and sunspots, follow a "biased" random walk. The simple relationship was

$$R/S = (a*N)^H$$

    where a is a constant, N is the number of observations, and H is the Hurst exponent.

Peters conducted R/S analyses on many different time series, including those for economic indicators, for Treasury bill yields, for S&P 500 returns over many different intervals, and for individual shares. In almost all situations, the R/S analysis indicated persistence (i.e., autocorrelation and fractal features), which is not consistent with the underlying independence and random-walk assumptions of the EMH. The Hurst exponent was developed for range changes in the water level of the Nile River. A river level is somewhat analogous to a stock price level in that it rises in some years and falls in others, but once in a great while there is a major event, say a 100-year flood, that surprises everyone with its intensity and size and goes far beyond the usual ranges of water-level expectations. This is precisely the type of action seen in financial asset price bubbles and crashes, in which the usual expected price ranges and growth trends are far exceeded. Buchanan (2013, pp. 162–165) provides a clear discussion of the Hurst method.

Some reservations against use of R/S analysis are to be found in Lo and MacKinlay (1999, p. 148) and also in the earlier work of Mandelbrot (1972). See Greene and Fielitz (1977), Campbell et al. (1997, p. 63), Lobato and Savin (1998), and Lo and MacKinlay (1999, p. 166) for criticisms of R/S analysis. Related material also includes Poterba and Summers (1988), Lo (1991), Mills (1993, p. 8), and Mantegna and Stanley (2000, p. 45).

23. For example, Fama and French (1996) posited a three-factor (FF3) model as an extension of the original CAPM approach. In addition to the excess market return of the standard CAPM, the FF3 multifactor approach adds the return on small stocks minus the return on big stocks (SMB), and the return on value stocks minus the return on growth stocks (HML, high minus low book/market). "Value" stocks have relatively high ratios of book value to market cap (>70th percentile); "growth" stocks are in the lowest (<30th percentile). Although Fama and French develop factor portfolios using firm characteristics, Chen et al. (1986) specify macroeconomic variables as factors. Estrada (2005, Ch. 8) provides an overview of the three-factor model approach. In the April 2010 GMO Quarterly Letter (www. GMO.com), Jeremy Grantham takes issue with the Fama and French as well as the Graham and Dodd approach to securities analysis. See also Zwieg (2018).

Turner and Weigel (1990) also cast doubt upon the assumption that returns follow a normal distribution, $N(0, \sigma^2)$, with mean zero and variance σ^2. In fact, more observations than in the normal were observed by these studies to be on the negative left-hand side of the distribution, and the peak around the mean was higher than would be predicted by a normal distribution, a condition called leptokurtosis. Such a condition may be what it seems, but it may also be caused by changes in the distribution over time. Friedman and Laibson (1989), who studied quarterly S&P 500 returns from 1946 through 1988, however, concluded that significant leptokurtosis "appears regardless of the period chosen." And Hall (2001, p. 2) says, "Most suggestions of irrationality appear to deal with mistakes in probability rather than mistakes in marginal utility...rational beliefs about probabilities are only loosely constrained in a nonstationary world."

Arbitrage pricing theory (APT), which was developed by Ross (1976), takes a somewhat different approach. As Campbell et al. (1997, p. 156) explain, the CAPM "is an equilibrium theory where the expected return of a given asset is a linear function of its covariance with the return of the market portfolio...APT... is an asset pricing theory where in the absence of asymptotic arbitrage the expected return of a given asset is determined by its covariances with multiple factors." Ross is quoted in Dunbar (2000, p. 71) as saying, "Whatever the systematic risks in the market, arbitrage will force excess expected returns to be proportional to the exposure to those risks."

Cuthbertson and Nitzsche (2004, p. 181) indicate that "APT implies that the return on a security can be broken down into an expected return and an unexpected, 'surprise' or 'news' component." Armitage (2005, p. 53) adds that APT shows "relations between expected returns that result from an absence of arbitrage opportunities, rather than from the maximisation of investor utility." This makes the APT approach more general than, but still consistent with that of the CAPM.

24. Fama and French (1992) marked a turning point in the theoretical and practical viability of the CAPM in suggesting that there is no link between risk as measured by volatility and return. Subsequently, Fama and French (2015) introduced a five-factor model that tries to explain stock returns by adding factors of profitability and investment to the original three factors. But the new model still doesn't fully account for the better performance of the small caps. Thaler (2015, p. 229) observes that "it is difficult to tell a plausible story in which highly profitable firms are riskier than firms losing money."

25. For instance, mortgage-backed securities indices had not been notably volatile just prior to the collapse that began in late 2006, but that didn't prevent them from soon thereafter falling by more than half. And in the cases of Bear Stearns and Lehman, balance sheet leverage at greater than 30 to 1 meant that only a 3% or so decrease in valuation of the securities on the balance sheet was sufficient to totally wipe out equity.

26. Follows Bookstaber (2017, p. 16).

27. Campbell et al. (1997, p. 283) similarly say "that the stock market is too volatile to be consistent with the view that stock prices are optimal forecasts of future dividends discounted at a constant rate."

28. Such "excess volatility" was also found in British stock prices from 1870 to 1990 and in the German stock market, 1876–1990. See De Long and Grossman (1993) who say that for the British market, "the strongest evidence against the simple constant required rate of return dividend-discount model is found in the pre-World War I experience." See De Long and Becht (1992) on the German market.

29. Bernstein (2007, p. 70). In Christensen and Prabhala (1998) the relation between implied and realized volatility is analyzed and it is found that "implied volatility outperforms past volatility in forecasting...."

30. LeRoy and Parke (1992) make a correction to Shiller's 1981 paper. They note that some data transformation that ensures that the appropriate variables are stationary must be found, but that Shiller's fitted log-linear trend method will still be nonstationary. A critique is also provided by Smant (2003), who cites the work on variance-bound tests done by Kleidon (1986). Smant suggests that Shiller's measurements of variance are not significant to the behavior of stock market prices because variance-bound tests must be applied to dividends and prices in a cross-sectional framework, not a time-series variance framework, as Shiller has done. That is because the expected probability distribution of future dividends changes over time and is conditional on the information set available at each subsequent time, t. But even if Smant's view is accepted, Shiller's concern that bubbles create social welfare, savings and investment, and policy dis-

tortions nevertheless remains valid. A review of policy implications appears in Hunter et al. (2003 [2005]).

31. All of this is consistent with the Gopikrishnan et al. (1998) study of 40 million stock trading data points in which an asymptotic power-law behavior for the cumulative distribution found. See also Mantegna (1991), Cont et al. (1997), Scalas and Kim (2006), and Gerow and Keane (2012).

32. Mantegna and Stanley (2000, p. 33) have observed that "[S]table non-Gaussian random processes have infinite variance, whereas the Gaussian process is the only stable process with finite variance." Taylor (2005, pp. 73–6) notes that the infinite-variance stable distribution advocated by Mandelbrot is used by few researchers, with most studies based on variations of the normal that sometimes include gamma and lognormal versions. The reason is that such variations have the high kurtosis and approximate symmetry that appears to characterize the distribution of daily returns. Hagerman (1978), for example, argues that monthly returns distributions are nearly normal.

However, the underlying data cover all types of market conditions and are not specific as to periods that might contain "bubbles" and "crashes." And near-normal distributions are not likely to reveal the power-law fractal nature of stock price patterns that are evident from visual inspection. That is, the characteristics of price charts taken over a period of five minutes are not readily distinguishable from those of charts taken over five months if time-scale information, as shown in Fig. 6.3, is not separately revealed.

Also, see Ané and Geman (2000), in which it is shown that normality of asset returns can be recovered through a stochastic time change. An example of "tail risk" given by Mandelbrot is that if the DJIA followed a normal distribution, it should have moved by more than 7% only once in every 300,000 years, yet it did so 48 times in the twentieth century. See also Orlowski (2012) and "In Plato's Cave," *The Economist*, January 22, 2009.

33. Critics such as in Campbell et al. (1997, p. 19) have for example, argued that such stable distributions

> *imply that sample estimates of the variance and higher moments of returns will tend to increase as the sample size increases, whereas in practice these estimates seem to converge. Second, they imply that long-horizon returns will be just as non-normal as short-horizon returns...In practice the evidence for non-normality is much weaker for long-horizon returns than for short-horizon returns.*

See also Weatherall (2013, p. 124).

34. Mantegna and Stanley (2000, p. 60) and Jovanovic and Schinckus (2017, p. 1) write: "Financial economists' insistence on maintaining the Gaussian distribution hypothesis meets with incomprehension among econophysicists."

35. These are generally based on the autoregressive conditional heteroskedastic (ARCH) techniques that were originated by Engle (1982). Such models imply unevenly spread regression error terms, $\varepsilon_{r,}$, and see market volatility as being conditional upon previous levels. Note that Conrad and Kaul (1988) found "variation through time in expected returns is well characterized by a stationary first-order autoregressive process...the degree of variation in expected returns also changes systematically over time."

36. From Mauboussin (2006, p. 39): "extreme days (up and down) come in bunches." Also, Vandewalle et al. (1999) find a tendency for volatility to cluster

around crashes. This clustering tendency is implemented in the WABSI and WACSI measures described in Chap. 10. Tsay (2005, p. 99) writes that "volatility evolves over time in a continuous manner – that is, volatility jumps are rare... volatility does not diverge to infinity." However, especially for 2008–2009, Figs. 8.5 and 10.4 visually contradict this view.

37. Studies such as by Rahman and Saadi (2008) and Cunningham (1993) indicate that the random-walk hypothesis cannot be confirmed through use of unit root tests for efficient markets because such tests (e.g., Samuelson-Fama and augmented Dickey-Fuller) are unable to "discriminate between a fully deterministic times series, generated from a nonlinear (chaotic) process, and a random walk."

   Mills (1993, pp. 139–41) explains that although generalized ARCH (GARCH) models have proven to be a popular method of modeling volatility in financial markets, they have limitations: GARCH models assume that only the magnitude and not the sign of unanticipated returns determines volatility and suggest different statistical properties for different time horizons, therefore failing, as Mantegna and Stanley (2000, p. 87) note, "to describe properly the scaling properties of pdfs at different time horizons." Ridley (1993) has further observed about GARCH, "All it means is that volatility is clustered. Prices tend to be volatile when they have just been volatile and not when they have not."

38. Poterba and Summers (1986) suggested that shocks to stock market volatility do not persist for long periods, having half-lives of less than six months. French et al. (1987) thereafter indicated that the expected market risk premium is positively related to the predictable volatility of stock returns. Investigation by Kim et al. (2004) also found a positive relationship between volatility and the equity premium.

   Adrian and Rosenberg (2005) developed a two-component (ICAPM framework) process for asset pricing purposes that allow short-lived volatility shocks (e.g., transitory liquidity events) to have different risk premiums than long-lived shocks to volatility (e.g., changes in economic outlook). They demonstrated that within an ICAPM framework there is strong cross-sectional evidence for the pricing of volatility of risk. And Schwert (1989a) observed that "[E]stimates of the standard deviation of monthly stock returns vary from two to twenty percent a month during the 1857-1987 period. Tests for whether differences this large could be attributable to estimation error strongly reject the hypothesis of constant variance."

39. Todorov and Tauchen (2010) found evidence for this. Todorov (2010) examines temporal variation in the variance risk premium and looks at jumps in stock prices and in volatility. See also Cartea and Karyampas (2009).

40. Advanced work on understanding volatility is centered at New York University's V-Lab (vlab.stern.nyu.edu), headed by Nobel Laureate Robert F. Engle. Cuthbertson and Nitzsche (2004) summarize: "{E}mpirically, the evidence for a link between stock market volatility and expected returns is not overly strong (p. 252)...Stock prices appear to be excessively volatile even when we allow time-varying discount rates and dividend forecasts (p. 295)." Munk (2013, pp. 14–6) reviews findings that stock volatility tends to be negatively correlated with returns, so that high volatility appears in periods of low returns and vice versa. In addition, while daily returns on market indexes tend to be negatively skewed, daily returns on individual stocks are roughly symmetric with zero skewness, stock dividends have different statistical properties than those of stock returns, and portfolio returns over short horizons exhibit positive autocorrelation (i.e., momentum). In the long run, however, particularly for indi-

vidual stocks more than for broad indices, there is mean reversion, with past returns tending to negatively predict returns over longer periods. Adrian and Rosenberg (2005) explain that "[M]ost studies...do not find a consistent significant relationship between risk and return...it is puzzling why the risk-return tradeoff is so difficult to detect empirically."

The average volatility for the S&P 500 for 2012 to 2016 was under 13% as compared to the annualized daily returns volatility of around 19% from 1930 to 2016. Table 5.1 shows that poor performance and high volatility tend to be followed by strong performance and low volatility. This, however, does not contradict the presentation of Fig. P1 which displays six-month rolling data, and not the long-term cyclical data shown here. See also Mackintosh (2018).

The Merrill Lynch Option Volatility Estimate (MOVE) Index does for bonds what the VIX does for stocks.

41. See "In the Shadows of Black Monday" by Christopher Cole of Artemis Capital Management in *Zero Hedge*, October 21, 2017.

42. This was seen when the DJIA lost 7% in two days, one of which (5 February 2018) saw the largest-ever one-day point drop of 1175.21 points. The S&P 500 fell 7.79% from 2872.87 on 26 January to 2648.94 on 5 February. Meanwhile, the VIX streaked from around 11 to 50 as the heavily-traded XIV inverse ETF collapsed to near zero. Grant's Interest Rate Observer, May 5, 2017, called such instruments portfolio insurance of the twenty-first century.

43. Cootner (1962) first linked the random-walk model to information and economic equilibrium, thereby setting the stage for the EMH.

44. Wilmott and Orrell (2017, p. 12).

45. Skidelsky (2009, p. 85). For insurance-type markets, risks can be probabilistically reflected from historical data. But the irreducible uncertainty of financial markets can never allow for such calculations.

46. Redleaf and Vigilante (2010, p. 73) say "[I]nvestors are paid for being right, not for the possibility of being wrong." See also Redleaf and Vigilante (2010, p. 55). Cooper (2008) emphasizes the weakness of the assumption that markets move toward an optimal state of equilibrium. Keynes and Minsky, who espoused a no-equilibrium theory, are cited as predecessors. It is noted that use of Gaussian returns distributions and the EMH approach leads to a situation in which assets will appear to be riskier after a steep decline, whereas they are, of course, riskier prior to the decline's occurrence. Lo (2012) writes, "During periods of market dislocation – when fear rules the day – investors will reduce their holdings of risky assets and move into safer investments. This will have the effect of reducing the average return on risky assets and increasing the average return on safer ones, exactly the opposite of what rational finance predicts."

47. Malkiel in a Bloomberg's Masters in Business interview with Barry Ritholtz, May 28, 2016, said that markets are efficient in the sense that new information is quickly reflected in stock prices. In Malkiel (2015, p. 108) he writes, "Markets can be highly efficient even if they make errors...Markets are not always or even usually correct."

48. Paraphrase of Bernstein (2004, p. 50).

49. See also Jensen (1968) and Chan and Lakonishok (2004), in which it was shown that US mutual fund managers consistently underperformed the S&P 500 (i.e., they were unable to systematically generate abnormal returns). The coefficient has come to be known as "Jensen's *alpha*." Strasburg and Pulliam (2011) discuss hedge fund herding. The increasing scarcity of *alpha* is described in Segal (2013).

50. Perhaps most damning, however, is the view expressed in Mandelbrot and Hudson (2004, p. 237):

> *Continuity is a fundamental assumption of conventional finance. The mathematics of Bachelier, Markowitz, Sharpe, and Black-Scholes all assume continuous change from one price to the next. Without that their formulae simply do not work...Alas, the assumption is false and so the math is wrong. Financial prices certainly jump, skip, and leap – up and down.*

Although Bernstein (2005) views the EMH/CAPM framework and the Black-Scholes option pricing model as remarkable advances in the way we now understand capital risks and allocation strategies, Triana (2009) and Haug and Taleb (2009) have much frostier views.

51. Thaler (2016) writes that "[I]t is an error because...the path is also not likely to be the result of maximizing some well-formed objective function..." Lowenstein (2000, p. 74) attributes the Shiller quote to Summers, but a check of original source Donnelly (1987) provides the proper attribution as shown. Shiller (1992, p. 2) contains the same thought. And Buiter (2009) follows similarly, writing with regard to the crash episode that began in 2007, "The EMH is surely the most notable empirical fatality of the financial crisis. By implication, the complete markets macroeconomics of Lucas, Woodford et al. is the most prominent theoretical fatality. The future surely belongs to behavioural approaches....Confusing the equilibrium of a decentralized market economy, competitive or otherwise, with the outcome of a mathematical programming exercise should no longer be acceptable." See also *The Economist*, July 16, 2009, in which "What Went Wrong with Economics" is surveyed in three articles.

52. In Gray and Vogel (2016, p. 65). (No relation.)

53. This was later followed by the suggestion in Fama and French (2008) that momentum investing is an embarrassment to the EMH and that momentum is the "premier anomaly."

Mehrling (2005, p. 91) writes, "...Fama's allegiance was always more to efficient markets than to any particular theory of expected return. In time, he would give up CAPM to save efficient markets even as his erstwhile colleague Fischer Black would do the opposite." Fox (2009) reviews the history of efficient markets and the rational expectations approach. See also Clement (2007) in which Fama says "The word 'bubble' drives me nuts" and explains that the fatal problem in the CAPM is its reliance on *beta* (volatility of an individual stock relative to overall market volatility). In Silver (2012, p. 347) Fama says with regard to bubbles that "the term has lost its meaning...A bubble is something that has a predictable ending. If you can't tell you're in a bubble, it's not a bubble." After sharing the 2013 Nobel award with Robert J. Shiller and Lars Peter Hansen, Fama again in an interview (Sommer 2013) says that he doesn't know what a bubble is. And in Appelbaum (2013), he says that it is impossible to consistently identify asset bubbles before a collapse.

54. Fabozzi et al. (2014, pp. 7–10).

55. On probabilistic predictions, Fischer Black in Black (1986) wrote "Noise makes it very difficult to test either practical or academic theories about the way that financial or economic markets work. We are forced to act largely in the dark."

56. See also Lo and Merton (2009) and Fabozzi et al. (2014).

References

Adrian, T., & Rosenberg, J. (2005, 2008). Stock Returns and Volatility: Pricing the Long-Run and Short-Run Components of Market Risk. *Federal Reserve Bank of New York and Journal of Finance, 63*(6), 2997–3030.

Ané, T., & Geman, H. (2000). Order Flow, Transaction Clock, and Normality of Asset Returns. *Journal of Finance, 55*(5), 2259–2284.

Appelbaum, B. (2013, October 15). Economists Clash on Theory, but Will Still Share the Nobel. *New York Times.*

Armitage, S. (2005). *The Cost of Capital: Intermediate Theory.* New York: Cambridge University Press.

Asness, C., & Liew, J. (2014, March). The Great Divide. *Institutional Investor.*

Bailey, R. E. (2005). *The Economics of Financial Markets.* Cambridge: Cambridge University Press.

Bak, P. (1996). *How Nature Works: The Science of Self-Organized Criticality.* New York: Springer-Verlag.

Baker-Said, S. (2008, May). Flight of the Black Swan. *Bloomberg Markets.*

Bates, D. S. (1996). Jumps and Stochastic Volatility: Exchange Rate Processes Implicit in Deutsche Mark Options. *Review of Financial Studies, 9*(1), 69–108.

Beechey, M., Gruen, D., & Vickery, J. (2000). *The Efficient Market Hypothesis: A Survey* (Research Discussion Paper, 2000-01). Federal Reserve Bank of Australia.

Bernstein, P. L. (2004). What's It All About, Alpha? *Institutional Investor.*

Bernstein, P. L. (2005a). Capital Ideas: From the Past to the Future. *Financial Analysts Journal, 61*(6), 55–59.

Bernstein, P. L. (2007). *Capital Ideas Evolving.* Hoboken: Wiley.

Black, F. (1986). Noise. *Journal of Finance, 41*(3), 529–534.

Black, F., Jensen, M. C., & Scholes, M. (1972). The Capital Asset Pricing Model: Some Empirical Tests. In M. C. Jensen (Ed.), *Studies in the Theory of Capital Markets.* New York: Praeger.

Bookstaber, R. (2017). *The End of Theory: Financial Crises, the Failure of Economics, and the Sweep of Human Interaction.* Princeton: Princeton University Press.

Buchanan, M. (2013). *Forecast: What Physics, Meteorology, and the Natural Sciences Can Teach Us About Economics.* New York: Bloomsbury.

Buiter, W. H. (2009, March 3). The Unfortunate Uselessness of Most 'State of the Art' Academic Monetary Economics. *Financial Times.*

Burton, J. (1998). Revisiting the Capital Asset Pricing Model. *Dow Jones Asset Manager.* http://www.stanford.edu/~wfsharpe/art/djam/djam.htm

Campbell, J. Y., Lo, A. W., & MacKinlay, A. C. (1997). *The Econometrics of Financial Markets.* Princeton: Princeton University Press.

Cartea, A., & Karyampas, D. (2009). The Relationship Between the Volatility of Returns and the Number of Jumps in Financial Markets. Birkbeck Working Paper 0914, Birkbeck, University of London. Available at http://www.ems.bbk.ac.uk/research/wp/PDF/BWPEF0914.pdf

Chan, L., & Lakonishok, J. (2004). Value and Growth Investing: Review and Update. *Financial Analysts Journal, 60*(1), 71–86.

Chen, N., Roll, R., & Ross, S. (1986). Economic Forces and the Stock Market. *Journal of Business, 59*(3), 383–403.

Christensen, B. J., & Prabhala, N. R. (1998). The Relation Between Implied and Realized Volatility. *Journal of Financial Economics, 50,* 125.

Chua, D. B., Kritzman, M., & Page, S. (2009). The Myth of Diversification. *Journal of Portfolio Management, 36*(1), 26–35.

Clement, D. (2007). Interview with Eugene Fama. *The Region*, Federal Reserve Bank of Minneapolis. Available at www.minneapolisfed.org/publications_papers/pub_display.cfm?id=1134

Conrad, J., & Kaul, G. (1988, October). Time-Variation in Expected Returns. *Journal of Business, 61*(4), 409–425.

Cont, R., Potters, M., & Bouchaud, J-P. (1997). Scaling in Stock Market Data: Stable Laws and Beyond. Available at http://arxiv.org/pdf/cond-mat/9705087.pdf

Cooper, G. (2008). *The Origin of Financial Crises: Central Banks, Credit Bubbles, and the Efficient Market Fallacy*. New York/Petersfield: Vintage Paperback/Harriman House.

Cootner, P. H. (1962). Stock Prices: Random vs Systematic Changes. *Industrial Management Review, 3*(2), 24–45.

Coval, J. D., Hirshleifer, D. A., & Shumway, T. G. (2002). Can Individual Investors Beat the Market? Harvard NOM Working Paper, No. 02-45. Cambridge, MA: Harvard University.

Cunningham, S. R. (1993, Fall). Unit Root Testing: A Critique from Chaos Theory. *Review of Financial Economics, 3*(1), 1–18.

Cuthbertson, K., & Nitzsche, D. (2004). *Quantitative Financial Economics* (2nd ed.). Chichester: Wiley.

De Long, J. B., & Becht, M. (1992). *'Excess Volatility' and the German Stock Market, 1876–1990*. NBER Working Paper No. 4054. Available at www.j-bradford-delong.net/pdf_files/German_Volatility.pdf

De Long, J. B., & Grossman, R. S. (1993). 'Excess Volatility' on the London Stock Market, 1870–1990. Working Paper, Department of Economics, Harvard University. Available at www.j-bradford-delong.net/pdf_files/London_Volatility.pdf

Donnelly, B. (1987, October 23). Efficient-Market Theorists Are Puzzled by Recent Gyrations in Stock Market. *Wall Street Journal*.

Dugan, I. J. (2005, August 31). Sharpe Point: Risk Gauge Is Misused. *Wall Street Journal*.

Dunbar, N. (2000). *Inventing Money: The Story of Long-Term Capital Management and the Legends Behind It*. Chichester: Wiley.

Engle, R. F. (1982). Autoregressive Conditional Heteroscedasticity with Estimates of the Variance of U.K. Inflation. *Econometrica, 50*, 987–1008.

Estrada, J. (2005). *Finance in a Nutshell*. London: Pearson/FT Prentice Hall.

Fabozzi, F. J., Focardi, S. M., & Jonas, C. (2014). Investment Management: A Science to Teach or an Art to Learn? *Research Foundation Review 2015*. CFA Institute Research Foundation at www.CFApubs.org/doi/pdf/10.2470

Fama, E. F. (1970, May). Efficient Capital Markets: A Review of Theory and Empirical Work. *Journal of Finance, 25*(2), 383–417.

Fama, E. F. (1991). Efficient Capital Markets: II. *Journal of Finance, XLVI*(5), 1575–1617.

Fama, E. F., & French, K. (1992, June). The Cross-Section of Expected Stock Returns. *Journal of Finance, 47*(2), 427–465.

Fama, E. F., & French, K. (1996). Multifactor Explanations of Asset Pricing Anomalies. *Journal of Finance, 51*(1), 55.

Fama, E. F., & French, K. (2008). Dissecting Anomalies. *Journal of Finance, 63*(4), 1653–1678.

Fama, E. F., & French, K. (2015). A Five-Factor Asset Pricing Model. *Journal of Financial Economics, 116*(1), 1–22.

Fama, E. F., & Litterman, R. (2012, November/December). An Experienced View on Markets and Investing. *Financial Analysts Journal, 68*(6), 1–5.

Fox, J. (2009). *The Myth of the Rational Market: A History of Risk, Reward, and Delusion on Wall Street.* New York: HarperCollins.

French, K. R., Schwert, G. W., & Stambaugh, R. F. (1987). Expected Stock Returns and Volatility. *Journal of Financial Economics, 19*, 3–29.

Friedman, B. M., & Laibson, D. I. (1989). Economic Implications of Extraordinary Movements in Stock Prices. *Brookings Papers on Economic Activity.* Washington, DC: Brookings Institute.

Gerow, A., & Keane, M. T. (2012). Mining the Web for the 'Voice of the Herd' to Track Stock Market Bubbles. Available at http://arxiv.org/abs/1212.2676v1

Gopikrishnan, P., Meyer, M., Amaral, L. A. N., & Stanley, H. E. (1998). Inverse Cubic Law for the Distribution of Stock Price Variations. *The European Physical Journal, 3*, 139–140.

Gray, W. R., & Vogel, J. R. (2016). *Quantitative Momentum.* Hoboken: Wiley.

Greene, M., & Fielitz, B. (1977). Long-Term Dependence in Common Stock Returns. *Journal of Financial Economics, 4*, 339–349.

Greenwald, B. C. N., Kahn, J., Sonkin, P. D., & van Biema, M. (2001). *Value Investing: From Graham to Buffett and Beyond.* New York: Wiley (Paperback edition).

Gulko, L. (2005). Efficient Irrational Markets. *Journal of Portfolio Management, 31*(2), 64–72.

Hagerman, R. L. (1978). More Evidence on the Distribution of Security Returns. *Journal of Finance, 33*(4), 1213–1221.

Hall, R. E. (2001). Struggling to Understand the Stock Market. *American Economic Review, 91*(2), 1–11.

Hassett, K. A. (2002). *Bubbleology: The New Science of Stock Market Winners and Losers.* New York: Crown.

Haug, E. S., & Taleb, N. N. (2009, February 26). Why We Have Never Used the Black-Scholes-Merton Option Pricing Formula (Fifth Version). Available at SSRN: http://ssrn.com/abstract=1012075

Heston, S. L. (1993). A Closed-Form Solution for Options with Stochastic Volatility with Applications to Bond and Currency Options. *Review of Financial Studies, 6*(2), 327–343.

Hunter, W. C., Kaufman, G. G., & Pomerleano, M. (Eds.). (2003). *Asset Price Bubbles: The Implications for Monetary, Regulatory, and International Policies.* Cambridge, MA: MIT Press. Paperback edition, 2005.

Jensen, M. C. (1968). The Performance of Mutual Funds in the Period 1945–1964. *Journal of Finance, 23*(2), 389–416.

Jensen, M. C. (1972). *Studies in the Theory of Capital Markets.* New York: Praeger.

Jensen, M. C. (1978). Some Anomalous Evidence Regarding Market Efficiency. *Journal of Financial Economics, 6*(2–3), 95–101.

Jovanovic, F., & Schinckus, C. (2017). *Econophysics and Financial Economics: An Emerging Dialog.* New York: Oxford University Press.

Kaizoji, T., & Sornette, D. (2008). Market Bubbles and Crashes. MPRA Paper 15204, University Library Munich, Germany and Available at http://arxiv.org/pdf/0812.2449

Kim, C.-J., Morley, J. C., & Nelson, C. R. (2004). Is There a Positive Relationship Between Stock Market Volatility and the Equity Premium? *Journal of Money, Credit and Banking, 36*(3), 339–360.

Kleidon, A. W. (1986, October). Variance Bounds Tests and Stock Price Valuation Models. *Journal of Political Economy, 94*, 953–1001.

LeRoy, S. F., & Parke, W. R. (1992, September). Stock Price Volatility: Tests Based on the Geometric Random Walk. *American Economic Review, 82*, 981–992.

Lewis, M. (2010). *The Big Short: Inside the Doomsday Machine.* New York: W. W. Norton.

Lintner, J. (1965). The Valuation of Risk Assets and the Selection of Risk Investments in Stock Portfolios and Capital Budgets. *Review of Economic Statistics, 47*, 13–37.

Lo, A. W. (1991). Long-Term Memory in Stock Market Prices. *Econometrica, 59*, 1279–1313.

Lo, A. W. (2004). The Adaptive Markets Hypothesis. *Journal of Portfolio Management, 30*(5), 15–29.

Lo, A. W. (2012). Adaptive Markets and the New World Order. *Financial Analysts Journal, 68*(2), 18–29.

Lo, A. W. (2017). *Adaptive Markets: Financial Evolution at the Speed of Thought.* Princeton: Princeton University Press.

Lo, A. W., & MacKinlay, A. C. (1999). *A Non-random Walk Down Wall Street.* Princeton: Princeton University Press.

Lo, A. W., & Merton, R. C. (2009). Preface to the Annual Review of Financial Economics. *Annual Review of Financial Economics, 1*, 01–17. Palo Alto: Annual Reviews.

Lobato, I. N., & Savin, N. E. (1998, July). Real and Spurious Long Memory Properties of Stock Market Data. *The Journal of Business and Economic Statistics, 16*, 261–268.

Lorie, J. H., & Hamilton, M. T. (1973). *The Stock Market: Theories and Evidence.* Homewood: Richard D. Irwin.

Lowenstein, R. (2000). *When Genius Failed: The Rise and Fall of Long-Term Capital Management.* New York: Random House.

Malkiel, B. G. (1999). *A Random Walk Down Wall Street* (7th ed., 8th ed. (2003), 9th ed. (2007), 11th ed. (2015)). New York: W.W. Norton.

Malkiel, B. G. (2003). The Efficient Market Hypothesis and Its Critics. *Journal of Economic Perspectives, 17*(1), 59–82.

Mandelbrot, B. (1972). Statistical Methodology for Non-periodic Cycles: From Covariance to R/S Analysis. *Annals of Economic and Social Measurement, 1*, 259–290.

Mandelbrot, B., & Hudson, R. L. (2004). *The (Mis)Behavior of Markets: A Fractal View of Risk, Ruin, and Reward.* New York: Basic Books.

Mantegna, R. N. (1991). Lévy Walks and Enhanced Diffusion in Milan Stock Exchange. *Physica A, 179*(2), 232–242.

Mantegna, R. N., & Stanley, H. E. (2000). *An Introduction to Econophysics: Correlations and Complexity in Finance.* Cambridge: Cambridge University Press.

Markowitz, H. M. (1952). Portfolio Selection. *Journal of Finance, 7*, 77–91.

Mauboussin, M. J. (2006). More Than You Know: Finding Financial Wisdom in Unconventional Places. New York: Columbia University Press.

Mehrling, P. (2005). *Fischer Black and the Revolutionary Idea of Finance.* Hoboken: Wiley.

Merton, R. C. (1992). *Continuous-Time Finance* (Rev. ed.). Oxford: Blackwell.

Mills, T. C. (1993). *The Econometric Modelling of Financial Time Series.* Cambridge: Cambridge University Press.

Modigliani, F., & Pogue, G. A. (1974, March/April). An Introduction to Risk and Return. *Financial Analysts Journal, 30*(2), 68–80.

Montier, J. (2002). *Behavioural Finance: Insights into Irrational Minds and Markets.* Chichester/Hoboken: Wiley.

Mood, A. (1940). The Distribution Theory of Runs. *Annals of Mathematical Statistics, 11,* 367–392.

Mossin, J. (1966). Equilibrium in a Capital Asset Market. *Econometrica, 34,* 768–783.

Munk, C. (2013). *Financial Asset Pricing Theory.* Oxford: Oxford University Press.

Orlowski, L. T. (2012). Financial Crisis and Extreme Market Risks: Evidence from Europe. *Review of Financial Economics, 21*(3), 120–130.

Peters, E. E. (1989, July/August). Fractal Structure in the Capital Markets. *Financial Analysts Journal, 45*(4), 32–37.

Peters, E. E. (1991). A Chaotic Attractor for the S&P 500. *Financial Analysts Journal, 47*(2), 55–81.

Peters, E. E. (1994). *Fractal Market Analysis: Applying Chaos Theory to Investment and Economics.* New York: Wiley.

Peters, E. E. (1996). *Chaos and Order in the Capital Markets: A New View of Cycles, Prices, and Market Volatility* (2nd ed.). New York: Wiley.

Poterba, J., & Summers, L. H. (1986). The Persistence of Volatility and Stock Market Fluctuations. *American Economic Review, 76.*

Poterba, J., & Summers, L. H. (1988). Mean Reversion in Stock Returns: Evidence and Implications. *Journal of Financial Economics, 22*(1), 27–59.

Prechter, R. R., Jr. (2016). *The Socionomic Theory of Finance.* Gainesville: Socionomics Institute Press.

Radner, R. (1968, January). Competitive Equilibrium Under Uncertainty. *Econometrica, 36*(1), 31–58.

Rahman, A., & Saadi, S. (2008). Random Walk and Breaking Trend in Financial Series: An Econometric Critique of Unit Root Tests. *Review of Financial Economics, 17*(3), 204–212.

Redleaf, A., & Vigilante, R. (2010). *Panic: The Betrayal of Capitalism by Wall Street and Washington.* Minneapolis: Richard Vigilante Books.

Ridley, M. (1993, October 9). Frontiers of Finance: On the Edge. *The Economist.*

Rockel, N. (2010, May). Evolutionary Road: The Enduring Popularity of MPT Hasn't Stopped Practitioners from Trying to Improve It. *Institutional Investor.*

Ross, S. M. (1976). The Arbitrage Theory of Capital Asset Pricing. *Journal of Economic Theory, 13,* 341–360.

Ross, S. M. (2003). *An Elementary Introduction to Mathematical Finance, Options and Other Topics* (2nd ed.). New York/Cambridge: Cambridge University Press.

Scalas, E., & Kim, K. (2006). The Art of Fitting financial Time Series with Lévy Stable Distributions. MPRA Paper No. 336 Available at http://mpra.ub.uni-muenchen.de/336/

Schwert, G. W. (1989a, May). Business Cycles, Financial Crises, and Stock Volatility. Working Paper No. 2957, NBER.

Segal, J. (2013, September). Is Alpha Dead? *Institutional Investor.*

Sharpe, W. F. (1964). Capital Asset Prices: A Theory of Market Equilibrium Under Conditions of Risk. *Journal of Finance, 19,* 425–442.

Shiller, R. J. (1992). *Market Volatility.* Cambridge, MA: MIT Press.

Shiller, R. J. (2000, 2005, 2015). *Irrational Exuberance.* Princeton: Princeton University Press (3rd ed, 2015).

Shleifer, A. (2000). *Inefficient Markets: An Introduction to Behavioral Finance.* Oxford: Oxford University Press.

Silver, N. (2012). *The Signal and the Noise: Why So Many Predictions Fail – But Some Don't.* New York: Penguin.

Skidelsky, R. (2009). *Keynes: The Return of the Master.* New York: Public Affairs (Perseus).

Smant, D. J. C. (2003). The Variance-Bound Fallacy. Rotterdam: Erasmus University, Rotterdam School of Economics. Available at www.few.eur.nl/few/people/smant

Sommer, J. (2013, October 27). Eugene Fama, King of Predictable Markets. *New York Times.*

Statman, M. (1995). Behavioral Finance Versus Standard Finance. In *Behavioral Finance and Decision Theory in Investment Management.* Charlottesville: Association for Investment Management and Research.

Strasburg, J., & Pulliam, S. (2011, January 14). Hedge Funds' Pack Behavior Magnifies Swings in Market. *Wall Street Journal.*

Summers, L. H. (1986). Does the Stock Market Rationally Reflect Fundamental Values? *Journal of Finance, 41*(3), 591–602.

Taylor, S. (2005). *Asset Price Dynamics, Volatility, and Prediction.* Princeton: Princeton University Press.

Taylor, L. (2010). *Maynard's Revenge: The Collapse of Free Market Macroeconomics.* Cambridge, MA: Harvard University Press.

Thaler, R. H. (2015). *Misbehaving: The Making of Behavioral Economics.* New York: W.W. Norton.

Thaler, R. H. (2016, July). Behavioral Economics: Past, Present, and Future. *American Economic Review, 106*(7), 1577–1600.

Tobin, J. (1958, February). Liquidity Preference as Behavior Toward Risk. *Review of Economic Studies, 25*(67), 65–86.

Todorov, V. (2010). Variance Risk Premium Dynamics: The Role of Jumps. *Review of Financial Studies, 23*(1), 345–383.

Todorov, V., & Tauchen, G. (2010). Volatility Jumps. Working Paper, Northwestern University, Kellogg School of Management, Evanston.

Treynor, J. L. (1965, January/February). How to Rate Management of Investment Funds. *Harvard Business Review, 43.*

Triana, P. (2009). *Lecturing Birds on Flying: Can Mathematical Theories Destroy the Financial Markets?* Hoboken: Wiley.

Tsay, R. (2005). *Analysis of Financial Time Series* (2nd ed.). Hoboken: Wiley.

Turner, A. L., & Weigel, E. J. (1990). "An Analysis of Stock Market Volatility," Russell Research Commentaries. Tacoma: Frank Russell Company.

Vandewalle, N., Ausloos, M., Boveroux, P., & Minguet, A. (1999). Visualizing the Log-Periodic Pattern Before Crashes. *European Physical Journal B, 9*(2), 355–359.

Vogel, H. L., & Werner, R. A. (2015, March). An Analytical Review of Volatility Metrics for Bubbles and Crashes. *International Review of Financial Analysis, 38,* 15–28.

Wallace, C. (2010, May). Mind Over Markets. *Institutional Investor.*

Weatherall, J. O. (2013). *The Physics of Wall Street: A Brief History of Predicting the Unpredictable.* Boston: Houghton Mifflin Harcourt.

Willoughby, J. (2010, July 26). Did Investors Learn Anything from 2008's Crash? *Barron's.*

Wilmott, P., & Orrell, D. (2017). *The Money Formula: Dodgy Finance, Psuedo Science, and How Mathematicians Took Over the Markets.* Hoboken: Wiley.

CHAPTER 6

Rationality Rules

Of potential relevance to the study of extreme market events are the many models that emerged during the years of research and controversy surrounding the EMH/CAPM. These appear in the literature with colorful bubble name adjectives such as "rational," "exploding," "intrinsic," "churning," and "collapsing," though most begin with neoclassical assumptions of financial theory.[1]

Substantial theoretical assumptions and econometric contortions are needed to fit "bubbles" into a conventional rational valuation-model framework. One such crucial assumption in traditional models takes the existence of arbitrage and the law of one price (LOOP) as a given feature. This law—which need not apply intertemporally and/or if buyers have less than perfect information—says that in efficient markets all identical goods must have one price and, if not, sellers and buyers will cause convergence toward such a price.[2] It then follows that markets with arbitrage cannot be markets that are in equilibrium.

6.1 RATIONAL EXPECTATIONS

Muth (1961) was the first to explicitly propose a rational expectations hypothesis (REH) approach, which then gained publicity in the 1970s and 1980s as a potentially useful way to model expectations of future events.[3] According to the approach—which was largely contra to the Keynesian macroeconomic analyses that had developed in the 1930s—the outcome of an economic event depends partly upon what people expect to happen. The larger importance, however, as Mehrling (2005, p. 210) writes, is that "[T]he hypothesis of rational expectations was for macroeconomics what the hypothesis of efficient markets was for finance...rational expectations thus undermined existing models."

Economists such as Milton Friedman in his permanent income theory of consumption and indeed Keynes himself had implicitly used expectations about the future ("waves of optimism and pessimism") as determinants of business

© The Author(s) 2018
H. L. Vogel, *Financial Market Bubbles and Crashes, Second Edition*,
https://doi.org/10.1007/978-3-319-71528-5_6

cycle activities. But proponents of the rational expectations theory—in attempting to be in agreement with previously developed models of perfect competition—prioritized expectations aspects as these also provided a building block for the random-walk and efficient-market hypotheses.[4]

At its core is the concept that rational people adjust their behavior to the government's announced economic policies. In extending this approach to stock price behavior, rational expectations theory would, for example, say that investors are likely to buy or sell shares based on what they expect the Fed will do with interest rates. And under rational expectations it is assumed that actual outcomes do not differ systematically or predictably from what was expected and that people do not make systematic errors when predicting the future. In other words, the expected value of a variable is equal to the value predicted by the model, plus a random error term.[5]

This REH approach proved to be an early favorite of bubble modelers because it was fully consistent with the random-walk/EMH line of thinking—which was to specify the conditions under which bubbles cannot form. The framework was also appealing because it didn't necessarily preclude a stock's price from increasing exponentially (even if dividends were assumed to be constant). After all, individuals might be willing to pay more than the present discounted value of expected dividends because they anticipated that the price would continue to rise (i.e., via "momentum, also known as relative performance strength") and thereby to generate capital gains that precisely offset the low dividend price ratio.

In addition, the theory could be readily adapted (using notions of what are known as "sunspot" equilibria and overlapping generation models) to include features in which—as in the Dutch tulip mania and the South Sea Bubbles—subjective factors appeared to have great influence and "prices change simply because they are expected to." That is, prophecies become *self-fulfilling*.[6]

However, as later sections on behavioral finance suggest, psychological factors (animal spirits, fears, etc.) are always present in pricing, preference, and production decisions and thus should not be stripped away from models that are designed to describe the real world.[7]

And so, as reasonable as it might seem at first glance, the REH approach eventually came to be criticized as much for its reliance on questionable underlying econometric and rationality assumptions as for its uncompelling results. The implications, for instance, are different if it's assumed that *most* investors remain rational most of the time or if they *all* behave rationally most of the time or if they *all* behave rationally *all* of the time.[8] The traditional economic approaches, including some elements of behavioral finance, don't adequately portray the essence of trading in financial markets.[9]

Such objections were taken more seriously only after many papers incorporating REH features had already been published. Blanchard and Watson (1982)—although noting that "arbitrage does not by itself prevent bubbles"—were apparently the first to introduce the notion of rational expectations bubbles to explain how observed prices might over extended time intervals deviate from fundamentally determined prices. Since then the majority of the bubble model literature still implicitly leaned on if not explicitly adopted the REH and its presumed axioms.

That the RE approach precludes the occurrence of bubbles and that the major assumptions (i.e., homogeneous, costless, and immediate information) are problematic is by now not a new insight. Indeed, it should be recognized that the goal of RE theories is not necessarily to describe how markets actually work but to instead describe how they would work if such simplifying assumptions are made. The RE approach thus defines in detail the environment in which there would be no bubbles and it defines those conditions which must be violated for bubbles to potentially be formed.

But beyond the generation of articles in prestigious journals, of what use is such theory in the normally tumultuous real world of trading and investments in which none of the assumptions hold true? Can this theory be applied so as to characterize, measure, explore causality, and forecast the occurrence of extreme market events? The value of a theory, it has been argued, lies not in the realism of its assumptions but in the quality of its predictions and in its simplicity.[10] The RE approach provides little in the way of predictive capabilities and is certainly not simple to apply.

6.2   ASSET BUBBLE AND CRASH ANALYSES

Financial asset bubbles are broadly seen as inflations of price beyond what would be expected based on fundamental economic features alone. But as Schaller and van Norden (1997) have remarked, there is still "no consensus on the correct model of fundamentals." And Bhar and Malliaris (2005) say that "the existence of bubbles is inherently an empirical issue that has not been settled yet."[11]

Herrera and Perry (2003, p. 131) write that studies generally attempt to define and then to analyze a bubble (B_t) "as the difference between the fundamentals-determined price (P^{pv}) and the observed price (P_t)...the fundamentals price can be expressed as the sum of discounted expected future cash flows – or dividends – to the holder of the asset so that $P_t = P^{pv} + B_t$," where B_t, "if it exists, can be expected to grow at the real rate of interest."

A key presumption in all such studies, however, is that investors have a solid grip on what the fundamental values actually *are*. Value investing expert Professor Bruce Greenwald of Columbia University has nonetheless said (in *Columbia Business School Alumni News*, July 20, 2005),

> *The DCF/CAPM methodology that business schools teach is a theoretically elegant formulation. But in practice, the margin of error makes it worthless for investing. These models depend not only on near-term cash flows, which can be projected reliably, but also on long-term cash flows and terminal values, which cannot. Terminal values rely on highly subjective assumptions of costs of capital and growth rates. Any error, however slight, in these variables can dramatically throw off valuations... Furthermore, DCF models ignore balance sheets, throwing away some of the most tangible, reliable and therefore valuable information available.[12]*

Yet the predominant neoclassical framework upon which almost all bubble studies depend is expressed in the overview by Campbell (2000):

> *In the absence of arbitrage opportunities, there exists a 'stochastic discount factor' that relates payoffs to market prices for all assets in the economy. This can be understood as an application of the Arrow-Debreu model of general equilibrium to financial markets. A state price exists for each state of nature at each date, and the market price of any financial asset is just the sum of its possible future payoffs, weighted by the appropriate state prices... if markets are complete then the stochastic discount factor is unique. If the stochastic discount factor is linearly related to a set of common shocks, then asset returns can be described by a linear factor model. If the economy has a representative agent with a well-defined utility function, then the SDF is related to the marginal utility of aggregate consumption.*[13]

Mixed into this academic mumbo jumbo are a lot of "ifs." In real life markets are not ever complete—that is, having a price today for every good and for all dates and contingencies. Markets, in fact, exist and operate only because of the presence of imperfect and asymmetrically held information. It seems that particularly in bubbles and crashes, utility functions may very well be confused, unstable (as in Fig. 1.2), conflicted ("should I join the crowd or stay out," etc.), and also nonlinear.

The basic starting point is usually an equation (or variant) of the form $P_t = E_t \sum_{i=1}^{\infty} \frac{D_{t+1}}{(1+R)^i}$, with the expected discounted future price assumed to have a limit of zero. If this assumption does not hold, and future prices are expected to grow forever at the rate of interest, a bubble term B_t that satisfies $B_t = E_t[B_{t+1}/(1+R)]$ is then added to the right-hand side of the previous equation. In a more abbreviated form, this can also be written as $B_t = \delta \cdot E_t[B_{t+1}]$, with δ the discount factor < 1.

This is the essence of the basic REH model, in which there are an infinite number of solutions and both a deterministic and a stochastic term (even though the stochastic term is not a logical necessity). As McQueen and Thorley (1994) write, "any price of the form, $p_t = p_t^* + b_t$ where $E_t[b_{t+1}] = (1 + r_{t+1})b_t$ is a solution to the equilibrium condition...Thus, the market price can deviate from the fundamental value by a rational speculative bubble factor, bt, if, on average, the factor grows at the required rate of return."[14]

What lies at the heart of this approach (with T representing the time at the end of the asset's life) is the following: If a bubble grows at a rate r_b such that $b_T = b_t (1 + r_b)^{T-t}$, and this rate of growth is below the discount rate so that $r_b < r$, then the bubble's present value is zero and the bubble cannot exist. But if the bubble's growth rate is above the discount rate so that $r_b > r$, the bubble's present value is infinite and, again, the bubble cannot exist because it would then outgrow the aggregate wealth of the economy.

Thus, for a finitely lived asset the only way in which the bubble component can survive without bursting is only if $r_b = r$, which means that the bubble's expected rate of growth is exactly equal to the asset's required rate of return. As suggested by Allen et al. (1993), the only way that a bubble can exist in the price of a finitely-lived asset without common knowledge and with binding short-sale constraints is if agents are asymmetrically informed about the asset's terminal dividend.

An unexpected by-product of the multiple equilibrium solutions that come out of REH models, says the survey by Adam and Szafarz (1992), is that deviations from the expected discounted value of dividends "could be interpreted as 'bubbles'...as reflecting financial market crazes, self-fulfilling prophecies and sunspots." Even they, however, note "that RE bubbles are only unambiguously defined within the context of a specific model. Their definition is not robust to small changes in model specification." There is, in other words, "an absence of a general definition for bubbles...researchers working with the same data base and identical models will not necessarily detect the 'same' bubbles." Also, "traditional bubbles seem to belong to the nonrational category and most RE bubbles can have shapes that have nothing to do with the popular view."

The key disconnect between what happens in the real world and in the theoretical is that theoretical models usually take for granted what has long been considered the fundamental law of economics—the arbitrage law of one price (LOOP). However, as Montier (2002, p. xv) observes, "arbitrage is not riskless, as so easily assumed in the traditional approach. Since this is the mechanism by which markets are forced to equilibrate, its absence suggests that markets and their 'fundamentals' can be divorced for long periods of time."

Effective arbitrage is often absent because there is a separation of information between the arbitrageurs and the providers of capital. Here the semantical trap is that if arbitrage is strictly defined as being a riskless and costless way to achieve profits that exceed the risk-free rate of return, then if there is any risk or cost there is no true arbitrage and some other description ought to be used.

Despite seemingly obvious opportunities, there have been notable instances in which arbitrage has gone missing. This is seen in equity carve-outs (e.g., 3Com/Palm), in parent company puzzles, (e.g., GM/Hughes Electronics), in closed-end mutual funds, in situations with twin securities (e.g., Royal Dutch/Shell and Unilever), and in discrepancies between cash and contract expiration prices in futures trading.[15] Many such discrepancies from a parity price dictated by LOOP can often be plus or minus 20% or more, which is far in excess of transaction costs for such large, liquid stocks traded on several international exchanges. Arbitrage or hedging breaks down in extreme market events because there is virtually always a substantial liquidity imbalance between the positions on one side as compared to those on the other.

That markets may not function anywhere near the ideal theoretical conditions is explained in Shleifer and Vishny (1997). Arbitrage will, indeed, always in reality be constrained by limits on time and/or capital, thereby making it "ineffective in extreme circumstances." But it is also constrained by the structural, regulatory, and sometimes political frictions that accompany the practice of short-selling—in which the financial asset is borrowed (for a fee) and time-sequentially sold first and bought back later (i.e., "covered"). Although there is nothing inherently nefarious and strange about this rather common practice, it has often in crises been incorrectly blamed by the public or demonized by politicians for causing and/or intensifying crashes.[16]

The apparent malleability and uncertainty surrounding the REH approach to "bubbles" is further underscored in Hamilton and Whiteman (1985), who plainly say that "many of the existing tests for the presence of speculative bubbles are not statistically valid...all such tests are subject to the admonition that what appears to be a speculative bubble could instead have arisen from rational agents responding solely to economic fundamentals not observed by the econometrician." As Froot and Obstfeld (1991) summarize, "econometric tests have not produced persuasive evidence that rational bubbles can help explain stock prices."

Rational Bubbles and Crashes

Rational speculative bubbles are described by Santoni (1987) as a condition that "might cause a persistent deviation in stock prices from the price consistent with the fundamentals." Other studies, such as that by McQueen and Thorley (1994), argue that even though investors might recognize prices as being in excess of fundamental values, they rationally remain in the market, believing that the bubble will continue to grow and thereby provide large positive returns. Hamilton and Whiteman (1985) argue that expectations leading to self-fulfilling speculative bubbles are consistent with rational, informed behavior.

Another example of hairsplitting appears in Hardouvelis (1988), who finds that a rational speculative bubble is characterized by the size of its expected rate of growth so that a rational speculative bubble is a special case of a speculative bubble. Here investors know that a bubble might end with a crash. But they nonetheless remain in the market because there appears to be a high probability that the bubble will continue to grow and therefore provide them with excess expected returns that are large enough to compensate for the probability of a crash and a large one-time negative return.[17] The implication (of such an implicit hazard-rate function) is that the bubble premium above the risk-free rate increases during the bubble's lifetime.[18]

In such studies, the term "rational" is used because the underlying model specifications are in sync with the theory of rational expectations and constant expected returns. Economic explanations of price bubbles have generally been divided by their differing assumptions concerning investor rationality.[19]

An extreme position is that of Tirole (1982), who says that "bubbles rely on the myopia of traders and that they disappear if traders adopt a truly dynamic maximizing behavior...speculation relies on inconsistent plans and is ruled out by rational expectations...in a fully dynamic REE [rational expectations equilibrium], bubbles do not exist." The exception, Tirole (p. 1179) then adds, is that "price bubbles may still exist with an infinite number of traders, e.g., with overlapping generations."

Thus, with overlapping generation (OLG) models and no informational imperfections, bubbles can develop in a dynamically inefficient economy. But rational bubbles cannot occur in assets that have a finite life because no rational trader will, in the period just prior to the end of the asset's life, willingly pay any more than the asset's discounted terminal value. In effect, Tirole presents a strict set of particular conditions under which no bubbles can form.

Santos and Woodford (1997) also "show the nonexistence of asset pricing bubbles under fairly general assumptions...known examples of bubbles depend on rather special circumstances." It is argued that bubbles dependent on the existence of infinitely many traders are exceptional and fragile and unlikely to survive. Yet Allen and Gorton (1993) adopt a different approach and "assume all agents are rational but they populate an imperfect world which is characterized by asymmetric information...asymmetric information can lead to firms making inefficient investment decisions."[20] Their model suggests that portfolio managers are instead "churning their clients' portfolios in the hope of a speculative profit," hence the possibility of "churning bubbles."

Allen et al. (1993) discuss how under rational expectations "bubbles can still exist when there is a finite horizon provided there are an infinite number of trading opportunities." Their model provides an example "in which the market price of a security is above the present value of its future dividends even though every agent is rational and knows the dividends with certainty. The reason is that agents do not know other agents' beliefs." Here, the fundamental value is the price at which every agent would willingly hold or buy the asset even if forced to do so forever.

Perhaps the most important assumption of most models—and one that is most at odds with the inductive approach of Werner (2005) and with what happens in the real world of asymmetrical information—is presented by Blanchard and Watson (1982), who say that "at least after having observed the price, all agents have the same information....bubbles can exist even in this case and...these bubbles would remain even if agents had differential information."[21] But "[T]o be rational, such an increase in the price must continue forever, making such a deterministic bubble implausible."[22]

A review of the theory of rational bubbles is given in Diba and Grossman (1987, 1988), who wrote that "[P]ositive rational bubbles are empirically plausible only if, despite explosive conditional expectations, the probability is small that a rational bubble would become arbitrarily large." Diba (1990, p. 23) also says, "...the proposition that such bubbles are present in long time series of U.S. aggregate stock prices is tenuous." Equilibrium-based model relating to share turnover is also explored in Scheinkman and Xiong (2003). And Wu (1997) suggests that estimated rational stochastic bubble components may explain much of the deviation of stock prices from simple present-value models.

Brunnermeier (2001, p. xii), meanwhile, provides a review of the field focusing "exclusively on models that assume that all agents are rational and act in their own self-interest." Citing earlier studies by LeRoy and Porter (1981) and Shiller (1989), he goes on (p. 55) to say,

...Commonly known bubbles generally do not arise in equilibrium...One can envision a situation where everybody knows that the price is above the fundamental value, that is, the bubble is mutual knowledge, yet each individual does not know that the others know it too.

Breaks in the rational bubble approach are nonetheless seen in the earlier cited work of Noguchi (1994) and also of Asako (1991) with regard to the Japanese land inflation of the late 1980s. Although Asako begins with a fairly conventional REH overlapping generations approach, he appears in the end to encounter difficulty in accepting that investors are always rational. And Noguchi (1994) shows (Tables 2.1 and 2.2) how investors reacted rationally (but not in the rational valuation sense) to the financial market disequilibrium caused by a huge flood of bank credit that could not be readily absorbed by the real (nonfinancial) economy.

As will be further illustrated, it seems that the rational bubble approach tends to readily disintegrate into definitional circularities that can never serve as a sound theoretical base. Although it is entirely plausible to have some rational investors participate in an irrational environment and although rational behavior within speculative bubbles is possible, the very idea of a bubble requires that the vast majority of investors—even those who begin by being rational—are inevitably swept up in the excitement of the moment (and of the price movement). The resulting auto- and cross-correlations (i.e., synchronizations) among speculators become, in the words of Townsend (1983), a game of "forecasting the forecasts of others."

Also, because pervasive emotionality is found to always accompany what is informally recognized in retrospect as having been a bubble, a rational bubble cannot exist as an apt description of reality. Professional money managers, for example, may be entirely rational in their ulterior economic motives for needing to participate in a bubble's price momentum: They are afraid of losing investor accounts, of being embarrassed by underperformance relative to their peer group (index tracking error risk), or of losing bonuses or jobs. But those are emotional issues different from what the "rational bubble" literature has typically explored.[23] "After a bubble has continued for a while, many people have become committed to the investments – emotionally and reputationally as well as financially," says Shiller (2002a, p. 21).

Of course, the market doesn't know or care about your reasons or motives for trading. When you buy a stock at a vastly inflated price relative to its fundamental value—whatever that value is or however it is determined—you may be an investor whose motives are entirely rational for many reasons outside of or apart from the specific valuation issues related to that particular trade. Perhaps your underperforming portfolio mix, for example, is too heavily weighted in the wrong industry sectors and you need to quickly rebalance. Emphasis is then not on buying shares of companies prospectively earning the highest long-term returns on invested capital (ROIC), but instead on beating an index short-term. So, despite what you think are high prices, it may still be quite rational (and legally defensible as "prudent") to join the herd. The only (inherently imperfect information) problem then is that you may not know when to get out!

By participating in this way you are further contributing in either bubble or crash mode, to the observed irrationality or emotionality, in either bubble or crash mode, of the market itself. In joining the manic crowd and adding to the non-Walrasian quantity-rationed disequilibrium (i.e., the "short-side determines the price")—for all intents and purposes and for all the present and future bubble economists to forever see and study—you've left a measurable pricing footprint in the data snow of the market.

Other Studies

It is proposed in Adam and Szafarz (1992) that rational bubbles can exhibit an infinite variety of shapes, including those that may not follow the popular definition of a bubble and with many of the traditional bubbles belonging to the nonrational category. In assuming that an asset's fundamental value can actually be determined, the overview by Flood and Garber (1994) shows that models used to test for the presence of bubbles are generally inadequate for the purpose of distinguishing between a bubble and a change in market fundamentals. And to this end, a cointegration test which rejects the bubble hypothesis as based on the Shiller (1992) data for stock prices and dividends was developed by Taylor and Peel (1998).

The papers by McQueen and Thorley (1994) and by Chan et al. (1998) are also of interest. In the first paper, the researchers test duration dependence by transforming returns into series of run lengths on positive and negative observed abnormal returns and find that as the length of the run of positive abnormal returns increases, the probability that the run will end *decreases* (i.e., there is a negative hazard function). This, they find, is consistent with the existence of bubbles (and also with the research of Sect. 6.4).[24]

In the second paper, tests are also conducted for duration dependence and conditional negative skewness in runs of positive returns for Asian stock markets. This study provides only marginal support for the existence of rational speculative bubbles in the six Asian markets analyzed.

The analysis of the 1990s TMT bubble in Lee (2004, pp. 39–65) is complementary in that it distinguishes "cyclical" from "structural" bubbles, that is, those in which the bubble lasts long enough and is large enough to spur substantial investment and development in sectors ancillary to the focus of the bubble itself. Haacke (2004) similarly attempts to differentiate between speculative price bubbles that do not produce anything and investment bubbles in which real businesses are built. And Bohl (2001) reviews attempts to find bubbles and bubble thresholds in securities price series data. After sophisticated statistical tests, he finds evidence in favor of present-value models (but without supporting the Evans (1991) hypothesis which posits the existence of periodically collapsing bubbles).[25]

A survey by LeRoy (2004) concludes that "[W]ithin the neoclassical paradigm there is no obvious way to derail the chain of reasoning that excluded bubbles. An alternative to the full neoclassical paradigm is to think about bubbles in a rational-agent setting...but to break off the analysis arbitrarily at some point." Friedman and Abraham (2009) use this breakoff approach by assuming a model that is not always in equilibrium and that makes risk exposure responsive to a payoff gradient that incorporates lessons learned from historical losses. Thus, when losses have been small for a long time, riskier portfolio profiles are adopted.

The presence of bubbles in the bull markets of the 1920s and 1980s is further examined by Santoni (1987), who uses a runs test in which the number of sequential observations that are greater than or less than the sample mean is analyzed. Both the EMH and random-walk theories of course imply that observed changes in stock prices are not correlated with one another, whereas the existence of a bubble would suggest the opposite. Santoni concludes that the behavior of stock prices during the 1920s and 1980s does not support the existence of bubbles. The findings of Santoni thus oppose McQueen's and Thorley's.

Blanchard and Watson search for bubbles in the gold market using runs and tail tests to analyze the distribution of changes in prices. Runs will tend to be longer than for a purely random sequence, making the total number of runs smaller over the sample—the same idea that is later explored in Sect. 10.4. And crashes will result in a distribution with fat tails generated by large outliers. Although results from their runs tests reveal no evidence indicating the presence of bubbles, their tail and variance bounds tests do suggest the presence of bubbles.[26]

West's approach, however, differs in that it attempts to test a no-bubble hypothesis separately from a no-misspecification hypothesis. Using long-term annual data for the S&P 500 and the DJIA, he rejects the hypothesis of no speculative bubble, but fails to reject the hypothesis of no model misspecification—all of which in plain English means that he thinks there is evidence of a bubble but he's not quite sure what it is or how it might be statistically characterized.

In Froot and Obstfeld (1991), the presence of a specific type of rational bubble depends exclusively on aggregate dividends. Such bubbles are "intrinsic" because all of their variability is derived in a nonlinear deterministic way from economic fundamentals (i.e., the level of real dividends) and none is from extraneous factors. The claim is that these intrinsic bubbles provide a more plausible empirical account of deviations from present-value pricing than do the traditional examples of rational bubbles. Their estimates "reveal a strong nonlinear relationship between prices and dividends, which can be interpreted as a rejection of the hypothesis that there is no bubble." The rational bubble framework is further linked to credit expansion factors in Martin and Ventura (2015).

Several studies have also applied similar techniques to other asset classes. Meese (1986), for instance, found mixed evidence for bubbles in the foreign exchange markets, saying, "[R]ationality of both behavior and of expectations often does not imply that the price of an asset be equal to its fundamental value...there can be rational deviations of the price from this value." And Woo's 1987 study suggests the existence of speculative bubbles in the bilateral exchange rate of the US dollar and other major currencies and finds that bubbles occur only when fundamentals change as a result of uncertainty in the foreign exchange markets. Wu (1995), however, casts doubt on these claims.

Evidence of speculative bubbles in agricultural commodities appears in Gutierrez (2013), and a paper by Etienne et al. (2014) found that over the long term, agricultural markets experienced episodes of bubble behavior, but for only relatively brief periods. Blanchard (1979) was among the first to develop a rational expectations model involving gold. Johansen and Sornette (1999d) also found speculative bubbles in gold that led up to crashes, and Miller and Ratti (2009) suggested the presence of oil price bubbles since the early 2000s. In addition, both Srivastava and Satchell (2012) and Kräussl et al. (2016) examined the possibility of art market bubbles and provided evidence of their existence.[27]

Although most of these studies come at the problem from an REH perspective, some of them employ notions of behavioral finance—a rapidly expanding and useful field, but one still in need of a unifying theory. An example is from Smith et al. (1988), in which 14 of 22 behavioral experiments exhibited "price bubbles followed by crashes relative to intrinsic dividend value...." Some of these laboratory experiments suggested convergence to rational expectations, and in a later paper, Porter and Smith (1992) found that "while bubbles almost always occur with inexperienced traders, bubbles are dampened with experienced traders."[28] At least in experimental settings, it seems that asset markets tend to exhibit bubbles and crashes.

Critics of the EMH and CAPM often note that market participants all have differing time horizons: The day trader usually speculates on technical price chart movements that are of little or no consequence to fundamentals-driven long-term institutional investors. De Grauwe and Grimaldi (2003) found in computer simulations that interactions of the two groups can spontaneously create bubbles and crashes. Issues concerning the synchronization of trading are explored in Abreu and Brunnermeier (2001), in Brunnermeier and Nagel (2004), and in Temin and Voth (2004).

A newer offshoot of behavioral finance is known as evolutionary finance and is based on time-series analysis of mutation and selection rather than on the cross-sectional analysis of returns as in mean-variance optimization (MVO) and CAPM theory. For instance, Evstigneev et al. (2006) demonstrate that a stock market is "evolutionary stable if and only if stocks are evaluated by expected relative dividends." And Hens and Schenk-Hoppé (2001) analyze the evolution of portfolio rules in incomplete markets.[29]

Still, none of these studies use the approach of the present research, the goal of which is to identify and measure extreme market events using an elasticity of price variance concept. As shall be seen, by this means, the equity risk premium

(ERP) elasticity of variance inductively captures both the underlying funda-mental value relationships and also the psychological/emotional features that are present in all bubbles and crashes.[30]

A representative selected summary of the studies mentioned in this and the following sections appears in Table 6.1.

Table 6.1 Representative studies of bubbles, crashes, and tests

Models	Approach	Type/comment
Bubbles		
Adam and Szafarz (1992)	RE	Survey
Allen et al. (1993)	RE	Asymmetric information
Angeletos and La'O (2013)	RE with Walrasian unique equilibrium	Shocks akin to sunspots, extrinsic shocks = "sentiments"
Asako (1991)	RE with OLG model	Explores Japanese land bubble and concludes it was not always rational
Blanchard and Watson (1982)	RE with periodically collapsing bubbles	Launched series of bubble articles
Campbell (2000)		Survey
Diba and Grossman (1988)	Rational bubble component	Explosive conditional expectations
Froot and Obstfeld (1991)	Intrinsic—i.e., modified RE bubbles driven by fundamentals	Separates present-value and bubble components of stock prices
Hardouvelis (1988)	Bubble premium	It's rational to stay in market if it seems highly probable that a bubble will grow
Kodres and Pritsker (2002)	REH and financial contagion	Contagion and exposures to shared macroeconomic risks and RE equilibrium
Lux and Sornette (2002)	REH	Fat tails and power laws suggest bubbles are a special case of multiplicative stochastic processes
Martin and Ventura (2015)	Rational bubble framework	Closed economy credit bubbles
Meese (1986)	"Fundamentals are just part of the story"	Finds bubbles in FX markets
Santos and Woodford (1997)	Intertemporal competitive equilibrium	Bubbles only under special circumstances
Shiller (1981)	Price and dividend series do not grow by the same amounts—variance bounds violated	Began new branch of investigation
Tirole (1982)	RE equilibrium and OLGs	No bubbles in infinite-horizon models with finite number of agents, but bubbles with infinite number of agents (OLG)
Crashes		
Brunnermeier (2001)	REH	Four different crash category models

(*continued*)

Table 6.1   (continued)

Models	Approach	Type/comment
Frankel (2008)	Adaptive expectations	Rational and naïve investors interact
Gennotte and Leland (1990)	RE and low liquidity	Asymmetric info causes low liquidity/equilibrium-based
Lee (1998)	Information avalanches	Agents learn from the action of others
Shiller et al. (1996)	Survey of changes in expectations	Nikkei crash due to changes in price expectations
Tests		
Caginalp et al. (2000)	Price momentum	Behavioral finance/experimental
Evans (1991)	Econometric weaknesses	Survey/tests unable to detect a class of rational bubbles
Flood and Hodrick (1990)	Self-fulfilling prophecy (i.e., sunspots) within an RE framework	Survey/tests are misspecified
McQueen and Thorley (1994)	Rational speculative bubbles and duration of runs	High probability of returns compensates for probability of a crash
West (1987)	Hausman spec test compares expected PDV parameters	Bubbles exist
West (1988b)	Standard models do not explain volatility	Volatility survey

A similar but more detailed table appears in the appendix to Taipalus (2012)

Testing Methods

General tests for bubbles, as discussed in Van Norden (1996), began to appear in papers such as those of Meese (1986) and West (1987). But beginning in the early 1990s, such tests became more specific, yielding information about the kind of behavior that produces significant evidence of bubbles. Yet, as Froot and Obstfeld (1991) have observed, "…general specification tests have been employed in the hope that bubbles can be detected without the need to take a stand on a specific bubble form. Even though these tests may have low power, they nevertheless reject the no-bubble null hypothesis frequently. However, they cannot reveal the precise source of rejection…"

In referring to the REH approach, Flood and Hodrick (1990) suggest that testing for (rational) bubbles is difficult because, given that "…the current price depends on the expectations of the future price and the expectation of the future price depends on the current price, the simple theory cannot determine the market price." They contend that "no econometric test has yet demonstrated that bubbles are present in the data…Bubble tests require a well-specified model of equilibrium expected return that has yet to be developed, and this makes inference about bubbles quite tenuous."[31]

Homm and Breitung (2012) review several tests for rational bubbles and assess their power properties. As rational bubbles supposedly lead to an explosive component in stock prices, "a change from a random walk to an explosive regime is considered to be an indication for the emergence of a speculative bubble." Chow-type break test procedures were found to perform relatively well in detecting such regime switches.

The literature on testing for bubbles also includes a regression method developed by Scott (1985) to determine whether aggregate stock prices are excessively volatile.[32] Sola and Driffill (1998) showed that in representing a time series of dividends, what is known as a Markov-switching model works better than other representations such as were used, for instance, in Froot and Obstfeld (1991).[33] Many rational bubble testing procedures, including those in Diba and Grossman (1986), Evans (1991), and Charemza and Deadman (1995), also used so-called unit root tests in which a discrete-time autoregressive process of order p is specified. Sophisticated econometric tests also appear in Voth (2003), who in using a price/dividend ratio found no bubble in the German stock market of 1926–1927.[34]

Indirect tests, according to Brooks and Katsaris (2003), are "based on the identification of bubbles through an examination of the distributional properties of actual prices (or returns) and fundamental values." This is in contrast to direct tests, which "examine the presence of specific forms of speculative bubbles by identifying the presence of bubble-like behaviour in financial and macroeconomic data."[35] Brooks and Katsaris say that generally, the "direct tests find mixed evidence of speculative bubbles...[and]...assume that bubble crashes are exogenous events."

Even from these limited examples, however, it might already be surmised that test procedures and results are often highly sensitive to the form of the underlying equilibrium model being propositioned.[36] Many economic time series are not stationary as their means and variances wander over the entire length of the series.[37] Much of the work on testing for bubbles is, accordingly, tied in some way or another to the stationarity issue—which is of far less concern when analyzing data on returns than on prices.[38]

A volatility-related approach is presented in Jarrow et al. (2011). This paper modeled a risky asset's price with a stochastic differential equation as applied to a volatility estimation method. The method appears to lead to the detection of asset bubbles in real time.

Chaos theory has also been applied in the testing of bubbles and their related aspects. An important study of this type, for example, is that by Park and Whang (1999) in which what is known as a Lyapunov-exponent test is used to distinguish between random-walk models and those generated by a chaotic system. For various stock price indexes, the authors are able to strongly reject the random-walk hypothesis and to suggest chaotic behavior, whereas such behavior is not indicated for foreign exchange and interest-rate series.

Another pertinent approach, used by Serletis and Dormaar (1996) to test for chaos in futures markets, employs the Lyapunov-exponent estimating methodology (for short data sets) that was developed by Nychka et al. (1992). Serletis and Dormaar detected chaos (i.e., positiveness of the dominant

Lyapunov exponent) in only two of the 13 weekly futures markets analyzed (Australian dollar and Japanese yen). As they note, "the implication would be that profitable nonlinearity-based trading rules exist...raising questions about the efficient market hypothesis."

Studies of bubbles using chaos concepts have, furthermore, been combined with the rational expectations approach. Of particular interest, because of the juxtaposition of rational expectations and elements of chaos theory, is a study by Johansen and Sornette (1999b), in which it was found, through application of a proposed rational expectations model, that in emerging Latin American market bubbles and crashes, log-periodic power laws adequately describe the bubbles.

Flow of Funds Factors

Perhaps bubbles might be better understood not through ever more complicated attempts at model gymnastics but instead through simple analysis of the flow of funds factors that influence relative supply and demand for shares. Evans (2003, p. 1) used this idea to investigate the great rise in US equity prices between 1982 and 2000 and concluded that "sizable international and domestic demand flows in the face of a shrinking supply of corporate equity via share repurchases, leveraged buyouts and merger activity," contributed importantly to the bubble environment. For this way of thinking, the necessary condition for a bubble to emerge is, as Binswanger (1999, p. 189) has noted, that there be at least a constant if not a shrinking net supply of equity. Reductions of asset floats (i.e., tradeable shares or net supply) were shown by Hong et al. (2006) to be related to bubble formations and high volatility.

From 1982 onward, as net share supply began to shrink, US households had also begun to massively channel savings into equities through mutual fund purchases (to a much greater extent than through pension funds). And international capital flows began to favor US financial markets and products. Especially during the 1990s, for instance, the large Japanese market was not at all competitive in attracting new inflows of capital, while European markets were choppy, and other Asian markets were still relatively small and experiencing sporadic bouts of disintermediation.

The Fed's flow of funds data, illustrated in Fig. 6.1, indicate the extent of shrinkage of corporate equity outstanding—enabled and encouraged by the November 1982 liberalization of SEC Rule 10b-18 concerning corporate share repurchases—and mutual fund growth trends. Rest-of-world (ROW) net equity purchases were also relatively large in the second half of the 1990s and then again in 2004. The great equity shrinkage—meaning fewer new issues and more corporate share repurchases—continued up through the market's peak in 2007, when despite aggressive capitalization reductions, stock prices nevertheless continued to decline severely into the market's low of March 2009.[39]

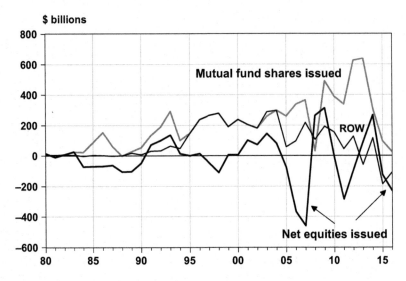

Fig. 6.1 Flow of funds accounts of the United States, net equities and mutual fund shares issued, and net rest-of-world (ROW) US equities purchased, 1980–2016. (Data Source: US Federal Reserve System, Board of Governors, Tables F.223 and F.224 in Financial Accounts of the United States—Z.1 releases)

Net share reductions tend to accompany market peaks because that's when corporations are relatively flush with excess cash from operations and, along with other market participants, are most optimistic about their own prospects. In the yield-chasing years, this effect was enhanced by near-zero interest rates which enabled share buybacks to be financed with low-cost borrowings. Total US corporation share repurchases between 2009 and 2017 summed to more than $4 trillion, thus providing a cushion against any market corrections and also support for rising equity prices.[40]

Crashes

Brunnermeier (2001, p. 166) approaches bubbles and crashes with a focus on presumptions as to how rational agents would be expected to behave and then groups theoretical models that purport to explain crashes into four categories.

1. Liquidity-shortage models
2. Multiple equilibria and sunspot models
3. Bursting bubble models
4. Lumpy information aggregation models

All of these models "differ in their prediction of the price path after a crash. Depending on the model, the crash can be a correction and the stock market can remain low for a substantial amount of time or it can immediately bounce back." As has already been suggested, however, the assumption that all agents behave "rationally" at such emotionally intense market-pricing junctures is arguable.

Lee (1998) sees "discrepancies of financial data from the standard theory drawing from rational expectations" and instead focuses on market microstructure theories that attempt to explain price movements in terms of financial market trading arrangements. The concept is that "[D]ue to information aggregations failure, hidden information gets accumulated in the market which may be revealed by a small trigger, yielding a high volatility in the absence of an accompanying event." In the Lee model, agents learn from the action of other people's choices, which is, in other words, herding in a crash. Even if agents are rational, Lee says, a "crash may happen due to a failure in information aggregation."

Crash events have also been extensively explored by Johansen and Sornette (1999a, b, c, d) (J&S) who demonstrated that unusual outcomes—a one-day 22.6% decline in the Dow-Jones Industrials on October 19, 1987, followed by a one-day rebound on October 21 of 9.7%—cannot be truly captured by standard statistical distribution theories. Through this body of work, highlighted in Sornette (2003a, p. 50), even the relatively rare daily advances and declines of 5% or so for the major stock market indexes occur far more frequently than would be expected by going very far out on the tails of, say, a Lévy distribution model. For instance, using the normal (Gaussian) types of distributions or standard variants thereof, "a daily return amplitude of more than 4% should be typically observed only once in 63 years, while a return amplitude of more than 5% should never be seen in our limited history." Yet in late 2008, there were several days in which many markets moved 4% a day in either direction.

These studies on crashes (including several additional models surveyed in Brunnermeier 2001, pp. 165–89) suggest that although independence between successive returns may be the proper way to describe markets most of the time, large declines may not be independent, that is, there are "pockets of predictability." J&S label such large changes in returns as "outliers" that operate on a different event scale and that are to be diagnosed and analyzed using nonparametric power laws (described below).

Indeed, according to J&S, crashes do not lie in the fat tails of a distribution used to describe noncrisis market activities, but are instead actually generated from an entirely different distribution—that is, one that an exponential or even a stretched exponential does not explain.[41] As discussed in Montier (2002, p. 141), this is important "because it means that we can focus on techniques that isolate crash periods rather than worrying about the whole distribution." According to this line of reasoning, traditional models cannot reveal the true nature of the market because crashes behave much more analogously to earthquakes, turbulence in fluids, and other such physical crises than to the models based on random walk, EMH, or other similarly constructed statistical concepts.[42]

J&S and other researchers including Lux (1995) adopt a probabilistic approach, defining the hazard rate that a crash will occur in the next measurement interval as a probability conditional on the fact that a crash has not yet happened. In this respect, the hazard rate can be taken as a type of proxy for the entropy state of the system (explained below).[43] Frankel (2008), meanwhile, develops a theory explaining how crashes can occur without fundamental news through the interaction of rational and naïve investors.

An overview of the different theoretical approaches to bubbles is presented in Table 6.2, where the deductively derived REH is compared to the inductively derived variance elasticity theory that is later developed. Although the prevalent REH depends on the empirically questionable assumption of "rationality," the proposed (in Part III) variance elasticity theory does not require any such presuppositions as it is based on the readily observed and demonstrable fact that the variance of price changes (and thus of returns) will, in all extreme events, always tend to increase (e.g., Fig. P2) as compared to its recent history.

Table 6.2 Bubble theory approaches compared

	REH	Behavioral finance	Chaos	Variance elasticity[a]
Key concept	Rational investors, EUH	Bounded rationality, people herd, anchor, etc.	Prices are attracted onto a new trajectory	Asymmetric information, incomplete markets
Model implementation	Net PV + "bubble" component	Searches for anomalies	Seeks sensitive dependence on initial conditions	Quantity is short-sided, thus expands price variance
Equilibrium	Walrasian	Not applicable	Conditional dynamic stability, depends on parameters and time	Never happens in real world, by this theory, improbable
Pros	Fits with traditional EMH/CAPM	Realistically describes human behavior	Conforms to visual aspects, power laws, fractal nature of price changes	No axioms need be assumed. Conforms to power laws and fractals and consistent with short-side rationing. Picks up human behavior aspects. Provides consistent statistical measurements across time and price scales. Relationships to different economic measures and ERPs[b] are enabled

(*continued*)

Table 6.2   (continued)

	REH	Behavioral finance	Chaos	Variance elasticity[a]
Cons	Not a good practical description. Requires assumption of rational man axiom. Empirically indecisive	Difficult to link to economic models	Not consistent with OLG[c] and long-term mean-reversion models	Is new and not yet empirically well developed. Nonlinear curve fitting required. Highly significant parameters (1%, 5%) not often estimated

Malliaris (2012) breaks this literature into four categories:

- Papers that assume all investors to be rational and have identical information. In these, finite bubbles cannot exist;

- Investors have rational expectations but asymmetric information. Bubbles might develop more easily under such conditions;

- Investors might be either rational or behavioral in reactions and bubbles can last a long time;

- Traders have heterogeneous beliefs and bubbles can emerge

[a]Concept developed in Chap. 10

[b]Equity risk premium

[c]Overlapping generations

6.3   Math Takes Over

Power Laws

As has been seen, a mainstay of recent stock price research is that returns may belong to a family of what are known as stable Paretian distributions. These distributions are characterized by undefined (or infinite) variance and were described by Mandelbrot (1960, 1964). Mandelbrot's early work on fractals (preceded by R.N. Elliott in the 1930s) made it clear that in terms of financial market behavior during bubbles and crashes, the complex patterns appear to be like those seen in many other large-scale catastrophic events.[44]

Such events are governed by power laws—fractal scalings in Mandelbrot's geometry—that are known and described mathematically as $1/f$ noise (or fractals in time, where f represents frequency).[45] The patterns are similarly found in a variation of Pareto's study of income distributions (that in discrete form sometimes goes by the name of Zipf's law) as shown in Fig. 6.2.[46] Pareto observed that the frequency of occurrence of some event (P)—taken as a function of the rank (i) when the rank is determined by the frequency of occurrence—is a power-law function $P_i \sim 1/i^\alpha$ with the exponent α close to unity. Indeed, were the largest price changes in the S&P 500 measured over a day, a week, a year, or a decade to be ranked in descending order, the same type of power-law pattern would be seen.

Fig. 6.2 Pareto (Zipf's) law conceptualized (Prob[X > x] ~ $x^{-\alpha}$). In actuality, the representation is concave to the origin, that is, it is depressed (i.e., sags) in the middle

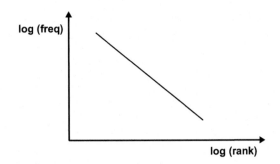

Although the underlying mechanisms that generate them are not well understood, such power-law relationships have been useful in describing a wide variety of natural and financial phenomena including earthquakes (e.g., for every hundred quakes of magnitude five on the Richter scale, there might be ten of magnitude six and one of magnitude seven) and the number of months in which variations in commodity or stock price series were of a certain amount.[47] Small variations would be common whereas large variations would be relatively scarce.

Given that Mandelbrot (1964) had found stock market returns to have fat-tailed distributions—which implies the presence of form invariance under addition and thus self-similarity—the applicability to all of financial economics is obvious.[48] That is, if, as is suspected, market bubble-characteristic behavior does indeed follow a power law, then bubbles—like seacoast lines viewed from different elevations—must also be fractal, exhibiting self-similarity (or self-affinity) on different scales.[49]

Conversely, if bubbles are in fact fractal, they must then demonstrate autoregressive features and be misspecified in using random-walk/Brownian motion models. As Mandelbrot and Hudson (2004, p. 169) assert, in economics, "time, not space, is the scaling factor." Under certain circumstances, bubbles can, they say (p. 203), "be entirely rational and flow from the entwined effects of long-term dependence and discontinuity."

Look, for example, at the two stock price charts of 1990s tech favorite Cisco Systems that are shown in Fig. 6.3. If you hide the bottom *x*-axis dates, the self-similarity on different time scales is impressive, even though on the top left is a *monthly* chart dating from 1991 through 2000, on the top right is a *daily* chart from 1998:06 through 1999:06, and on the bottom is a 100-*minute* chart for April 8, 2008, between 12:51 and 14:31 hours. Such self-similarities on different time scales are often easy to spot on charts of actively traded indexes and stocks.

As shall be seen in the chapters that follow, the fractal, power law, and scaling aspects are all tied to the self-organizing behavior of crowds – that is, to the herding that is the hallmark of all extreme market events.[50] As Strogatz (2003, p. 255) writes,

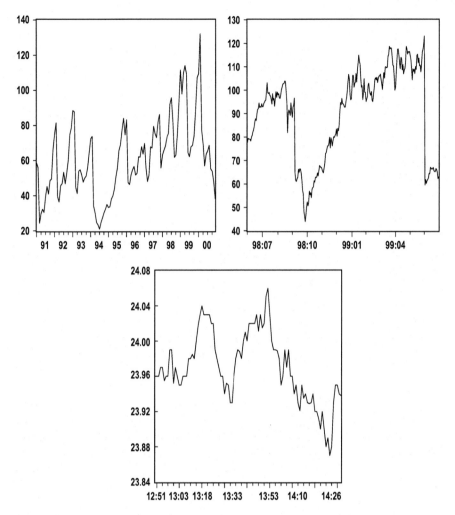

Fig. 6.3   Cisco Systems, Inc. (CSCO) share prices in $US, monthly 1991 through 2000, left; daily, 1998:06 through 1999:06, middle; and 100 minutes, April 8, 2008, bottom. (Source data: Yahoo.com and Bloomberg)

> *[From] a purely mathematical perspective, a power law signifies nothing in particu-lar…[But]…power laws hint that a system may be organizing itself. They arise at phase transitions, when a system is poised at the brink, teetering between order and chaos. They arise in fractals, when an arbitrarily small piece of a complex shape is a microcosm of the whole.*

Chaos Concepts

From visual inspection alone, it appears that prices in bubbles (and crashes) are being pulled magnetically toward a trajectory—an attractor of some sort. Despite occasional sell-offs (collapsing bubbles, perhaps), the price continues to persistently approximate (i.e., trace) such an attractor's path: Attractors occupy only certain zones within a bounded phase space, with a chaotic attractor showing zones of recurrent behavior that is reproducible.[51]

Is there order behind the disorder that characterizes the behavior of share prices in the midst of a bubble and its subsequent demise? Chaos is a dynamical systems theory that is based on nonlinear relationships, often simple but ironically deterministic, as in the case of the famous logistics equation $x_{t+1} = kx_t(1-x_t)$, where k is the control parameter, a positive real number. Such deterministic systems create apparent randomness but depend on neither noise in the time-series data nor complexity.[52]

Nonetheless, the systems are able to spawn time series that, as Silverberg and Lehnert (1996, p. 59) explain, "mimic the properties of a stochastic process even though they are generated deterministically. The standard methods of linear time-series analysis are not, in general, sufficient to distinguish the two types of mechanisms."[53]

As Brock (2000) explains, "[C]haos theory is the study of deterministic difference (differential) equations that display Sensitive Dependence on Initial Conditions (SDIC) to generate time paths that look like random behavior... nonlinear prediction methods can do a good job on short term predictions when chaos or other nonlinearity is present."[54]

Given the somewhat controversial and conflicting evidence of chaotic behavior presented in various studies of economic time series, applications in this area are far from foolproof. Mills (1993, p. 126) provides important caveats in suggesting that such tests are designed to distinguish between linear and nonlinear *stochastic* dynamics, but that they are not as yet capable of distinguishing nonlinear stochastic dynamics from *deterministic* chaotic dynamics. "[T]he presence of important non-linear dynamics may...make standard linear rational expectations models quite misleading."

According to Brock (2000), "... the evidence is weak for financial data and for macroeconomic data for the presence of chaos which can be short term predicted..." Possible pitfalls in the application of chaos concepts also appear in the study of Ramsey et al. (1990), in which tests using the typically small data sets available to economists and conducted through an analysis of correlation dimension characteristics, showed no evidence of the presence of simple chaotic attractors.[55]

In all, it seems that many of the studies attempting to find chaotic attractors in market price data series might not be looking in the right places; perhaps such attractors might be more readily revealed in trading volume or variance elasticity series.

Brownian Motions

The wide assortments of scholarly theories and tests have more recently been augmented by the deeply mathematical—but nonetheless still faultily rooted rational, EMH, and equilibrium-seeking—approaches to options and other derivatives pricing models that have emerged from the early 1970s' pioneering work of Fischer Black, Myron Scholes, and Robert C. Merton.[56] Models of stochastic processes based on Brownian motion – originally a descrption of how gas molecules in a closed container randomly bump into each other—also serve as a way to mathematically describe random walks.[57] In these, the emphasis has been on development of arbitrage and hedging strategies and tactics, volatility relationships, and only incidentally on studies of extreme events.

However, the most fundamental and damaging aspect of trying to apply Brownian motion analysis to financial—and to even science-based research—is that Brownian motion approaches (and extensions, including fractional and multifractional versions fBm, mBm), are all based on assumptions of a closed system that has been largely isolated from the variability and fluctuations of the surrounding environment. Remove this isolation assumption—meaning that people influence other people, that there is herding and memory of previous price levels and investment performance outcomes, that there are important anomalies (see Chap. 7)—and the entire random-walk/stochastic modeling and Markowitz mean-variance and diversification framework collapses into an analytical abyss.[58]

Volatility has been turned into an asset class. But there nonetheless remain prominent and knowledgeable skeptics about the usefulness of all the fancy math.[59] The models themselves, no matter how smartly designed, all unavoidably and invisibly include what's known as "model risk" wherein variance is neither constant nor consistently predictable.[60]

6.4   Conclusions

Economists have spent substantial time and effort in attempts to understand asset price bubbles. The literature is by now voluminous and divides generally into rational expectations and behavioral approaches. The differences often hinge on the distinctions, explained by Friedman (1979), between information *exploitation* and information *availability*. Brav and Heaton (2002) write,

> *Inside a rational expectations world, rational investors make optimal statistical decisions …about which they have all relevant structural knowledge…Outside a rational expectations world, rational investors still make optimal statistical decisions, but they lack critical structural knowledge.*

Many different aspects have been (sometimes) exhaustingly investigated, but the major quarrel, says Brunnermeier (2001, p. 47),

> *…relates to the question of whether large changes in prices are due to shifts in the fundamentals or departures of the asset price from fundamental value. The difficulty lies in determining the fundamental value of an asset … (which) is generally not exogenously given; it is endogenously determined in equilibrium. This fundamental value determines whether a bubble occurred at all and which component of the price is due to a bubble.[61]*

The vast literature is thus fixated on equilibrium modeling that has extended from the highly conditional mathematics of the 1950s Arrow-Debreu efficient-market framework (using Brouwer's theorem) to the 1960s and 1970s rational expectations approach of Robert Lucas and Roy Radner (which fortified Arrow-Debreu by incorporating aspects of uncertainty and expectations).[62]

As presented, however, in Jovanovic et al. (2017, p. 98), econophysics alternatively suggests that financial equilibrium is an entirely false will-of-the-wisp premise. "...econophysicists do not reject the concept of equilibrium, but they do not assume a convergence toward such a state....equilibrium is considered merely a *potential* state of the entire system" because there's no empirical evidence in support of it being the final state of the system.[63]

No wonder, then, that Loeys and Panigirtzoglou (2006) appear to be exasperated when writing,

> *The detection of bubbles is difficult simply because there is no objective way to measure fundamentals...econometric tests of asset price bubbles have been developed in the finance literature. However, all suffer from the fact that they assume implicitly or explicitly a particular model of fundamentals. That is, they do not simply test the hypothesis of an asset price bubble but rather the joint hypothesis of an asset price bubble and a particular model of fundamentals.*

And concerning rational expectations and the EMH approaches in which price equals fundamental value, Evans (2003, pp. 38–62) comments that the theories "are enlightening" only because they inform "us of how markets would operate if they were indeed efficient."

Dividend payouts appear on the average to advance over time at a relatively steady growth rate and without notable volatility as compared to stock prices. But the observed long-run variance of stock market returns (or prices) as graphed against trends in expected (or potentially available) dividend payouts provides a striking display of the difficulties in relating price volatility to such "fundamentals."[64] The characteristics that have in the early literature attracted greatest attention have instead involved the distribution of price variations (returns) and the correlation between successive price variations.

The central concept of "modern" finance, according to Mandelbrot and Hudson (2004, pp. 9–12), is that "[P]rices are not predictable, but their fluctuations can be described by the mathematical laws of chance. Therefore, their risk is measurable, and manageable...price changes are not independent of each other...price series have a 'memory,' of sorts...price changes are very far from following the bell curve."[65]

Nevertheless, "bubble" articles in the literature have been largely based on the REH assumptions, with most positing a fundamental value term that takes some form of discounted present value of expected dividends and growth and then adds to this a bubble component.[66] Well-intentioned attempts to explain bubble phenomena with such models have largely turned out to be merely armchair thought experiments with little or no practical relevance.[67] "Rationality is...an a priori assumption rather than a description of the world..."[68] "[H]igh intelligence does not make people immune to biases...*rationality* should be distinguished from intelligence."[69] And as extreme market events unfold, behavior that had once seemed irrational, now seems rational.

Yet the foundation for the conventional equilibrium asset pricing models indeed *depends* on the notion of rational expectations, which by itself is usually a necessary but not a sufficient condition for market efficiency. The random-walk hypothesis, it seems, may at best hold true only over the short run.[70]

Marginal utility theory, according to Cochrane (2005), also does not provide new insights.[71] "Since consumption and risk aversion do not change much day to day, we might expect the random walk view to hold pretty well on a day-to-day basis...However, more recently, evidence has accumulated that long-horizon excess returns are quite predictable, and to some this evidence indicates that the whole enterprise of economic explanation of asset returns is flawed."[72]

As for such predictability, Fama and French (1988) found that forecast power appears to increase with the return horizon as "[D]ividend yields typically explain less than 5 percent of the variances of monthly or quarterly returns... (and) often explain more than 25 percent of the variances of 2–4 year returns." But Campbell et al. (1997, p. 260) noted "that rational bubbles cannot explain the observed predictability of stock returns. Bubbles create volatility in prices without creating predictability in returns." As Gilchrist et al. (2004) wrote, "Research on asset prices increasingly challenges the view that asset prices equal fundamental value."[73]

By and large, historical descriptions and explanations of bubbles may be broadly grouped into three categories.[74] The first and most popular in the vast literature of 1970–2000 or so (and as surveyed in Chap. 5) is that market efficiency and rational expectations are prevalent. In these models of relatively pure rationality, bubbles and crashes are viewed as aberrations, perversions, or corruptions of the basic theoretical foundation. The second category is that bubbles and crashes are episodes of temporary irrationality and are as such disruptions to mostly steady market trends. The third category, which includes the Kindleberger and Minsky views, relies on mechanical analogies in which exogenous and always unanticipated systemic "shocks" trigger extreme events. Shocks might include excessive credit (e.g., central bank quantitative easing announcements) for market melt-ups and excessive debt burdens and bank failures for meltdowns.

Gurkaynak (2005) indeed concludes that "[F]or each paper that finds evidence of bubbles, there is another one that fits the data equally well without allowing for a bubble. We are still unable to distinguish bubbles from time-varying or regime-switching fundamentals, while many small sample econometrics problems of bubble tests remain unresolved."

And from a psychologists perspective, Nobelist Daniel Kahneman (2013, p. 269, 140, 182) explains that "people are neither fully rational nor completely selfish, and their tastes are anything but stable...[T]he emotional tail wags the rational dog...[O]ur mind is strongly biased toward causal explanations"[75] An approach that hews much closer to the emotional and psychological impetus for trading and speculation and that uses methods that are mainly inductive—not deductive—is thus provided by the behavioral finance research reviewed in the next chapter.[76]

As finance theory pioneer Fischer Black, quoted by Derman (2004, p. 171), has said, "Certain economic quantities are so hard to estimate that I call them 'unobservables'." One such unobservable is *expected return*, the amount by which people expect to profit when buying a security. "So much of finance, from Markowitz on deals with this quantity unquestioningly," says Derman. Yet, wrote Fischer Black, "Our estimates of expected return are so poor they are almost laughable."[77]

That seems to say it all.[78]

NOTES

1. Assumptions are that agents are risk-neutral, have rational expectations, and require a constant (real) rate of return on the asset, $E_t R_{t+i} = k$. The Euler equation is then $P_t = \delta(E_t P_{t+1} + E_t D_{t+1})$, where P is the price, D is the dividends, E is the mathematical expectations operator, and $\delta = 1/(1 + k)$ is the discounting factor. Cuthbertson and Nitzsche (2004, p. 398) explain: "The price you are prepared to pay today for a stock depends on the price you think you can obtain at some point in the future. But the latter depends on the expected price even further in the future...[T]he Euler equation does not rule out the possibility that the price may contain an explosive bubble." An Euler equation is a general theorem of the calculus that appears as $x_1 f_1 + x_2 f_2 = k f(x_1, x_2)$.

   After repeated forward substitutions and the assumption that what is known as a transversality condition holds (i.e., $\lim(\delta^n E_t D_{t+n} = 0$ as $n \to \infty)$, the formulation of a "rational bubble" that satisfies the Euler equation is expressed as:

   $$P_t = \sum_{i=1}^{\infty} \delta^i E_t D_{t+1} + B_t = P_t^f + B_t \text{, where } B_t \text{ is the "rational bubble," and "the}$$

   actual market price P_t deviates from its fundamental value, P_t^f by the amount of the rational bubble B_t" (p. 399). As Bailey (2005, p. 241) writes, this suggests that "asset prices need not equal the NPV of future payoffs but can become any one of an infinite number of values according to the size of the bubble. The 'bubble' term captures all the speculative and self-fulfilling aspects of potentially wild asset price changes."

   According to Cuthbertson and Nitzsche (2004, p. 401), individuals will pay prices above the fundamental price "as long as the bubble element yields them the required rate of return next period *and is expected to persist*...[I]n the real world, rational bubbles can really only exist if each individual's horizon is shorter than the time period when the bubble is expected to burst...[O]ne would pay a price above the fundamental value because one believes that someone else will pay an even greater price in the future...investors are myopic."

   From this point onward, however, assumptions and complications with the various rational bubble models begin to compound in terms of both model-specification complexities and problematic econometric testing assumptions. Cuthbertson and Nitzsche (2004, p. 408), for example, include in their list of econometric challenges:

- Potentially nonstationary series using finite data sets
- Behavior of asymptotic test statistics in the presence of explosive regressors
- Obtaining precise estimates of nonlinear parameters
- Corrections for heteroscedasticity and moving average errors
- Difficulties in specification of correct equilibrium modes of expected returns

Poundstone (2010, p. 9) questions entirely the notion that prices of anything can be firmly established over time. "Relative valuations are stable and coherent, while actual dollar amounts can be wildly arbitrary." And Prechter writes in the April 2011 *Elliott Wave Theorist* that "the stock market never attaches to any benchmark of value, be it dividends, earnings, book values or the bond/stock yield spread. It is ceaselessly dynamic." By illustration, over the past century, the price of $1 worth of S&P annual earnings based on trailing 12-month P/E ratios has ranged from around six times to more than 50 times (excluding rare years of losses when the ratio is infinite). Similarly, the price of $1 worth of annual DJIA dividends has had a range of 14 times and for book value around 19 times. In the 1940s and the early 1980s, $1 worth of S&P 400 book value was priced around $1.50 and, in the early 2000s, around $9.00. Poundstone (2010, p. 263) makes the same point.

2. To take account of the cost of money and uncertainty of payoff, the general mathematical representation of the LOOP is simply stated as $p_{t+1} = f(m_t, p_t)$, where m_t are discount factors and parameters and p_t are prices (with p_{t+1} being the price one period ahead).

3. Interest in the rational expectations school of thought continued to grow and peaked in the 1980s, although it was not until 1995 that Robert Lucas, Jr., a leader in the field, was awarded the Bank of Sweden Prize in Economic Sciences in Memory of Alfred Nobel. But another Nobel Laureate, Gary Becker, says in O'Grady (2009), "There is a lot of debate in economics about whether we can understand bubbles within a rational framework." And Garrison (2001) provides a detailed review of why RE doesn't work from the Austrian school's perspective. As Stiglitz (1990) explains with regard to the large body of work on rational expectations, the underlying issue is the movement of asset prices over time:

> If the asset price increased more slowly than the discount factor, eventually the terminal price became of negligible importance as viewed from today. Under such circumstances, the value of the asset had to be just equal to the discounted value of the stream of returns it generated, and no bubbles could exist. But as long as no one in the economy has an infinite planning horizon, there was nothing to ensure that this condition on prices (called the transversality condition) would be satisfied...If, for some asset, the rate of price increase equals (or exceeds) the rate of interest, then the share of the value of all assets accounted for by this asset would grow without bound, a condition inconsistent with long run equilibrium.

4. Evans (2003, p. 15) mentions this, and in Chap. 2, drawing on the comprehensive Raines and Leathers (2000), he surveys and compares competing theories. Keynes, for instance, is shown to be unsurprised by volatile departures from "intrinsic" values, and Toporowski (1999) views the market in nonequilibrium terms antithetical to the EMH approaches.

5. The Turnovsky (1996, pp. 59-60) representation of the rational expectations hypothesis is not much different from those used by others. Predictions generated by this model are conditional on information available at the time of prediction, with purely random price fluctuations around the forecast shown by the error term, e_t, which has zero mean. Turnovsky 1996, p. 137) writes that "most rational expectations models have been associated with saddlepoint behavior. That is, the dynamic system in which they are embedded involves both unstable and stable roots."

6. The quotation is from Azariadis (1981). Theoretical embellishments include overlapping generation (OLG) models that take account of presumed intertemporal optimizing changes of consumer utility functions, but that also include what are known as "sunspot" equilibria, the meaning of which, according to Azariadis and Guesnerie (1986),

   is still open to interpretation. One may view "sunspots" as a convenient label for a host of psychological factors ("animal spirits," fears, Bayesian learning theories, etc.) that are unrelated to the preferences, endowment or production set of any individual, and yet come to influence the forecasts and actions of economic decision-makers...these factors have some pertinence for the explanation of...the Dutch tulip mania...and the Great Depression....Whatever it may denote, the concept of sunspot equilibrium seems to be of central importance for a thorough understanding of rational expectations as an equilibrium construct.

   This says that in some circumstances economic fundamentals alone will not be sufficient to determine equilibrium allocations and that psychological factors (i.e., extraneous variables or "sunspots") eventually do matter. How investors interpret, feel about, and react to fundamentals may thus be important. Thus, following Tirole (1982), Blanchard and Fischer (1989, pp. 218–223) explain that "bubbles cannot arise when there is a finite number of individuals who have infinite horizons...if bubbles can exist in a general equilibrium, it must be because new players come into the game over time." Duffy and Fisher (2005) advise that the "difficulty lies in identifying sunspot variables and isolating their effects from those of the fundamentals." Their lab experiment found direct evidence of sunspot equilibria in a closed-book call market in which price determination is centralized. Such equilibria are sensitive to the flow of information. As an aside, the phrase "self-fulfilling prophecy" was coined by sociologist Robert K. Merton (and father of financial economist Robert C. Merton) in the *Antioch Review*, 1948. See Dunbar (2000, p. 19). In the article by Cass and Shell (1983), a sunspot is something that is intrinsically irrelevant but nonetheless influences prices. Benhabib et al. (2015) formalize a Keynesian rational expectations model showing that aggregate demand driven by sentiments (i.e., "animal spirits") can generate output fluctuations and boom-bust cycles.

7. Kurz (1994) proposes that "the theory of expectations be reformulated under the assumption that agents do not know the structural relations (such as equilibrium prices) of the economy."

8. Different implications of rationality assumptions appear in Kindleberger and Aliber (2011, p. 40). Maddala (2001, p. 420) shows that Muth required the prediction error, $(e)_t = y_t - y_t^*$, to be unbiased, with $E(\varepsilon)_t = 0$. He also required that the prediction error be *uncorrelated* with the entire information set that is available to the forecaster at the time the prediction is made. It would seem at

the outset that the use of such rational expectations models for the purpose of studying bubbles is already doomed to failure by this very assumption, which requires that at the inception of every new trade, automaton-like investors immediately erase from their memories any and all past information and emotions relating to previous trades. Evans (1991) explains the econometric weaknesses of REH studies.

Several additional objections to the REH approach are raised because, for this approach to work, rather severe restrictive assumptions are required. For example, commonly shared information ought to be held unanimously and all relationships are assumed to be linear. But in a world in which information appears to be far from being perfectly distributed and relationships are probably far from linear, these model restrictions alone appear ab initio to limit practical applications. Lovell (1986) is also a skeptic, finding in a study of business firms that "the variance of anticipations is larger than the variance of the realizations, which is inconsistent with the rational expectations hypothesis...if the cumulative evidence is to be believed, we are compelled to conclude that expectations are a rich and varied phenomenon that is not adequately captured by the concept of rational expectations."

The Cagan (1956) model of hyperinflation is an early example suggesting that adaptive inflation expectations can be "rational," but only under special assumptions. The Cagan REH approach allows, for example, according to Blanchard and Fischer (1989, pp. 218–23), "that the announcement of a future increase in the money stock itself increases the price level today. Real money balances decrease, and the price level slowly increases to its new higher level over time. Inflation therefore takes place in advance of the increase in the money stock."

9. Tuckett (2011, p. x). Meltzer (1982) also wrote: "The models used to illustrate rational expectations typically endow people with more information than they usually have."

10. The question and the arguments harken back to Friedman's *Essays in Positive Economics* (1953) in which Keynes is quoted as saying that positive economics deals with what is not what ought to be. See also Brock (1991).

Again, Shiller (2002b) places rational expectations in historical perspective:

> *The efficient markets theory reached its height of dominance in academic circles around the 1970s. At that time, the rational expectations revolution in economic theory was in its first blush of enthusiasm...Prominent finance models of the 1970s related speculative asset prices to economic fundamentals, using rational expectations to tie together finance and the entire economy in one elegant theory...*
>
> *...efficient markets theory may lead to drastically incorrect interpretations of events such as major stock market bubbles.* (p. 31)

11. Surveys in this area include Camerer (1989), Flood and Hodrick (1990), and Campbell (2000).

12. According to Greenwald et al. (2001, pp. 148–9), a further implication with respect to the EMH/CAPM is that "value investors reject both parts of the theory. They think stock selection does matter, and they do not accept the definition of risk as simply relative volatility...volatility is not the only and perhaps not even the best measure of risk." Ederington and Guan (2005), in fact, indicate that adjusted mean absolute deviation might be a better measure. Also, in a

BusinessWeek interview (April 9, 2007) with Peter Bernstein, Professor Elroy Dimson is quoted as saying "Risk means more things can happen than will happen." This quotation also appears in Bernstein (2005b, p. 47) and is from Dimson's earlier work. See also Zhang et al. (2016). The DCF methodology is also flawed because both the cash flow estimates and discount-rate assumptions are highly uncertain (i.e., stochastic).

   Taleb (2007, p. 161) emphasizes that when making forecasts, "variability matters." Bogle (2008) highlights the work of economist Frank H. Knight, who made the first distinction between the terms "risk"—a measureable quantity in which probabilities and distributions are known—and "uncertainty," which is immeasurable and thus not subject to probabilities. And commodity trader, Richard Dennis, is quoted in Covel (2007, p. 23) as saying, "One man's volatility is another man's profit."

13. Hansen and Renault (2009) describe pricing kernels or stochastic discount factors as being used to represent valuation operators. Such operators are built as "mappings that assign prices that trade in competitive markets to payoffs on portfolios of assets." This is all related to the law of one price.

14. See also Miao (2014).

15. See Henriques (2008).

16. Among the many studies of short-selling bans and regulations, see Saffi and Sigurdsson (2011), Beber and Pagano (2013), and Jain et al. (2013). Napoleon labeled short-sellers "enemies of the state," England banned the practice from 1733 until the middle of the nineteenth century, and short-selling was illegal in New York State in the early 1800s. See Surowiecki (2004, p. 225).

17. Tirole (1982) adds, "the price has to grow faster during the duration of the bubble...for the asset holders to be compensated for the probability of a crash." McQueen and Thorley (1994) similarly say, "The probability of a high return exactly compensates investors for the probability of a crash; the model shows the rationality of staying in the market despite the overvaluation."

18. Using traditional methods—in which the number of positive abnormal returns within a period suspected of containing bubbles is counted—Hardouvelis (1988) further notes that "[I]nstead of testing directly the null hypothesis of speculative bubbles, they test the null hypothesis that stock prices are priced rationally, and then interpret a possible rejection of this null hypothesis as evidence that speculative bubbles may be present. Since these methods are indirect, they have very little power to detect speculative bubbles." See also Scheinkman and Xiong (2003).

19. This appears in Gay et al. (1994).

20. Hillier (1997, pp. 3–5) explains that asymmetric information problems fall into three categories: selection of projects, hidden actions, and costly state verification.

21. They go on to show that "[T]he simplest is that of a deterministic bubble, $c_t = c_0 \theta^{-t}$." In this case the higher price is justified by the higher capital gain and the deviations grow exponentially.

22. In comparing the Blanchard and Watson (1982) to the Abreu and Brunnermeier (2003) approach, Chamley (2004, p. 383) explains that in "Blanchard, the growth rate of the bubble price must be higher than the market rate to compensate for the probability of the crash, as all agents are informed." But in Abreu

and Brunnermeier, "the growth rate of the price bubble does not need to be as high, because only a fraction of the agents are informed."

23. As Jeremy Grantham said in GMO's January 2005 *Quarterly Letter* (p. 5), "one of the paradoxes...is that reducing or avoiding real risk in portfolios can seriously increase career and business risk, which rises with any deviation from standard behavior." Hong et al. (2000) cited in Cassidy (2009a, p. 178) found that "being bold and good does not significantly improve an analyst's future career prospects." A similar finding for fund managers appears in Chevalier and Ellison (1999). See also Guerrieri and Kondor (2012) and Sato (2016).

   Grantham, in the GMO October 2006 *Quarterly Letter* (p. 4) and in *Barron's* of November 6, 2006, later observes that "Great Lakes Dock & Dredge, Hartford Steam Boiler and Twin Disc Clutch made clients feel much worse, apparently, than losing the same money in Avon, IBM and Johnson & Johnson." The implication is that investment in the most popular stocks carries a lower career risk even though the losses may be the same with less popular names. In the GMO April 2007 *Quarterly Letter*, he observes that the necessary conditions for bubbles to form are that "the fundamental economic conditions must appear to be excellent...and liquidity must be generous in quantity and price: it must be easy and cheap to leverage." He calls the early 2007 experience the "first truly global bubble" in which the risk premiums for the three major asset classes—stocks, bonds, and real estate—reached historic lows everywhere.

24. In using equal-weighted and value-weighted monthly data of major exchange indices, Harman (2000, p. 266) questions whether duration dependence tests have the power adequate to detect speculative bubbles in stock prices. "[T]he type of hazard function used and the frequency at which returns were measured had an effect on the results." Serial dependence is covered by Kritzman (1994). Another study relevant to duration dependence by Harman and Zuehlke (2004) points to "some troublesome issues" and "calls into question the efficacy of using hazard models to test for speculative bubbles."

25. Pierdzioch (2010) found that periodically collapsing bubbles in the pre-WWI German stock market cannot be ruled out.

26. Other papers that touch on the topic of runs tests include Blanchard and Watson (1982), Meese (1986), West (1987), and Woo (1987).

27. See Gerlis (2014a, b) about art as an investable asset. See also Ekelund (2017).

28. Nobel Laureate Vernon Smith began experimental economics in Smith (1962). An example of its application is in Henker and Owen (2008). Laboratory asset market experiments by Lei et al. (2001) suggest (counterintuitively and unrealistically, in my opinion) that even when speculation is not possible, bubbles and crashes still emerge. Gjerstad and Smith (2009) write, "Bubbles can arise when some agents buy not on fundamental value, but on price trend or momentum. If momentum traders have more liquidity, they can sustain a bubble longer." Smith's laboratory approach also suggests that people who experience bubbles more than once tend to learn from their first-round experience, with later bubbles not as pronounced. This is discussed in Hussam et al. (2008) and in Caginalp et al. (2000). Greenwood and Nagel (2008), also showed that more experienced fund managers in the TMT bubble were better at recognizing the bubble and avoiding it than were the younger ones. Experiments in Haruvy et al. (2007) indicate that

individuals hold beliefs conditioned on past trends and that traders don't initially anticipate market downturns. Palan (2009) surveys experimental economics literature and suggests that the efficiency of markets might be improved through the use of derivative forward-looking options. Poundstone (2010, p. 263) cites similar experiments by Colin Camerer. See also Ackert et al. (2009) and Andrade et al. (2016) on types of recently seen films affecting subsequent trading activity.

29. Several Ph.D. dissertations have focused on bubbles include Harman (2000), who analyzes "characteristics of securities to determine whether bubbles form more readily in the prices of some securities than in the prices of others." Harman examines bubbles from the standpoint of institutional investors and finds "evidence of skewness, kurtosis, and serial dependence in returns that is consistent with asset price bubbles." She also finds that "investor herding is present during periods identified as having characteristics consistent with speculative bubbles," that "investors herd on both positive and negative returns," and that there is evidence "of a positive relationship between changes in institutional ownership and measures of abnormal volume." Other dissertations of interest include those of Golden (1995), Aksoy (1997), Porras-Gonzalez (2000), Ali (2003), and Smith (2003).

30. The definitional approach that comes mathematically closest to the current work was provided by Watanabe et al. (2007), in which divergent and convergent expressions of recent prices are exponentially fitted for the purpose of defining bubbles and crashes emanating from the TMT mania of the late 1990s. The Watanabe approach, however, is entirely mechanistic and, like vector autoregression models, atheoretical.

31. West (1987) tests for bubbles using the specification test of Hausman by comparing two sets of estimated parameters that calculate the expected present discounted value (PDV) of a stock's dividend stream. The null hypothesis is that prices are in accord with a standard EMH model. "Speculative bubbles are tested for, then, by seeing whether the two sets of estimates are the same...The data reject the null hypothesis of no bubbles." Another approach is shown in Engsted and Tanggaard (2004), who constructed a test for speculative bubbles based on the price/dividend ratio, with the idea that if there are no bubbles, the P/D ratio can be decomposed into different covariances. The results suggest that "up to the late 1980s, there are not strong indications of bubbles in U.S. stock prices. However, by including data from the 1990s, there is some evidence of the presence of speculative bubbles."

32. Dezhbakhsh and Demirguc-Kunt (1990) applied what is known as a regression equation specification error test (RESET) even though the test, because of its behavioral symmetry, admittedly does not discriminate between bubbles and fads. Additional tests for self-fulfilling speculative price bubbles, discussed in Hamilton (1986), may also be applicable here. Fukuta (2002) examines via cointegration techniques two necessary conditions for the absence of rational bubbles while assuming that the discount rate is stationary.

33. With the Sola and Driffill approach, the explanatory importance of a bubble in accounting for the divergence of stock price trends from expected dividend trends is relatively low. A Markov-switching unit root test approach for detecting periodically collapsing bubbles is further explored by Hall et al. (1999), who propose use of a generalized Dickey-Fuller procedure to identify collapsing peri-

ods from expanding ones. On regime switching see also Driffill and Sola (2001). Evans (1991) examines pitfalls in testing for explosive bubbles. Charemza and Deadman (1995) highlight the failure of unit root testing, and Psaradakis et al. (2001) note that "tests for unit roots and cointegration may fail to detect the presence of explosive rational bubbles that collapse periodically." On using unit root tests (augmented Dickey-Fuller), see also Hamilton and Whiteman (1985), Campbell and Perron (1991), Craine (1993), and Taipalus (2012).

34. Cointegration, for example, is a method for analyzing long-run relationships between nonstationary variables and has often been used to test the rational expectations and market efficiency hypotheses. The methodology is covered by Dickey et al. (1991) and by Maddala and Kim (1999). Cointegration aspects of bubbles are noted in Campbell and Shiller (1987), Froot and Obstfeld (1991), Barsky and DeLong (1993), and Gujarati (1995, p. 726). From Sarno and Taylor (1999):

> If stock prices and dividends are realizations of I(1) (difference-stationary) processes, then in the absence of bubbles the standard present value model of stock prices implies cointegration between the stock price and dividend series...If the stock price series contains an explosive bubble term, however, which is not by definition in the dividend price series, then this will drive a wedge between prices and dividends so that they will not be cointegrated.

The vector autoregression (VAR) approach, as described by Maddala (2001, p. 544), "is a multiple time-series generalization...easy to estimate because we can use the OLS [ordinary least squares] method."

35. Such direct tests, focused on the presence of deterministic bubbles, include those found in Flood and Garber (1980), McQueen and Thorley (1994), Van Norden (1996), and Schaller and van Norden (1997).

36. A test that does not require a detailed specification of the underlying equilibrium model was designed by Diba and Grossman (1988). In this study, the explosive price action of a rational bubble is such that prices and fundamentals follow a different path, that is, prices and fundamentals will not be cointegrated. The advantage of this approach is that the researcher does not have to specify all the details of the equilibrium model. Still, the main drawback of the Diba and Grossman method is that it will generally have difficulty in discovering bubbles that successively grow over time and partially burst.

West (1987) provides a specification test for rational speculative bubbles based on estimates of the underlying equilibrium model using two different techniques. From Engsted and Tanggaard (2002):

> ...one technique gives consistent estimates of the model parameters both with and without bubbles. The other technique gives consistent estimates if there are no bubbles, but inconsistent estimates if there is a bubble (provided the bubble is correlated with fundamentals). Thus, under the null hypothesis of no bubbles, the two sets of estimates should be equal. If the null is rejected, it indicates the presence of bubbles. A drawback of this test is that it requires detailed specification of the underlying equilibrium model, so <u>rejection of the no bubble hypothesis may not be due to bubbles but may instead be due to imposition of the wrong model.</u>

37. As implied in Greene (2003, p. 631) and also Mills (1990, p. 69), stationarity guarantees that all moments such as the mean and variance exist, are indepen-

dent of time, and are finite. See also Gujarati (1995, p. 719), Hendry (1995, p. 44), and Favero (2001, p. 39).

38. Econometricians have thus devised tests for stationarity, among which the unit root test is perhaps the most popular. In West's tests, for instance, a model using discounted stock dividends requires a specific assumption about whether the discount rate is stationary or time-varying (and also a model of what generates such variation), whereas in the Diba and Grossman (1988) approach it doesn't matter whether the discount factor applied to future dividends varies as long as the series itself is stationary.

39. In media-related stocks, Time Warner had responded to the 2006 breakup threat by corporate activist Carl Icahn by repurchasing $20 billion worth of shares at prices around $18. By 2008, the remaining shares had traded down to $9. Percentage declines of Viacom and CBS shares in the face of sizable repurchase programs were even steeper. And from 2006 onward GE had been repurchasing nearly $25 billion of shares at as high as $40 in 2007/2008, but this didn't prevent shares from falling to $13 in late 2008. At the urging of activist Trian Fund, GE then from 2014-17 wasted $29 billion on share repurchases at prices averaging $30, more than double the early 2018 price. GE was then unable to comfortably support pension liabilities and an already reduced dividend. See also Grullon and Michaely (2002).

40. Higher regulatory and other related costs, meanwhile diminished the number of IPOs even as mergers and private equity takeovers reduced the number of domestic companies listed on U. S. exchanges from a peak of 8,025 in 1996 to 4,333 in 2016.

41. See Laherrère and Sornette (1998) and Chang and Feigenbaum (2006).

42. Malliaris (2012) breaks this literature into four categories:
    a) Papers that assume all investors to be rational and have identical information. In these, finite bubbles cannot exist;
    b) Investors have rational expectations but asymmetric information. Bubbles might develop more easily under such conditions;
    c) Investors might be either rational or behavioral in reactions and bubbles can last a long time;
    d) Traders have heterogeneous beliefs and bubbles can emerge.

43. Sornette (2003a, p. 153) suggests, "The market return from today to tomorrow is proportional to the crash hazard rate…the higher the risk of a crash, the larger is the price return. In essence, investors must be compensated by a higher return in order to be induced to hold an asset that might crash."

44. About Elliott's work, see the February and June 1999 *Scientific American* and also Elliott (1938), who apparently was first to describe stock market price patterns as being "fractal." Prechter (2004) says that such self-similarity at different scales was foreshadowed by Goethe in 1790 and then by the mathematician Georg Cantor a hundred years later. The basic Elliott idea can be described as follows: A line of length c is partitioned into segment lengths a and b. The ratio of the first segment, a, to the second, b, is made equal to the ratio of the second segment, b, to the total, c. The equation is then $a/b = b/(a+b) = b/c$. Setting $b = 1$ as the scale of measurement, the equation becomes $a = 1/(a + 1)$, or $a^2 + a - 1 = 0$. The two solutions for a are then 0.618 (the "golden mean") and −1.618. See also Chap. 10, note 15 and Sornette (2003b) and Gresnigt et al. (2015) in which crashes are modeled as being akin to earthquakes.

45. Bourke (1998) describes $1/f$ noise.

46. Pareto (Zipf's) law has also been used to compare the number of cities in the world and the number of inhabitants. The income or revenue of a company as a function of the rank is another example of the law, which as Li (1999) has noted should be called Pareto's law because Pareto observed this at the end of the 1800s.

47. See Pierce (1980, p. 87), Farmer and Lillo (2004), and Gabaix (2009).

48. There may be instances in which a function seems to follow a power law (i.e., be exponential) but in actuality does not. But a study by Ijiri and Simon (1974) showed that rejecting the Pareto law (i.e., a power law) in favor of a downwardly concave relationship between log-size and log-rank is consistent with positively autocorrelated growth rates. This would then suggest that a power law might still be used as an approximation and that autocorrelation might be more broadly applied. Among the papers in this area are those by Laherrère and Sornette (1998), Li (1999), Rousseau (1999), Urzua (2000), and Limpert et al. (2001).

    Skepticism as to the full applicability of power laws to a wide variety of physical and economic data is also the theme of Laherrère and Sornette (1998), who instead propose use of a complementary alternative known as a stretched exponential family of probability density functions (pdfs). The problem is that such log-log plots "often display linearity over a limited range of scales and/or exhibit noticeable curvature." In their comparisons of fit, they found that stretched exponential pdfs "account remarkably well for the center of most analyzed distributions...and have a tail that is 'fatter' than the exponential but much less so than a pure power law distribution...being economical in their number of adjustable parameters." See also Geraskin and Fantazzini (2013).

49. From West (2017, p. 142): "...it turns out that the patterns of fluctuations in financial markets...are simply nonlinearly scaled versions of one another...the behavior of the stock market is a self-similar fractal pattern that repeats itself across all timescales following a power law that can be quantified by its exponent.

50. Bikhchandani and Sharma (2001) provide an overview of herding. However, the best contextually developed sources are Prechter (2001, 2016). Mass psychology leading toward herding and synchronicity is covered by Strogatz (2003, pp. 1–3).

51. An attractor, as Hilborn (2000, p. 22) explains, "is that set of points to which trajectories approach as the number of iterations goes to infinity." The trajectory or orbit is the sequence of position values as measured over time and is analogous to, say, the path of a planet orbiting the sun. Williams (1997, p. 14) has additionally advised that "chaos analysis can reveal the time-limits of reliable predictions and can identify conditions where long-term forecasting is largely meaningless." There is indeed a value to knowing ahead of time when something cannot be predicted, but chaos theory is weak in revealing details of a particular underlying physical law or governing equation.

52. Serletis (1996) adds that "chaotic processes have first and second moment properties that are the same as for white noise processes."

53. Chaos theory methods, according to Hsieh (1991), make possible the description of a rich variety of nonlinear situations that are commonly found in financial market economics. Says Serletis (1996, p. 211), "[T]he existence of chaos creates the possibility that profitable nonlinearity-based trading rules may exist, raising questions about the efficient markets hypothesis."

54. Serletis: "The most important tool for diagnosing the presence of sensitive dependence on initial conditions (and thereby chaoticity) is provided by the

dominant Lyapunov exponent. The exponent measures the average exponential divergence or convergence between (state-space) trajectories that have 'infinitesimally' small differences in their initial conditions. A positive Lyapunov exponent is an operational definition of chaotic behavior."

Lyapunov-exponent methods are widely used in searching for such attractors. These exponents are based on the idea that in time-series regions governed by chaos, the most significant feature is sensitive dependence on initial conditions (SDIC). This means that even a small change at the beginning of the data series results in enormous changes down the line. But it also means that long-term forecasts cannot be made.

Bulow and Klemperer (1994) explain frenzies by focusing on the idea that "in the real world, buyers and sellers can choose *when* to trade...A further result is that the price path is highly sensitive to small changes in the underlying demand structure." See also Williams (1997, pp. 355–70) and Theiler et al. (1992).

55. Liu et al. (1992) found that the correlation exponent test of chaos theory could distinguish white noise from chaos (but could not distinguish white noise from chaos mixed with a small amount of white noise). Their paper advises instead that the well-known BDS test (Brock et al. 1996) is perhaps more effective in distinguishing between linear and nonlinear stochastic processes. The classic papers of Grassberger and Procaccia (1983a, b) showed how the correlation dimension could be used to detect attractors in both standard and lagged phase space. See also Takens (1981), Wolf et al. (1985), Rasband (1990, p. 75), and Hilborn (2000, p. 376). Gleick (1987) provides a popular overview.

As for the BDS test, Serletis and Dormaar (1996, p. 116) nevertheless say, "The BDS test does not currently provide a direct test for nonlinearity or for chaos, because the sampling distribution of the test statistic is not known (either in finite samples or asymptotically) under the null hypothesis of nonlinearity, linearity, or chaos. It is, however, possible to use the BDS test to produce indirect evidence about nonlinear dependence...which is necessary but not sufficient for chaos." See also Brock (1986).

56. See Black and Scholes (1973) and Merton (1973).

57. Falconer (2013, p. 87). Very small such random steps taken rapidly at small intervals t with length $\sqrt{t}$ lead to a fractal Brownian motion form. See also Hassler (2016), Cox and Hobson (2005), Heston et al. (2007), Jarrow et al. (2010, 2011), Cieplinski et al. (2012), and Herzog (2015). Brownian noise is, of course, the random walk under a different name. It is an example of a martingale process, in which the best forecast of x_{t+1} that could be determined on the basis of current information, Ω_t, equals x_t.

58. The EMH construct crumbles when the correlations among the returns of individual securities and different asset classes rise toward unity, as they alway do in extreme events (e.g., Fig. 2.8).

59. Dardik (2017, p. 130) writes in relation to science in general that "[M]athematics does not work where there is high variability, or a high degree of complexity, within or across scales." That is, for instance, bubbles and crashes.

60. Wilmott and Orrell (2017, pp. 140–7) write: "...it is no longer correct to say that the volatility is a single parameter– it is a whole series of separate parameters, which apply to different prices and dates." Bookstaber (2017, pp. 17–8) adds that markets are not ergodic, a term that describes a process that doesn't vary with time or experience and continues to follow the same probabilities as in

the past. "This works for physics. And for the game of roulette…Our world is not ergodic – yet economists treat it as though it is."

61. Brunnermeier (2001, p. 59) adds: "…almost all bubbles can be ruled out in a symmetric information setting."

62. Buchanan (2013, pp. 29–49) provides a concise history of equilibrium-thinking economics and of the different meanings ascribed to the word "efficiency."

63. See also McCauley (2004, p. 6) and Farmer and Geanakoplos (2009, p. 17). Wilmott and Orrell (2017) also question the notion of equilibrium.

64. Spotton and Rowley (1998) write that the simple premise that "fundamental" present value of discounted stream of dividends and earnings governs asset and prices is a corresponding

> *implicitly compromised by the severity of its main requirements for constituents and a corresponding reliance on supplemental assumptions (representative individuals, atomistic markets, very rapid and sensitive adjustments…and an effective and immediate…dynamic process of arbitrage)…Trading risk against anticipated return, the rational investors choose current portfolios, seemingly free from the activities of others…the commitment to EMH often stems from a prior conviction that efficiency is clearly desirable…rather than from a clear evidential basis.*

The random-walk/EMH approach and the presumed rationality of investors in the REH are actually separate issues that are not necessarily linked, even though the two notions often confusingly appear together in the literature.

65. Taylor (2005, p. 69) agrees, writing, "It is very clear that the returns-generating process is not even approximately Gaussian." And in Baker-Said (2008), Taleb explains that quant models typically make at least four errors: (a) *narrativity*, in which people hedge for what makes sense even though things that can happen don't make sense at the time; (b) *low volatility*, in which the mistake is that low volatility does not mean low risk; (c) *blindfoldedness*, in which most people take risks even when they don't know what risks they are incurring; and (d) *stress testing*, in which the most dangerous unforeseen events are not tested.

Patterson (2010b, p. 57) writes that Lévy studied distributions in which a single sample made an important change to the curve. Fox (2009, p. 7) writes that Henri Poincaré, the great French mathematician and thesis supervisor of Bachelier, thought with regard to the Gaussian distribution that "caution needed to be exercised in applying it to human behavior." Jovanovic and Schinckus (2017, p. 2) recall that a French banker's assistant, Jules Regnault, in 1863 first began to represent market variations using a random-walk approach.

66. The belief remains that there is an equilibrium "fundamental" value that might somehow be found if only the right models were to be specified. Gilles and LeRoy (1992) indicate that the difficulties already begin with coming to an understanding of what is meant by the terms "fundamental" and "speculative bubble." A source of the confusion, they say, is that "fundamental" is used to describe "sunspot as well as bubble equilibria." See also Allen et al. (1993) and Brunnermeier (2001, p. 50), who say that sunspots "serve as a coordination device for the agents in the economy to select a particular static price equilibrium."

Bailey (2005, Chapter 1) describes markets that can be "efficient" in several different ways: allocative, operational, informational, and portfolio structure. And Bray (1985) says that "Employing the rational expectations hypothesis imposes two logical requirements, that objective probability distributions exist, and that rational expectations equilibrium exists."

67. Robert Lucas, Jr., a pioneer proponent of the REH, in fact later found the theory to be flawed because it is not reasonable to believe that humans are perfectly rational or perfectly informed. Much of this theory "worked" only after making such idealistic assumptions. In the strict Lucas REH approach, there are no bubbles and banking crises.

68. Kindleberger (1996, [1989], p. 21).

69. Kahneman (2013, pp. 49, 411). "The only test of rationality is not whether a person's beliefs and preferences are reasonable, but whether they are internally consistent."

70. Lim (2015, p. 139 and 155).

71. In an overview of modern financial economics, Cochrane (2005, p. 4) states that if the marginal utility of consumption, c, in period $t+1$ versus that in period t is taken into account, it can be shown that "bubbles"—"in which the prices grow so fast that people will buy now just to resell at higher prices later, even if there are no dividends"—are ruled out (p. 25). By contrast, the portfolio approach to asset pricing as in the CAPM and ICAPM relies heavily on the assumption that the investor has no non-asset income (p. 36)...the CAPM and ICAPM are not *alternatives* to the consumption-based model: "they are *special cases* of that model" (p. 169). Even Fama and French (2004) conclude that the early versions of the CAPM have "never been an empirical success...[T]he problems are serious enough to invalidate most applications of the CAPM."

72. From Cochrane (2005, p. 23). Barberis et al. (2001) develop a model in which investors derive direct utility not only from consumption but also from fluctuations in wealth. Their model allows for changes in risk aversion, incorporates aspects of prospect theory from behavioral finance, and also helps to explain excess volatility, predictability of returns, and a low correlation with consumption growth.

73. Bailey (2005, p. 65) adds: "Without a criterion for separating what is fundamental from what is not, the distinctiveness of the EMH evaporates."

74. As per Prechter (2016, pp. 506–10).

75. The emotional tail is explored in a somewhat different context by Haidt (2001).

76. See Forbes (2009). Bookstaber (2017, p. 183) writes that with a deductive approach "[Y]ou could be only somewhat right, and you can find many ways to be completely and precisely wrong."

77. The quotation also appears in Mehrling (2005, p. 13) and in Triana (2009, p. 53). Bernstein (2007, p. 214) adds that when Black moved from MIT near Boston to Goldman Sachs in New York in 1984, he said, "The market appears a lot more efficient on the banks of the Charles River than it does on the banks of the Hudson." The quote is also in Mehrling, p. 246. Sharpe would also obviously agree with the sentiment. In a discussion with Bernstein (2007, p. 94), Sharpe says, "...how in the world can you measure expectations, which are a look forward, not backward? You cannot just look at history and deduce much about what expectations have been – or would be. The whole matter revolves around the future. Therefore, the historical data on which we all depend so heavily may be useless for asset pricing."

Lowenstein (2008a) similarly writes, "Modern finance is an antiseptic discipline; it eschews anecdotes and examples, which are messy and possibly misleading — but nonetheless real. It favors abstraction, which is perfect but theoretical. Rather than evaluate financial assets case by case, financial models rely on the notion of randomness, which has huge implications for diversification. It means two investments are safer than one, three safer than two."

78. In commenting on the EMH, Buchan (1997, p. 240) says, "The efficient-markets doctrine is merely another attempt to apply rational laws to an arena that is self-evidently irrational. A market cannot operate by laws, for the laws would be discovered, and it would cease to be a market."

REFERENCES

Abreu, D., & Brunnermeier, M. K. (2003). Bubbles and Crashes. *Econometrica, 71,* 173.

Ackert, L. F., Charupat, N., Deaves, R., & Kluger, B. D. (2009). Probability Judgment Error and Speculation in Laboratory Asset Market Bubbles. *Journal of Financial and Quantitative Analysis, 44*(3), 719–744.

Adam, M. C., & Szafarz, A. (1992). Speculative Bubbles and Financial Markets. *Oxford Economic Papers, 44,* 626.

Ahamed, L. (2009). *Lords of Finance: The Bankers Who Broke the World.* New York: Penguin.

Aksoy, L. (1997). A Nash Equilibrium Solution for Stock Market Crashes. Unpublished PhD Dissertation, City University of New York.

Ali, M. F. (2003). Stock Market Bubbles, Time-Varying Risk Premia, and Monetary Policy. Unpublished PhD Dissertation, George Mason University.

Allen, F., & Gorton, G. (1993). Churning Bubbles. *Review of Economic Studies, 60*(4), 813–836.

Allen, F., Morris, S., & Postlewaite, A. (1993). Finite Bubbles with Short Sale Constraints and Asymmetric Information. *Journal of Economic Theory, 61,* 206.

Andrade, E. B., Odean, T., & Lin, S. (2016). "Bubbling with Excitement: An Experiment, " *Review of Finance,* 20(2)(March)

Angeletos, G.-M., & La'O, J. (2013). Sentiments. *Econometrica, 81*(2), 739–779.

Asako, K. (1991). The Land Price Bubble in Japan. *Ricerche Economiche, XLV*(2–3).

Azariadis, C. (1981). Self-Fulfilling Prophecies. *Journal of Economic Theory, 25*(3), 380–396.

Azariadis, C., & Guesnerie, R. (1986). Sunspots and Cycles. *Review of Economic Studies, 53*(5), 725–737.

Bailey, R. E. (2005). *The Economics of Financial Markets.* Cambridge: Cambridge University Press.

Baker-Said, S. (2008, May). Flight of the Black Swan. *Bloomberg Markets.*

Barberis, N., Huang, M., & Santos, T. (2001). Prospect Theory and Asset Prices. *Quarterly Journal of Economics, CXVI*(1), 1–53.

Barsky, R. B., & DeLong, J. B. (1993). Why Does the Stock Market Fluctuate? *Quarterly Journal of Economics, 108*(2), 291.

Beber, A., & Pagano, M. (2013). Short-Selling Bans Around the World: Evidence from the 2007–09 Crisis. *Journal of Finance, 68*(1), 343–381.

Benhabib, J., Wang, P., & Wen, Y. (2015). Sentiments and Aggregate Demand Fluctuations. *Econometrica, 83*(2), 549–585.

Bernstein, P. L. (2005b). *Capital Ideas: The Improbable Origins of Modern Wall Street.* Hoboken: Wiley (Paperback ed.).

Bernstein, P. L. (2007). *Capital Ideas Evolving.* Hoboken: Wiley.

Bhar, R., & Malliaris, A. G. (2005). Are There Rational Bubbles in the U.S. Stock Market? Overview and a New Test. In Malliaris (2005).

Bikhchandani, S., & Sharma, S. (2001). Herd Behavior in Financial Markets. *IMF Staff Papers, 47*(3), 279–310. Washington, DC: IMF.

Binswanger, M. (1999). *Stock Markets, Speculative Bubbles and Economic Growth.* Aldershot: Edward Elgar.

Black, F., & Scholes, M. (1973). The Pricing of Options and Corporate Liabilities. *Journal of Political Economy, 81*(3), 637.

Blanchard, O. J. (1979). Speculative Bubbles, Crashes and Rational Expectations. *Economics Letters, 3*(4).

Blanchard, O. J., & Fischer, S. (1989). *Lectures on Macroeconomics.* Cambridge, MA: MIT Press.

Blanchard, O. J., & Watson, M. W. (1982). Bubbles, Rational Expectations, and Financial Markets. In P. Wachtel (Ed.), *Crises in the Economic and Financial Structure.* Lexington: Lexington Books.

Bogle, J. C. (2008). Black Monday and Black Swans. *Financial Analysts Journal, 64*(2), 30.

Bohl, M. T. (2001). Periodically Collapsing Bubbles in the U.S. Stock Market. Working Paper Series, No. 6. Frankfurt: European University.

Bookstaber, R. (2017). *The End of Theory: Financial Crises, the Failure of Economics, and the Sweep of Human Interaction.* Princeton: Princeton University Press.

Bourke, P. (1998). Generating Noise with Different Power Spectra Laws. Available at http://astronomy.swin.edu.au/~pbourke/fractals/noise/

Brav, A., & Heaton, J. B. (2002). Competing Theories of Financial Anomalies. *Review of Financial Studies, 15*(2), 575.

Bray, M. (1985). Rational Expectations, Information and Asset Markets: An Introduction. *Oxford Economic Papers*, New Series, *37*(2)161–195.

Brock, W. A. (1986). Distinguishing Random and Deterministic Systems. *Journal of Economic Theory, 40*, 168–195. (Abridged version).

Brock, W. A. (1991). Causality, Chaos, Explanation, and Prediction in Economics and Finance. In J. Casti & A. Karlqvist (Eds.), *Beyond Belief: Randomness, Predition, and Explanation in Science.* Boca Raton: FL. CRC Press.

Brock, W. A. (2000). Chaos Theory. In Smelser and Baltsis (2001) (Eds.), *International Encyclopedia of the Social and Behavioral Sciences.* London: Elsevier.

Brock, W. A., Decehert, J. A., Scheinkman, J. A., & LeBaron, B. (1996). A Test for Independence Based on the Correlation Dimension. *Econometric Reviews, 15*(3), 197.

Brooks, C., & Katsaris, A. (2003). *Regime Switching Models of Speculative Bubbles with Volume: An Empirical Investigation of the S&P 500 Composite Index.* Reading: IMSA.

Brunnermeier, M. K. (2001). *Asset Pricing Under Asymmetric Information: Bubbles, Crashes, Technical Analysis, and Herding.* New York: Oxford University Press.

Brunnermeier, M. K., & Nagel, S. (2004, October). Hedge Funds and the Technology Bubble. *Journal of Finance, LIX*(6) and AFA 2004 San Diego Meetings; EFA 2003 Annual Conference Paper No. 446. Available at http://ssrn.com/abstract=423940

Buchan, J. (1997). *Frozen Desire: The Meaning of Money*. New York: Farrar Straus Giroux.

Buchanan, M. (2013). *Forecast: What Physics, Meteorology, and the Natural Sciences Can Teach Us About Economics*. New York: Bloomsbury.

Bulow, J., & Klemperer, P. (1994). Rational Frenzies and Crashes. *Journal of Political Economy, 102*(1), 1–23.

Cagan, P. (1956). The Monetary Dynamics of Hyperinflation. In M. Friedman (Ed.), *Studies in the Quantity Theory of Money*. Chicago: University of Chicago Press.

Caginalp, G., Porter, D., & Smith, V. L. (2000). Overreactions, Momentum, Liquidity, and Price Bubbles in Laboratory and Field Asset Markets. *Journal of Psychology and Financial Markets, 1*(1), 24.

Camerer, C. F. (1989). An Experimental Test of Several Generalized Utility Theories. *Journal of Risk and Uncertainty, 2*, 61.

Campbell, J. Y. (2000). Asset Pricing at the Millennium. *Journal of Finance, 55*, 1515.

Campbell, J. Y., & Perron, P. (1991). *Pitfalls and Opportunities: What Macroeconomists Should Know About Unit Roots*. NBER Technical Working Paper No. 100 in Macroeconomics Annual 1991, National Bureau of Economic Research. Cambridge, MA: MIT Press.

Campbell, J. Y., & Shiller, R. J. (1987). Cointegration and Tests of Present Value Models. *Journal of Political Economy, 95*(5), 1062–1088.

Campbell, J. Y., Lo, A. W., & MacKinlay, A. C. (1997). *The Econometrics of Financial Markets*. Princeton: Princeton University Press.

Case, K., & Shiller, R. J. (1989). The Efficiency of the Market for Single-Family Homes. *American Economic Review, 79*(1), 125–137.

Cass, D., & Shell, K. (1983). Do Sunspots Matter? *Journal of Political Economy, 91*(2), 193–227.

Cassidy, J. (2009). *How Markets Fail: The Logic of Economic Calamities*. New York: Farrar, Straus and Giroux.

Casti, J., & Karlqvist, A. (Eds.). (1991). *Beyond Belief: Randomness, Prediction, and Explanation in Science*. Boca Raton: CRC Press.

Chamley, C. P. (2004). *Rational Herds: Economic Models of Social Learning*. New York: Cambridge University Press.

Chan, K., McQueen, G., & Thorley, S. (1998). Are There Rational Speculative Bubbles in Asian Stock Markets? *Pacific-Basin Finance Journal, 6*, 125.

Chang, G., & Feigenbaum, J. (2006). A Bayesian Analysis of Log-Periodic Precursors to Financial Crashes. *Quantitative Finance, 6*, 15.

Charemza, W. W., & Deadman, D. F. (1995). Speculative Bubbles with Stochastic Explosive Roots: The Failure of Unit Root Testing. *Journal of Empirical Finance, 2*, 153.

Chevalier, J., & Ellison, G. (1999). Career Concerns of Mutual Fund Managers. *Quarterly Journal of Economics, 114*(2), 389–432.

Cieplinski, T., Dominiczak, A., & Kutner, R. (2012). Short Comprehensive Report on the Non-Brownian Stochastic Dynamics at Financial and Commodity Markets. *Acta Physica Polonica A, 121*, B-24.

Cochrane, J. H. (2005). *Asset Pricing* (Rev. ed.). Princeton: Princeton University Press.

Cootner, P. H. (Ed.). (1964). *The Random Character of Stock Market Prices*. Cambridge, MA: MIT Press.

Covel, M. W. (2007). *The Complete Turtle Trader: The Legend, the Lessons, the Results*. New York: HarperCollins.

Cox, A., & Hobson, D. (2005). Local Martingales, Bubbles and Option Prices. *Finance and Stochastics, 9,* 477.

Craine, R. (1993). Rational Bubbles: A Test. *Journal of Economic Dynamics and Control, 17,* 829.

Cuthbertson, K., & Nitzsche, D. (2004). *Quantitative Financial Economics* (2nd ed.). Chichester: Wiley.

Dardik, I. (2017). *The Nature of Nature: The Discovery of SuperWaves and How It Changes Everything.* New York: Rodale.

De Grauwe, P., & Grimaldi, M. (2003). *Bubbling and Crashing Exchange Rates.* CESIfo Working Paper No. 1045. Leuven, Belgium: Catholic University of Leuven.

Derman, E. (2004). *My Life As a Quant: Reflections on Physics and Finance.* New York: Wiley.

Dezhbakhsh, H., & Demirguc-Kunt, A. (1990, March). On the Presence of Speculative Bubbles in Stock Prices. *Journal of Financial and Quantitative Analysis, 25,* 101.

Diba, B. T. (1990). Bubbles and Stock-Price Volatility. In G. P. Dwyer Jr. & R. W. Hafer (Eds.), *The Stock Market: Bubbles, Volatility, and Chaos.* Norwell: Kluwer Academic.

Diba, B. T., & Grossman, H. I. (1987, August). On the Inception of Rational Bubbles. *Quarterly Journal of Economics, 102*(409).

Diba, B. T., & Grossman, H. I. (1988, September). The Theory of Rational Bubbles in Stock Prices. *Economic Journal, 98,* 746.

Dickey, D. A., Jansen, D. W., & Thornton, D. L. (1991). A Primer on Cointegration with an Application to Money and Income. In *Federal Reserve Bank of St. Louis Review.* St. Louis: Federal Reserve Bank.

Driffill, J., & Sola, M. (2001). Irreversible Investment and Changes in Regime. Economic and Social Research Council Working Paper. Birkbeck College, University of London. Available at http://www.econ.bbk.ac.uk//research/macro/macro.htm

Duffy, J., & Fisher, E. O'N. (2005). Sunspots in the Laboratory. *American Economic Review, 95*(3), 510.

Dunbar, N. (2000). *Inventing Money: The Story of Long-Term Capital Management and the Legends Behind It.* Chichester: Wiley.

Dwyer, G. P., Jr., & Hafer, R. W. (Eds.). (1990). *The Stock Market: Bubbles, Volatility, and Chaos.* Norwell: Kluwer Academic Press. Also in *Proceedings of the Thirteenth Annual Economic Policy Conference* of the Federal Reserve Bank of St. Louis.

Ederington, L. H., & Guan, W. (2005, Spring/Summer). Measuring Historical Volatility. *Journal of Applied Finance.*

Ekelund, R. B., Jr. (2017). *The Economics of American Art: Issues, Artists and Market Institutions.* New York: Oxford University Press.

Elliott, R. N. (1938). *The Wave Principle.* Gainesville: New Classics Library.

Engsted, T., & Tanggaard, C. (2002). A New Test for Speculative Bubbles Based on Return Variance Composition. Working Paper Series, No. 106. Aarhus, Denmark: University of Aarhus.

Engsted, T., & Tanggaard, C. (2004). *Speculative Bubbles in Stock Prices? Tests Based on the price-dividend Ratio* (Working Paper Series). Aarhus: University of Aarhus.

Etienne, X. L., Irwin, S. H., & Garcia, P. (2014, April). Bubbles in Food Commodity Markets: Four Decades of Evidence. *Journal of International Money and Finance, 42,* 129.

Evanoff, D. D., Kaufman, G. G., & Malliaris, A. G. (Eds.). (2012). *New Perspectives on Asset Price Bubbles: Theory, Evidence, and Policy*. New York: Oxford University Press.

Evans, G. W. (1991). Pitfalls in Testing for Explosive Bubbles in Asset Prices. *American Economic Review, 81*, 922–930.

Evans, L. L., Jr. (2003). *Why the Bubble Burst: US Stock Market Performance Since 1982*. Cheltenham: Edward Elgar.

Evstigneev, I. V., Hens, T., & Schenk-Hoppé, K. R. (2006). Evolutionary Stable Stock Markets. *Economic Theory, 27*(2), 449–468.

Falconer, K. (2013). *Fractals: A Very Short Introduction*. Oxford: Oxford University Press.

Fama, E. F., & French, K. (1988). Dividend Yields and Expected Stock Returns. *Journal of Financial Economics, 22*, 3.

Fama, E. F., & French, K. (2004, Summer). The Capital Asset Pricing Model: Theory and Evidence. *Journal of Economic Perspectives, 18*(3).

Farmer, J. D., & Geanakoplos, J (2009). The Virtues and Vices of Equilibrium and the Future of Financial Economics. Working paper. Cowles Foundation ad available at: https://arxiv.org/pdf/0803.2996.pdf/

Farmer, J. D., & Lillo, F. (2004). On the Origin of Power Law Tails in Price Fluctuations. *Quantitative Finance, 4*(1), 7.

Favero, C. A. (2001). *Applied Macroeconometrics*. Oxford: Oxford University Press.

Flood, R. P., & Garber, P. M. (1980). Market Fundamentals Versus Price-Level Bubbles: The First Tests. *Journal of Political Economy, 88*, 745.

Flood, R. P., & Garber, P. M. (Eds.). (1994). *Speculative Bubbles, Speculative Attacks and Policy Switching*. Cambridge, MA: MIT Press.

Flood, R. P., & Hodrick, R. J. (1990). On Testing for Speculative Bubbles. *Journal of Economic Perspectives, 4*(2), 85–101.

Forbes, W. (2009). *Behavioural Finance*. Chichester: Wiley.

Fox, J. (2009). *The Myth of the Rational Market: A History of Risk, Reward, and Delusion on Wall Street*. New York: HarperCollins.

Frankel, D. M. (2008). Adaptive Expectations and Stock Market Crashes. *International Economic Review, 49*(2), 595–619.

Friedman, M. (1953). *Essays in Positive Economics*. Chicago: University of Chicago Press.

Friedman, M. (Ed.). (1956). *Studies in the Quantity Theory of Money*. Chicago: University of Chicago Press.

Friedman, B. M. (1979). Optimal Expectations and the Extreme Information Assumption of Rational Expectations' Macromodel. *Journal of Monetary Economics, 5*(1), 23.

Friedman, D., & Abraham, R. (2009, April). Bubbles and Crashes: Gradient Dynamics in Financial Markets. *Journal of Dynamics & Control, 33*, 922.

Froot, K. A., & Obstfeld, M. (1991). Intrinsic Bubbles: The Case of Stock Prices. *American Economic Review, 81*(5).

Fukuta, Y. (2002). A Test for Rational Bubbles in Stock Prices. *Empirical Economics, 27*(4), 587–600.

Gabaix, X. (2009). Power Laws in Economics and Finance. *Annual Review of Economics, 1*, 255–293.

Galbraith, J. K. (1988). *The Great Crash, 1929* (2nd ed.). Boston: Houghton-Mifflin.

Garrison, R. W. (2001). *Time and Money: The Macroeconomics of Capital Structure*. London/New York: Routledge.

Gay, G., Kale, J., Kolb, R., & Noe, T. (1994). (Micro) Fads in Asset Prices: Evidence from the Futures Market. *Journal of Futures Markets, 14*, 637.

Gennotte, G., & Leland, H. (1990). "Market Liquidity, Hedging, and Crashes," *American Economic Review*, 80(5)(December).

Geraskin, P., & Fantazzini, D. (2013). Everything You Always Wanted to Know About Log-Periodic Power Laws for Bubble Modeling But Were Afraid to Ask. *The European Journal of Finance, 19*(5), 366–391.

Gerlis, M. (2014a). *Art as an Investment? A Survey of Comparative Assets*. London: Lund Humphries.

Gerlis, M. (2014b, January 14). Is Collecting Art As Profitable as It Is Painted? *Financial Times*.

Gilchrist, S., Himmelberg, C. P., and Huberman, G. (2004). *Do Stock Price Bubbles Influence Corporate Investment?* Staff Report No. 177. Federal Reserve Bank of New York.

Gilles, C., & LeRoy, S. F. (1992). Bubbles and Charges. *International Economic Review, 33*(2), 323–339.

Gjerstad, S. D., & Smith, V. L. (2009, April 6). From Bubble to Depression? *Wall Street Journal*.

Glassman, J. K., & Hassett, K. A. (1999). *Dow 36,000: The New Strategy for Profiting from the Coming Rise in the Stock Market*. New York: Times Books.

Gleick, J. (1987). *Chaos: Making a New Science*. New York: Penguin.

Golden, D. P. (1995). Three Essays on the Theory of Speculative Bubbles. Unpublished PhD dissertation, University of North Carolina at Chapel Hill.

Grassberger, P., & Procaccia, I. (1983a). Characterization of Strange Attractors. *Physical Review Letters, 50*(5), 346.

Grassberger, P., & Procaccia, I. (1983b). Measuring the Strangeness of Strange Attractors. *Physica D, 9*, 189.

Greene, W. H. (2003). *Econometric Analysis* (5th ed.). Upper Saddle River: Prentice Hall.

Greenwald, B. C. N., Kahn, J., Sonkin, P. D., & van Biema, M. (2001). *Value Investing: From Graham to Buffett and Beyond*. New York: Wiley (Paperback ed.).

Greenwood, R., & Nagel, S, (2008). Inexperienced Investors and Bubbles. Available at http://faculty-gsb.stanford.edu/nagel/pdfs/Mfage.pdf

Gresnigt, F., Kole, E., & Franses, P. H. (2015, July). Interpreting Financial Market Crashes as Earthquakes: A New Early Warning System for Medium Term Crashes. *Journal of Banking & Finance, 56*, 123.

Grullon, G., & Michaely, R. (2002). Dividends, Share Repurchases, and the Substitution Hypothesis. *Journal of Finance, 57*(4), 1649.

Guerrieri, V., & Kondor, P. (2012). Fund Managers, Career Concerns, and Asset Price Volatility. *American Economic Review, 102*(5), 1986.

Gujarati, D. N. (1995). *Basic Econometrics* (3rd Int. ed.). New York: McGraw-Hill.

Gurkaynak, R. S. (2005). *Econometric Tests of Asset Price Bubbles: Taking Stock*. Washington, DC: Federal Reserve.

Gutierrez, L. (2013). Speculative Bubbles in Agricultural Commodity Markets. *European Review of Agricultural Economics, 40*(2), 217–238.

Haacke, C. (2004). *Frenzy: Bubbles, Busts and How to Come Out Ahead*. New York: Palgrave Macmillan.

Haidt, J. (2001). "The Emotional Dog and its Rational Tail," *Psychological Review*, 108.

Hall, S. G., Psaradakis, Z., & Sola, M. (1999). Detecting Periodically Collapsing Bubbles: A Markov-Switching Unit Root Test. *Journal of Applied Econometrics, 14*, 143.

Hamilton, J. D. (1986, October). On Testing for Self-Fulfilling Speculative Price Bubbles. *International Economic Review, 27*, 545.

Hamilton, J. D., & Whiteman, C. H. (1985). The Observable Implications of Self-Fulfilling Expectations. *Journal of Monetary Economics, 16*, 353.

Hansen, L. P., & Renault, E. (2009). Pricing Kernels and Stochastic Discount Factors. In *Encyclopedia of Quantitative Finance*. Chicago: University of Chicago.

Hardouvelis, G. (1988, Summer). Evidence on Stock Market Speculative Bubbles: Japan, the United States, and Great Britain. *Federal Reserve Bank of New York Quarterly Review*.

Harman, Y. S. (2000). *Bubbles, Fads, and the Psychology of Investors*. Unpublished PhD Dissertation, Florida State University.

Harman, Y. S., & Zuehlke, T. W. (2004). Duration Dependence Testing for Speculative Bubbles. *Journal of Economics and Finance, 28*(2), 147.

Haruvy, E., Lahav, Y., & Noussair, C. N. (2007). Traders' Expectations in Asset Markets: Experimental Evidence. *American Economic Review, 97*(5), 1901–1920.

Hassler, U. (2016). *Stochastic Processes and Calculus: An Elementary Introduction with Applications*. Heidelberg: Springer.

Hendry, D. F. (1995). *Dynamic Econometrics*. Oxford: Oxford University Press.

Henker, J., & Owen, S. A. (2008). Bursting Bubbles: Linking Experimental Financial Market Results to Field Market Data. *Journal of Behavioral Finance, 9*(1), 5.

Henriques, D. B. (2008, March 28). Odd Crop Prices Defy Economics. *New York Times*.

Hens, T., & Schenk-Hoppé, K. R. (2001). Evolution of Portfolio Rules in Incomplete Markets. Working Paper Series ISSN 1424-0459, No. 74. Zurich: University of Zurich. Available at http://www.iew.unizh.ch/wp/iewwp074.pdf

Herrera, S., & Perry, G. E. (2003). Tropical Bubbles: Asset Prices in Latin America, 1980–2001. In Hunter et al. (2003 [2005]).

Herzog, B. (2015). An Econophysics Model of Financial Bubbles. *Natural Science, 7*, 55.

Heston, S. I., Loewenstein, M., & Willard, G. A. (2007). Options and Bubbles. *Review of Financial Studies, 20*(2), 359.

Hilborn, R. C. (2000). *Chaos and Nonlinear Dynamics: An Introduction for Scientists and Engineers* (2nd ed.). Oxford/New York: Oxford University Press.

Hillier, B. (1997). *The Economics of Asymmetric Information*. New York: St. Martin's Press.

Homm, U., & Breitung, J. (2012). Testing for Speculative Bubbles in Stock Markets: A Comparison of Alternative Methods. *Journal of Financial Econometrics, 10*(1), 198–231.

Hong, H., Kubik, J. D., & Solomon, A. (2000). Security Analysts' Career Concerns and Herding of Earnings Forecasts. *RAND Journal of Economics, 31*(1), 121–144.

Hong, H., Scheinkman, J. A., & Xiong, W. (2006). Asset Float and Speculative Bubbles. *Journal of Finance, LXI*(3), 1073–1117.

Hsieh, D. (1991). Chaos and Nonlinear Dynamics: Application to Financial Markets. *Journal of Finance, 46*, 1839–1877.

Hunter, W. C., Kaufman, G. G., & Pomerleano, M. (Eds.). (2003). *Asset Price Bubbles: The Implications for Monetary, Regulatory, and International Policies.* Cambridge, MA: MIT Press (Paperback ed., 2005).

Hussam, R. N., Porter, D., & Smith, V. L. (2008). Thar She Blows: Can Bubbles Be Rekindled with Experienced Subjects? *American Economic Review, 98*(3), 924–937.

Ijiri, Y., & Simon, H. A. (1974). Interpretations of Departures from the Pareto Curve Firm-Size Distributions. *Journal of Political Economy, 82,* 315.

Jain A., Jain, P. K., McInish, T. H., & McKenzie, M. (2013). Worldwide Reach of Short-Selling Regulations. *Journal of Financial Economics, 109*(1), 177–197.

Jarrow, R. A., Protter, P., & Shimbo, K. (2010). Asset Price Bubbles in Incomplete Markets. *Mathematical Finance, 20*(2), 145–185.

Jarrow, R. A., Kchia, Y., & Protter, P. (2011). How to Detect an Asset Bubble. *SIAM Journal on Financial Mathematics, 2*(1), 839.

Johansen, A., & Sornette, D. (1999a). Critical Crashes. *Risk, 12*(1), 91–94.

Johansen, A., & Sornette, D. (1999b). Log-Periodic Power Law Bubbles in Latin-American and Asian Markets and Correlated Anti-Bubbles in Western Stock Markets: An Empirical Study. Economics Working Paper, St. Louis: Washington University.

Johansen, A., & Sornette, D. (1999c). Modeling the Stock Market Prior to Large Crashes. *European Physics Journal B, 9,* 167.

Johansen, A., & Sornette, D. (1999d). Financial 'Anti-Bubbles': Log-Periodicity in Gold and Nikkei Collapses. *International Journal of Modern Physics C, 10*(4), 563–575.

Jovanovic, F., & Schinckus, C. (2017). *Econophysics and Financial Economics: An Emerging Dialog.* New York: Oxford University Press.

Kahneman, D. (2013). *Thinking, Fast and Slow.* New York: Farrar, Straus and Giroux.

Kindleberger, C. (1996[1989]). *Manias, Panics, and Crashes: A History of Financial Crises* (3rd ed.). New York: Wiley. (2nd ed., 1989).

Kindleberger, C., & Aliber, R. Z. (2011). *Manias, Panics, and Crashes: A History of Financial Crises* (6th ed.). Houndmills: Palgrave Macmillan.

Kodres, L., & Pritsker, M. (2002). A Rational Expectations Model of Financial Contagion," *Journal of Finance, 57*(2).

Kräussl, R., Lehnert, T., & Martelin, N. (2016, January). Is There a Bubble in the Art Market? *Journal of Empirical Finance, 35,* 99.

Kritzman, M. (1994, March/April). About Serial Dependence. *Financial Analysts Journal, 50*(2).

Kurz, M. (1994). On the Structure and Diversity of Rational Beliefs. *Journal of Economic Theory, 4*(6), 877–900.

Laherrère, J., & Sornette, D. (1998). Stretched Exponential Distributions in Nature and Economy: 'Fat Tails' with Characteristic Scales. *European Physical Journal, B2,* 525–539. Available at http://xxx.lanl.gov/abs/cond-mat/9801293

Lee, I. H. (1998). Market Crashes and Informational Avalanches. *Review of Economic Studies, 65,* 741.

Lee, T. (2004). *Why the Markets Went Crazy.* New York: Palgrave Macmillan.

Lei, V., Noussair, C. N., & Plott, C. R. (2001). Nonspeculative Bubbles in Experimental Asset Markets: Lack of Common Knowledge of Rationality vs. Actual Irrationality. *Econometrica, 69*(4), 831.

LeRoy, S. F. (2004). Rational Exuberance. *Journal of Economic Literature, 42*(3), 783.

LeRoy, S. F., & Porter, R. D. (1981). The Present Value Relation: Tests Based on Implied Variance Bonds. *Econometrica, 64.*

Li, W. (1999). *Zipf's Law Web site.* Available at http://linkage.rockefeller.edu/wli/zipf/

Lillo, F., & Mantegna, R. N. (2000). Symmetry Alterations of Ensemble Return Distribution in Crash and Rally Days of Financial Markets. *European Physical Journal B, 15,* 603.

Lim, K. G. (2015). *Financial Valuation and Econometrics* (2nd ed.). Singapore: World Scientific.

Limpert, E., Stahel, W. A., & Abbt, M. (2001). Lognormal Distributions across the Sciences: Keys and Clues. *Bioscience, 51*(5), 341–352.

Liu, T., Granger, C. W. J., & Heller, P. (1992). Using the Correlation Exponent to Decide Whether an Economic Time Series Is Chaotic. *Journal of Applied Econometrics, 7,* S25–S39.

Loeys, J., & Panigirtzoglou, N. (2006, Winter). Are Alternatives the Next Bubble? *Journal of Alternative Investments, 9*(3).

Lovell, M. C. (1986, March). Tests of the Rational Expectations Hypothesis. *American Economic Review.*

Lowenstein, R. (2008, September 6). Long-Term Capital: It's a Short-Term Memory. *New York Times.*

Lux, T. (1995). Herd Behavior, Bubbles and Crashes. *Economic Journal: The Journal of the Royal Economic Society, 105,* 881.

Lux, T., & Sornette, D. (2002). On Rational Bubbles and Fat Tails. *Journal of Money, Credit and Banking, 34*(3), 589–610.

Maddala, G. S. (2001). *Introduction to Econometrics* (3rd ed.). Chichester: Wiley.

Maddala, G. S., & Kim, I. (1999). *Unit Roots, Cointegration, and Structural Change.* Cambridge: Cambridge University Press.

Malliaris, A. G. (2012). Asset Price Bubbles and Central Bank Policies. In Evanoff et al. (2012).

Mandelbrot, B. (1960). The Pareto-Lévy Law and the Distribution of Income. *International Economic Review, 1,* 79.

Mandelbrot, B. (1964). The Variation of Certain Speculative Prices. In P. Cootner (Ed.), *The Random Character of Stock Prices.* Cambridge, MA: MIT Press.

Mandelbrot, B., & Hudson, R. L. (2004). *The (Mis)Behavior of Markets: A Fractal View of Risk, Ruin, and Reward.* New York: Basic Books.

Martin, A., & Ventura, J. (2015). The International Transmission of Credit Bubbles: Theory and Policy. *Journal of Monetary Economics, 76*(Supplement), S37–S56.

McCauley, J. L. (2004). *Dynamics of Markets: Econophysics and Finance.* Cambridge: Cambridge University Press.

McQueen, G., & Thorley, S. (1994). Bubbles, Stock Returns, and Duration Dependence. *Journal of Financial and Quantitative Analysis, 29,* 379.

Meese, R. A. (1986). Testing for Bubbles in Exchange Markets: A Case of Sparkling Rates? *Journal of Political Economy, 94,* 345.

Mehrling, P. (2005). *Fischer Black and the Revolutionary Idea of Finance.* Hoboken: Wiley.

Meltzer, A. H. (1982). Rational Expectations, Risk, Uncertainty, and Market Responses. Available at http://repository.cmu.edu/tepper

Merton, R. C. (1973). Theory of Rational Option Pricing. *Bell Journal of Economics and Management Science (The Rand Corporation), 4*(1), 141–183.

Miao, J. (2014). Introduction to Economic Theory of Bubbles. *Journal of Mathematical Economics, 53,* 130.

Miller, J. I., & Ratti, R. A. (2009). Crude Oil and Stock Markets: Stability, Instability, and Bubbles. *Energy Economics, 31*(4), 559–568.

Mills, T. C. (1990). *Time Series Techniques for Economists.* Cambridge: Cambridge University.

Mills, T. C. (1993). *The Econometric Modelling of Financial Time Series.* Cambridge: Cambridge University Press.

Montier, J. (2002). *Behavioural Finance: Insights into Irrational Minds and Markets.* Chichester/Hoboken: Wiley.

Muth, J. A. (1961). Rational Expectations and the Theory of Price Movements. *Econometrica, 29*(6), 315–335.

Napier, R. (2007). *Anatomy of the Bear: Lessons from Wall Street's Four Great Bottoms* (2nd ed.). Petersfield: Harriman House.

Noguchi, Y. (1994). The 'Bubble' and Economic Policies in the 1980s. *Journal of Japanese Studies, 20*(2), 291–329.

Nychka, D. W., Ellner, S., Gallant, A. R., & McCaffrey, D. (1992). Finding Chaos in Noisy Systems. *Journal of the Royal Statistical Society B, 54,* 399–426.

O'Grady, M. A. (2009, March 21). Now Is No Time to Give Up on Markets. *Wall Street Journal.*

Palan, S. (2009). *Bubbles and Crashes in Experimental Asset Markets.* Berlin: Springer-Verlag.

Park, J. Y., & Whang, Y. J. (1999). Random Walk or Chaos: A Formal Test on the Lyapunov Exponent. Working Paper No. 9, Institute of Economic Research, Seoul National University.

Patterson, S. (2010). *The Quants: How a New Breed of Math Whizzes Conquered Wall Street and Nearly Destroyed It.* New York: Crown (Random House).

Pierce, J. R. (1980). *An Introduction to Information Theory: Symbols, Signals and Noise* (2nd. Rev. ed.). New York: Dover.

Pierdzioch, C. (2010). Periodically Collapsing Bubbles in the German Stock Market, 1876–1913. *Applied Economics Letters, 17*(9), 907–908.

Porras-Gonzalez, E. R. (2000). Speculative Bubbles and Tests of the Contagion Mechanism in Financial Markets. Unpublished PhD Dissertation, Florida Atlantic University.

Porter, D., & Smith, V. L. (1992). Price Expectations in Experimental Asset Markets with Futures Contracting. Social Science Working Paper 827. Pasadena: California Institute of Technology. Available at http://www.hss.caltech.edu/SSPapers/sswp827.pdf

Poundstone, W. (2010). *Priceless: The Myth of Fair Value.* New York: Hill and Wang. (Farrar, Straus and Giroux).

Prechter, R. R., Jr. (2001). Unconscious Herding Behavior as the Psychological Basis of Financial Market Trends and Patterns. *Journal of Psychology and Financial Markets, 2*(3), 120.

Prechter, R. R., Jr. (2004). The Fractal Nature of the Stock Market. In *The Colours of Infinity: The Beauty, and Power of Fractals.* London: Clear Books.

Prechter, R. R., Jr. (2016). *The Socionomic Theory of Finance.* Gainesville: Socionomics Institute Press.

Psaradakis, Z., Sola, M., & Spagnolo, F. (2001). A Simple Procedure for Detecting Periodically Collapsing Rational Bubbles. *Economic Letters, 72,* and Birkbeck College Working Paper.

Raines, J. P., & Leathers, C. G. (2000). *Economists and the Stock Market: Speculative Theories of Stock Market Fluctuations.* Aldershot: Elgar.

Ramsey, J. B., Sayers, C. L., & Rothman, P. (1990). The Statistical Properties of Dimension Calculations Using Small Data Sets: Some Economic Applications. *International Economic Review, 31*(4), 991–1020.

Rasband, S. N. (1990). *Chaotic Dynamics of Nonlinear Systems.* New York: Wiley.

Rousseau, R. (1999). *A Weak Goodness-of-Fit Test for Rank-Frequency Distributions.* In C. Macias-Chapula (Ed.), Proceedings of the Seventh Conference of the International Society for Scientometrics and Informetrics, Universidad de Colima, Mexico.

Saffi, P. A. C., & Sigurdsson, K. (2011). Price Efficiency and Short Selling. *Review of Financial Studies, 24*(3), 821–852.

Santoni, G. J. (1987). The Great Bull Markets of 1924–1929 and 1982–1987: Speculative Bubbles or Economic Fundamentals? *Federal Reserve Bank of St. Louis Review.*

Santos, M. S., & Woodford, M. (1997). Rational Asset Pricing Bubbles. *Econometrica, 65,* 19.

Sarno, L., & Taylor, M. P. (1999). Moral Hazard, Asset Price Bubbles, Capital Flows, and the East Asian Crisis: The First Tests. *Journal of International Money and Finance, 18,* 637.

Sato, Y. (2016). "Fund Tournaments and Asset Bubbles," *Review of Finance,* 20(4) (July).

Schaller, H., & van Norden, S. (1997). Fads or Bubbles? Working Paper 97-92, Bank of Canada. Available at http://www.bankofcanada.ca/en/res/wp/1997/wp97-2.html

Scheinkman, J. A., & Xiong, W. (2003). Overconfidence and Speculative Bubbles. *Journal of Political Economy, 111*(6), 1183.

Scott, L. O. (1985). The Present Value Model of Stock Prices: Regression Tests and Monte Carlo Results. *Review of Economics and Statistics, 67,* 599–605.

Serletis, A. (1996). Is There Chaos in Economic Time Series? *Canadian Journal of Economics, 29*(Special Issue – Part 1), S210–S212.

Serletis, A., & Dormaar, P. (1996). Chaos and Nonlinear Dynamics in Futures Markets. In W. A. Barnett et al. (Eds.), *Nonlinear Dynamics and Economics.* Cambridge: Cambridge University Press.

Shiller, R. J. (1981). Do Stock Prices Move Too Much to Be Justified by Subsequent Movements in Dividends? *American Economic Review, 71*(3), 421–436.

Shiller, R. J. (1989). Comovements in Stock Prices and Comovements in Dividends. *Journal of Finance, 44*(3), 719–729.

Shiller, R. J. (1992). *Market Volatility.* Cambridge, MA: MIT Press.

Shiller, R. J. (2002a). Bubbles, Human Judgment, and Expert Opinion. *Financial Analysts Journal, 58*(3), 18.

Shiller, R. J. (2002b, October). *From Efficient Market Theory to Behavioral Finance.* Cowles Foundation Discussion Paper No. 1385. New Haven: Cowles Foundation for Research in Economics, Yale University. Available at http://cowles.econ.yale.edu/

Shiller, R. J., Kon-Ya, F., & Tsutsui, Y. (1996). Why Did the Nikkei Crash? Expanding the Scope of Expectations Data Collection. *Review of Economics and Statistics, 78*(1), 156–164.

Shleifer, A., & Vishny, R. W. (1997). The Limits of Arbitrage. *Journal of Finance, 52*(1), 35–55.

Silverberg, G., & Lehnert, D. (1996). Evolutionary Chaos: Growth Fluctuations in a Schumpeterian Model of Creative Destruction. In W. A. Barnett, A. P. Kirman, & M. Salmon (Eds.), *Nonlinear Dynamics and Economics*. Cambridge: Cambridge University Press.

Smelser, N. J., & Baltsis, P. B. (Eds.). (2001). *International Encyclopedia of the Social and Behavioral Sciences*. London: Elsevier.

Smith, V. L. (1962). An Experimental Study of Competitive Market Behavior. *Journal of Political Economy, 70*(3), 322–323.

Smith, C. W. (2003). Bubbles and Stock Market Behavior, Rational and Irrational. Unpublished PhD Dissertation, State University of New York at Binghamton.

Smith, V. L., Suchanek, G. L., & Williams, A. W. (1988). Bubbles, Crashes, and Endogenous Expectations in Experimental Spot Asset Markets. *Econometrica, 56*(5), 1119–1151.

Sola, M., & Driffill, J. (1998). Intrinsic Bubbles and Regime Switching. *Journal of Monetary Economics, 42*(2), 357–373.

Sornette, D. (2003a). *Why Stock Markets Crash: Critical Events in Complex Financial Systems*. Princeton: Princeton University Press.

Sornette, D. (2003b). Critical Market Crashes. *Physics Reports, 378*(1), 1–98.

Spotton, B., & Rowley, R. (1998). Efficient Markets, Fundamentals, and Crashes: American Theories of Financial Crises and Market Volatility. *American Journal of Economics and Sociology, 57*(4), 663–690.

Srivastava, N., & Satchell, S. (2012). *Are There Bubbles in the Art Market? The Detection of Bubbles When Fair Value Is Unobservable*. Birkbeck Working Papers in Economics and Finance, 1209 (April).

Stiglitz, J. E. (1990). Symposium on Bubbles. *Journal of Economic Perspectives, 4*(2), 13–18.

Strogatz, S. (2003). *Sync: The Emerging Science of Spontaneous Order*. New York: Hyperion.

Surowiecki, J. (2004). *The Wisdom of Crowds*. New York: Doubleday.

Taipalus, K. (2012). Detecting Asset Price Bubbles with Time-Series Methods. *Helsinki, Bank of Finland, Scientific Monograph E*, 47-2012.

Takens, F. (1981). Dynamical Systems and Turbulence. In D. A. Rand & L. S. Young (Eds.), *Lecture Notes in Mathematics*. Berlin: Springer-Verlag.

Taleb, N. N. (2007). *The Black Swan*. New York: Random House.

Taylor, S. (2005). *Asset Price Dynamics, Volatility, and Prediction*. Princeton: Princeton University Press.

Taylor, M. P., & Peel, D. A. (1998). Periodically Collapsing Stock Price Bubbles: A Robust Test. *Economics Letters, 61*, 221–228.

Temin, P., & Voth, H.-J. (2004). Riding the South Sea Bubble. *American Economic Review, 94*(5), 1654–1668.

Theiler, J. B., Galdrikian, A., Longtin, S., Eubank, S., & Farmer, J. D. (1992). Using Surrogate Data to Detect Nonlinearity in Time Series. In M. Casdagli & S. Eubank (Eds.), *Nonlinear Modeling and Forecasting*. Redwood City: Addison-Wesley.

Tirole, J. (1982). On the Possibility of Speculation Under Rational Expectations. *Econometrica, 50*(5), 1163.

Toporowski, J. (1999). *The End of Finance: Capital Market Inflation, Financial Derivatives and Pension Fund Capitalism*. London: Routledge.

Townsend, R. M. (1983). Forecasting the Forecasts of Others. *Journal of Political Economy, 91*(4), 546.

Triana, P. (2009). *Lecturing Birds on Flying: Can Mathematical Theories Destroy the Financial Markets?* Hoboken: Wiley.

Tuckett, D. (2011). *Minding the Markets: An Emotional Finance View of Financial Instability.* London: Palgrave/Macmillan.

Turnovsky, S. J. (1996). *Methods of Macroeconomic Dynamics.* Cambridge, MA: MIT Press.

Urzua, C. M. (2000). A Simple and Efficient Test for Zipf's Law. *Economic Letters, 66,* 257.

Van Norden, S. (1996). Regime-Switching as a Test for Exchange Rate Bubbles. *Journal of Applied Econometrics, 11*(3), 219–251.

Voth, H.-J. (2003). With a Bang, Not a Whimper: Pricking Germany's 'Stock Market Bubble' in 1927 and the Slide into Depression. *Journal of Economic History, 63*(1), 65–99.

Wachtel, P. (Ed.). (1982). *Crises in the Economic and Financial Structure.* Lexington: Lexington Books.

Watanabe, K., Takayasu, H., & Takayasu, M. (2007). A Mathematical Definition of the Financial Bubbles and Crashes. *Physica A, 383,* 120–124.

Werner, R. A. (2005). *New Paradigm in Macroeconomics: Solving the Riddle of Japanese Macroeconomic Performance.* Houndmills: Palgrave Macmillan.

West, K. D. (1987). A Specification Test for Speculative Bubbles. *Quarterly Journal of Economics, 102,* 553.

West, K. D. (1988). Bubbles, Fads and Stock Volatility Tests: A Partial Evaluation. *Journal of Finance, 43*(3), 639.

West, G. (2017). *Scale: The Universal Laws of Growth, Innovation, and Sustainability.* New York: Penguin/Random House.

White, E. N. (Ed.). (1990). *Crashes and Panics: The Lessons from History.* Homewood: Dow-Jones-Irwin.

Williams, G. P. (1997). *Chaos Theory Tamed.* Washington, DC: Joseph Henry Press/National Academy Press.

Wilmott, P., & Orrell, D. (2017). *The Money Formula: Dodgy Finance, Psuedo Science, and How Mathematicians Took Over the Markets.* Hoboken: Wiley.

Wolf, A., Swift, J. B., Swinney, H. L., & Vastano, J. A. (1985). Determining Lyapunov Exponents from a Time Series. *Physica D, 16*(3), 285–317.

Woo, W. T. (1987). Some Evidence of Speculative Bubbles in the Foreign Exchange Markets. *Journal of Money, Credit and Banking, 19*(4), 499.

Wu, Y. (1995). Are There Rational Bubbles in Foreign Exchange Markets? Evidence from An Alternative Test. *Journal of International Money and Finance, 14*(1), 27–46.

Wu, Y. (1997). Rational Bubbles in the Stock Market: Accounting for the U.S. Stock-Price Volatility. *Economic Inquiry, 35*(2), 309–319.

Zhang, F. X., Green, J., & Hand, J. (2016). Errors and Questionable Judgments in Analysts' DCF Models. *Review of Accounting Studies, 21*(2), 596–632.

CHAPTER 7

Behavioral Beats

Dilbert cartoonist and persuasion theorist Scott Adams has observed that "people are never rational. They rationalize. So after the fact they tell you why they did something."[1]

Economists, however, with obviously a less refined sense of irony or humor, generally posit that it's rational for people to behave rationally when it comes to investments and money. It's a splendid idea. The only problem is that psychologists and other observers, including socionomists, have found that the idea does not go far as a description of how humans actually behave. As legendary fund manager, Sir John Templeton, said, "Bull markets are born on pessimism, grow on skepticism, mature on optimism, and die on euphoria."

7.1 OVERVIEW

Behavioral finance—a theoretical mix of economics and psychology—can be generally viewed as a "bounded rationality" alternative to the expected utility hypothesis (EUH) that underlies the random-walk/EMH approach to decision-making under uncertainty. As Barberis and Thaler (2002) explained:

> *Behavioral finance argues that some financial phenomena can plausibly be understood using models in which some agents are not fully rational. The field has two building blocks: limits to arbitrage, which argues that it can be difficult for rational traders to undo the dislocations caused by less rational traders; and psychology, which catalogues the kinds of deviations from full rationality we might expect to see.*

Statman goes so far as to say (in Statman 1995) that "behavioral finance is a replacement for standard finance as a descriptive theory" and notes (in Statman 1999) that risk premiums "may be affected by more than attitudes toward risk."

© The Author(s) 2018
H. L. Vogel, *Financial Market Bubbles and Crashes, Second Edition,*
https://doi.org/10.1007/978-3-319-71528-5_7

Academic work began with studies by Tversky and Kahneman (1981) and later by De Bondt and Thaler (1986), among others. What has been discovered is that people don't necessarily react quickly or rationally to changes in trends at or near the time that the trends change.

Behavioral finance instead finds that people generally prefer to go on believing what they have believed and thus want to believe because it's easier not to have to frequently rethink and then revise basic assumptions and behaviors. For a change in beliefs and behaviors to occur, there must often be overwhelming confirmation that the prior beliefs and behaviors are no longer proper or acceptable in the new environment.[2]

Kahneman and Tversky (K&T) demonstrated that our utilities are not determined by overall wealth, but by gains and losses that are relative to some reference point. The asymmetry between gains and losses is the key feature of K&T's prospect theory: Herein, losses loom larger than gains and produce a kinked function—meaning that most investors are risk-averse when presented with a sure gain, whereas when presented with a sure loss they will become risk takers.[3] In other words, the underlying utility functions are not as in most conventional models based on consumption or wealth, but instead on returns on assets as measured in relative, not absolute, terms. The theory indicates how people actually make money-related decisions.[4]

Thus, as found by Shefrin and Statman (1985), the purchase price of a stock is a natural reference point for judging gains and losses; investors then have a disposition (i.e., there is a "disposition effect") to sell winning stocks too early and hold losing stocks too long. Several other studies such as those by Odean (1998) and Weber and Camerer (1998) largely confirm this, finding respectively that investors harvest their profitable stock investments at a much higher rate than their unprofitable ones and tend to sell less when the price is below the purchase price than when it is above the purchase price.

Behavioral economists suggest that this loss aversion bias is tied to an endowment effect, which says that investors have a propensity to overvalue what they already own. Investors "lose the ability to think rationally when the time comes to sell."[5]

Nobel Laureate Herbert Simon early resisted the strict rationality approach adopted by the neoclassicists. Simon alternatively believed that individuals use mental shortcuts (i.e., heuristics) to make quick and intuitive decisions and that rationality as expressed through the weighing of choices based on calculations of expected utilities does not well-characterize most economic behavior. According to Simon, people are "boundedly rational."[6]

Indeed, Kahneman and Tversky (1979) found that departures from rationality follow systematic patterns in what Ariely (2008, p. xxx) calls predictable irrationality.[7] "The exact same choice presented or 'framed' in different setup," say K&T, "would elicit different decisions, a finding that traditional economic theory could not explain." By thus framing a question or a choice, the outcome is prejudiced.

Even so, the behavioralist approach has not been fully embraced. Manne (2006), for example, writes that "behavioralists did not – and do not – have a general theory that can explain why financial markets work as well as they do. Some close approximation of the efficient market theory is still the most accurate and useful model of the stock market that we have." Frydman and Goldberg (2011) further condemn the behavioralists for their attempts to portray asset-pricing decisions through the application of mechanical rules.[8] And Pixley (2012, p. 61) finds fault with the cognitive psychologist's comparisons of gambling risks with business decision-making because "known chances do not exist in economics."

In addition, Cochrane (2011) views abstract arguments between "rational" and "behavioral" approaches as being pointless because discount rates play such an important role in pricing and in the distortion of expectations. The central idea of "behavioral" asset pricing is that people's expectations are wrong. Behavioral theories are also discount-rate theories because "[A] distorted probability with risk-free discounting is mathematically equivalent to a different discount rate...behavioral research so far largely ties prices to other prices."

Tuckett (2011, pp. 13–14), however, writes that "agents can only be rational in those limited instances where the choice context is stable...in financial markets, it is often not so sure what a fully rational action might be...behavioural economics has largely been a matter of contesting whether or not economic agents are rational." Tuckett thus argues that simple decision rules and emotions facilitate efficient decision-making in the uncertain and urgent situations that appear in bubbles and crashes.

In socionomic terms Prechter (2016, p. 111) writes that "how people feel is the primary cause of how people act." Here, for financial assets, social mood and herding are the hidden engines behind buy and sell decisions. As Kahneman (2013, p. 69) further suggests, "...when in a good mood, people become more intuitive and more creative but also less vigilant and more prone to logical errors...the environment is safe, and it is all right to let one's guard down."[9]

Because people seem to react nonlinearly and are not risk-averse at all times, markets are not efficient—in other words, all new information is not immediately discounted or reflected in prices.[10] Yet once the new information becomes overwhelmingly obvious, people act on the information that they have up to that point ignored. This implies that the present is influenced, sometimes with a considerable lag, by the past (and in violation of the *iid* EMH modeling assumption).

Behavioral theories are based on the concepts of mental frames, loss aversion, and heuristics, says De Bondt (1995, 2012):

...despite its many insights, modern finance offers only a set of asset-pricing theories for which no empirical support exists and a set of empirical facts for which no theory exists....theorists blame the data.[11]

7.2   BIASES, VIOLATIONS, AND CORRELATIONS

In reviewing the behavioral approach, Montier (2002) observes (p. 25) that "symmetry of attitude towards risk is the working assumption of virtually all standard finance." But as has been already suggested in earlier chapters, when it comes to money and credit transactions, little or no symmetry is to be found. Behavioral finance instead enlists well-documented psychological traits to replace the assumption that rational man is always trying to maximize the (expected) utility of wealth. The major traits, seen among a wide variety of investors and investment styles, are related to the tendency of people to be habitually optimistic and overconfident in their own abilities to handle risk and beat the markets. In addition, people tend to weigh the most recent news, either good or bad, with more significance than is actually warranted.[12]

The underlying behaviors can be labeled and classified as:

- *Cognitive dissonance*: This is "the mental conflict that people experience when they are presented with evidence that their beliefs or assumptions are wrong. People have an incredible degree of self-denial."
- *Confirmation bias*: This "is the technical name for people's desire to find information that agrees with their existing view. Any information that conflicts with the null is ignored, whilst information that reinforces the null is over-weighted."[13]
- *Conservation bias*: "This is a tendency to cling tenaciously to a view or forecast. Once a position has been stated most people find it hard to move away from that view. When movement does occur it's only very slowly (this creates under-reaction to events)." By another name, it's also a *status quo/validity delusion (clinging) bias*, as people prefer things to stay the same and do nothing even when evidence is contradictory.[14]
- *Anchoring*: "It is well known that when people are asked to form a quantitative assessment their views can be influenced by suggestions. When faced with uncertainty people will grasp at straws in order to find a basis for the view...The value of the stock market is inherently ambiguous...In the absence of any solid information, past prices are likely to act as anchors for today's prices."
- *Ambiguity aversion*: As seen above, this is related to anchoring and refers to the notion that "people are exceptionally afraid of financial situations involving ambiguity."
- *Availability bias*: This follows the early research of Tversky and Kahneman (1974) in which heuristics (rules of thumb) are used by decision-makers "who assess the frequency of class or the probability of an event by the ease with which instances or occurrences can be brought to mind." For example, it is easier to recall and adapt to information that has just been read in the *Financial Times* or *Wall Street Journal* or that is seen on a financial television show than to an item on a stock that is buried deep in an obscure report.
- *Contextual definitions*: This refers to the notion that there can be no such thing as context-free decision-making, because the way in which a

question or situation is framed by context determines the way in which questions are answered or situations are handled.

- *Framing*: People tend to employ simple abstractions in thinking about complex events or ideas.
- *Self-attribution bias*: When good things happen to you, it's the result of something that you did; when bad things happen, it's because of something someone else did or didn't do. This bias becomes especially prominent and pernicious in periods of great economic distress and/or market crashes, when vituperative blame and aspersions are cast in a society-wide breakdown of trust accompanied by a search for scapegoats.
- *Hindsight bias*: After the fact, people tend to think that they always knew the outcome was likely.
- *Dynamic prospects*: By extension of prospect theory, this was originally designed to explain responses to one-shot games in which a second chance is not permitted. This was later applied to investment decision-making and it suggests that the perception of risk changes depending upon prior outcomes. It has been found that people were more willing to take a gamble if they had previously won money than if they had lost money.[15] Risk perception is thus not a statistically stationary feature and as such it violates a significant presumption underlying the efficient-market hypothesis. And it illustrates how and why investors might, in the face of relatively high P/E ratios and other financial indicators of pricing extremes, continue buying shares.

Dynamic prospect behavior in effect says that participants in a bubble become progressively bolder (less risk-averse) as time goes on. Their utility functions, as illustrated in Fig. 1.2, appear to collectively change from a position of risk aversion to what perhaps could be more appropriately called risk obliviousness (or complacency). One consequence in practice is that investors often appear (as they lose their conservation bias) to react most strongly to the latest bits of information even as they suffer from information overload. "[P]eople value changes not states....people worry far more about gains and losses than they do about levels."[16]

Violations of the EMH's stationarity, symmetry, and rational expectations assumptions are also explored by Montier (2002, p. 28). And studies such as those by Erb et al. (1994) and Ang and Chen (2002) found that markets react asymmetrically and thus contravene a key MPT assumption—that of constant correlations. The Erb paper found that when both the US and German markets are rising, the correlation is just 8.6%. But when both markets are falling, the correlation jumps to 52%.[17] Such asymmetric correlations indicate that the value of portfolio diversification as specified by the CAPM is overrated and that investors react (behave) asymmetrically to gains versus losses.

7.3   RESPONSE INVERSION AND FEEDBACK

The possibility that there are situations in which demand rises with price was early identified by economist Thorstein Veblen (1899), who understood such situations to be an artifact of "conspicuous consumption" by the wealthy. To the wealthy, the visibly high price of an object generates the demand for it because affordability of the object is used as an indicator of economic status. In this, scarcity value also plays a role, as does the rate of change in the price (particularly) of financial assets. It is the price change relative to where the asset was bought or sold (its return), not its absolute value, that is always a trader's dominant concern.[18]

Nonacademic practitioners have expanded on this notion, examining the behavioral aspects of transactions in ways that nevertheless provide keen insights and perspectives. Most economic theory, for instance, presumes that price signals as determined by supply and demand schedules operate in the same way whether the market is for goods and services or for financial assets. Prechter (1999, Ch. 20), however, makes an important distinction between the two:

> *When the price of a good or service rises, fewer people buy it, and when its price falls, more people buy it. This response allows pricing to keep supply and demand in balance. In contrast, when the price of an investment rises, more people buy it, and when its price falls, fewer people buy it… In economic matters, rising prices repel buyers; in investment matters, rising prices attract buyers…In the product marketplace, the consumer wants prices lower while the producer wants them higher…In the world of investments, however, the consumer (who buys it) and the producer (who creates and wants to sell more of it) both want prices higher. Rather than become excited to buy as prices fall, as consumers of goods and services do, investors become excited to buy as prices rise.[19]*

This different mentality with respect to financial transactions has many different sources, but the most basic is that:

> *Producers and consumers make rational decisions based on what the prices are; speculators make impulsive decisions based on the belief, hope or fear that prices will change. Each speculator cares only about the future direction and extent of price change, not present level.…Stock is not a good or service to be utilized or consumed; stock is simply traded…In financial markets, there is no opposition of forces among producers and consumers…it means that the market has no state of equilibrium at all…prices fluctuate independently of corporate valuation measures.* (Prechter 2016, chapter 12)

Such differences in trading responses are further explained by Tuckett (2011, pp. 19–21):

- Financial assets tend over time to exhibit volatile valuations, going up or down a lot over time, sometimes even coming to be worth nothing.

- Financial assets are "*abstract* in the sense that they cannot be enjoyed for themselves. They have no value other than what they can be exchanged for." Purchase of a television set can be enjoyed without ever again giving a thought to price fluctuations, whereas prices of financial assets are always on the minds of active buyers and sellers. As such, financial assets "are never really bought or sold. The original decision to buy has to be made again and again and again for as long as one holds the stock...[A] decision to sell may shortly create regret and a wish to reverse it."
- Financial assets have no intrinsic values and are based on inherently uncertain views of expected future values.

In brief, the price of a share depends in part on what everyone else believes it to be worth, and over time physical products will mostly lose value whereas financial assets have the potential to gain value.[20]

The relation of all this to bubble and crash environments is that:

Booms last longer because optimism is fed by slowly rising emotions involving hope and greed, which, because they are tempered by caution, can reach maximum intensity only over a long period of time and fulfillment only after prolonged effort. Busts are swifter because pessimism is fed by fast-flaming emotions such as fear and anger, which can be realized in a flash of destructive action. (Prechter 1995 [2001], pp. 280–81)

7.4   Herding

Herding is seen in many species, including the human, because it is a means of self-preservation. Fears of ostracism and of appearing to be uninformed, wrong, stupid, or plain crazy create social pressures that make it extremely difficult for most individuals and institutions to persist in going against the grain and thus to buy near bottoms and sell near tops. In joining with the crowd's view, the stress of dissonance is relieved and the fears largely eliminated. And through what's been called an "availability cascade," people then begin to believe whatever it is that others believe and assess a proposition's truth by its familiarity.[21] Substantial social-environment and price-to-value uncertainty is thus a necessary precondition of herding. Blame it all on our mirror neurons.[22]

Testing as to whether individuals suppress their beliefs in favor of the market consensus (i.e., following the herd) during periods of unusual, stressful market movements was presented by Christie and Huang (1995). Because individual assets differ in their sensitivity to market returns, rational asset-pricing models would predict that during such movements, large changes in market return should be reflected in an increase of dispersion, as defined by the cross-sectional standard deviations of returns. Their tests found an increase in dispersions, a result consistent with rational pricing rather than herding behavior.

This finding was, however, contradicted by Nofsinger and Sias (1999), who concluded that individual investors engage in what is called feedback trading, a type of herding. It seems that investors do indeed engage in this type of herding—for example, basing their mutual fund purchase decisions on prior performance information by flocking to funds showing the highest recent returns. Positive feedback amplified by publicity is an important component of asset price bubble creation. Investors evidently derive comfort and reassurance from joining the crowd.[23]

Herding, Sornette (2003a) writes, is the "collective coherent motion of large numbers of self-propelled organisms" which has also been observed in many financial activities including analyst recommendations, earnings forecasts, and portfolio stock choices. Essentially, "the less information you have, the stronger is your incentive to follow the consensus."[24]

Herding in finance can be subdivided into the following somewhat overlapping categories:

- *Informational cascades,* which occur when "individuals choose to ignore or downplay their private information and instead jump on the bandwagon by mimicking the actions of individuals who acted previously."[25]
- *Reputational herding,* which occurs when people follow what others of high reputation are saying and doing.
- *Investigative herding,* which occurs when an analyst investigates something in anticipation that it will also be investigated by others.
- *Empirical herding,* which refers to herding without any specific model or explanation except perhaps that shares are to be bought because of price momentum created by others doing the same.

Of these, informational cascades might have the greatest influence over the choices that investors make. If so, then the behavioral finance (and also socionomics) approach is preferable to that of rational expectations. For, as Bikhchandani et al. (1992) write, "...conformist behaviors can be fragile and idiosyncratic because cascades start readily on the basis of even a small amount of information. There are many models that have unstable equilibria for some parameter values...fragility arises *systematically* because cascades bring about precarious equilibria." Cascades have been known to affect the behavior of even rational people and lead to their participation in bubbles (or crashes), because there are times when people need to rely on the judgment of others.[26]

Another way to understand herding can be gleaned from studies of the so-called winner's curse, first named in a paper by Capen et al. (1971) and covered in Thaler (1992). Theory would advocate that all bidders are rational and that the winner's curse—of bidding at auction a price that is higher than an asset's true value—cannot happen.

Yet, as Thaler (1992, p. 51) explained: "[A]n increase in the number of other bidders implies that to win the auction you must bid more aggressively, but their presence also increases the chance that if you win, you will have over-estimated the value of the object for sale – suggesting that you should bid less aggressively." Environments in which there are lots of bidders always character-ize bubbles (even though having many bidders does not necessarily contradict rationality or signal irrationality).

That investor as well as portfolio diversity is an essential feature for markets to be efficient and rational—that is, it's possible to have rational markets even when individual participants are irrational—has been posited by Vaga (1990), Peters (1994, pp. 46–50), and Mauboussin (2006, p. 83).[27] This occurs, says Mauboussin, only when individual investors are not "irrational in the same way at the same time." However, collective irrationality at the same time is in fact what's seen in all extreme market events.

In summary, herding theories fall into six major categories:[28]

- *Social-psychological* such as fashions and fads
- *Information cascades* which include feedback loops that can especially appear in crashes
- *Ethological* as with flocks of birds and swarms of bees
- *Econophysics* which uses mechanical analogies that include avalanches and sandpiles
- *Medical* as with disease epidemics and infections
- *Socionomic*, which is not tied to notions of equilibrium, rationality, or utility maximization

Of these, social-psychological studies – showing how ideas and fads are contagiously propagated – and socionomics are the only ones that provide the conceptual degrees of freedom necessary to fully capture what happens in the real world as it pertains to bubbles and crashes. Information contagion requires, according to Berger (2016, pp. 22–4, 105), most if not all of the following:

- *Social Currency*—in which people talk about a product, service, or a stock because they wish to appear smart, hip, rich, and tuned-in rather than dumb, dull, poor, boring, and cluless.
- *Triggers*—from which words, objects, and situations trigger thoughts of related things.
- *Emotion*—in which messages and ideas awake and stir an easily shared emotional response that thereby deepens and reinforces social connec-tions, opinions, and attitudes.
- *Public*—in which widespread media coverage and conversation leads to mimicry and herding.
- *Practical Value*—in which products or services or stocks appear to pro-vide something of value.
- *Stories*—which are vessels for the transmission of information and ideas.

To see the relevance to extreme market events, think of the many bubbles described in Chapter 2 and the more recent rise of Bitcoin (Fig. 8.7). All or most of these elements were present and active in every bubble episode and in crashes too.[29]

7.5   ANOMALIES

Unsolved anomalies in the financial markets—defined by Brav and Heaton (2002) as "a documented pattern of price behavior that is inconsistent with the predictions of traditional efficient markets, rational expectations asset pricing theory"—are numerous. One of the most curiously fascinating but not widely known calendar anomalies was discussed by the late market analyst Paul Macrae Montgomery (1942–2014), who compiled a record of significant financial events that occurred on or about the autumnal equinox (September 21 give or take a day or two).

1893: Panic forces NYSE to shut down
1929: Dow-Jones Utility Index was last major average to peak before the Great Crash
1931: British pound taken off gold standard and devalued 28%
1978 and 1979: October "massacres" began
1980: Gold stocks and many oil stocks peaked
1981: Treasury note and bond yields peaked at 17% and 15%, respectively, and ended 35-year bond bear market
1992: Britain forces to withdraw from European Exchange Rate Mechanism
1997: Asian currency-related collapse
1998: Long-Term Capital Management dissolved
2008: Lehman Brothers collapses causing market chaos

Markets, it appears, are (also according to master technician W. D. Gann) more likely to reverse around this date than any other of the year![30]

Thaler (1992) covers many more of the major anomalies that have been discovered: The January effect, in which most of the gains are made in the first week of the month and the first month of the year; specific differences in the average return experienced on different days of the week and at different times of the trading day; steep discounts to net asset values of closed-end mutual funds; and evidence of long-run mean reversion of stock price returns—which shouldn't occur if the market is truly a random walk.[31]

Momentum strategies that involve ranking the performance of assets as based on their previous (usually 12-month look-back) returns have also been shown to be anomalous.[32] Shares of the largest firms perform much better relative to those of small companies in the last quarter of the year and relatively worse in the first quarter.[33] Weather-induced mood changes appear to affect trading decisions, with market returns higher on sunny days.[34] Reversal in returns, wherein last month's or week's winners are next month's or week's losers and vice versa has also been verified.[35]

But perhaps the most debilitating to EMH and MPT proponents is the evidence that low-risk portfolios (i.e., those with low volatility) outperform those with high volatility—all of which flies in the face of the underlying economic theory dictating that greater risk must be compensated by greater rewards (i.e., expected returns).[36] There is thus a *beta* anomaly in that low *beta* stocks tend to outperform high *beta* stocks and high *beta* is associated with low *alpha*.[37] Getting better performance (in "value" versus "growth" stocks) while even taking on less risk totally upends the EMH thinking. What a deal!

7.6   CONCLUSIONS

It is increasingly evident that a more promising overall approach—one that much more closely aligns with the emotional and psychological impetus for trading and speculation—is provided by behavioral finance and socionomic research, which uses methods that are mainly inductive, not deductive.

There is, moreover, an emerging recognition of linkages between the work of behavioral economists and that of scientists who study the brain's activity centers.[38] Plainly, when emotional intensity waxes, rationality wanes. "Intense emotion drowns out rational thought."[39] The madness of mobs rules the moment.[40]

The pillars of economic theory—its core premises—are that (a) people constrained to a budget optimize (i.e., decide via rational expectations) in making affordable choices and (b) that in competitive markets fluctuating prices take aim at an "equilibrium" point at which supply equals demand.[41] As the following pages suggest, these premises are not effectively descriptive or prescriptive in the not-so-rare occurrences of extreme market events.

The one behavioral certainty is that nothing attracts a crowd like a crowd.

NOTES

1. Taranto (2016).
2. This perhaps incidentally provides an explanation for why many financial economists, like dogs chewing on a favorite old bone, still continue to analyze minutia of the efficient-market hypothesis. Behavioralists would say this is mistaken focus on sunk costs. See also Conlisk (1996), Dhami (2016) on bounded rationality, Warneryd (2001), and Scherbina and Schlusche (2014).
3. Akerlof (2002) has suggested that such asymmetry is also seen in macroeconomic relationships. Kim and Nofsinger (2007) discuss how the behavior of Japanese investors differed in bull and bear markets and they "identify some striking differences in investing behavior." Adriani and Deidda (2004) illustrate that sellers, who "are informed about their own quality and have the same information as the buyers regarding other sellers," can engage in "a signaling game."

4. A related regret theory, posited by Bailey (2005, p. 100), even suggests that decision-makers compare outcomes "that might have occurred but didn't." When winning, people are proud and likely to boast. When losing from having made a bad decision, holding onto loses and hoping for recovery implies that feelings of regret can be avoided.

5. See also Peterson (2007, pp. 203–4).

6. See Poundstone (2010, pp. 51–2) and Simon's 1945 book, *Administrative Behavior: A Study of Decision-Making Processes*, New York: Macmillan.

7. Ariely (2008) writes "that we are not only irrational, but *predictably irrational* – that our irrationality happens the same way, again and again....we are far less rational than standard economic theory assumes. Moreover, these irrational behaviors of ours are neither random nor senseless. They are systematic, and since we repeat them again and again, predictable." Wallace (2010) writes of how behavioral finance ideas are being practically applied to actual portfolio management. In this piece, Eugene Fama is quoted, saying, "...the behavioralists haven't replaced the EMH with a single, comprehensive explanation of their own."

Research recounted by Blakeslee (2003) also suggests that economic decisions are at least in part governed by brain chemistry and by individual biological makeup rather than rationality and economic logic. Work by Burnham (2007) goes against the classical economic presumptions in supporting the idea that people strive more for relative than for absolute prosperity. See also Hotz (2008), covering research on trading activity as it relates to levels of testosterone and cortisol.

An overview of this "neuroeconomics" is given in "Why Logic Often Takes a Backseat," *BusinessWeek*, March 28, 2005, in Parisi and Smith (2005), and in Cassidy (2006), who noted that "economists were obliged to exclude from their analyses many phenomena that didn't fit the rational-actor framework, such as stock-market bubbles, drug addiction, and compulsive shopping." Gao and Schmidt (2005) add that in neoclassical models, "the representative agent is presumed to be a perfectly rational man who behaves according to expected utility theory in order to realize his maximal utility. He is an unbiased Bayesian forecaster, always serious-minded, and never subject to psychological effects. He optimizes, but otherwise his behavior is like a black box." See also Goode (2002) and Milgrom and Stokey (1982) concerning the no-speculation theorem, which says that if all traders are rational and the current allocation is *ex ante* Pareto efficient, then new asymmetric information will not lead to trading.

Another branch is "neurofinance," which indicates that the primal pleasure circuits in the brain (*nucleus accumbens*) often override the seat of reason in the frontal cortex. Levy (2006) says, "...stocks, like sex, sometimes drive us crazy."

Cowen (2006) writes "that people are not consistent or fully rational decision makers," and it has been "found that brains assess risk and return separately, rather than making a single calculation of what economists call expected utility." Following research outlined by LeDoux (2004), Taleb (2005, p. 38) similarly notes that "both risk detection and risk avoidance are not mediated in the 'thinking' part of the brain but largely in the emotional one...rational thinking has little, very little, to do with risk avoidance." Andrew Lo in a *PBS NewsHour* of January 9, 2009, said, "Neuroscientists have shown that financial gain triggers the exact same reward circuitry in the brain that cocaine does: It makes you relax and be a lot less concerned about risk." See also Loewenstein (2000) on visceral factors and emotions and Coates (2012a, b). A thorough overview appears in Dhami (2016).

In terms of socionomics, Prechter (2004) writes: "...consumers judge prices for bread and shoes consciously and reasonably according to their needs and means. When human beings value financial assets, they must contend with a debilitating lack of knowledge and feelings of uncertainty. They contend with these obstacles to a great degree by forming judgments in sympathy with or in reaction to the opinions and behavior of others. This surrender of responsibility makes them participants in a collective, which is not a reasoning entity....shared mood trends and collective behavior appear to derive from a herding impulse governed by the phylogenetically ancient, pre-reasoning portions of the brain... it is maladaptive to forming successful expectations concerning future financial valuation...Social mood change does not necessarily affect every individual involved, but in the aggregate, the people participating in markets act as a crowd...just like a crowd, Wall Street feeds off its own frenzies." In a later *Market Perspective* interview (February 23, 2006), he adds: "The markets aren't merely an intellectual exercise. They're an emotional one as well." See also Prechter and Parker (2007), which expands on this theme, saying, "...herds are ruled by the majority, not the wise...The rational areas of the brain...provide rationalization for the emotional behavior in question."

Zweig (2010) points to a *Current Biology* journal study showing that "that the value you place on something is likely to go up when other people tell you it is worth more than you thought, and down when others say it is worth less." This means that people are inclined to go along with the crowd not only for the sense of safety in numbers but also because it gives pleasure by activating a part of the brain that specializes in processing rewards. Glimcher (2003), Peterson (2007), Burnham (2008), and Shermer (2008) provide additional references.

Several other studies indicate that other nonrational factors might also affect emotional behavior, psychology, and therefore trading decisions. Kamstra et al. (2003), for instance found that different amounts of daylight in different seasons might affect average returns, Hirshleifer and Shumway (2003) found that "sunshine is strongly significantly correlated with stock returns." Dichev and Janes (2003) showed that average returns around new moon dates are almost twice those around full moon dates. Yuan et al. (2006) found "strong global evidence that stock returns are lower on days around a full moon than on days around a new moon...findings are thus not consistent with the predictions of traditional asset pricing theories that assume fully rational investors." Sias (2007) shows an end-of-quarter month anomaly. Novy-Marx (2014) writes that predictive regressions indicate that things like El Niño currents, sunspot activity, and conjunctions of the planets have significant power in predicting anomalies. And Krivelyova and Robotti (2003) write that "[U]nusually high levels of geomagnetic activity have a negative, statistically and economically significant effect on the following week's stock returns for all U.S. stock market indices...substantially higher returns around the world during periods of quiet geomagnetic activity." Shefrin (2002) provides a general overview of behavioral finance.

How people make decisions is covered in Lehrer (2009), who writes (p. xv) that the assumption of human rationality is wrong. "It's not how the brain works...we weren't designed to be rational creatures." See also note 22.

8. Frydman and Goldberg (2011) explain that imperfect knowledge is inescapable and they find faults in both the REH and behavioral approaches, noting (p. 4) that "extant economic models fail to account for swings in asset prices and risk because they rest on irreparably flawed foundations...their use by market participants...has no scientific basis." As for the behavioralists (p. 3), they also presume that "irrational individuals' decisions...can be adequately portrayed with mechanical rules." Loewenstein and Willard (2006) further suggest that it is logically flawed to claim that behavioral biases will affect asset prices if there is limited liability of investors, interest rates are endogenous to the economy (i.e., determined by supply and demand for capital), and if a budget constraint is satisfied (i.e., excessive consumption or investment is balanced by increased borrowing). Fama (1998) defends the EMH in noting that behavioralists rarely provide any specific statistical models as alternatives.

9. A study by Kaplanski et al. (2015) found that "noneconomic factors affect return and risk expectations, where the return effect is more profound."

10. Cutler et al. (1989) found that "large market moves often occur on days without any identifiable major news releases," which "casts doubt on the view that stock price movements are fully explicable by news about future cash flows and discount rates." For the majority of the 50 largest changes in stock prices between 1946 and 1987, news was not responsible for the changes. Romer (1993) also addresses this issue. Roll (1984, 1988) finds that the correlations (adjusted R-squared) of stock returns and news events are rather small—perhaps 0.35 with monthly data and 0.20 with daily data. Buchanan (2008) discusses research by Joulin et al. (2008), indicating that most sudden, large price jumps are *not* linked to news items per se. Tetlock (2011) finds that "individual investors overreact to stale information, leading to temporary movements" in related stock prices. Prechter (2016) provides more detail and Kahneman (2013, p. 75) describes the underlying psychology, writing "all headlines do is satisfy our need for coherence: a large event is supposed to have consequences, and consequences need causes to explain them.' See also Funke and Matsuda (2006).

11. According to De Bondt (1995), theorists blame the data for being noisy and containing measurement error, survivorship bias, and selection bias. If the data are few, they cannot be properly tested, and if numerous, the data are mined. Dimson et al. (2002) further observe that total returns, including those from reinvested income, are overstated by historical indices because of contamination by survivorship bias.

12. See also Camerer et al. (2004), Tvede (1999), and Forbes (2009) who provide an overview of psychology as applied to trading, and Kahneman (2013).

13. As Bogle (2008) puts it, most people, in both their investment and political ideas, "search for the facts that confirm our beliefs (reinforcement bias), not for the facts that would negate them." A related behavioral concept is "disaster myopia," in which people find it difficult to imagine that very bad things might happen. See also Friesen et al. (2009).

14. Samuelson and Zeckhauser (1988).

15. Thaler and Johnson (1990).

16. Quote from Montier (2002, p. 21). Kahneman and Tversky (2000) suggest that people tend to give zero weight to relatively unlikely but possible outcomes and to give a weight of one to relatively certain but not guaranteed outcomes, that is, people tend to exaggerate the true probabilities. The weighting function is accordingly nonlinear and asymmetric, which indicates that if people do indeed behave in this manner perhaps a nonlinear dynamics (i.e., chaos) theoretical approach—as, for example, surveyed in Barnett and Serletis (2000)—may be the one most consistent with the precepts of behavioral finance. See also Ziemba and Ziemba (2007) and Chap. 6 on chaos.

17. As found by Ang and Chen, correlations conditional on downside movements (for both a US equity portfolio and the US equity market) are on average 11.6% higher than that implied by a normal distribution, whereas correlations conditional on upside movements cannot be statistically distinguished from those implied by a normal distribution. See Chap. 3 on correlations.

18. Cooper (2008, pp. 7–8) and Wilmott and Orrell (2017, p. 154).

19. If so, then stocks and other readily tradable assets are sometimes almost like what economists call Giffen (or experience) goods, which are those for which a rise in price makes people demand more rather than less of them—that is, the price elasticity of demand is positive rather than negative, as is the case with most utilitarian products and services. Cassidy (2009, p. 36) writes that Adam Smith had not intended the notion of an "invisible hand" to be applied to financial transactions.

20. See Surowiecki (2004, pp. 246–47).

21. An availability cascade, as described in Kuran and Sunstein (1999), "is a self-reinforcing process of collective belief formation by which an expressed perception triggers…increasing plausibility." The effect is obviously seen also in politics.

22. First discovered in the early 1990s, mirror neurons operate in the subconscious mind and enable us, as a matter of survival, to mimic and to feel the emotions of others in the community. Pradeep (2010, p. 99) explains that mirror neurons "absorb the culture, experiences, feelings, and actions of those around you – and you are changed…{M}irror neurons for emotion reading and empathy reside in two areas deep inside the cortex: the insula and the anterior cingulate cortex." "Crowds," as Futia (2009, p. 24) says, "suppress the dissenting views of non-members and amplify the consensus views of their members." Strogatz (2003, p. 262) writes that "…the signs of human sync are inescapable: the herd mentality of stock traders and the resultant booms and crashes in the market; the brutal stupidity of mobs; the political and business oversights cause by 'group think'… are all instances of sync at the level of the group." See also note 7.

23. See Patel et al. (1991), Topol (1991), Lakonishok et al. (1992), Sirri and Tufano (1998), and Youssefmir et al. (1998). Former Fed Chairman Greenspan in Greenspan (2007, p. 16) also wrote, "All people appear motivated by an inbred striving for self-esteem that is in large part fostered by the approval of others." This is consistent with Greenspan (2013), in which he expressed acceptance of aspects of behavioral finance and indeed sounded like a socionomist writing (p. 9): "…markets are prone to wild and even deranging mood swings that are uncoupled from any underlying rational basis."

24. Higher prices begetting higher demand has been described as a positive self-reinforcing feedback loop associated with herding behavior. See Sornette (2003, pp. 94–6) and Nofsinger and Sias (1999).

25. Alevy et al. (2007) explain that an information cascade occurs when "individuals rationally choose identical actions despite having different private information… The homogeneity of a herd may arise through other than informational means such as payoff externalities, preferences for conformity, or sanctions." A bibliography on information cascades appears at www.info-cascades.info.

26. See Chap. 10, note 13.

27. If everyone "diversifies" into the same assets at the same time, as happens in bubbles, then no one is diversified. One hundred seventy years ago, Mackay (1841, pp. xix–xx) certainly had it right when he observed that "…whole communities suddenly fix their minds upon one object and go mad in its pursuit… Men, it has been well said, think in herds; it will be seen that they go mad in herds, while they only recover their senses slowly, and one by one." Along similar lines, a paper by Asparouhova et al. (2011) characterizes bubbles and crashes as tension between social and individual rationality. Scharfstein and Stein (1990) explore the forces that lead to herding behavior and how it can be rational from a fund manager's point of view.

28. Categorization is by Parker in Chap. 34 in Prechter (2016).

29. Kaminsky and Reinhart (2000) and Kaminsky et al. (2003) examine patterns of fundamentals-based contagion.

30. Events cataloged by Montgomery appear in Forsyth (2009). A Yale study on neuroanatomy relating such seasonal anomalies to changes in human blood chemistry at specific times of the year is summarized in "Do the Seasons Affect How We Think?," available at http://yalemedicine.org/info/health.aspx?Cont entTypeId=6&ContentId=707839 and Feb. 8, 2016, edition of *Proceedings of the National Academy of Sciences*.

31. The January effect was covered in Rozeff and Kinney (1976), and French (1980) studied the weekend effect, finding that the average return on Monday is low. However, the formal study of seasonal stock price movements dates back to Wachtel (1942). Ariel (1987) presented an end-of-month (monthly) effect, which was also analyzed by Rosenberg (2004). Booth and Keim (2000) find that "the January effect is alive and well, but difficult to capture." Hensel and Ziemba (2000) conclude that there is a small-cap effect in the second half of December that may be exploitable in the future market. They also found a significant seasonality in S&P 500 returns for February 1928 to June 1993, with January, March, May, and July showing above-average turn-of-the-month (TOM) returns. Also, "[I]n every month, the mean daily returns during TOM were higher than the average daily return." This appears in Ziemba (2012). TOM effects are also covered in Hensel et al. (2000). Haug and Hirschey (2006) found the "January effect in small-cap stock returns is remarkably consistent over time…continues to present a serious challenge to the efficient market hypothesis." Hulbert (2017), though, suggests that the January Barometer has been right only 64% of the time since 1972, which conflicts with Yale Hirsch's *Stock Trader's Almanac* report that the Barometer has since 1950 been far more accurate than that. Keloharju et al. (2016) examine seasonal return anomalies. And Jacobsen and Bouman (2002) found a strong seasonal return

effect based on the idea of "Sell in May and go away" (or Halloween indicator). Xie et al. (2016) suggested that "the Halloween effect" is actually a 'news effect' or efficient market in disguise.

On the same subject, McConnell and Xu (2008) found that the turn-of-the-month effect "is not confined to small-capitalization or low-price stocks, to calendar year-ends or quarter-ends, or to the United States...it occurs in 31 of the 35 countries examined." The accrual anomaly shows that companies using the most aggressive accounting policies for earnings had stock prices that were later most likely to fall and those with the least aggressive policies tended to rise. See "Fuzzy Numbers," *BusinessWeek*, October 4, 2004, and Sloan (1996). Richardson (2004) describes a Friday announcement effect in which "20% of earnings that came out on Fridays were more likely to be negative than those announced on other weekdays and 25% more likely to fall below analysts' forecasts." The famous Palm/3Com anomaly is noted in Varian (2005) and analyzed in Cochrane (2003) and at gsbwww.uchicago.edu/fac/john.cochrane/ research/papers/.

Shleifer (2000) reviews anomalies and the case against the EMH and in favor of the behavioral finance approach, and mean reversion is discussed in Goetzmann (1993) and Cecchetti et al. (1990). Using long-term data, Goetzmann found "evidence of a persistent mean-reverting component in stock prices." Cecchetti et al. found that "negative serial correlation in long horizon stock returns is consistent with an equilibrium model of asset pricing." Prechter and Parker (2007), however, note that "...there is no stock-price mean that isn't arbitrary or constantly changing, so stock prices have nothing constant to which to revert." That is, financial markets do not revert to anything. Anomalies and liquidity effects are also discussed in Gromb and Vayanos (2010).

Hall (2001, p. 4) also writes, "Modern financial economics speaks of the puzzle of time-varying risk premiums, not a clear finding of irrationality...No new information about the fundamentals of the economy became evident on the days in October 1929 and October 1987 when the market fell remarkably. Interpretation of these kinds of events takes us squarely back to the issue of how people estimate probabilities in a nonstationary world."

32. Momentum at the individual stock level has been studied by Jegadeesh and Titman (1993) and for a wide variety of asset classes by Asness et al. (2013). Miffre and Rallis (2007) showed that momentum strategies earn significant excess returns.

33. See Hulbert (2016) and Ackert and Athanassakos (2000). A possible reason for this is that because of the way money managers are incentivized, they have greatest risk tolerance in January and least in Q4.

34. See Saunders (1993), Hirshleifer and Shumway (2003), Sias (2007), Novy-Marx (2014), Goetzmann et al. (2015), and Keloharju et al. (2016).

35. See Lehmann (1990), Jegadeesh (1990), and Gray and Vogel (2016, pp. 80–92).

36. Li et al. (2016) and Hou et al. (2015).

37. See Frazzini and Pederson (2014) and Fama and French (2016), who address this anomaly with a five-factor model that uses profitability and investments as additional factors helping to explain the low average returns of high *beta* shares.

38. Experiments (reported in the March 2009 *Proceedings of the National Academy of Sciences USA*) have shown that the central location for the "money illusion"

that is characteristic of bubbles and crashes is in the brain's ventromedial pre-frontal cortex (VMPFC). This area lights up in subjects who encounter a large amount of money and reacts with other parts of the brain that govern fear (the amygdala) and greed (the *nucleus accumbens*). The primitive limbic system over-rides the neocortex. See Stix (2009) and note 7. As to why and when people change their minds and switch preferences (e.g., from bullish to bearish or vice versa), see Lichtenstein and Slovic (1973).

39. Paraphrase from Marah Boyesen presentation at Socionomics Summit 2013.
40. On this see Surowiecki (2004) and Lo (2017).
41. Thaler (2015, p. 5).

REFERENCES

Ackert, L. F., & Athanassakos, G. (2000). Institutional Investors, Analyst Following, and the January Anomaly. *Journal of Business Finance & Accounting, 27*(3–4), 469–485.

Adriani, F., & Deidda, L. G. (2004). Few Bad Apples or Plenty of Lemons: Which Makes It Harder to Market Plums? Working Paper CRENoS 200413, Cagliari: Centre for North South Economic Research. Available at www.crenos.it/working/pdf/04-13.pdf

Akerlof, G. A. (2002, June). Behavioral Macroeconomics & Macroeconomic Behavior. *American Economic Review, 92*(3).

Alevy, J. E., Haigh, M. S., & List, J. A. (2007). Information Cascades: Evidence from a Field Experiment with Financial Market Professionals. *Journal of Finance, 62*(1), 151–180.

Ang, A., & Chen, J. (2002). Asymmetric Correlations of Equity Portfolios. *Journal of Financial Economics, 63*(3).

Ariel, R. A. (1987). A Monthly Effect in Stock Returns. *Journal of Financial Economics, 18*(1), 161–174.

Ariely, D. (2008). *Predictably Irrational: The Hidden Forces that Shape Our Decisions.* New York: HarperCollins.

Arnott, R. D. (2004, October). Blinded by Theory? *Institutional Investor* and *Journal of Portfolio Management*, 30th Anniversary Issue.

Asness, C., Moskowitz, T., & Pedersen, L. (2013). Value and Momentum Everywhere. *Journal of Finance, 68*(3), 929–985.

Asparouhova, E., Bossaerts, P., & Tran, A. (2011). Market Bubbles and Crashes as an Expression of Tension Between Social and Individual Rationality: Experiments. Working Paper, University of Utah.

Bailey, R. E. (2005). *The Economics of Financial Markets.* Cambridge: Cambridge University Press.

Barberis, N., & Thaler, R. (2002). A Survey of Behavioral Finance. In G. M. Constantinides, M. Harris, and R. M. Stulz. (2003), (Eds.), *Handbook of the Economics of Finance.* Amsterdam: Elsevier Science, Ltd., and also in Thaler (2005).

Barnett, W. A., & Serletis, A. (2000). Martingales, Nonlinearity, and Chaos. *Journal of Economic Dynamics and Control,24*, 703–724, and Available at wuecon.wustl.edu/~barnett/Papers.html

Berger, J. (2016). *Contagious: Why Things Catch On.* New York: Simon & Schuster (Paperback edition).

Bikhchandani, S., Hirshleifer, D., & Welch, I. (1992). A Theory of Fads, Fashion, Custom, and Cultural Change as Informational Cascades. *Journal of Political Economy, 100*(5), 992–1026.

Blakeslee, S. (2003, June 17). Brain Experts Now Follow the Money. *New York Times.*

Bogle, J. C. (2008, March/April). Black Monday and Black Swans. *Financial Analysts Journal, 64*(2).

Booth, D. G., & Keim, D. B. (2000). Is There Still a January Effect? In D. B. Keim & W. T. Ziemba (Eds.), *Security Market Imperfections in Worldwide Equity Markets.* Cambridge/New-York/Melbourne: Cambridge University Press.

Brav, A., & Heaton, J. B. (2002). Competing Theories of Financial Anomalies. *Review of Financial Studies, 15*(2), 575.

Buchanan, M. (2008, July 19). Crazy Money. *New Scientist.*

Burnham, T. C. (2007, September 22). High-Testosterone Men Reject Low Ultimatum Game Offers. *Proceedings of the Royal Society B, 274*(1623).

Burnham, T. C. (2008). *Mean Markets and Lizard Brains: How to Profit from the New Science of Irrationality* (Rev. ed.). Hoboken: Wiley.

Camerer, C. F., Lowenstein, G., & Rabin, M. (Eds.). (2004). *Advances of Behavioral Economics.* Princeton: Princeton University Press. (Russell Sage Foundation).

Capen, E. C., Clapp, R. V., & Campbell, W. M. (1971, June). Competitive Bidding in High-Risk Situations. *Journal of Petroleum Technology, 23.*

Cassidy, J. (2006, September 18). Mind Games: What Neuroeconomics Tells Us About Money and the Brain. *The New Yorker.*

Cassidy, J. (2009). *How Markets Fail: The Logic of Economic Calamities.* New York: Farrar, Straus and Giroux.

Cecchetti, S. G., Lam, P. K., & Mark, N. C. (1990, June). Mean Reversion in Equilibrium Asset Prices. *American Economic Review, 80*(3).

Christie, W., & Huang, R. (1995). Following the Pied Piper: Do Individual Returns Herd Around the Market? *Financial Analysts Journal, 51*(4), 31.

Coates, J. (2012a, June 10). The Biology of Bubble and Crash. *New York Times.*

Coates, J. (2012b). *The Hour Between Dog and Wolf: Risk Taking, Gut Feelings, and the Biology of Boom and Bust.* New York: Penguin.

Cochrane, J. H. (2003). Stocks as Money: Convenience Yield and the Tech Stock Bubble. In Hunter et al. (2003 [2005]).

Cochrane, J. H. (2011, August). Discount Rates. *Journal of Finance, 66*(4).

Conlisk, J. (1996). Why Bounded Rationality? *Journal of Economic Literature, 34.*

Cooper, G. (2008). *The Origin of Financial Crises: Central Banks, Credit Bubbles, and the Efficient Market Fallacy.* New York: Harriman House (Vintage paperback).

Cowen, T. (2006, April 20). Enter the Neuro-Economists: Why Do Investors Do What They Do? *New York Times.*

Cutler, D. M., Poterba, J. M., & Summers, L. H. (1989, Spring). What Moves Stock Prices? *Journal of Portfolio Management, 15*(3).

De Bondt, W. (1995). Investor Psychology and the Dynamics of Security Prices. In *Behavioral Finance and Decision Theory in Investment Management.* Charlottesville: Association for Investment Management and Research.

De Bondt, W. (2012). Asset Bubbles: Insights from Behavioral Finance. In Evanoff et al. (2012).

De Bondt, W., & Thaler, R. (1986). Does the Stock Market Overreact? *Journal of Finance, 60.*

Dhami, S. (2016). *The Foundations of Behavioral Economic Analysis*. New York: Oxford University Press.

Dichev, I. D., & Janes, T. D. (2003). Lunar Cycle Effects in Stock Returns. *Journal of Private Equity, 6*(4). Available at http://ssrn.com/abstract=281665

Dimson, E., Marsh, P., & Staunton, M. (2002, September). Global Evidence on the Equity Risk Premium. *Journal of Applied Corporate Finance*.

Erb, C., Harvey, C., & Viskanta, T. (1994). Forecasting International Equity Correlations. *Financial Analysts Journal, 50*(6), 32–45.

Evanoff, D. D., Kaufman, G. G., & Malliaris, A. G. (Eds.). (2012). *New Perspectives on Asset Price Bubbles: Theory, Evidence, and Policy*. New York: Oxford University Press.

Fama, E. F. (1998). Market Efficiency, Long Run Returns, and Behavioral Finance. *Journal of Financial Economics, 49*.

Fama, E. F., & French, K. (2016). Dissecting Anomalies with a Five-Factor Model. *Review of Financial Studies, 29*(1), 69–103.

Forbes, W. (2009). *Behavioural Finance*. Chichester: Wiley.

Forsyth, R. W. (2009, September 22). Autumnal Equinox – Paul Montgomery. *Barron's*.

Frazzini, A., & Pederson, L. H. (2014). Betting Against Beta. *Journal of Financial Economics, 111*(1), 1–25.

French, K. R. (1980). Stock Returns and the Weekend Effect. *Journal of Financial Economics, 81*(1), 55–69.

Friesen, G. C., Weller, P. A., & Dunham, L. M. (2009). Price Trends and Patterns in Technical Analysis: A Theoretical and Empirical Examination. *Journal of Banking & Finance, 33*(6), 1089–1100.

Frydman, R., & Goldberg, M. D. (2011). *Beyond Mechanical Markets: Asset Price Swings, Risk, and the Role of the State*. Princeton: Princeton University Press.

Funke, N., & Matsuda, A. (2006). Macroeconomic News and Stock Returns in the United States and Germany. *German Economic Review, 7*(2), 189–210.

Futia, C. (2009). *The Art of Contrarian Trading: How to Profit from Crowd Behavior in the Financial Markets*. Hoboken: John Wiley & Sons.

Gao, L., & Schmidt, U. (2005). Self is Never Neutral: Why Economic Agents Behave Irrationally. *Journal of Behavioral Finance, 6*(1), 27–37.

Glimcher, P. W. (2003). *Decisions, Uncertainty, and the Brain: The Science of Neuroeconomics*. Cambridge, MA: MIT Press.

Goetzmann, W. N. (1993, April). Patterns in Three Centuries of Stock Market Prices. *Journal of Business, 66*.

Goetzmann, W. N., Kim, D., & Wang, Q. (2015). Weather-Induced Mood, Institutional Investors, and Stock Returns. *Review of Financial Studies, 28*(1).

Goode, E. (2002, November 5). On Profit, Loss and the Mysteries of the Mind. *New York Times*.

Gray, W. R., & Vogel, J. R. (2016). *Quantitative Momentum*. Hoboken: Wiley.

Greenspan, A. (2007). *The Age of Turbulence: Adventures in a New World*. New York: Penguin.

Greenspan, A. (2013). *The Map and the Territory: Risk, Human Nature, and the Future of Forecasting*. New York: Penguin.

Gromb, D., & Vayanos, D. (2010, December). Limits of Arbitrage. *Annual Review of Financial Economics*, (2).

Hall, R. E. (2001, May). Struggling to Understand the Stock Market. *American Economic Review*, 91(2).

Haug, M., & Hirschey, M. (2006). The January Effect. *Financial Analysts Journal,* *62*(5).

Hensel, C. R., & Ziemba, W. T. (2000). Anticipation of the January Small Firm Effect in the US Futures Markets. In D. B. Keim & W. T. Ziemba (Eds.), *Security Market Imperfections in Worldwide Equity Markets.* New York: CambridgeUniversity Press.

Hensel, C. R., Sick, G. A., & Ziemba, W. T. (2000). A Long Term Examination of the Turn-of-the-Month Effect in the S&P 500. In D. B. Keim & W. T. Ziemba (Eds.), *Security Market Imperfections in Worldwide Equity Markets.* Cambridge University Press.

Hirshleifer, D., & Shumway, T. (2003). Good Day Sunshine: Stock Returns and the Weather. *Journal of Finance, 58*(3), 1009–1032.

Hotz, R. L. (2008, April 18). Testosterone May Fuel Stock-Market Success, or Make Traders Tipsy. *Wall Street Journal.*

Hou, K., Xue, C., & Zhang, L. (2015, March). Digesting Anomalies: An Investment Approach. *Review of Financial Studies, 28*(3).

Hulbert, M. (2016, October 10). Why Large Stocks Wake Up at This Time of Year. *Wall Street Journal.*

Hulbert, M. (2017, January 9). Sorry, the 'January Barometer' Is a Market Myth. *Wall Street Journal.*

Hunter, W. C., Kaufman, G. G., & Pomerleano, M. (Eds.). (2003). *Asset Price Bubbles: The Implications for Monetary, Regulatory, and International Policies.* Cambridge, MA: MIT Press (Paperback edition, 2005).

Jacobsen, B., & Bouman, S. (2002). The Halloween Indicator, 'Sell in May and Go Away' Another Puzzle. *American Economic Review, 92*(5), 1618–1635.

Jegadeesh, N. (1990, July). Evidence of Predictable Behavior of Security Returns. *Journal of Finance, 45*(3).

Jegadeesh, N., & Titman, S. (1993). Returns to Buying Winners and Selling Losers: Implications for Stock Market Efficiency. *Journal of Finance, 48*(1), 65–91.

Joulin, A., Lefevre, A., Grunberg, D., & Bouchaud, J-P. (2008, March). Stock Price Jumps: News and Volume Play a Minor Role. *Physics and Society.* Available at www.arxiv.org/abs/0803.1769 and *Wilmott,* Sept/Oct 2008.

Kahneman, D. (2013). *Thinking, Fast and Slow.* New York: Farrar, Straus and Giroux.

Kahneman, D., & Tversky, A. (1979). Prospect Theory: An Analysis of Decision Under Risk. *Econometrica, 47.*

Kahneman, D., & Tversky, A. (2000). *Choices, Values and Frames.* Cambridge: Cambridge University Press.

Kaminsky, G. L., & Reinhart, C. (2000). On Crises, Contagion, and Confusion. *Journal of International Economics, 51*(1).

Kaminsky, G. L., Reinhart, C., & Végh, C. A. (2003). The Unholy Trinity of Financial Contagion. *Journal of Economic Perspectives, 17*(4), 51–74.

Kamstra, M. L., Kramer, L., & Levi, M. (2003). Winter Blues: A SAD Stock Market Cycle. *American Economic Review, 93*(1), 324–343.

Kaplanski, G., Levy, H., Veld, C., & Veld-Merkoulova, Y. (2015). Do Happy People Make Optimistic Investors? *Journal of Financial and Quantitative Analysis, 50*(1-2), 145–168.

Keim, D. B., & Ziemba, W. T. (Eds.). (2000). *Security Market Imperfections in Worldwide Equity Markets.* Cambridge: Cambridge University Press.

Keloharju, M., Linnainmaa, J. T., & Nyberg, P. (2016, August). Return Seasonalities. *Journal of Finance, 71*(4).

Kim, K. A., & Nofsinger, J. R. (2007). The Behavior of Japanese Individual Investors During Bull and Bear Markets. *Journal of Behavioral Finance, 8*(3), 138–153.

Krivelyova, A., & Robotti, C. (2003). Playing the Field: Geomagnetic Storms and the Stock Market. Working Paper 2003-5b, Federal Reserve Bank of Atlanta. Available at http://www.frbatlanta.org/filelegacydocs/wp0305b.pdf

Kuran, T., & Sunstein, C. R. (1999, April). Availability Cascades and Risk Regulation. *Stanford Law Review, 51*(4).

Lakonishok, J., Shleifer, A., & Vishny, R. W. (1992). The Impact of Institutional Trading on Stock Prices. *Journal of Financial Economics, 32*(1), 23–43.

LeDoux, J. E. (2004). *The Emotional Brain.* London: Orion Books (Paperback edition).

Lehmann, B. N. (1990). Fads, Martingales, and Market Efficiency. *Quarterly Journal of Economics, 105*(1), 1.

Lehrer, J. (2009). *How We Decide.* Boston: Houghton Mifflin Harcourt.

Levy, A. (2006, March). Mapping the Traders' Brain. *Bloomberg Markets Magazine.* Available at http://www-psych.stanford.edu/~span/Press/neurofinance.pdf

Li, X., Sullivan, R. N., & Garcia-Feijóo, L. (2016). The Low-Volatility Anomaly: Market Evidence on Systematic Risk vs. Mispricing. *Financial Analysts Journal, 72*(1), 36–47.

Lichtenstein, S., & Slovic, P. (1973). Response-Induced Reversals of Preference in Gambling: An Extended Replication in Las Vegas. *Journal of Experimental Psychology, 101*(1).

Lo, A. W. (2017). *Adaptive Markets: Financial Evolution at the Speed of Thought.* Princeton: Princeton University Press.

Loewenstein, G. F. (2000). Emotions in Economic Theory and Economic Behavior. *American Economic Review, 90*(2), 426–432.

Loewenstein, M., & Willard, G. A. (2006, January). The Limits of Investor Behavior. *Journal of Finance, 61*(1).

Mackay, C. (1841). *Extraordinary Popular Delusions and the Madness of Crowds* (1995 ed). New York: John Wiley & Sons.

Manne, H. G. (2006). Efficient Markets. The Welfare of American Investors. Available at www.wku.edu/~brian.goff/Efficient%20Markets%20Manne.doc

Mauboussin, M. J. (2006). *More Than You Know: Finding Financial Wisdom in Unconventional Places.* New York: Columbia University Press.

McConnell, J. J., & Xu, W. (2008, March/April). Equity Returns at the Turn of the Month. *Financial Analysts Journal, 64*(2).

Miffre, J., & Rallis, G. (2007). Momentum Strategies in Commodity Futures Markets. *Journal of Banking and Finance, 31*, 1863–1886.

Milgrom, P., & Stokey, N. (1982). Information, Trade and Common Knowledge. *Journal of Economic Theory, 26*, 17–27.

Montier, J. (2002). *Behavioural Finance: Insights into Irrational Minds and Markets.* Chichester/Hoboken: Wiley.

Nofsinger, J. R., & Sias, R. W. (1999). Herding and Feedback Trading by Institutional and Individual Investors. *Journal of Finance, 53*.

Novy-Marx, R. (2014, May). Predicting Anomaly Performance with Politics, the Weather, Global Warming, Sunspots, and the Stars. *Journal of Financial Economics, 112*(2).

Odean, T. (1998). Volume, Volatility, Price, and Profit When all Traders Are Above Average. *Journal of Finance, 53*(6), 1887–1934.

Parisi, F., & Smith, V. L. (2005). *The Law and Economics of Irrational Behavior.* Stanford: Stanford University Press.

Patel, J., Zeckhauser, R., & Hendricks, D. (1991). The Rationality Struggle: Illustrations from Financial Markets. *American Economic Review, 81,* 232–236.

Peters, E. E. (1994). *Fractal Market Analysis: Applying Chaos Theory to Investment and Economics.* New York: Wiley.

Peterson, R. L. (2007). *Inside the Investor's Brain: The Power of Mind Over Money.* Hoboken: Wiley.

Pixley, J. (2012). *Emotions in Finance: Booms, Busts and Uncertainty* (2nd ed.). Cambridge: Cambridge University Press.

Poundstone, W. (2010). *Priceless: The Myth of Fair Value.* New York: Hill and Wang (Farrar, Straus and Giroux).

Pradeep, A. K. (2010). *The Buying Brain: Secrets to Selling to the Subconscious Mind.* Hoboken: Wiley.

Prechter, R. R., Jr. (1995 [2001]). *At the Crest of the Tidal Wave.* Gainesville: New Classics Library.

Prechter, R. R., Jr. (1999). *The Wave Principle of Human Social Behavior and the New Science of Socionomics.* Gainesville: New Classics Library.

Prechter, R. R., Jr. (2004). The Fractal Nature of the Stock Market. In *The Colours of Infinity: The Beauty, and Power of Fractals.* London: Clear Books.

Prechter, R. R., Jr. (2016). *The Socionomic Theory of Finance.* Gainesville: Socionomics Institute Press.

Prechter, R. R., Jr., & Parker, W. D. (2007). The Financial/Economic Dichotomy in Social Behavioral Dynamics: The Socionomic Perspective. *Journal of Behavioral Finance, 8*(1).

Richardson, K. (2004, September 24). Friday's a Good Day for Bad News After All. *Wall Street Journal.*

Roll, R. (1984). Orange Juice and Weather. *American Economic Review, 74.*

Roll, R. (1988). R². *Journal of Finance, 43*(3)

Romer, D. H. (1993). Rational Asset-Price Movements Without News. *American Economic Review, 83*(5).

Rosenberg, M. (2004, Fall). The Monthly Effect in Stock Returns and Conditional Heteroscedasticity. *The American Economist, XLVIII*(2).

Rozeff, M. S., & Kinney, W. R., Jr. (1976). Capital Market Seasonality: The Case of Stock Returns. *Journal of Financial Economics, 3*(4), 379–402.

Samuelson, W., & Zeckhauser, R. (1988). Status Quo Bias in Decision Making. *Journal of Risk and Uncertainty, 1,* 7–59.

Saunders, E. M., Jr. (1993, December). Stock Prices and Wall Street Weather. *American Economic Review, 83*(5).

Scharfstein, D. S., & Stein, J. C. (1990, June). Herd Behavior and Investment. *American Economic Review, 90*(3).

Scherbina, A., & Schlusche, B. (2014). Asset Price Bubbles: A Survey. *Quantitative Finance, 14*(4), 589–604.

Shefrin, H. (2002). *Beyond Greed and Fear: Understanding Behavioral Finance and the Psychology of Investing.* New York: Oxford University Press.

Shefrin, H., & Statman, M. (1985). The Disposition to Sell Winners Too Early and Ride Losers Too Long. *Journal of Finance, 40.*

Shermer, M. (2008). *The Mind of the Market.* New York: Times Books (Henry Holt).

Shleifer, A. (2000). *Inefficient Markets: An Introduction to Behavioral Finance*. Oxford: Oxford University Press.

Sias, R. (2007, March/April). Causes and Seasonality of Momentum Profits. *Financial Analysts Journal, 63*(2).

Sirri, E. R., & Tufano, P. (1998). Costly Search and Mutual Fund Flows. *Journal of Finance, 53*, 1589–1622.

Sloan, R. G. (1996, July). Do Stock Prices Fully Reflect Information in Accruals and Cash Flows About Future Earnings. *Accounting* Review, *7*(3).

Sornette, D. (2003). *Why Stock Markets Crash: Critical Events in Complex Financial Systems*. Princeton: Princeton University Press.

Statman, M. (1995). Behavioral Finance Versus Standard Finance. In *Behavioral Finance and Decision Theory in Investment Management*. Charlottesville: Association for Investment Management and Research.

Statman, M. (1999, November/December). Behavioral Finance: Past Battles and Future Engagements. *Financial Analysts Journal, 55*(6).

Stix, G. (2009, July). The Science of Bubbles & Busts. *Scientific American*.

Strogatz, S. (2003). *Sync: The Emerging Science of Spontaneous Order*. New York: Hyperion.

Surowiecki, J. (2004). *The Wisdom of Crowds*. New York: Doubleday.

Taleb, N. N. (2005). *Fooled by Randomness*. New York: Random House (2nd Paperback edition).

Taranto, J. (2016, August 20). Dilbert Explains Donald Trump. *Wall Street Journal*.

Tetlock, P. (2011, January). All the News That's Fit to Reprint: Do Investors React to Stale Information? *Review of Financial Studies*.

Thaler, R. H. (1992). *The Winner's Curse: Paradoxes and Anomalies of Economic Life*. Princeton: Princeton University Press.

Thaler, R. H. (Ed.). (2005). *Advances in Behavioral Finance* (Vol. II). Princeton: Princeton University Press.

Thaler, R. H. (2015). *Misbehaving: The Making of Behavioral Economics*. New York: W.W. Norton.

Thaler, R., & Johnson, E. (1990, June). Gambling with the House Money and Trying to Break Even. *Management Science, 36*(6).

Topol, R. (1991). Bubbles and Volatility of Stock Prices: Effect of Mimetic Contagion. *The Economic Journal, 101*(407), 786–800.

Tuckett, D. (2011). *Minding the Markets: An Emotional Finance View of Financial Instability*. London: Palgrave Macmillan.

Tvede, L. (1999). *The Psychology of Finance*. Chichester: Wiley.

Tversky, A., & Kahneman, D. (1974). *Judgment Under Uncertainty: Heuristics and Biases. Science*.

Tversky, A., & Kahneman, D. (1981, January). The Framing of Decisions and the Psychology of Choice. *Science, 211*.

Vaga, T. (1990, November/December). The Coherent Market Hypothesis. *Financial Analysts Journal, 45*(6).

Varian, H. R. (2005, March 10). Five Years After Nasdaq Hit Its Peak, Some Lessons Learned. *New York Times*.

Veblen, T. (1899). *The Theory of the Leisure Class*. New York: Macmillan (Paperback, New American Library, 1953).

Wachtel, S. B. (1942, April). Certain Observations on Seasonal Movements in Stock Prices. *Journal of Business, 15*(2).

Wallace, C. (2010, May). Mind Over Markets. *Institutional Investor.*

Warneryd, K.-E. (2001). *Stock Market Psychology: How People Value and Trade Stocks.* Cheltenham: Elgar.

Weber, M., & Camerer, C. (1998). The Disposition Effect in Securities Trading: An Experimental Analysis. *Journal of Economic Behavior and Organization, 33.*

Wilmott, P., & Orrell, D. (2017). *The Money Formula: Dodgy Finance, Psuedo Science, and How Mathematicians Took Over the Markets.* Hoboken: Wiley.

Xie, H., Qin, Q., & Wang, S. (2016, November). The Halloween Effect a New Puzzle? Evidence from Price Gap. *Review of Economics and Finance, 6.*

Youssefmir, M., Huberman, B. A., & Hogg, T. (1998). Bubbles and Market Crashes. *Computational Economics, 12.*

Yuan, K., Zheng, L., & Zhu, Q. (2006). Are Investors Moonstruck? Lunar Phases and Stock Returns. *Journal of Empirical Finance, 13*(1).

Ziemba, W. T. (Ed.). (2012). *Calendar Anomalies and Arbitrage.* Hackensack/ Singapore: World Scientific.

Ziemba, R. E. S., & Ziemba, W. T. (2007). *Scenarios for Risk Management and Global Investment Strategies.* Chichester: Wiley.

Zweig, J. (2010, June 19). So That's Why Investors Can't Think for Themselves. *Wall Street Journal.*

PART III

Theories Present and Future

The review in Part II suggested that traditional models and approaches, though appealing and successful in some limited applications, are unable to adequately or satisfyingly describe bubble and crash events. This part begins with an overview of the central role played by the equity risk premium, which provides the main, but perhaps not the only, reference series that can be used in developing an elasticity-of-variance (EOV) concept. EOV enables the empirical identification and strength measurement of bubbles and crashes and is applicable in forecasting.

In this wide-ranging coverage, the main departure from neoclassical Walrasian economic theories of equilibrium is that—especially in bubbles and crashes—holding quantity desired is much more what drives the process than price received or offered. The works of Bénassy and Malinvaud provide the theoretical underpinning for this approach.

It is then shown that bubbles and crashes can be empirically described when the elasticity-of-variance measurements within any period follow an exponential-like path and form "microbubbles" and "microcrashes." The more such micro events occur within a sample period, the stronger is the entire event. As the sampling period can be as brief as minutes or as long as months or years, the theory is time-scale independent and consistent with the idea that market price patterns are fractal.

It is shown that the standard equity risk premium contains a behavioral risk premium component that can be estimated from transactions volume changes. A behavioral risk premium appears to have primary significance only during the extreme events known as bubbles and crashes.

CHAPTER 8

Bubble Dynamics

8.1 BUILDING BLOCKS

Share prices are normally expected to trend gradually higher as a reflection of the growth of fundamental economic features that include earnings and dividends. Those features are, in turn, driven over the long run by rising productivity (i.e., technological innovations) and expanding populations. In bubbles, however, the rate of increase in the realized current price runs ahead faster than even the rising but highly uncertain changes in expected earnings and dividend streams. The relationship between the risk premium and the price variance thus changes conspicuously and capriciously.

In any market, there are two moving pieces to watch. The first is the change in expected earnings and dividends—the "fundamentals"—and the second is the valuation applied to the fundamentals. It is, for example, entirely possible that earnings and dividends rise as expected but that share prices do not, or it could be the other way around. The valuation aspect is what makes the difference and what makes forecasting always so devilishly tricky. That's because valuation changes as a function of investor psychology, interest rates, political events, and other such things.

No matter the reasons, however, valuation shifts are manifested by changes in the risk premium. When optimism is prevalent, the risk premium is low, and vice versa. Movement in the risk premium in either direction will thus, often at great relative speed, act to either amplify or dampen any price changes that are based purely on the slower-moving fundamental factors.[1]

This is where the short-side rationing theory of Malinvaud and Bénassy enters. If prices rise proportionately more than the risk premium falls, it is a clear sign that investors and speculators *want and need* to acquire more shares in their portfolios. Prices are being bid up because expected returns now begin to include a *behavioral* as well as a monetary payoff component (see Chap. 9).

Similarly, in crashes the inverse is seen as investors dump shares into the market in far greater proportion than would be called for by a rising monetary

© The Author(s) 2018
H. L. Vogel, *Financial Market Bubbles and Crashes, Second Edition,*
https://doi.org/10.1007/978-3-319-71528-5_8

(i.e., financial) risk premium alone. All of this short-side quantity-determined action shows up in price *variance* bounds being violated to the upside in both bubbles and crashes.[2] In the continuous-time processes that are used to represent asset price trajectories, variation is unbounded.[3]

One way to capture this short-side rationing aspect—and also to avoid the econometric difficulties of equation identification when dealing with prices and quantities—is to simply define a bubble or a crash in terms of variance elasticities. When variance rises proportionately more than the equity risk premium falls (or rises, in crashes), previous price boundaries are violated to the upside (downside in crashes). And this change in the elasticity is the tip-off that something important and different is—for whatever reasons (interest rates, credit availability, investor psychology, dynamic hedging strategies, etc.)—happening.

Different authors will of course model the variance of a stock's price, $\sigma^2 = Var$ $(p_t - p_{t-1})$ differently and cope with series stationarity concerns in assorted ways. But it is sufficient to describe variance bounds (i.e., barriers) as starting to be broken when the historical average variance as computed over the selected time scale is exceeded with increasing frequency and magnitude. More frequency and magnitude must then arithmetically generate a statistically identifiable upward curve whose parameters can be estimated using common econometric methods. With variance elasticity as the central concept, the issue of whether variance bounds actually exist or how they are defined is then largely tangential and inconsequential.

In sum, it is the change of price level that adjusts to changes in the risk premium, but *it is the change in variance that gauges the pressure on quantity demanded or supplied.* Changes in variance are thus the *process* through which the short-side rationing effect is most directly expressed. Unlike the situation described by neoclassical economics, in extreme events considerations of price become secondary to quantity.[4]

8.2   EQUITY RISK PREMIUMS

The one thing (beyond exponentiality) that is readily observed in all bubble and crash experiences is that price return variance rises substantively relative to its previous pre-bubble (or crash) baseline. To be more informative, however, this rise in variance needs a frame of reference. Although not without measurement problems of its own, the equity risk premium (ERP) is able to provide such a reference. That's because the ERP reveals the market's collective attitudinal balance toward acceptance of risk: It drives the quantities of shares that participants will want to hold and it is relatively the easiest to empirically implement because a long and consistently defined series is readily available.[5]

A much more workable definition of a bubble—an elasticity concept—can then be derived by analyzing how much the return variance rises in relation to a decline in the ERP. To this end, it is helpful to first provide a deeper exploration of the nature of the ERP itself, even while recognizing that the ERP literature has little to say on the subject of bubbles and crashes and does not at all aim to explain them.[6]

Definitions

The market risk premium is the return that stock investors want beyond the risk-free rate of return. It can be viewed as being the extra return that investors demand for holding stocks instead of Treasury bills and bonds. Given a bond's fixed-interest and repayment-of-principal-at-maturity features, returns on bonds would over the long run normally be more predictable than for stocks.[7] In the language of the CAPM, the ERP is a premium for bearing *nondiversifiable* aggregate risk.[8]

The equity risk premium is also describable from both a historical *ex post* and a forward-looking *ex ante* point of view.[9] Because the ERP determines the rate at which investors discount future cash flows derived from market portfolios, it determines the return on common stocks, typically defined as

$$R_t = \left(R_t \,/\, R_{t-1} \right)$$

where R_t is the return in period t and P_t and P_{t-1} are, respectively, the prices in the current and immediately prior periods. (If dividends in period t, D_t, are also to be included, R_t then becomes $((P_t + D_t)/P_{t-1})$.[10]

After this, however, a description of the ERP and its relationship to other economic features tends to become rather fluid. Entire books on the subject (e.g., Mehra 2008; Hammond et al. 2011) have been filled with discussions of its various connections to consumption decisions, utility functions, and other such factors. Nevertheless, recognized limitations aside, the ERP is central to the investment process and at the least is something that can be defined and measured relatively well in retrospect. Long-term equity and bond risk premiums are shown in Fig. 8.1.

Estimation Problems

ERP Forecasts of the *ex ante* premium, though not directly observable, are always important to what happens in the stock market.[11] A falling *ex ante* ERP implies that the discount rate applied to the sum of expected dividends has dropped, thereby raising the present level of stock prices. The equity premium, according to Jagannathan et al. (2000), has averaged around four percentage points for the last two centuries and around seven percentage points for the span from 1926 to 1999.

Even this, however, has turned out to be controversial, with economists pondering what is known as the equity premium puzzle.[12] Numerous studies have proposed that the size of the equity premium for holding stocks rather than bonds ought to be much smaller than the real (inflation-adjusted) 4% or so actually averaged over the long run (1871–2007, Table 8.2). Indeed, this perceived large gap between returns on equity and those on fixed-income assets suggests that the rate of return on stocks should be lower or the rate of return on fixed-income assets higher or both.[13]

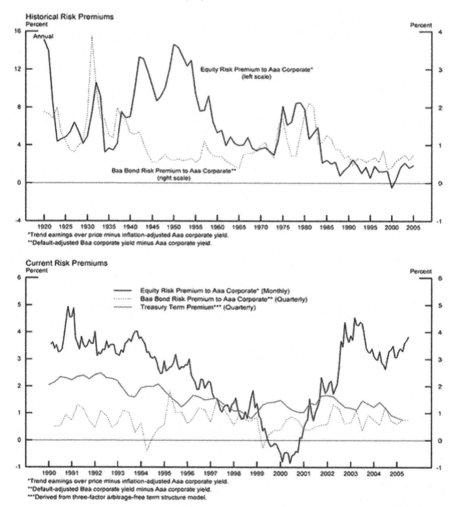

Fig. 8.1 Estimated equity and bond risk premiums, long term and short term, 1920–2005 (Source: Kohn (2005). Note dips to below zero circa 2000. Updated annual equity risk premium data for the S&P 500 is available from the website of NYU Professor Aswath Damodaran available at http://pages.stern.nyu.edu/~adamodar/New_Home_Page/datafile/implpr.html)

In all, estimation of an ERP series is not as simple as it might at first appear (and possible alternatives present similar difficulties and deficiencies). The series are sensitive to the length of the period over which the sample is taken, are probably nonstationary, inherently contain survival biases, and vary somewhat depending on whether the estimate is made using arithmetic or geometric averages.[14] For the United States and the United Kingdom, the arithmetic average has historically been around 2% above the downward-biased geometric.[15] To illustrate, the geometric average of 2 and 18 is $(2 \times 18)^{1/2} = 6$, but the arithmetic average is $(2 + 18)/2 = 10$.[16]

There is also a difference when the underlying risk-free rate is based on one-month Treasury bills or on 20-year bonds, the approach taken by Ibbotson Associates, an often-used compiler of ERP data.[17] In bubbles and crashes further distortions might also occur from the likely feedback effects on the risk-free rates.[18]

However, whether taken from either an *ex post* or *ex ante* perspective, analysis of ERPs is inescapably tied to aspects of price-change volatility.[19] The implication is that as volatility rises, the expected market risk premium normally ought to also correspondingly rise (a crash) or fall (a bubble). But because volatility tends to vary over time and to cluster, it is both autoregressive and persistent.[20]

Although various definitions of ERPs have appeared in the literature, there is no single approach that is demonstrably better than the others, for, as Damodaran (2002, p. 158) explains,

> *the expected return on any investment can be written as the sum of the risk-free rate and an extra return to compensate for the risk. The disagreement, in both theoretical and practical terms, remains on how to measure this risk, and how to convert the risk measure into an expected return that compensates for risk...*[21]

The ERP clearly plays a central role in corporate finance and investment as it propels future equity returns and is a major determinant of the cost of capital as well as a proxy for time preference. The problem is that—whether looking to the past, the present, or the future—it is difficult to measure. The historic mean turns out to be an unreliable estimate of the expected premium (and making the expected ERP conditional on various factors in the past doesn't necessarily lead to dependable forecasts).[22]

Consistently estimated historic ERPs and returns are indicated for the United States for several defined periods in Tables 8.1 and 8.2.[23] By comparison, the master work done by Dimson, Marsh, and Staunton in this area shows that between 1900 and 2005, annual real equity returns for the United States averaged approximately 6.50%, with the United Kingdom at 5.50%, Japan at 4.50%, and France, Germany, Switzerland, and Spain ranging between 3.10%

Table 8.1 Historical risk premiums for the United States in percent, selected time periods

	Stocks vs. T-bills		Stocks vs. Treasury bonds	
	Arithmetic	*Geometric*	*Arithmetic*	*Geometric*
1928–2017	8.09%	6.26%	6.38%	4.77%
1968–2017	6.58	5.28	4.24	3.29
2008–2017	9.85	8.01	5.98	4.56

Source: http://pages.stern.nyu.edu/~adamodar/pc/datasets/histretSP.xls. See also Damodaran (2002, p. 162)

Table 8.2 Historical returns and equity premiums, 1802–December 2004

| | Real return | | | | | | Stock minus return on | | | |
| | Stocks | | Bonds | | Bills | | Bonds | | Bills | |
Period	Comp.	Arith.	Comp.	Arith.	Comp.	Arith.	Comp.	Arith.	Comp.	Arith.
1802–2004	6.8%	8.4%	3.5%	3.9%	2.8%	3.0%	3.3%	4.5%	4.0%	5.4%
1871–2004	6.7	8.4	2.9	3.2	1.7	1.8	3.9	5.2	5.0	6.6
Major subperiods										
1802–1870	7.0%	8.3%	4.8%	5.1%	5.1%	5.4%	2.2%	3.2%	1.9%	2.9%
1871–1925	6.6	7.9	3.7	3.9	3.2	3.3	2.9	4.0	3.5	4.7
1926–2004	6.8	8.8	2.3	2.8	0.7	0.8	4.6	6.0	6.1	8.0

Zweig (2009) raises serious questions about methodological flaws in the sample of stocks used for calculations prior to 1870

Note: Comp. = compound; Arith. = arithmetic

Sources: Data for 1802–1871 are from Schwert (1990); data for 1871–1925 are from Cowles (1938); data for 1926–2004 are from the CRSP capitalization-weighted indexes of all NYSE, Amex, and NASDAQ stocks

Source: Siegel, J. J. (2001). *Equity Risk Premium Forum, Historical Results I*. Philadelphia: University of Pennsylvania, Wharton School, November 2001, AIMR (Charlottesville, VA), and Siegel (2005)

and 4.50%. Annual stock and bond returns for the U.S., 1928–2017, appear in Fig. 8.2.[24]

However, even though it's useful to know a bit about such ERP characteristics, what's instead more important to the EOV approach being developed here is the direction of change as dictated by basic economic principles and definitions: In a bubble risk premiums shrink and in a crash they grow. And because credit spreads in fixed-income markets and cap (capitalization) rates in real estate move and respond in the same manner as do equity risk premiums, credit spreads and cap rates are accordingly appropriate alternatives to ERPs.[25] This key summary for risk premium directional behavior in bubbles and crashes is shown in Table 8.3.

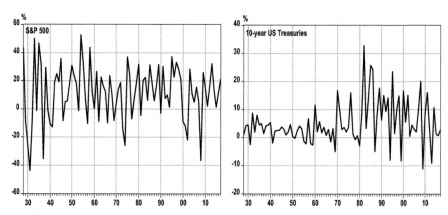

Fig. 8.2 Annual returns on the S&P 500 (left panel) and on ten-year US Treasuries (right panel), 1928–2017. (Source data: Aswath Damodaran, adamodar@stern.nyu.edu)

Table 8.3 Bubbles and crashes (inverse bubbles), direction of movement

	Bubbles	Crashes
Risk premium	↓	↑
Volatility	↑	↑

Stock Indexes Estimation problems are not confined only to the ERP series. The underlying stock market indexes are also not consistent over time as there is a survival bias as well as a replacement bias: Failed company shares don't trade and are dropped out. And replacement bias occurs when one S&P 500 company merges with another or when fast-growing companies replace older, stodgier companies as components. Of the 500 names back in 1957 fewer than 120 are today the same.

For instance, in the DJIA of early 2004, AT&T, Kodak, and International Paper were replaced by AIG, Pfizer, and Verizon; in early 2008, Altria Group and Honeywell were replaced by Bank of America and Chevron; in 2013 Bank of America, Alcoa, and Hewlett-Packard were replaced by Goldman Sachs, Visa, and Nike; and in 2015 Apple replaced AT&T. The replacements are (sometimes erroneously) presumed to have higher growth rates than the ones that have been removed, to have a larger following by investors, and to sport higher price-earnings multiples. It's as if the index averages were ingesting steroids.[26] Even so, however, such features are often seen only after the replacements have already achieved the bulk of their potential popularity and gains and might be approaching if not already past their prime.

As for the S&P 500, which represents about 75% of the value of the US market, the critics reviewed in Blake (2002) suggest that this benchmark "has become grossly distorted by concentration, warping the market it's meant to mirror...In bull markets a handful of big stocks utterly dominate the 500, forcing passive and active investors alike to channel more and more money into those companies to keep up with the index, creating a vicious cycle as the chosen shares, and thus the index itself, rise ever higher...the index became a contributing factor to the bubble."[27] (Others, however, counter that "manias don't need benchmarks to thrive.")

The realism and adequacy of the basic assumptions that are customarily made in CAPM or APT models may be further questioned in terms of the changing diversity of the market portfolio over time. In the technology asset bubble of the late 1990s, when the NASDAQ Index soared to over 5000, most large and small investors were, in actuality, not well diversified at all, but instead were heavily concentrated in technology-related stocks (see Fig. 2.8).

This is typical bubble behavior in which one asset class—be it bulbs, railroads, Florida real estate, or new technology—becomes of dominant interest. In the 1970s, for example, two OPEC-induced increases in the price per barrel of oil caused the percentage of total S&P 500 Index capitalization represented by energy-related shares to more than double in the course of around ten years. By 1980, energy shares had accounted for 27.1% of the S&P 500 Index (31% in November 1980), but five years on only 12.8%.

Twenty years later the same degree of concentration was again seen in the tech and financial stock representations within the S&P 500 as these sectors together accounted for almost 45% of the S&P's market value. In June 2000, near the peak, the top 25 S&P 500 stocks, or 5%, accounted for 44% of the index's capitalization. Similarly, at one point in the takeover of Mannesmann by Vodafone, the combined company, accounted for 16% of the FTSE-100 capitalization.[28] Alternative, broader-based capitalization-weighted indexes such as the Wilshire 5000 or the Russell 3000 normally have only somewhat less (6–8%) contemporaneous value concentration in the top 25 names than do the S&P 500 or FTSE-100.

Evidently, the extent of the market portfolio's diversification is not stable over time. And because of this, in a bubble episode, the market portfolio's ability to reduce exposure to firm-specific risk is markedly diminished.[29] In the theoretical terms of the CAPM, what you get is more risk for the same expected return or, equivalently, a lower return for taking the same risk.

There may be long periods (e.g., 1995–early 2000) when it may actually in a bubble episode be less risky in practical terms to join the crowd and to concentrate the portfolio. A portfolio manager who in such episodes remains as diversified as is suggested by the ideal CAPM strategy risks severe under-performance as measured against peers, becomes a pariah in the investment community as funds under management are taken away, and incurs the risk of job loss.[30] Given that the primary incentive is to retain clients and fees, it is thus common for fund managers to be constrained to "style boxes" which are designed to keep performance somewhat aligned with related (average) benchmarks. Maximization of absolute returns is then a secondary consideration as the bubble environment forces the marginal investor that the theory so neatly posits to behave as and in fact become the average investor.

Indeed, as the peak is approached speculators and investors become increasingly indistinguishable—both being caught up by the emotions and temptations of the moment. All participants not only become less diversified through ever more urgent purchases of high-covariance stocks but also become less concerned about risks. Especially near a bubble's extreme, it thus appears that the higher the volatility of returns, the *more* desirable the asset becomes (as buying on dips up until then has repeatedly been well-rewarded).[31]

The implicit assumption in all of the conventional treatments is, of course, that investors are "rational." Sometimes, however, they clearly are not and there have been occasions, such as the bubble peak of early 2000, when share prices have been bid so high that the risk premium drops into negative territory—i.e., below the risk-free rate.[32] This, of course, doesn't make any sense at all because in the event of bankruptcy shareholders are residual claimants; they are the last to be paid and face the greatest risk of total loss.

All of this agrees with Cochrane (2005, p. 392) who, following Fama and French (1989), says:

> *Expected returns vary over business cycles; it takes a higher risk premium to get people to hold stocks at the bottom of a recession. When expected returns go up, prices go down. We see the low prices, followed by the higher returns expected and required by the market...Higher prices reflect low risk premia, lower expected excess returns.* (p. 400)

In other words, "high stock price/dividend, price/earnings, or market/book ratios are on average followed by years of poor returns...[h]igh credit spreads (low prices) on low-grade debt are followed, on average, by good returns on that debt." These outcomes hold across all markets.[33]

The situation from a behavioral and socionomic standpoint evolves as investors, despite (and probably because of) the rise of prices, become ever greedier and less risk-averse.[34] This aspect of dynamic prospect theory suggests that even when actual riskiness remains unchanged or increases, *attitudes* toward risk always adjust and vary and are dependent upon past experiences. The market is perceived as less risky if it has risen significantly from the price at which the investor bought in, hence the decline in the implied premiums.

8.3   ELASTICITY, EQUILIBRIUM, AND EXPONENTIALITY

Risk premiums are just the first of several building blocks that form a new approach that can discern when and where a bubble (or crash) might form and persist (i.e., continue to inflate). The indexation and measurement of sample path lengths are another step toward development in this direction.

TPUTs and Path Lengths

Within the confines of discrete-time analysis, the goal is to find a means for bubble episodes to be described, defined, and distinguished from ordinary non-bubble rising market trends. In such non-bubble situations, the market can, for whatever fundamental reasons, rise without an increase in variance or a decrease in the risk premium.

In bubbles, however, short-side rationing causes variances to rise even as risk premiums decline. As speculative enthusiasm spreads, fundamental concerns about preservation of capital and incurrence of risk (and debt) fade into the background, while trading volumes and number of transactions per unit time (TPUT)—in violation of the basic EMH/REH tenets—rise. And many participants will reach the point where it becomes psychologically and fiscally more important (and/or prudent) for them to buy into the game than to worry about potential asset overvaluations or losses somewhere further down the road.

In all instances in which the term bubble has been applied, no exceptions to such behavioral features—whether pertaining to tulip bulbs of the 1600s or to tech stocks of the 1990s—have ever been observed. Bull markets, according to a famous adage, climb a "wall of worry," at the top of which prospects for further gains are seemingly so bright and worriless that stocks appear to be approximately no riskier than Treasuries and gilts.

In contrast, no such high-activity variance effects and artifacts would appear in non-crash market declines, which are characterized by subdued investor sentiment conditions and lethargic trading. In such declines, investors are not panicked and the prevailing psychology is that of complacent acceptance of worsening conditions, of denial of loss ("it's only on paper"), or of casting fate to the winds of whatever will be will be. Prices decline on the proverbial "slope of hope."

The key to making distinctions between bubbles and non-bubbles and also crashes and non-crashes thus follows naturally. In non-bubble (or non-crash) markets, little relative variation over time in either return variances or in ERPs would be expected: A ratio of change in one series to change in the other ought to be fairly stable, as rising prices in non-bubble markets are carried by actual demonstrations of real earnings and dividend growth rather than just by rank, liquidity-driven speculations.

In bubble markets, though, an ascending variance accompanied by a declining risk premium will show a rising variance-to-ERP change ratio (also seen in the diverging indexed path lenths traversed by the two series). First, the variance rises as eager (i.e., quantity short-rationed) bidders more fearlessly pursue shares with intensified aggressiveness, thereby pushing upward and expanding the range of price variation that had previously been established as a price barrier or price-range boundary.

The motivation is explained by Buchan (1997, p. 110):

> *The great stock-market bull seeks to condense the future into a few days, to discount the long march of history, and capture the present value of all future riches.*[35]

Second, liquidity (and rising underlying collateral value) effects will generally make it easier and less costly to borrow and to trade, thereby reducing the actual as well as the perceived riskiness of participating in equities (or other bubbling assets). The traders' consensus is often that if anything should inconceivably go wrong the central bank will ultimately bail everyone out.[36]

Still, any rapid modification of the variance-to-ERP change ratio signals that something out of the ordinary—a bubble or a crash—might be either imminent or have already begun (and with feedback of one series on the other).

This view also ties directly into the classic but oversimplified growth valuation formula, known as the Gordon model (Gordon 1962), which says that

$P = D/(r^e - g^e)$, where P is the price, D is the dividend, r^e is the expected *constant* discount factor, and g^e is the expected constant growth rate (of per share dividends).[37] Even small changes in expected growth rates—for whatever justified or unjustified reasons or narratives—are then immediately reflected in rather large changes in stock prices.[38] If so, then price variance is the statistical artifact that must be expanded early and quickly.[39]

The salient feature is that it does not take much of a revision in expected growth—especially when it is amplified by changes in risk premiums—to produce a large gain or loss in price: A bubble (or crash) first reveals itself through the unmistakable stretch (or skid) marks on price variance as the previous upper (or lower) bounds on price are challenged and then ultimately exceeded. Although the focus on variance is nothing new in theories of financial economics, the relationship of changes in variance to changes in equity risk premiums, as far as is known, has yet to be investigated.[40] A viable way to explore this relationship is through elasticity comparisons.

Elasticity

The measure of elasticity of price variance with respect to ERP, ε_{erp}, has a conventional definition, relating the percent change of variance between t and $t + 1$ to the percent change in ERP over the same period. As usual, ε_{erp} is expressed as a delta from time t to $t+1$:

$$\epsilon_{erp} = \frac{\dfrac{\Delta\,\mathrm{var}}{\mathrm{var}}}{\dfrac{\Delta\,\mathrm{erp}}{\mathrm{erp}}} = \frac{\mathrm{erp}}{\mathrm{var}} * \frac{\Delta\,\mathrm{var}}{\Delta\,\mathrm{erp}}$$

The exogenous energy here emanates from a change in ERP, with the change in variance being the response. The elasticity approach *allows the variance when the ERP is 6% to be analyzed in the same way as when, say, the ERP is 2%.*

This elasticity is also a pressure gauge of the amount of short-side rationed quantity that price change alone would not adequately reveal.[41] In other words, when the market's collective ERP assumption—its risk appetite—changes, adjustments in the short-rationed *quantities* that will then be wanted and needed are made through buying and selling. In bubbles and crashes, the adjustment is large enough so as to be manifested via large gains in price variance; that is, the variance becomes highly elastic.[42]

The display in Fig. 8.3 illustrates. As in elementary economics, demand schedule D is plotted on the conventional price (p) and quantity (q) axes.

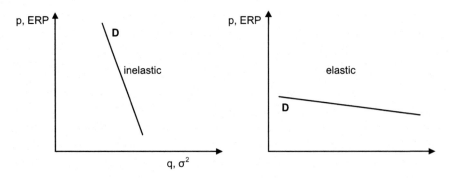

Fig. 8.3 Elasticity concept illustrated

(A strong case could also admittedly be made here for transposition of the axes and lines; either way, the story is the same.)

The left-hand panel shows an almost inelastic (i.e., nearly vertical) situation where even a relatively large change in price results in only a small change of the quantity demanded. Good examples would be tickets for a major Olympics event, a Super Bowl, or a World Cup Final, where even a 30% rise in the price would not likely much reduce the quantity demanded. In contrast, the demand schedule in the right-hand panel depicts an almost infinite elasticity (i.e., nearly horizontal) in which the quantity demanded has great sensitivity to even small changes in price.

Comparably, if the same axis for price now represents the equity risk premium (ERP) and the same axis for quantity now represents the variance (σ^2), it can be seen that, as in the right panel, a small change in the ERP—whether due to an earnings or takeover announcement, a change in Fed policy, or whatever—results in a large change in the variance: As the line flattens, the ERP elasticity of variance tends toward infinity.

Here, the boundary of stock price variation is being expanded faster (in percentage terms) than the ERP is expanding its own range of movement (to the downside in a bubble, upside in a crash). None of this can happen unless traders and investors are aggressively and persistently willing to "pay up," or "sell down." It is thus the market action itself that defines and contours an extreme event episode.

For any period this elasticity can also be seen as a kind of inverse of the usual Sharpe ratio. Whereas the Sharpe ratio takes the risk premium per unit of standard deviation, this elasticity concept in a way turns the Sharpe ratio on its head and takes the percentage change in variance (i.e., standard deviation squared) for each unit of percentage change in risk premium.[43] Estimates of such a series of point elasticities are shown in Fig. 8.4.

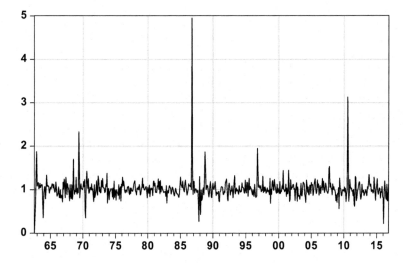

Fig. 8.4 ERP elasticity of variance for indexed 12-observation samples, S&P 500, 1962:08–2016:11[44]

Equilibrium

The subject of economic "equilibrium" has been extensively studied, predominantly from a neoclassical Walrasian point of view in which markets are assumed to be complete and perfect information is available to all participants without any distributional asymmetries.[45] In such models, important real-world issues concerning the costs and incentives involved in the acquisition and processing of new information are largely assumed away or ignored.[46] Although an empirically workable definition of such an equilibrium condition has apparently not been established and tested, it can be defined by its features—namely, that the ERP elasticity of variance must be *precisely* 1.0—which for all practical purposes would never occur.[47]

Compare, also, this notion by Merton (1992, p. 477), which requires that "The capital market is always in equilibrium (i.e., there is no trading at nonequilibrium prices)."[48] In the harsh reality of markets, this basic assumption of the CAPM does not ring true. As any securities trader can attest, markets are *never* in full equilibrium as markets are part of an open-ended, nondeterministic process.[49]

In the EMH/CAPM view, yes indeed, there is a price at which buyers and sellers will agree to trade. But, how deep is the market? What kind of equilibrium can this be (in terms of Malinvaud's rationed markets) if it is only a trade that clears the market of a thousand shares when the mutual fund has another ten million for sale hovering in the background and unknown to the buyer of the first thousand?[50]

Is price truly the *only* issue and motive of the buyer or the seller or are other psychological imperatives—job security, good relative performance at the end of the quarter, "window dressing," client-complaint intensity, bragging rights—affecting the bids and offers that are accepted? "[D]emand will equal supply *if and only if* everyone had perfect information." In the real world of trading that will never happen because information is never perfectly or symmetrically distributed and is costly to obtain, absorb, and process. Disequilibrium is far likelier than equilibrium.[51] "Stability can never be a destination, only a journey to instability."[52]

None of this, however, would appear in the neoclassical economist's Walrasian framework, which does not have any particular relevance to the analysis of bubbles and crashes except for as a point of departure.[53]

From the Bénassy point of view, "...the Walrasian story is clearly incomplete...The consequences of abandoning the assumption that all markets clear at all times turns out to be quite far-reaching:

- Transactions cannot be all equal to demands and supplies expressed on markets. As a consequence some agents experience rationing and quantity signals are formed in addition to price signals.
- Demands and supplies must be substantially modified on account of these quantity signals. Walrasian demand, which takes only prices into account, must be replaced by a more general *effective demand*, which takes into account both price and quantity signals." As a result, "some demands and supplies cannot be satisfied in the exchange process and some agents must be rationed."[54]

This rationing feature is what emerges most forcefully in support of the EOV approach. That's because rationing in markets provides the underlying rationale and thrust for the characteristic features (including much higher rates of trading activity) that are always seen in extreme market events. The main point is further clarified by Malinvaud, who writes:

> *Purchase (or sale) is the quantity actually traded, whereas demand (or supply) is the quantity that the individual would like to trade in this market. In a Walrasian equilibrium in which prices are supposed to have adjusted, demand is equal to purchase or supply to sale. But in an equilibrium with fixed prices and quantity adjustments, the equality no longer holds... What kind of general properties must demand-supply and purchase-sale satisfy in order that the resulting state be called an equilibrium?*[55]

What therefore occurs in bubbles is that there are, in Malinvaud's descriptions, an increasing number of "rationed buyers." These are defined as individuals whose purchases are smaller than their demand. Similarly, in crashes there are an increasing number of "rationed sellers" whose sales are smaller than their supply.

More concisely,

With imperfect information markets do not clear. This includes the market for money and credit. Markets that do not clear are rationed. Rationed markets are determined by quantities *not prices, according to the 'short-side' principle: whichever quantity of demand or supply is smaller will determine the outcome...there is no guarantee that equilibrium will be obtained. It would be pure chance if demand equaled supply.*[56]

In bubbles the rationed buyer readily meets asking prices and then, to obtain the full quantity that is desired, must bid even higher, thereby extending prices beyond the previously established boundaries and thus also increasing the variance of prices.[57] And in crashes the variance of prices and returns is similarly expanded, only now with returns to the downside as rationed sellers hit every bid and then sell more even lower so as to trade the quantity, à la Malinvaud, that they would *like* to trade.[58] As such, this behavior reveals that for whatever psychological and emotional reasons, financial market traders are actually not buying or selling as based on "fundamental" valuations but instead only on their projections and *expectation* of what *future* prices will likely be.

The degree of urgency with which this is done is then often reflected in price discontinuities (or jumps) that appear on a chart as gaps—with, say, a trade at $12.60 followed the very next instant by a trade at $14.10 (or, in a crash, $9.75). This indicates that at many interim prices there may be no trades at all.[59]

In brief, the rationing described by Bénassy and Malinvaud provides a model of transaction behavior that appears to be much more pragmatic than that offered by the Walrasian hypothesis of *tâtonnement*. Individuals will never uniformly confront the same known set of prices, and information is always *asymmetrically* distributed and not instantly understood or analyzed properly by all participants at the same time. Whenever large price jumps occur, linear extrapolations from recent experiences become irrelevant for predictive purposes. And not all exchanges occur at a single point; there will always be some agents who are rationed.[60]

The only thing that then makes bubbles and crashes different from "normal" markets is that the number of rationed buyers (or sellers) is compounded. This increase in short-rationed buying (or selling) happens when utility functions of individual agents *are not being independently determined* and when, at the same time, the functions are changing shape from risk aversion to what might be called collective risk obliviousness (Fig. 1.2).

All of this provides the basis for "herding" during extreme market events. In this, it is important to understand that in reality, "you don't trade the markets, you trade your beliefs about the markets."[61] "[B]elief in the power of the stock market is vital to sustaining it."[62]

A cogent theory of bubbles and crashes must therefore take account of *disequilibrium* conditions rather than of the equilibrium conditions posited by the emotionally sterile EMH/CAPM and REH approaches in which—except for under highly selective assumptions—bubbles and crashes can never occur and do not exist. In these older theories, asymmetric and imperfect information is treated as an improbable aberration rather than the virtually universal condition that it actually is.

Exponentiality

The power-law and fractal characteristics of stock return distributions that were found by Mandelbrot are mathematically described through exponential expressions. Without the steady or rising rate of price change—that is, exponentiality—an uptrend fails to show the price-change acceleration seen in all bubbles.[63] So, at the heart of any bubble description, there must somewhere be an exponential component that is driven by and reflects short-side quantity rationing. It might even be said that, essentially, extreme market events are all about such exponentiality.[64]

Exponentiality implies that a higher-order curve—an attractor, in the language of chaos theory—is being traced for a relatively long time. Parabolic curves, which have higher-order algebraic characteristics as well (i.e., nonlinear growth), are therefore also effectively a part of the family of exponentials, taken broadly. Thus, when Wall Streeters describe a steep price gain as "parabolic," they are generally on the right track. Enormously large numbers can be generated if even small exponents in either of these higher-order expressions are compounded often enough. Idealized versions of exponential and parabolic curves are represented in the panels of Fig. 8.5.[65]

The exponentiality concept is further illustrated in Fig. 8.6. In the left panel, there is no acceleration. Only if the percent change from period to period is the same as or larger than that of the previous period (i.e., the quantity is growing at least in proportion to itself) can there be exponentiality or parabolicity. As in

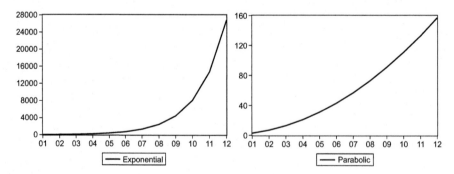

Fig. 8.5 Idealized examples of exponential (left) and parabolic curves

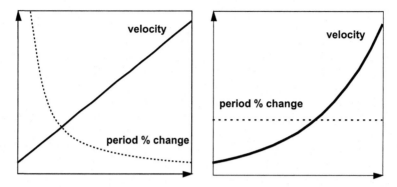

Fig. 8.6   Idealized rate-of-change curves, left panel, declining; right panel, steady

the right panel, a constant percentage change from period t to period $t + 1$ is all that's needed to generate the characteristic curvature.[66]

However, exponentiality in price change (or returns) alone is only a necessary but not sufficient condition for defining a bubble. The main and unique insight is that—as short-side rationing pressure intensifies—the *elasticity* of price variance begins to rise exponentially toward infinity.

In trading terms, existing supply is readily absorbed by eager buyers. And previous highs in price that had functioned as reflecting barriers are now easily penetrated and then greatly and rapidly exceeded (for chartists, a "breakout"). As historically new high prices are registered, the supply of shares (sellers) often becomes even smaller, as every previous buyer is now sitting on a profit and the surrounding euphoria discourages early selling.

An important aspect is that bubbles appear to be born amid prevalent skepticism, despair, or sideways-market complacencies and to end with a spontaneous and infectious upsurge of enthusiasm. This suggests that curves describing bubbles ought to go from being relatively flat and approximately linear to a near-vertical nonlinear climax.

Illustrative price charts of spectacular speculative vehicles, which gained more than fifteen-fold in less than a year, are displayed in Fig. 8.7. The Bitcoin episode—and the shares of largely worthless companies rising sharply in value by merely adding words relating to blockchain and crypto to their names—greatly resembled what had occurred in the TMT bubble of the late 1990s.

The Shanghai Stock Exchange Composite Index, which between 2004 and 2007 tripled in 18 months with a sixfold increase in average daily trading volume, is shown in Fig. 8.8. (The subsequent 2015 Shanghai bubble and crash appears in Fig. 1.3.) These charts are strikingly exponential and/or parabolic in appearance and are obviously not unique to one national index or time.[67]

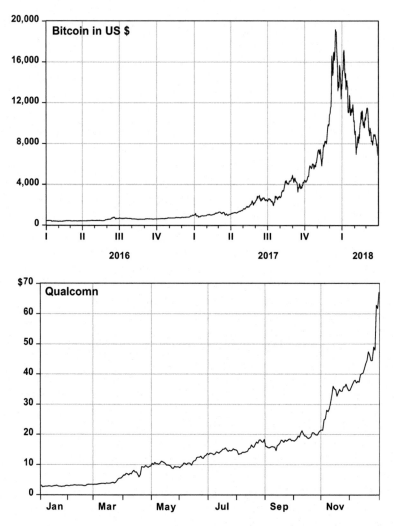

Fig. 8.7 Bitcoin USD daily prices, 2016:01–2018:03 and daily closing prices of Qualcomm shares (QCOM: Nasdaq), 1999.[68] (Source data: Investing.com, Yahoo)

Nevertheless, such *exponential price changes alone do not necessarily qualify as or represent an asset price bubble.* The extreme price moves provide necessary but not sufficient conditions: It is instead the ERP elasticity of variance, based on the underlying steep end-of-pattern price moves that here defines a bubble (crash).

8.4   Transactions Volume Aspects

The EOV approach at this point requires that additional elements be included. The related Wall Street aphorisms are that "volume precedes price," and that "in price there is information, but in volume truth."[69] Indeed, volume—as an indicator of the conviction of the marketplace—is tied directly to the short-side rationed approach.[70]

Fig. 8.8   Shanghai Stock Exchange Composite Index, monthly, and trading volume in millions of shares, 2004 to 2008. (Source data: Bloomberg index identifier, SHCOMP. The index peaked at 6092.06 on October 16, 2007, and fell to 1706.70 on November 4, 2008. See also previous Fig. 1.3, which shows a 2015 peak of around 5200, or 800 points below that of 2007)[71]

In the real world, price-change action is the most visible manifestation of what a financial market bubble is all about. But it is not the only one. No bubble would be fully identifiable were it not for the dramatic increase in share trading (transactions volume) and number of transactions per unit time (TPUT) as compared to conditions in a market unaffected by bubble psychology.

To grow to maturity, a bubble requires that, like moths to a flame, ever more people (both individuals and professionals)—perhaps with little or no regard for the rising risk—are attracted to trading and investment activity in the bubble's asset class. Volume is an indicator of market psychology because it reflects the relative societal mood and degree of emotional commitment by buyers and sellers that underlie significant price changes.

Experience in the Taiwan (TSE) market, recounted by Champion (1998, pp. 12–15), explains the typical extremes to which trading volume in a bubble will grow.

During the last quarter of 1989, total trading on the TSE had reached $309 billion, more than the total amount traded in the entire previous year…and trading on a busy day…was greater than the sum total of all stock trades in 1985…The fact that this level of trading was taking place in the shares of the relatively small number of companies listed on the Taiwan Stock Exchange made the statistics even more amazing…every single share of stock that was available to trade in Taiwan changed hands approximately every 15 days. By contrast, turnover of shares on the New York Stock Exchange peaked at just under 100% (i.e., one time per year) just before the 1987

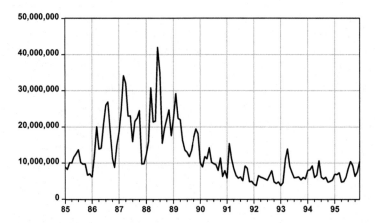

Fig. 8.9 Tokyo Stock Exchange, first section, monthly trading volume in thousands of shares, 1985:01–1995:12. (Source: Tokyo Stock Exchange)

market crash...After the crash, the annual turnover level in New York stayed near 40% for several years.

The Tokyo Stock Exchange experience of 1986 to 1988, depicted in Fig. 8.9, similarly shows average daily volume rising threefold in two years (1986–1988)—but by not as much as was the volume expansion for the Shanghai Composite Index from mid-2005 to early 2007 in previous Fig. 8.8.[72]

Statistically significant increases in the number of shares traded per unit time and the number of transactions per unit time typically accompany price bubbles. And conversely, a subsequent decline in volume is normally characteristic of a falling market—that is, up until the capitulation stage is entered.[73]

8.5   CONCLUSIONS

Theoretical work of Bénassy and Malinvaud suggests that there is no such thing as market equilibrium and that, therefore, equilibrium-assuming constructs (e.g., the EMH/CAPM framework) provide few or no insights as to how bubbles and crashes are formed and sustained.

The preliminary work in this chapter has been used to explore the idea that all bubbles (and crashes) are a manifestation of short-side quantity rationing that leaves trading-related statistical artifacts in its wake. The ERP elasticity-of-variance definition provides a direct way (i.e., unencumbered by difficult econometric supply/demand equation identification problems) to detect the urgency with which traders adjust the quantities that they, for whatever reasons—economic, psychological, sociological, and so on—at the moment, desire to hold.

The most important aspect is that variance bounds are expanded (broken) to the upside as price changes begin to follow an exponential trajectory. But this alone does not constitute a bubble because, in almost all such circumstances, as equity risk premiums fall, prices rise. It is instead proposed that a much more viable definition of a bubble is obtained when the variance in percentage terms rises *faster* than the ERP declines. Constant growth rates of earnings, dividends, and/or share prices would not and should not be expected to generate this type of *variance boundary* expansion effect.

This chapter has considered changes in the elasticity of variance (i.e., volatility with respect to changes in the equity risk premium). Yet there is also another, heretofore, largely unexplored aspect and extension—the behavioral risk premium—which (covered in the next chapter) has great bearing and affect in bubbles and crashes. The ultimate goal is to define bubble episodes through such elasticity, exponentiality, and behavioral risk characteristics.

NOTES

1. Cochrane (2005, p. 451) writes, "most returns and price variation come from variations in *risk premia*, not variations in expected cash flows, interest rates, etc....variation in priced risk comes from nonmarket factors...*virtually all variation in price/dividend ratios has reflected varying expected excess returns*" (p. 397). Greenspan (2013, p. 5) writes, "Risk taking and avoiding it is at the root of almost all financial decisions."
2. Explored in studies by Shiller (1981), LeRoy and Porter (1981), Kelidon (1986), West (1988a), Smant (2003), Engel (2005), and Lansing (2010b).
3. West (1988b) introduces volatility bounds that are valid when there is a unit root in the dividend-payment stream series. Some studies question whether volatility bounds exist and there is an arbitrary element in the sense that the bound will depend on the length of the historical period over which it is measured. Neftci (2000, p. 52) explains unbounded variation in asset price trajectories modeled as continuous-time processes.
4. See also Shiller (1981, 1992), French et al. (1987), and Kurz et al. (2005), in which it is suggested that "the dynamics of diverse beliefs is the primary propagation mechanism of volatility in asset markets." Bernstein (2007, p. 71) writes that it all boils down to the idea that beliefs may be rational, but the real world is too nonstationary, fast-moving, and complex for investors to cope.
5. Although many series might conceivably serve as viable references against which to relate variance changes, such series are generally inconsistently defined and reported. See Noguchi (1994), Werner (2005, pp. 232–3), and Posen (2003).

   All of the securities and economic data needed for this study are readily available from government bureaus and the Federal Reserve Banks of New York and St. Louis. Other sources include World Financial Data, Inc. (www.worldfindata. com), the NYSE, AMEX, NASDAQ, Bloomberg, Thomson Datastream, or the often-cited files of the University of Chicago's Center for Research in Security Prices (CRSP). The main empirical work uses both the Ibbotson and CRSP data sets, which can reach back as far as the year 1900 with annual, quarterly, monthly, and sometimes daily data on the S&P 500 and the Dow-Jones Industrials, and as far as 1926 with at least monthly estimates of equity risk premiums from Ibbotson based on US Treasury bonds and bills. Yahoo Finance provides daily closing price data starting in 1950 and is another source. An even longer monthly historical database for NYSE returns stretching from 1815 to 1925 appears in Goetzmann et al. (2001). See also Jorion and Goetzmann (1999).

6. Aspects of the equity risk premium are covered in depth by Goetzmann and Ibbotson (2006) and by Mehra (2008). Keim and Stambaugh (1986) found that three *ex ante* observable variables, including yield differences, affect the risk premiums of stocks and bonds. See also Bleiberg (2018).

7. In his biography of the late financial economics pioneer, Fischer Black, Mehrling (2005, p. 10) makes the concept of risk premiums clear:

> *The return associated with a given risk is the price of that risk, the price that needs to be paid in order to induce people to take it...risk is the cost of reward.*

And Siegel (2005, p. 65) says, "...risk premiums exist because individuals are assumed to have declining marginal utility of consumption."

8. For instance, in terms of one simple variation of the CAPM, the ERP relationship can be generally represented as:

$$E(R_t) = R_f + \beta(\text{risk premium}),$$

where $E(R_t)$ is the expected return in time, t, R_f is the risk-free rate, and β is the beta of the security relative to the market.

Cochrane (2005, pp. xiv–xv) observes that, "the risk premium on stocks – the expected return less interest rates – is much larger than the interest rate, and varies a good deal more than interest rates. This means that attempts to line investment up with interest rates are pretty hopeless – most variation in the cost of capital comes from the varying risk premium."

9. Ibbotson and Chen (2003) write that ERP studies make estimates using four different approaches:
   - historical returns between stocks and bonds,
   - fundamental information such as earnings, dividends, or overall economic productivity,
   - demand-side models that derive expected equity returns through the payoff demanded by investors for bearing the risk of equity investments,

Opinions of investors and financial professionals through broad survey Montier (2002) calculates a top-down implied equity risk premium (ERP) by taking current dividend yield on the market plus the long-term growth rate of nominal GDP minus the current ten-year bond yield. A second measure uses a bottom-up approach, calculating a current payout ratio multiplied by the long-term earnings growth forecast. "[T]he implied ERP does drop during long bull markets during which inves-tors build up a store of gains, and then the ERP starts to rise as prices start to drop." This view is consistent with what has occurred at some market peaks such as prior to the crash of 1987 and in early 2000, when the implied ERP declined to virtually zero (or even slightly below as per Arnott 2004).

10. Hamilton (1994, p. 37) equivalently represents the total return of this "market fundamentals" model as $R_t = (P_{t+1} - P_t)/ P_t + (D_t / P_t)$. He notes (pp. 41–2), however, that when the expression is modified to include expectations and the solution is bounded, phenomena such as speculative bubbles may be ruled out.

11. In forecasting (see Chap. 10), calculation of an *implied* risk premium series is of particular interest. The formula is illustrated by Damodaran (2002, pp. 171–5):

    Value = Expected dividends next period /
    (Required return on equity – Expected growth rate).

    If, for example, the S&P 500 Index is at 1000 and the expected dividend yield equivalently represents the total return of this "market on."

    Generally, the implied risk premium series is different from the historical premium and expectations are unobservable and can only be estimated.

12. Explained in Grant and Quiggin (2001) and in Siegel (2005) and originated in Mehra and Prescott (1985). Barro (2006), as based on Rietz (1988), seems to have a solution to the puzzle by "bringing in low-probability economic disasters, such as the Great Depression."

13. In the classic study by Dimson et al. (2007, p. 469), the authors write that this is "a quantitative puzzle about the magnitude, rather than the sign, of the risk premium. Ironically…this puzzle has grown yet more quantitatively puzzling... This leads us back to the second possible resolution to the puzzle, namely that the historical premium may be misleading."

    Gomes (2008, p. 159) says that the puzzle reveals "a fundamental weakness in the ability of extant economic models to price non-hedgeable risk." The puzzle, Mandelbrot and Hudson (2004, p. 231) say, is explained away by the problem assuming "wrongly that the bell curve is a realistic yardstick for measuring the risk," and that it is not the average stock market performance but the extremes of profit or loss that matter most to investors. Mandelbrot posits that the market is thus much riskier than the standard models implicitly have assumed. Cochrane (2005, Ch. 21) writes of the puzzle and its relation to observed stable consumption patterns and to the CAPM. He says (p. 465), "The equity premium puzzle asks whether the market premium itself makes any sense." Donaldson et al. (2010) use a joint distribution of the dividend yield, return volatility, and realized excess returns and find that "the equity premium lies within 50 basis points of 3.5%, a range much narrower than was achieved in previous studies."

    Armitage (2005, p. 47) notes that the risk-free rate and the market risk premium are exogenous to the model. Moreover (p. 98), "A higher expected premium requires either a fall in the value of the stock market (which increases dividend yield), or higher forecast growth, or a lower risk-free rate." Taleb (2005, p. 280) suggests that "little consideration was given to the possibility that the premium may have been an optical illusion owing to the survivorship bias."

    Gala (2008, p. 403) writes: "Accounting for the historically low correlation between equity returns and aggregate consumption growth makes the puzzle worse: only with implausible large risk aversion might one reconcile the observed equity premium." See also Kocherlakota (1996) and Cogley and Sargent (2008).

    In view of the market movements as of 2008–09 the entire puzzle literature probably needs to be rethought because by that time US Treasuries had outperformed stocks over the preceding 10-, 20-, and 30-year periods and the 40-year returns were about equal. See *BusinessWeek*, October 5, 2009, and Tables 1.2, 8.1, and 8.2. The *Wall Street Journal* article by T. Lauricella of December 21, 2009, discusses how the first decade of the 2000s generated the worst performance by equities (−0.5%) of all decades since the 1830s, including the Great Depression decade of the 1930s (−0.2%).

Although market imperfections are often given as a reason for the observed discrepancies, such flaws do not by themselves provide a convincing rationale for the observed changes of the ERP in recent decades.

14. See Cornell (1999).

15. Armitage (2005, p. 88).

16. Poundstone (2005, pp. 190–201) explains the implications of using geometric versus arithmetic averages. The geometric and average means are only the same when all averaged values are identical. But because the geometric mean is otherwise lower, it is "a more conservative way of valuing risky assets." The geometric mean can also be estimated by taking the arithmetic mean minus one-half the variance. Standard mean-variance analysis does not account for compounding of returns and this makes a substantial difference in the ultimate outcome as variance alone is not a perfect measure of risk.

    What is known as the Kelly criterion is important in portfolio selection, as it states, "When faced with a choice of wagers or investments, choose the one with the highest geometric mean of outcomes." This criterion selects the portfolio that is "best." The salient features are that it produces maximum return with zero risk of ruin. However, it was (as described in Poundstone, pp. 208–29) the subject of great debate, with economists such as Samuelson and Merton finding it to be incorrect but with other practitioners finding it to be sensible. Poundstone (p. 294) makes one other important point in favor of its use, writing, "The Kelly Criterion tells *exactly* how far a trade can go before tumbling into the abyss. Mean-variance and VaR do not." See also Armitage (2005, p. 88), Covel (2007, pp. 57–69), and Patterson (2008).

17. The problem with the 20-year bond is that it is a compromise: the 30-year bond, the true trading benchmark for much of the data history, only began to be regularly issued by the Treasury in 1977 and its issuance was suspended in October 2001, only to be reinstated in February 2006.

18. Lee (2004, pp. 71–5) argues that relating equity valuations to the "risk-free" rate on long-term government bonds may be misleading, especially in the midst of a structural financial bubble in which feedback effects create overvaluations of bonds themselves. From 1926 to the present, as Siegel (2005, p. 63) notes, "the premium can differ by 3.5 percentage points depending on whether long-or-short-dated securities are used or arithmetic or geometric returns are calculated."

19. A paper by French et al. (1987) is illustrative. This study showed that the expected market risk premium—defined as the expected return on a stock portfolio minus the Treasury bill yield—"is positively related to the predictable volatility of stock returns" and "that unexpected stock market returns are negatively related to the unexpected change in the volatility of stock returns. This negative relation provides indirect evidence of a positive relation between expected risk premiums and volatility."

    The basis for separating returns into expected and unexpected terms is the Wold decomposition theorem as explained, for example, in Greene (2003, p. 620) and used in Neftci (2000, p. 109).

20. Far as is known, none of the classic studies, including those by Engle (1982), Poterba and Summers (1988), or Schwert (1989b), nor any subsequently have approached the analysis of bubbles (and crashes) through analysis of elasticity of variance with respect to the equity risk premium or credit spreads.

21. Damodaran (2002, pp. 158–61) continues:

competing models of risk ranging from the capital asset pricing model to multifactor models...notwithstanding their different conclusions, they all share some common views about risk...they all define risk in terms of variance in actual returns around an expected return: thus an investment is riskless when actual returns are always equal to the expected return... they all argue that risk has to be measured from the perspective of the marginal investor in an asset, and that this marginal investor is well diversified. Therefore...it is only the risk that an investment adds on to a diversified portfolio that should be measured and compensated..."The risk-free rate chosen in computing the premium has to be consistent with the risk-free rate used to compute expected returns."

An example of top-down and bottom-up ERP definitions is provided in Montier (2002). A simple bottom-up definition is (1-D/P)g, where the current payout ratio is multiplied by the long-term earnings growth forecast.

22. Dimson et al. (2002a, pp. 1–17) write that although the magnitude of the equity risk premium is central to corporate finance and investment—it "drives future equity returns and is the key determinant of the cost of capital – ...it is not clear how big the equity premium has been in the past, or how large it is today." Armitage (2005, pp. 88, 96) says: "The underlying assumptions that justify using the long-run historic premium as a forecast are that realized returns will tend to reflect *ex ante* expected returns, and that the *ex ante* expected return is constant over time...{but}...the historic mean provides an unreliable estimate of the expected premium." Furthermore, "the expected equity premium is an elusive number; it is unobservable, it probably varies over time and across investors...", (p. 119).

Arnott and Bernstein (2002) conclude that "the long-term forward-looking risk premium is nowhere near the level of the past: today it may well be near zero, perhaps even negative." They are aware, in fact, of the confusion that results because there is a "difference between the *observed* excess return and the *prospective* risk premium, two fundamentally different concepts that, unfortunately, carry the same label – risk premium."

Duarte and Rosa (2013) survey a wide variety of 29 ERP estimation models, the weighted average of which suggested that the ERP as of December 2012 was at an historic high and that the market thus ought to trend higher over the subsequent years. It appears that the high ERP was "due to exceptionally low Treasury yields at all foreseeable horizons." The S&P did in fact rise to an intraday high of 1687.18 from a December 31, 2012, closing at 1426.19 (about 18.3%) over the next five months to May 22, 2013.

23. A review of issues concerning the equity risk premium appears in Armitage (2005, Ch. 5). It is noted (p. 96) that estimates of the premium, as studied by Carleton and Lakonishok (1985), are very sensitive to the estimation period chosen. *Ex ante* one-year and ten-year horizon risk premiums, based on a survey of chief financial officers, are estimated by Graham and Harvey (2001, 2003). Variation may be larger than had been previously documented. A 300-year chart in Ferguson (2001, p. 303) shows that for the United Kingdom, the *ex post* returns on stocks over bonds ranged widely from approximately −6% in the late 1930s to +16% at the end of the 1940s. See also Falkenstein (2009).

24. ERP and stock price index series have long been mainstays in financial economics research. In the United Kingdom the primary source is the *Equity Gilt Study* (now produced by Barclays Capital), and in the United States it has been the *Stocks, Bonds, Bills and Inflation Yearbook* (SBBI) previously published by Ibbotson Associates (and as based on CRSP data). Data sets including equity

risk premiums are available from several additional sources or can be approximated as in Chap. 10.

25. Credit spreads will always narrow during times when speculative confidence is high and widen as pessimism and fear become dominant. Credit default swaps might theoretically also provide an alternative, but their history does not extend back far enough for long-term studies and the reliability and availability of the pricing data are inferior to that for credit spreads. The differences for real estate are relative illiquidity, absence of instantly available quotations, large size of unit transactions, and impossibility of physical conveyance of properties. The Florida land boom of the 1920s is of interest here. See Crossen (2005) and also Foster (2000).

26. Another example: On June 1, 2009, the deeply troubled Citigroup and bankrupt General Motors were replaced in the DJIA by Cisco and Travelers. Hulbert (2009) observes that removal of IBM from the DJIA in 1939, just before the company enjoyed a long period of high growth, may have significantly held down the overall average. With IBM included, recovery back to the 1929 peak of 381.17 on September 3 would have been much faster. IBM was again included in the DJIA in 1979. See also Siegel and Schwartz (2006) on S&P 500 changes.

27. Basak and Pavlova (2013) show that "institutions tilt their portfolios towards stocks that compose their benchmark indexes." The effect amplifies changes in the index and sector concentration.

28. See Lee (2004, p. 133) and Blake (2002) writing about the S&P 500, which represents about 75% of the value of the US market. Critics suggest that this benchmark "has become grossly distorted by concentration, warping the market it's meant to mirror...In bull markets a handful of big stocks utterly dominate the 500, forcing passive and active investors alike to channel more and more money into those companies to keep up with the index, creating a vicious cycle as the chosen shares, and thus the index itself, rise ever higher...the index became a contributing factor to the bubble." (Others, however, counter that "manias don't need benchmarks to thrive.")

29. Merton (1992, p. 31) has observed, "The greatest benefits in risk reduction come from adding a security to the portfolio whose realized return tends to be higher when the return on the rest of the portfolio is lower." That does not happen in the real world of a major index like the S&P.

30. No such risks, which take on exaggerated importance as bubbles become explosive, are at all captured in the rigid but mathematically indisputable and elegant CAPM calculations of risk as measured by standard deviations of returns.

31. In bubbles speculators see declines only as opportunities to buy and nearly everyone, despite some efforts at resistance, is ultimately forced by the surrounding-market psychology and professional portfolio performance obligations (i.e., to be fully or almost fully invested in equities and to meet or beat index performance) to become a speculator. If correct, however, that would be in egregious violation of the basic assumptions of modern portfolio theory. It might then also be asked how appropriate for application to bubble (or crash) market episodes is typical measurement of riskiness as expressed through volatility of returns.

32. Arnott (2004, pp. 116–20) writes,

There is no reason, beyond finance theory, to believe that a temporary negative risk premium should be impossible. Only finance theory suggests that this should not be possible (if investors are rational, if there are not taxes, if utility functions flatten, with increasing wealth, and so forth)...At the start of 2000, stock market yields were a scant 1.1 percent, while the TIPS [Treasury Inflation Protection Securities] yield was 4.4 percent. Earnings and dividends would have needed to grow 3.3 percentage points per year (triple the real growth rate of the prior century) for stocks to merely match the total return of TIPS. Was there a negative risk premium (at least for broad stock market averages, relative to TIPS) at the beginning of 2000? In my own view, the answer to this is obviously yes – but no one wanted to believe it.

Fund manager Jeremy Grantham is also quoted in Strauss (2008) as saying, "At the center of this crisis was a bubble in risk-taking. The risk premiums dropped off the cosmic scale, the lowest ever recorded...between June of '06 and June of '07, people were actually paying for the privilege of taking risk."

Yet Glassman and Hassett (1999a, b) contended that investors ought to apply a lower or even zero risk premium to stocks versus bonds and that by their doing so, share prices ought to be much higher. The risk premium at that time, though, was in retrospect apparently not high enough. In the two years following the time around which this book was released, all the major averages (DJIA, S&P 500, and NASDAQ) experienced declines of more than 35%. At the closing highs, the DJIA peaked at 11,722.98 on January 14, 2000, the NASDAQ at 5048.62 on March 10, 2000, the S&P 500 at 1527.46 on March 24, 2000 (with an almost-as-high close of 1520.77 on September 1, 2000), and the DJ Wilshire 5000 at 14,751.64 on March 24, 2000. However, the S&P intraday high on March 24, 2000, was 1552.87 and above the year's next intraday high of 1530.09 on September 1, 2000.

33. The wording closely follows that in a Cochrane article, "Why Identifying a Bubble Is So Much Trouble," that appeared on Bloomberg.com, September 21, 2011.
34. A chart in Montier (2002, p. 126) depicts how implied risk premiums calculated with both top-down and bottom-up methods not only are cyclical but have declined during times (e.g., 1998–2000) that are generally seen as including price bubble episodes.
35. Also in Chancellor (1999, p. 26).
36. In Fed Chairman Greenspan's days, this was often referred to as the "Greenspan put." Ferguson (2001, p. 305) identifies the basis for this as being the Fed's injection of liquidity in the October 1987 crash and the subsequent similar handling of the financial crises of 1997 and 1998. However, in the *Wall Street Journal* of August 30, 2007, Greg Ip writes, "Neither Mr. Bernanke nor his closest colleagues, some of whom served under Mr. Greenspan, believe there ever was a 'Greenspan put'." Fleckenstein and Sheehan (2008), however, write of evidence to the contrary. They also suggest (p. 20) that Greenspan recognized and spoke of bubbles at a 1994 FOMC meeting. Greenspan defends his policies and strategies in Ip (2008).
37. See William C. Hunter, George G. Kaufman, and Michael Pomerleano, eds., *Asset Price Bubbles: The Implications for Monetary, Regulatory, and International Policies*, p. 232 (article by Chirinko 2003 and also in Cochrane 2005, p. 410).
38. For instance, in this simple model, with r^e at 7% and g^f at 3%, just a 1% downward revision of growth expectations results in a 20% decline in the stock's price. Professor Greenwald of Columbia University, however, notes that the Gordon

model is greatly oversimplified, because growth requires new cash investments. See also Siegel (2014, p. 145).

39. Cuthbertson et al. (1999) decomposed the variance of unexpected real UK stock returns into components due to revisions in expected dividends and in discount rates and found that "the contribution of news about future discount rates is about four times that of news about future dividends, with no significant covariance between them."

40. Shiller's seminal 1981 paper employed an important volatility concept that compared the actual price today, P_t, to the price, P_t^*, that long-ago investors with perfect foresight might have paid had they been able to precisely forecast dividends. Cuthbertson and Nitzsche (2004, p. 258) indicate that under the EMH/rational valuations model, and assuming a constant discount factor, $\mathrm{var}(P_t^*) \geq \mathrm{var}(P_t)$. Shiller found that stock prices in the United States (Fig. 5.4) have been excessively volatile and in violation of the variance bound. This calls the rational valuation approach into question. Other, later, studies also found such violations. Important variance-bound theories include the Sharpe ratio as a special case of Hansen-Jagannathan bounds. See Cuthbertson and Nitzsche (2004, pp. 325–27).

41. As the elasticities vary with time, a linear rather than a log-linear model, which imposes constant elasticities, might be preferable, per Verbeek (2004, p. 53).

42. The market's proximity to a critical point at which a melt-up or melt-down might begin is suggested too by the degree of sensitivity. See Bak (1996) on sand-pile avalanches and self-organized critical points.

43. Ziemba (2005) writes of the limitations of the Sharpe ratio, which he says might be misleading if investment returns are skewed to the high side. That is "[B]ecause it is based on mean-variance theory, and thus is basically valid only for quadratic preferences or normal distributions…Typically the Sharpe ratio is computed using arithmetic returns…mean-variance analysis and the capital asset pricing model are based on arithmetic means. These are static, one-period theories. For asset returns over time, however, the geometric mean is a more accurate measure of average performance because the arithmetic mean is biased upward." The MAR ratio, devised by Managed Accounts Reports, LLC, also provides a measure of risk-adjusted reward. This ratio takes the annual return and divides it by the maximum drawdown in the period using month-end data. Thus a return of 30%, with a maximum drawdown of 20%, would have a MAR ratio of 1.5.

44. Although it's possible to index the entire ERP and variance series to their first data points (series indexing), the method here is to index to the beginning of each sample (sample indexing).

45. One of many discussions on the famous Arrow-Debreu equilibrium model appears, for example, in Rubinstein (1975). See also Radner (1968).

46. See Grossman and Stiglitz (1980).

47. In physics, the absolute or perfect equilibrium temperature corresponds to −459 °F, −273 °C, and 0 ° on the Kelvin scale (K). Quasi-equilibrium conditions, which are like Schumpeter's "neighborhoods" of equilibrium (see note 49).

Bubbles and crashes do not and cannot be sustained when in any given sample can also be defined and are discussed in this book's first edition. Period the directional changes in ERP and variance are persistently about evenly split between ups and downs. Such a balance reflects collective indecisiveness and emotional equanimity. In traders' talk it constitutes a "slow" market, one in which time seems to stand still and traders are bored, inactive, and complacent. It is thus a state of *quasi-equilibrium*, which is, of course, different from the Walrasian or other types of equilibria that have been often implied in theoretical economics. In contrast, bubble and crash markets are "fast" and traders are active.

48. Gao and Schmidt (2005) write that "the so-called long-run equilibrium in financial markets is not defined, and financial markets are always in a non-deterministic, irreversible, and open-ended process." Anecdotal evidence (gleaned through my own futures trading experiences) suggests that when markets are in near quasi-equilibrium quiet periods, floor traders (the "locals") such as those that had existed in the futures pits at the Chicago Merc and elsewhere often instigated brief flurries of furious buying or selling based on reactions to fleeting rumors of dubious origins or on fanciful observations, many of which they may sometimes fabricated themselves. The locals abhorred the relative quietude of near equilibrium conditions (in which they cannot make any money) and they actually purposely pushed the markets away from it whenever they could. This is much smaller in relative scale but similar to the creation of high volumes of buying by supposedly "informed" traders who, in the 1920s, hoped to stimulate further buying by those less "informed." See Thomas and Morgan Witts (1979).

49. Schumpeter (1939, p. 70) describes equilibrium for the overall economy in terms consistent with the present analysis and inconsistent with Merton's. Schumpeter says, "...we will, for our purpose, recognize existence of equilibrium *only at those discrete points on the time scale at which the system approaches a state which would, if reached, fulfill equilibrium conditions.* And since the system in practice never actually reaches such a state, we shall consider, instead of equilibrium points, ranges within which the system as a whole is more nearly in equilibrium than it is outside of them. Those ranges...we call *neighborhoods of equilibrium.*"

   More broadly, Pearce (1992, p. 129) defines equilibrium as denoting "... a state in which the agent is under no pressures or has no incentive to alter the current levels or states of economic action..."

50. Large funds such as Fidelity in Boston often require weeks or months of accumulation or distribution of shares to reach their ultimate desired holding quantities. In practice there is nothing neoclassically "instantaneous" about any of this. See also Huang and Werner (2000).

51. Quotes and paraphrase from Werner (2005, p. 19). [P]erfect information does not exist, and (p. 193) "[I]mperfect information appears to be pervasive...This has major implications for Walrasian models of market clearing...If we relax the assumption of perfect information...there is no guarantee that any market will clear...disequilibrium is therefore far likelier than equilibrium." With regard to auctions, he writes (p. 327) that "...there are market outcomes, but they are not equilibrium outcomes....the very definition of such equilibrium requires perfect information." "Disequilibrium economics," (p. 194) "is clearly more relevant to the real world."

   In real world, market equilibrium is always improbable because things are always changing. Technology advances, earnings estimates and interest rates rise or fall, people move and/or transfer jobs, the population grows in number but gets older or younger, there are major wars and minor disputes among nations, fads come and go, and so on. As Dardik (2017) posits, motion is waves waving in waves.

52. From Pimco manager Paul McCulley as noted in Mansharamani (2011, p. 33).

53. Walrasian general equilibrium is an integral part of the neoclassical framework. The Walrasian paradigm, as described by Barron et al. (2006, pp. 7–9), assumes that:

    - There are m individuals (agents) in the economy, and T commodities, each indexed and with each individual having the exclusive right to determine the use of that commodity.
    - All exchanges occur at a single point in time.
    - Each individual confronts the same known set of prices at which exchange can occur.
    - Purchase and sale prices are identical for each commodity. This means that there are no price spreads.

54. Bénassy (1986, pp. 4–5).

55. Malinvaud (1985, pp. 12–14) then answers the question, saying that there are three such properties:

    The first one needs no discussion, namely that trades balance: for each commodity the sum of purchases equals the sum of sales

    The second property states a consistency between the two concepts that relate to the intervention of any individual on any market: his purchase cannot exceed his demand and his sale exceed his supply...

    The third property states a consistency between the situations of various individuals intervening in the same market: if there is a rationed buyer in a market, there cannot be a rationed seller in the same market, and vice versa. *Again, this is a quite natural hypothesis because, in any given market, a rationed buyer and a rationed seller would have the chance to make a mutually advantageous trade.*

56. From Werner (2005, pp. 27 and 326).

57. From Brunnermeier (2001, p. 1): Prices are both "an index of scarcity or bargaining power, and a conveyor of information."

58. The implication for both bubbles and crashes, as Muellbauer and Portes (1978) recognize, is that "[A]n agent who is rationed as a buyer or seller on one market and cannot transact his notional excess demand...will in general alter his behaviour on other markets."

59. Such price jumps are also akin to sandpile or snow avalanches or earthquakes that appear in nature in what are known as self-organized critical systems (SOCs) and are universally characterized by power-law distributions. Such systems may go for long periods in conditions that seem to be at or close to equilibrium. This "equilibrium" is then punctuated by a burst of activity. As Bak (1996, p. 59) puts it, "A single grain of sand might cause an avalanche involving the entire pile. A small change in the configuration might cause what would otherwise be an insignificant event to become a catastrophe." Punctuated equilibrium is a core concept of large system dynamics. More on the SOC approach appears in Scheinkman and Woodford (1994) and in Bak (1996, p. 184). See also Prechter (2016) and Dardik (2017).

60. The times of greatest "short-side" pressures are on approach to major price tops or bottoms—often the times of greatest volatility and turbulence. It is the quietest of periods—somewhere in a neighborhood about midway between peaks and troughs—where such pressures are minimal (Chap. 9).

    Quandt and Rosen (1986) write that "failure of markets to clear is generally viewed as concomitant with the failure of some agents to optimize, a notion that is heretical according to the neoclassical religion." Grossman and Stiglitz (1980) noted that "assumptions that all markets, including that for information, are always in equilibrium and always perfectly arbitraged are inconsistent when arbitrage is costly... [B]ecause information is costly, prices cannot perfectly reflect the information that is available." See also Brunnermeier (2001), Bailey (2005), and Gromb and Vayanos (2010).

61. Tharp (2013, p. xxviii).

62. Goetzmann (2016b, p. 404).

63. This was even implicitly recognized in the simplest price model of the landmark Blanchard and Watson (1982) study.

64. In attempting to classify speculative peaks, Roehner (2002, p. 130) implements the same exponentiality concept but with price changes alone rather than with the ERP elasticity of variance that is used here and that was developed before I become aware of Roehner's work.

65. Distinctions between the exponential and parabolic do not appear to make any difference as to the conclusions to be drawn. There's also a difference between substantive and statistical significance. Even small exponents compound to substantive effects. See also Martenson (2011, p. 30).

66. If functions are presumed to be continuous, the mathematical description is simple and straightforward. The continuous relationship between the natural logarithm and exponential functions is $e^{\ln t} = t$ for $t > 0$. Similarly, $\ln(e^{kt}) = kt$ for any t and estimated parameter, k. The first derivative of y, dy/dt, equals $ke^{kt} = ky$. Also, recall that $\ln 1 = 0$ and that, for instance, with an equation such as $e^{6t} = 12$, the solution is $6\,t = \ln 12$, or $t = (\ln 12)/6 = 2.4849/6 = 0.414$. If the value of the parameter, k, in the expression $\exp(kt)$ is tiny, the exponential can appear to be close to the parabolic for a relatively long time. Nevertheless, the expression for an exponential always mathematically nests that of the parabolic.

Wilmott (2001, p. 143) notes that almost all partial differential equations in finance, including the Black-Scholes, are of the linear parabolic form.

67. Some parts of the exponential gains shown would be attributable to real fundamental factors and some to "bubble" action. Such real factors would include productivity and population growth.

68. An article on the *Seeking Alpha* (December 25, 2017) website "conservatively" predicted a price of $4 million per coin. Also, fundamental growth prospects for Qualcomm appeared to be rapidly improving. And in the case of Bitcoin, the underlying blockchain technology was truly innovative.

69. See Barron's online, "Getting Technical" column, March 15, 2006, and April 11, 2007. The same column of March 17, 2010, also written by Michel Kahn, quotes the classic Technical Analysis of Stock Trends by Edwards and Magee as saying that "Volume is of the utmost importance in all technical phenomena." The column further recalls that early master technician Richard Wyckoff referred to volume as the "cause" and price as the "effect."

70. Jones et al. (1994) find evidence of a "positive volume-volatility relationship" in which "it is the occurrence of transactions per se, and not their size, that generates volatility." Such a correlation has also been found by Karpoff (1987), Schwert (1989a, b), and Gallant et al. (1992).

71. On Shanghai Barboza (2007) writes: "Perhaps the most remarkable sign of the recent irrational exuberance underpinning China's stock markets was that during the last year, when a company announced bad news, its stock price shot through

the roof." The impact of news on markets is covered in Cutler et al. (1989) and Joulin et al. (2008).

72. Barboza (2007) writes, "Trading volumes have been so high that the Shanghai Stock Exchange recently worried that the country's electronic trading system could be destabilized." However, the Chinese market, which rose to new heights in 2007, was influenced by a whole complex of factors. Barboza (2008) recounts how much sentiment soured after prices dropped by 45% in just a few months.

73. Ying (1966) found that large increases in volume are usually followed by large price changes, Lee and Swaminathan (2000) show that past trading volume provides an important link to momentum and value strategies, and Morgan (1976) found that variance of returns is positively correlated with volume and that volume is associated with systematic risk. Trading volume, as explored by Shalen (1993), is also often posited as a proxy for the degree of disagreement of opinion among investors. Brown et al. (2009) found that "trading-volume measures may proxy for a number of factors including liquidity, momentum, and information." See also Chen et al. (2000), Amihud (2002), Scheinkman and Xiong (2003), Hong and Stein (2007), Santoli (2011).

Blume et al. (1994) found that volume holds significant explanatory power. Huddart et al. (2005) found (unsurprisingly to professional traders and technical market analysts) that trading volume rises substantially when prices break above or below previously established trading ranges. "This finding is difficult to reconcile with rational economic motives for trade and instead seems most consistent with behavioral research suggesting that investors focus on current prices relative to previous price extremes." Lobato and Velasco (2000) found that trading volume and volatility exhibit long memory.

Brooks (1998) found that measures of market volume do not improve volatility forecast accuracy, even though a study by Brooks and Katsaris (2003), in looking for periodic collapsing bubbles, found that "abnormal volume is a predictor and a classifier of returns because it can provide information to investors about the belief of the market in the future of the bubble…"

The concept of on-balance volume (OBV), which probably originated in 1940 under the name "accumulative volume," was then further developed and popularized by Joseph Granville in the 1960s (Granville 1963) and by trade-volume charts, popularized by Richard W. Arms, Jr. in the 1970s. These are germane to the notion of "short-side rationing" and serve also as background for the behavioral risk-premium concept that is developed in Chap. 9.

OBV begins with the assumption that volume precedes price and it attempts to measure the level of accumulation or distribution of shares. The Arms Index, also known as the TRIN Index, is named after its creator and is an indicator that uses advancing and declining stocks and their volume to measure market supply and demand. The formula can be applied over short (even intraday) or long time periods and is simply

$$TRIN = \frac{\left(\# \, advancing \, issues \, / \, \# \, declining \, issues\right)}{\left(advancing \, volume \, / \, declining \, volume\right)}$$

See Arms (1989, 2008).

REFERENCES

Amihud, Y. (2002). Illiquidity and Stock Returns: Cross-Section and Time-Series Effects. *Journal of Financial Markets, 5,* 31–56.

Armitage, S. (2005). *The Cost of Capital: Intermediate Theory.* New York: Cambridge University Press.

Arms, R. W., Jr. (1989). *The Arms Index (TRIN).* Homewood: Dow Jones-Irwin.

Arms, R. W., Jr., (2008, March 31). Whiplashed? That's a Bullish Sign. *Barron's.*

Arnott, R. D. (2004, October). Blinded by Theory? *Institutional Investor* and *Journal of Portfolio Management,* 30th Anniversary Issue.

Arnott, R. D., & Bernstein, P. L. (2002). What Risk Premium Is Normal? *Financial Analysts Journal, 58*(2), 64–85.

Bailey, R. E. (2005). *The Economics of Financial Markets.* Cambridge: Cambridge University Press.

Bak, P. (1996). *How Nature Works: The Science of Self-Organized Criticality.* New York: Springer-Verlag.

Barboza, D. (2007, February 28). A Shock Wave from Shanghai. *New York Times.*

Barboza, D. (2008, April 2). To See a Stock Market Bubble Bursting, Look at Shanghai. *New York Times.*

Barro, R. J. (2006, August). Rare Disasters and Asset Markets in the Twentieth Century. *Quarterly Journal of Economics, 121*(3), 823–866.

Barron, J. M., Ewing, B. T., & Lynch, G. J. (2006). *Understanding Macroeconomic Theory.* New York/London: Routledge.

Basak, S., & Pavlova, A. (2013). Asset Prices and Institutional Investors. *American Economic Review, 103*(5), 1728–1758.

Bénassy, J.-P. (1986). *Macroeconomics: An Introduction to the Non-Walrasian Approach.* Orlando: Academic Press.

Bernstein, P. L. (2007). *Capital Ideas Evolving.* Hoboken: Wiley.

Blake, R. (2002, May). Is Time Running Out for the S&P 500? *Institutional Investor.*

Blanchard, O. J., & Watson, M. W. (1982). Bubbles, Rational Expectations, and Financial Markets. In P. Wachtel (Ed.), *Crises in the Economic and Financial Structure.* Lexington: Lexington Books.

Bleiberg, S. D. (2018). "The Limits of Modern Portfolio Theory," *Barron's,* April 13.

Blume, L., Easley, D., & O'Hara, M. (1994). Market Statistics and Technical Analysis: The Role of Trading Volume. *Journal of Finance, 49*(1), 153–181.

Brooks, C. (1998). Forecasting Stock Return Volatility: Does Volume Help? *Journal of Forecasting, 17,* 59–80.

Brooks, C., & Katsaris, A. (2003). *Regime Switching Models of Speculative Bubbles with Volume: An Empirical Investigation of the S&P 500 Composite Index.* Reading: IMSA.

Brown, J. H., Crocker, D. K., & Foerster, S. R. (2009). Trading Volume and Stock Investments. *Financial Analysts Journal, 65*(2), 67–84.

Brunnermeier, M. K. (2001). *Asset Pricing Under Asymmetric Information: Bubbles, Crashes, Technical Analysis, and Herding.* New York: Oxford University Press.

Buchan, J. (1997). *Frozen Desire: The Meaning of Money.* New York: Farrar Straus Giroux.

Carleton, W. T., & Lakonishok, J. (1985). Risk and Return on Equity: The Use and Misuse of Historical Estimates. *Financial Analysts Journal, 30*(1), 38–47.

Champion, S. R. (1998). *The Great Taiwan Bubble: The Rise and Fall of an Emerging Stock Market*. Berkeley: Pacific View Press.

Chancellor, E. (1999). *Devil Take the Hindmost: A History of Financial Speculation*. New York: Farrar, Straus, Giroux.

Chen, J., Hong, H., & Stein, J. C. (2000). Forecasting Crashes: Trading Volume, Past Returns and Conditional Skewness in Stock Prices. NBER Working Paper No. 7687.

Chirinko, R. S. (2003 [2005]). Comments on: 'Stocks as Money,' and 'Bubble Psychology.' In Hunter et al. (2003).

Cochrane, J. H. (2005). *Asset Pricing* (Revised ed.). Princeton: Princeton University Press.

Cogley, T., & Sargent, T. J. (2008). The Market Price of Risk and the Equity Premium: A Legacy of the Great Depression? *Journal of Monetary Economics, 55*(3), 454–476.

Cornell, B. (1999). *The Equity Risk Premium*. New York: Wiley.

Covel, M. W. (2007). *The Complete Turtle Trader: The Legend, the Lessons, the Results*. New York: HarperCollins.

Cowles, A. (1938). *Common-Stock Indexes, 1871–1937*. Bloomington: Principia Press.

Crossen, C. (2005, August 3). Land in 1920s Florida Was So Hot, People Sold Underwater Lots. *Wall Street Journal*.

Cuthbertson, K., & Nitzsche, D. (2004). *Quantitative Financial Economics* (2nd ed.). Chichester: Wiley.

Cuthbertson, K., Hayes, S., & Nitzsche, D. (1999). Explaining Movements in UK Stock Prices. *The Quarterly Review of Economics and Finance, 39*(1), 1–19.

Cutler, D. M., Poterba, J. M., & Summers, L. H. (1989). What Moves Stock Prices? *Journal of Portfolio Management, 15*(3), 4–12.

Damodaran, A. (2002). *Investment Valuation: Tools and Techniques for Determining the Value of Any Asset* (2nd ed.). New York: Wiley.

Dardik, I. (2017). *The Nature of Nature: The Discovery of SuperWaves and How It Changes Everything*. New York: Rodale.

Dimson, E., Marsh, P., & Staunton, M. (2002a). Global Evidence on the Equity Risk Premium. *Journal of Applied Corporate Finance, 15*(4), 27–38.

Dimson, E., Marsh, P., & Staunton, M. (2007). *The Worldwide Equity Premium: A Smaller Puzzle*. London: London Business School. Available at http://www.london.edu/assets/documents/PDF/The_Worldwide_EquityPremium.pdf.

Donaldson, R. G., Kamstra, M. J., & Kramer, L. A. (2010). Estimating the Equity Premium. *Journal of Financial and Quantitative Analysis, 45*(4), 813–846.

Duarte, F., & Rosa, C. (2013, May 8). Are Stocks Cheap? A Review of the Evidence, Liberty Street Economics, New York Federal Reserve, 691.

Engel, C. (2005). Some New Variance Bounds for Asset Prices. *Journal of Money, Credit, and Banking, 37*(5), 949–955.

Engle, R. F. (1982). Autoregressive Conditional Heteroskedasticity with Estimates of the Variance of U.K. Inflation. *Econometrica, 50*, 987–1008.

Falkenstein, E. (2009). *Finding Alpha: The Search for Alpha When Risk and Return Break Down*. Hoboken: Wiley.

Fama, E. F., & French, K. (1989). Business Conditions and Expected Returns on Stocks and Bonds. *Journal of Financial Economics, 25*, 23–49.

Ferguson, N. (2001). *The Cash Nexus: Money and Power in the Modern World 1700–2000*. New York: Basic Books.

Fleckenstein, W. A., & Sheehan, F. (2008). *Greenspan's Bubbles: The Age of Ignorance at the Federal Reserve*. New York: McGraw-Hill.

Foster, M. S. (2000). *Castles in the Sand: The Life and Times of Carl Graham Fisher*. Gainesville: University Press of Florida.

French, K. R., Schwert, G. W., & Stambaugh, R. F. (1987). Expected Stock Returns and Volatility. *Journal of Financial Economics, 19*(1), 3–29.

Gala, V. D. (2008). Discussion: Cash Flow Risk, Discounting Risk, and the Equity Premium Puzzle. In R. Mehra (Ed.), *Handbook of the Equity Risk Premium*. Amsterdam: Elsevier.

Gallant, R. A., Rossi, P. E., & Tauchen, G. (1992). Stock Prices and Volume. *The Review of Financial Studies, 5*(2), 199–242.

Gao, L., & Schmidt, U. (2005). Self Is Never Neutral: Why Economic Agents Behave Irrationally. *Journal of Behavioral Finance, 6*(1), 27–37.

Glassman, J. K., & Hassett, K. A. (1999a). *Dow 36,000: The New Strategy for Profiting from the Coming Rise in the Stock Market*. New York: Times Books.

Glassman, J. K., & Hassett, K. A. (1999b, March 17). Stock Prices Are Still Far Too Low. *Wall Street Journal*.

Goetzmann, W. N. (2016b). *Money Changes Everything: How Finance Made Civilization Possible*. Princeton, NJ: Princeton University Press.

Goetzmann, W. N., & Ibbotson, R. G. (Eds.). (2006). *The Equity Risk Premium: Essays and Explorations*. Oxford: Oxford University Press.

Goetzmann, W. N., Ibbotson, R. G., & Peng, L. (2001). A New Historical Database for the NYSE 1815 to 1925: Performance and Predictability. *Journal of Financial Markets, 4*, 1–32.

Gomes, F. (2008). Discussion: Equity Premia with Benchmark Levels of Consumption: Closed-Form Results. In R. Mehra (Ed.), *Handbook of the Equity Risk Premium*. Amsterdam: Elsevier.

Gordon, M. J. (1962). *The Investment, Financing and Valuation of the Corporation*. Homewood: Irwin.

Graham, J. R., & Harvey, C. R. (2001, 2003). Expectations of Equity Risk Premia, Volatility and Asymmetry. (Working Paper 8678, NBER and Working Paper). Durham: Duke University.

Grant, S., & Quiggin, J. (2001). The Risk Premium for Equity Explanations and Implications. Working Paper No 2001-89. School of Economics, Australian National University.

Granville, J. E. (1963). *Granville's New Key to Stock Market Profits*. Englewood Cliffs: Prentice-Hall.

Greene, W. H. (2003). *Econometric Analysis* (5th ed.). Upper Saddle River: Prentice Hall.

Greenspan, A. (2013). *The Map and the Territory: Risk, Human Nature, and the Future of Forecasting*. New York: Penguin.

Gromb, D., & Vayanos, D. (2010). Limits of Arbitrage. *Annual Review of Financial Economics, 2*, 251–275.

Grossman, S. J., & Stiglitz, J. E. (1980). On the Impossibility of Informationally Efficient Markets. *American Economic Review, 70*(3), 393–408.

Hamilton, J. D. (1994). *Time Series Analysis*. Princeton: Princeton University Press.

Hammond, P. B., Jr., Leibowitz, M. L., and Siegel, L B., eds. (2011). *Rethinking the Equity Risk Premium*. Charlottesville, VA: CFA Research Institute.

Hong, H., & Stein, J. C. (2007). Disagreement and the Stock Market. *Journal of Economic Perspectives, 21*(2), 109–128.

Huang, K. X. D., & Werner, J. (2000). Asset Price Bubbles in Arrow-Debreu and Sequential Equilibrium. *Economic Theory, 15*, 253–278.

Huddart, S., Lang, M., & Yetman, M. (2005). Psychological Factors, Stock Price Paths, and Trading Volume. Working Paper, Pennsylvania State University. Available at http://www.smeal.psu.edu/faculty/huddart/Papers/HuLaYe.pdf

Hulbert, M. (2009, April 26). 25 Years to Bounce Back? Try 4 ½. *New York Times.*

Hunter, W. C., Kaufman, G. G., & Pomerleano, M. (Eds.). (2003). *Asset Price Bubbles: The Implications for Monetary, Regulatory, and International Policies.* Cambridge, MA: MIT Press (Paperback edition, 2005).

Ibbotson, R. G., & Chen, P. (2003). Long-Run Stock Returns: Participating in the Real Economy. *Financial Analysts Journal, 59*(1), 88–98.

Ip, G. (2008, April 8). His Legacy Tarnished, Greenspan Goes on Defensive. *Wall Street Journal.*

Jagannathan, R., McGrattan, E. R., & Scherbina, A. (2000). The Declining U.S. Equity Premium. *Federal Reserve Bank Quarterly Review, 24*(4), 3–19.

Jones, C., Kaul, G., & Lipson, M. (1994). Transactions, Volume, and Volatility. *Review of Financial Studies, 7*(4), 631–651.

Jorion, P., & Goetzmann, W. N. (1999). Global Stock Markets in the Twentieth Century. *Journal of Finance, 54*, 953–980.

Joulin, A., Lefevre, A., Grunberg, D., & Bouchaud, J.-P. (2008, March). Stock Price Jumps: News and Volume Play a Minor Role. *Physics and Society.* Available at www.arxiv.org/abs/0803.1769 and *Wilmott,* Sept/Oct 2008.

Karpoff, J. M. (1987). The Relation Between Price Changes and Trading Volume: A Survey. *Journal of Financial and Quantitative Analysis, 22*, 109–126.

Keim, D. B., & Stambaugh, R. F. (1986). Predicting Returns in the Bond and Stock Markets. *Journal of Financial Economics, 17*(2), 357–390.

Kleidon, A. W. (1986). Variance Bounds Tests and Stock Price Valuation Models. *Journal of Political Economy, 94*, 953–1001.

Kocherlakota, N. R. (1996). The Equity Premium: It's Still a Puzzle. *Journal of Economic Literature, 34*(1), 42–71.

Kohn, D. (2005). *Monetary Policy Perspectives on Risk Premiums in Financial Markets.* Washington, DC: Financial Market Risk Premiums Conference, Federal Reserve Board.

Kurz, M., Jin, H., & Motolese, M. (2005). Determinants of Stock Market Volatility and Risk Premia. *Annals of Finance, 1*(2), 109–147.

Lansing, K. J. (2010). Some New Variance Bounds for Asset Prices: A Comment, Federal Reserve Bank of San Francisco, 2010:29.

Lee, T. (2004). *Why the Markets Went Crazy.* New York: Palgrave Macmillan.

Lee, C. M. C., & Swaminathan, B. (2000). Price Momentum and Trading Volume. *Journal of Finance, LV*(5), 2017–2067.

LeRoy, S. F., & Porter, R. D. (1981). The Present Value Relation: Tests Based on Implied Variance Bonds. *Econometrica, 64*, 555–574.

Lobato, I. N., & Velasco, C. (2000). Long Memory in Stock-Market Trading. *Journal of Business & Economic Statistics, 18*(4), 410–427.

Malinvaud, E. (1985). *The Theory of Unemployment Reconsidered* (2nd ed.). New York/London: Blackwell.

Mandelbrot, B., & Hudson, R. L. (2004). *The (Mis)Behavior of Markets: A Fractal View of Risk, Ruin, and Reward.* New York: Basic Books.

Mansharamani, V. (2011). *Boombustology: Spotting Financial Bubbles Before They Burst.* Hoboken: Wiley.

Martenson, C. (2011). *The Crash Course: The Unsustainable Future of Our Economy, Energy, and Environment.* Hoboken: Wiley.

Mehra, R. (Ed.). (2008). *Handbook of the Equity Risk Premium.* Amsterdam: Elsevier.

Mehra, R., & Prescott, E. C. (1985). The Equity Premium: A Puzzle. *Journal of Monetary Economics, 15*(2), 145–161.

Mehrling, P. (2005). *Fischer Black and the Revolutionary Idea of Finance.* Hoboken: Wiley.

Merton, R. C. (1992). *Continuous-Time Finance* (rev ed.). Oxford: Blackwell.

Montier, J. (2002). *Behavioural Finance: Insights into Irrational Minds and Markets.* Chichester/Hoboken: Wiley.

Morgan, I. G. (1976). Stock Prices and Heteroscedasticity. *Journal of Business, 49*(4), 496–508.

Muellbauer, J., & Portes, R. D. (1978). Macroeconomic Models with Quantity Rationing. *Economic Journal, 88*(4), 788–821.

Neftci, S. N. (2000). *An Introduction to the Mathematics of Financial Derivatives* (2nd ed.). San Diego/London: Academic Press.

Noguchi, Y. (1994). The 'Bubble' and Economic Policies in the 1980s. *Journal of Japanese Studies, 20*(2), 291–329.

Patterson, S. (2008, March 22). Old Pros Size Up the Game. *Wall Street Journal.*

Pearce, D. W. (Ed.). (1992). *The MIT Dictionary of Modern Economics* (4th ed.). Cambridge, MA: MIT Press.

Posen, A. S. (2003). It Takes More Than a Bubble to Be Japan. WP 03-9, Institute for International Economics. Available at http://www.petersoninstitute.org/publications/wp/03-9.pdf

Poterba, J., & Summers, L. H. (1988). Mean Reversion in Stock Returns: Evidence and Implications. *Journal of Financial Economics, 22*(1), 27–59.

Poundstone, W. (2005). *Fortune's Formula: The Untold Story of the Scientific Betting System That Beat the Casinos and Wall Street.* New York: Hill and Wang (Farrar, Straus and Giroux).

Prechter, R. R., Jr. (2016). *The Socionomic Theory of Finance.* Gainesville: Socionomics Institute Press.

Quandt, R. E., & Rosen, H. S. (1986). Unemployment, Disequilibrium and the Short Run Phillips Curve: An Econometric Approach. *Journal of Applied Econometrics, 1,* 235–253.

Radner, R. (1968). Competitive Equilibrium Under Uncertainty. *Econometrica, 36*(1), 31–58.

Rietz, T. A. (1988). The Equity Risk Premium: A Solution. *Journal of Monetary Economics, XXII,* 117–131.

Roehner, B. M. (2002). *Patterns of Speculation: A Study in Observational Econophysics.* Cambridge: Cambridge University Press.

Rubinstein, M. (1975). Securities Market Efficiency in an Arrow-Debreu Economy. *American Economic Review, 65*(5), 812–824.

Santoli, M. (2011, April 11). What Is Low Volume Telling Us? *Barron's.*

Scheinkman, J. A., & Woodford, M. (1994). Self-Organized Criticality and Economic Fluctuations. *American Economic Review, 84*(2), 417–421.

Scheinkman, J. A., & Xiong, W. (2003). Overconfidence and Speculative Bubbles. *Journal of Political Economy, 111*(6), 1183–1219.

Schumpeter, J. A. (1939). *Business Cycles: A Theoretical, Historical, and Statistical Analysis of the Capitalist Process.* New York: McGraw-Hill.

Schwert, G. W. (1989a, May). *Business Cycles, Financial Crises, and Stock Volatility* (Working Paper No. 2957). NBER.

Schwert, G. W. (1989b). Why Does Stock Market Volatility Change Over Time? *Journal of Finance, 44*(5), 1115–1153.

Schwert, G. W. (1990). Stock Volatility and the Crash of '87. *Review of Financial Studies, 3*(1), 77–102.

Shalen, C. T. (1993). Volume Volatility, and the Dispersion of Beliefs. *Review of Financial Studies, 6*(2) (April).

Shiller, R. J. (1981). Do Stock Prices Move Too Much to Be Justified by Subsequent Movements in Dividends? *American Economic Review, 71*(3), 421–436.

Shiller, R. J. (1992). *Market Volatility.* Cambridge, MA: MIT Press.

Siegel, J. J. (2005). Perspectives on the Equity Risk Premium. *Financial Analysts Journal, 61*(6), 61–73.

Siegel, J. J. (2008, 2014). *Stocks for the Long Run* (4th and 5th ed). New York: McGraw-Hill.

Siegel, J. J., & Schwartz, D. (2006). Long-Term Returns on the Original S&P 500 Companies. *Financial Analysts Journal, 52*(1), 18–31.

Smant, D. J. C. (2003). *The Variance-Bound Fallacy.* Rotterdam: Erasmus University, Rotterdam School of Economics. Available at www.few.eur.nl/few/people/smant

Strauss, L. C. (2008, October 13). Still Holding Back. *Barron's.*

Taleb, N. N. (2005). *Fooled by Randomness.* New York: Random House (2nd paperback ed.).

Tharp, V. K. (2013). *Trading Beyond the Matrix.* Hoboken: Wiley.

Thomas, G., & Morgan Witts, M. (1979). *The Day the Bubble Burst.* New York: Doubleday.

Verbeek, M. (2004). *A Guide to Modern Econometrics* (2nd ed.). Chichester: Wiley.

Werner, R. A. (2005). *New Paradigm in Macroeconomics: Solving the Riddle of Japanese Macroeconomic Performance.* Houndmills: Palgrave Macmillan.

West, K. D. (1988a). Dividend Innovations and Stock Price Volatility. *Econometrica, 56*(1), 37–61.

West, K. D. (1988b). Bubbles, Fads and Stock Volatility Tests: A Partial Evaluation. *Journal of Finance, 43*(3), 639–655.

Wilmott, P. (2001). *Paul Wilmott Introduces Quantitative Finance.* Chichester: Wiley.

Ying, C. C. (1966). Stock Market Prices and Volumes of Sales. *Econometrica, 34,* 676–685.

Ziemba, W. T. (2005, Fall). The Symmetric Downside-Risk Sharpe Ratio. *Journal of Portfolio Management,* 108–122.

Zweig, J. (2009, July 11). Does Stock-Market Data Really Go Back 200 Years? *Wall Street Journal.*

CHAPTER 9

Behavioral Risk Features

9.1 BEHAVIORAL RISK PREMIUM

Anyone who has traded—not on hypothetical papers but in the real world—with real money at stake and deep-seated emotions stirred will immediately recognize that in the heat of battle it's difficult *not* to buy at the top just as it is difficult *not* to sell (or to buy) at the bottom. In the real world, no one buys into the market at or near the top expecting a lower return. No! There's instead a fear of missing out. At the top, the expected return for many if not most (or average) participants is *high*, just as at the bottom participants dump shares willy-nilly because they expect a *low* or negative return and decide they had better sell before prices fall some more and the expected returns shrink still further.[1]

These behavioral aspects are in direct opposition to the dominant theories of modern finance which posit that investors largely follow a rational expectations model, movement toward "equilibrium" is always the direction of change, and arbitrage is smooth, riskless, and executable. The traditional models, moreover, focus mostly on ebbs and flows of economic activity and ignore or purposely overlook (for purposes of simplification) the banking and commercial and industrial balance sheet conditions that might facilitate or impede such flows.[2] Therefore, as mathematically neat as the coldly precise standard theory has been, it is still lacking when it comes to describing bubbles and baths (crashes). And it is clueless when it comes to explaining that economically based transactions for everyday goods and services differ greatly from those in the financial markets, where cognitive uncertainty and herding are dominant.

9.2 TWO-COMPONENT PREMIUMS

All of the preceding rational expectations literature, it seems, takes the equity risk premium as a uniform piece reflective only of financial features and without regard to any behavioral features. As traditionally described, the ERP is

© The Author(s) 2018

H. L. Vogel, *Financial Market Bubbles and Crashes, Second Edition*,
https://doi.org/10.1007/978-3-319-71528-5_9

one-dimensional; it covers only the readily quantifiable elements of discount rates, money supply changes, dividends, and P/E ratios (and indirectly, consumption and utility preferences).

In relatively "normal" trending or sideways markets, and for most practical intents and purposes, this usually works reasonably well enough as an approximation. But it breaks down at the extremes, where many amorphous behavioral/psychological aspects readily trump the pure financials and thereby directly influence expectations. In brief, the standard conceptualization of the ERP is too rigid and particularly unrepresentative of what happens in bubbles and crashes.

One way to possibly broaden and supplement the conventional theory to account for what is seen at the real-world extremes is to thus propose that there are actually two different risk premiums in operation at the same time. That is, the well-known equity risk premium (ERP)—puzzles, warts, and all—ought to be thought of as having two components, financial (FRP) and behavioral (BRP). For both the FRP and the BRP, a high and rising premium in a "crash" must for instance come from the perception that, for whatever reasons, there lurks an imminent and rising potential for loss that necessitates adjustment to a more riskaverse position.[3]

This BRP may be fashioned in a way that parallels that of the FRP. The BRP is simply the expected return on behavior that is in excess of the risk-free behavioral return. Quantification of this BRP—which only comes to the forefront at market extremes when herding, greed, fear, and other such high-anxiety psychological factors are in command—is not as easy as for the FRP.[4] But it can be done.

The trickiest part is finding representative quantities for a risk-free BRP that play a role equivalent to that of Treasury bills in calculations of the FRP. And this is where the previously developed notions of quasi-equilibrium (Chap. 8, notes 47 and 49) are useful, even though the case has already been made that because of short-side quantity rationing and imperfect information, markets are never truly in equilibrium; markets are only relatively quieter at some times than at others. The quietest times are those at which the behavioral risk premium is minimal and in a state that has been earlier described as akin to quasi-equilibrium.

9.3   High-Anxiety Smiles

Because any BRP is likely to be substantially different when the financial risk premium is 5% than when it is 10%, it is also useful to contemporaneously measure BRP relative to the FRP as a ratio of BRP to FRP. This proposed concept is illustrated in Fig. 9.1.[5] The drawing resembles (and is inspired by) the volatility "smiles" (plotting implied volatilities against strike prices) that are used in option-pricing theory.

If such a theoretical proposition is indeed correct, the smile ought to be "crooked" (i.e., asymmetrical, or somewhat like a reclining capital letter J).

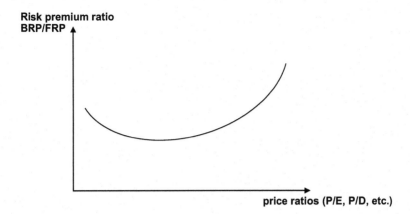

Fig. 9.1 Two-dimensional BRP/FRP smile; idealized concept

That's because the BRP is high at *both* high-anxiety extremes (i.e., bubbles and crashes) and low in the relatively tranquil middle range. The BRP/FRP ratios at the ends—high over a high (FRP) at low prices and high over a low (FRP) at high prices—ought thus to generate the asymmetry of the proposed smile.

This appearance would also be reinforced by the fact that transactions per unit time—the BRP proxy explained in greater detail below—are limited in the most severe of market crashes by illiquidity gaps, trading shutdowns (e.g., NYSE-mandated "cooling-off" periods), short-sale bans, and total market closures in which you cannot get out no matter what your degree of desperation to do so.[6] In contrast, though, stock markets have never been known to close when prices were zooming higher (i.e., in Wall Street lingo, "melting up" or in a "moonshot"): Only commodity futures trading is halted when daily prices move "limit up" or "limit down."[7] New York Stock Exchange "circuit breaker" rules (e.g., Rule 80B) are thus asymmetric as they are intended to slow crashes, not bubbles.[8]

In brief, at the extremes, the BRP is a measure of the urgency with which people respond to overall movement and price-change momentum.[9] As there is a cost of inaction, the impulsive urgency is to either buy in as prices bubble up or sell out as prices crash down. And in reflecting the short-side rationing principle, the focus increasingly shifts from sensitivity to prices paid (or received in crashes) and fundamental valuation metrics, to sensitivity to desired quantities held.[10] Under extreme conditions, *time* is of the essence and is the distinguishing feature. At such junctures, in the parlance of traders, we see a "fast" market, which is the opposite of the dull, tranquil, or "slow" markets characterized earlier as being in a state of quasi-equilibrium.

The middle of the smile represents normally trending, non-bubble, or non crash conditions in which the BRP *relative* to the FRP is not notably high. In this middle region, there is no sense of or need for urgency or a call to action.

The FRP accounts for nearly the entire risk premium. And within this middle region, investors have plenty of time to be "rational" and carefully analytical; to weigh potential risks and take them into full account; to conduct in-depth interviews of company and industry executives and experts; to meticulously study fundamentals such as balance sheets, income statements, and growth prospects; to plow through dense analysts' reports; and to deliberate earnestly with portfolio selection committees.

Yet once price-change exponentiality becomes more obvious, the BRP becomes relatively more important. As the bubble top (or crash bottom) approaches, this BRP is rising, whereas the FRP, as has been shown in conventional theory, goes low (high in crashes).

It is thus suggested that at any single point in time the *full* equity risk premium ought to be decomposed and understood to be a combination of the FRP and the BRP as in the following expressions:

$$Bubbles: \text{ERP} = \text{FRP} - \text{BRP},$$

$$Crashes: \text{ERP} = \text{FRP} + \text{BRP}.$$

Plainly, if you are running a fund and want to earn a bonus and keep your job, your psychological risk premium (as compared to the FRP at that time) is relatively high and rising on approach to extremes: As everyone else begins to outperform your fund due to concentration in momentum sectors, the imperative— "rationality" notwithstanding—is that you'd better climb aboard (or in crashes, run toward cash). It has been shown, for instance, that portfolio managers who have underperformed their benchmark indexes will in the last quarter of the year then take on more risk in hope of catching up to their peers.[11] Thus, in the real world of professional investment management, a *loss* of 15% in a market also down 15% will not typically trigger significant withdrawals and/or redemptions of funds (assets under management, AUM). But should a benchmark index be *up* 15% and the portfolio up by only 7%, AUM will most likely shrink rather quickly.[12]

Even some of the world's largest, savviest, and normally most successful fund managers have sometimes faced situations in which they are known to have succumbed to such pressures. Perhaps the most onerous part of an under-performing portfolio manager's job is explaining to clients the reasons (i.e., excuses) for losses and/or relative underperformance.[13]

Indeed, at the approaching bubble extreme (top), it is generally perceived that the biggest risk is in being *out* of or short the market, or of being stuck in boring old risk-free treasuries making 4% annually when everyone else is frol-icking—making 4% a week, a day, and sometimes even an hour. So powerful and entrenched is the grip of this behavioral ("buy the dip") component on the psyche of traders, that on the first significant downdraft of an embryonic bear market, it is typical for professional investors and media pundits to sternly advise "Don't Panic!"–even though if you're ever going to panic this is by far the best time at which to do it.

Similarly, in approaching a crash low, as a fund manager you start to appear rather foolish holding onto positions that have already lost 30%, 70%, or sometimes 98% or more (think Enron or WorldCom, for examples). The impulse then is to capitulate ("Help, get me out!"), just as at the approaching peak it's "Get me in!" At such emotionally charged moments, the behavioral aversion to risk of loss of bonus or job, or of relative performance standings (for marketing to attract new funds), or of shame and ridicule, or of not being part of the crowd, would be much higher than in the slow-moving quasi-equilibrium periods when the psychological pressure is relatively muted and contained.[14]

This thus suggests that the required return in bubble and crash environments comes to include payoffs not only in slow-moving streams of long-term monetary dividends but also in psychological and emotional dividends that are potentially large, fast-moving, and immediately rewarding. Such nearly instant expected gratification—by its very "instantness"—does not require any significant time discounting and therefore looms large as a component of the total combined monetary *and* nonmonetary rewards: For the behavioral nonmonetary payoffs, no one expects to discount over many years and to estimate terminal values that are far into the future. The crucial necessity is to hang onto your job, your assets under management, and your relative peer performance (benchmark) comparisons *now!*

From this perspective, it makes sense that variance bounds are violated: The monetary dividend alone does not move fast, but an expected dividend *including* a behavioral dimension does have the potential to move fast because the time factor is "telescoped."

9.4   TRANSACTIONS PER UNIT TIME

Data for testing of behavioral features are obviously not as easy to obtain as for the ERP or money supply. For one thing, there is no immediately available behavioral risk-free rate as there is with the ERP in the form of nearly continuous quotes on T-bills.[15]

But actions speak louder than words and the information that is closest to what is needed to test the BRP/ERP ratio is most readily available in the form of transactions volume data. More specifically, this comes in the form of transactions per unit time (TPUT) as adjusted for total shares outstanding for all companies that are index components. TPUT is an indicator of the *urgency* that is present as extremes are approached and short-side rationed quantity pressures intensify.[16] The higher the adjusted TPUT, the higher the BRP.[17]

Unfortunately, though, complications abound. Whereas market melt-ups will rarely result in market closures the same is not true under crash or near-crash conditions, when liquidity disappears (e.g., brokers cannot be reached and computer systems fail) and the market freezes or seizes to the point that regulations have often mandated (cooling-off period) shutdowns.[18] With markets closed, no trades can be completed even though the need of most participants to trade is then at its utmost.

Another important complication is that no pure long-term series of trading volumes or numbers of shares traded per unit time for components of the S&P 500 is available. The closest proxy for this is activity on the NYSE.

TPUT in particular has been greatly enhanced by vast investments in new trading-platform technologies that have been developed since the 1990s.[19] As of the early 2000s, transactions per unit time have also risen because of switchover in American markets to decimal from fractional (i.e., mostly one-eighth) pricing spreads, which has notably diminished the average number of shares that are completed per trade (on the NYSE from around 1205 in 1999 to under 331 by 2005). Seasonality will be seen in the next to last week of every quarter, when the "triple witch" (now quadruple) expiration of options increases activity. Seasonality will also appear as an anomaly in end-of-quarter month returns.[20] And stock splits, mergers, option grants, spin-offs and carve-outs, secondary financings, and a greater number of companies listed have further on a net basis (and despite many large recent share buyback programs) added to total NYSE-company shares outstanding.

The extraordinary growth of NYSE TPUT beginning circa 1994 and shown in Fig. 9.2a is striking. By 2005, more than 100 million trades, a 20-fold rise in ten years, were being executed each month.[21] Figure 9.2b shows the annualized monthly trades as a percentage of total monthly NYSE shares listed.

Unusually slow and quiet trading periods of quasi-equilibrium would likely be the regions where the best approximations to a risk-free behavioral benchmark might be found.[22]

The use of TPUT variance as a first approximation to a behavioral risk-free point of reference is obviously not as clean and precise as that which can be derived from a continuously quoted Treasury bill rate that is available at any time.[23] But establishment of such a proxy, which plays a role analogous to the

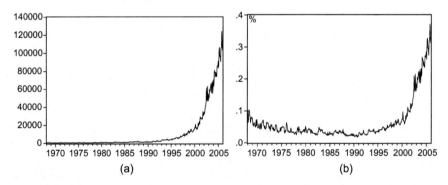

Fig. 9.2 (a) Average number of trades per month (in 000s), NYSE, 1968–2005; (b) monthly number of trades as percentage of NYSE-listed company shares, 1968:01–2005:12, with small (3%) change in listed share base series, 1977. (Source data: NYSE)

financial risk-free rate, now makes it possible to see if there is any evidence that the crooked smile might actually exist.

In what follows, BRP proxies—essentially the variances of NYSE transactions per unit time adjusted for the number of shares listed—have for each available month of data been converted to an annual average estimate to enable comparison with annual five-year trailing averages for P/E, P/S, and P/B ratios of the S&P 500 Index. Such comparisons are displayed in the scatter diagrams of Fig. 9.3. As can immediately be seen, the high price ratios of the 1990s are dominant, making the smile unconvincing; high price levels are accompanied by high variances and low prices by low variances, giving an appearance that is not much different from that of Fig. 9.2b.

Comparison of *annual* ERPs to *annual* BRPs, as shown in the upper-panel scatter diagram of Fig. 9.4 again appears to more reveal the extraordinarily high (technology-enhanced) transactions volume increases seen in the late 1990s than the hypothesized underlying reclining J-curve relationship.[24]

In addition, though, because an ERP of 3% in an 8% T-bill environment is not, for example, the same as an ERP of 3% in a 3% T-bill environment, it is necessary to make one further adjustment by taking annual ERPs as a percent of the annual T-bill rate of each year, respectively. From 1968 to 2002, this percentage has ranged from between 25.6 and 138.8, with a mean of 60.8, and a median of 56.8.[25] The lower display of Fig. 9.4 thus shows the BRP-to-ERP ratio as compared to the P/E ratio, with the ERP adjusted for concurrent T bill rates and the BRP adjusted for the number of listed NYSE shares.

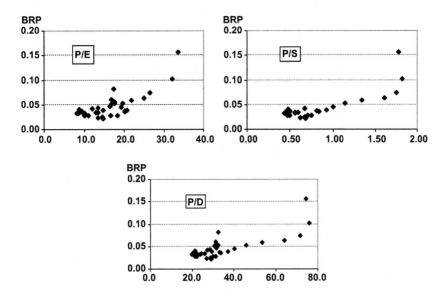

Fig. 9.3 Variance of shares outstanding-adjusted TPUT for NYSE (vertical axis) compared against S&P 500 P/E, P/S, and P/D ratios (horizontal axis) annually, 1968–2002 (P/S from 1976)

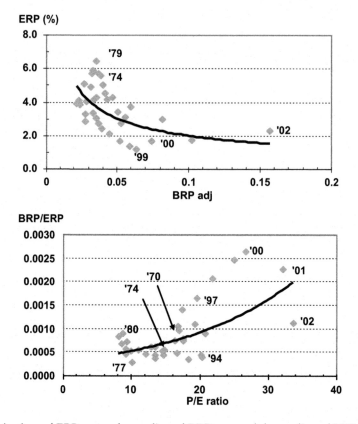

Fig. 9.4 Annual ERP versus share-adjusted BRP, top, and share-adjusted BRP/T-bill-adjusted ERP versus five-year trailing average S&P 500 P/E ratios, bottom, 1968–2002. (Source data: Annual ERP data are from NYU finance Professor Damodaran's website: http://pages.stern.nyu.edu/~adamodar/)

The lower graph's curve (fitted to the dots) roughly resembles the reclining J-curve shape that had been hypothesized (and it also appears much the same when BRP/ERP is plotted against P/S or P/B ratios). It can now be seen that the BRP/ERP level for the low-market year of 2002 is almost the same as for other low-market years such as 1970 and that these levels are only slightly above the level of the major low-market year 1974. This would not be readily suspected from viewing the traces shown in previous Fig. 9.3. Also, the market peak in 2000 has a high (actually the highest) BRP/ERP level.[26]

The little upward curve or hooklike cluster at the left-hand start of the J-curve (see the point for 1980) is also intriguing. It is consistent with the earlier idea that TPUT in crashes is restrained by the absence of liquidity to a greater extent than in bubbles: Liquidity in selling is never the same as liquidity in buying.

At a minimum, the experiments described in this section appear to support the notion that bubbles (and crashes) are characterized by increases in both trading volumes and thus transactions per unit time. Both aspects are useful for purposes of identification and benchmarking.

9.5   CONCLUSIONS

This chapter suggests that an equity risk premium actually involves two components—one is financial and the other is behavioral. Especially in bubbles and crashes, the behavioral aspect gains relative importance and eventually comes to rule.

Consequently, the equity risk premium estimates used in the preceding literature are imperfectly specified. In normally trending markets this is probably not an issue of great significance. But this changes as extreme events unfold and intensify. The greater the intensity of a bubble or crash, the greater is the effect of the behavioral component.

The BRP concept may also prospectively provide a theoretical bridge to the more conventional approaches in that the definition of expected returns and payoffs is broadened to include features and incentives that go beyond just the usual financial considerations of capital gains, dividends, and earnings growth rates.

NOTES

1. As early as 1934, Graham and Dodd (1934, p. 12) wrote in their first edition, speculators are "most optimistic when prices are highest and most despondent when they are at bottom."

   Empirically, this can be seen from commercial surveys such as those of *Investors Intelligence*, in reports from Market Vane's *Bullish Consensus* that measure percentages of bullish or bearish opinions, and in Shiller's *Crash Confidence Index*, a monthly survey of individual and institutional investors as to their level of confidence that the market *won't* crash in the next six months. Its all-time high was in 2006, according to Shiller in, "An Echo Chamber of Boom and Bust," *New York Times*, August 30, 2009. At the tops, the percentages of bulls are always high: at the bottoms, bears predominate. For example, according to the *Investors Intelligence* surveys of more than 100 independent investment advisory newsletters, bullish readings of above 60% and bearish readings above 55% are rare. Bullish readings surged near the 1999 peak to above 60%, with a previous high prior to the crash in 1987. Two bearish readings above 55% were seen in 1994, just prior to the start of the late 1990s uptrend. See also Evans (2003, p. 4).
2. Gjerstad and Smith (2014, p. 15).
3. See Cochrane (2005, p. 480), consistent with Kahneman, who, in Schrage (2003) said, "What actually happens with fear is that probability doesn't matter very much." Prechter (1999, pp. 395–7) would add, "Hope tends to build slowly, while fear often crystallizes swiftly." He has also said (*Perspectives*, 2004,

Elliott Wave International, Gainesville, GA; www.elliottwave.com) that "Fear does not need a period of dissipation as does hope." Greenspan (2008) makes the same point, writing, "The most credible explanation of why risk manage-ment based on state-of-the-art statistical models can perform so poorly is that the underlying data used to estimate a model's structure are drawn generally from both periods of euphoria and periods of fear, that is, from regimes with importantly different dynamics...The contraction phase of credit and business cycles, driven by fear, have historically been far shorter and far more abrupt than the expansion phase, which is driven by a slow but cumulative build-up of euphoria." From Greenspan (2009b): "Bubbles seem to require prolonged periods of prosperity, damped inflation and low long-term interest rates. Euphoria-driven bubbles do not arise in inflation-racked or unsuccessful econo-mies. I do not recall bubbles emerging in the former Soviet Union." Loewenstein (2000) suggests that "[V]isceral factors have important, but often underappre-ciated, consequences for behavior."

4. Bank of England Working Paper 283 by Gai and Vause (2005) appeared with a related concept that measures changes of investors' risk appetites as distin-guished from risk premiums and risk aversion. Their conclusion—that risk appe-tite fluctuates within a fairly narrow range during normal times but falls sharply during crises—is entirely consistent with the approach taken here. Their work seems particularly applicable to crash episodes.

5. As in derivatives pricing, the drawing could be extended to a three-dimensional representation, which would show price ratios (e.g., P/E, P/S, or P/B) on one axis, the FRP on another, and the BRP on the third. References on volatility smiles include Wilmott et al. (1995), Neftci (2000), Hull (2003), and Gatheral (2006).

6. Klingaman (1989, p. 263), concerning the Crash of 1929 (re: October 24), makes this clear: "The most horrifying hour came between 11:15 and 12:15 when numerous stocks could find no buyers *at any price*. These were the dreaded 'air pockets,' when prices shot straight down in a devastating free fall into an abyss that seemingly had no bottom." Klingaman (p. 230) shows that just six weeks prior there had been great *reluctance* to sell. Absence of liquidity thus does not imply just low prices; it may imply that there is *no* price.

7. Commodity markets may halt trading when daily "limit up" restrictions are reached, but the markets themselves remain open during those times. NYSE regulations for trading halts are asymmetrical as the halt-trading rules, which are adjusted regularly for changes in index levels, are designed to cushion crashes only. There are no equivalent rules to dampen steep rises, though there is a program-trading collar that says that in the event of a predetermined gain in the DJIA (150 points in Q4, 2005), all index arbitrage buy orders of the S&P 500 stocks must be stabilizing for the remainder of the day.

8. The rules, installed in response to market breaks in October 1987, were first adopted in October 1988 and were designed to reduce market volatility and promote investor confidence. The revised halt provisions and circuit-breaker levels for a market-wide trading halt were set at 10%, 20%, and 30% of the DJIA calculated at the beginning of each calendar quarter.

9. This idea, though independently arrived at, fits well with the findings of Jones et al. (1994), in which it is explained that volatility is correlated with the number of transactions but not as much with the size of each trading order. It also meshes with Derman (2002), who shows that "short-term stock speculators will expect returns proportional to the temperature of a stock, where temperature is

defined as the product of the stock's traditional volatility and the square root of its trading frequency."

10. All of this is equally applicable to individual stocks or other assets or sectors.

11. See Chevalier and Ellison (1999, 1997).

12. See Van Vliet (2017).

13. In the two years preceding the TMT mania's peak of early 2000, Tiger Fund's master, Julian Robertson, suffered such poor performance, in part from steadfast commitment to value stock investing, that he closed the fund and returned the remaining money (around $5 billion) to its outside investors. Gray and Vogel (2016, p. 35) posit that long-term value investing is better than growth investing but is often not feasible as a business model. Quantum Fund's George Soros dumped 5000 S&P 500 futures contracts on October 22, 1987, just days after the "crash" of October 19. See "A Bad Two Weeks," *Barron's*, p. 35, November 2, 1987, in which the fund's two-week loss was estimated at $840 million. Even legendary Warren Buffett's Berkshire, according to *Barron's* (October 13, 2008), apparently made at least a short-term mistake in the crash of 2008 by selling long-dated put options, a bullish bet, on some $40 billion of equity indexes that included the S&P 500. Lauricella (2008) recounts the errors made by fund manager William H. Miller in his Legg Mason Value Trust. See also Guerrieri and Kondor (2012). Tuckett (2011, pp. 78–9) describes how portfolio managers have to not only convince themselves that they are correct but also convince employers and clients "...your employer might panic or your clients might panic" even if you don't...[M]any players in the market don't have the luxury...of taking a long-term view, even if they think they ought to." Futia (2009, p. 131) adds, "The social and financial pressure an investment crowd can exert on disbelievers cannot be overestimated."

14. Olson (2006) notes that emotions are associated with a person, thing, or specific event, fluctuate more than mood, and do not last as long as moods, which are vaguely expressed. This ties directly to the socionomic approach as described in Prechter (2016).

15. Qualitative investor surveys mentioned in Shiller (2000 [2005]) might be a possible source of behavioral data, as might studies of bullish and bearish sentiments published by several commercial-service vendors. For instance, the Daily Sentiment Index from MBH Commodity Advisors (www.trade-futures) for commodities. Huang et al. (2015) and Da et al. (2015) explore sentiment and asset pricing using different sentiment indicators.

16. The Chicago Board Options Exchange's put-call option volatility index known as the VIX might provide another alternative: It is generally seen to be high, above 50 in crashes, and low, between 10 and 15, in complacent or bullish markets. The VIX is considered a leading benchmark of market sentiment and measures the market's expectation of 30-day volatility implicit in the prices of near-term options. VIX options began trading in February 2006. VIX cannot be traded directly.

17. Psychologists might find other measures. Related market microstructure literature includes Admati and Pfleiderer (1988), Gallant et al. (1992), Brennan and Subrahmanyam (1996), and Madhavan (2000). See also Spencer (2000, Chs. 4–6) and Vives (2008). Jarrow (1992) investigates market manipulation.

18. The closing of India's market on May 18, 2009, after the Sensex had run up 17.3% in less than a minute of trading was a rare exception.

19. By 2008, trading technology had improved to such an extent that on September 16, 2008, exchange transactions volume for the troubled insurance giant AIG reached a one-day record of 1.18 billion shares. That's for a single listing and not counting trades in the other 2000 or so listed securities. A record of 10.27 billion shares was printed on the NYSE Composite on September 17, 2008. However, this was surpassed on October 10, 2008, its most volatile day ever, with a new record of 11.16 billion shares. Another high-volume (the "flash-crash") day was on May 6, 2010, with 10.3 billion exchange shares (19 billion in all) traded. See Browning et al. (2008), Lauricella and Strasburg (2010), and Patterson (2010a), who writes of the parallels to October 1987; Peltz (2010), who describes high-frequency trading; and Lauricella and Patterson (2010). A joint report of the SEC and Commodity Futures Trading Commission, *Findings Regarding the Market Events of May 6, 2010*, was released on September 30, 2010. The more recent emergence of algorithmic private-trading dark pools, which provide anonymous and quick access to liquidity, further distorts TPUT data. As Patterson (2012, p. 6) writes, 10–15% of all trading in 2011 was in dark pools. See also Bowley (2011) and Levisohn (2017) on risks from algorithmic trading and dates of subsequent flash-crash episodes, for example, August 2007's "quant quake" and one on August 24, 2015.

20. See section 7.4 on anomalies, Sias (2007), and Gray and Vogel (2016, pp. 113–5).

21. Only annual, not monthly, data on total NYSE shares listed are available prior to 1994 and, for the analysis that follows, these annual data have been interpolated, with a one-twelfth addition of the year-to-year difference added each month to provide monthly estimates prior to 1994.

22. Periods of quasi-equilibrium exhibit, in terms of annualized monthly number of trades as a percentage of NYSE shares traded, much lower price variance than as measured over all bubble and non-bubble periods combined.

23. For such estimates, it remains an open empirical question whether it is better to average the variances taken over the entire series or whether, because of technological and other changes, this behavioral variance benchmark ought to be based only on the most recent quasi-equilibrium periods that have been identified.

24. Unlike the previously used ERP data from Ibbotson, these ERPs are based on a dividend-discount model taken from New York University Professor Damodaran's website, www.Damodaran.com.

25. More detail appears in Table 9.2 in this first edition of this book.

26. The same data are further analyzed via a simple OLS regression (35 observations, 1968–2002) which takes the trailing five-year S&P 500 P/E ratio against the FRP and BRP. Both the FRP and BRP coefficients (–2.7 and 117.2, respectively) are significant with a p-value of 0,0. The adjusted R-sq. was 0.87 and the F-stat was 0.0, but with a DW statistic of 1.08, serial correlation is evident.

    The negative sign of the FRP consistent with standard theory—the lower the FRP, the higher the P/E ratio. However, the positive sign for the BRP is more ambiguous given that a high BRP should lead to a high P/E ratio in bubbles (which is acceptable), but perhaps a bit less so in crashes given the trading cutoff limitations that would have a dampening effect on the available data. Much of this would also depend on whether the crash was accompanied or followed closely by a steep S&P 500-component earnings decline, in which case P/E ratios might also be high and ultimately infinite. That there are many more annual data points extending over bubble than crash periods might further distort the regression's results.

REFERENCES

Admati, A. R., & Pfleiderer, P. (1988). A Theory of Intraday Patterns: Volume and Price Variability. *Review of Financial Studies, 1*(1), 3–40.

Bowley, G. (2011, January 1). The New Speed of Money, Reshaping Markets. *New York Times.*

Brennan, M., & Subrahmanyam, A. (1996). Market Microstructure and Asset Pricing: On the Compensation for Illiquidity in Stock Returns. *Journal of Financial Economics, 41*, 441–464.

Browning, E. S., Gullapalli, D., & Karmin, C. (2008, October 11). Wild Day Caps Worst Week Ever for Stocks. *Wall Street Journal.*

Chevalier, J., & Ellison, G. (1997). Risk Taking by Mutual Funds as a Response to Incentives. *Journal of Political Economy, 105*(6), 1167–1200.

Chevalier, J., & Ellison, G. (1999). Career Concerns of Mutual Fund Managers. *Quarterly Journal of Economics, 114*(2), 389–432.

Cochrane, J. H. (2005). *Asset Pricing* (Rev. ed.). Princeton: Princeton University Press.

Da, Z., Engelberg, J., & Gao, P. (2015). The Sum of All FEARS Investor Sentiment and Asset Prices. *Review of Financial Studies, 28*(1), 1–32.

Derman, E. (2002). The Perception of Time, Risk and Return during Periods of Speculation. *Quantitative Finance, 2* (see also, stacks.iop.org/Quant/2/282).

Evans, L. L., Jr. (2003). *Why the Bubble Burst: US Stock Market Performance Since 1982.* Cheltenham: Edward Elgar.

Futia, C. (2009). *The Art of Contrarian Trading: How to Profit from Crowd Behavior in the Financial Markets.* Hoboken: Wiley.

Gai, P. & Vause, N. (2005, November). Measuring Investors' Risk Appetite. Working Paper 283, Bank of England.

Gallant, R. A., Rossi, P. E., & Tauchen, G. (1992). Stock Prices and Volume. *The Review of Financial Studies, 5*, 199–242.

Gatheral, J. (2006). *The Volatility Surface: A Practioner's Guide.* Hoboken: John Wiley.

Gjerstad, S. D., & Smith, V. L. (2014). *Rethinking Housing Bubbles.* New York: Cambridge University Press.

Graham, B., & Dodd, D. (1934). *Security Analysis.* New York: McGraw-Hill.

Gray, W. R., & Vogel, J. R. (2016). *Quantitative Momentum.* Hoboken: Wiley.

Greenspan, A. (2008, March 16). We Will Never Have a Perfect Model of Risk. *Financial Times.*

Greenspan, A. (2009b, March 27). We Need a Better Cushion Against Risk. *Financial Times.*

Guerrieri, V., & Kondor, P. (2012). Fund Managers, Career Concerns, and Asset Price volatility. *American Economic Review, 102*(5), 1986–2017.

Huang, D., Jiang, F., Tu, J., & Zhou, G. (2015). Investor Sentiment Aligned: A Powerful Predictor of Stock Returns. *Review of Financial Studies, 28*(3), 791–837.

Hull, J. (2003). *Options, Futures and Other Derivative Securities* (5th ed.). Upper Saddle River: Prentice-Hall.

Jarrow, R. A. (1992). Market Manipulation, Bubbles, Corners, and Short-Squeezes. *Journal of Financial and Quantitative Analysis, 27*(3), 311–336.

Jones, C., Kaul, G., & Lipson, M. (1994). Transactions, Volume, and Volatility. *Review of Financial Studies, 7*(4), 631–651.

Klingaman, W. K. (1989). *1929: The Year of the Great Crash.* New York: Harper & Row.

Lauricella, T. (2008, December 11). The Stock Picker's Defeat. *Wall Street Journal.*

Lauricella, T., & Patterson, S. (2010, August 6). Legacy of the 'Flash Crash': Enduring Worries of Repeat. *Wall Street Journal*.

Lauricella, T., & Strasburg, J. (2010, September 2). SEC Probes Canceled Trades. *Wall Street Journal*.

Levisohn, B. (2017, October 16). Black Monday 2.0: the Next Machine-Driven Meltdown. *Barron's*.

Loewenstein, G. F. (2000). Emotions in Economic Theory and Economic Behavior. *American Economic Review, 90*(2), 426–432.

Madhavan, A. (2000). Market Microstructure: A Survey. *Journal of Financial Markets, 3*, 205–258.

Neftci, S. N. (2000). *An Introduction to the Mathematics of Financial Derivatives* (2nd ed.). San Diego/London: Academic Press.

Olson, K. R. (2006). A Literature Review of Social Mood. *Journal of Behavioral Finance, 7*(4), 193–203.

Patterson, S. (2010a). "How the 'Flash Crash' Echoed Black Monday, *Wall Street Journal*, May 17.

Patterson, S. (2012). *Dark Pools: High-Speed Traders, A.I. Bandits, and the Threat to the Global Financial System*. New York: Crown Business/Random House.

Peltz, M. (2010, June). Inside The Machine. *Institutional Investor*.

Prechter, R. R., Jr. (1999). *The Wave Principle of Human Social Behavior and the New Science of Socionomics*. Gainesville: New Classics Library.

Prechter, R. R., Jr. (2016). *The Socionomic Theory of Finance*. Gainesville: Socionomics Institute Press.

Schrage, M. (2003). Daniel Kahneman: The Thought Leader Interview, *Business+Strategy*. Booz, Allen, & Hamilton and http://ebusiness.mit.edu/schrage/Articles/DanielKahnemanInterview.pdf

Shiller, R. J. (2000, 2005, 2015). *Irrational Exuberance* (3rd ed.). Princeton: Princeton University Press.

Sias, R. (2007). Causes and Seasonality of Momentum Profits. *Financial Analysts Journal, 63*(2), 48–54.

Spencer, P. D. (2000). *The Structure and Regulation of Financial Markets*. Oxford: Oxford University Press.

Tuckett, D. (2011). *Minding the Markets: An Emotional Finance View of Financial Instability*. London: Palgrave/Macmillan.

Van Vliet, P. (2017). *High Returns from Low Risk: A Remarkable Stock Market Paradox*. Hoboken: Wiley.

Vives, X. (2008). *Information and Learning in Markets: The Impact of Market Microstructure*. Princeton: Princeton University Press.

Wilmott, P., Howison, S., & Dewynne, J. (1995). *The Mathematics of Financial Derivatives*. New York: Cambridge University Press.

CHAPTER 10

Estimating and Forecasting

The basic elements needed for defining and finding bubbles and crashes are now in place and this chapter collates and summarizes the concepts that have earlier been developed. The result is a practical empirical method that enables extreme events to be statistically defined, detected, and tested by applying the elasticity-of-variance approach to real-world data. Given the fractal, scaled nature of financial markets, all bubbles and crashes are comprised of what can be called microbubbles and microcrashes.

10.1 PRELIMINARIES

At Peaks and Troughs

Elasticity of variance is the centerpiece of bubble and crash definitions because it directly reflects the emotionally and psychologically driven short-side rationing that is always experienced in extreme market episodes. As such, the EOV approach circumvents the fuzziness that is an inherent component of the rational expectations, efficient markets, and "intrinsic value" constructs. It also does not require the use of arcane econometric techniques. The sequence of events that characterizes what happens in bubbles and crashes from the viewpoint of elasticity of variance is traced in Fig. 10.1.

At the approach to a bubble's peak, equity risk premiums are low, volatility of returns is high, and expectations for future returns are commonly high. Relatively few participants are worried about low or no dividend yields and capital losses. The focus is on capital gains. And almost everyone either wants to or *must* enter into the game.

At this stage, "rational" models typically based on the standard economic supply and demand framework as properly applied to markets for goods and services—but improperly to financial markets—might advise that investors generally ought to be scared of price heights. Behavioral and socionomic finance, however, posits that most market participants are not scared at all:

© The Author(s) 2018
H. L. Vogel, *Financial Market Bubbles and Crashes, Second Edition*,
https://doi.org/10.1007/978-3-319-71528-5_10

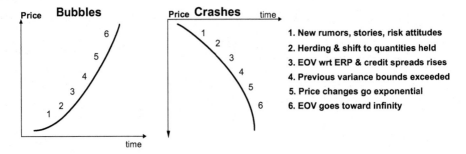

Fig. 10.1   Idealized EOV sequence of steps for both bubbles and crashes

The Siren's song is loudest at the top. A bull market "climbs a wall of worry" and a bear market "slides a slope of hope."[1]

By definition, the time of the least worry and most extended enthusiasm is at the peak, around which it seems that almost everyone becomes an "investor" for the long term (i.e., "at the top of the stairs, there are no bears."). And the trough is the time when hope for a sturdy recovery has been largely abandoned or exhausted—either through a long, agonizing collapse on low volume that typically marks a major bottom or through a rapid-selling capitulation crash.[2]

The market thus invites your participation to play at the most dangerous time and is most dissuasive when the actual (as opposed to the perceived) risk is least.

The direction of movement for the ERP (or credit spread) and volatility whenever a major top or bottom is approached is represented in previous Table 8.3. In a bubble, volatility rises and the ERP declines, whereas in a crash (i.e., anti-bubble, or inverse bubble), both ERP and volatility rise. The practical issue for the active portfolio manager may then be to forecast volatility. But based on a survey by Poon and Granger (2005), this often seems more an art than a science.[3]

Runs

Early random-walk theorists—beginning with the idea used by Mood (1940) and extended by Fama (1965)—often used runs tests to determine whether the null hypothesis, that k is drawn randomly, could be accepted.[4] The rationale is that a random walk is defined if successive price changes are independent. What's being sought is a telltale, distinctive, statistical signature of a random walk. Recall that for strict random walkers bubbles and crashes cannot and do not exist.[5]

Nevertheless, it happens that analysis of such sequential runs—which are uninterrupted sequences of either positive or negative price changes—can prospectively provide interesting econometric insights (serial and/or autocorrelation metrics) because a distinguishing characteristic of all bubble and crash episodes is that day after day or week after week, prices persistently climb or drop with hardly any respite (i.e., "corrections").[6]

For instance, three runs would be $+ + + - - +$. The first run has three elements of one attribute ($+ + +$), followed by a second run with two elements of
an opposite attribute ($-$), followed by a third run with one element ($+$).[7] A so-
called runs test, also known as the Geary (1970) nonparametric test, was one
handy method for answering the question of whether a certain number of runs,
k, within a sample's observations are too many or too few as compared with the
number of runs expected in a strictly random sequence of observations.

In normally trending, non-extreme markets test results (depending on the
confidence level chosen) might be close to random. However, the statistical
earmark or signature of an extreme event would be provided by convergence
to a sample-run number of one with a sample's variance of length going toward
zero. In other words, as a bubble (or crash) strengthens there's ultimately only
one run in the sample—for instance, 1111111...—and, at the limit, the length
of runs in a sample doesn't vary. It becomes one long string of consecutive
positive returns, up and up and up (or in a crash, down and down and down).[8]

But when the number of up and down runs in a sample period are about
evenly balanced, a largely trendless price pattern and what might be called a
quasi-equilibrium condition is suggested.[9]

Important (and slightly anticipatory) directional changes in markets are
indicated by relative lows in average run length-variance illustrated in Fig. 10.2.
This can be seen when the tech bubble approached peak intensity circa 1999
and the crash low was nigh in 2009. In both instances the average run-length
variance fell well below the long-run average of 4.63 for 48-period samples.[10]

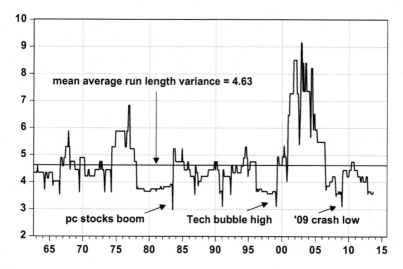

Fig. 10.2   Average run-length variance per sample, 48-month rolling samples of S&P
500 monthly returns, *entire* data set, 1968:02 to 2017:10. The S&P 500's steep
18-month climb of 37.9% from 153 in June 1984 to 211 by December 1985 was led by
the personal computer stocks (e.g., Microsoft's 1986 IPO), which were bid up aggressively (i.e., were "bubbly")[11]

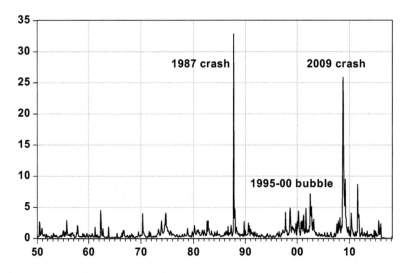

Fig. 10.3 Monthly variance of S&P 500 returns, as based on daily intra-month price changes, 1950:01 to 2018:03

But market peaks may also be broadly classified into two major types. The first is a relatively gentle rollover, in which most market participants are not even aware that the top has already been largely formed. That usually happens when a few major and highly regarded generals in the great army of stocks remain strong, still buoying the market indexes even as the lower-ranked shares of the privates, sergeants, and lieutenants weaken.[12] In this type, the number of runs per sample period window will gradually begin to increase and the average length of positive runs decrease, the reverse of the buildup to the periods immediately preceding the peak.[13]

The other major type of top occurs when, instead of a gentle rollover, there is almost instantaneous reversal in the polarity of the price-change sequences from a few long positive runs to a few long negative runs.[14] The result appears as a price spike, after which crash conditions may quickly follow.

Variance

Variance of equity market returns and exponentiality are central to understanding what occurs in extreme market events. As can be seen from Fig. 10.3, variance (or its square root, volatility) always rises/spikes as bubbles and as crashes approach maximum intensity. This characteristic is important and useful for identification and measurement of such extreme market events.

10.2   EOV BUBBLES AND CRASHES

The empirical elements needed to find and to define bubbles and crashes through notions of elasticity of variance now lead to more formal definitions.

Greater elasticity indicates that higher prices are not being resisted by and/ or are not deterring potential buyers, that is, the price boundary per ERP unit change is being expanded as buyers willingly meet the asking price (and beyond). If this weren't so, prices would stagnate or fall and a sideways or perhaps downward pattern would be evident. Similarly, in crashes, the price boundary per ERP unit change is also being expanded but this time to the downside as sellers willingly hit the quoted bids and begin, as in a cascade, to accept bids that are even lower. In brief, short-side rationing motivates and propels the action.

An important aspect in all of this is recognition that the sample elasticities in *both* bubbles and crashes will exhibit the *same* directional movement toward infinity, with the distinguishing attribute being that for the former, the net arithmetic sign of the sample's elasticity is negative and for the latter it is positive (Table 10.1).

By thus combining the notions of elasticity, exponentiality, and consecutive pairing, a statistically workable definition of bubbles and crashes becomes viable. The resulting elasticity-of-variance (EOV) definition is empirically practical, consistent with what is observed in the real world, and also with the fractal (and power law) nature of stock price changes. Because of such fractal self-similarity (Fig. 10.4)—as seen in nature in the forms of tree and arterial branches and galactic spirals—the methodology may be applied to any chosen scale of time, be it monthly, daily, or hourly.[15]

With the EOV approach, earnings growth expectations and other such "fundamental" input factors are in the background and interest rates are indirectly embedded in the equity risk premium calculation. EOV is instead based on measurement of the market's *reaction* to news and fundamentals and not on the news and fundamentals in and of themselves.

It is in this way somewhat akin to the convexity concept that is used to describe the price sensitivy of fixedincome seurities to changes in required yields: A positive convexity indicates that the price of a bond will rise faster than the rate at which market yields decline and will fall in price more slowly than the rate at which yields rise. EOV may thus be interpreted as convexity of equities.[16]

Hence, the market reveals and expresses bubble and crash events through relatively excessive stock price variance: The market directly reveals when something unusual is probably happening.

Table 10.1   Signs of sample variance and ERP directional changes as related to market conditions

	(1) Bubbles	*(2)* Crashes	*(3)* Slowly rising market	*(4)* Slowly declining market
Variance	+	+	− or =	− or =
ERP	−	+	−	+
Net sign	−	+	+	−

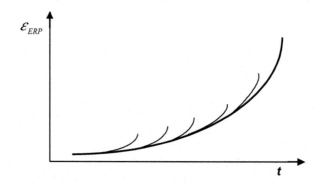

Fig. 10.4 Fractal microbubbles (and microcrashes) conceptualized. The main exponential (dark) curve is composed of smaller, clustered exponential samples, that is, "microbubbles" and "microcrashes." As time, t, progresses, the ERP elasticity of variance goes to infinity

EOV bubble definition: On any given fixed scale of measurement, the elasticities of variance with respect to the equity risk premiums (credit spreads, or cap ratios in real estate) in the selected interval follow an exponentially rising pattern that can be called a "microbubble." All bubbles of a larger scale are comprised of a series (or clusters) of such microbubbles.[17]

EOV crash definition: On any fixed scale of measurement, the elasticities of variance with respect to the equity risk premiums (credit spreads, or cap ratios in real estate) in the selected interval follow an exponentially rising pattern (the same as in bubbles), only with the net arithmetic sign in front of the estimated coefficient positive instead of negative. These can be called "microcrashes," and all larger crashes are comprised of a series (or clusters) of such microcrashes.

10.3   EMPIRICAL RESULTS

The EOV method as applied to centered rolling samples of 12 months leads to weighted average bubble and crash strength indicators (WABSI and WACSI) as illustrated in the panels of Fig. 10.5.[18] The strongest of such bubbles often tend to develop just after severe market corrections and/or crashes, though that did not happen in 1987. The correction/crash of nearly 20% in the summer of 2011 (see Chap. 3, note 8) was, however, followed by a strong bubble that was probably a consequence of intense QE policy interventions and other such central bank efforts to lower interest rates and thereby "stimulate" the economy.

From this it may be understood that by the present definitions and methodology, rising (falling) prices are merely a necessary but not sufficient condition to create bubbles (crashes), which here require a rising string of percentage gains in price variance that are greater than the percentage declines (rises) in ERPs (or credit spreads or cap rates).

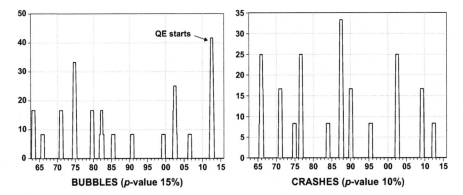

Fig. 10.5 EOV time-centered unweighted bubble and crash strength indicators, 12-month rolling samples, left panel bubbles, right panel, crashes, data, 1962:08 to 2018:03. Lower *p*-values suggest greater likelihood that event occurred. The 1987 crash stands out for its strength. The lag in seeing event results is twice the sample size; here the lag is 24 months

Still, for proper interpretation further historical context is required. For instance, the weaker than expected WABSI readings of the late 1990s in particular might plausibly be attributed to the bubble-dampening concurrence of several incidents from mid-1997 to near the end of 1998. This was a period that included Asian currency devaluations (Thailand, Korea, Indonesia, etc.), the Long-Term Capital Management meltdown crisis, and the destabilization of Russia's currency. All of these contributed to pronounced worldwide market weaknesses that would have sapped the strength of even the strongest of bubbles.[19] To some degree, these events undoubtedly cooled or restrained temporarily the speculative TMT (tech, media, telecom) fever that was still propagating.[20]

10.4   PREDICTABILITY AND FORECASTING

Predictability[21]

In has been earlier suggested in Figs. 1.4 and 1.6 that it is possible to generally assess—from stock market capitalizations to GDP, wealth as a percent of disposable personal income, and debt as a percentage of GDP—that valuations are relatively high or low (i.e., plus or minus one standard deviation away from the means). Shiller's CAPE ratio of Fig. 1.5 and Treasury bond yields versus earnings yields on stocks (BSEYD) as displayed in Fig. 3.4 also point to broad areas of relatively low or high valuations. The problem, however, is that all such deviations, especially those in bubbles, can persist for very long periods and sometimes go to what retrospectively will be seen as absurd extremes. Being too early, as has been noted, is being wrong: Being too early can be as wealth-destructive as being too late. At best, these charts show broad zones in which investors ought at a minimum to be alert to the heightened possibility of reversals from bull to bear or vice versa. But the timing of such reversals yet remains unspecified and frustratingly imprecise. In this respect, it's important to consider that bubbles are unlikely to begin to inflate when money/credit/liquidity is tight and crashes are not likely to occur when those conditions are easy.

On the whole, though, mainstream theory—steeped as it is in the flawed neoclassical efficient markets and rational expectations approach—cannot at all help with timing of exit or entry.[22]

Predictability, say Schaller and van Norden (1997),

> *"has two main interpretations. The first…is that financial markets are rational and efficient and that discount rates vary over time in a predictable manner. The second…is that there may be some element of apparent irrationality in financial markets in the form of fads or bubbles."* Yet, *"excess returns are predictable and can be explained quite well by a relatively small number of independent variables."*

However, if such excess returns were so predictable professional money managers would rarely suffer losses and chronic underperformance relative to benchmarks.

The deeper problem, though, is that:

> *Traditional…theory relies heavily on the economy remaining in an approximately equilibrium state. The serious challenge is to be able to predict outlying, major transitions, critical points, and…[the] record has mostly been pretty dismal.*[23]

Important attempts at predictability have also been developed by Didier Sornette, formerly a professor of geophysics and a prolific student of bubbles and crashes, who wrote:

> *… extreme events should be considered to be rather frequent and to result from the same organization principle(s) as those generating other events: because they belong to the same statistical distribution, this suggests common generating mechanism(s). In this view, a great earthquake is just an earthquake that started small … and did not stop…*[24]

The elasticity-of-variance approach has features somewhat similar to those used by Sornette's Financial Crisis Observatory computers at ETH Zurich, which search major asset classes for faster-thanexponential price movement and accelerating oscillations and then assess the probabilities of a crash.[25]

Yet there are significant differences too: EOV is relatively simple to understand and implement, it is economically grounded, as elasticities with respect to interest rates are implicitly embedded in equity risk premiums, credit spreads, and cap rates. EOV is, furthermore, based on and triggered by mood-driven short-side rationing behavior and also credit availability beyond what can be readily absorbed by GDP growth. And best of all, EOV is not mechanistically described by equations that are largely untethered to any economic and financial relationships.[26]

If the random walk's basic presumption that previous-period returns are independent and incapable of predicting current and future returns (i.e., are *iid*), there would be scant evidence of serial correlation of returns from one period to the next. Yet as Fig. 10.6 suggests there are times—as in the mid-1960s to the early 1970s—when today's returns predicted positive future returns (i.e., there were long runs) and other periods when today's positive return was followed by tomorrow's negative one (e.g., from around 2004 and 2006). This aspect compares with Fig. 10.7, in which daily returns for the same daily data series are centered on zero, but with the record 22.6% drop of October 19, 1987, clearly visible. Random-walk proponents were, it seems, misleadingly fixated on Fig. 10.7 instead of Fig. 10.6.

Forecasting[27]

To be able to know at the earliest possible stage that a bubble (or crash) either has already begun or is likely to soon begin is extremely valuable, and the methods developed here have the potential to facilitate such informational extraction.

The conventional approach to forecasting is represented by the following from Armitage (2005, p. 60):

Fig. 10.6 First-order autocorrelations, 500-day rolling sample windows for S&P 500 data, January 3, 1950, to March 29, 2018. Horizontal lines above/below these lines are 1.6 times the standard deviation of the autocorrelation coefficient series. In Normal distributions, points above/below these lines would occur in around 5% of instances. Similar to Lo (2017, p. 281), who used CRSP data from 1928 to December 2014 and a 750-day roll. A pure random walk would show fluctuations predominantly around zero, with no significant deviations

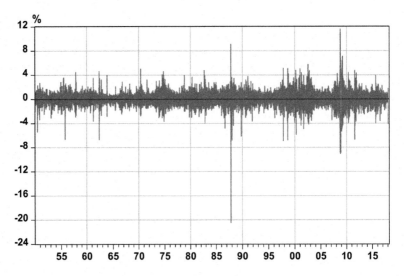

Fig. 10.7 Daily percent changes in the S&P 500, January 3, 1950, to March 29, 2018

> *...the market premium can be forecast to an extent....it has been found that a relatively high dividend yield for the stock market is followed by relatively high observed premiums. So dividend yield on the market can be used to estimate the* ex ante *premium at a given time.*

This is correct as far as it goes, but again, how high is high and low is low and for how much time must an investor be exposed to risky market gyrations before the forecast comes true?

The good news is that all of the data elements needed to apply the EOV methodology to forecasting of bubbles and crashes are widely available in the form of estimates of earnings, volatilities, and interest rates. For instance, earnings forecasts for all stocks in the S&P 500 (and/or other market indexes) for 12 months ahead are generated by many Wall Street firms and funds and are also aggregated and published in the *S&P Analysts' Handbook: Monthly Supplement*. These earnings estimates (along with dividend payout estimates) provide the basis for roll-ahead calculations of an expected-return series for 12–18 months into the future.

To then obtain an *ex ante* (i.e., forecast) risk premium series, forward-looking current Treasury bill and/or bond auction interest rates (taken from off the yield curve) are then subtracted from expected earnings plus dividend returns.

The last required element for forecasting is a forward-looking series on variance. The implied volatility (square root of variance) data generated in the call options market is such a source, with history available on Bloomberg terminals under SPX [Index] HIVG [Go]. For example, the implied annualized volatility for the end of October 1996 was 16.63%.

These raw *ex ante* data, when processed without any modification to the previously developed programs, may then be used in predicting the likelihood of bubbles and crashes. As always, the underlying earnings and dividend growth estimates, implied option market volatilities, and future interest-rate assumptions will be subject to error and change and will therefore produce imperfect predictions. Nevertheless, the resulting forecasts ought to be at least as consistently reliable as those made by other methods.[28]

In the end, as major directional changes approach, the market itself (*sui generis*)—starting with relatively persistent gains in EOV—sends timing signals.[29]

As extreme events unfold, the market's price elasticity of variance starts moving toward infinity, more noticeable and frequent violations of recent variance bounds (OK, technical chart analysis breakouts) are seen across a widening sample of stocks, positions in favored or unfavored sectors become more concentrated and correlated, the average length of runs (positive or negative as the case may be) increases, and the variance of the sampled length of runs goes toward zero. This means that diversity of opinion about a market's (or a sector's) direction disappears (goes toward zero) even as performance time horizons are foreshortened.

10.5 Conclusions

For a bubble to form, a necessary but not sufficient condition is the occurrence of a relatively rapid rise of prices (with no extended intervening phase of declining prices). For a crash, a necessary but not sufficient condition is a relatively rapid decline of prices (with no extended intervening phase of rising prices).

In addition, it appears that microbubble clusters tend to (but need not always) be quickly followed by crashes, that crashes have a tendency to (but need not always) be followed by bubbles, and that the ends of recessions also often coincide with and/or are closely followed by bubbles (Fig. 10.5, Tables 2.3 and 3.1). Streaks of consecutive days up also will tend to occur near the start and end of bubbles, and, similarly, streaks of consecutive days down will often occur at the start and end of crashes.

This chapter has explored changes in the elasticity of variance with respect to changes in the equity risk premium. The ultimate goal has been to define bubble (and crash) episodes through such elasticity characteristics.

The works of Bénassy and Malinvaud suggest that market equilibrium exists in theory only and that therefore the equilibrium-assuming framework (e.g., the EMH/CAPM) provides little or no insight as to how bubbles and crashes are formed and sustained. The random-walk/EMH approach (Chap. 5), thus presents a hollow theory "whose only prediction is that it cannot predict."[30] As shown in Fig. 10.6, autocorrelation of period-to-period returns is a common feature that over the decades has drifted from positive to negative and back again, thereby rendering the main random-walk assumption as false.

All bubbles (and crashes) are instead a manifestation of short-side quantity rationing that leaves trading-related statistical artifacts in its wake. The ERP elasticity-of-variance definition provides a direct way (i.e., unencumbered by difficult econometric problems) to detect the urgency with which traders adjust the quantities that they, for whatever reasons—economic, psychological, sociological, and so on—at the moment, desire to hold.

Consequently, extreme market events may be empirically and statistically defined as being a collection of consecutive rolling sample periods in which the elasticity itself—the ERP elasticity of variance—rises exponentially. This definition thereby captures both the economic *and* the behavioral features that are seen in all extreme events as they unfold in the quantity-driven real-world environment of incomplete markets with asymmetric information.[31]

In all extreme market events variance bounds are expanded (broken) as price changes begin to follow an exponential trajectory. This alone, however, does not constitute a bubble because, in almost all such circumstances, as prices rise (fall), equity risk premiums fall (rise). To define bubbles and crashes, variance must rise *faster* than the ERP declines (or rises in crashes). Relatively constant or fairly steady growth rates (or declines) of earnings, dividends, and/or share prices would not and should not be expected to generate this type of *variance boundary* expansion effect.

This simple elasticity concept thus enables extreme market events occurring at different times in history and on different time scales to be measured and compared to each other and to be tested for cyclicity and for other statistical features. The underlying econometric philosophy is that expressed by Kennedy (2008, p. 363), who writes that "an approximate answer to the right question is worth a great deal more than a precise answer to the wrong question."

Paraphrasing Keynes: "Would you rather be elegant and precisely wrong, or messy and vaguely right?"[32]

NOTES

1. This aphorism is attributable (in 1985) to market technical analyst Robert Prechter, Jr. See Prechter (2003, p. 63) and Prechter (2016).
2. A slow Roehner-style collapse description (see Chaps. 1, 2, and 3) is compatible with Napier (2007, p. 286), who found that the four major bottoms of the twentieth century—1921, 1932, 1949, and 1982—were all characterized by such slow collapses on low volume, with good news being ignored and Tobin's Q ratios at around 0.3. Less important lows are likely to be made through capitulative selling. Visual comparisons of bubbles and crashes are also shown in Kaizoji and Sornette (2008).
3. Poon and Granger (2005, p. 45) compared 93 studies of volatility forecasting testing methods. They found "that option-implied volatility provides more accurate forecasts than time-series models. Among the time-series models, no

model is a clear winner, but historical volatility ranked as being the best forecasting method." See also Benzoni et al. (2010).

4. See note 8.

5. At the time when runs were first studied there was no purpose or thought given to using such tests for experiments about bubbles. Runs and duration dependence tests were first used to study bubbles by McQueen and Thorley (1994). Duration dependence indicates an inverse relation between the probability of a run ending and the length of the run. Tirole (1985) writes that if a data series does not contain these elements, it probably does not describe a bubble.

6. According to the late expert market technician, Paul Montgomery, such streaks tend to occur at the start, midpoint, or end of a move. Such episodes occurred just prior to the early-November 2016 US presidential election when the S&P 500 lost 3.1% over nine consecutive days—the longest-run slide since December 1980. Another that extended to after this election was the 16.5% rise of the Russell 2000 Index that began from the low of November 3 and ran for 15 days—the longest streak since a 15-day +6.1% gain ending February 6, 1996. The DJIA also rose (3.9%) for 12 days ending February 27, 2017—the longest run since the 13-day streak at the start of January 1987. The longest 14-day stretch occurred in June 1897—90 years prior. Through the end of February 2017, the S&P 500 had gone 95 trading days without more than a 1% daily decline. Trading for 80 or more consecutive days without a 1% decline occurred only six times since 1980. And as of October 5, 2017, the S&P 500 had run for six consecutive days to all-time closing highs (2552.07), the longest such streak since 1997. The S&P 500 did not experience a single decline of five percent or more in 2017 and until February 2018, it hadn't lost at least 2% in a day since September 2016.

7. To study autocorrelation, the early random-walk experimenters used the Geary nonparametric test (Geary 1970). The Geary definition of a run differs slightly wherein a run is defined as a *set* of *adjacent* positive changes (negative for crashes)—that is, as being at least two consecutive signs (elements) of the same type instead of a sequence containing only one such element. To see the difference, take a sequence of + + − + + + − − + −. Geary would label this as three positive runs (and three negative runs), whereas the alternative definition counts this only as two positive runs because only the adjacent positives bunched together are considered as being part of the same run. Despite the difference in definition, the results and conclusions are largely the same either way.

Treynor (1998) writes: "If a bubble is some self-reinforcing, self-perpetuating mechanism that prevents successive security price changes from being random, then an up-day in the market would be more likely to be followed by another up-day than by a down-day....Bubbles should be distinguished by a disproportionate number of up-days (in the case of bull markets) or down-days (in the case of bear markets)."

Gujarati (2003, p. 465) explains that in such nonparametric tests, "we make no assumptions about the (probability) distributions from which the observations are drawn."

8. Autocorrelation is the one feature that all bubbles must have in order to be called "bubbles." If there weren't a preponderance of positive correlations in

actual price series (inflation-detrended) of financial assets or in positive returns (percentage changes of prices), there would be a trading range, not a bubble.

The basic question is whether a certain number of runs, *k*, within a sample's observations are too many or too few as compared with the number of runs expected in a strictly random sequence of observations. The rationale is that a random walk is defined if successive price changes are independent. The null of randomness is only accepted at the 95% confidence level if the number of runs, *k*, lies within the interval $E(k) \pm 1.96\sigma k$. Blanchard and Watson (1982) also looked at runs and "attribute runs in price innovations to bubbles." See also McQueen and Thorley (1994).

9. Quasi-equilibrium measures, including the spread between the numbers of up and down runs in a sample, were more extensively examined in the first edition of this book. See also Chapter 8, note 47.

10. Although I developed these ideas independently, I later found a paper by O'Brien and Dyck (1985) that describes a similar procedure "based on a weighted linear combination of the variances of run lengths of successes and failures."

11. Empirical investigation of this proposition required that a program (using EViews) be designed to take a sample of total monthly returns on the S&P 500, count the number of positive runs in each sample, calculate the average run length in each sample, find the variance of run length in the sample, and then roll ahead by one period. The same can also be done for crashes with consecutive negative runs. The program is set up as follows: Say a sample includes ten observations, with 1 designating a positive return and 0 being either zero or negative. If a runs sequence is 1,0,0,1,1,1,0,1,1,0, then there are two positive consecutive runs in this sample, 1, 1, 1 and 1, 1. The average length of runs is (3+2)/2 = 2.5 and the variance is 0.5. The program's output confirmed this proposition.

12. Browning (2007a) writes, "Big multinationals gradually take over leadership from the smaller, more-volatile stocks...with a small band of highly admired issues leading the gains." The identification of two types of peaks, rollover and spike, is also discussed in Roehner (2002, pp. 157–76).

13. Although applicability of runs analysis for the purpose of statistically defining and measuring bubbles and crashes prior to their occurrence is limited, launch- and peak-zone conditions also have distinctive statistical signatures. For a "launch zone," the following, nearly simultaneous or coincidental conditions, ought to appear:
    - The expected *number* of runs, $E(k)_t$, in samples rolling forward is beginning to decrease (ultimately to a limit of one run that extends over the whole sample),
    - The rate of change toward a *smaller* expected *number* of runs remains the same or is increasing.
    - The average *length* of runs, $E[L_t]$, is increasing.
    - The rate of change toward *greater* average length of runs remains the same or is increasing, that is, $[E(L)_t - E(L)_{t-1}]/E(L)_t \geq 0$.
    - The variance of the *length* of runs, σ_L^2, is decreasing.

14. As a bubble approaches its maximum, peak-zone conditions would induce fewer directional reversals (surprises) in the price movements; up becomes even more up until, in the ultimate extreme (which doesn't always happen), all prices

changes are sequentially straight-up. This leads to the notion that several differ-ent peaks might thus be defined:

- a peak in actual price per share or in index reading, which is the usual definition;
- a peak in share (i.e., percentage) of total capitalization (price multiplied by number of shares outstanding) traded per unit time;
- a point when changes in the expected number of runs for samples stop decreasing and the average length of runs stops increasing;
- a point when the variance of the length of runs in the samples, σ_L^2, stops decreasing.

Not all of these "peaks" must necessarily occur (and actually couldn't occur) at the same time. The last two items call attention to factors that speak to the internal process and structure of a financial market bubble much in the same way that stock market technicians sometimes speak of "orthodox" (i.e., end-of-pattern) peaks. On this, see Frost and Prechter (1978), Casti (2002), and Livio (2002).

These criteria can by extension be used to assert that the maximal internal strength of a bubble is in the range of time—call it a "peaking zone"—in which all of the following appear:

- the average (or expected) length of the runs is longest;
- the rate of change of the average length of runs is highest;
- the decrease in the variance of the length of runs, σ_L^2, is at a maximum;
- the expected number of runs approaches and is closest to one.

Such "peaking zone" conditions must collectively come close in time to that of the actual price peak. Theoretically, the actual price peak should never be registered *after all* of these conditions have already occurred. The conditions further suggest the presence of an internal and partially hidden market dynamic within the wild price and volume performance that is typically observed when-ever bubbles are nearing the point of maximum intensity.

15. Methodological details for finding EOV bubbles are:

   Step 1: *Elasticity calculations and quasi-equilibrium sample counting*
   - Select sample size and data granularity (monthly, daily, etc.).
   - Calibrate (i.e., index) ERP and variance series to the first observation of each sample period.
   - Calculate *point* elasticities of variance with respect to ERP for each sample.

   Step 2: *Exponential curve fitting—finding bubbles (and crashes)*
   - Fit exponential curves that estimate a trajectory of changes in variance elasticity over each sample period's interval (using the elasticities derived in step 1).
   - In both bubbles and crashes, variance elasticities in the interval will trace an exponential trajectory with statistically significant parameters. If the main parameter is not significantly different from zero, there is no micro-bubble in that sample (because $y = e^0 = 1$). Sign criteria are used for sepa-rating variance elasticities of bubbles from those of crashes.

   Step 3: *Finding microbubble WABSIs, clusters, and time-centering*
   - Reset the sample counter again. Count the number of times that a micro-bubble appears within the sample and calculate this as a percentage of total sample size, S. Let m equal the number of in-sample estimated

microbubbles. The maximum is 100% (100* *m/S when m = S*), which gives an evenly weighted (and simple) bubble-strength indicator (WABSI).

- Time-center microbubbles for alignment with actual calendar time because samples are sequentially anchored to an initially fixed date and samples of different lengths (i.e., numbers of observations) span different ranges of time. For instance, sample number 68 containing 30 observations extends all the way out to calendar-time 98, whereas sample number 68 containing 12 observations extends only to calendar-time 80.

16. In comparing convexity for bonds and stocks, both entail a second derivative concept, for bonds the rate of change of duration and for stocks the rate of change of variance. For bonds, a) long-maturity issues show more price movement and convexity than short-maturity issues; b) low-coupon issues have higher duration, convexity, and sensitivity to changes in market yield than high-coupon issues; and c) loweryielding bond prices move more than higher-yielding bond prices. For stocks, a) equities are normally like long-maturity bonds, as valuation depends on long-term estimated cash flows; b) equities normally have relatively low-coupons in the form of dividends; and c) earnings yields (the inverse of P/E ratios) are low in bubbles and may also be low in crashes if earnings evaporate.

17. The exponential expression to be fitted is $y = e^{kt}$, and the parabolic is $y = k_1 t^2 + k_2 t + k_3$, where k_i are the coefficients. The null hypothesis is that the estimated parameter, k, is zero. Shreve (2008, p. 272) describes a constant elasticity-of-variance (CEV) model in which $\sigma(t, x) = \sigma x^{\delta - 1}$ depends on x but not on t. In time-series econometrics, a move toward infinity would suggest presence of a unit root in which the series "explodes." See also note 15 and the first edition's Appendix A. The notion is consistent with what is known as momentum investing. As per Gray and Vogel (2016, p. 39), momentum investing "is purely focused on prices…[and] is a better alternative to growth investing, which considers both fundamentals and prices." See also Jegadeesh and Titman (1993, 2001).

18. An even weighting for each microbubble or microcrash found in each sample interval is the simplest to implement. However, a *cluster-weighted* scheme might sometimes provide an alternative. That is because a single *stand-alone* microbubble episode—a flare-up within a sample interval—would not necessarily provide autoregressiveness sufficient to build from a small price-change event to a much larger one. But successive pairings or clusterings of microbubbles nested as in Fig. 10.4 nevertheless have the potential to cumulatively over time reflect—as the elasticity of variance goes toward infinity—price moves of enormous magnitude.

19. Collyns and Senhadji (2003, p. 104) write, "Regional stock prices generally fell sharply from mid 1997 through the end of 1998, the crisis period. Korea, Malaysia, and Thailand suffered declines of more than 70 percent, while the other five countries suffered declines of more than 50 percent from the peak."

20. Around 1995 the long-term productivity trend appeared to slope notably higher, moving from linear average growth of around 1.2% a year to a new rate of nearly 2.7% a year. In referring to this period, Western (2004, p. 16) observed that "[S]tock prices rose sixfold in this decade while labor productivity only doubled." The arguable nature of the productivity gain from 1995 onward, as frequently cited by Fed Chairman Greenspan, was—according to material

shown in Fleckenstein and Sheehan (2008, p. 102) and based on work by James Grant's *Interest Rate Observer* newsletter—measured using faulty data. In actuality, the only important productivity improvements were registered in computer-related businesses.

21. Cuthbertson and Nitzsche (2004, pp. 81–112) review predictability and cite Pesaran and Timmermann (1994). See also Ferson and Harvey (1991). Ang and Bekaert (2007) suggest that "statistical inference at long horizons critically depends on the choice of standard errors...there is some evidence for long horizon predictability, but it disappears when we correct for heteroskedasticity and remove the moving average structure..." They also find that "the most robust predictive variable for future excess returns is the short rate, but it is significant only at short horizons," and that "the dividend yield's predictive power to forecast future dividend growth is not robust across sample periods or countries."

22. Socionomics provides a firm theoretical foundation but is also imprecise as to timing.

23. West (2017, p. 383).

24. The focus of this work is on self-organized criticality likened to what happens in mountain avalanches, beach sandpiles, and earthquakes. All such events enter with increasing probability into a transition phase and approach a tipping point—in market terms, the start of a crash. Unusually large outliers are called dragon-kings (i.e., they are dominant in size and uniquely identifiable) that adhere to the statistical properties of power laws, are scale-invariant, self-similar, and thus fractal. Sornette's work is also associated with the black swan events of Taleb (2007).

25. Sornette (2009). Sornette's methods and predictions can be seen at www.er.ethz.ch/financial-crisis-observatory.html.

26. On this, see Prechter (2016).

27. On economic forecasting and predictability, Cochrane (2005, p. 465) says

> *that a model has yet to be devised that explains high market Sharpe ratios, a high level of volatility of stock returns with low and relatively constant interest rates, and relatively low-variance consumption....When prices are high relative to dividends (or earnings, cash flow, book value, or some other divisor), one of three things must be true: (1) Investors expect dividends to rise in the future. (2) Investors expect returns to be low in the future. Future cash flows are discounted at a lower than usual rate, leading to higher prices. (3) Investors expect prices to rise forever., giving an adequate return even if there is no growth in dividends...If the price/dividend ratio is high, either dividends must rise, prices must decline, or the price/dividend ratio must grow explosively...Are prices high now because investors expect future earnings, dividends, etc. to rise, because they expect low returns in the future, or because they expect prices to go on rising forever?*

> *"...high prices today correspond to low excess returns in the future."* (p. 465)

28. In an experiment of this type, *ex post* data was first used to find bubbles. A second run then substituted *ex ante* data in the last years of the sample. The out-

comes were compared and it was found that the *ex post* data bubble occurred at nearly the same point in time as the *ex ante*, but that the *ex post* was stronger.

29. The background conditions must be ripe in terms of social mood, wealth ratios, and credit conditions. A sentiment-based forecasting approach is provided by Da et al. (2015), who used daily Internet search volume to reveal sentiment. Huang et al. (2015) also proposed a new investor sentiment index that they suggest is a "powerful predictor of stock returns."

30. Wilmott and Orrell (2017, p. 68).

31. Quantity-rationed effects may also be seen in some theories concerning behavior of foreign exchange rates. Dornbusch (1976), for example, says, "An initial overshooting of exchange rates is shown to derive from the differential adjustment speed of markets." See also Woo (1987) for an REH approach to finding FX bubbles.

32. This appears in Thaler (1992, p. 198) who contrasts simple rational models to complicated behavioral models and paraphrases Keynes as covered by Skidelsky (2009).

REFERENCES

Ang, A., & Bekaert, G. (2007). Stock Return Predictability: Is It There? *Review of Financial Studies, 20*(3), 651–707.

Armitage, S. (2005). *The Cost of Capital: Intermediate Theory*. New York: Cambridge University Press.

Benzoni, L., Collin-Dufresne, P., & Goldstein, R. S. (2010). *Explaining Asset Pricing Puzzles Associated with the 1987 Market Crash*. Working Paper 2010–10, Federal Reserve Bank of Chicago.

Blanchard, O. J., & Watson, M. W. (1982). Bubbles, Rational Expectations, and Financial Markets. In P. Wachtel (Ed.), *Crises in the Economic and Financial Structure*. Lexington: Lexington Books.

Browning, E. S. (2007a, July 30). Analysts Debate If Bull Market Has Peaked. *Wall Street Journal*.

Casti, J. (2002, August 31). I Know What You'll Do Next Summer. *New Scientist*.

Cochrane, J. H. (2005). *Asset Pricing* (revised ed.). Princeton: Princeton University Press.

Collyns, C., & Senhadji, A. (2003). Lending Booms, Real Estate Bubbles, and the Asian Crisis. In Hunter et al. (2003).

Cuthbertson, K., & Nitzsche, D. (2004). *Quantitative Financial Economics* (2nd ed.). West Sussex: Wiley.

Da, Z., Engelberg, J., & Gao, P. (2015). The Sum of All FEARS Investor Sentiment and Asset Prices. *Review of Financial Studies, 28*(1), 1–32.

Dornbusch, R. (1976). Expectations and Exchange Rate Dynamics. *Journal of Political Economy, 84*(6), 1161–1176.

Fama, E. F. (1965). The Behavior of Stock-Market Prices. *The Journal of Business, 38*(1), 34–105.

Ferson, W., & Harvey, C. (1991). Sources of Predictability in Portfolio Returns. *Financial Analysts Journal, 47*(3), 49–56.

Fleckenstein, W. A., & Sheehan, F. (2008). *Greenspan's Bubbles: The Age of Ignorance at the Federal Reserve*. New York: McGraw-Hill.

Frost, A. J., & Prechter, R. R. (1978). *Elliot Wave Principle*. Chappaqua: New Classics Library.

Geary, R. C. (1970). Relative Efficiency of Count of Sign Changes for Assessing Residual Autoregression in Least Squares Regression. *Biometrika, 57*(1), 123–127.

Gray, W. R., & Vogel, J. R. (2016). *Quantitative Momentum*. Hoboken: Wiley.

Gujarati, D. N. (2003). *Basic Econometrics*, 4th (international) ed. New York: McGraw-Hill.

Huang, D., Jiang, F., Tu, J., & Zhou, G. (2015). Investor Sentiment Aligned: A Powerful Predictor of Stock Returns. *Review of Financial Studies, 28*(3), 791–837.

Hunter, W. C., Kaufman, G. G., & Pomerleano, M. (Eds.). (2003). *Asset Price Bubbles: The Implications for Monetary, Regulatory, and International Policies*. Cambridge, MA: MIT Press (Paperback edition, 2005).

Jagadeesh, N., & Titman, S. (1993). Returns to Buying Winners and Selling Losers: Implications for Stock Market Efficiency. *Journal of Finance, 48*(1), 65–91.

Jagadeesh, N., & Titman, S. (2001). Profitability of Momentum Strategies: An Evaluation of Alternative Explanations. *Journal of Finance, 56*(2), 699–720.

Kaizoji, T., & Sornette, D. (2008). *Market Bubbles and Crashes*. MPRA Paper 15204, University Library Munich, Germany. http://arxiv.org/pdf/0812.2449

Kennedy, P. (2003, 2008). *A Guide to Econometrics* (6th ed.). Malden/Oxford: Blackwell.

Livio, M. (2002). *The Golden Ratio*. New York: Random House/Broadway Books.

Lo, A. W. (2017). *Adaptive Markets: Financial Evolution at the Speed of Thought*. Princeton: Princeton University Press.

McQueen, G., & Thorley, S. (1994). Bubbles, Stock Returns, and Duration Dependence. *Journal of Financial and Quantitative Analysis, 29*(3), 379–401.

Mood, A. (1940). The Distribution Theory of Runs. *Annals of Mathematical Statistics, 11*, 367–392.

Napier, R. (2007). *Anatomy of the Bear: Lessons from Wall Street's Four Great Bottoms* (2nd ed.). Hampshire: Harriman House.

O'Brien, P. C., & Dyck, P. J. (1985). A Runs Test Based on Run Lengths. *Biometrics, 41*(1), 237–244.

Pesaran, M. H., & Timmermann, A. (1994). Forecasting Stock Returns: An Examination of Stock Market Trading in the Presence of Transaction Costs. *Journal of Forecasting, 13*(4), 335–367.

Poon, S., & Granger, C. (2005). Practical Issues in Forecasting Volatility. *Financial Analysts Journal, 61*(1), 45–56.

Prechter, R. R, Jr. (2003). Conquer the Crash. West Sussex: Wiley.

Prechter, R. R, Jr. (2016). The Socionomic Theory of Finance. Gainesville: Socionomics Institute Press.

Roehner, B. M. (2002). *Patterns of Speculation: A Study in Observational Econophysics*. Cambridge, UK: Cambridge University Press.

Schaller, H., & van Norden, S. (1997). *Fads or Bubbles?* Working Paper 97–2, Bank of Canada. http://www.bankofcanada.ca/en/res/wp/1997/wp97-2.html

Shreve, S. E. (2008). *Stochastic Calculus for Finance II: Continuous Time Models*. New York: Springer.

Skidelsky, R. (2009). *Keynes: The Return of the Master*. New York: Public Affairs (Perseus).

Sornette, D. (2009). Dragon-Kings, Black Swans and the Prediction of Crises. *International Journal of Terraspace Science and Engineering*, 2(1), 1–18. arXiv:0907.4290.

Taleb, N. N. (2007). *The Black Swan*. New York: Random House.

Thaler, R. H. (1992). *The Winner's Curse: Paradoxes and Anomalies of Economic Life*. Princeton: Princeton University Press.

Tirole, J. (1985). Asset Bubbles and Overlapping Generations. *Econometrica, 53*(6), 1499–1528.

Treynor, J. L. (1998). Bulls, Bears, and Market Bubbles. *Financial Analysts Journal, 54*(2), 69–74.

Wachtel, P. (Ed.). (1982). *Crises in the Economic and Financial Structure*. Lexington: Lexington Books.

West, G. (2017). *Scale: The Universal Laws of Growth, Innovation, and Sustainability*. New York: Penguin/Random House.

Western, D. L. (2004). *Booms, Bubbles and Busts in US Stock Markets*. New York: Routledge.

Wilmott, P., & Orrell, D. (2017). *The Money Formula: Dodgy Finance, Pseudo Science, and How Mathematicians Took Over the Markets*. Hoboken: Wiley.

Woo, W. T. (1987). Some Evidence of Speculative Bubbles in the Foreign Exchange Markets. *Journal of Money, Credit and Banking, 19*(4), 499–514.

PART IV

Roundup

As the previous pages have shown, the subject of financial market bubbles and crashes is broad and deep. This last section summarizes the major points and suggests directions for further research.

CHAPTER 11

Financial Asset Bubble Theory

Financial asset price bubbles are not unique to any time or place. For at least the last 400 years they have been experienced in many different nations and cultures. And had extensive money and credit creation and recording systems existed in earlier times, we can surmise that bubbles would have occurred then too.

Price bubble effects and artifacts have been seen in everything from stocks and bonds to tulip bulbs, real estate, gold, art, and all other types of commodities and asset classes. Yet there have often been relatively long periods without any important bubbles or crashes and other periods in which such episodes—in effect volatility clusters—have appeared rather frequently. The transition from tranquil to bubble-condition trading is *always* accompanied by availability of money and credit that is in excess of what is required in the conduct of GDP transactions.

Even so, however, for all the work on trying to understand such phenomena by parsing price changes into fundamental value and bubble components, there has been virtually no progress to date. "Distinguishing bubbles from increases in asset prices driven by fundamentals (or sensible beliefs about the future development of fundamentals) is no easy matter."[1]

That is not for lack of effort, though. All sorts of bubble studies and approaches have been undertaken and all sorts of nomenclature invented. Rational bubbles and expectations, intrinsic bubbles, churning bubbles, collapsing bubbles, regime switches, and many other variants have all become parts of this jargon.

The problem stems principally, it seems, from the attempt to shoehorn "bubbles" into the convenient and comfortable neoclassical rational expectations framework, which is readily expressed in terms of the random walk, efficient markets, and CAPM theories. In such conceptualizations, investors behave rationally, arbitrage is riskless and readily executed, information is close

© The Author(s) 2018

H. L. Vogel, *Financial Market Bubbles and Crashes, Second Edition,*
https://doi.org/10.1007/978-3-319-71528-5_11

to instantly assimilated and evenly distributed, and movement is always toward a state of equilibrium.[2] Within this idealistic construct, bubbles and crashes do not and cannot exist, there is nothing to talk about, and the case is closed.

Stiglitz (1990) writes that "bubble-like phenomena present a challenge to the foundations of the economics theory of rational individual behavior and general equilibrium (including macroeconomic) models based on those foundations." Thaler (1992, p. 61) says that "It is important to keep in mind that rationality is an assumption in economics, not a demonstrated fact."

A dictionary (*American Heritage*) definition of the adjective "rational" describes having or exercising the ability to reason and being sane and of sound mind. And, in this sense, it may at times be quite rational to join the crowd, even with the knowledge that prices are far above "intrinsic" value. But rationality, however it's defined, is a nonindependent variable in itself. The traditional rational expectations approach to understanding bubbles and crashes—with rationality assumed to be a constant—thus contains from the start so many potential pitfalls and flaws as to be unworkable.

As behavioral finance experiments have already shown—especially when in the midst of extreme market events—investors and traders alike seem to cue off many different types of payoffs that are inclusive of but not restricted to only those presumed in the emotionally sterile environments of the traditional models. Hence, participants might behave "rationally," but in ways that are far from those depicted in most such primarily deductive approaches and studies.

A most important neoclassical assumption that is often violated in the real world of trading is the law of one price (LOOP), which takes the presence of risk-free arbitrage as the bedrock feature of financial economics. Logical as it is, though, the LOOP does not always enable the prediction of linkages among asset prices. That's because real-world arbitrage is constrained by availability of time and/or capital and markets are incomplete and operate with asymmetric information. The greater such incompleteness and asymmetry, the less likely it is that the LOOP will be functional. In fact, in the absence of asymmetry and imperfect information, there would be no market activity at all.[3]

It is this limitation on arbitrage—when combined with the behavioral aspects of herding and nonindependence of individual utility functions—that opens the way for bubbles and crashes to form.[4]

Even worse: The fatal flaw in the vast conventional literature is the presumption that financial asset prices respond in the same way to supply and demand forces and incentives as do common economic items like corn chips, cars, computers, and coats.

But as is definitively shown in socionomics, financial market asset price determination is the inverse of that for everyday economic items: For financial assets riding on a wave of easy credit availability, higher prices attract *more* bidding, and with credit tightening, lower prices lead to *more* selling. Prices for economic products and services are normally tethered to a cost to manufacture and serve; financial asset prices are in contrast not tethered to any particular cost.[5] These prices are instead set by the cumulative expression of the crowd's expectations and imaginations.

Hence, for financial assets there is no such thing as equilibrium and therefore no equilibrium price.[6] The Bénassy and Malinvaud studies imply that short-side quantity rationing is an operating feature of all markets all of the time and that this becomes a particularly prominent and important feature during extreme market events.

Short-side quantity rationing is central to understanding that as bubbles and crashes advance toward their ultimate reversals, investors increasingly abandon—and are indeed forced by competitive performance and behavioral pressures to abandon—their focus on "fundamental" valuation analysis and on metrics that typically would include price-earnings and cash flow ratios, potential earnings growth rates, and dividends. The focus instead turns to portfolio quantities of the relevant assets held or not held and away from income statements to balance sheets. In trading, considerations of price thus begin to take a backseat to considerations of quantity.

It would be unfair and improper to dismiss entirely the framework that has been explored and developed in the voluminous REH and CAPM body of work. Those theories are what they are and, as long as the underlying assumptions and limitations are understood, they may provide apt descriptions for some thought experiments, circumstances, and purposes.

But, certainly, those do not include bubbles and crashes. If we are to understand what is happening to the hearts, minds, stomachs, and wallets of real people under extreme conditions, a new and different line of attack and set of analytic tools is needed.

Although the EOV approach differs from the conventional, it nevertheless remains consistent with the notions of intertemporal consumption and utility preferences, discount factors, and risk premiums—all of the standard building blocks of modern financial economics. In essence, EOV may be broadly characterized as a type of liquidity theory of asset pricing that renders the vast historical body of literature on bubbles and crashes devoid of redeeming practical relevance.

Also, by broadening the concept of "risk premium" to include nonfinancial behavioral features, greater depth and perspective is gained about not only what happens in bubbles and crashes but also what happens when conditions are not extreme. Dividends thus ought not to only be measured in terms of single-dimensional monetary payoffs.[7]

Risk, moreover, can be time-shifted and redistributed but never entirely eliminated. In the context of the broader financial market ecosystem, someone somewhere will always be left, as they say, holding the bag (of risk). And in extreme event conditions this can lead to unknown, unpredictable, and unhedgeable repercussions and consequences for everyone else.

Autocorrelation of period-to-period returns is a common feature that over the decades has drifted (Fig. 10.6) from positive to negative and back again and thereby rendered the main random-walk models ineffectual.

11.1   Research Results

From all this, it is hoped that a new financial asset bubble theory will emerge.[8] The approach adheres to the advice given by Morrison (1991) who wrote: "... progress comes by a new method of attack, not by pursuing with added vigor what worked before... [T]he trick is to observe behavior in the real world and similar behavior in a computation and then identify these as equivalent within a certain range of scales and to a limited level of precision."[9]

There's no mystery involved in comparing changes in the variance of the S&P 500 or any other actively traded index to changes in the ERPs or credit spreads or cap rates. The changes in variance are an immediate and direct expression of the intensity of short-side rationing and are manifestations of both fundamental *and* psychological/emotional factors. With this methodology it is possible to measure and directly compare the strengths of bubbles and crashes of different times, financial asset types (including foreign exchange), and time scales. In both bubbles and crashes, short-side quantity rationing is seen in action.

This approach is, furthermore, entirely consistent with the way in which the real world of investments operates. Herding, anomalies, portfolio manager behavioral incentives, and fractal, exponential, and fat-tailed characteristics are all embodied, explained, and accounted for.

With the bubble and crash strength indicators that have been developed, it is then a straightforward step to explore the influence of various measures of monetary liquidity and credit creation. No monetary economist would be surprised that excessive monetary liquidity and/or credit extension is a concomitant driving force in the creation and sustenance of bubbles and that relative stringency may be a factor in triggering crashes. As economist Henry Kaufman has said, "Money matters, but credit counts."[10]

The experiments here suggest that the chain of events leading up to a bubble begins with enlargements of nonborrowed reserves, which when transformed into consumer, commercial, and business loans leads to a positive-mood environment. If such credit creation then reaches the point where it is in excess of what is needed for real GDP transactions, the excess spills over into incremental new demand for financial assets, especially onto the stock market, but often also onto real estate (and art, gold, and other commodities and collectibles) as well.[11]

Similar experiments pertaining to crashes, however, suggest that the mechanism behind them is different. For these, a slowing or reversal in the rate of new credit creation causes a premium to be placed on cash, so that financially leveraged assets must then be quickly (i.e., force) liquidated. When, as is typical in crashes and panics, it becomes difficult or impossible to dispose of and therefore conveniently convert the lowest-quality assets into cash, the contagious sense of urgency ("dumping") spreads to those assets of higher quality for which bids relatively close to previous prices are still available. As a result, the directions of price changes of *all* assets—and also of individuals' utility functions *and* time horizons—then tend to become highly synchronized.

Synchronization then leaves no place to hide.[12]

11.2   Knowns and Conjectures

The key facts, important unknowns, and conjectures as interpreted through the concepts and ideas presented in this book may then be summarized as follows:

Knowns

- Bubbles and crashes are fairly common occurrences in the history of markets and economic development. They appear in all societies, cultures, and asset classes.
- Speculation is a feature of all bubbles and crashes, but speculation alone is not sufficient to cause them.
- Credit availability for non-GDP-related transactions fuels bubbles. Availability of money and credit beyond what is needed to finance real growth of GDP tends to stimulate and sustain speculative activity, which eventually becomes so widespread and intense that it turns into an asset price bubble.
- When readily available cash and credit is no longer adequate to service previously accumulated debt repayment obligations, forced rapid liquidations and crashes become inescapable.
- Credit has generally not heretofore been given enough credit (i.e., emphasis) in the preponderance of financial and economic models.
- Traditional highly model-and-test-specific analytical approaches are fundamentally defective and have little practical relevance.[13]
- Arbitrage and the LOOP are not always possible and practicable.
- Bubbles and crashes both appear to be characterized (visually and thus mathematically) by exponential and/or parabolic trajectories. Crashes, however, are practically by definition, always characterized by relatively rapid price changes.
- Bubbles and crashes are processes rather than events per se and all bubbles and crashes are thus, like the overall market, fractal in nature and composed of "microbubbles" and "microcrashes."
- In extreme market events, utility preferences of participants tend to become synchronized (i.e., nonindependent) and there is lessening of diversity in terms of expected-return time horizons, opinions, and types of assets held. That is, directional price changes of assets approach a correlation limit of 1.0 and diversity of opinion goes to a limit of zero.
- Deep fundamental analysis and industry knowledge—which is expensive and time-consuming to acquire—can generate above-average returns but requires a patient long-term perspective.[14]
- As bubbles transition to crashes, fear of missing out (FOMO) is replaced by fear of staying in (FOSI).

Conjectures

- Short-side rationing is the key mechanism behind the formation and propagation of bubbles and crashes, with the result that considerations of current price (and of fundamental values) take a backseat to considerations of desired quantities held.
- The degree of urgency in reaching the desired quantities is—assuming that markets remain open and functional—reflected in measures of transactions per unit time and trading volume.
- It matters little whether the dominant attributed "cause" of a bubble or crash is fundamental, technical, psychological, political, or any combination of these as the market's artifacts and the responses of investors and traders are what actually matters most.
- A behavioral risk premium—which enlarges and becomes important in bubbles and crashes—may be approximated and respectively subtracted from or added to a financial risk premium component to form the full ERP.
- Entropy, in the sense of information probability and exhaustion of energy capable of doing additional work—that is, in financial economics, money and credit available for speculation—is a largely unexplored but potentially important concept in thinking about these processes.[15]

11.3   FURTHER RESEARCH DIRECTIONS

Much remains to be done. From an empirical standpoint, more extensive experiments on different time scales (weekly, daily, and hourly) as well as on different definitions of ERPs, credit spreads, and cap rates as applied to other asset classes would likely support the EOV short-rationed approach. Empirical extensions might include tests of different leads or lags and of threshold conditions.

Trading volume and number of trades per unit time data should also become more integrated in studies of bubbles and crashes. For instance, are microbubbles and microcrashes detectable in trading volume or transactions per unit time data?

The notion of a behavioral risk premium, tied to transactions per unit time, has the further potential to seed a whole new branch of market microstructure studies. Such behavioral risk premiums may be linkable to the already extensive practical experience and literature on derivatives and options.

From the standpoint of forecasting, it would be useful to establish whether there is cyclicity to bubbles. With reasonably reliable forecasts of monetary liquidity and credit creation, it theoretically ought to be possible to identify an impending bubble (and/or crash) episode earlier on.[16]

Surely there will be important further ties to the topic of synchrony and the ways in which herding—which is the default behavior of individuals in the face of uncertainty—occurs. Indeed, bubbles in bonds, real estate, and housing appear to be related to each other and governed by the same collective psychologies and tied to the same financial discounting and money/credit mechanisms as is seen in stocks. Yet much less is known of bubbles in other asset classes.[17]

When it comes to the financial market price-moving effects of herding and mass psychology, the underlying explanations are best provided by a socionomic theory of finance. Herding and social mood changes drive market manias—both positive and negative—and are reflected by and are consistent with the fractal nature of markets and also short-rationed and nonlinear (exponential) trading behavior.

This is complicated stuff. By studying it, we rediscover "that price and value is not always one-and-the-same thing."[18] We come to appreciate that "[B]ubbles lie at the intersection between finance, economics, and psychology."[19] We find that the market "is actually played in a third dimension of the emotions and a fourth dimension of dreams."[20]

It happens that "investing success is not a function of what you buy – but what you pay."[21] We find that Frederick Lewis Allen was on target in writing that "[P]rosperity is more than an economic condition; it is a state of mind."[22] And, "...we do not live in a clockwork universe."[23]

The common wisdom that a bubble cannot be precisely described but that people know one when they see one is actually not far from the truth. In extreme market events the visual and emotional impressions and expressions of price-change exponentiality and of herding are not figments of the imagination.

NOTES

1. Voth (2003).
2. The inescapable problem with all of the REH-based approaches is their need to join the concept of efficient markets with market-equilibrium models. But it may be inferred from the current project that financial and macroeconomic market equilibrium does not exist and that all attempts to portray equilibrium will therefore be defective. As Sharpe has noted in Burton (1998), "The CAPM was and is a theory of equilibrium."
3. From Werner (2005, pp. 20–5).
4. The limitations were first discussed in Shleifer and Vishny (1997).
5. Exceptions would be luxury goods for which the price is much above the item's production cost. People demand more such so-called Giffen goods at higher prices because of other perceived psychological benefits tied to markers of above-average wealth. See Prechter (2016).
6. See note 2.
7. Beyond the monetary returns, a mainstream participant in bubbles and crashes also expects to receive and/or requires an almost immediate (and therefore largely undiscounted and full) psychological reward that may include good near-term investment performance that leads to client approbation and attraction of additional assets under management, comfort in following or being with the herd, better job security, a higher bonus, and adulatory media coverage.

8. The term "bubbleology" or "bubblemetrics" might be an alternative name for financial asset bubble theory. However, the terms are not easy to pronounce, are not elegant and sophisticated, and do not reflect the full scope of the theory, which includes crashes as well.

9. Morrison (1991, pp. 272 and 304–8).

10. Alan Abelson column in *Barron's*, April 2, 2007.

11. When it comes to commodities, however, it is important to distinguish between nonrenewables such as oil, in which the supply is consumed almost immediately after being refined, and those that are primarily renewable, convertible into other forms, and/or storable such as gold (e.g., bars, jewelry, coins). Some commodities may have characteristics of both, but the key in applying the proposed approach is to understand that with a quickly consumed nonrenewable, the mortal risk for industries such as airlines or trucking is in *not* owning or controlling the supply. In such instances, the resulting commodity risk premium (CRP) then performs inversely to the usual ERP.

12. As explained in Khandani and Lo (2007), even quantitatively driven black box, hedge funds were found, in the August 2007 subprime-related market disruption, to have been using trading algorithms that were for the most part similarly constructed. Consequently, they ended up holding and then later disgorging many of the same securities. Koedijk and Slager (2011) relate this to the importance of belief systems to pension funds.

13. That's because in all situations, markets are incomplete, information is asymmetrically held and not uniformly distributed, and equilibrium is never attained.

14. Campanella et al. (2016) support the assertion that "fundamental analysis does help predict abnormal returns."

15. It has been said that energy is equivalent to money and that all economic activity is based on the use of time and energy. Entropy is highest when the distribution of occurrences is uniform. See McFarland (2016, pp. 33 and 62).

16. As William Dudley, former New York Fed President, said, "…we try to identify bubbles in real time, try to develop tools to address those bubbles, try to use those tools when appropriate to limit the size of those bubbles and, therefore, try to limit the damage when those bubbles burst." See Jarrow et al. (2011) and Goldstein (2010).

17. Real estate bubbles often lag those in stocks and bonds, usually by several years. The Florida land boom of the 1920s appears to have been an exception.

There is no convenient long-running housing risk premium series with which to test for residential real estate bubbles. Rich and Leonhardt (2005) suggest that recent trading in real estate was similar to that of dot-com stocks in the late 1990s. In the United States household assets in real estate as a percent of GDP reached a new high of around 140% in 2005 as compared to below 100% in 1995. See Shiller (2002) and Abelson (2005), and also column of December 5, 2005. Existing home prices divided by median family incomes further suggested the probability of housing bubble conditions circa 2005. Low long-term interest rates around the world appear to have contributed to sizable housing price upsurges in the United Kingdom, Spain, Australia, and China. Hilsenrath and Barta (2005), show that the three-year change in home prices to early 2005 was 95% in South Africa, 68% in Shanghai (China), 63% in Spain, 56% in Australia, and 50% in the United Kingdom as compared to 29% in the United States over the same period. See also Ip (2005) and Barth (2009). Mayer and Sinai (2005), however, argued that there was no housing bubble.

18. De Bondt (2003, p. 206).
19. Garber (2000, p. ix).
20. Appears in Biggs (2006, p. 93) and originally in Winkleman (1932).
21. Attributable to Howard Marks of Oaktree Capital Management as quoted by Doug Kass of Seabreeze Partners in Strauss (2014).
22. Allen (1931, p. 281).
23. Dardik (2017, p. 108).

REFERENCES

Abelson, A. (2005, January 31). Unhappy Ending? *Barron's*.
Allen, F. L. (1931). *Only Yesterday: An Informal History of the 1920s*. New York: Harper Perennial.
Barth, J. R. (2009). *The Rise and Fall of the U. S. Mortgage and Credit Markets*. Hoboken: Wiley (with Milken Institute).
Biggs, B. (2006). *HedgeHogging*. Hoboken: Wiley.
Burton, J. (1998). Revisiting the Capital Asset Pricing Model. *Dow Jones Asset Manager*. http://www.stanford.edu/~wfsharpe/art/djam/djam.htm
Campanella, F., Mustilli, M., & D'Angelo, E. (2016, February). Efficient Market Hypothesis and Fundamental Analysis: An Empirical Test in the European Securities Market. *Review of Economics and Finance*, 6.
Dardik, I. (2017). *The Nature of Nature: The Discovery of SuperWaves and How It Changes Everything*. New York: Rodale.
De Bondt, W. (2003). *Bubble Psychology*. In Hunter et al. (2003 [2005]).
Garber, P. M. (2000). *Famous First Bubbles: The Fundamentals of Early Manias*. Cambridge, MA: MIT Press.
Goldstein, J. (2010, April 9). Interview with William Dudley. *Planet Money*.
Hilsenrath, J. E., & Barta, P. (2005, June 16). Amid Low Rates, Home Prices Rise Across the Global Village. *Wall Street Journal*.
Ip, G. (2005, June 9). In Treating U.S. After Bubble, Fed Helped Create New Threats. *Wall Street Journal*.
Jarrow, R. A., Kchia, Y., & Protter, P. (2011). How to Detect an Asset Bubble. *SIAM Journal on Financial Mathematics*, 2(1), 839–865.
Khandani, A. E., & Lo, A. W. (2007). What Happened to the Quants in August 2007? Working Paper, MIT Sloan School of Management. Available at http://web.mit.edu/alo/www/
Koedijk, K., & Slager, A. (2011). *Investment Beliefs: A Positive Approach to Institutional Investing*. Houndmills: Palgrave Macmillan.
Mayer, C., & Sinai, T. (2005, September 19). Bubble Trouble? Not Likely. *Wall Street Journal*.
McFarland, D. (2016). *The Biological Bases of Economic Behaviour: A Concise Introduction*. New York: Palgrave Macmillan.
Morrison, F. (1991). *The Art of Modeling Dynamic Systems: Forecasting for Chaos Randomness, and Determinism*. New York: Wiley Interscience, Wiley.
Prechter, R. R., Jr. (2016). *The Socionomic Theory of Finance*. Gainesville: Socionomics Institute Press.

Rich, M., & Leonhardt, D. (2005, March 25). Trading Places: Real Estate Instead of Dot-coms. *New York Times*.

Shiller, R. J. (2002, December 17). Safe as Houses? *Wall Street Journal*.

Shleifer, A., & Vishny, R. W. (1997, March). The Limits of Arbitrage. *Journal of Finance*, 52(1).

Skypala, P. (2014, September 1). Ditch the Hokum on Asset Diversification. *Financial Times*.

Stiglitz, J. E. (1990, Spring). Symposium on Bubbles. *Journal of Economic Perspectives*, 4(2).

Strauss, L. C. (2014, April 26). Preparing for the Bubble to Burst. *Barron's*.

Thaler, R. H. (1992). *The Winner's Curse: Paradoxes and Anomalies of Economic Life*. Princeton: Princeton University Press.

Voth, H.-J. (2003). With a Bang, Not a Whimper: Pricking Germany's 'Stock Market Bubble' in 1927 and the Slide into Depression. *Journal of Economic History*, 63(1), 65–99.

Werner, R. A. (2005). *New Paradigm in Macroeconomics: Solving the Riddle of Japanese Macroeconomic Performance*. Houndmills: Palgrave Macmillan.

Winkleman, B. F. (1932). *Ten Years of Wall Street*. New York: John Winston Company.

GLOSSARY

ABS Asset-backed security.

Alpha On a traded investment such as a stock, alpha is the difference between the actual returns earned and the return that would have been expected given its risk. It generally measures how much better than the market the investment is performing after adjustment for risk.

ARM Adjustable rate mortgage.

Autocorrelation The correlation of different lagged observations in a time series, such when the current observation, t, is correlated with the immediately previous observation, $t - 1$.

Autoregression A model in which observation, x_t, is postulated to be a linear function of previous (i.e., lagged) values in the time series.

Bear market After the 1987 crash, the media began to refer to any decline of more than 20% from a peak as being a bear market. The definition, however, is rather imprecise and depends also on the amount of time in which the declines occur. A better definition would include the time element and perhaps the effects on investor psychology and mood.

Behavioral finance and economics Involves research on social, emotional, and cognitive factors to explain behavior of investors, borrowers, and consumers with regard to buying and selling decisions for goods, services, or financial assets. First developed in the 1970s, this approach brings aspects and insights of psychology into the analysis of economic decision-making and, as such, is concerned with the bounds of rationality that must be considered when taking features such as selfishness and self-control into account.

Beta It generally refers to a regression of stock returns against returns on a broad market index, often the S&P 500. The slope of the regression line is the beta. The chief drawback is that beta is a backward-looking measure.

© The Author(s) 2018

383

H. L. Vogel, *Financial Market Bubbles and Crashes, Second Edition,*
https://doi.org/10.1007/978-3-319-71528-5

Black-Scholes theory "It's an equation that prices options on common stock and provides a methodology to value options on securities generally. It can be used to measure risk and transfer risk," Myron Scholes, *New York Times* Magazine interview, May 17, 2009. But, as noted by Wilmott and Orrell (2017, p. 156), "the expected return doesn't affect the value of an option."

Capital asset pricing model (CAPM) A model based on the idea that rational investors will optimize expected returns on portfolios through diversification. It assumes that investors are risk-averse, so that of two assets that offer the same return, the preference will be for the less risky (i.e., less volatile) one, as measured by mean return and standard deviation. It says that investors will take on additional risk only if they are compensated by higher expected returns. It is also a model for pricing individual securities. An asset is theoretically priced correctly when its observed price is the same as the calculated expected return based on discounted expected cash flows. The market beta is used to calculate the expected return of an individual security. An important aspect is that even though risk is minimized by building a portfolio of low- or no-covariance stocks or assets, covariance is variable over time.

CDO Collateralized debt obligation.

Chaos theory A theory that mathematically describes the behavior of systems whose states evolve with time and that are highly sensitive to initial conditions. The behavior of chaotic systems appears to be random even though the systems are deterministic—that is, the future changes are fully defined by initial conditions. Chaotic behavior may be observed in nature, for instance, in weather systems, electrical circuits, lasers, and chemical reactions. The word chaos is misleading, as it suggests total disorder, whereas the theory suggest that the systems are following a predetermined path.

Cointegration Refers to time series that, when linearly combined, are stationary.The term implies the existence of a stationary long-term relationship, such as between GDP and disposable personal income. However, the statistical techniques, studied in the 1980s by Nobel laureates Clive Granger and Robert Engle, are not intended to model short-run adjustments. See Engle and Granger (1987).

Complete markets Markets in which all types of transactions are possible and there are no impediments to trading at any time.

Deflation A contraction in the volume of credit and money relative to available goods. Falling prices are caused by de-leveraging, bankruptcy, destruction of debt, and contraction of bank lending.

Depression Defined by Barro and Ursua (2009) as a 10% decline in real per capita GDP.

Econometrics A term that was first used in the 1930s, it now generally refers to statistical and analytical techniques that enable economists to draw inferences and make forecasts based on estimated relationships that are suggested by economic theory. In the end, it is a mixture of art and science.

Efficient market hypothesis (EMH) This hypothesis, developed by Eugene Fama in the early 1960s, asserts that markets are "efficient" in that trading and prices reflect information that is already known. It is closely related to the random walk concept and suggests that it is impossible to consistently outperform the market. The EMH requires that agents have rational expectations.

Elasticity An estimate of responsiveness, it is used to indicate the expected percentage change of one observation in a time series as compared to the percentage change in the observations in another time series. For instance, if there is a 1% change in the quantity of an item demanded—up or down—as compared to a percentage change in incomes (or some other factor), elasticity, ε_i, may be stated as $\varepsilon_i = \dfrac{\%\ \text{change in quantity demanded}}{\%\ \text{change in income}}$ This is the income elasticity of demand. All other things being equal, demand would normally be expected to rise with an increase in income and decline with an increase in price. For example, if demand declined 8% when price rose 4%, the price elasticity of demand would be -2.0.

Equilibrium Generally, an economic situation in which there is minimal incentive or pressure to either buy or sell. It can be likened to physical equilibrium, in which a body at rest stays at rest.

Equity risk premium (ERP) Determined by taking the average return on an asset over a given period and subtracting the risk-free return available during that period. A risk-free return is often represented by the return generated by investments in US Treasury securities. Historical ERPs do not generally provide reliable forecasts of future ERPs, as companies and indeed the entire economy are always changing in structure and composition due to technological innovations, population growth, and policy decisions.

Exponential Describes growth or decay that is mathematically proportional to a current value. With exponential growth, the larger a quantity gets, the faster it grows.

Fed funds rate The overnight interest rate at which banks lend funds at the Federal Reserve to other depository institutions. The rate is used by the Fed to regulate money supply and influence the growth path of the US economy.

Fractal Self-similarity across different times or distance scales. An example is a tree, whose branches resemble the whole in detailed structure.

iid Independent and identically distributed.

Martingale In probability theory, it models a fair game in which knowledge of past events never helps predict the mean of future outcomes. It represents a sequence of random variables—that is, stochastic process—for which at a particular time the expectations of the next value in the sequence equal the present observed value conditional on knowledge of all prior observed values.

MBS Mortgage-backed security

Mean Also known as the average and mathematically represented as μ. For example, the arithmetic mean, or average, of $1 + 4 + 10$ equals 5 (i.e., 15 divided by 3). There is also a geometric mean, for example, the geometric average of 2 and 18 is $(2 \times 18)^{1/2} = 6$.

Moral hazard A situation in which those institutions and people that are partly insulated from bearing the full consequences of their risk-taking behave differently than they would otherwise. Hence, for example, banks and brokerages might (and actually have) taken more risks than otherwise because of the sense that if something went wrong on their bets (subprime, CDOs, etc.), they could always count on the Federal Reserve to bail them out. Such bailouts encourage more risky lending in the future. Moral hazard is related to information asymmetry. In effect, moral hazard privatizes gains and socializes losses.

Neoclassical economics A mainstream economics approach that analyzes prices, outputs, and income distributions as the result of economic behavior based on rational choice and on participants maximizing monetary utility. A major point of criticism is that this approach does not explain actual economic situations but instead provides a normative description of what ought to be rather than what is. It relies largely on equilibrium concepts borrowed from nineteenth-century physics.

Nonborrowed reserves Banks are required by regulation to set aside (i.e., hold) a minimum of customer deposits and notes to satisfy potential withdrawal demands. Holdings that are in excess of reserves requirements are excess reserves, and free or nonborrowed reserves are the margin by which excess reserves exceed borrowings.

Nonlinear dynamics A way of representing movements through time or space that is not linear and that may therefore exhibit completely unpredictable behavior that might seem to be random. It is generally another name for chaos theory.

Normal distribution Also known as a Gaussian distribution, the normal probability distribution is in the shape of a bell curve and is the most common used of all continuous distributions. When the normal distribution is standardized, it has parameters with a mean (or average, μ) that is zero and a variance, σ^2, that is one and is written as $N(0, \sigma^2)$.

p-value or probability value The probability of obtaining a result that is as extreme as the one actually observed. Generally, the null hypothesis is rejected if the p-value is less than or equal to the significance level used in the statistical experiment. For example, if the null hypothesis is that a coefficient is zero, and the p-value for an estimated coefficient is close to zero, it is unlikely that the coefficient is zero and the null is rejected.

Pareto distribution Named after economist Vilfredo Pareto, who used a probability distribution to describe allocation of wealth. The distribution showed that in any society the larger portion of wealth is owned by a smaller percentage of individuals. This type of relationship may also be used to describe many natural, social, and economic phenomena and is more generally known as a power law.

Pdf Probability density (or distribution) function.

Power law See Pareto distribution.

Price-earnings (P/E) ratio Price per share divided by earnings per share. Similar ratios can be constructed for book value per share, sales per share, and dividends per share.

Probability distribution Describes a range of possible values that a random variable might attain. A common example would be the normal (also known as Gaussian) distribution, which has the shape of a bell.

Q-ratio The q-ratio, developed by economist James Tobin in 1969, compares the market equity value of stocks to their equity (replacement) book value. As used here, the ratio is calculated as the value of the stock market divided by corporate net worth. It was extensively discussed in Smithers and Wright (2000), and shows significant spikes in 1929 and 1999, years of major valuation peaks.

Quantitative easing (QE) Essentially a central bank monetary policy that typically entails purchases of government-issued debt securities for the purpose of driving long-term interest rates down and increasing the supply of money. This supposedly increases bank lending activity and liquidity, and is thereby expected to spur economic growth. However, QE policies also will usually lead to a currency's exchange rate depreciation and to a heightened risk of inflated prices.

Quasi-equilibrium A temporary situation defined in this book as arithmetically describing a dull trading environment in which, regardless of magnitude, the *numbers* of up and down movements of price or volume or variance or ERP are equal within the sample period. It is proposed that there are four forms of such quasi-equilibrium: weak, strong, super-strong, and absolute (perfect).

Random variable Variables that take on probabilistically determined values that are either discrete or continuous. Discrete refers to a set of specific values with some probability greater than zero, whereas continuous refers to a range of values that have a probability of greater than zero. The toss of a fair coin would, for instance, result in a discrete value of one-half for heads and one-half for tails.

Random walk A theory that asset prices are unpredictable and follow a pattern that might describe a drunkard staggering around randomly. More formally, it says that the current period's price, X_t, is $X_t = \mu + X_{t-1} + \varepsilon_t$ with $E[\varepsilon_t] = 0$ for all t, and with drift μ an arbitrary parameter, in what is known as a stochastic process. This is also characterized by the path traced by a molecule moving in a gas or liquid (the so-called Brownian motion). The topic is related to diffusion processes, Markov chains, and martingales, which assume that the best forecast for tomorrow is provided by today's price. The random walk idea as applied to stocks can be linked to Bachelier's French doctoral thesis of 1900 and to Samuelson (1965). See Efficient Market Hypothesis.

Recession Informally defined as two consecutive quarters of decline in Gross Domestic Product (GDP), but actually determined by declines in a host of factors such as payrolls, average number of hours worked, and retail sales. Timing is determined by economists at the National Bureau of Economic Research (NBER).

Regression analysis A technique for analyzing numerical data that includes a dependent variable and one or more independent (explanatory) variables. In the regression equation, the dependent variable is modeled as a function of the independent variables and an error term and the corresponding parameters of the independent variables are estimated and are statistically significant with a designated probability. See p-value or probability value.

Sharpe ratio Measures reward as related to variability (i.e., risk). It is mathematically described as the expected return in excess of the risk-free return divided by the variability (i.e., standard deviation), σ. In symbols,

$$S = \frac{E\left[R - R_f\right]}{\sigma}.$$

Socionomics A theory of market, economic, and social behavior that does not depend on neoclassical presumptions and notions of mechanistic causality, equilibrium, random walks, the efficient-market hypothesis, monetary policy decisions, or exogenous shocks to describe and explain why and how markets, fads, and fashions come and go. Socionomics is based on many psychological and philosophical predecessor concepts, on links to neurological structures of the brain, and on the fractal nature of human progress that is traced by market price movements. Changes in social mood are seen to precede societal actions. At the heart of socionomics is the observation that standard supply and demand concepts in markets for utilitarian goods and services are misapplied to financial markets in which rising prices attract more buying and falling prices more selling. Ralph N. Elliott in the late 1930s, Benoit Mandelbrot in the 1960s and 1970s, and Robert R. Prechter, Jr. in the late 1970s through the early 2000s all made important contributions. Prechter (2016, p. 113) summarizes socionomics as "the study of social mood and its influence over social attitudes and actions."

Stable distribution A probability distribution that departs from the normal in that it has infinite variance and is compatible with the fractal notion of self-similarity. Its probability density function is usually not expressible.

Stationarity Generally refers to a series of investment returns measured at progressive points in time for which the mean and variance of the returns are the same, no matter the point in time at which the series is measured. More technically, a series is said to be strictly stationary if the joint distribution of returns is identical under any shift of time. A series is weakly stationary if both the mean and covariance between returns at different times are time-invariant. With weak stationarity, a time plot of data would show values that fluctuated with constant variation around a fixed level.

t-statistic A significance test used for evaluating whether the mean of a population is likely to be a specified value, or to determine whether the means of two populations are likely to be equal. See *p*-value.

Time series A series of values of a variable quantity recorded at regular intervals of time.

Trajectory The path that a moving object or time series follows as it progresses through space or time.

Unit root In statistics, a test of whether a time series variable is non-stationary and possesses a unit root, with the null hypothesis being that a unit root is present. A process with a characteristic equation larger than 1 is explosive. Also involves distinctions between difference-stationary and trend-stationary processes.

Utility A measure of the relative satisfaction derived from consumption of various goods and services. In neoclassical economics, individuals are described as being rational when they maximize expected monetary utility.

Variance Generally, a measure of fluctuation or dispersion from a fixed numerical benchmark. In a sample, the averaged difference of an observation from the mean (i.e., average) of the sample. Variance is mathematically denoted as σ^2.

Volatility The square root of variance times the square root of elapsed time, t. For instance, using historical daily returns, the standard deviation of returns (or square root of their variance) might be 0.002, and assuming that there are 250 trading days in a calendar year, an approximation of annual volatility will be $0.002 \sqrt{250} = 31.62\%$. Implied volatility is generally used as a pricing metric for options.

Walras Léon Walras was a nineteenth-century French economist who is most closely associated with the development of general equilibrium theory.

Zombie banks Banks that are technically insolvent and that ought to be closed but, due to government or other supports and dodgy accounting, are allowed to live (i.e., continue to operate and to make loans) even though they should be dead. The expression was first used in an academic paper written in 1987 by Professor Edward J. Kane.

REFERENCES

Abarbanel, H. D. I. (1995). *Analysis of Observed Chaotic Data*. New York: Springer-Verlag.

Abelson, A. (2005, January 31). Unhappy Ending? *Barron's*.

Abelson, A. (2006, January 30). Fun and Games. *Barron's*.

Abhyankar, A., Copeland, L. S., & Wong, W. (1997). Uncovering Nonlinear Structure in Real-Time Stock-Market Indexes. *Journal of Business and Economic Statistics, 15*, 1–14.

Abken, P. A. (1988). Stock Market Activity in October 1987: The Brady, CFTC & SEC Reports. *Economic Review. LXXIII*(3). FRB of Atlanta.

Abreu, D., & Brunnermeier, M. K. (2002). Synchronization Risk and Delayed Arbitrage. *Journal of Financial Economics, 66*(2), 341–360.

Abreu, D., & Brunnermeier, M. K. (2003). Bubbles and Crashes. *Econometrica, 71*, 173–204.

Acharya, V. V., & Naqvi, H. (2012). Bank Liquidity and Bubbles: Why Central Banks Should Lean Against Liquidity, in Evanoff et al. (2012).

Acharya, V. V., & Thakor, A. V. (2016). The Dark Side of Liquidity Creation: Leverage and Systemic Risk. *Journal of Financial Intermediation, 28*, 4–21.

Ackert, L. F., & Athanassakos, G. (2000). Institutional Investors, Analyst Following, and the January Anomaly. *Journal of Business Finance & Accounting, 27*(3–4), 469–485.

Ackert, L. F., Charupat, N., Deaves, R., & Kluger, B. D. (2009). Probability Judgment Error and Speculation in Laboratory Asset Market Bubbles. *Journal of Financial and Quantitative Analysis, 44*(3), 719–744.

Adam, M. C., & Szafarz, A. (1992). Speculative Bubbles and Financial Markets. *Oxford Economic Papers, 44*.

Adebambo, B., Brockman, P., & Yan, X. (2015). Anticipating the 2007–2008 Financial Crisis: Who Kew What and When Did They Know It? *Journal of Financial and Quantitative Analysis, 60*(4).

Admati, A. R., & Pfleiderer, P. (1988). A Theory of Intraday Patterns: Volume and Price Variability. *Review of Financial Studies, 1*(1), 3–40.

© The Author(s) 2018

H. L. Vogel, *Financial Market Bubbles and Crashes, Second Edition*,

https://doi.org/10.1007/978-3-319-71528-5

Adrangi, B., Chatrath, A., Macri, J., & Raffiee, K. (2016). The US Monetary Base and Major World Equity Markets: An Empirical Investigation. *Review of Economics and Finance, 6.*

Adrian, T., & Rosenberg, J. (2005, 2008). Stock Returns and Volatility: Pricing the Long-Run and Short-Run Components of Market Risk. *Federal Reserve Bank of New York and Journal of Finance, 63*(6), 2997–3030.

Adrian, T., & Shin, H. S. (2008). Liquidity, Monetary Policy, and Financial Cycles. *Current Issues in Economics and Finance, 14*(1). Federal Reserve Bank of New York. Available at http://www.newyorkfed.org/research/current_issues/ci14-1.pdf

Adrian, T., & Shin, H. S. (2010). Liquidity and Leverage. *Journal of Financial Intermediation, 19*(3), 418–437. Federal Reserve Bank of New York.

Adriani, F., & Deidda, L. G. (2004). Few Bad Apples or Plenty of Lemons: Which Makes It Harder to Market Plums? *Working Paper CRENoS 200413.* Cagliari: Centre for North South Economic Research. Available at www.crenos.it/working/pdf/04-13.pdf

Ahamed, L. (2009). *Lords of Finance: The Bankers Who Broke the World.* New York: Penguin.

Akerlof, G. A. (2002). Behavioral Macroeconomics & Macroeconomic Behavior. *American Economic Review, 92*(3), 411–433.

Akerlof, G. A., & Shiller, R. J. (2009). *Animal Spirits.* Princeton: Princeton University Press.

Aksoy, L. (1997). *A Nash Equilibrium Solution for Stock Market Crashes.* Unpublished Ph.D. Dissertation, City University of New York.

Alevy, J. E., Haigh, M. S., & List, J. A. (2007). Information Cascades: Evidence from a Field Experiment with Financial Market Professionals. *Journal of Finance, 62*(1), 151–180.

Alexander, C. (2001). *Market Models: A Guide to Financial Data Analysis.* Chichester: Wiley.

Ali, M. F. (2003). *Stock Market Bubbles, Time-Varying Risk Premia, and Monetary Policy.* Unpublished Ph.D. Dissertation, George Mason University.

Allen, F. L. (1931). *Only Yesterday: An Informal History of the 1920s.* New York: Harper Perennial.

Allen, F., & Gale, D. (2000). Bubbles and Crises. *Economic Journal, 110,* 236–255.

Allen, F., & Gale, D. (2007). *Understanding Financial Crises.* New York: Oxford University Press.

Allen, F., & Gorton, G. (1993). Churning Bubbles. *Review of Economic Studies, 60*(4), 813–836.

Allen, F., Morris, S., & Postlewaite, A. (1993). Finite Bubbles with Short Sale Constraints and Asymmetric Information. *Journal of Economic Theory, 61,* 206–229.

Allen, F., Babus, A., & Carletti, E. (2009). Financial Crises: Theory and Evidence. In *Annual Review of Financial Economics* (Vol. 1). Palo Alto: Annual Reviews.

Allen, F., Carletti, E., Krahnen, J. P., & Tyrell, M. (2011). *Liquidity and Crises.* New York: Oxford University Press.

Allison, J. A. (2012). The Fed's Fatal Conceit. *Cato Journal, 32*(2), 265–278.

Almgren, R., & Chriss, N. (2000). Optimal Execution of Portfolio Transactions. *Journal of Risk, 3,* 5–40.

Almgren, R., Thum, C., Hauptmann, E., & Li, H. (2005). *Direct Estimation of Equity Market Impact.* Available at http://www.math.nyu.edu/~almgren/papers/costestim.pdf

Alpert, B. (2008, July 14). The Numbers Speak for Themselves. *Barron's*.

Amihud, Y. (2002). Illiquidity and Stock Returns: Cross-Section and Time-Series Effects. *Journal of Financial Markets, 5*, 31–56.

Amihud, Y., Mendelson, H., & Pedersen, L. H. (2005). Liquidity and Asset Prices. *Foundations and Trends in Finance, 1*(4), 269–364.

Anand, P. (1993). *Foundations of Rational Choice Under Risk*. Oxford: Oxford University Press.

Anderson, B. M. (1949). *Economics and the Public Welfare: Financial and Economic History of the United States, 1914–1946*. Princeton: D. Van Nostrand.

Anderson, J. (2008, February 19). Wall Street Banks Confront a String of Write-Downs. *New York Times*.

Anderson, A. M., & Dyl, E. A. (2007). Trading Volume: NASDAQ and the NYSE. *Financial Analysts Journal, 63*(3), 79–86.

Andrade, E. B., Odean, T., & Lin, S. (2016). Bubbling with Excitement: An Experiment. *Review of Finance, 20*(2), 447–466.

Ané, T., & Geman, H. (2000). Order Flow, Transaction Clock, and Normality of Asset Returns. *Journal of Finance, 55*(5), 2259–2284.

Ang, A., & Bekaert, G. (2007). Stock Return Predictability: Is It There? *Review of Financial Studies, 20*(3), 651–707.

Ang, A., & Chen, J. (2002). Asymmetric Correlations of Equity Portfolios. *Journal of Financial Economics, 63*(3), 443–494.

Angeletos, G.-M., & La'O, J. (2013). Sentiments. *Econometrica, 81*(2), 739–779.

Appelbaum, B. (2011, March 25). Fed to Take a Step Out From Behind the Veil. *New York Times*.

Appelbaum, B. (2012, January 13). Inside the Fed in '06: Coming Crisis and Banter. *New York Times*.

Appelbaum, B. (2013a, October 15). Economists Clash on Theory, But Will Still Share the Nobel. *New York Times*.

Appelbaum, B. (2013b, January 18). Days Before 2007 Crisis, Fed Officials Doubted Need to Act. *New York Times*.

Appelbaum, B. (2015, March 5). In Eye of Economic Storm, the Fed Blinked. *New York Times*.

Appelbaum, B. (2018, January 10). Fed Is Urged to Rewrite Its Playbook. *New York Times*.

Appelbaum, B., Ewing, J., Tabuchi, H., & Thomas, L. Jr. (2013, May 29). Central Banks Act with a New Boldness to Revitalize Economies. *New York Times*.

Appley, M. H. (Ed.). (1971). *Adaptation-Level Theory*. New York: Academic.

Arestis, P., & Karakitsos, E. (2004). *The Post Bubble US Economy*. Houndmills: Palgrave Macmillan.

Ariel, R. A. (1987). A Monthly Effect in Stock Returns. *Journal of Financial Economics, 18*(1), 161–174.

Ariely, D. (2008). *Predictably Irrational: The Hidden Forces That Shape Our Decisions*. New York: HarperCollins.

Armitage, S. (2005). *The Cost of Capital: Intermediate Theory*. New York: Cambridge University Press.

Arms, R. W., Jr. (1989). *The Arms Index (TRIN)*. Homewood: Dow Jones-Irwin.

Arms, R. W., Jr., (2008, March 31). Whiplashed? That's a Bullish Sign. *Barron's*.

Arnhart, L. (1998). *Darwinian Natural Right: The Biological Ethics of Human Nature*. Albany: State University of New York Press.

Arnhart, L. (2003). Human Nature Is Here to Stay. *The New Atlantis, 2*, 65–78.

Arnott, R. D. (2004). Blinded by Theory? *Institutional Investor, October and Journal of Portfolio Management*, 30th Anniversary Issue.

Arnott, R. D., & Bernstein, P. L. (2002). What Risk Premium Is Normal? *Financial Analysts Journal, 58*(2), 64–85.

Asako, K. (1991). The Land Price Bubble in Japan. *Ricerche Economiche, XLV*(2–3), 451–468.

Asness, C., & Liew, J. (2014, March). The Great Divide. *Institutional Investor.*

Asness, C., Moskowitz, T., & Pedersen, L. (2013). Value and Momentum Everywhere. *Journal of Finance, 68*(3), 929–985.

Asparouhova, E., Bossaerts, P., & Tran, A. (2011). *Market Bubbles and Crashes as an Expression of Tension Between Social and Individual Rationality: Experiments* (Working Paper). University of Utah.

Auerbach, R. D. (2008). *Deception and Abuse at the Fed: Henry B. Gonzales Battles Alan Greenspan's Bank.* Austin: University of Texas Press.

Auerswald, P. E. (2016). *The Code Economy: A forty Thousand Year History of Algorithms and Work.* New York: Oxford University Press.

Authers, J. (2010). *The Fearful Rise of Markets: Global Bubbles, Synchronized Meltdowns, and How to Prevent Them in the Future.* Saddle Brook: FT Press.

Ayres, R. U. (2014). *The Bubble Economy: Is Sustainable Growth Possible?* Cambridge, MA: MIT Press.

Azariadis, C. (1981). Self-Fulfilling Prophecies. *Journal of Economic Theory, 25*(3), 380–396.

Azariadis, C., & Guesnerie, R. (1986). Sunspots and Cycles. *Review of Economic Studies, 53*(5), 725–738.

Bagehot, W. (1873). *Lombard Street: A Description of the Money Market.* New York: Scribner, Armstrong & Co.

Bailey, N. T. (1957). *The Mathematical Theory of Epidemics.* London: C. Griffin.

Bailey, R. E. (2005). *The Economics of Financial Markets.* Cambridge: Cambridge University Press.

Bajaj, V., & Leonhardt, D. (2008, December 18). Tax Break May Have Helped Cause Housing Bubble. *New York Times.*

Bak, P. (1996). *How Nature Works: The Science of Self-Organized Criticality.* New York: Springer-Verlag.

Baker-Said, S. (2008, May). Flight of the Black Swan. *Bloomberg Markets.*

Balen, M. (2003). *The Secret History of the South Sea Bubble: The World's First Great Financial Scandal.* New York: HarperCollins (Fourth Estate). Also under the title, *The King, the Crook, & the Gambler.*

Balke, N. S., & Fomby, T. B. (1997). Threshold Cointegration. *International Economic Review, 38*, 627–645.

Barberis, N., & Thaler, R. (2002). A Survey of Behavioral Finance. In G. M. Constantinides, M. Harris, & R. M. Stulz (2003), Eds., *Handbook of the Economics of Finance.* Amsterdam: Elsevier Science, Ltd., and also in Thaler (2005).

Barberis, N., Huang, M., & Santos, T. (2001). Prospect Theory and Asset Prices. *Quarterly Journal of Economics, CXVI*(1), 1–54.

Barboza, D. (2007, February 28). A Shock Wave from Shanghai. *New York Times.*

Barboza, D. (2008, April 2). To See a Stock Market Bubble Bursting, Look at Shanghai. *New York Times.*

Barboza, D. (2010, March 5). Market Defies Fear of Real Estate Bubble in China. *New York Times.*

Barboza, D. (2015a, July 13). China's Incendiary Market Is Fanned by Borrowers and Manipulation. *New York Times*.

Barboza, D. (2015b, July 7). Chinese Investors Who Borrowed Are Hit Hard by Market Turn. *New York Times*.

Barlevy, G. (2007). Economic Theory and Asset Bubbles. *Economic Perspectives*, Federal Reserve Bank of Chicago, Third Quarter.

Barlevy, G. (2008). *A Leverage-Based Model of Speculative Bubbles* (Working Paper 2008-01). Federal Reserve Bank of Chicago.

Barlevy, G. (2012). Rethinking Theoretical Models of Bubbles, in Evanoff et al. (2012).

Barlevy, G. (2015). Bubbles and Fools. *Economic Perspectives, Q2*. Chicago: Federal Reserve Bank of Chicago.

Barlevy, G., & Fisher, J. D. M. (2010). *Mortgage Choices and Housing Speculation*. Chicago: Federal Reserve Bank of Chicago.

Barndorff-Nielsen, O. E., & Veraart, A. E. D. (2013). Stochastic Volatility of Volatility and Variance Risk Premia. *Journal of Financial Econometrics, 11*(1), 1–46.

Barnett, W. A., & Serletis, A. (2000). Martingales, Nonlinearity, and Chaos. *Journal of Economic Dynamics and Control, 24*, 703–724. Available at wuecon.wustl. edu/~barnett/Papers.html

Barnett, W. A., Kirman, A. P., & Salmon, M. (Eds.). (1996). *Nonlinear Dynamics and Economics*. Cambridge: Cambridge University Press.

Baron, J. (1988). *Thinking and Deciding*. Cambridge: Cambridge University Press.

Barro, R. J. (2006). Rare Disasters and Asset Markets in the Twentieth Century. *Quarterly Journal of Economics, 121*(3), 823–866.

Barro, R. J. (2009, March 4). What Are the Odds of a Depression? *Wall Street Journal*.

Barro, R. J., & Ursua, J. F. (2009, May 5). Pandemics and Depressions. *Wall Street Journal*.

Barron, J. M., Ewing, B. T., & Lynch, G. J. (2006). *Understanding Macroeconomic Theory*. New York/London: Routledge.

Barsky, R. B., & DeLong, J. B. (1993). Why Does the Stock Market Fluctuate? *Quarterly Journal of Economics, 108*(2), 291–311.

Barth, J. R. (2009). *The Rise and Fall of the U.S. Mortgage and Credit Markets*. Hoboken: Wiley (with Milken Institute).

Bary, A. (2008, June 23). Bye, Bubble? The Price of Oil May Be Peaking. *Barron's*.

Basak, S., & Pavlova, A. (2013). Asset Prices and Institutional Investors. *American Economic Review, 103*(5), 1728–1758.

Bates, D. S. (1991). The Crash of '87: Was It Expected? The Evidence from Options Markets. *Journal of Finance, 46*(3), 1009–1044.

Bates, D. S. (1996). Jumps and Stochastic Volatility: Exchange Rate Processes Implicit in Deutsche Mark Options. *Review of Financial Studies, 9*(1), 69–107.

Baumol, W. J., & Benhabib, J. (1989). Chaos: Significance, Mechanism, and Economic Applications. *Journal of Economic Perspectives, 3*(1), 77–105.

Beber, A., & Pagano, M. (2013). Short-Selling Bans Around the World: Evidence from the 2007–09 Crisis. *Journal of Finance, 68*(1), 343–381.

Beckman, R. (1988). *Crashes: Why They Happen – What to Do*. London: Sidgwick & Jackson Ltd.

Beechey, M., Gruen, D., & Vickery, J. (2000). *The Efficient Market Hypothesis: A Survey* (Research Discussion Paper, 2000-01). Federal Reserve Bank of Australia.

Bekaert, G., Hodrick, R. J., & Zhang, X. (2012). Aggregate Idiosyncratic Volatility. *Journal of Financial and Quantitative Analysis, 47*(6), 1155–1185.

Bénassy, J.-P. (1986). *Macroeconomics: An Introduction to the Non-Walrasian Approach.* Orlando: Academic.

Benhabib, J., Wang, P., & Wen, Y. (2015). Sentiments and Aggregate Demand Fluctuations. *Econometrica, 83*(2), 549–585.

Benmelech, E., & Bergman, N. K. (2012). Credit Traps. *American Economic Review, 102*(6), 3004–3032.

Ben-Naim, A. (2012). *Entropy and the Second Law: Interpretation and Miss-Interpretations.* Singapore: World Scientific.

Benzoni, L., Collin-Dufresne, P., & Goldstein, R. S. (2010). *Explaining Asset Pricing Puzzles Associated with the 1987 Market Crash* (Working Paper 2010-10). Federal Reserve Bank of Chicago.

Berge, T. J., & Jorda, O. (2010, August 9). *Future Recession Risks.* San Francisco: Economic Letter, Federal Reserve Board of San Francisco.

Berger, J. (2016). *Contagious: Why Things Catch On.* New York: Simon & Schuster (Paperback edition).

Berman, D. K., Angwin, J., & Cummins, C. (2002, December 23). As Market Bubble Neared End, Bogus Swaps Provided a Lift. *Wall Street Journal.*

Bernanke, B. S. (1983). Nonmonetary Effects of the Financial Crisis in the Propagation of the Great Depression. *American Economic Review, 73*(3), 257–276.

Bernanke, B. S. (2003). *Monetary Policy and the Stock Market: Some Empirical Results.* Banking and Finance Lecture, Widener University, Chester, October 2 and at London School of Economics, London, October 9. Available at http://www.federalreserve.gov/boarddocs/speeches/2003/20031002/default.htm

Bernanke, B. S. (2015a). *The Courage to Act: A Memoir of a Crisis and Its Aftermath.* New York: W. W. Norton.

Bernanke, B. S. (2015b, October 5). How the Fed Saved the Economy. *Wall Street Journal.*

Bernanke, B. S., & Gertler, M. (1989). Agency Costs, Net Worth, and Business Fluctuations. *American Economic Review, 79*(1), 14–31.

Bernanke, B. S., & Gertler, M. (1999, 2000, August). *Monetary Policy and Asset Price Volatility.* Federal Reserve Bank of Kansas City, Presented at Jackson Hole, Wyoming Conference. Available at www.kc.frb.org and 2000, NBER Working Paper No. 7559.

Bernanke, B. S., & Kuttner, K. (2005). What Explains the Stock Market's Reaction to Federal Reserve Policy? *Journal of Finance, 60*(3), 1221–1257.

Bernanke, B. S., & Reinhart, V. R. (2004). Conducting Monetary Policy at Very Low Short-Term Interest Rates. *American Economic Review, 94*(2), 85–90.

Bernanke, B. S., Gertler, M., & Gilchrist, S. (1996). The Financial Accelerator and the Flight to Quality. *Review of Economics and Statistics, 78*(1), 1–15.

Bernasek, A. (2013, August 4). What the Nation Got for $800 Billion. *New York Times.*

Bernholz, P. (2003). *Monetary Regimes and Inflation.* Cheltenham: Edward Elgar.

Bernstein, P. L. (1996). *Against the Gods: The Remarkable Story of Risk.* New York: Wiley.

Bernstein, P. L. (2004, May). What's It All About, Alpha? *Institutional Investor.*

Bernstein, P. L. (2005a, November/December). Capital Ideas: From the Past to the Future. *Financial Analysts Journal, 61*(6).

Bernstein, P. L. (2005b). *Capital Ideas: The Improbable Origins of Modern Wall Street.* Hoboken, NJ: Wiley, paperback ed.

Bernstein, P. L. (2007). *Capital Ideas Evolving.* Hoboken: Wiley.

Bernstein, J., & Eisinger, J. (2010, August 26). *Banks' Self-Dealing Super-Charged Financial Crisis.* Available at www.propublica.org/article/banks-self-dealing-super-charged-financial-crisis

Bezemer, D. J. (2009). 'No One Saw This Coming': *Understanding Financial Crisis Through Accounting Models* (MRA Paper No. 15892). Available at http://mpra.ub.uni-muenchen.de/15892/

Bhar, R., & Malliaris, A. G. (2005). *Are There Rational Bubbles in the U.S. Stock Market? Overview and a New Test,* in Malliaris (2005).

Bhidé, A., & Phelps, E. (2013, July 16). Central Banking Needs Rethinking. *Wall Street Journal.*

Bierens, H. J. (2004). *Introduction to the Mathematical and Statistical Foundations of Econometrics.* New York: Cambridge University Press.

Bierman, H., Jr. (1991). *The Great Myths of 1929 and the Lessons to Be Learned.* Westport: Greenwood Press.

Bierman, H., Jr. (1995). Bubbles, Theory, and Market Timing. *Journal of Portfolio Management, 22*(1), 54–56.

Biggs, B. (2006). *HedgeHogging.* Hoboken: Wiley.

Bikhchandani, S., & Sharma, S. (2001). *Herd Behavior in Financial Markets* (IMF Staff Papers, 47(3)). Washington, DC: IMF.

Bikhchandani, S., Hirshleifer, D., & Welch, I. (1992). A Theory of Fads, Fashion, Custom, and Cultural Change as Informational Cascades. *Journal of Political Economy, 100*(5), 992–1026.

Binder, S., & Spindel, M. (2017). *The Myth of Independence: How Congress Governs the Federal Reserve.* Princeton: Princeton University Press.

Binswanger, M. (1999). *Stock Markets, Speculative Bubbles and Economic Growth.* Aldershot: Edward Elgar Publishing.

Bissonnette, Z. (2015). *The Great Beanie Baby Bubble: Mass Delusion and the Dark Side of Cute.* New York: Portfolio/Penguin.

Bitmead, A., Durand, R. B., & Ng, H. G. (2004). Bubblelepsy: The Behavioral Wellspring of the Internet Stock Phenomenon. *Journal of Behavioral Finance, 5*(3), 252–267.

Black, F. (1986). Noise. *Journal of Finance, 41*(3), 529–534.

Black, F. (1988). An Equilibrium Model of the Crash. In *NBER Macroeconomics Annual* (Vol. 3). Cambridge, MA: MIT Press.

Black, F., & Scholes, M. (1973). The Pricing of Options and Corporate Liabilities. *Journal of Political Economy, 81*(3), 637–654.

Black, F., Jensen, M. C., & Scholes, M. (1972). The Capital Asset Pricing Model: Some Empirical Tests. In M. C. Jensen (Ed.), *Studies in the Theory of Capital Markets.* New York: Praeger.

Blackstone, B., & Walker, M. (2012, October 3). How ECB Chief Outflanked German Foe in Fight for Euro. *Wall Street Journal.*

Blackstone, B., & Wessel, D. (2013, January 9). Button-Down Central Bank Bets It All. *Wall Street Journal.*

Blake, R. (2002, May). Is Time Running Out for the S&P 500? *Institutional Investor*.

Blakeslee, S. (2003, June 17). Brain Experts Now Follow the Money. *New York Times*.

Blanchard, O. J. (1979). Speculative Bubbles, Crashes and Rational Expectations. *Economics Letters, 3*(4).

Blanchard, O. J. (1993). Movements in the Equity Premium. *Brookings Papers on Economic Activity, 2*.

Blanchard, O. J., & Fischer, S. (1989). *Lectures on Macroeconomics*. Cambridge, MA: MIT Press.

Blanchard, O. J., & Watson, M. W. (1982). Bubbles, Rational Expectations, and Financial Markets. In P. Wachtel (Ed.), *Crises in the Economic and Financial Structure*. Lexington: Lexington Books.

Blankmeyer, E. (1999). The Heisenberg Principle in Economics. In *Economics Working Paper Archive at WUSTL*. San Marcos: Southwest Texas State University.

Bleiberg, S. D. (2018, April 13). The Limits of Modern Portfolio Theory. *Barron's*.

Blinder, A. S. (2008, June 15). Two Bubbles, Two Paths. *New York Times*.

Blinder, A. S. (2013). *After the Music Stopped: The Financial Crisis, The Response, and the Work Ahead*. New York: Penguin Press.

Blume, L., Easley, D., & O'Hara, M. (1994). Market Statistics and Technical Analysis: The Role of Trading Volume. *Journal of Finance, 49*(1), 153–181.

Blumenstein, R. (2001, June 18). Web Overbuilt: How the Fiber Barons Plunged The Nation into a Telecom Glut. *Wall Street Journal*.

Blyth, M. (2013). *Austerity: The History of a Dangerous Idea*. New York: Oxford University Press.

Bogle, J. C. (2008). Black Monday and Black Swans. *Financial Analysts Journal, 64*(2), 30–40.

Bohl, M. T. (2001). *Periodically Collapsing Bubbles in the U.S. Stock Market* (Working Paper Series, No. 6). Frankfurt: European University.

Bookstaber, R. (2007). *A Demon of Our Own Design: Markets, Hedge Funds, and the Perils of Financial Innovation*. Hoboken: Wiley.

Bookstaber, R. (2017). *The End of Theory: Financial Crises, the Failure of Economics, and the Sweep of Human Interaction*. Princeton: Princeton University Press.

Booth, D. D. (2017). *Fed Up: An Insider's Take on Why the Federal Reserve Is Bad for America*. New York: Portfolio (Penguin).

Booth, D. G., & Keim, D. B. (2000). Is There Still a January Effect? In D. B. Keim & W. T. Ziemba (Eds.), *Security Market Imperfections in Worldwide Equity Markets*. Cambridge: Cambridge University Press.

Booth, G. G., & Gurun, U. G. (2004). *Financial Archaeology: Capitalism, Financial Markets, and Price Volatility* (Working Paper). East Lansing: Michigan State University.

Bordo, M. (2003). *Stock Market Crashes, Productivity Boom and Bush, and Recessions: Some Historical Evidence* (Unpublished). Washington, DC: International Monetary Fund, *World Economic Outlook*, Ch. 2.

Bordo, M. D., Cochrane, J. H., & Seru, A. (Eds.). (2018). *The Structural Foundations of Monetary Policy*. Stanford: Hoover Institution Press.

Bordo, M. D., & Wheelock, D. C. (1998). Price Stability and Financial Stability: the Historical Record. *Federal Reserve Bank of St. Louis Review, 80*(5).

Bose, M. (1988). *The Crash*. London: Bloomsbury Publishing.

Boswijk, H. P. (1994). Testing for an Unstable Root in Conditional and Structural–Error Correction Models. *Journal of Econometrics, 63*, 37–60.

Bouchaud, J.-P., & Potters, M. (2001). More Stylized Facts of Financial Markets: Leverage Effect and Downside Correlations. *Physica A, 299*, 60–70.

Bouchaud, J.-P., Matacz, A., & Potters, M. (2001). The Leverage Effect in Financial Markets: Retarded Volatility and Market Panic. *Physical Review Letters, 87*, 228701.

Bourke, P. (1998). *Generating Noise with Different Power Spectra Laws.* Available at http://astronomy.swin.edu.au/~pbourke/fractals/noise/

Bowley, G. (2011, January 1). The New Speed of Money, Reshaping Markets. *New York Times.*

Boyd, R. (2008). The Last Days of Bear Stearns. *Fortune, 157*(7), 40–43.

Brav, A., & Heaton, J. B. (2002). Competing Theories of Financial Anomalies. *Review of Financial Studies, 15*(2), 575–606.

Bray, M. (1985). Rational Expectations, Information and Asset Markets: An Introduction. *Oxford Economic Papers*, New Series, *37*(2), 161–195.

Brennan, M., & Subrahmanyam, A. (1996). Market Microstructure and Asset Pricing: On the Compensation for Illiquidity in Stock Returns. *Journal of Financial Economics, 41*, 464–441.

Brenner, R. (2002). *The Boom and the Bubble: The U.S. in the World Economy.* New York: Verso.

Brickman, P., & Campbell, D. T. (1971). Hedonic Relativism and Planning the Good Society. In M. H. Appley (Ed.), *Adaptation-Level Theory.* New York: Academic.

Brock, W. A. (1986). Distinguishing Random and Deterministic Systems. *Journal of Economic Theory, 40*, 168–195. [Abridged version].

Brock, W. A. (1991). Causality, Chaos, Explanation, and Prediction in Economics and Finance. In J. Casti & A. Karlqvist (Eds.), *Beyond Belief: Randomness, Prediction, and Explanation in Science.* Boca Raton: CRC Press.

Brock, W. A. (2000). Chaos Theory. In N. J. Smelser & P. B. Baltsis (2001) (Eds.), *International Encyclopedia of the Social and Behavioral Sciences.* London: Elsevier.

Brock, W. A., Decehert, J. A., Scheinkman, J. A., & LeBaron, B. (1996). A Test for Independence Based on the Correlation Dimension. *Econometric Review, 15*(3), 197–236.

Brooks, J. (1969). *Once in Golconda: A True Drama of Wall Street, 1920–1938.* New York: Wiley (Paperback edition, 1999).

Brooks, C. (1998). Forecasting Stock Return Volatility: Does Volume Help? *Journal of Forecasting, 17*, 59–80.

Brooks, C. (2002 [2008]). *Introductory Econometrics for Finance* (2nd ed.). Cambridge: Cambridge University Press.

Brooks, C., & Katsaris, A. (2003). *Regime Switching Models of Speculative Bubbles with Volume: An Empirical Investigation of the S&P 500 Composite Index.* Reading: IMSA.

Brown, T. A. (1997). Measuring Chaos Using the Lyapunov Exponent. In L. D. Kiel & E. W. Elliott (Eds.), *Chaos Theory in the Social Sciences: Foundations and Applications.* Ann Arbor: University of Michigan Press.

Brown, B. (2008). *Bubbles in Credit and Currency: How Hot Markets Cool Down.* New York: Palgrave Macmillan.

Brown, B. (2014). *Euro Crash: How Asset Price Inflation Destroys the Wealth of Nations* (3rd ed.). London: Palgrave Macmillan.

Brown, B. (2015). *A Global Monetary Plague: Asset Price Inflation and Federal Reserve Quantitative Easing.* London: Palgrave Macmillan.

Brown, R. L., Durbin, J., & Evans, J. M. (1975). Techniques for Testing the Constancy of Regression Relationships Over Time. *Journal of the Royal Statistical Society, Series B, 37,* 149–192.

Brown, J. H., Crocker, D. K., & Foerster, S. R. (2009). Trading Volume and Stock Investments. *Financial Analysts Journal, 65*(2), 67–84.

Browning, E. S. (2007a, July 30). Analysts Debate If Bull Market Has Peaked. *Wall Street Journal.*

Browning, E. S. (2007b, May 23). Why Market Optimists Say This Bull Has Legs. *Wall Street Journal.*

Browning, E. S. (2010, July 12). The Herd Instinct Takes Over. *Wall Street Journal.*

Browning, E. S. (2011a, October 10). Volatile Market Sends a Warning. *Wall Street Journal.*

Browning, E. S. (2011b, August 29). Fed Faces Old Foe as Hazard Returns. *Wall Street Journal.*

Browning, E. S., & Dugan, I. J. (2002, December 16). Aftermath of a Market Mania. *Wall Street Journal.*

Browning, E. S., & Lobb, A. (2008, October 10). Market's 7-Day Rout Leaves U.S. Reeling. *Wall Street Journal.*

Browning, E. S., Gullapalli, D., & Karmin, C. (2008, October 11). Wild Day Caps Worst Week Ever for Stocks. *Wall Street Journal.*

Bruner, R. F., & Carr, S. D. (2007). *The Panic of 1907: Lessons Learned from the Market's Perfect Storm.* Hoboken: Wiley.

Brunnermeier, M. K. (2001). *Asset Pricing Under Asymmetric Information: Bubbles, Crashes, Technical Analysis, and Herding.* New York: Oxford University Press.

Brunnermeier, M. K. (2008). Bubbles. In S. N. Durlauf & L. E. Bluem (Eds.), *New Palgrave Dictionary of Economics* (2nd ed.). London: Macmillan.

Brunnermeier, M. K., & Koby, Y. (2017). *The Reversal Interest Rate: The Effective Lower Bound of Monetary Policy.* Available at ir.princeton.edu/markus/publications/reversal-interest-rate-effectove-lower-bound-monetary-policy.

Brunnermeier, M. K., & Nagel, S. (2004, October). Hedge Funds and the Technology Bubble. *Journal of Finance, LIX*(6) and AFA 2004 San Diego Meetings; EFA 2003 Annual Conference Paper No. 446. Available at http://ssrn.com/abstract=423940

Buchan, J. (1997). *Frozen Desire: The Meaning of Money.* New York: Farrar Straus Giroux.

Buchanan, M. (2001). *Ubiquity: The Science of History or Why the World Is Simpler Than We Think.* New York: Crown.

Buchanan, M. (2008, July 19). Crazy Money. *New Scientist.*

Buchanan, M. (2013). *Forecast: What Physics, Meteorology, and the Natural Sciences Can Teach Us About Economics.* New York: Bloomsbury.

Buiter, W. H. (2009, March 3). The Unfortunate Uselessness of Most 'State of the Art' Academic Monetary Economics, *Financial Times.*

Buiter, W. H., & Sibert, A. (2004). *Deflationary Bubbles* (Working Paper No. W10642). NBER.

Bulow, J., & Klemperer, P. (1994). Rational Frenzies and Crashes. *Journal of Political Economy, 102*(1), 1–23.

Burnham, T. C. (2007). High-Testosterone Men Reject Low Ultimatum Game Offers. *Proceedings of the Royal Society B, 274*(1623), 2327–2330.

Burnham, T. C. (2008). *Mean Markets and Lizard Brains: How to Profit from the New Science of Irrationality* (rev ed.). Hoboken: Wiley.

Burton, J. (1998). Revisiting the Capital Asset Pricing Model. *Dow Jones Asset Manager.* http://www.stanford.edu/~wfsharpe/art/djam/djam.htm

Byun, K. J. (2010). The U.S. Housing Bubble and Bust: Impacts on Employment. *Monthly Labor Review, 133*, 3–17.

Cagan, P. (1956). The Monetary Dynamics of Hyperinflation. In M. Friedman (Ed.), *Studies in the Quantity Theory of Money.* Chicago: University of Chicago Press.

Caginalp, G., & Balenovich, D. (1999). *Asset Flow and Momentum: Deterministic and Stochastic Equations.* London: Proceedings of the The Royal Society of London. Series A.

Caginalp, G., Porter, D., & Smith, V. L. (2000). Overreactions, Momentum, Liquidity, and Price Bubbles in Laboratory and Field Asset Markets. *Journal of Psychology and Financial Markets, 1*(1), 24–48.

Caginalp, G., Porter, D., & Smith, V. L. (2001). Financial Bubbles: Excess Cash, Momentum, and Incomplete Information. *The Journal of Psychology and Financial Markets, 2*(2), 80–99. See also, *Journal of Behavioral Finance.*

Calomiris, C. W., & Haber, S. H. (2014). *Fragile By Design: The Political Origins of Banking Crises and Scarce Credit.* Princeton: Princeton University Press.

Calomiris, C. W., & Meltzer, A. (2016). Rules for the Lender of Last Resort: Introduction. *Journal of Financial Intermediation, 28*, 1–3.

Calomiris, C. W., Flandreau, M., & Laeven, L. (2016). Political Foundations of the Lender of Last Resort: A Global Historical Narrative. *Journal of Financial Intermediation, 28*, 48–65.

Calverley, J. P. (2004). *Bubbles and How to Survive Them.* London: Nicholas Brealey.

Camerer, C. F. (1989). An Experimental Test of Several Generalized Utility Theories. *Journal of Risk and Uncertainty, 2*, 61.

Camerer, C. F., Lowenstein, G., & Rabin, M. (Eds.). (2004). *Advances of Behavioral Economics.* Princeton: Princeton University Press (Russell Sage Foundation).

Campanella, F., Mustilli, M., & D'Angelo, E. (2016). Efficient Market Hypothesis and Fundamental Analysis: An Empirical Test in the European Securities Market. *Review of Economics and Finance, 6*, 27–42.

Campbell, J. Y. (2000). Asset Pricing at the Millennium. *Journal of Finance, 55*, 1515.

Campbell, J. Y., & Perron, P. (1991). *Pitfalls and Opportunities: What Macroeconomists Should Know About Unit Roots* (NBER Technical Working Paper No. 100). In *Macroeconomics Annual 1991*, National Bureau of Economic Research. Cambridge, MA: MIT Press.

Campbell, J. Y., & Shiller, R. J. (1987). Cointegration and Tests of Present Value Models. *Journal of Political Economy, 95*(5), 1062–1088.

Campbell, J. Y., Lo, A. W., & MacKinlay, A. C. (1997). *The Econometrics of Financial Markets.* Princeton: Princeton University Press.

Campbell, R., Koedijk, K., & Kofman, P. (2002). Increased Correlation in Bear Markets. *Financial Analysts Journal, 58*(1), 87–94.

Camplin, B., & Beighton, J. (2010). *Railway Mania.* Middlesbrough: Middlesbrough Institute of Modern Art.

Caner, M., & Hansen B. E. (1998). *Threshold Autoregression with a Near Unit Root* (Working Paper, No. 27). Madison: University of Wisconsin.

Capen, E. C., Clapp, R. V., & Campbell, W. M. (1971). Competitive Bidding in High-Risk Situations. *Journal of Petroleum Technology, 23*, 641–653.

Capie, F. H. (2007). *The Emergence of the Bank of England as a Mature Central Bank*, in Capie and Wood (2007).

Capie, F. H., & Wood, G. E. (2007). *The Lender of Last Resort*. London/New York: Routledge.

Caplin, A., & Leahy, J. (1994). Business as Usual, Market Crashes, and Wisdom After the Fact. *American Economic Review, 80*(3), 548.

Carleton, W. T., & Lakonishok, J. (1985). Risk and Return on Equity: The Use and Misuse of Historical Estimates. *Financial Analysts Journal, 30*(1), 38–47.

Carlson, M. A., & Wheelock, D. C. (2012). *The Lender of Last Resort: Lessons from the Fed's First 100 Years* (Working Paper 1012-056a). Federal Reserve Bank of St. Lois. Available at http://research.stlouisfed.org/wp/2012/2012-056.pdf

Carney, B. M. (2008a, October 18). Bernanke Is Fighting the Last War. *Wall Street Journal*.

Carney, B. M. (2008b, July 5). The Credit Crisis Is Going to Get Worse. *Wall Street Journal*.

Carney, B. M. (2013, February 23). Why the Euro Crisis Isn't Over. *Wall Street Journal*.

Carr, P., & Wu, L. (2009). Variance Risk Premia. *Review of Financial Studies, 22*(3), 1311–1341.

Cartea, A., & Karyampas, D. (2009). *The Relationship Between the Volatility of Returns and the Number of Jumps in Financial Markets* (Birkbeck Working Paper 0914). Birkbeck: University of London. Available at http://www.ems.bbk.ac.uk/research/wp/PDF/BWPEF0914.pdf

Caruana, J. (2003). *Banking Provisions and Asset Price Bubbles*, in Hunter et al. (2003 [2005]).

Casdagli, M. (1992). Chaos and Deterministic Versus Stochastic Nonlinear Modeling. *Journal of the Royal Statistical Society, Series B, 54*, 303–328.

Case, K. E., & Shiller, R. J. (1989). The Efficiency of the Market for Single-Family Homes. *American Economic Review, 79*(1), 125–137.

Case, K. E., & Shiller, R. J. (2003). Is There a Bubble in the Housing Market? *Brookings Papers on Economic Activity, 2*, 299–342.

Case, K. E., & Shiller, R. J. (2004, August 24). Mi Casa Es Su Housing Bubble. *Wall Street Journal*.

Cass, D., & Shell, K. (1983). Do Sunspots Matter? *Journal of Political Economy, 91*(2), 193–227.

Cassidy, J. (2002, November 11). The Next Crash. *The New Yorker*.

Cassidy, J. (2006, September 18). Mind Games: What Neuroeconomics Tells Us About Money and the Brain. *The New Yorker*.

Cassidy, J. (2008, March 31). Subprime Suspect. *The New Yorker*.

Cassidy, J. (2009a). *How Markets Fail: The Logic of Economic Calamities*. New York: Farrar, Straus and Giroux.

Cassidy, J. (2009b, October 5). Rational Irrationality. *The New Yorker*.

Casti, J. (2002, August 31). I Know What You'll Do Next Summer. *New Scientist*.

Casti, J., & Karlqvist, A. (Eds.). (1991). *Beyond Belief: Randomness, Prediction, and Explanation in Science*. Boca Raton: CRC Press.

Cecchetti, S. G. (2008). Asset Bubbles and the Fed. *Milken Institute Review*, Second Quarter.

Cecchetti, S. G., Lam, P. K., & Mark, N. C. (1990). Mean Reversion in Equilibrium Asset Prices. *American Economic Review, 80*(3), 398–418.

Cecchetti, S. G., Mohanty, M. S., & Zampolli, F. (2010, March). *The Future of Public Debt: Prospects and Implications* (BIS Working Papers, No. 300).

Černý, A. (2004). *Mathematical Techniques in Finance: Tools for Incomplete Markets.* Princeton: Princeton University Press.

Chambers, D., & Dimson, E. (Eds.). (2016). *Financial Market History: Reflections on the Past for Investors Today.* Charlottesville: CFA Institute Research Foundation. Available at http://www.cfapubs.org/doi/pdf/10.2470/rf.v2016.n3.1

Chamley, C. P. (2004). *Rational Herds: Economic Models of Social Learning.* New York: Cambridge University Press.

Champion, S. R. (1998). *The Great Taiwan Bubble: The Rise and Fall of an Emerging Stock Market.* Berkeley: Pacific View Press.

Chan, S. (2010, March 19). Greenspan Concedes That the Fed Failed to Gauge the Bubble. *New York Times.*

Chan, S. (2011, January 26). Financial Crisis Was Avoidable, Inquiry Finds. *New York Times.*

Chan, L., & Lakonishok, J. (2004). Value and Growth Investing: Review and Update. *Financial Analysts Journal, 60*(1), 71–86.

Chan, K., McQueen, G., & Thorley, S. (1998). Are There Rational Speculative Bubbles in Asian Stock Markets? *Pacific-Basin Finance Journal, 6,* 125.

Chancellor, E. (1999). *Devil Take the Hindmost: A History of Financial Speculation.* New York: Farrar, Straus, Giroux.

Chang, G., & Feigenbaum, J. (2006). A Bayesian Analysis of Log-Periodic Precursors to Financial Crashes. *Quantitative Finance, 6,* 15.

Chang, A. C., & Li, P. (2015). *Is Economics Research Replicable? Sixty published Papers from Thirteen Journals Say "Usually Not"* (Discussion Series 2015-083). Washington, DC: Board of Governors of the Federal Reserve System. Available at https://doi.org/10.17016/FEDS.2015.083

Charemza, W. W., & Deadman, D. F. (1995). Speculative Bubbles with Stochastic Explosive Roots: The Failure of Unit Root Testing. *Journal of Empirical Finance, 2,* 153.

Chari, V. V., & Kehoe, P. J. (2000) *Financial Crises as Herds* (Working Paper 600). Federal Reserve Bank of Minneapolis.

Chari, V. V., & Kehoe, P. J. (2003) *Financial Crises as Herds: Overturning the Critiques* (Staff Report 316). Federal Reserve Bank of Minneapolis.

Chari, V. V., Kehoe, P. J., & McGrattan, E. R. (2003). Accounting for the Great Depression. *Federal Reserve Bank of Minneapolis Quarterly Review, 27*(2), 22–27.

Chatfield, C. (2004). *The Analysis of Time Series: An Introduction* (6th ed.). Boca Raton: Chapman and Hall/CRC Press.

Chava, S., Gallmeyer, M., & Park, H. (2010). *Credit Conditions and Stock Return Volatility* (Working Paper). Georgia Institute of Technology.

Chen, N., Roll, R., & Ross, S. (1986). Economic Forces and the Stock Market. *Journal of Business, 59*(3), 383–403.

Chen, J., Hong, H., & Stein, J. C. (2000). *Forecasting Crashes: Trading Volume, Past Returns and Conditional Skewness in Stock Prices* (NBER Working Paper No. 7687).

Chen, H., Cúrdia, V., & Ferrero, A. (2011, December). The Macroeconomic Effects of Large-Scale Asset Purchase Programs. *Federal Reserve Bank of New York Staff Report* No. 527.

Chernow, R. (2009, October 23). Everyman's Financial Meltdown. *New York Times.*

Chevalier, J., & Ellison, G. (1997). Risk Taking by Mutual Funds as a Response to Incentives. *Journal of Political Economy, 105*(6), 1167–1200.

Chevalier, J., & Ellison, G. (1999). Career Concerns of Mutual Fund Managers. *Quarterly Journal of Economics, 114*(2), 389–432.

Chirinko, R. S. (2003 [2005]). *Comments on: 'Stocks as Money,' and 'Bubble Psychology',* in Hunter et al. (2003).

Christensen, B. J., & Prabhala, N. R. (1998). The Relation Between Implied and Realized Volatility. *Journal of Financial Economics, 50,* 125.

Christie, W., & Huang, R. (1995). Following the Pied Piper: Do Individual Returns Herd Around the Market? *Financial Analysts Journal, 51*(4), 31.

Chua, D. B., Kritzman, M., & Page, S. (2009). The Myth of Diversification. *Journal of Portfolio Management, 36*(1), 26–35.

Cieplinski, T., Dominiczak, A., & Kutner, R. (2012). Short Comprehensive Report on the Non-Brownian Stochastic Dynamics at Financial and Commodity Markets. *Acta Physica Polonica A, 121,* B-24.

Clement, D. (2007). Interview with Eugene Fama. *The Region.* Federal Reserve Bank of Minneapolis. Available at www.minneapolisfed.org/publications_papers/pub_display.cfm?id=1134

Clews, R. (2002). Asset Prices and Inflation. *Bank of England Quarterly Bulletin* (Summer).

Coakley, J., Hadass, L., & Wood, A. (2007). Post-IPO Operating Performance, Venture Capital and the Bubble Years. *Journal of Business Finance and Accounting, 34*(9–10), 1423–1446.

Coates, J. (2012a, June 10). The Biology of Bubble and Crash. *New York Times.*

Coates, J. (2012b). *The Hour Between Dog and Wolf: Risk Taking, Gut Feelings, and the Biology of Boom and Bust.* New York: Penguin.

Cochrane, J. H. (2003). *Stocks as Money: Convenience Yield and the Tech Stock Bubble,* in Hunter et al. (2003 [2005]).

Cochrane, J. H. (2005). *Asset Pricing* (rev ed.). Princeton: Princeton University Press.

Cochrane, J. H. (2011). Discount Rates. *Journal of Finance, 66*(4), 1047–1108.

Cochrane, J. H. (2012, September 1). The Federal Reserve: From Central Bank to Central Planner. *Wall Street Journal.*

Cochrane, J. H. (2013, August 27). The Danger of an All-Powerful Federal Reserve. *Wall Street Journal.*

Cochrane, J. H. (2018). Lessons from the Quiet Zero Lower Bound. In M. D. Bordo et al. (2018).

Cogley, T., & Sargent, T. J. (2008). The Market Price of Risk and the Equity Premium: A Legacy of the Great Depression? *Journal of Monetary Economics, 55*(3), 454–476.

Cohan, W. D. (2010). Merrill Lynch's $50 Billion Feud. *Fortune, 161*(6).

Cohan, W. D. (2012, April). How We Got the Crash Wrong. *Atlantic Monthly.*

Cohen, E. E. (1992). *Athenian Economy and Society: A Banking Perspective.* Princeton: Princeton University Press.

Cohen, B. (1997). *The Edge of Chaos: Financial Booms, Bubbles, Crashes and Chaos.* Chichester: Wiley.

Colander, D. (Ed.). (2006). *Post Walrasian Macroeconomics: Beyond the Dynamic Stochastic General Equilibrium Model.* New York: Cambridge University Press.

Cole, C. (2014). Volatility: The Market Price of Uncertainty. *CFA Institute: Conference Proceedings Quarterly, 1.*

Cole, H. L., & Ohanian, L. E. (1999). The Great Depression in the United States From a Neoclassical Perspective. *Federal Reserve Bank of Minneapolis Quarterly Review, 23*(1), 2–24.

Collyns, C., & Senhadji, A. (2003). *Lending Booms, Real Estate Bubbles, and the Asian Crisis*, in Hunter et al. (2003).

Colvin, G. (2010). Alan Greenspan Fights Back. *Fortune, 161*(3), 60–64.

Congdon, T., & Hanke, S. H. (2017, March 14). More Bank Capital Could Kill the Economy. *Wall Street Journal.*

Conlisk, J. (1996). Why Bounded Rationality? *Journal of Economic Literature, 34,* 669–700.

Conrad, J., & Kaul, G. (1988). Time-Variation in Expected Returns. *Journal of Business, 61*(4), 409–425.

Cont, R., Potters, M, & Bouchaud, J.-P. (1997). Scaling in Stock Market Data: Stable Laws and Beyond. Available at http://arxiv.org/pdf/cond-mat/9705087.pdf

Conti-Brown, P. (2016). *The Power and Independence of the Federal Reserve.* Princeton: Princeton University Press.

Cooper, G. (2008). *The Origin of Financial Crises: Central Banks, Credit Bubbles, and the Efficient Market Fallacy.* New York/Petersfield: Vintage Paperback/Harriman House.

Cootner, P. H. (1962). Stock Prices: Random vs Systematic Changes. *Industrial Management Review, 3*(2), 24–45.

Cootner, P. H. (Ed.). (1964). *The Random Character of Stock Market Prices.* Cambridge, MA: MIT Press.

Corcoran, C. M. (2007). *Long/Short Market Dynamics: Trading Strategies in Today's Markets.* Chichester: Wiley.

Corkery, M. (2010, March 16). Lehman Whistle-Blower's Fate: Fired. *Wall Street Journal.*

Cornell, B. (1999). *The Equity Risk Premium.* New York: Wiley.

Corsi, F., & Sornette, D. (2014). Follow the Money: The Monetary Roots of Bubbles and Crashes. *International Review of Financial Analysis, 32,* 47–59.

Corzo, T., Prat, M., & Vaquero, E. (2014). Behavioral Finance in Joseph de la Vega's Confusion de Confusiones. *Journal of Behavioral Finance, 15*(4), 341–350.

Coval, J.D., Hirshleifer, D. A., & Shumway, T. G. (2002). *Can Individual Investors Beat the Market?* (Harvard NOM Working Paper, No. 02-45). Cambridge, MA: Harvard University.

Covel, M. W. (2007). *The Complete Turtle Trader: The Legend, the Lessons, the Results.* New York: HarperCollins.

Cowen, T. (2006, April 20). Enter the Neuro-Economists: Why Do Investors Do What They Do? *New York Times.*

Cowles, A. (1938). *Common-Stock Indexes, 1871–1937.* Bloomington: Principia Press.

Cowles, A. (1960). A Revision of Previous Conclusions Regarding Stock Price Behavior. *Econometrica, 28*(4), 909–915.

Cowles, V. (2002). *The Great Swindle: The Story of the South Sea Bubble.* Hong Kong: Hindsight Books. [Copyright H. Crowley 1960].

Cox, A., & Hobson, D. (2005). Local Martingales, Bubbles and Option Prices. *Finance and Stochastics, 9,* 477.

Craig, S., & Protess, B. (2011, February 10). Morgan Stanley and Citi Were Closer to Brink Than Thought. *New York Times.*

Craig, S., McCracken, J., Luccehtti, A., & Kelly, K. (2008, December 29). The Weekend That Wall Street Died. *Wall Street Journal.*

Craine, R. (1993). Rational Bubbles: A Test. *Journal of Economic Dynamics and Control,* *17,* 829.

Crossen, C. (2005, August 3). Land in 1920s Florida Was So Hot, People Sold Underwater Lots. *Wall Street Journal.*

Crovitz, L. G. (2009, January 26). Bad News Is Better Than No News. *Wall Street Journal.*

Crudele, J. (2006, June 20). The Day I Met the Plunge Protection Team. *New York Post.*

Cunningham, S. R. (1993). Unit Root Testing: A Critique from Chaos Theory. *Review of Financial Economics, 3*(1), 1–18.

Cuthbertson, K., & Nitzsche, D. (2004). *Quantitative Financial Economics* (2nd ed.). West Sussex: Wiley.

Cuthbertson, K., Hayes, S., & Nitzsche, D. (1999). Explaining Movements in UK Stock Prices. *The Quarterly Review of Economics and Finance, 39*(1), 1–19.

Cutler, D. M., Poterba, J. M., & Summers, L. H. (1989). What Moves Stock Prices? *Journal of Portfolio Management, 15*(3), 4–12.

Cutler, D. M., Poterba, J. M., & Summers, L. H. (1991). Speculative Dynamics. *Review of Economic Studies, 58,* 529–546.

Da, Z., Engelberg, J., & Gao, P. (2015). The Sum of All FEARS Investor Sentiment and Asset Prices. *Review of Financial Studies, 28*(1), 1–32.

Dale, R. (2004, 2012). *The First Crash: Lessons from the South Sea Bubble.* Princeton: Princeton University Press.

Dale, R. S., Johnson, J. E. V., & Tang, L. (2005). Financial Markets Can Go Mad: Evidence of Irrational Behaviour During the South Sea Bubble. *Economic History Review, LVIII*(2), 233–271.

Daley, D. J., & Gani, J. (1999). *Epidemic Modelling.* Cambridge: Cambridge University Press.

Damodaran, A. (1999). *Estimating Equity Risk Premiums* (Working Paper). New York: New York University.

Damodaran, A. (2002). *Investment Valuation: Tools and Techniques for Determining the Value of Any Asset* (2nd ed.). New York: Wiley.

Dardik, I. (2017). *The Nature of Nature: The Discovery of SuperWaves and How It Changes Everything.* New York: Rodale.

Das, S. (2006). *Traders Guns & Money.* Harlow: Prentice-Hall/Pearson.

Dash, M. (1999). *Tulipomania: The Story of the World's Most Coveted Flower and the Extraordinary Passions It Aroused.* New York: Crown Publishing.

Dash, E. & Creswell, J. (2008, November 23). Citigroup Pays for a Rush to Risk. *New York Times.*

Davidson, J. N. (1999). *Courtesans & Fishcakes: The Consuming Passions of Classical Athens.* New York: HarperPerennial.

Davidson, K., & McGrane, V. (2015, July 14). Janet Yellen's Fed Flounders in Political Arena. *Wall Street Journal.*

Davidson, J. D., & Rees-Mogg, W. (1992). *The Great Reckoning.* London: Sidgwick & Jackson.

Davies, G. (2002). *A History of Money: From Ancient Times to the Present Day* (3rd ed.). Cardiff: University of Wales Press.

Davis, B. (2011a, June 27). China Risks Being Next Property-Bubble Blow Up. *Wall Street Journal.*

Davis, B. (2011b, June 9). The Great Property Bubble of China May Be Popping. *Wall Street Journal*.

De Bondt, W. (1995). Investor Psychology and the Dynamics of Security Prices. In *Behavioral Finance and Decision Theory in Investment Management*. Charlottesville: Association for Investment Management and Research.

De Bondt, W. (2003). *Bubble Psychology*, in Hunter et al. (2003 [2005]).

De Bondt, W. (2012). *Asset Bubbles: Insights from Behavioral Finance*, in Evanoff et al. (2012).

De Bondt, W., & Thaler, R. (1986). Does the Stock Market Overreact? *Journal of Finance, 60*.

De Grauwe, P. (1990). *Deterministic Chaos in the Foreign Exchange Markets* (Discussion Paper 370). London: Centre for Economic Policy Research.

De Grauwe, P., & Grimaldi, M. (2003). *Bubbling and Crashing Exchange Rates* (CESIfo Working Paper, 1045). Leuven: Catholic University of Leuven.

De Long, J. B., & Becht, M. (1992). *'Excess Volatility' and the German Stock Market, 1876–1990* (NBER Working Paper No. 4054). Available at www.j-bradford-delong. net/pdf_files/German_Volatility.pdf

De Long, J. B., & Grossman, R. S. (1993). *'Excess Volatility' on the London Stock Market, 1870–1990* (Working Paper). Department of Economics, Harvard University. Available at www.j-bradford-delong.net/pdf_files/London_Volatility.pdf

De Long, J. B., & Shleifer, A. (1991). The Stock Market Bubble of 1929: Evidence from Closed-End Mutual Funds. *Journal of Economic History, 51*, 675–700.

De Soto, J. H. (2006). *Money, Bank Credit, and Economic Cycles* (trans: Stroup, M. A.). Auburn: Ludwig von Mises Institute.

Dechert, W. D. (Ed.). (1996). *Chaos Theory in Economic Methods, Models and Evidence*. Cheltenham: Elgar.

Deidda, L. G., & Fattouh, B. (2005). *Banks, Financial Markets and Growth* (Working Paper 2005/11). London: SOAS, University of London and CRENoS. Available at www.crenos.it/working/pdf/05-11.pdf

Dent, H. S., Jr. (2006). *The Next Great Bubble Boom: How to Profit from the Greatest Boom in History, 2006–2010*. New York: Simon & Schuster (Free Press).

Dent, H. S., Jr. (2016). *The Sale of a Lifetime: How the Great Bubble Burst of 2017–2019 Can Make You Rich*. New York: Penguin/Random House.

Dent, H. S., Jr., & Pancholi, A. (2017). *Zero Hour*. New York: Portfolio/Penguin.

Der Hovanesian, M. (2008, November 24). Sex, Lies, and Mortgage Deals. *Business Week*.

Derman, E. (2002). The Perception of Time, Risk and Return During Periods of Speculation. *Quantitative Finance, 2* (see also, stacks.iop.org/Quant/2/282).

Derman, E. (2004). *My Life as a Quant: Reflections on Physics and Finance*. New York: Wiley.

Derman, E. (2011). *Models Behaving Badly: Why Confusing Illusion with Reality Can Lead to Disaster, on Wall Street and in Life*. New York: Free Press.

Detken, C., & Smets, F. (2004, May). *Asset Price Booms and Monetary Policy* (Working Paper Series No. 364). () Frankfurt: European Central Bank. Available at www.ecb. int

Dewey, J. (1922). *Human Nature and Conduct: An Introduction to Social Psychology*. New York: Modern Library.

Dezhbakhsh, H., & Demirguc-Kunt, A. (1990). On the Presence of Speculative Bubbles in Stock Prices. *Journal of Financial and Quantitative Analysis, 25,* 101–112.

Dhami, S. (2016). *The Foundations of Behavioral Economic Analysis.* New York: Oxford University Press.

Dholakia, N., & Turcan, R. V. (2014). *Toward a Metatheory of Economic Bubbles: Socio-Political and Cultural Perspectives.* New York: Palgrave Macmillan.

Diamond, D. W. (1997). Liquidity, Banks, and Markets. *Journal of Political Economy, 105*(5), 928–956.

Diba, B. T. (1990). Bubbles and Stock-Price Volatility. In G. P. Dwyer Jr. & R. W. Hafer (Eds.), *The Stock Market: Bubbles, Volatility, and Chaos.* Norwell: Kluwer Academic.

Diba, B. T., & Grossman, H. I. (1985). *The Impossibility of Rational Bubbles* (NBER Working Paper, w1615).

Diba, B. T., & Grossman, H. I. (1987, August). On the Inception of Rational Bubbles. *Quarterly Journal of Economics, 102*(409).

Diba, B. T., & Grossman, H. I. (1988). The Theory of Rational Bubbles in Stock Prices. *Economic Journal, 98,* 746.

Dichev, I. D., & Janes, T. D. (2003). Lunar Cycle Effects in Stock Returns. *Journal of Private Equity, 6*(4). Available at http://ssrn.com/abstract=281665

Dickey, D. A., & Fuller, W. A. (1981). Likelihood Ratio Statistics for Autoregressive Time Series with a Unit Root. *Econometrica, 49*(4), 1057–1072.

Dickey, D. A., Jansen, D. W., & Thornton, D. L. (1991). *A Primer on Cointegration with an Application to Money and Income.* Federal Reserve Bank of St. Louis *Review.* St. Louis: Federal Reserve Bank.

Diebold, F. X., & Nason, J. M. (1990). Nonparametric Exchange Rate Prediction. *Journal of International Economics, 28,* 315–332.

DiMartino, D., & Duca, J. V. (2007). The Rise and Fall of Subprime Mortgages. *Federal Reserve Bank of Dallas Economic Letter, 2*(11), 1–8.

Dimson, E., Marsh, P., & Staunton, M. (2001). *Millennium Book II: 101 Years of Investment Returns.* London: ABN-Amro, London Business School, and also in Bradfield et al. (2002). *The Attractiveness of the Equity Market as Signaled by the Market Risk Premium.* Houghton. Available at www.cadiz.co.za/research_docs/X0010054.pdf

Dimson, E., Marsh, P., & Staunton, M. (2002a, September). Global Evidence on the Equity Risk Premium. *Journal of Applied Corporate Finance.*

Dimson, E., Marsh, P., & Staunton, M. (2002b). *Triumph of the Optimists: 101 Years of Global Investment Returns.* Princeton: Princeton University Press.

Dimson, E., Marsh, P., & Staunton, M. (2007). *The Worldwide Equity Premium: A Smaller Puzzle.* London: London Business School. Available at http://www.london.edu/assets/documents/PDF/The_Worldwide_EquityPremium.pdf

Doherty, J. (2008, May 26). The Sad Story of Auction-Rate Securities. *Barron's.*

Dominguez, K. M., Fair, R. C., & Shapiro, M. D. (1988). Forecasting the Depression: Harvard Versus Yale. *American Economic Review, 78*(4), 595–612.

Donaldson, R. G., Kamstra, M. J., & Kramer, L. A. (2010). Estimating the Equity Premium. *Journal of Financial and Quantitative Analysis, 45*(4), 813–846.

Donkin, R. A. (2003). *Between East and West: The Moluccas and the Traffic in Spices Up to the Arrival of Europeans.* Darby: Diane Publishing Company and American Philosophical Society.

Donnelly, B. (1987, October 23). Efficient-Market Theorists Are Puzzled by Recent Gyrations in Stock Market. *Wall Street Journal*.

Dornbusch, R. (1976). Expectations and Exchange Rate Dynamics. *Journal of Political Economy, 84*(6), 1161–1176.

Dovern, J., Fritsche, U., Loungani, P., & Tamirisa, N. (2013). *Information Rigidities in Economic Growth Forecasts: Evidence from a Large International Panel* (IMF Working Paper, WP/13/56). http://www.imf.org/external/pubs/ft/wp/2013/wp1356.pdf

Dowd, K., & Hutchinson, M. (2010). *Alchemists of Loss: How Modern Finance and Government Intervention Crashed the Financial System*. Chichester: Wiley.

Dreazen, Y. J. (2002, September 26). Wildly Optimistic Data Drove Telecoms to Build Fiber Glut. *Wall Street Journal*.

Driffill, J., & Sola, M. (2001). *Irreversible Investment and Changes in Regime*. Economic and Social Research Council Working Paper, Birkbeck College, University of London. Available at http://www.econ.bbk.ac.uk//research/macro/macro.htm

Duarte, F., & Rosa, C. (2013, May 8). Are Stocks Cheap? A Review of the Evidence. *Liberty Street Economics, 691*. New York Federal Reserve.

Dubecq, S., Mojon, B., & Ragot, X. (2010). *Fuzzy Capital Requirements, Risk-Shifting and the Risk Taking Channel of Monetary Policy*. Paper Presented at American Economic Association Annual Meeting, Denver, 2011.

Dudley, W. C. (2010). *Asset Bubbles and the Implications for Central Bank Policy*. Federal Reserve Bank of New York. Available at http://www.newyorkfed.org/newsevents/speeches/2010/dud100407.html

Duffy, J., & Fisher, E. O. N. (2005). Sunspots in the Laboratory. *American Economic Review, 95*(3), 510.

Dufwenberg, M., Lindqvist, T., & Moore, E. (2005). Bubbles and Experience: An Experiment. *American Economic Review, 95*(5), 1731–1737.

Dugan, I. J. (2005, August 31). Sharpe Point: Risk Gauge Is Misused. *Wall Street Journal*.

Duhigg, C. (2008, October 4). Pressured to Take More Risk, Fannie Reached a Tipping Point. *New York Times*.

Dunbar, N. (2000). *Inventing Money: The Story of Long-Term Capital Management and the Legends Behind It*. West Sussex: Wiley.

Dunbar, N. (2011). *The Devil's Derivatives: The Untold Story of the Slick Traders and Hapless Regulators Who Almost Blew Up Wall Street*. Boston: Harvard Business School Publishing.

Durant, W. (1944). *Caesar and Christ: A History of Roman Civilization and of Christianity from Their Beginnings to A.D. 325*. New York: Simon & Schuster.

Durham, J. B. (2001). *The Effect of Monetary Policy on Monthly and Quarterly Stock Market Returns: Cross-Country Evidence and Sensitivity Analyses*. Washington, DC: Federal Reserve, Board of Governors.

Durham, J. B. (2003). *Does Monetary Policy Affect Stock Prices and Treasury Yields? An Error Correction and Simultaneous Equation Approach*. Washington, DC: Federal Reserve, Board of Governors.

Dvorak, P., & Warnock, E. (2013a, November 18). Japan's Banks Find It Hard to Lend Easy Money. *Wall Street Journal*.

Dvorak, P., & Warnock, E. (2013b, March 21). Stagnant Japan Rolls Dice on New Era of Easy Money. *Wall Street Journal*.

Dwyer, G. P., Jr., & Hafer, R. W. (Eds.) (1990). *The Stock Market: Bubbles, Volatility, and Chaos.* Norwell: Kluwer Academic Press. Also in Proceedings of the Thirteenth Annual Economic Policy Conference of the Federal Reserve Bank of St. Louis.

Eavis, P. (2015, December 18). A Missed Opportunity of Ultra-Cheap Money. *New York Times.*

Economic Planning Agency. (1992). *Kokumin keizai keisan nenpo* [National Account Statistics]. Economic Planning Agency.

Ederington, L. H., & Guan, W. (2005). Measuring Historical Volatility. *Journal of Applied Finance* (Spring/Summer).

Ekelund, R. B., Jr. (2017). *The Economics of American Art: Issues, Artists and Market Institutions.* New York: Oxford University Press.

Elliott, R. N. (1938). *The Wave Principle.* Gainesville: New Classics Library.

Enders, W. (2004). *Applied Econometric Time Series* (2nd ed.). New York: Wiley.

Engel, C. (2005). Some New Variance Bounds for Asset Prices. *Journal of Money, Credit, and Banking, 37*(5), 949–955.

Engle, R. F. (1982). Autoregressive Conditional Heteroskedasticity with Estimates of the Variance of U.K. Inflation. *Econometrica, 50,* 987–1008.

Engle, R. F. (2002). New Frontiers for ARCH Models. *Journal of Applied Econometrics, 17*(5), 425–446.

Engle, R. F., & Granger, C. W. J. (1987). Co-integration and Error Correction: Representation, Estimation, and Testing. *Econometrica, 55*(2), 251–276.

Engsted, T., & Tanggaard, C. (2002). *A New Test for Speculative Bubbles Based on Return Variance Composition* (Working Paper Series, No. 106). Aarhus: University of Aarhus.

Engsted, T., & Tanggaard, C. (2004). *Speculative Bubbles in Stock Prices? Tests Based on the Price-Dividend Ratio* (Working Paper Series). Aarhus: University of Aarhus.

Engstrom, E. (2014, May 7). Forecasting Stock Market Crashes Is Hard – Especially Future Ones: Can Option Prices Help? *Fed Notes.* Available at http://www.federalreserve.gov/econresdata/notes/feds-notes/2014/forecasting-stock-market-crashes-is-hard-especially-future-ones-20140507.html

Erb, C., Harvey, C., & Viskanta, T. (1994). Forecasting International Equity Correlations. *Financial Analysts Journal, 50*(6), 32–45.

Estrada, J. (2005). *Finance in a Nutshell.* London: Pearson/FT Prentice Hall.

Estrella, A., & Mishkin, F. S. (1996). The Yield Curve as a Predictor of U.S. Recessions. *Current Issues in Finance and Economics, 2*(7), 1–6. Federal Reserve Bank of New York.

Etienne, X. L., Irwin, S. H., & Garcia, P. (2014). Bubbles in Food Commodity Markets: Four Decades of Evidence. *Journal of International Money and Finance, 42,* 129.

Evanoff, D. D., Kaufman, G. G., & Malliaris, A. G. (Eds.). (2012). *New Perspectives on Asset Price Bubbles: Theory, Evidence, and Policy.* New York: Oxford University Press.

Evans, G. W. (1991). Pitfalls in Testing for Explosive Bubbles in Asset Prices. *American Economic Review, 81,* 922–930.

Evans, L. L., Jr. (2003). *Why the Bubble Burst: US Stock Market Performance Since 1982.* Cheltenham: Edward Elgar.

Evans, T., Heine, M, & Herr, H. (2007). *Elements of a Monetary Theory of Production,* in Heim and Truger, eds. (2007).

Evstigneev, I. V., Hens, T., & Schenk-Hoppé, K. R. (2006). Evolutionary Stable Stock Markets. *Economic Theory, 27*(2), 449–468.

Ewing, J. (2010, July 12). Crisis Awaits World's Banks as Trillions Come Due. *New York Times.*

Ewing, J. (2014, September 3). Europe Crisis Is Resistant to Medicine of Low Rates. *New York Times*.

Fabozzi, F. J., Focardi, S. M., & Kolm, P. N. (2006). *Financial Modeling of the Equity Market: From CAPM to Cointegration*. Hoboken: Wiley.

Fabozzi, F. J., Focardi, S. M., & Jonas, C. (2014). *Investment Management: A Science to Teach or an Art to Learn? Research Foundation Review 2015*. CFA Institute Research Foundation at www.CFApubs.org/doi/pdf/10.2470

Fackler, M. (2008, December 19). Japan Offers a Possible Road Map for U.S. Economy. *New York Times*.

Fair, R. C. (2012). Analyzing Macroeconomic Forecastability. *Journal of forecasting, 31*, 99–108.

Fairless, T. (2016, December 7). Ceiling Closes In on ECBs Bond Buying. *Wall Street Journal*.

Falconer, K. (2013). *Fractals: A Very Short Introduction*. Oxford: Oxford University Press.

Falkenstein, E. (2009). *Finding Alpha: The Search for Alpha When Risk and Return Break Down*. Hoboken: Wiley.

Fama, E. F. (1965). The Behavior of Stock-Market Prices. *The Journal of Business, 38*(1), 34–105.

Fama, E. F. (1970). Efficient Capital Markets: A Review of Theory and Empirical Work. *Journal of Finance, 25*(2), 383–417.

Fama, E. F. (1991). Efficient Capital Markets: II. *Journal of Finance, XLVI*(5), 1575–1617.

Fama, E. F., & French, K. (1988). Dividend Yields and Expected Stock Returns. *Journal of Financial Economics, 22*, 3.

Fama, E. F., & French, K. (1989). Business Conditions and Expected Returns on Stocks and Bonds. *Journal of Financial Economics, 25*, 23–49.

Fama, E. F., & French, K. (1992). The Cross-Section of Expected Stock Returns. *Journal of Finance, 47*(2), 427–465.

Fama, E. F., & French, K. (1996). Multifactor Explanations of Asset Pricing Anomalies. *Journal of Finance, 51*(1), 55.

Fama, E. F., & French, K. (1998). Market Efficiency, Long Run Returns, and Behavioral Finance. *Journal of Financial Economics, 49*, 283–306.

Fama, E. F., & French, K. (2004). The Capital Asset Pricing Model: Theory and Evidence. *Journal of Economic Perspectives, 18*(3), 25–46.

Fama, E. F., & French, K. (2008). Dissecting Anomalies. *Journal of Finance, 63*(4), 1653–1678.

Fama, E. F., & French, K. (2015). A Five-Factor Asset Pricing Model. *Journal of Financial Economics, 116*(1), 1–22.

Fama, E. F., & French, K. (2016). Dissecting Anomalies with a Five-Factor Model. *Review of Financial Studies, 29*(1), 69–103.

Fama, E. F., & Litterman, R. (2012). An Experienced View on Markets and Investing. *Financial Analysts Journal, 68*(6), 1–5.

Farmer, J. D., & Geanakoplos, J. (2009). *The Virtues and Vices of Equilibrium and the Future of Financial Economics* (Working Paper). Cowles Foundation ad. Available at https://arxiv.org/pdf/0803.2996.pdf

Farmer, J. D., & Lillo, F. (2004). On the Origin of Power Law Tails in Price Fluctuations. *Quantitative Finance, 4*(1), 7.

Farmer, J. D., Gillemot, L., Lillo, F., Mike, S., & Sen, A. (2004). *What Really Causes Large Price Changes?* Available at arxiv.org/pdf/cond-mat/0312703.pdf

Favero, C. A. (2001). *Applied Macroeconometrics*. Oxford: Oxford University Press.

Fawley, B. W., & Neely, C. J. (2013). Four Stories of Quantitative Easing. *Federal Reserve Bank of St. Louis Review, 95*(1), 51–88.

Feigenbaum, J. A. (2001). A Statistical Analysis of Log-Periodic Precursors to Financial Crashes. *Quantitative Finance, 1*(3), 346–360.

Ferguson, N. (2001). *The Cash Nexus: Money and Power in the Modern World 1700–2000.* New York: Basic Books.

Ferguson, N (2008a, 2009). *The Ascent of Money: A Financial History of the World.* New York: Penguin.

Ferguson, N. (2008b, December). Wall Street Lays Another Egg. *Vanity Fair.*

Ferguson, N. (2009, May 17). Diminished Returns. *New York Times.*

Ferreira, S., & Karali, B. (2017). Do Earthquakes Shake Stock Markets? *PLoS ONE, 10*(7), e0133319. https://doi.org/10.1371/journal.pone.0133319

Ferson, W., & Harvey, C. (1991). Sources of Predictability in Portfolio Returns. *Financial Analysts Journal, 47*(3), 49–56.

Fieler, S., & Bell, J. (2011, April 6). Our Unaccountable Fed. *Wall Street Journal.*

Fischer, S. (1999). *On the Need for an International Lender of Last Resort.* Delivered at the American Economic Association and American Finance Association meeting, January 3, 1999, and in Capie, F. H., & Wood, G. E., eds., *The Lender of Last Resort.* London: Routledge.

Fleckenstein, W. A., & Sheehan, F. (2008). *Greenspan's Bubbles: The Age of Ignorance at the Federal Reserve.* New York: McGraw-Hill.

Flood, R. P., & Garber, P. M. (1980). Market Fundamentals Versus Price-Level Bubbles: The First Tests. *Journal of Political Economy, 88,* 745.

Flood, R. P., & Garber, P. M. (Eds.). (1994). *Speculative Bubbles, Speculative Attacks and Policy Switching.* Cambridge, MA: MIT Press.

Flood, R. P., & Hodrick, R. J. (1990). On Testing for Speculative Bubbles. *Journal of Economic Perspectives, 4*(2), 85–101.

Flood, R. P., & Hodrick, R. J. (1991). *Asset Price Volatility, Bubbles, and Process Switching,* in Flood and Garber (1994).

Flood, R., Hodrick, R., & Kaplan, P. (1986). *An Evaluation of Recent Evidence on Stock Market Bubbles* (NBER Working Paper #1971). In Flood, R. P., & Garber, P. M. (1994). *Speculative Bubbles, Attacks and Policy Switching.* Cambridge, MA: MIT Press.

Floridi, L. (Ed.). (2016). *The Routledge Handbook of Philosophy of Information.* New York: Routledge.

Fong, D., & Wei, L. (2016, October 8). Fears Rise of China Housing Bubble. *Wall Street Journal.*

Forbes, W. (2009). *Behavioural Finance.* Wiley: Chichester.

Forsyth, R. W. (2009, September 22). Autumnal Equinox – Paul Montgomery. *Barron's.*

Foster, M. S. (2000). *Castles in the Sand: The Life and Times of Carl Graham Fisher.* Gainesville: University Press of Florida.

Fox, J. (2009). *The Myth of the Rational Market: A History of Risk, Reward, and Delusion on Wall Street.* New York: HarperCollins.

Frank, R. H. (2008, October 4). Pursuit of an Edge, in Steroids or Stocks. *New York Times.*

Frankel, D. M. (2008). Adaptive Expectations and Stock Market Crashes. *International Economic Review, 49*(2), 595–619.

Franses, P. H. (1998). *Time Series Models for Business and Economic Forecasting.* Cambridge: Cambridge University Press.

Frazzini, A., & Pederson, L. H. (2014). Betting Against Beta. *Journal of Financial Economics, 111*(1), 1–25.

Freeman, J. (2016, September 1). The 5,000-Year Government Debt Bubble. *Wall Street Journal.*

Frehen, R. G. P., Goetzmann, W. N., & Rouwenhorst, K. G. (2009). *New Evidence on the First Financial Bubble* (Yale ICF Working Paper No. 09-04). Available at SSRN https://ssrn.com/abstract=1371007

Frehen, R. G. P., Goeztmann, W. N., & Rowenhorst, K. (2013). New Evidence on the First Financial Bubble. *Journal of financial Economics, 108*(3), 585–607 and Yale ICF Working Paper No. 09-04. Available at SSRN: http://ssrn.com/abstract=1371007

French, K. R. (1980). Stock Returns and the Weekend Effect. *Journal of Financial Economics, 81*(1), 55–70.

French, D. E. (2006). The Dutch Monetary Environment During Tulipmania. *Quarterly Journal of Austrian Economics, 9*(1), 3–14.

French, D. E. (2009). *Early Speculative Bubbles and Increases in the Supply of Money* (2nd ed.). Auburn: Ludwig von Mises Institute.

French, K. R., & Poterba, J. M. (1991). Were Japanese Stock Prices Too High? *Journal of Financial Economics, 29,* 337.

French, K. R., Schwert, G. W., & Stambaugh, R. F. (1987). Expected Stock Returns and Volatility. *Journal of Financial Economics, 19,* 3–29.

Friedman, M. (1953). *Essays in Positive Economics.* Chicago: University of Chicago Press.

Friedman, M. (Ed.). (1956). *Studies in the Quantity Theory of Money.* Chicago: University of Chicago Press.

Friedman, B. M. (1979). Optimal Expectations and the Extreme Information Assumption of Rational Expectations' Macromodel. *Journal of Monetary Economics, 5*(1), 23.

Friedman, D., & Abraham, R. (2009). Bubbles and Crashes: Gradient Dynamics in Financial Markets. *Journal of Dynamics & Control, 33,* 922.

Friedman, B. M., & Laibson, D. I. (1989). Economic Implications of Extraordinary Movements in Stock Prices. In *Brookings Papers on Economic Activity.* Washington, DC: Brookings Institute.

Friedman, M., & Schwartz, J. (1963). *A Monetary History of the United States: 1867–1960.* Princeton: Princeton University Press.

Friesen, G. C., Weller, P. A., & Dunham, L. M. (2009). Price Trends and Patterns in Technical Analysis: A Theoretical and Empirical Examination. *Journal of Banking & Finance, 33*(6), 1089–1100.

Fromson, B. D. (1997, February 23). Plunge Protection Team. *Washington Post.*

Froot, K. A., & Obstfeld, M. (1991). Intrinsic Bubbles: The Case of Stock Prices. *American Economic Review, 81*(5), 1189–1214.

Frost, A. J., & Prechter, R. R. (1978). *Elliot Wave Principle.* Chappaqua: New Classics Library.

Frydman, R., & Goldberg, M. D. (2011). *Beyond Mechanical Markets: Asset Price Swings, Risk, and the Role of the State.* Princeton: Princeton University Press.

Fukuta, Y. (2002). A Test for Rational Bubbles in Stock Prices. *Empirical Economics,* *27*(4), 587–600.

Funke, N., & Matsuda, A. (2006). Macroeconomic News and Stock Returns in the United States and Germany. *German Economic Review, 7*(2), 189–210.

Furnham, A., & Argyle, M. (1998). *The Psychology of Money.* New York: Routledge.

Futia, C. (2009). *The Art of Contrarian Trading: How to Profit from Crowd Behavior in the Financial Markets.* Hoboken: Wiley.

Gabaix, X. (2009). Power Laws in Economics and Finance. *Annual Review of Economics, 1,* 255–293.

Gagnon, J., Raskin, M., Remache, J., & Sack, B. (2011, May). Large-Scale Asset Purchases by the Federal Reserve: Did They Work? Federal Reserve Bank of New York. *Economic Policy Review, 17.* Available at www.newyorkfed.org/research/staff_reports/sr441.html

Gai, P., & Vause, N. (2005, November). *Measuring Investors' Risk Appetite* (Working Paper 283). Bank of England.

Gala, V. D. (2008). Discussion: Cash Flow Risk, Discounting Risk, and the Equity Premium Puzzle. In R. Mehra (Ed.), *Handbook of the Equity Risk Premium.* Amsterdam: Elsevier.

Galbraith, J. K. (1944). *A Short History of Financial Euphoria.* New York: Penguin (Paper 1993).

Galbraith, J. K. (1988). *The Great Crash, 1929* (2nd ed.). Boston: Houghton-Mifflin.

Gallant, R. A., Rossi, P. E., & Tauchen, G. (1992). Stock Prices and Volume. *The Review of Financial Studies, 5,* 199–242.

Gallin, J. (2004). *The Long-Run Relationship Between House Prices and Rents* (Working Paper 2004-50). Washington, DC: Federal Reserve Board.

Gao, L., & Schmidt, U. (2005). Self Is Never Neutral: Why Economic Agents Behave Irrationally. *Journal of Behavioral Finance, 6*(1), 27–37.

Garbade, K. D., & Silber, W. L. (1979). Structural Organization of Secondary Markets: Clearing Frequency, Dealer Activity and Liquidity Risk. *Journal of Finance, 34,* 577–593.

Garber, P. M. (1989). Tulipmania. *Journal of Political Economy, 97*(3), 535–560.

Garber, P. M. (1990). Who Put the Mania in Tulipmania?, in White, ed. (1990).

Garber, P. M. (2000). *Famous First Bubbles: The Fundamentals of Early Manias.* Cambridge, MA: MIT Press.

Garnsey, P., & Saller, R. (1987). *The Roman Empire: Economy, Society and Culture.* Berkeley: University of California Press.

Garrison, R. W. (2001). *Time and Money: The Macroeconomics of Capital Structure.* London/New York: Routledge.

Garside, W. R. (2007). The Great Depression, 1929–33. In M. J. Oliver & D. H. Aldcroft (Eds.), *Economic Disasters of the Twentieth Century.* Cheltenham: Edward Elgar.

Gascoigne, B. (2003). *The Dynasties of China: A History.* New York: Carroll and Graf.

Gasparino, C. (2005). *Blood on the Street.* New York: Free Press.

Gasparino, C. (2009). *The Sellout: How Three Decades of Wall Street Greed and Government Mismanagement Destroyed the Global Financial System.* New York: HarperBusiness.

Gatheral, J. (2006). *The Volatility Surface: A Practitioner's Guide.* Hoboken: Wiley.

Gatheral, J., Jaisson, T., & Rosenbaum, M. (2014). *Volatility Is Rough.* Available at https://ssrn.com/abstract=2509457

Gay, G., Kale, J., Kolb, R., & Noe, T. (1994). (Micro) Fads in Asset Prices: Evidence from the Futures Market. *Journal of Futures Markets, 14,* 637.

Geanakoplos, J. (2012). *Leverage and Bubbles: The Need to Manage the Leverage Cycle,* in Evanoff et al. (2012).

Geanakoplos, J., Magill, M., & Quinzii, M. (2002). *Demography and the Long-Run Predictability of the Stock Market* (Discussion Paper No. 1380). New Haven: Yale University, Cowles Foundation, and Research Paper No. C02-21, University of Southern California (Davis).

Geary, R. C. (1970). Relative Efficiency of Count of Sign Changes for Assessing Residual Autoregression in Least Squares Regression. *Biometrika, 57*(1), 123–127.

Gehring, W. J., & Willoughby, A. R. (2002). The Medial Frontal Cortex and the Rapid Processing of Monetary Gains and Losses. *Science, 295,* 2279–2282.

Geisst, C. R. (2004). *Wall Street: A History from Its Beginnings to the Fall of Enron.* Oxford: Oxford University Press.

Gennotte, G., & Leland, H. (1990). Market Liquidity, Hedging, and Crashes. *American Economic Review, 80*(5), 999–1021.

George, D. A. R. (2007). Consolations for the Economist: The Future of Economic Orthodoxy. *Journal of Economic Surveys, 21*(3), 417–425.

Georgescu-Roegen, N. (1971). *The Entropy Law and the Economic Process.* Cambridge, MA: Harvard University Press.

Geraskin, P., & Fantazzini, D. (2013). Everything You Always Wanted to Know About Log-Periodic Power Laws for Bubble Modeling but Were Afraid to Ask. *The European Journal of Finance, 19*(5), 366–391.

Gerding, E. F. (2013). *Law, Bubbles, and Financial Regulation.* New York: Routledge.

Gerlis, M. (2014a). *Art as an Investment? A Survey of Comparative Assets.* London: Lund Humphries.

Gerlis, M. (2014b, January 14). Is Collecting Art As Profitable as It Is Painted? *Financial Times.*

Gernet, J. (1982). *A History of Chinese Civilization* (trans: Foster, J. R.). Cambridge: Cambridge University Press.

Gerow, A., & Keane, M. T. (2012). *Mining the Web for the 'Voice of the Herd' to Track Stock Market Bubbles.* Available at http://arxiv.org/abs/1212.2676v1

Ghysels, E., Swanson, N. R., & Watson, M. W. (Eds.). (2001). *Essays in Econometrics: Collected Papers of Clive W. J. Granger.* New York: Cambridge University Press.

Gilchrist, S., & Leahy, J. V. (2002). Monetary Policy and Asset Prices. *Journal of Monetary Economics, 49,* 75–97.

Gilchrist, S., & Zakrajsek, E. (2012). Credit Spreads and Business Cycle Fluctuations. *American Economic Review, 102*(4), 1692–1720.

Gilchrist, S., Himmelberg, C. P., & Huberman, G. (2004). *Do Stock Price Bubbles Influence Corporate Investment?* (Staff Report No. 177). Federal Reserve Bank of New York.

Gilchrist, S., López-Salido, D., & Zakrajšek, E. (2015). Monetary Policy and Real Borrowing Costs at the Zero Lower Bound. *American Economic Journal: Macroeconomics, 7*(1), 77–109.

Giles, C. (2014, June 25). Crashing the Party: The Central Bank Has New Tools to Stop Bubbles. *Financial Times.*

Gilles, C., & LeRoy, S. F. (1992). Bubbles and Charges. *International Economic Review, 33*(2), 323–339.

Gjerstad, S. D., & Smith, V. L. (2009, April 6). From Bubble to Depression? *Wall Street Journal.*

Gjerstad, S. D., & Smith, V. L. (2014). *Rethinking Housing Bubbles*. New York: Cambridge University Press.

Gladwell, M. (2002). *The Tipping Point: How Little Things Can Make a Big Difference*. New York: Little Brown.

Glassman, J. K., & Hassett, K. A. (1999a). *Dow 36,000: The New Strategy for Profiting from the Coming Rise in the Stock Market*. New York: Times Books.

Glassman, J. K., & Hassett, K. A. (1999b, March 17). Stock Prices Are Still Far Too Low. *Wall Street Journal*.

Gleeson, J. (1999). *Millionaire: The Philanderer, Gambler, and Duelist Who Invented Modern Finance*. New York: Simon & Schuster/Touchstone.

Gleick, J. (1987). *Chaos: Making a New Science*. New York: Penguin.

Glimcher, P. W. (2003). *Decisions, Uncertainty, and the Brain: The Science of Neuroeconomics*. Cambridge, MA: MIT Press.

Goetzmann, W. N. (1993). Patterns in Three Centuries of Stock Market Prices. *Journal of Business, 66*, 249–270.

Goetzmann, W. N. (2016a). Bubble Investing: Learning from History. In D. Chambers & E. Dimson (Eds.), *Financial Market History*. Charlottesville, VA: CFA Research Foundation.

Goetzmann, W. N. (2016b). *Money Changes Everything: How Finance Made Civilization Possible*. Princeton: Princeton University Press.

Goetzmann, W. N., & Ibbotson, R. G. (Eds.). (2006). *The Equity Risk Premium: Essays and Explorations*. Oxford: Oxford University Press.

Goetzmann, W. N., Ibbotson, R. G., & Peng, L. (2001). A New Historical Database for the NYSE 1815 to 1925: Performance and Predictability. *Journal of Financial Markets, 4*, 1–32.

Goetzmann, W. N., Labio, C., Rouwenhorst, K. G., & Young, T. G. (Eds.). (2013). *The Great Mirror of Folly*. New Haven: Yale University Press.

Goetzmann, W. N., Kim, D., & Wang, Q. (2015). Weather-Induced Mood, Institutional Investors, and Stock Returns. *Review of Financial Studies, 28*(1), 73–111.

Golden, D. P. (1995). *Three Essays on the Theory of Speculative Bubbles*. Unpublished Ph.D. Dissertation, University of North Carolina at Chapel Hill.

Goldgar, A. (2007). *Tulipmania: Money, Honor, and Knowledge in the Dutch Golden Age*. Chicago: University of Chicago Press.

Goldman, S. (1953). *Information Theory*. New York: Prentice-Hall.

Goldstein, J. (2010, April 9). Interview with William Dudley, *Planet Money*.

Gomes, F. (2008). Discussion: Equity Premia with Benchmark Levels of Consumption: Closed-Form Results. In R. Mehra (Ed.), *Handbook of the Equity Risk Premium*. Amsterdam: Elsevier.

Gongloff, M. (2008, March 17). Crunch Proves a Test of Faith for Street Strong. *Wall Street Journal*.

Gonzalez, L., Hoang, P., Powell, J. G., & Shi, J. (2006). Defining and Dating Bull and Bear Markets: Two Centuries of Evidence. *Multinational Finance Journal, 10*(1/2), 81–116.

Goode, E. (2002, November 5). On Profit, Loss and the Mysteries of the Mind. *New York Times*.

Goodfriend, M. (2003). *Interest Rate Policy Should Not React Directly to Asset Prices*, in Hunter et al. (2003).

Goodhart, C. A. E. (2007). Myths About the Lender of Last Resort. In F. H. Capie & G. E. Wood (Eds.), *The Lender of Last Resort*. London: Routledge.

Goodhart, C. A. E. (2011). The Changing Role of Central Banks. *Financial History Review, 18*(2), 135–154.

Goodman, P. S. (2008, October 8). Taking Hard New Look at a Greenspan Legacy. *New York Times.*

Goodman, P. S., & Morgenson, G. (2008, December 27). Saying Yes, WaMu Built Empire on Shaky Loans. *New York Times.*

Gopikrishnan, P., Meyer, M., Amaral, L. A. N., & Stanley, H. E. (1998). Inverse Cubic Law for the Distribution of Stock Price Variations. *The European Physical Journal, 3,* 139–140.

Gordon, M. J. (1962). *The Investment, Financing and Valuation of the Corporation.* Homewood: Irwin.

Gorton, G. B. (1988). Banking Panics and Business Cycles. *Oxford Economic Papers, 40.*

Gorton, G. B. (2008). Information, Liquidity, and the (Ongoing) Panic of 2007. *American Economic Review, Papers and Proceedings, 99*(2), 567–572.

Gorton, G. B. (2010). *Slapped by The Invisible Hand: The Panic of 2007.* New York: Oxford University Press.

Gouldey, B. K., & Thies, C. F. (2012). Asset Bubbles and Supply Failures: Where Are the Qualified Sellers? *Cato Journal, 32*(3), 513–538.

Graham, B., & Dodd, D. (1934). *Security Analysis.* New York: McGraw-Hill.

Graham, J. R., & Harvey, C. R. (2001, 2003). *Expectations of Equity Risk Premia, Volatility and Asymmetry* (Working Paper 8678, NBER and Working Paper). Durham: Duke University.

Gramm, P., & Solon, M. (2013, August 12). The Clinton-Era Roots of the Financial Crisis. *Wall Street Journal.*

Granger, C. W. J. (1981). Some Properties of Time Series Data and Their Use in Econometric Model Specification. *Journal of Econometrics, 16,* 121–130.

Granger, C. W. J., & Joyeux, R. (1981). An Introduction to Long-Memory Time Series and Fractional Differencing. *Journal of Time Series Analysis, 1,* 15–30.

Granger, C.W. J., & Yoon, G. (2002). *Hidden Cointegration.* Presented at *Royal Economic Society,* 92, Annual Conference.

Grant, J. (1996). *The Trouble With Prosperity: The Loss of Fear, the Rise of Speculation, and the Risk.* New York: Times Books (Random House).

Grant, J. (2008). *Mr. Market Miscalculates: The Bubble Years and Beyond.* Mount Jackson: Axios Press.

Grant, J. (2014). *The Forgotten Depression –1921: The Crash That Cured Itself.* New York: Simon & Schuster.

Grant, J. (2016, September 10). Hostage to a Bull Market. *Wall Street Journal.*

Grant, S., & Quiggin, J. (2001). *The Risk Premium for Equity Explanations and Implications* (Working Paper no. 2001-89). School of Economics, Australian National University.

Grantham, J. (2014, May 5). Jeremy Grantham Remains Bullish on Stocks. *Barron's.*

Granville, J. E. (1963). *Granville's New Key to Stock Market Profits.* Englewood Cliffs: Prentice-Hall.

Granville, K. (2017, June 15). A President at War with the Fed, 5 Decades Back. *New York Times.*

Grassberger, P., & Procaccia, I. (1983a). Characterization of Strange Attractors. *Physical Review Letters, 50*(5), 346.

Grassberger, P., & Procaccia, I. (1983b). Measuring the Strangeness of Strange Attractors. *Physica D, 9,* 189.

Gray, W. R., & Vogel, J. R. (2016). *Quantitative Momentum*. Hoboken: Wiley.

Greene, W. H. (2003). *Econometric Analysis* (5th ed.). Upper Saddle River: Prentice Hall.

Greene, M., & Fielitz, B. (1977). Long-Term Dependence in Common Stock Returns. *Journal of Financial Economics, 4*, 339–349.

Greenspan, A. (1999, August 27). New Challenges for Monetary Policy. Presented at the FRB Kansas, *Jackson Hole Symposium*.

Greenspan, A. (2004). Risk and Uncertainty in Monetary Policy. *American Economic Review, 94*(2), 33–40.

Greenspan, A. (2007). *The Age of Turbulence: Adventures in a New World*. New York: Penguin.

Greenspan, A. (2008, March 16). We Will Never Have a Perfect Model of Risk. *Financial Times*.

Greenspan, A. (2009a, March 11). The Fed Didn't Cause the Housing Bubble. *Wall Street Journal*.

Greenspan, A. (2009b, March 27). We Need a Better Cushion Against Risk. *Financial Times*.

Greenspan, A. (2013). *The Map and the Territory: Risk, Human Nature, and the Future of Forecasting*. New York: Penguin.

Greenwald, B. C. N., Kahn, J., Sonkin, P. D., & van Biema, M. (2001). *Value Investing: From Graham to Buffett and Beyond*. New York: Wiley (Paperback edition).

Greenwood, R., & Nagel, S. (2008). *Inexperienced Investors and Bubbles*. Available at http://faculty-gsb.stanford.edu/nagel/pdfs/Mfage.pdf

Gresnigt, F., Kole, E., & Franses, P. H. (2015). Interpreting Financial Market Crashes as Earthquakes: A New Early Warning System for Medium Term Crashes. *Journal of Banking & Finance, 56*, 123.

Griffin, G. E. (2002). *The Creature from Jekyll Island: A Second Look at the Federal Reserve* (4th ed.). Westlake Village: American Media.

Gromb, D., & Vayanos, D. (2010). Limits of Arbitrage. *Annual Review of Financial Economics, 2*, 251–275.

Gross, D. (2002). The Fiber-Optic Network Bubble: Back to the Future. *Milken Institute Review* (First Quarter).

Grossman, S. J., & Stiglitz, J. E. (1980). On the Impossibility of Informationally Efficient Markets. *American Economic Review, 70*(3), 393–408.

Grullon, G., & Michaely, R. (2002). Dividends, Share Repurchases, and the Substitution Hypothesis. *Journal of Finance, 57*, 1649.

Guerrieri, V., & Kondor, P. (2012). Fund Managers, Career Concerns, and Asset Price volatility. *American Economic Review, 102*(5), 1986–2017.

Guha, K. (2008, May 16). Troubled by Bubbles. *Financial Times*.

Guiso, L., Sapienza, P., & Zingales, L. (2008). Trusting the Stock Market. *Journal of Finance, 63*(6), 2557–2600.

Gujarati, D. N. (1995). *Basic Econometrics* (3rd (international) ed.). New York: McGraw-Hill.

Gujarati, D. N. (2003). *Basic Econometrics* (4th (international) ed.). New York: McGraw-Hill.

Gulko, L. (2005). Efficient Irrational Markets. *Journal of Portfolio Management, 31*(2), 64–72.

Gurkaynak, R. S. (2005). *Econometric Tests of Asset Price Bubbles: Taking Stock*. Washington, DC: Federal Reserve.

Gutierrez, L. (2013). Speculative Bubbles in Agricultural Commodity Markets. *European Review of Agricultural Economics, 40*(2), 217–238.

Haacke, C. (2004). *Frenzy: Bubbles, Busts and How to Come Out Ahead.* New York: Palgrave Macmillan.

Hagerman, R. L. (1978). More Evidence on the Distribution of Security Returns. *Journal of Finance, 33*(4), 1213–1221.

Hagerty, J. R., Simon, R., & Paletta, D. (2008, September 8). U.S. Seizes Mortgage Giants. *Wall Street Journal.*

Haidt, J. (2001). The Emotional Dog and Its Rational Tail. *Psychological Review, 108.*

Halbfinger, D. M., & Powell, M. (2010, August 24). As HUD Chief, Cuomo Earns A Mixed Score. *New York Times.*

Hale, D. (2007, July 31). The Best Economy Ever. *Wall Street Journal.*

Hall, R. E. (2001). Struggling to Understand the Stock Market. *American Economic Review, 91*(2), 1–11.

Hall, S. G., Psaradakis, Z., & Sola, M. (1999). Detecting Periodically Collapsing Bubbles: A Markov-Switching Unit Root Test. *Journal of Applied Econometrics, 14,* 143–154.

Hammond, P. B., Jr., Leibowitz, M. L., & Siegel, L. B. (2011). *Rethinking the Equity Risk Premium.* Charlottsville: CFA Institute.

Hamilton, J. D. (1986). On Testing for Self-Fulfilling Speculative Price Bubbles. *International Economic Review, 27,* 545–552.

Hamilton, J. D. (1994). *Time Series Analysis.* Princeton: Princeton University Press.

Hamilton, J. D., & Lin, G. (1996). Stock Market Volatility and the Business Cycle. *Journal of Applied Econometrics, 11*(5), 573–593.

Hamilton, J. D., & Whiteman, C. H. (1985). The Observable Implications of Self-Fulfilling Expectations. *Journal of Monetary Economics, 16,* 353–373.

Hamilton, J. D., & Wu, J. C. (2012). The Effectiveness of Alternative Monetary Policy Tools in a Zero Lower Bound Environment. *Journal of Money, Credit and Banking, 44,* 3–46.

Hansell, S. (2008, September 18). How Wall Street Lied to Its Computers. *New York Times.*

Hansen, B. E. (1992). Testing for Parameter Instability in Linear Models. *Journal of Policy Modeling, 14*(4), 517–533.

Hansen, L. P., & Renault, E. (2009). Pricing Kernels and Stochastic Discount Factors. *Encyclopedia of Quantitative Finance,* University of Chicago.

Harcourt, G. C. (2007). *What Is the Cambridge Approach to Economics?,* in Heim and Truger, eds. (2007).

Hardouvelis, G. (1988). Evidence on Stock Market Speculative Bubbles: Japan, the United States, and Great Britain. *Federal Reserve Bank of New York Quarterly Review* (Summer).

Hargreaves, C. P. (1994). A Review of Methods of Estimating Cointegration Relationships. In C. P. Hargreaves (Ed.), *Nonstationary Time Series Analysis and Cointegration.* New York: Oxford University Press.

Harman, Y. S. (2000). *Bubbles, Fads, and the Psychology of Investors.* Unpublished Ph.D. Dissertation, Florida State University.

Harman, Y. S., & Zuehlke, T. W. (2004). Duration Dependence Testing for Speculative Bubbles. *Journal of Economics and Finance, 28*(2), 147–154.

Harrison, P. (1998). Similarities in the Distribution of Stock Market Price Changes Between the Eighteenth and Twentieth Centuries. *Journal of Business, 71*(1), 55–79.

Harrison, M. J., & Kreps, D. (1978). Speculative Investor Behavior in a Stock Market with Heterogeneous Expectations. *Quarterly Journal of Economics, 89*, 519–542.

Hartcher, P. (2006). *Bubble Man.* New York: W. W. Norton.

Haruvy, E., Lahav, Y., & Noussair, C. N. (2007). Traders' Expectations in Asset Markets: Experimental Evidence. *American Economic Review, 97*(5), 1901–1920.

Hassett, K. A. (2002). *Bubbleology: The New Science of Stock Market Winners and Losers.* New York: Crown.

Hassler, U. (2016). *Stochastic Processes and Calculus: An Elementary Introduction with Applications.* Heidelberg: Springer.

Haug, M., & Hirschey, M. (2006). The January Effect. *Financial Analysts Journal, 62*(5), 78–88.

Haug, E. S., & Taleb, N. N. (2009). *Why We Have Never Used the Black-Scholes-Merton Option Pricing Formula.* (Fifth Version) (26 February). Available at SSRN: https://ssrn.com/abstract=1012075

Hayford, M. D., & Malliaris, A. G. (2005). *Is the Federal Reserve Stock Market Bubble-Neutral?,* in Malliaris (2005).

Heim, E., & Truger, A. (Eds.). (2007). *Money, Distribution and Economic Policy: Alternatives to Orthodox Macroeconomics.* Cheltenham: Edward Elgar.

Heller, R. (2017). Monetary Mischief and the Debt Trap. *Cato Journal, 37*(2), 247–261.

Hendricks, V. F. (2015). *Bubble Studies: The Brass Tacks.* London: Bloomsbury. *Leading Frontier Research in the Humanities,* (September).

Hendricks, V. F., & Rendsvig, R. K. (2016). The Philosophy of Distributed Information. In L. Floridi (Ed.), *The Routledge Handbook of Philosophy of Information.* New York: Routledge.

Hendry, D. F. (1995). *Dynamic Econometrics.* Oxford: Oxford University Press.

Hendry, D., & Mizon, G. E. (2013). *Unpredictability in Economic Analysis, Econometric Modeling and Forecasting* (Working Paper No. 2013-W04). Oxford.

Henker, J., & Owen, S. A. (2008). Bursting Bubbles: Linking Experimental Financial Market Results to Field Market Data. *Journal of Behavioral Finance, 9*(1), 5–14.

Henriques, D. B. (2008, March 28). Odd Crop Prices Defy Economics. *New York Times.*

Henriques, D. B. (2017). *Anatomy of a Crash: A First-Class Catastrophe.* New York: Holt.

Henriques, D. B., & Kouwe, Z. (2008, December 11). Prominent Trader Accused of Defrauding Clients. *New York Times.*

Hens, T., & Schenk-Hoppé, K. R. (2001). *Evolution of Portfolio Rules in Incomplete Markets* (Working Paper Series ISSN 1424-0459, No. 74). Zurich: University of Zurich. Available at http://www.iew.unizh.ch/wp/iewwp074.pdf

Hensel, C. R., Sick, G. A., & Ziemba, W. T. (2000). A Long Term Examination of the Turn-of-the-Month Effect in the S&P 500. In D. B. Keim & W. T. Ziemba (Eds.), *Security Market Imperfections in Worldwide Equity Markets.* Cambridge: Cambridge University Press.

Hensel, C. R., & Ziemba, W. T. (2000). Anticipation of the January Small Firm Effect in the US Futures Markets. In D. B. Keim & W. T. Ziemba (Eds.), *Security Market Imperfections in Worldwide Equity Markets.* New York: Cambridge University Press.

Herrera, S., & Perry, G. E. (2003). *Tropical Bubbles: Asset Prices in Latin America, 1980–2001,* in Hunter et al. (2003 [2005]).

Herzog, B. (2015). An Econophysics Model of Financial Bubbles. *Natural Science, 7,* 55–63.

Heston, S. L. (1993). A Closed-Form Solution for Options with Stochastic Volatility with Applications to Bond and Currency Options. *Review of Financial Studies, 6*(2), 327–343.

Heston, S. I., Loewenstein, M., & Willard, G. A. (2007). Options and Bubbles. *Review of Financial Studies, 20*(2), 359–390.

Hilborn, R. C. (2000). *Chaos and Nonlinear Dynamics: An Introduction for Scientists and Engineers* (2nd ed.). Oxford/New York: Oxford University Press.

Hillier, B. (1997). *The Economics of Asymmetric Information.* New York: St. Martin's Press.

Hilsenrath, J. E. (2004, October 18). As Two Economists Debate Markets, The Tide Shifts. *Wall Street Journal.*

Hilsenrath, J. E. (2009, December 2). Fed Debates New Role: Bubble Fighter. *Wall Street Journal.*

Hilsenrath, J. E. (2010a, July 26). Deflation Defies Expectations – And Solutions. *Wall Street Journal.*

Hilsenrath, J. E. (2010b, June 18). Fed Deputy Says Rules Changed Too Slowly. *Wall Street Journal.*

Hilsenrath, J. E. (2012a, December 31). Fed's Computer Models Pose Problems. *Wall Street Journal.*

Hilsenrath, J. E. (2012b, September 28). How Bernanke Pulled the Fed His Way. *Wall Street Journal.*

Hilsenrath, J. E. (2013, December 17). Meltdown Averted, Bernanke Struggled to Stoke Growth. *Wall Street Journal.*

Hilsenrath, J. E. (2017, September 23). What We Know About Financial Bubbles: Bubbles Aren't Necessarily Bad Things. *Wall Street Journal.*

Hilsenrath, J. E., & Barta, P. (2005, June 16). Amid Low Rates, Home Prices Rise Across the Global Village. *Wall Street Journal.*

Hilsenrath, J., & Blackstone, B. (2012, December 11). Inside the Risky Bets of Central Banks. *Wall Street Journal.*

Hilsenrath, J. E., & Fujikawa, M. (2011, March 1). Japan's Bernanke Hits Out at His Critics in the West. *Wall Street Journal.*

Hilsenrath, J. E., & Harrison, D. (2015, December 12). Fed's Unsolved Puzzle: How to Deflate Bubbles. *Wall Street Journal.*

Hilsenrath, J. E., Solomon, D., & Paletta, D. (2008, November 10). Paulson, Bernanke Strained for Consensus in Bailout. *Wall Street Journal.*

Himmelberg, C., Mayer, C., & Sinai, T. (2005). Assessing High House Prices: Bubbles, Fundamentals and Misperceptions. *Journal of Economic Perspectives, 19*(4), 67–92.

Hirshleifer, D., & Shumway, T. (2003). Good Day Sunshine: Stock Returns and the Weather. *Journal of Finance, 58*(3), 1009–1032.

Hobusch, E., Nikolova, I., Mironenko, A., Edilashvili, T., & Zulfiquar, M. (2014/15). *Interest Rate Policy Changes as a Trigger of a Financial Crisis* (WS 2014/15). Rhine-Waal University Faculty of Society and Economics.

Hodrick, L. S., & Moulton, P. C. (2009). Liquidity: Considerations of a Portfolio Manager. *Financial Management, 38*(1), 59–74.

Holmes, S. A. (1999, September 30). Fannie Mae Eases Credit to Aid Mortgage Lending. *New York Times.*

Homm, U., & Breitung, J. (2012). Testing for Speculative Bubbles in Stock Markets: A Comparison of Alternative Methods. *Journal of Financial Econometrics, 10*(1), 198–231.

Hong, H., & Sraer, D. (2012). *Quiet Bubbles* (NBER Working Paper 18547). Available at www.nber.org/papers/w18547

Hong, H., & Stein, J. C. (2007). Disagreement and the Stock Market. *Journal of Economic Perspectives, 21*(2), 109–128.

Hong, H., Kubik, J. D., & Solomon, A. (2000). Security Analysts' Career Concerns and Herding of Earnings Forecasts. *RAND Journal of Economics, 31*(1), 121–144.

Hong, H., Scheinkman, J. A., & Xiong, W. (2006). Asset Float and Speculative Bubbles. *Journal of Finance, LXI*(3), 1073–1117.

Hoshi, T., & Kashyap, A. (1999). The Japanese Banking Crisis: Where Did It Come From and How Will It End? *NBER Macroeconomics Annual.* Cambridge, MA: MIT Press and in Evanoff et al. (2012).

Hotz, R L. (2008, April 18). Testosterone May Fuel Stock-Market Success, or Make Traders Tipsy. *Wall Street Journal.*

Hou, K., Xue, C., & Zhang, L. (2015). Digesting Anomalies: An Investment Approach. *Review of Financial Studies, 28*(3), 650–705.

Housel, M. (2010, September 28). A Tale of Two Bubbles. Available at www.fool.com/investing/general.

Howe, R. H. (1915). *The Evolution of Banking: A Study of the Development of the Credit System.* Chicago: C. H. Kerr & Company.

Hsieh, D. (1991). Chaos and Nonlinear Dynamics: Application to Financial Markets. *Journal of Finance, 46*, 1839–1877.

Huang, K. X. D., & Werner, J. (2000). Asset Price Bubbles in Arrow-Debreu and Sequential Equilibrium. *Economic Theory, 15*, 253–278.

Huang, D., Jiang, F., Tu, J., & Zhou, G. (2015). Investor Sentiment Aligned: A Powerful Predictor of Stock Returns. *Review of Financial Studies, 28*(3), 791–837.

Huddart, S., Lang, M., & Yetman, M. (2005). *Psychological Factors, Stock Price Paths, and Trading Volume.* Working paper, Pennsylvania State University. Available at http://www.smeal.psu.edu/faculty/huddart/Papers/HuLaYe.pdf

Hughes, R. (2011). *Rome: A Cultural and Personal History.* New York: Random House/Vintage.

Hulbert, M. (2002, December 1). 16-Year Slump? If So, Blame It on the Boomers. *New York Times.*

Hulbert, M. (2009, April 26). 25 Years to Bounce Back? Try 4 ½. *New York Times.*

Hulbert, M. (2016, October 10). Why Large Stocks Wake Up at This Time of Year. *Wall Street Journal.*

Hulbert, M. (2017, January 9). Sorry, the 'January Barometer' Is a Market Myth. *Wall Street Journal.*

Hull, J. (2003). *Options, Futures and Other Derivative Securities* (5th ed.). Upper Saddle River: Prentice-Hall.

Hunter, W. C., Kaufman, G. G., & Pomerleano, M. (Eds.). (2003). *Asset Price Bubbles: The Implications for Monetary, Regulatory, and International Policies.* Cambridge, MA: MIT Press (Paperback edition, 2005).

Hussam, R. N., Porter, D., & Smith, V. L. (2008). Thar She Blows: Can Bubbles Be Rekindled with Experienced Subjects? *American Economic Review, 98*(3), 924–937.

Huszar, A. (2013, November 12). Confessions of a Quantitative Easer. *Wall Street Journal.*

Hyerczyk, J. A. (1998). *Pattern, Price and Time: Using Gann Theory in Trading Systems.* New York: Wiley.

Ibbotson, R. G. (2004). *Stocks, Bonds, Bills, and Inflation.* Chicago: Ibbotson Associates.

Ibbotson, R. G., & Chen, P. (2003). Long-Run Stock Returns: Participating in the Real Economy. *Financial Analysts Journal, 59*(1), 88–98.

Ijiri, Y., & Simon, H. A. (1974). Interpretations of Departures from the Pareto Curve Firm-Size Distributions. *Journal of Political Economy, 82,* 315–331.

International Monetary Fund [IMF]. (2003). When Bubbles Burst. *World Economic Report.* Washington, DC: IMF.

Ip, G. (2004, November 18). Fed Chief's Style: Devour the Data, Beware of Dogma. *Wall Street Journal.*

Ip, G. (2005a, June 9). In Treating U.S. After Bubble, Fed Helped Create New Threats. *Wall Street Journal.*

Ip, G. (2005b, December 7). Long Study of Great Depression Has Shaped Bernanke's Views. *Wall Street Journal.*

Ip, G. (2007, August 30). Bernanke Breaks Greenspan Mold. *Wall Street Journal.*

Ip, G. (2008, April 8). His Legacy Tarnished, Greenspan Goes on Defensive. *Wall Street Journal.*

Ip, G., & Hilsenrath, J. E. (2007, August 7). How Credit Got So Easy and Why It's Tightening. *Wall Street Journal.*

Ip, G., Hagerty, J. R., & Karp, J. (2008, March 19). Housing Bust Fuels Blame Game. *Wall Street Journal.*

Irwin, N. (2014, July 8). From Stocks to Farmland, All's Booming or Bubbling. *New York Times.*

Isenberg, C. (1992). *The Science of Soap Films and Soap Bubbles.* New York: Dover.

Ito, T., & Iwaisako, T. (1996). *Explaining Asset Bubbles in Japan.* Bank of Japan, *Monetary and Economic Studies,* 14 (July), and Working Paper No. 5358. NBER. org.

Jacobs, B. I. (1999). *Capital Ideas and Market Realities: Option Replication, Investor Behavior, and Stock Market Crashes.* Oxford: Blackwell.

Jacobs, L. R., & King, D. S. (2016). *Fed Power: How Finance Wins.* New York: Oxford University Press.

Jacobsen, B., & Bouman, S. (2002). The Halloween Indicator, 'Sell in May and Go Away' Another Puzzle. *American Economic Review, 92*(5), 1618–1635.

Jagannathan, R., McGrattan, E. R., & Scherbina, A. (2000). The Declining U.S. Equity Premium. *Federal Reserve Bank Quarterly Review, 24*(4), 3–19.

Jain A., Jain, P. K., McInish, T. H., & McKenzie, M. (2013). Worldwide Reach of Short-Selling Regulations. *Journal of Financial Economics, 109*(1), 177–197.

Janszen, E. (2008, February). The Next Bubble: Priming the Markets for Tomorrow's Big Crash. *Harper's Magazine.*

Jaroncinski, M., & Smets, F. R. (2008, July/August). House Prices and the Stance of Monetary Policy. *Review,* Federal Reserve Bank of St. Louis.

Jarrow, R. A. (1992). Market Manipulation, Bubbles, Corners, and Short-Squeezes. *Journal of Financial and Quantitative Analysis, 27*(3), 311–336.

Jarrow, R. A., Protter, P., & Shimbo, K. (2010). Asset Price Bubbles in Incomplete Markets. *Mathematical Finance, 20*(2), 145–185.

Jarrow, R. A., Kchia, Y., & Protter, P. (2011). How to Detect an Asset Bubble. *SIAM Journal on Financial Mathematics, 2*(1), 839–865.

Jegadeesh, N. (1990). Evidence of Predictable Behavior of Security Returns. *Journal of Finance, 45*(3), 81–898.

Jegadeesh, N., & Titman, S. (1993). Returns to Buying Winners and Selling Losers: Implications for Stock Market Efficiency. *Journal of Fiinance, 48*(1), 65–91.

Jegadeesh, N., & Titman, S. (2001). Profitability of Momentum Strategies: An Evaluation of Alternative Explanations. *Journal of Finance, 56*(2), 699–720.

Jenkins, H. W., Jr. (2010, December 22). Next, an Aircraft Bubble? *Wall Street Journal.*

Jensen, M. C. (1968). The Performance of Mutual Funds in the Period 1945–1964. *Journal of Finance, 23*(2), 389–416.

Jensen, M. C. (1972). *Studies in the Theory of Capital Markets.* New York: Praeger.

Jensen, M. C. (1978). Some Anomalous Evidence Regarding Market Efficiency. *Journal of Financial Economics, 6*(2–3), 95–101.

Johansen, S. (1991). Estimation and Hypothesis Testing of Cointegration Vectors in Gaussian Vector Autoregression Models. *Econometrica, 59*(6), 1551–1580.

Johansen, A., & Sornette, D. (1998). Stock Market Crashes Are Outliers. *European Physical Journal B, 1,* 141–143.

Johansen, A., & Sornette, D. (1999a). Critical Crashes. *Risk, 12*(1), 91–94.

Johansen, A., & Sornette, D. (1999b). *Log-Periodic Power Law Bubbles in Latin-American and Asian Markets and Correlated Anti-Bubbles in Western Stock Markets: An Empirical Study* (Economics Working Paper). St. Louis: Washington University.

Johansen, A., & Sornette, D. (1999c). Modeling the Stock Market Prior to large Crashes. *European Physics Journal B, 9,* 167–174.

Johansen, A., & Sornette, D. (1999d). Financial 'Anti-Bubbles': Log-Periodicity in Gold and Nikkei Collapses. *International Journal of Modern Physics C, 10*(4), 563–575.

Johnson, P. (1991). *Modern Times: The World From the Twenties to the Nineties* (rev ed.). New York: Perennial Classics/HarperCollins.

Johnston, J., & DiNardo, J. (1997). *Econometric Methods* (4th ed.). New York: McGraw-Hill.

Jones, C., Kaul, G., & Lipson, M. (1994). Transactions, Volume, and Volatility. *Review of Financial Studies, 7*(4), 631–651.

Jordá, Ò., Schularick, M., & Taylor, A. M. (2014). *The Great Mortgaging: Housing Finance, Crises, and Business Cycles* (Working Paper 2014-23). Federal Reserve Bank of San Francisco. Available at http://www.frbsf.org/economic-research/publications/working-papers/wp2014-23.pdf

Jordá, Ò., Schularick, M., & Taylor, A. M. (2015). Leveraged Bubbles. *Journal of Monetary Economics, 76*(Supplement), S1–S20.

Jorion, P., & Goetzmann, W. N. (1999). Global Stock Markets in the Twentieth Century. *Journal of Finance, 54,* 953–980.

Joulin, A., Lefevre, A., Grunberg, D., & Bouchaud, J.-P. (2008). Stock Price Jumps: News and Volume Play a Minor Role. *Physics and Society.* Available at www.arxiv.org/abs/0803.1769 and *Wilmott,* September/October

Jovanovic, F., & Schinckus, C. (2017). *Econophysics and Financial Economics: An Emerging Dialog.* New York: Oxford University Press.

Juglar, C. (1966). *A Brief History of Panics and Their Periodical Occurrence in the United States* (3rd ed.). New York: A. M. Kelley. Reprint of the 1916 Edition Translated by DeC. W. Thom.

Justiniano, A., Primiceri, G. F., & Tambalotti, A. (2015, February). Credit Supply and the Housing Boom. *Federal Reserve Bank of New York Staff Reports,* no. 709.

Kahneman, D. (2013). *Thinking, Fast and Slow.* New York: Farrar, Straus and Giroux.

Kahneman, D., & Tversky, A. (1979). Prospect Theory: An Analysis of Decision Under Risk. *Econometrica, 47,* 263–291.

Kahneman, D., & Tversky, A. (2000). *Choices, Values and Frames.* Cambridge: Cambridge University Press.

Kaizoji, T., & Sornette, D. (2008). *Market Bubbles and Crashes* (MPRA Paper 15204). University Library Munich. Available at http://arxiv.org/pdf/0812.2449

Kamarck, A. M. (2001). *Economics for the Twenty-First Century.* Aldershot: Ashgate.

Kaminska, I. (2012, July 3). The Base Money Confusion. *FT Alphaville.*

Kaminsky, G. L., & Reinhart, C. (2000). On Crises, Contagion, and Confusion. *Journal of International Economics, 51*(1), 145–168.

Kaminsky, G. L., Reinhart, C., & Végh, C. A. (2003). The Unholy Trinity of Financial Contagion. *Journal of Economic Perspectives, 17*(4), 51–74.

Kamstra, M. L., Kramer, L., & Levi, M. (2003). Winter Blues: A SAD Stock Market Cycle. *American Economic Review, 93*(1), 324–333.

Kantchev, G., Whittall, C., & Inada, M. (2016, August 8). Are Negative Rates Backfiring? Here's Some Early Evidence. *Wall Street Journal.*

Kantz, H., & Schreiber, T. (2004). *Nonlinear Times Series Analysis* (2nd ed.). Cambridge: Cambridge University Press.

Kaplan, D. A. (2011, July 25). Don't Call It The Next Tech Bubble – Yet. *Fortune, 164*(2).

Kaplanski, G., Levy, H., Veld, C., & Veld-Merkoulova, Y. (2015). Do Happy People Make Optimistic Investors? *Journal of Financial and Quantitative Analysis, 50*(1–2), 145–168.

Karpoff, J. M. (1987). The Relation Between Price Changes and Trading Volume: A Survey. *Journal of Financial and Quantitative Analysis, 22,* 109–126.

Kaufman, H. (2009, October 10). The Real Threat to Fed Independence. *Wall Street Journal.*

Keay, J. (2006). *The Spice Route: A History.* Berkeley: University of California Press.

Keen, S. (1995). Finance and Economic Breakdown: Modelling Minsky's Financial Instability Hypothesis. *Journal of Post Keynesian Economics, 174*(4), 607.

Keim, D. B., & Stambaugh, R. F. (1986). Predicting Returns in the Bond and Stock Markets. *Journal of Financial Economics, 17*(2), 357–390.

Keim, D. B., & Ziemba, W. T. (Eds.). (2000). *Security Market Imperfections in Worldwide Equity Markets.* Cambridge: Cambridge University Press.

Kelly, K. (2008a, May 29). Bear Stearns Neared Collapse Twice in Frenzied Final Week. *Wall Street Journal.*

Kelly, K. (2008b, May 28). Fear, Rumors Touched Off Fatal Run on Bear Stearns. *Wall Street Journal.*

Kelly, K. (2008c, May 27). Lost Opportunities Haunt Final Days of Bear Stearns. *Wall Street Journal.*

Kelly, K. (2009a, May 9). Inside the Fall of Bear Stearns. *Wall Street Journal.*

Kelly, K. (2009b). *Street Fighters: The Last 72 Hours of Bear Stearns, the Toughest Firm on Wall Street.* New York: Portfolio/Penguin.

Kelly, K., Ng, S., & Strasburg, J. (2008, March 13). In Dealing With Bear Stearns, Wall Street Plays Guardedly. *Wall Street Journal.*

Keloharju, M., Linnainmaa, J. T., & Nyberg, P. (2016). Return Seasonalities. *Journal of Finance, 71*(4), 1557–1590.

Kennedy, P. (2003, 2008). *A Guide to Econometrics* (6th ed.). Malden/Oxford: Blackwell.

Kenourgios, D., Samitas, A., & Paltalidis, N. (2011). Financial Crises and Stock Market Contagion in a Multivariate Time-Varying Asymmetric Framework. *Journal of International Financial Markets, Institutions & Money, 21*, 92–106.

Keuzenkamp, H. A. (2000). *Probability, Econometrics and Truth: The Methodology of Econometrics.* New York/Cambridge: Cambridge University Press.

Keynes, J. M. (1926). *The End of Laissez-Faire.* Amherst/New York: Prometheus (Paperback, 2004).

Keynes, J. M. (1936). *The General Theory of Employment, Interest, and Money.* London: Macmillan; and San Diego: Harcourt Brace 1964 Reprint.

Khandani, A. E., & Lo, A. W. (2007). *What Happened to the Quants in August 2007?* (Working Paper). MIT Sloan School of Management. Available at http://web.mit.edu/alo/www/

Kim, K. A., & Nofsinger, J. R. (2007). The Behavior of Japanese Individual Investors During Bull and Bear Markets. *Journal of Behavioral Finance, 8*(3), 138–153.

Kim, C.-J., Morley, J. C., & Nelson, C. R. (2004). Is There a Positive Relationship Between Stock Market Volatility and the Equity Premium? *Journal of Money, Credit and Banking, 36*(3), 339–360.

Kindleberger, C. (1987). Bubbles. In J. Eatwell, M. Milgate, & P. Newman (Eds.), *The New Palgrave: A Dictionary of Economics.* London: Macmillan.

Kindleberger, C. (1996 [1989]). *Manias, Panics, and Crashes: A History of Financial Crises* (3rd ed.). New York: Wiley. (2nd Ed., 1989).

Kindleberger, C., & Aliber, R. Z. (2011). *Manias, Panics, and Crashes: A History of Financial Crises* (6th ed.). Houndmills: Palgrave Macmillan.

King, M. (2016). *The End of Alchemy: Money, Banking and the Future of the Global Economy.* New York: W.W. Norton.

Kirkland, R. (2007, July 12). The Greatest Economic Boom Ever. *Fortune.*

Kiyotaki, N., & Moore, J. (1997). Credit Cycles. *Journal of Political Economy, 105*(2), 211–248.

Kleidon, A. W. (1986). Variance Bounds Tests and Stock Price Valuation Models. *Journal of Political Economy, 94,* 953–1001.

Klein, M. (2001). *Rainbow's End: The Crash of 1929.* New York: Oxford University Press.

Klingaman, W. K. (1989). *1929: The Year of the Great Crash.* New York: Harper & Row.

Knee, J. (2006). *The Accidental Investment Banker: Inside the Decade That Transformed Wall Street.* New York: Oxford University Press.

Knight, T. (2014). *Panic, Prosperity, and Progress: Five Centuries of History and the Markets.* Hoboken: Wiley.

Knoop, T. A. (2008). *Modern Financial Macroeconomics: Panics, Crashes, and Crises.* Oxford: Blackwell.

Kocherlakota, N. R. (1996). The Equity Premium: It's Still a Puzzle. *Journal of Economic Literature, 34*(1), 42–71.

Kocherlakota, N. R. (2009, April). *Bursting Bubbles: Consequences and Cures.* Federal Reserve Bank of Minneapolis and IMF Conference, Washington, DC.

Kodres, L., & Pritsker, M. (2002). A Rational Expectations Model of Financial Contagion. *Journal of Finance, 57*(2), 769–799.

Koedijk, K., & Slager, A. (2011). *Investment Beliefs: A Positive Approach to Institutional Investing.* Houndmills: Palgrave Macmillan.

Kohn, D. (2005). *Monetary Policy Perspectives on Risk Premiums in Financial Markets.* Washington, DC: Financial Market Risk Premiums Conference, Federal Reserve Board.

Koivu, M., Pennanen, T., & Ziemba, W. T. (2005). Cointegration Analysis of the Fed Model. *Finance Research Letters, 2,* 248–259.

Kolata, G. (Ed.). (2013). *The New York Times Book of Mathamatics.* New York: Sterling.

Koo, R. C. (2010). Lessons from Japan: Fighting a Balance Sheet Recession. *CFA Institute Conference Proceedings Quarterly, 27*(4), 28–39.

Krainer, J. (2003). House Price Bubbles. *Economic Letter* (#2003-06), Federal Reserve Bank of San Francisco.

Kräussl, R., Lehnert, T., & Martelin, N. (2016). Is There a Bubble in the Art Market? *Journal of Empirical Finance, 35,* 99–109.

Krishnamurthy, A., & Vissing-Jorgensen, A. (2013). *The Ins and Outs of LSAPs.* http://kansascityfed.org/publicat/sympos/2013/2013Krishnamurthy.pdf

Kritzman, M. (1994). About Serial Dependence. *Financial Analysts Journal, 50*(2), 19–22.

Krivelyova, A., & Robotti, C. (2003). *Playing the Field: Geomagnetic Storms and the Stock Market* (Working Paper 2003-5b). Federal Reserve Bank of Atlanta. Available at http://www.frbatlanta.org/filelegacydocs/wp0305b.pdf

Kroszner, R. S. (2003 [2005]). Asset Price Bubbles, Information, and Public Policy, in Hunter et al. (2003).

Kroszner, R. S. (2016, October 8). Sebastian Mallaby's Biography Shows That Alan Greenspan Foresaw the Housing Crisis. *Wall Street Journal.*

Krueger, A. B. (2005, April 28). Economists Try to Explain Why Bubbles Happen. *New York Times.*

Kruger, R. (2003). *All Under Heaven: A Complete History of China.* Chichester: Wiley.

Kuran, T., & Sunstein, C. R. (1999). Availability Cascades and Risk Regulation. *Stanford Law Review, 51*(4), 683–768.

Kurz, M. (1994). On the Structure and Diversity of Rational Beliefs. *Journal of Economic Theory, 4*(6), 877–900.

Kurz, M., Jin, H., & Motolese, M. (2005). Determinants of Stock Market Volatility and Risk Premia. *Annals of Finance, 1*(2), 109–147.

Kuttner, K. N. (2012). Monetary Policy and Asset Price Volatility, in Evanoff et al. (2012).

Lacker, J. M. (2012). Understanding the Interventionist Impulse of the Modern Central Bank. *Cato Journal, 32*(2), 247–253.

Lahart, J. (2007, August 18). In Time of Tumult, Obscure Economist Gains Currency. *Wall Street Journal.*

Lahart, J. (2008a, May 16). Bernanke's Bubble Laboratory. *Wall Street Journal.*

Lahart, J. (2008b, October 17). Fed Rethinks Stance on Popping Bubbles. *Wall Street Journal.*

Lahart, J. (2008c, May 27). High Oil Prices Spur Thoughts About Bubbles, But This Might Be Misguided. *Wall Street Journal.*

Laherrère, J. & Sornette, D. (1998). Stretched Exponential Distributions in Nature and Economy: 'Fat Tails' with Characteristic Scales. *European Physical Journal, B2,* 525–539. Available at http://xxx.lanl.gov/abs/cond-mat/9801293

Laing, J. R. (1991, July 29). Efficient Chaos or, Things They Never Taught in Business School. *Barron's.*

Laing, J. R. (2003, January 20). The Debt Bomb. *Barron's.*

Laing, J. R. (2008, July 14). Botton's Up: This Real-Estate Rout May Be Short-Lived *Barron's*.

Laing, J. R. (2013, June 24). Where Will It End? *Barron's*.

Laise, E. (2010, March 13). The Professor Who Chases Financial Bubbles. *Wall Street Journal*.

Lakonishok, J., Shleifer, A., & Vishny, R. W. (1992). The Impact of Institutional Trading on Stock Prices. *Journal of Financial Economics, 32*, 23–44.

Lansing, K. J. (2010a). Rational and Near-Rational Bubbles Without Drift. *Economic Journal, 120*(549), 1149–1174.

Lansing, K. J. (2010b). Some New Variance Bounds for Asset Prices: A Comment. *Federal Reserve Bank of San Francisco, 29*.

Laperriere, A. (2008, April 3). Questions for the Fed. *Wall Street Journal*.

Lattman, P. (2011, May 12). Howard Marks's Missives, Now for the Masses. *New York Times*.

Lattman, P., Smith, R., & Strasburg, J. (2008, March 14). Carlyle Fund in Free Fall as Its Banks Get Nervous. *Wall Street Journal*.

Lauricella, T. (2008, December 11). The Stock Picker's Defeat. *Wall Street Journal*.

Lauricella, T. (2009, July 10). Failure of a Fail-Safe Strategy Sends Investors Scrambling. *Wall Street Journal*.

Lauricella, T., & Patterson, S. (2010, August 6). Legacy of the 'Flash Crash': Enduring Worries of Repeat. *Wall Street Journal*.

Lauricella, T., & Strasburg, J. (2010, September 2). SEC Probes Canceled Trades. *Wall Street Journal*.

Le Bon, G. (1895). *The Crowd: A Study of the Popular Mind*. Available at digireads.com, 2009 ed.

Leamer, E. E. (2007). Housing Is the Business Cycle. In *Housing, Housing Finance, and Monetary Policy*. Kansas City: Federal Reserve Bank of Kansas City.

LeBaron, B. (1994). Chaos and Nonlinear Forecastability in Economics and Finance. *Philosophical Transactions of the Royal Society of London. Series A, 348*. Available at http://129.3.20.41/eps/fin/papers/9411/9411001.pdf

LeBor, A. (2013). *Tower of Basel: The Shadowy History of the Secret Bank that Runs the World*. New York: PublicAffairs/Perseus.

LeDoux, J. E. (2004). *The Emotional Brain*. London: Orion Books (Paperback edition).

Lee, I. H. (1998a). Market Crashes and Informational Avalanches. *Review of Economic Studies, 65*, 741–759.

Lee, R. (1998b). *What Is an Exchange?* New York: Oxford University Press.

Lee, T. (2004). *Why the Markets Went Crazy*. New York: Palgrave Macmillan.

Lee, C. M. C., & Swaminathan, B. (2000). Price Momentum and Trading Volume. *Journal of Finance, LV*(5), 2017–2069.

Lefèvre, E. (1923). *Reminiscences of a Stock Operator*. New York: George H. Doran. Reprinted 1980 by Fraser Publishing, Burlington VT.

Lehmann, B. N. (1990). Fads, Martingales, and Market Efficiency. *Quarterly Journal of Economics, 105*(1), 1–28.

Lehrer, J. (2009). *How We Decide*. Boston: Houghton Mifflin Harcourt.

Lei, V., Noussair, C. N., & Plott, C. R. (2001). Nonspeculative Bubbles in Experimental Asset Markets: Lack of Common Knowledge of Rationality vs. Actual Irrationality. *Econometrica, 69*(4), 831–859.

Leland, H. E., & Rubinstein, M. (1988). Comments on the Market Crash: Six Months After. *Journal of Economic Perspectives, 2*(3), 45–50.

Leonhardt, D. (2008, September 30). Lessons From a Crisis: When Trust Vanishes, Worry. *New York Times.*

Leonhardt, D. (2010, January 6). If Fed Missed This Bubble, Will It See a New One? *New York Times.*

LeRoy, S. F. (2004). Rational Exuberance. *Journal of Economic Literature, 42*(3), 783–804.

LeRoy, S. F., & Parke, W. R. (1992). Stock Price Volatility: Tests Based on the Geometric Random Walk. *American Economic Review, 82*, 981–992.

LeRoy, S. F., & Porter, R. D. (1981). The Present Value Relation: Tests Based on Implied Variance Bonds. *Econometrica, 64*, 555–574.

Levisohn, B. (2017, October 16). Black Monday 2.0: The Next Machine-Driven Meltdown. *Barron's.*

Levy, A. (2006, March). Mapping the Traders' Brain. *Bloomberg Markets Magazine.* Available at http://www-psych.stanford.edu/~span/Press/neurofinance.pdf

Lewis, M. (2007, August 26). In Nature's Casino. *New York Times.*

Lewis, M. (2010). *The Big Short: Inside the Doomsday Machine.* New York: W. W. Norton.

Lhabitant, F.-S., & Gregoriou, G. N. (Eds.). (2008). *Stock Market Liquidity: Implications for Market Microstructure and Asset Pricing.* Hoboken: Wiley.

Li, W. (1999). *Zipf's Law Web Site.* Available at http://linkage.rockefeller.edu/wli/zipf/

Li, D. (2000). On Default Correlation: A Copula Function Approach. *Journal of Fixed Income, 9*(4), 43–54.

Li, X., Sullivan, R. N., & Garcia-Feijóo, L. (2016). The Low-Volatility Anomaly: Market Evidence on Systematic Risk vs. Mispricing. *Financial Analysts Journal, 72*(1), 36–47.

Lichtenstein, S., & Slovic, P. (1973). Response Induced Reversals of Preference in Gambling: An Extended Replication in Las Vegas. *Journal of Experimental Psychology, 101*(1), 16–20.

Lillo, F., & Mantegna, R. N. (2000). Symmetry Alterations of Ensemble Return Distribution in Crash and Rally Days of Financial Markets. *European Physical Journal B, 15*, 603–606.

Lim, K. G. (2015). *Financial Valuation and Econometrics* (2nd ed.). Singapore: World Scientific.

Limpert, E., Stahel, W. A., & Abbt, M. (2001). Lognormal Distributions Across the Sciences: Keys and Clues. *Bioscience, 51*(5), 341–352.

Lintner, J. (1965). The Valuation of Risk Assets and the Selection of Risk Investments in Stock Portfolios and Capital Budgets. *Review of Economic Statistics, 47*, 13–37.

Liu, T., Granger, C. W. J., & Heller, P. (1992). Using the Correlation Exponent to Decide Whether an Economic Time Series Is Chaotic. *Journal of Applied Econometrics, 7*(S1), S25–S39.

Livio, M. (2002). *The Golden Ratio.* New York: Random House/Broadway Books.

Lleo, S., & Ziemba, W. T. (2012). Stock Market Crashes in 2007–2009: Were We Able to Predict Them? *Quantitative Finance, 12*, 1161–1187.

Lleo, S., & Ziemba, W. T. (2015). Some Historical Perspectives on the Bond-Stock Yield Model for Crash Prediction Around the World. *International Journal of Forecasting, 31*, 399–425.

Lleo, S., & Ziemba, W. T. (2017). *Can Warren Buffett Forecast Equity Market Corrections?* Available at https://ssrn.com/abstract=2630068 or https://doi.org/10.2139/ssrn.2630068

Lo, A. W. (1991). Long-Term Memory in Stock Market Prices. *Econometrica, 59*, 1279–1313.

Lo, A. W. (2004). The Adaptive Markets Hypothesis. *Journal of Portfolio Management, 30*(5), 15–29.

Lo, A. W. (2012). Adaptive Markets and the New World Order. *Financial Analysts Journal, 68*(2), 18–29.

Lo, A. W. (2017). *Adaptive Markets: Financial Evolution at the Speed of Thought.* Princeton: Princeton University Press.

Lo, A. W., & Hasanhodzic, J. (2009). *The Heretics of Finance: Conversations with Leading Practitioners of Technical Analysis.* New York: Bloomberg Press.

Lo, A. W., & MacKinlay, A. C. (1999). *A Non-Random Walk Down Wall Street.* Princeton: Princeton University Press.

Lo, A. W., & Merton, R. C. (2009). Preface to the Annual Review of Financial Economics. In *Annual Review of Financial Economics* (Vol. 1). Palo Alto: Annual Reviews.

Lo, A. W., Mamaysky, H., & Wang, J. (2000). Foundations of Technical Analysis: Computational Algorithms, Statistical Inference, and Empirical Implementation. *Journal of Finance, 55*(4), 1705–1765.

Lobato, I. N., & Savin, N. E. (1998). Real and Spurious Long Memory Properties of Stock Market Data. *The Journal of Business and Economic Statistics, 16*, 261–268.

Lobato, I. N., & Velasco, C. (2000). Long Memory in Stock-Market Trading. *Journal of Business & Economic Statistics, 18*(4), 410–427.

Loewenstein, G. F. (2000). Emotions in Economic Theory and Economic Behavior. *American Economic Review, 90*(2), 426–432.

Loewenstein, M., & Willard, G. A. (2006). The Limits of Investor Behavior. *Journal of Finance, 61*(1), 231–258.

Loeys, J., & Panigirtzoglou, N. (2006). Are Alternatives the Next Bubble? *Journal of Alternative Investments, 9*(3), 54–76.

Lohr, S. (2008, November 5). In Modeling Risk, the Human Factor Was Left Out. *New York Times.*

Lohr, S. (2009, September 13). Wall Street's Math Wizards Forgot a Few Variables. *New York Times.*

Lorie, J. H., & Hamilton, M. T. (1973). *The Stock Market: Theories and Evidence.* Homewood: Richard D. Irwin.

Lovell, M. C. (1986, March). Tests of the Rational Expectations Hypothesis. *American Economic Review.*

Lowenstein, R. (2000). *When Genius Failed: The Rise and Fall of Long-Term Capital Management.* New York: Random House.

Lowenstein, R. (2004). *Origins of the Crash: The Great Bubble and Its Undoing.* New York: Penguin Group.

Lowenstein, R. (2008a, September 6). Long-Term Capital: It's a Short-Term Memory. *New York Times.*

Lowenstein, R. (2008b, April 27). Triple-A Failure: The Ratings Game. *New York Times.*

Lowenstein, R. (2016). *America's Bank: The Epic Struggle to Create the Federal Reserve.* New York: Penguin Paperback.

Lucchetti, A. (2007, October 16). After Crash, NYSE Got the Message(s). *Wall Street Journal*.

Lux, T. (1995). Herd Behavior, Bubbles and Crashes. *Economic Journal: The Journal of the Royal Economic Society, 105*, 881–896.

Lux, T., & Sornette, D. (2002). On Rational Bubbles and Fat Tails. *Journal of Money, Credit and Banking, 34*(3), 589–610.

Lybeck, J. A. (2011). *A Global History of the Financial Crash of 2007–10*. Cambridge: Cambridge University Press.

Lyons, J., & Hong, S. (2016, November 1). Series of Bubbles Rattles China. *Wall Street Journal*.

Lyons, J., & Inada, M. (2017, February 27). The World's Most Radical Experiment in Monetary Policy Isn't Working. *Wall Street Journal*.

Machina, M. J. (1987). *Choice Under Uncertainty. Journal of Economic Perspectives, 1*, 121–154.

Machlup, F. (1940). *Stock Market, Credit, and Capital Formation*. London: William Hodge and Company. Available at www.Mises.org

Mackay, C. (1841). *Extraordinary Popular Delusions and the Madness of Crowds* (1995th ed.). New York: Wiley.

MacKintosh, J. (2017, September 22). $2 Trillion Later, Does the Fed Even Know if Quantitative Easing Worked? *Wall Street Journal*.

Maddala, G. S. (2001). *Introduction to Econometrics* (3rd ed.). West Sussex: Wiley.

Maddala, G. S., & Kim, I. (1999). *Unit Roots, Cointegration, and Structural Change*. Cambridge: Cambridge University Press.

Maddison, A. (2003). *The World Economy: Historical Statistics*. Paris: OECD.

Madhavan, A. (2000). Market Microstructure: A Survey. *Journal of Financial Markets, 3*, 205–258.

Malinvaud, E. (1985). *The Theory of Unemployment Reconsidered* (2nd ed.). New York/ London: Blackwell.

Malkiel, B. G. (1999). *A Random Walk Down Wall Street*, 7th ed., 8th ed. (2003), 9th ed. (2007, 11th ed. (2015). New York: W.W. Norton

Malkiel, B. G. (2003). The Efficient Market Hypothesis and Its Critics. *Journal of Economic Perspectives, 17*(1), 59–82.

Mallaby, S. (2016). *The Man Who Knew: The Life and Times of Alan Greenspan*. New York: Penguin/Random House.

Mallaby, S. (2017, June 24). The Fed Should Surprise Us. *Wall Street Journal*.

Malliaris, A. G. (2005). *Economic Uncertainty, Instability and Asset Bubbles: Selected Essays*. Hackensack: World Scientific.

Malliaris, A. G., (2012). Asset Price Bubbles and Central Bank Policies, in Evanoff et al. (2012) ed.

Malliaris, A. G., & Urrutia, J. L. (1992). The International Crash of October 1987: Causality Tests. *Journal of Financial and Quantitative Analysis, 27*(3), 353–364.

Malpass, D. (2011, September 21). The Fed 'Twist' That Won't Dance. *Wall Street Journal*.

Malpass, D. (2015, January 22). The World's Monetary Dead End. *Wall Street Journal*.

Mandel, J. (1964). *The Statistical Analysis of Experimental Data*. New York: Dover.

Mandelbrot, B. (1960). The Pareto-Lévy Law and the Distribution of Income. *International Economic Review, 1*, 79–106.

Mandelbrot, B. (1964). The Variation of Certain Speculative Prices. In P. Cootner (Ed.), *The Random Character of Stock Prices*. Cambridge, MA: MIT Press.

Mandelbrot, B. (1972). Statistical Methodology for Non-Periodic Cycles: From Covariance to R/S Analysis. *Annals of Economic and Social Measurement, 1,* 259–290.

Mandelbrot, B., & Hudson, R. L. (2004). *The (Mis)Behavior of Markets: A Fractal View of Risk, Ruin, and Reward.* New York: Basic Books.

Manne, H. G. (2006). *Efficient Markets.* The Welfare of American Investors. Available at www.wku.edu/~brian.goff/Efficient%20Markets%20Manne.doc

Mansharamani, V. (2011). *Boombustology: Spotting Financial Bubbles Before They Burst.* Hoboken: Wiley.

Mantegna, R. N. (1991). Lévy Walks and Enhanced Diffusion in Milan Stock Exchange. *Physica A, 179*(2), 232–242.

Mantegna, R. N., & Stanley, H. E. (2000). *An Introduction to Econophysics: Correlations and Complexity in Finance.* Cambridge: Cambridge University Press.

Markowitz, H. M. (1952). Portfolio Selection. *Journal of Finance, 7,* 77–91.

Martenson, C. (2011). *The Crash Course: The Unsustainable Future of Our Economy, Energy, and Environment.* Hoboken: Wiley.

Martin, F. (2015). *Money: The Unauthorized Biography – From Coinage to Cryptocurrencies.* New York: Random House/Vintage (Paperback edition).

Martin, A., & Ventura, J. (2015). The International Transmission of Credit Bubbles: Theory and Policy. *Journal of Monetary Economics, 76*(Supplement), 37–56.

Mathews, P. H. (2006). Who Is Post Walrasian Man?, in Colander, D. (2006).

Mauboussin, M. J. (2006). *More Than You Know: Finding Financial Wisdom in Unconventional Places.* New York: Columbia University Press.

Mayer, T. (1999). *Monetary Policy and the Great Inflation in the United States: The Federal Reserve and the Failure of Macroeconomic Policy, 1965–1979.* Cheltenham: Edward Elgar.

Mayer, M. (2001). *The Fed: The Inside Story of How the World's Most Powerful Financial Institution Moves the Markets.* New York: Free Press (Simon & Schuster).

Mayer, C., & Sinai, T. (2005, September 19). Bubble Trouble? Not Likely. *Wall Street Journal.*

Mayo, M. (2011). *Exile on Wall Street: One Analysts Fight to Save the Big Banks from Themselves.* Hoboken: Wiley.

McCarthy, J., & Peach, R. W. (2004, December). *Are Home Prices the Next 'Bubble'?* Federal Reserve Bank of New York, *Economic Policy Review.*

McCauley, J. L. (2004). *Dynamics of Markets: Econophysics and Finance.* Cambridge: Cambridge University Press.

McConnell, J. J., & Xu, W. (2008). Equity Returns at the Turn of the Month. *Financial Analysts Journal, 64*(2), 49–64.

McDonald, L. G., & Robinson, P. (2009). *A Colossal Failure of Common Sense: The Inside Story of the Collapse of Lehman Brothers.* New York: Crown.

McFarland, D. (2016). *The Biological Bases of Economic Behaviour: A Concise Introduction.* New York: Palgrave Macmillan.

McGrattan, E. R., & Prescott, E. C. (2000). Is the Stock Market Overvalued? *Federal Reserve Bank of Minneapolis Quarterly Review, 24*(4), 20–40.

McGrattan, E. R., & Prescott, E. C. (2003). *Testing for Stock Market Overvaluation/Undervaluation,* in Hunter et al. (2003 [2005]).

McGregor, J. (1991, December 19). China Cancels Its Red-Hot Stamp Market, But Traders Hope Crackdown Will Pass. *Wall Street Journal.*

McKinnon, R. I. (2013, July 30). The Near-Zero Interest Rate Trap. *Wall Street Journal*.

McLean, B., & Nocera, J. (2010). *All the Devils Are Here*. New York: Penguin Group (Portfolio).

McQueen, G., & Thorley, S. (1994). Bubbles, Stock Returns, and Duration Dependence. *Journal of Financial and Quantitative Analysis, 29*(3), 379–401.

Medio, A. (1992). *Chaotic Dynamics: Theory and Applications to Economics*. Cambridge: Cambridge University Press.

Meese, R. A. (1986). Testing for Bubbles in Exchange Markets: A Case of Sparkling Rates? *Journal of Political Economy, 94*, 345–373.

Meese, R. A., & Rose, A. K. (1990). Nonlinear, Nonparametric, Nonessential Exchange Rate Estimation. *American Economic Review, 80*, 192–196.

Mehra, R. (Ed.). (2008). *Handbook of the Equity Risk Premium*. Amsterdam: Elsevier.

Mehra, R., & Prescott, E. C. (1985). The Equity Premium: A Puzzle. *Journal of Monetary Economics, 15*(2), 145–161.

Mehrling, P. (2005). *Fischer Black and the Revolutionary Idea of Finance*. Hoboken: Wiley.

Mehrling, P. (2011). *The New Lombard Street: How the Fed Became the Dealer of Last Resort*. Princeton: Princeton University Press.

Meltzer, A. H. (1982). *Rational Expectations, Risk, Uncertainty, and Market Responses*. Available at http://repository.cmu.edu/tepper

Meltzer, A. H. (2003). *Rational and Nonrational Bubbles*, in Hunter et al. (2003 [2005]).

Meltzer, A. H. (2009, May 4). Inflation Nation. *New York Times*.

Meltzer, A. H. (2012). Federal Reserve Policy in the Great Recession. *Cato Journal, 32*(2), 255–263.

Meltzer, A. H. (2013). *What's Wrong with the Fed: What Would Restore Independence?* American Economic Association Meeting, January. Available at www.aeaweb.org/aea/2013conference/program/meetingpapers.php and *Cato Journal, 33*(3), Fall.

Merton, R. C. (1973). Theory of Rational Option Pricing. *Bell Journal of Economics and Management Science (The Rand Corporation), 4*(1), 141–183.

Merton, R. C. (1992). *Continuous-Time Finance* (rev ed.). Oxford: Blackwell.

Miao, J. (2014). Introduction to Economic Theory of Bubbles. *Journal of Mathematical Economics, 53*, 130–136.

Michaelson, J. C. (2010, August 11). The High Costs of Very Low Interest Rates. *Wall Street Journal*.

Micklethwait, J. (2016, March). Jamie Dimon on Finance: 'Who Owns the Future?' *Bloomberg Markets, 25*(1).

Miffre, J., & Rallis, G. (2007). Momentum Strategies in Commodity Futures Markets. *Journal of Banking and Finance, 31*, 1863–1886.

Milgrom, P., & Stokey, N. (1982). Information, Trade and Common Knowledge. *Journal of Economic Theory, 26*, 17–27.

Miller, R. M. (2002). *Experimental Economics: How We Can Build Better Financial Markets*. Hoboken: Wiley.

Miller, J. I., & Ratti, R. A. (2009). Crude Oil and Stock Markets: Stability, Instability, and Bubbles. *Energy Economics, 31*(4), 559–568.

Mills, T. C. (1990). *Time Series Techniques for Economists*. Cambridge: Cambridge University Press.

Mills, T. C. (1993). *The Econometric Modelling of Financial Time Series*. Cambridge: Cambridge University Press.

Mills, T. C., & Markellos, R. N. (2008). *The Econometric Modelling of Financial Time Series* (3rd ed.). Cambridge: Cambridge University Press.

Milne, A. (2009). *The Fall of the House of Credit*. Cambridge: Cambridge University Press.

Minsky, H. P. (2008). *Stabilizing an Unstable Economy*. New York: McGraw-Hill (1996), New Haven: Yale University Press.

Mirowski, P. (1989). *More Heat than Light: Economics as Social Physics, Physics as Nature's Economics*. New York: Cambridge University Press (Paperback edition, 1991).

Mishkin, F. S. (2003). U.S. Stock Market Crashes and Their Aftermath: Implications for Monetary Policy, in Hunter et al. (2003 [2005]).

Mishkin, F. S. (2008). *How Should We Respond to Asset Price Bubbles?* Board of Governors of the Federal Reserve System. Available at http://www.federalreserve.gov/newsevents/speech/mishkin20080515a.htm

Mishkin, F. S. (2009). Is Monetary Policy Effective During Financial Crises? Available at www.aeaweb.org/annual_mtg_papers/2009/

Mishkin, F. S., & White, E. N. (2003). Stock Market Bubbles: When Does Intervention Work? *Milken Institute Review*, Second Quarter.

Mitchell, H., Brown, R. L., & Easton, S. A. (2002). Old Volatility – ARCH effects in 19th Century Consol Data. *Applied Financial Economics, 12*(4), 301–307.

Modigliani, F., & Pogue, G. A. (1974). An Introduction to Risk and Return. *Financial Analysts Journal, 30*(2), 68–80.

Mollenkamp, C., & Ng, S. (2007, December 27). Wall Street Wizardry Amplified Credit Crisis. *Wall Street Journal*.

Mollenkamp, C., & Wei, L. (2010, July 8). To Fix Sour Property Deals, Lenders 'Extend and Pretend.' *Wall Street Journal*.

Mollenkamp, C., & Whitehouse, M. (2008, March 17). Banks Fear a Deepening of Turmoil. *Wall Street Journal*.

Mollenkamp, C., Ng, S., Pleven, L., & Smith, R. (2008, November 3). Behind AIG's Fall, Risk Models Failed to Pass Real-World Test. *Wall Street Journal*.

Montier, J. (2002). *Behavioural Finance: Insights into Irrational Minds and Markets*. Chichester/Hoboken: Wiley.

Montier, J. (2007). *Behavioural Investing: A Practitioners Guide to Applying Behavioural Finance*. Chichester/Hoboken: Wiley.

Mood, A. (1940). The Distribution Theory of Runs. *Annals of Mathematical Statistics, 11*, 367–392.

Mora, N. (2008). The Effect of Bank Credit on Asset Prices: Evidence from the Japanese Real Estate Boom During the 1980s. *Journal of Money, Credit and Banking, 40*(1), 57–87.

Morewood, S. (2007). The Demise of the Command Economies in the Soviet Union and Its Outer Empire. In M. J. Oliver & D. H. Aldcroft (Eds.), *Economic Disasters of the Twentieth Century*. Cheltenham: Edward Elgar.

Morgan, I. G. (1976). Stock Prices and Heteroscedasticity. *Journal of Business, 49*(4), 496–508.

Morgenson, G. (2008). *The Trillion Dollar Meltdown: Easy Money, High Rollers, and the Great Credit Crash*. New York: PublicAffairs (Perseus Book Group).

Morgenson, G. (2008a, November 8). How the Thundering Herd Faltered and Fell. *New York Times*.

Morgenson, G. (2008b, July 20). Given a Shovel, Americans Dig Deeper Into Debt. *New York Times*.

Morgenson, G. (2015, March 8). At the Fed in 2009, Rolling Dice in a Crisis. *New York Times*.

Morgenson, G., & Rosner, J. (2011). *Reckless Endangerment: How Outsized Ambition, Greed, and Corruption Led to Economic Armageddon*. New York: Times Books (Henry Holt).

Morgenson, G., & Story, L. (2009, December 24). Banks Bundled Bad Debt, Bet Against It and Won. *New York Times*.

Morris, C. R. (2017). *A Rabble of Dead Money: The Great Crash and the Global Depression, 1929–39*. New York: Public Affairs.

Morrison, F. (1991). *The Art of Modeling Dynamic Systems: Forecasting for Chaos Randomness, and Determinism*. New York: Wiley Interscience, Wiley.

Mossin, J. (1966). Equilibrium in a Capital Asset Market. *Econometrica, 34*, 768–783.

Muelbauer, J., Duca, J., & Murphy, A. (2011). Home Prices and Credit Constraints: Making Sense of the U.S. Experience. *Economic Journal, 121*(532).

Muellbauer, J., & Portes, R. D. (1978). Macroeconomic Models with Quantity Rationing. *Economic Journal, 88*(4), 788–821.

Munk, C. (2013). *Financial Asset Pricing Theory*. Oxford: Oxford University Press.

Murase, H. (2012). *Macroeconomics of Weak Corporate Governance: An alternative Theory of Japan's Lost Decade*. Japan Society of Monetary Economics. Available at http://www.jsmeweb.org/kinyu/pdf/journal/full-paper34en-murase.pdf

Muth, J. A. (1961). Rational Expectations and the Theory of Price Movements. *Econometrica, 29*(6), 315–335.

Nairn, A. (2001). *Engines that Move Markets: Technology Investing from Railroads to the Internet and Beyond*. Hoboken: Wiley.

Nakamichi, T., & Ito, T. (2015, March 11). BOJ Helps Tokyo Stocks to Soar. *Wall Street Journal*.

Napier, R. (2007). *Anatomy of the Bear: Lessons from Wall Street's Four Great Bottoms* (2nd ed.). Hampshire: Harriman House.

Nations, S. (2017). *A History of the United States in Five Crashes: Stock Meltdowns that Defined a Nation*. New York: William Morrow (HarperCollins).

Neal, L. D. (1990). How the South Sea Bubble Was Blown Up and Burst: A New Look at Old Data, in White (1990).

Neal, L. D. (1993). *The Rise of Financial Capitalism: International Capital Markets in the Age of Reason*. New York: Cambridge University Press.

Neal, L. D. (1998, May–June). The Financial Crisis of 1825 and the Restructuring of the British Financial System. *FRB St. Louis Review*.

Neal, L. D. (2015). *A Concise History of International Finance from Babylon to Bernanke*. Cambridge: Cambridge University Press.

Neftci, S. N. (2000). *An Introduction to the Mathematics of Financial Derivatives* (2nd ed.). San Diego/London: Academic.

Nesvetailova, A. (2010). *Financial Alchemy in Crisis: The Great Liquidity Illusion*. London: Pluto Press.

Newman, P., Milgate, M., & Eatwell, J. (Eds.). (1992). *The New Palgrave Dictionary of Money and Finance*. London: Macmillan Press.

Ng, S., & Pleven, L. (2009, February 5). An AIG Unit's Quest to Juice Profit. *Wall Street Journal*.

Ning, C., Xu, D., & Wirjanto, T. S. (2015). Is Volatility Clustering of Asset Returns Asymmetric? *Journal of Banking & Finance, 52*, 62–76.

Nocera, J. (1999). Do You Believe? How Yahoo! Became a Blue Chip. *Fortune, 139*(11), 76–92.

Nocera, J. (2008, October 1). As Credit Crisis Spiraled, Alarm Led to Action. *New York Times*.

Nocera, J. (2009a, February 28). Propping Up a House of Cards. *New York Times*.

Nocera, J. (2009b, January 2). Risk Mismanagement. *New York Times*.

Nocera, J. (2010, April 17). A Wall Street Invention That Let the Crisis Mutate. *New York Times*.

Nocera, J., & Andrews, E. L. (2008, October 22). Struggling to Keep Up as the Crisis Raced On. *New York Times*.

Nofsinger, J. R. (2005). Social Mood and Financial Economics. *Journal of Behavioral Finance, 6*(3), 144–160.

Nofsinger, J. R., & Sias, R. W. (1999). Herding and Feedback Trading by Institutional and Individual Investors. *Journal of Finance, 53*.

Noguchi, Y. (1994). The 'Bubble' and Economic Policies in the 1980s. *Journal of Japanese Studies, 20*(2), 291–329.

Norberg, J. (2009). *Financial Fiasco: How America's Infatuation with Homeownership and Easy Money Created the Economic Crisis*. Washington, DC: Cato Institute.

Norris, F. (1987, October 26). The Crash of 1987. *Barron's*.

Norris, F. (2008, October 31). A Monthlong Walk on the Wildest Side of the Stock Market. *New York Times*.

Norris, F. (2013, July 19). The Time Bernanke Got It Wrong. *New York Times*.

Novy-Marx, R. (2014). Predicting Anomaly Performance with Politics, the Weather, Global Warming, Sunspots, and the Stars. *Journal of Financial Economics, 112*(2), 137–146.

Nychka, D. W., Ellner, S., Gallant, A. R., & McCaffrey, D. (1992). Finding Chaos in Noisy Systems. *Journal of the Royal Statistical Society. B, 54*, 399–426.

O'Brien, P. C., & Dyck, P. J. (1985). A Runs Test Based on Run Lengths. *Biometrics, 41*(1), 237–244.

O'Driscoll, G. P., Jr. (2007, August 10). Our Subprime Fed. *Wall Street Journal*.

O'Driscoll, G. P., Jr. (2008, May 20). *Asset Bubbles and Their Consequences*. (Cato Institute Briefing Paper No. 103).

O'Driscoll, G. P., Jr. (2011, July 26). Why the Fed Is Not Independent. *Wall Street Journal*.

O'Grady, M. A. (2009, March 21). Now Is No Time to Give Up on Markets. *Wall Street Journal*.

O'Harrow, R., Jr., & Dennis, B. (2008a, December 30). A Crack in The System. *Washington Post*.

O'Harrow, R., Jr., & Dennis, B. (2008b, December 31). Downgrades and Downfall. *Washington Post*.

O'Harrow, R., Jr., & Dennis, B. (2008c, December 29). The Beautiful Machine: Greed on Wall Street and Blindness in Washington Certainly. *Washington Post*.

Oates, J. (1986). *Babylon* (rev ed.). New York: Thames and Hudson.

Odean, T. (1998). Volume, Volatility, Price, and Profit When All Traders Are Above Average. *Journal of Finance, 53*(6), 1887–1934.

Odlyzko, A. (2010). *Collective Hallucinations and Inefficient Markets: The British Railway Mania of the 1840s*. Minneapolis: University of Minnesota.

Ofek, E., & Richardson, M. (2001). *DotCom Mania: The Rise and Fall of Internet Stock Prices* (Working Paper, No. 8630). National Bureau of Economic Research.

Officer, R. R. (1972). The Distribution of Stock Returns. *Journal of the American Statistical Association, 67*(340), 807–812.

Ohanian, L. E. (2018). Should Policy Makers Worry About R-Star? In M. D. Bordo et al. (2018). *The Structural Foundations of Monetary Policy*. Stanford: Hoover Institution.

Oliver, M. J. (2007). Financial Crises. In M. J. Oliver & D. H. Aldcroft (Eds.), *Economic Disasters of the Twentieth Century*. Elgar: Cheltenham.

Oliver, M. J., & Aldcroft, D. H. (Eds.). (2007). *Economic Disasters of the Twentieth Century*. Cheltenham: Elgar.

Olson, K. R. (2006). A Literature Review of Social Mood. *Journal of Behavioral Finance, 7*(4), 193–203.

Onaran, Y. (2012). *Zombie Banks: How Broken Banks and Debtor Nations Are Crippling the Global Economy*. New York: Bloomberg Press/Wiley.

Orlowski, L. T. (2012). Financial Crisis and Extreme Market Risks: Evidence from Europe. *Review of Financial Economics, 21*(3), 120–130.

Overbye, D. (2009, March 10). They Tried to Outsmart Wall Street. *New York Times*.

Pagan, A. R., & Sossounov, K. (2003). A Simple Framework for Analyzing Bull and Bear Markets. *Journal of Applied Econometrics, 18*, 23–46.

Palan, S. (2009). *Bubbles and Crashes in Experimental Asset Markets*. Berlin: Springer-Verlag.

Pareto, V. (1982). *Cours d'Économie Politique*. Oeuvres Complètes. Geneva: Droz.

Parisi, F., & Smith, V. L. (2005). *The Law and Economics of Irrational Behavior*. Stanford, CA: Stanford University Press.

Park, J. Y., & Whang, Y. J. (1999). *Random Walk or Chaos: A Formal Test on the Lyapunov Exponent*. Working Paper No. 9. Institute of Economic Research, Seoul National University.

Parks, T. (2005). *Medici Money: Banking, Metaphysics, and Art in Fifteenth Century Florence*. New York: W. W. Norton.

Pastor, L., & Stambaugh, R. F. (2003). Liquidity Risk and Expected Stock Returns. *Journal of Political Economy, 111*(3), 642–685.

Pastor, L, & Stambaugh, R. F. (2011). *Are Stocks Really Less Volatile in the Long Run?* AFA 2010 Atlanta Meetings Paper (2011). Available at http://ssrn.com/abstract=1136847 and NBER Working Paper 14757.

Pastor, L., & Veronesi, P. (2008). *Technological Revolutions and Stock Prices* (NBER Working Paper No. 11876).

Patel, J., Zeckhauser, R., & Hendricks, D. (1991). The Rationality Struggle: Illustrations from Financial Markets. *American Economic Review, 81*, 232–236.

Patterson, K. (2000). *An Introduction to Applied Econometrics: A Time Series Approach*. New York: Palgrave Macmillan.

Patterson, S. (2008, March 22). Old Pros Size Up the Game. *Wall Street Journal*.

Patterson, S. (2010a, May 17). How the 'Flash Crash' Echoed Black Monday. *Wall Street Journal*.

Patterson, S. (2010b). *The Quants: How a New Breed of Math Whizzes Conquered Wall Street and Nearly Destroyed It*. New York: Crown (Random House).

Patterson, S. (2012). *Dark Pools: High-Speed Traders, A.I. Bandits, and the Threat to the Global Financial System*. New York: Crown Business/Random House.

Pattillo, C., Poirson, H., & Ricci, L. A. (2011). External Debt and Growth. *Review of Economics and Institutions, 2*(3), 1–30.

Paul, R. (2009). *End the Fed.* New York: Grand Central Publishing (Hachette).

Paumgarten, N. (2009, October 12). The Secret Cycle. *The New Yorker.*

Pearce, D. W. (Ed.). (1992). *The MIT Dictionary of Modern Economics* (4th ed.). Cambridge, MA: MIT Press.

Peltz, M. (2010, June). Inside The Machine. *Institutional Investor.*

Pepper, G., & Oliver, M. J. (2006). *The Liquidity Theory of Asset Prices.* Chichester: Wiley.

Perkins, A. B., & Perkins, M. C. (1999). *The Internet Bubble: Inside the Overvalued World of High-Tech Stocks – And What You Need to Know to Avoid the Coming Shakeout.* New York: HarperBusiness.

Pesaran, M. H., & Timmermann, A. (1994). Forecasting Stock Returns: An Examination of Stock Market Trading in the Presence of Transaction Costs. *Journal of Forecasting, 13*(4), 335–367.

Peters, E. E. (1989). Fractal Structure in the Capital Markets. *Financial Analysts Journal, 45*(4), 32–37.

Peters, E. E. (1991). A Chaotic Attractor for the S&P 500. *Financial Analysts Journal, 47*(2), 55–81.

Peters, E. E. (1994). *Fractal Market Analysis: Applying Chaos Theory to Investment and Economics.* New York: Wiley.

Peters, E. E. (1996). *Chaos and Order in the Capital Markets: A New View of Cycles, Prices, and Market Volatility* (2nd ed.). New York: Wiley.

Peterson, R. L. (2007). *Inside the Investor's Brain: The Power of Mind Over Money.* Hoboken: Wiley.

Phillips, P. C. B., & Perron, P. (1988). Testing for a Unit Root in Time Series Regression. *Biometrika, 75,* 335–346.

Pierce, J. R. (1980). *An Introduction to Information Theory: Symbols, Signals and Noise* (2nd, rev ed.). New York: Dover.

Pierdzioch, C. (2010). Periodically Collapsing Bubbles in the German Stock Market, 1876–1913. *Applied Economics Letters, 17*(9), 907–908.

Pixley, J. (2012). *Emotions in Finance: Booms, Busts and Uncertainty* (2nd ed.). Cambridge: Cambridge University Press.

Plosser, C. I. (2018). The Risks of a Fed Balance Sheet Unconstrained by Monetary Policy. In M. D. Bordo et al. (2018). *The Structural Foundations of Monetary Policy.* Stanford: Hoover Institution Press.

Pollock, A. J. (2016). Does the Federal Reserve Know What It's Doing? *Cato Journal, 36*(2), 385–392.

Poole, W. (2013). Prospects for and Ramifications of the Great Central Banking Unwind. *Financial Analysts Journal, 69*(6), 33–39.

Poon, S., & Granger, C. (2005). Practical Issues in Forecasting Volatility. *Financial Analysts Journal, 61*(1), 45–56.

Porras, E. R. (2016). *Bubbles and Contagion in Financial Markets, Vol 1: An Integrative View.* New York: Palgrave Macmillan.

Porras-Gonzalez, E. R. (2000). *Speculative Bubbles and Tests of the Contagion Mechanism in Financial Markets.* Unpublished Ph.D. Dissertation, Florida Atlantic University.

Porter, E. (2017, March 15). The Fed vs. the Angry Masses. *New York Times.*

Porter, D., & Smith, V. L. (1992). *Price Expectations in Experimental Asset Markets with Futures Contracting* (Social Science Working Paper 827). Pasadena: California Institute of Technology. Available at http://www.hss.caltech.edu/SSPapers/sswp827.pdf

Posen, A. S. (2003). *It Takes More than a Bubble to Be Japan* (WP 03-9). Institute for International Economics. Available at http://www.petersoninstitute.org/publications/wp/03-9.pdf

Posthumus, N. W. (1929). The Tulip Mania in Holland. *Journal of Economic and Business History.*

Poterba, J., & Summers, L. H. (1986). The Persistence of Volatility and Stock Market Fluctuations. *American Economic Review, 76.*

Poterba, J., & Summers, L. H. (1988). Mean Reversion in Stock Returns: Evidence and Implications. *Journal of Financial Economics, 22*(1), 27–59.

Potter, S. (2011). The Failure to Forecast the Great Recession. *Liberty Street Economics,* Federal Reserve Bank of New York. http://libertystreeteconomics.newyorkfed.org/2011/11/the-failure-to-forecast-the-great-recession.html#.U3aW3Kgo-Hs

Poundstone, W. (2005). *Fortune's Formula: The Untold Story of the Scientific Betting System That Beat the Casinos and Wall Street.* New York: Hill and Wang (Farrar, Straus and Giroux).

Poundstone, W. (2010). *Priceless: The Myth of Fair Value.* New York: Hill and Wang (Farrar, Straus and Giroux).

Pradeep, A. K. (2010). *The Buying Brain: Secrets to Selling to the Subconscious Mind.* Hoboken: Wiley.

Prechter, R. R, Jr. (1995 [2001]). *At the Crest of the Tidal Wave.* Gainesville: New Classics Library.

Prechter, R. R., Jr. (1999). *The Wave Principle of Human Social Behavior and the New Science of Socionomics.* Gainesville: New Classics Library.

Prechter, R. R., Jr. (2001). Unconscious Herding Behavior as the Psychological Basis of Financial Market Trends and Patterns. *Journal of Psychology and Financial Markets, 2*(3), 120–125.

Prechter, R. R., Jr. (2003). *Conquer the Crash.* West Sussex: Wiley.

Prechter, R. R., Jr. (2004). The Fractal Nature of the Stock Market. In *The Colours of Infinity: The Beauty, and Power of Fractals.* London: Clear Books.

Prechter, R. R., Jr. (2016). *The Socionomic Theory of Finance.* Gainesville: Socionomics Institute Press.

Prechter, R. R., Jr., & Parker, W. D. (2007). The Financial/Economic Dichotomy in Social Behavioral Dynamics: The Socionomic Perspective. *Journal of Behavioral Finance, 8*(1), 84–110.

Presscott, E. C. (1999). Some Observations on the Great Depression. *Federal Reserve Bank of Minneapolis Quarterly Review, 23*(1), 25–31.

Pribram, K. (1983). *A History of Economic Reasoning.* Baltimore: Johns Hopkins University Press.

Pringle, R. (2012). *The Money Trap: Escaping the Grip of Global Finance.* New York: Palgrave Macmillan.

Protter, P. (2012). A Mathematical Theory of Financial Bubbles. Available at https://doi.org/10.2139/ssrn.2115895

Psaradakis, Z., Sola, M., & Spagnolo, F. (2001). A Simple Procedure for Detecting Periodically Collapsing Rational Bubbles. *Economic Letters, 72,* and Birkbeck College Working Paper.

Pulliam, S., Ng, S., & Smith, R. (2008, April 16). Merrill Upped Ante as Boom as Mortgage Bonds Fizzled. *Wall Street Journal.*

Quandt, R. E., & Rosen, H. S. (1986). Unemployment, Disequilibrium and the Short Run Phillips Curve: An Econometric Approach. *Journal of Applied Econometrics, 1,* 235–253.

Radner, R. (1968). Competitive Equilibrium Under Uncertainty. *Econometrica, 36*(1), 31–58.

Rahman, A., & Saadi, S. (2008). Random Walk and Breaking Trend in Financial Series: An Econometric Critique of Unit Root Tests. *Review of Financial Economics, 17*(3), 204–212.

Raines, J. P., & Leathers, C. G. (2000). *Economists and the Stock Market: Speculative Theories of Stock Market Fluctuations.* Aldershot: Elgar.

Rajan, R. G. (2010). *Fault Lines: How Hidden Fractures Still Threaten the World Economy.* Princeton: Princeton University Press.

Ramsey, J. B. (1990). Economic and Financial Data as Nonlinear Processes. In G. P. Dwyer Jr. & R. W. Hafer (Eds.), *The Stock Market: Bubbles, Volatility, and Chaos.* Boston: Kluwer Academic.

Ramsey, J. B. (1996). If Nonlinear Models Cannot Forecast, What Use Are They? *Studies in Nonlinear Dynamics, 1*(2), 65–86.

Ramsey, J. B., Sayers, C. L., & Rothman, P. (1990). The Statistical Properties of Dimension Calculations Using Small Data Sets: Some Economic Applications. *International Economic Review, 31*(4), 991–1020.

Rao, P., & Griliches, Z. (1969). Small-Sample Properties of Several Two-Stage Regression Methods in the Context of Autocorrelated Error. *Journal of the American Statistical Association, 64*(325), 253–272.

Rapoport, A., & Wallsten, T. S. (1972). Individual Decision Behaviour. *Annual Review of Psychology, 21.*

Rappoport, P., & White, E. (1993). Was there a Bubble in the 1929 Stock Market? *Journal of Economic History, 53,* 549–574.

Rappoport, P., & White, E. (1994). Was the Crash of 1929 Expected? *American Economic Review, 84.*

Rasband, S. N. (1990). *Chaotic Dynamics of Nonlinear Systems.* New York: Wiley.

Rebello, J. (2005, March 7). Fed Officials Worried in 1999 About Managing Stock Bubble'. *Wal Street Journal.*

Reddy, S. (2008, September 22). Fed Could Suffer If New Role Clashes with Policy-Setting. *Wall Street Journal.*

Redleaf, A., & Vigilante, R. (2010). *Panic: The Betrayal of Capitalism by Wall Street and Washington.* Minneapolis: Richard Vigilante Books.

Reilly, D., & Mollenkamp, C. (2007, August 30). 'Conduits' in Need of a Fix. *Wall Street Journal.*

Reingold, D., & Reingold, J. (2006). *Confessions of a Wall Street Analyst.* New York: HarperCollins.

Reinhart, C. M., & Rogoff, K. S. (2008). *This Time It's Different: A Panoramic View of Eight Centuries of Financial Crises* (Working Paper 13882). NBER. Available at www.economics.harvard.edu/faculty/rogoff/Recent_Papers_Rogoff

Reinhart, C. M., & Rogoff, K. S. (2009). *This Time Is Different: Eight Centuries of Financial Folly.* Princeton: Princeton University Press.

Reinhart, C. M., Reinhart, V. R., & Rogoff, K. S. (2012). Public Debt Overhangs: Advanced-Economy Episodes Since 1800. *Journal of Economic Perspectives, 26*(3), 69–86.

Rich, M., & Leonhardt, D. (2005, March 25). Trading Places: Real Estate Instead of Dot-coms. *New York Times.*

Richardson, K. (2004, September 24). Friday's a Good Day for Bad News After All. *Wall Street Journal.*

Rickards, J. (2011). *Currency Wars: The Making of the Next Global Crisis.* New York: Portfolio/Penguin.

Rickards, J. (2014). *The Death of Money: The Coming Collapse of the Monetary System.* New York: Portfolio/Penguin.

Ridley, M. (1993, October 9). Frontiers of Finance: On the Edge. *The Economist.*

Rietz, T. A. (1988). The Equity Risk Premium: A Solution. *Journal of Monetary Economics, XXII,* 117–131.

Ritter, L. S., & Silber, W. L. (1974). *Principles of Money, Banking, and Financial Markets.* New York: Basic Books.

Roberts, R. (2008, October 3). How Government Stoked the Mania. *Wall Street Journal.*

Robinson, P. M. (1994). Efficient Tests of Nonstationary Hypothesis. *Journal of the American Statistical Association, 89,* 1420–1437.

Rockel, N. (2010, May). Evolutionary Road: The Enduring Popularity of MPT Hasn't Stopped Practitioners from Trying to Improve It. *Institutional Investor.*

Roehner, B. M. (2000). Identifying the Bottom Line After a Stock Market Crash. *International Journal of Modern Physics, C, 11*(1), 91–100.

Roehner, B. M. (2002). *Patterns of Speculation: A Study in Observational Econophysics.* Cambridge: Cambridge University Press.

Roll, R. (1984). Orange Juice and Weather. *American Economic Review, 74.*

Roll, R. (1988). R^2. *Journal of Finance, 43*(3), 541–566.

Roll, R. (2011). The Possible Misdiagnosis of a Crisis. *Financial Analysts Journal, 67*(2), 12–17.

Romer, D. H. (1993). Rational Asset-Price Movements Without News. *American Economic Review, 83*(5), 1112–1130.

Rosenberg, M. (2004). The Monthly Effect in Stock Returns and Conditional Heteroscedasticity. *The American Economist, XLVIII*(2), 67–73.

Rosenstein, M. T., Collins, J. J., & De Luca, C. J. (1993). A Practical Method for Calculating Largest Lyapunov Exponents from Small Data Sets. *Physica D, 65,* 117–134.

Ross, S. M. (1976). The Arbitrage Theory of Capital Asset Pricing. *Journal of Economic Theory, 13,* 341–360.

Ross, S. M. (2003). *An Elementary Introduction to Mathematical Finance, Options and Other Topics* (2nd ed.). New York/Cambridge: Cambridge University Press.

Rostovtzeff, M. (1941). *The Social and Economic History of the Roman Empire.* Oxford: Clarendon.

Rostovtzeff, M. (1953). *The Social and Economic History of the Hellenistic World* (Vol. 1). Oxford: Oxford University Press.

Roubini, N. (2006). Why Central Banks Should Burst Bubbles. *International Finance, 9*(1), 87–107.

Roubini, N., & Mihm, S. (2011). *Crisis Economics: A Crash Course in the Future of Finance.* New York: Penguin.

Rousseau, R. (1999). A Weak Goodness-of-Fit Test for Rank-Frequency Distributions. In C. Macias-Chapula (Ed.), *Proceedings of the Seventh Conference of the International Society for Scientometrics and Informetrics,* Universidad de Colima (Mexico).

Rozeff, M. S., & Kinney, W. R., Jr. (1976). Capital Market Seasonality: The Case of Stock Returns. *Journal of Financial Economics, 3*(4), 379–402.

Rubinstein, M. (1975). Securities Market Efficiency in an Arrow-Debreu Economy. *American Economic Review, 65*(5), 812–824.

Russolillo, S., & Kilgore, T. (2010, August 14). 'Hindenburg Omen' Flashes. *Wall Street Journal*.

Russollio, S. (2016, December 6). Greenspan's New Worrisome Gauge. *Wall Street Journal*.

Ryan-Collins, J., Greenham, T., Werner, R., & Jackson, A. (2011). *Where Does Money Come From?: A Guide to the UK Monetary and Banking System*. London: New Economics Foundation.

Rynecki, D. (2000, April 3). Market Madness: What the Hell Is Going On? *Fortune, 141*(7).

Saffi, P. A. C., & Sigurdsson, K. (2011). Price Efficiency and Short Selling. *Review of Financial Studies, 24*(3), 821–852.

Salmon, F. (2009). Recipe for Disaster: The Formula That Killed Wall Street. *Wired, 17*(3), 74–79.

Samuels, W. J., Biddle, J. F., & Davis, J. B. (Eds.). (2007). *A Companion to the History of Economic Thought*. Oxford: Blackwell.

Samuelson, P. A. (1965). Proof That Properly Anticipated Prices Fluctuate Randomly. *Industrial Management Review, 6,* 41–49.

Samuelson, W., & Zeckhauser, R. (1988). Status Quo Bias in Decision Making. *Journal of Risk and Uncertainty, 1,* 7–59.

Santoli, M. (2011, April 11). What Is Low Volume Telling Us? *Barron's*.

Santoni, G. J. (1987). The Great Bull Markets of 1924–1929 and 1982–1987: Speculative Bubbles or Economic Fundamentals? *Federal Reserve Bank of St. Louis Review*.

Santos, M. S., & Woodford, M. (1997). Rational Asset Pricing Bubbles. *Econometrica, 65,* 19–58.

Sargan, J. D., & Bhargava, A. S. (1983). Testing Residuals from Least-Squares Regression for Being Generated by the Gaussian Random Walk. *Econometrica, 51,* 153–174.

Sarno, L., & Taylor, M. P. (1999). Moral Hazard, Asset Price Bubbles, Capital Flows, and the East Asian Crisis: The First Tests. *Journal of International Money and Finance, 18,* 637–657.

Satchell, S., & Timmermann, A. (1996). *Daily Returns in International Stock Markets: Predictability, Nonlinearity, and Transaction Costs*, in Barnett et al. (1996).

Sato, Y. (2016). Fund Tournaments and Asset Bubbles. *Review of Finance, 20*(4), 1383–1426.

Saunders, E. M., Jr. (1993). Stock Prices and Wall Street Weather. *American Economic Review, 83*(5), 1337–1345.

Scalas, E., & Kim, K. (2006). *The Art of Fitting financial Time Series with Lévy Stable Distributions* (MPRA Paper No. 336). Available at http://mpra.ub.uni-muenchen. de/336/

Schacter, S., Hood, D., Gerin, W., & Adreassen, P. (1985). Was the South Sea Bubble a Random Walk? *Journal of Economic Behavior and Organization, 6,* 323–329.

Schaede, U. (1989). Forwards and Futures in Tokugawa-Period Japan: A New Perspective on the Dojima Rice Market. *Journal of Banking and Finance, 13,* 487–513.

Schaller, H., & van Norden, S. (1997). *Fads or Bubbles?* (Working Paper 97-2). Bank of Canada. Available at http://www.bankofcanada.ca/en/res/wp/1997/wp97-2.html

Scharfstein, D. S., & Stein, J. C. (1990, June). Herd Behavior and Investment. *American Economic Review, 90*(3).

Scheinkman, J. A. (2014). *Speculation, Trading, and Bubbles.* New York: Columbia University Press.

Scheinkman, J. A., & LeBaron, B. (1989). Nonlinear Dynamics and Stock Returns. *Journal of Business, 62,* 311–337.

Scheinkman, J. A., & Woodford, M. (1994). Self-Organized Criticality and Economic Fluctuations. *American Economic Review, 84*(2), 417–421.

Scheinkman, J. A., & Xiong, W. (2003). Overconfidence and Speculative Bubbles. *Journal of Political Economy, 111*(6), 1183–1219.

Scherbina, A., & Schlusche, B. (2014). Asset Price Bubbles: A Survey. *Quantitative Finance, 14*(4), 589–604.

Schlesinger, J. M., & Gruley, B. (2002, December 27). A Tale of a Broker and His Clients and an Era's End. *Wall Street Journal.*

Schlesinger, J. M., & Nakamichi, T. (2014, November 10). How BOJ's Kuroda Won the Vote for Stimulus Expansion. *Wall Street Journal.*

Schoemaker, P. J. H. (1982). The Expected Utility Model. *Journal of Economic Literature, 20.*

Schrage, M. (2003). Daniel Kahneman: The Thought Leader Interview. *Business+Strategy.* Booz, Allen, & Hamilton and http://ebusiness.mit.edu/schrage/Articles/DanielKahnemanInterview.pdf

Schularick, M., & Taylor, A. (2012). Credit Booms Gone Bust: Monetary Policy, Leverage Cycles and Financial Crises, 1870–2008. *American Economic Review, 102*(2), 1029–1061.

Schumpeter, J. A. (1934). *The Theory of Economic Development: An Inquiry into Profits, Capital, Credit, Interest and the Business Cycle* (trans: Opie, R.). Cambridge, MA: Harvard University Press edition, 1961.

Schumpeter, J. A. (1939). *Business Cycles: A Theoretical, Historical, and Statistical Analysis of the Capitalist Process.* New York: McGraw-Hill.

Schwager, J. (1993). *Market Wizards: Interviews with Top Traders.* New York: HarperCollins (Collins Business).

Schwartz, A. J. (1986). Real and Pseudo-Financial Crises. In F. H. Capie & G. E. Wood (Eds.), *The Lender of Last Resort.* London: Routledge.

Schwartz, A. J. (1995). Why Financial Stability Depends on Price Stability. *Economic Affair, 15*(4), 21–25.

Schwartz, D. G. (2006). *Roll the Bones: The History of Gambling.* New York: Gotham Books (Penguin Group).

Schwartz, N. D. (2008, March 16). Wait. Weren't These Safer Bets? *New York Times.*

Schwartz, N. D., & Creswell, J. (2008, March 23). What Created This Monster? *New York Times.*

Schwert, G. W. (1989a, May). *Business Cycles, Financial Crises, and Stock Volatility* (Working Paper No. 2957). NBER.

Schwert, G. W. (1989b). Why Does Stock Market Volatility Change Over Time? *Journal of Finance, 44*(5), 1115–1153.

Schwert, G. W. (1990). Stock Volatility and the Crash of '87. *Review of Financial Studies, 3*(1), 77–102.

Schwert, G. W. (2009). *Rolling Annualized Standard Deviation of S&P Daily Returns, 1928–2009*. Available at http://schwert.simon.rochester.edu/spvol.pdf

Scott, L. O. (1985). The Present Value Model of Stock Prices: Regression Tests and Monte Carlo Results. *Review of Economics and Statistics, 57*(November).

Segal, J. (2013, September). Is Alpha Dead? *Institutional Investor*.

Segaller, S. (1999). *Nerds 2.0.1: A Brief History of the Internet*. New York: TV Books.

Sender, H, Guerrera, F., Larsen, P. T., & Silverman, G. (2008, September 15). Broken Brothers: How Brinkmanship Was Not Enough to Save Lehman. *Financial Times*.

Serletis, A. (1996). "Is There Chaos in Economic Time Series?," *Canadian Journal of Economics*, 29 (Special Issue – Part 1) (April).

Serletis, A., & Dormaar, P. (1996). Chaos and Nonlinear Dynamics in Futures Markets. In Barnett et al., (Ed.), *Nonlinear Dynamics and Economics*. Cambridge: Cambridge University Press.

Shalen, C. T. (1993). Volume Volatility, and the Dispersion of Beliefs. *Review of Financial Studies, 6*(2)(April).

Shannon, C. E., & Weaver, W. (1949). *Mathematical Theory of Communications*. Urbana-Champaign: University of Illinois Press.

Sharma, R. (2015a, July 7). China's Stock Plunge Is Scarier Than Greek Debt Crisis. *Wall Street Journal*.

Sharma, R. (2015b, May 12). The Federal Reserve Asset Bubble Machine. *Wall Street Journal*.

Sharma, R. (2015c, January 16). How Spending Capped the Global Recovery. *Wall Street Journal*.

Sharpe, W. F. (1964). Capital Asset Prices: A Theory of Market Equilibrium Under Conditions of Risk. *Journal of Finance, 19*, 425–442.

Shefrin, H. (2002). *Beyond Greed and Fear: Understanding Behavioral Finance and the Psychology of Investing*. New York: Oxford University Press.

Shefrin, H., & Statman, M. (1985). The Disposition to Sell Winners Too Early and Ride Losers Too Long. *Journal of Finance, 40*, 777–790.

Sheng, A. (2009). *From Asian to Global Financial Crisis: An Asian Regulator's View of Unfettered Finance in the 1990s and 2000s*. New York: Cambridge University Press.

Shermer, M. (2008). *The Mind of the Market*. New York: Times Books (Henry Holt).

Shiller, R. J. (1981). Do Stock Prices Move Too Much to Be Justified by Subsequent Movements in Dividends? *American Economic Review, 71*(3), 421–436.

Shiller, R. J. (1989). Comovements in Stock Prices and Comovements in Dividends. *Journal of Finance, 44*(3), 719–729.

Shiller, R. J. (1992). *Market Volatility*. Cambridge, MA: MIT Press.

Shiller, R. J. (2000, 2005, 2015). *Irrational Exuberance* (3nd ed.). Princeton: Princeton University Press.

Shiller, R. J. (2002a). Bubbles, Human Judgment, and Expert Opinion. *Financial Analysts Journal, 58*(3), 18–26.

Shiller, R. J. (2002b, October). *From Efficient Market Theory to Behavioral Finance* (Cowles Foundation Discussion Paper No. 1385). New Haven: Cowles Foundation for Research in Economics, Yale University. Available at http://cowles.econ.yale.edu/

Shiller, R. J. (2002c, December 17). Safe as Houses? *Wall Street Journal*.

Shiller, R. J. (2006). Irrational Exuberance Revisited. In R. N. Sullivan & J. J. Diermeier (Eds.), *Global Perspectives on Investment Management*. CFA Institute: Charlottesville.

Shiller, R. J. (2008a, November 1). Challenging the Crowd in Whispers, Not Shouts. *New York Times.*

Shiller, R. J. (2008b, March 2). How a Bubble Stayed Under the Radar. *New York Times.*

Shiller, R. J. (2013, April 21). Before Housing Bubbles, There Was Land Fever. *New York Times.*

Shiller, R. J., Kon-Ya, F., & Tsutsui, Y. (1996). Why Did the Nikkei Crash? Expanding the Scope of Expectations Data Collection. *Review of Economics and Statistics, 78*(1), 156–164.

Shleifer, A. (2000). *Inefficient Markets: An Introduction to Behavioral Finance.* Oxford: Oxford University Press.

Shleifer, A., & Vishny, R. W. (1997). The Limits of Arbitrage. *Journal of Finance, 52*(1), 35–55.

Shreve, S. E. (2008). *Stochastic Calculus for Finance II: Continuous Time Models.* New York: Springer Science + Business Media.

Sias, R. (2007). Causes and Seasonality of Momentum Profits. *Financial Analysts Journal, 63*(2), 48–54.

Sichel, D. E. (1991). Business Cycle Duration Dependence: A Parametric Approach. *Review of Economics and Statistics, 73,* 254–260.

Siebert, H. (1999). *Some Lessons from the Japanese Bubble* (Kiel Working Paper No. 919). Kiel: Kiel Institute of World Economics. Available at http://opus.zbw-kiel. de/volltexte/2003/27/pdf/268909717.pdf

Siegel, J. J. (1992). Equity Risk Premia, Corporate Profit Forecasts, and Investor Sentiment Around the Stock Crash of October 1987. *Journal of Business, 65*(4), 557–570.

Siegel, J. J. (2001). *Equity Risk Premium Forum, Historical Results I.* Philadelphia: University of Pennsylvania, Wharton School, November 2001 and AIMR (Charlottesville).

Siegel, J. J. (2005). Perspectives on the Equity Risk Premium. *Financial Analysts Journal, 61*(6), 61–73.

Siegel, J. J. (2006, December 6). Irrational Exuberance, Reconsidered. *Wall Street Journal.*

Siegel, J. J. (2008, 2014). *Stocks for the Long Run,* 4th and 5th eds. New York: McGraw-Hill.

Siegel, J. J., & Schwartz, D. (2006). Long-Term Returns on the Original S&P 500 Companies. *Financial Analysts Journal, 52*(1), 18–31.

Siklos, P. L. (2017). *Central Banks into the Breach: From Triumph to Crisis and the Road Ahead.* Oxford: Oxford University Press.

Silber, W. L. (2012). *Volcker: The Triumph of Persistence.* New York: Bloomsbury Press.

Silver, N. (2012a). *The Signal and the Noise: Why So Many Predictions Fail – But Some Don't.* New York: Penguin.

Silver, N. (2012b, September 8). The Weatherman Is Not a Moron. *New York Times.*

Silverberg, G., & Lehnert, D. (1996). Evolutionary Chaos: Growth Fluctuations in a Schumpeterian Model of Creative Destruction. In W. A. Barnett, A. P. Kirman, & M. Salmon (Eds.), *Nonlinear Dynamics and Economics.* Cambridge: Cambridge University Press.

Singleton, J. (2011). *Central Banking in the Twentieth Century.* Cambridge: Cambridge University Press.

Sirri, E. R., & Tufano, P. (1998). Costly Search and Mutual Fund Flows. *Journal of Finance, 53,* 1589–1622.

Skidelsky, R. (2009). *Keynes: The Return of the Master*. New York: Public Affairs (Perseus).

Skypala, P. (2014, September 1). Ditch the Hokum on Asset Diversification. *Financial Times*.

Sloan, R. G. (1996). Do Stock Prices Fully Reflect Information in Accruals and Cash Flows About Future Earnings. *Accounting Review, 7*(3), 289–316.

Smant, D. J. C. (2003). *The Variance-Bound Fallacy*. Rotterdam: Erasmus University, Rotterdam School of Economics. Available at www.few.eur.nl/few/people/smant

Smelser, N. J., & Baltsis, P. B. (Eds.). (2001). *International Encyclopedia of the Social and Behavioral Sciences*. London: Elsevier.

Smick, D. M. (2008). *The World Is Curved: Hidden Dangers to the Global Economy*. New York: Penguin Portfolio.

Smith, E. L. (1924). *Common Stocks as Long-Term Investments*. New York: Macmillan.

Smith, V. L. (1962). An Experimental Study of Competitive Market Behavior. *Journal of Political Economy, 70*(3), 111–137.

Smith, C. W. (2003). *Bubbles and Stock Market Behavior, Rational and Irrational*. Unpublished Ph.D. Dissertation, State University of New York, Binghamton.

Smith, V. L., Suchanek, G. L., & Williams, A. W. (1988). Bubbles, Crashes, and Endogenous Expectations in Experimental Spot Asset Markets. *Econometrica, 56*(5), 1119–1151.

Smithers, A., & Wright, S. (2000). *Valuing Wall Street: Protecting Wealth in Turbulent Markets*. New York: McGraw-Hill.

Sobel, R. (1968). *The Great Bull Market: Wall Street in the 1920s*. New York: Norton.

Soble, J. (2016, February 16). Abenomics Hits a Wall. *New York Times*.

Sola, M., & Driffill, J. (1998). Intrinsic Bubbles and Regime Switching. *Journal of Monetary Economics, 42*(2), 357–373.

Sommer, J. (2013, October 27). Eugene Fama, King of Predictable Markets. *New York Times*.

Sommer, J. (2014, March 30). In Some Ways, It's Looking Like 1999 in the Stock Market. *New York Times*.

Sorkin, A. R. (2009). *Too Big to Fail: The Inside Story of How Wall Street and Washington Fought to Save the Financial System – And Themselves*. New York: Viking.

Sornette, D. (2003a). *Why Stock Markets Crash: Critical Events in Complex Financial Systems*. Princeton: Princeton University Press.

Sornette, D. (2003b). Critical Market Crashes. *Physics Reports, 378*(1), 1–98.

Sornette, D. (2009). Dragon-Kings, Black Swans and the Prediction of Crises. *International Journal of Terraspace Science and Engineering*. arXiv:0907.4290.

Spence, M., & Warsh, K. (2015, October 27). The Fed Has Hurt Business Investment. *Wall Street Journal*.

Spencer, P. D. (2000). *The Structure and Regulation of Financial Markets*. Oxford: Oxford University Press.

Spotton, B., & Rowley, R. (1998). Efficient Markets, Fundamentals, and Crashes: American Theories of Financial Crises and Market Volatility. *American Journal of Economics and Sociology, 57*(4), 663–690.

Srivastava, N., & Satchell, S. (2012, April). Are There Bubbles in the Art Market? The Detection of Bubbles When Fair Value Is Unobservable. *Birkbeck Working Papers in Economics and Finance, 1209*.

Statman, M. (1995). Behavioral Finance Versus Standard Finance. In *Behavioral Finance and Decision Theory in Investment Management*. Charlottesville: Association for Investment Management and Research.

Statman, M. (1999). Behavioral Finance: Past Battles and Future Engagements. *Financial Analysts Journal, 55*(6), 18–27.

Steil, B. (2012). What Should a Central Bank (Not) Do? *Cato Journal, 32*(2).

Steil, B., & Swartz, P. (2010, August 19). Bye-Bye to the Fed-Funds Rate. *Wall Street Journal*.

Stein, B. (2008, April 27). Wall Street, Run Amok. *New York Times*.

Sterge, A. J. (1989). On the Distribution of Financial Futures Price Changes. *Financial Analysts Journal, 45*(3), 75–78.

Stewart, I. (2004). The Nature of Fractal Geometry. In *The Colours of Infinity: The Beauty, and Power of Fractals*. London: Clear Books.

Stiglitz, J. E. (1990). Symposium on Bubbles. *Journal of Economic Perspectives, 4*(2), 13–18.

Stiglitz, J. E. (2003). *The Roaring Nineties: A New History of the World's Most Prosperous Decade*. New York: Norton.

Stiglitz, J. E., & Greenwald, B. (2003). *Towards a New Paradigm in Monetary Economics*. New York: Cambridge University Press.

Stiglitz, J. E., & Weiss, A. (1981). Credit Rationing in Markets with Imperfect Information. *American Economic Review, 71*(3), 393–410.

Stix, G. (2009, July). The Science of Bubbles & Busts. *Scientific American*.

Stock, J., & Watson, M. W. (1989). Testing for Common Trends. *Journal of the American Statistical Association, 83*, 1097–1107.

Stone, D., & Ziemba, W. T. (1993). Land and Stock Prices in Japan. *Journal of Economic Perspectives, 7*(3), 149–165.

Story, L. (2010a, December 12). A Secretive Banking Elite Rules Trading in Derivatives. *New York Times*.

Story, L. (2010b, August 10). Hidden From the Light: Regulators Unearth Merrill's Dodging of Risk Disclosures. *New York Times*.

Story, L., & Bowley, G. (2011, September 12). Market Swings Are Becoming New Standard. *New York Times*.

Stout, D. (2002, August 30). Greenspan Says Fed Could Not Prevent Market Bubble. *New York Times*.

Strasburg, J., & Pulliam, S. (2011, January 14). Hedge Funds' Pack Behavior Magnifies Swings in Market. *Wall Street Journal*.

Strauss, L. C. (2008, October 13). Still Holding Back. *Barron's*.

Strauss, L. C. (2014, April 26). Preparing for the Bubble to Burst. *Barron's*.

Strogatz, S. (2003). *Sync: The Emerging Science of Spontaneous Order*. New York: Hyperion.

Strumeyer, G. (2005). *Investing in Fixed Income Securities: Understanding the Bond Market*. Hoboken: Wiley.

Suhadolnik, N., Galimberti, J., & Da Silva, S. (2010). Robot Traders Can Prevent Extreme Events in Complex Stock Markets. *Physica A, 389*, 5182–5192.

Sullivan, R. N., & Diermeier, J. J. (Eds.). (2006). *Global Perspectives on Investment Management*. Charlottesville: CFA Institute.

Summers, L. H. (1986). Does the Stock Market Rationally Reflect Fundamental Values? *Journal of Finance, 41*(3), 591–602.

Summers, L. H. (2016, February 16). It's Time to Kill the $100 Bill. *The Washington Post.*

Summers, G. (2017). *The Everything Bubble: The Endgame for Central Banking.* North Charleston: CreateSpace Independent Publishing.

Surowiecki, J. (2004). *The Wisdom of Crowds.* New York: Doubleday.

Swanson, E. T., & Williams, J. C. (2012). *Measuring the Effect of the Zero Lower Bound on Medium-and Longer-Term Interest Rates*(Working Paper 2012-02). Federal Reserve Bank of San Francisco.

Swarup, B. (2014). *Money Mania: Booms, Panics and Busts from Ancient Rome to the Great Meltdown.* New York: Bloomsbury Press.

Sylla, R. (2001). The New Media Boom in Historical Perspective. *Prometheus, 19*(1), 17–26.

Taibbi, M. (2009, October 14). Wall Street's Naked Swindle. *Rolling Stone.*

Taipalus, K. (2012). *Detecting Asset Price Bubbles with Time-Series Methods.* Helsinki, Bank of Finland, Scientific Monograph E:47 – 2012.

Takens, F. (1981). Dynamical Systems and Turbulence. In D. A. Rand & L. S. Young (Eds.), *Lecture Notes in Mathematics.* Berlin: Springer-Verlag.

Taleb, N. N. (2004). Bleed or Blowup? Why Do We Prefer Asymmetric Payoffs? *Journal of Behavioral Finance, 5*(1), 2–7.

Taleb, N. N. (2005). *Fooled by Randomness.* New York: Random House (2nd Paperback edition).

Taleb, N. N. (2007). *The Black Swan.* New York: Random House.

Taleb, N. N. (2012). *Antifragile: Things That Gain from Disorder.* New York: Random House.

Tapia, J. A. (2014). *From the Oil Crisis to the Great Recession: Five Crises of the World Economy.* Paper Presented January 3 at the ASSA Annual Meeting in Philadelphia.

Taranto, J. (2016, August 20). Dilbert Explains Donald Trump. *Wall Street Journal.*

Taylor, T. J. (1996). Time Series, Stochastic and Chaotic. In W. A. Barnett, A. P. Kirman, & M. Salmon (Eds.), *Nonlinear Dynamics and Economics.* Cambridge: Cambridge University Press.

Taylor, S. (2005). *Asset Price Dynamics, Volatility, and Prediction.* Princeton: Princeton University Press.

Taylor, J. B. (2010a, January 11). The Fed and the Crisis: A Reply to Ben Bernanke. *Wall Street Journal.*

Taylor, L. (2010b). *Maynard's Revenge: The Collapse of Free Market Macroeconomics.* Cambridge, MA: Harvard University Press.

Taylor, J. B. (2012, March 29). The Dangers of an Interventionist Fed. *Wall Street Journal.*

Taylor, J. B. (2013, January 29). Fed Policy Is a Drag on the Economy. *Wall Street Journal.*

Taylor, J. B. (2016, December 21). The Case for a Rules-Based Fed. *Wall Street Journal.*

Taylor, J. B. (2018). Alternatives for Reserve Balances. In M. D. Bordo et al. (2018). *The Structural Foundations of Monetary Policy.* Stanford: Hoover Institution Press.

Taylor, M. P., & Peel, D. A. (1998). Periodically Collapsing Stock Price Bubbles: A Robust Test. *Economics Letters, 61,* 221–228.

Temin, P., & Voth, H.-J. (2004). Riding the South Sea Bubble. *American Economic Review, 94*(5), 1654–1668.

Tetlock, P. (2011, January). All the News That's Fit to Reprint: Do Investors React to Stale Information? *Review of Financial Studies.*

Tett, G. (2009). *Fool's Gold.* New York: Free Press.

Thaler, R. H. (1990). *Quasi Rational Economics.* New York: Sage.

Thaler, R. H. (1992). *The Winner's Curse: Paradoxes and Anomalies of Economic Life*. Princeton: Princeton University Press.

Thaler, R. H. (Ed.). (2005). *Advances in Behavioral Finance* (Vol. II). Princeton: Princeton University Press.

Thaler, R. H. (2016). Behavioral Economics: Past, Present, and Future. *American Economic Review, 106*(7), 1577–1600.

Thaler, R. H. (2015). *Misbehaving: The Making of Behavioral Economics*. New York: W.W. Norton.

Thaler, R., & Johnson, E. (1990, June). Gambling with the House Money and Trying to Break Even. *Management Science, 36*(6).

Tharp, V. K. (2013). *Trading Beyond the Matrix*. Hoboken: Wiley.

Theiler, J. B., Galdrikian, A., Longtin, S., Eubank, S., & Farmer, J. D. (1992). Using Surrogate Data to Detect Nonlinearity in Time Series. In M. Casdagli & S. Eubank (Eds.), *Nonlinear Modeling and Forecasting*. Redwood City: Addison-Wesley.

Thomas, D. L. (1967 [2001]). *The Plungers and the Peacocks: 170 Years of Wall Street*. New York/London: Texere Publishing.

Thomas, L., Jr. (2012, June 27). Spain Officials Hailed Banks as Crisis Built. *New York Times*.

Thomas, G., & Morgan Witts, M. (1979). *The Day the Bubble Burst*. New York: Doubleday.

Thompson, E. A. (2007). The Tulipmania: Fact or Artifact? *Public Choice, 130*(1–2), 99–114.

Thornton, D. L. (2017). Federal Reserve Mischief and the Credit Trap. *Cato Journal, 37*(2), 263–285.

Thurm, S., & Brown, K. (2002, October 18). Tech Will Be Back, Past Slumps Suggest, as Innovators Revive It. *Wall Street Journal*.

Tirole, J. (1982). On the Possibility of Speculation Under Rational Expectations. *Econometrica, 50*(5), 1163–1181.

Tirole, J. (1985). Asset Bubbles and Overlapping Generations. *Econometrica, 53*(6), 1499–1528.

Tobin, J. (1958). Liquidity Preference as Behavior Toward Risk. *Review of Economic Studies, 25*(67), 65–86.

Todd, W. F. (2017). The Fed's Failed Policies. *Cato Journal, 37*(2), 407–421.

Todorov, V. (2010). Variance Risk Premium Dynamics: The Role of Jumps. *Review of Financial Studies, 23*(1), 345–383.

Todorov, V., & Tauchen, G. (2010). *Volatility Jumps* (Working Paper). Northwestern University, Kellogg School of Management, Evanston.

Tognato, C. (2012). *Central Bank Independence: Cultural Codes and Symbolic Performance*. New York: Palgrave Macmillan.

Topol, R. (1991). Bubbles and Volatility of Stock Prices: Effect of Mimetic Contagion. *The Economic Journal, 101*(407), 786–800.

Toporowski, J. (1995). *The Economics of Financial Markets and the 1987 Crash*. Aldershot: Elgar Publishing, Ltd.

Toporowski, J. (1999). *The End of Finance: Capital Market Inflation, Financial Derivatives and Pension Fund Capitalism*. London: Routledge.

Townsend, R. M. (1983). Forecasting the Forecasts of Others. *Journal of Political Economy, 91*(4), 546–588.

Treynor, J. L. (1965). How to Rate Management of Investment Funds. *Harvard Business Review, 43*, 63–75.

Treynor, J. L. (1998). Bulls, Bears, and Market Bubbles. *Financial Analysts Journal,* 54(2), 69–74.

Triana, P. (2009). *Lecturing Birds on Flying: Can Mathematical Theories Destroy the Financial Markets?* Hoboken: Wiley.

Triana, P. (2012). *The Number That Killed Us: A Story of Modern Banking, Flawed Mathematics, and a Big Financial Crisis.* Hoboken: Wiley.

Trichet, J.-C. (2005). *Asset Price Bubbles and Monetary Policy.* Available at http://www.ecb.int/press/key/date/2005/html/sp050608.en.html

Tsay, R. (2005). *Analysis of Financial Time Series* (2nd ed.). Hoboken: Wiley.

Tuckett, D. (2011). *Minding the Markets: An Emotional Finance View of Financial Instability.* London: Palgrave Macmillan.

Tully, S. (2007, August 20). Why the Private Equity Bubble Is Bursting. *Fortune,* 156(4).

Turner, A. L. (2016). *Between Debt and the Devil: Money, Credit, and Fixing Global Finance.* Princeton: Princeton University Press.

Turner, A. L., & Weigel, E. J. (1990). An Analysis of Stock Market Volatility. In *Russell Research Commentaries.* Tacoma: Frank Russell Company.

Turnovsky, S. J. (1996). *Methods of Macroeconomic Dynamics.* Cambridge, MA: MIT Press.

Tvede, L. (1999). *The Psychology of Finance.* Chichester: Wiley.

Tversky, A., & Kahneman, D. (1974). *Judgment Under Uncertainty: Heuristics and Biases. Science.*

Tversky, A., & Kahneman, D. (1986, October). Rational Choice and the Framing of Decisions. *Journal of Business.*

Ursua, J. F., & Barro, R. J. (2009). *Stock-Market Crashes and Depressions* (Working Paper Series, No. w14760). Cambridge, MA: National Bureau of Economic Research.

Urzua, C. M. (2000). A Simple and Efficient Test for Zipf's Law. *Economic Letters, 66,* 257–260.

Vaga, T. (1990). The Coherent Market Hypothesis. *Financial Analysts Journal, 45*(6), 36–49.

Vaga, T. (1994). *Profiting From Chaos: Using Chaos Theory for Market Timing, Stock Selection, and Option Valuation.* New York: McGraw-Hill.

Valeyre, S., Grebenkov, D., Aboura, S., & Liu, Q. (2012). *The Reactive Volatility Model.* Available at SSRN: ssrn.com/abstract=2126483

Van Norden, S. (1996). Regime-Switching as a Test for Exchange Rate Bubbles. *Journal of Applied Econometrics, 11*(3), 219–251.

Van Overtveldt, J. (2009). *Bernanke's Test: Ben Bernanke, Alan Greenspan, and the Drama of the Central Banker.* Chicago: Agate.

Van Vactor, S. A. (2010). *Introduction to the Global Oil and Gas Business.* Tulsa: PennWell.

Van Vliet, P. (2017). *High Returns from Low Risk: A Remarkable Stock Market Paradox.* Hoboken: Wiley.

Vandewalle, N., Ausloos, M., Boveroux, P., & Minguet, A. (1998a). How the Financial Crash of October 1997 Could Have Been Predicted. *European Physical Journal B, 4*(2), 139–141.

Vandewalle, N., Ausloos, M., Boveroux, P., & Minguet, A. (1998b). The Crash of October 1987 Seen as a Phase Transition: Amplitude and Universality. *Physica A, 255*(1), 201–210.

Vandewalle, N., Ausloos, M., Boveroux, P., & Minguet, A. (1999). Visualizing the Log-Periodic Pattern Before Crashes. *European Physical Journal B, 9*(2), 355–359.

Varchaver, N. (2008, April 28). What Warren Thinks.... *Fortune 157*(8).

Varian, H. R. (2005, March 10). Five Years After Nasdaq Hit Its Peak, Some Lessons Learned. *New York Times.*

Veblen, T. (1899). *The Theory of the Leisure Class.* New York: Macmillan (Paperback, New American Library, 1953).

Verbeek, M. (2004). *A Guide to Modern Econometrics* (2nd ed.). Chichester: Wiley.

Vigna, P. (2016, March 26). Mervyn King on the Limits of Central Banks. *Wall Street Journal.*

Vincent, M. (2010, February 12). Baby-boomers, Bubbles and Emerging Markets. *Financial Times.*

Vines, S. (2005). *Market Panic: Wild Gyrations, Risks, and Opportunities in Stock Markets.* Singapore: Wiley (Paperback edition).

Visco, I. (2003). *Comments on Recent Experiences with Asset Price Bubbles,* in Hunter et al. (2003).

Vives, X. (2008). *Information and Learning in Markets: The Impact of Market Microstructure.* Princeton: Princeton University Press.

Vogel, H. L. (2016). *Travel Industry Economics: A Guide for Financial Analysis.* New York/Cham: Springer International Publishing.

Vogel, H. L. (2017). Are There Any Laws and Constants in Economics? A Brief Comparison to the Sciences. *Journal of Contemporary Management, 6*(1), 73–88.

Vogel, H. L., & Werner, R. A. (2015). An Analytical Review of Volatility Metrics for Bubbles and Crashes. *International Review of Financial Analysis, 38,* 15–28.

Voit, J. (2003). *The Statistical Mechanics of Financial Markets* (2nd ed.). Berlin-Heidelberg: Springer-Verlag.

Von Mises, L. (1979, 2006). *Economic Policy: Thoughts for Today and Tomorrow* (3rd ed.). Chicago: Regenery/Gateway. Available at http://books.google.com/books/download

Von Mises, L. (1996). *Human Action* (4th rev ed.). San Francisco: Fox & Wilkes.

Voth, H.-J. (2000). *A Tale of Five Bubbles – Asset price Inflation and Central Bank Policy in Historical Perspective* (Discussion Paper 416). Canberra: Australian National University. http://econrsss.anu.edu.au

Voth, H.-J. (2003). With a Bang, Not a Whimper: Pricking Germany's 'Stock Market Bubble' in 1927 and the Slide Into Depression. *Journal of Economic History, 63*(1), 65–99.

Wachtel, S. B. (1942). Certain Observations on Seasonal Movements in Stock Prices. *Journal of Business, 15*(2), 184–193.

Wachtel, P. (Ed.). (1982). *Crises in the Economic and Financial Structure.* Lexington: Lexington Books.

Wallace, C. (2010, May). Mind Over Markets. *Institutional Investor.*

Wallison, P. J. (2014, January 6). The Bubble Is Back. *New York Times.*

Wallison, P. J. (2015, November 5). Bernanke and the Slow-Growth Crew. *Wall Street Journal.*

Wang, P., & Wen, Y. (2009). *Speculative Bubbles and Financial Crisis* (Working Paper 2009-029B). Federal Reserve Bank of St. Louis.

Wapshott, N. (2011). *Keynes Hayek: The Clash That Defined Modern Economics.* New York: W.W. Norton.

Warburton, P. (2000). *Debt and Delusion: Central Bank Follies That Threaten Economic Disaster*. London: Penguin.

Warneryd, K.-E. (2001). *Stock Market Psychology: How People Value and Trade Stocks*. Cheltenham: Elgar.

Watanabe, K., Takayasu, H., & Takayasu, M. (2007). A Mathematical Definition of the Financial Bubbles and Crashes. *Physica A, 283*.

Weatherall, J. O. (2013). *The Physics of Wall Street: A Brief History of Predicting the Unpredictable*. Boston: Houghton Mifflin Harcourt.

Weber, M., & Camerer, C. (1998). The Disposition Effect in Securities Trading: An Experimental Analysis. *Journal of Economic Behavior and Organization, 33*, 167–184.

Weil, J. (2007, August 22). Wells Fargo Gorges on Mark-to-Make-Believe Gains. *Bloomberg.com*.

Weisman, S. R. (2008, May 28). With Bold Steps, Fed Chief Quiets Some Criticism. *New York Times*.

Wen, K. (1996). Continuous-Time Chaos in Stock Market Dynamics. In W. A. Barnett, A. P. Kirman, & M. Salmon (Eds.), *Nonlinear Dynamics and Economics*. Cambridge: Cambridge University Press.

Werner, R. A. (2003). *Princes of the Yen: Japan's Central Bankers and the Transformation of the Economy*. Armonk/New York/London: M. E. Sharpe (East Gate Books).

Werner, R. A. (2005). *New Paradigm in Macroeconomics: Solving the Riddle of Japanese Macroeconomic Performance*. Houndmills: Palgrave Macmillan.

Werner, R. A. (2007). *The Link Between Fiscal and Monetary Policy – Lessons for Germany from Japan*, in Heim and Truger, eds. (2007).

Werner, R. A. (2014a). Can Banks Individually Create Money Out of Nothing?—The Theories and the Empirical Evidence. *International Review of Financial Analysis, 36*, 1–19.

Werner, R. A. (2014b). How Do Banks Create Money, and Why Can Other Firms Not Do the Same? An Explanation for the Coexistence of Lending and Deposit-Taking. *International Review of Financial Analysis, 36*, 71–77.

Werner, R. A. (2016). A Lost Century in Economics: Three Theories of Banking and the Conclusive Evidence. *International Review of Financial Analysis, 46*, 361–379.

Wessel, D. (2008, May 29). Lessons from the Housing Bubble. *Wall Street Journal*.

Wessel, D. (2009). *In Fed We Trust: Ben Bernanke's War on the Great Panic*. New York: Crown/Random House.

Wessel, D. (2010, January 14). Bernanke's Puzzling Bubble Logic. *Wall Street Journal*.

Wessel, D., & Frangos, A. (2013, July 9). Central Bankers Hone Tools to Pop Bubbles. *Wall Street Journal*.

West, K. D. (1987). A Specification Test for Speculative Bubbles. *Quarterly Journal of Economics, 102*, 553–580.

West, K. D. (1988a). Dividend Innovations and Stock Price Volatility. *Econometrica, 56*(1), 37–61.

West, K. D. (1988b). Bubbles, Fads and Stock Volatility Tests: A Partial Evaluation. *Journal of Finance, 43*(3), 639–655.

West, M. D. (2000). Private Ordering at the World's First Futures Exchange. *Michigan Law Review, 98*(8), 2574–2615.

West, G. (2017). *Scale: The Universal Laws of Growth, Innovation, and Sustainability*. New York: Penguin/Random House.

Western, D. L. (2004). *Booms, Bubbles and Busts in US Stock Markets*. New York: Routledge.

White, E. N. (Ed.). (1990). *Crashes and Panics: The Lessons from History*. Homewood: Dow-Jones-Irwin.

White, W. R. (2009). *Should Monetary Policy "Lean or Clean?"* http://dallasfed.org/assets/documents/institute/wpapers/2009/0034

White, L. J. (2011). Preventing Bubbles: What Role for Financial Regulation? *Cato Journal, 31*(3), 603–619.

White, W. R. (2012). *Ultra Easy Monetary Policy and the Law of Unintended Consequences* (Working Paper No. 126). Globalization and Monetary Policy Institute, Federal Reserve Bank of Dallas. www.dallasfed.org/assets/documents/institute/wpapers/2012/0126.pdf

Wiewiura, J. S., & Hendricks, V. F. (2017, January). Informational Pathologies and Interest Bubbles: Exploring the Structural Mobilization of Knowledge, Ignorance, and Slack. *New Media and Society*.https://doi.org/10.1177/1461444816686095

Wigmore, B. A. (1985). *The Crash and Its Aftermath: A History of Securities Markets in the United States, 1929–1933*. Westport: Greenwood Press.

Williams, G. P. (1997). *Chaos Theory Tamed*. Washington, DC: Joseph Henry Press/National Academy Press.

Williamson, E. (2008, March 24). Political Pendulum Swings Toward Stricter Regulation. *Wall Street Journal*.

Williamson, S. D. (2015a, July). *Current Federal Reserve Policy Under the Lens of Economic History: A Review Essay* (Working Paper 2015-015A). Federal Reserve Bank of St. Louis.

Williamson, S. D. (2015b). Monetary Policy Normalization in the United States. *Federal Reserve Bank of St. Louis Review, Q2, 97*(2), 87–108.

Williamson, S. D. (2017). Quantitative Easing: Does This Tool Work? *The Regional Economist*, Third Quarter. www.stlouisfed.org

Willoughby, J. (2010, July 26). Did Investors Learn Anything from 2008's Crash? *Barron's*.

Wilmott, P. (2001). *Paul Wilmott Introduces Quantitative Finance*. Chichester: Wiley.

Wilmott, P., & Orrell, D. (2017). *The Money Formula: Dodgy Finance, Pseudo Science, and How Mathematicians Took Over the Markets*. Hoboken: Wiley.

Wilmott, P., Howison, S., & Dewynne, J. (1995). *The Mathematics of Financial Derivatives*. New York: Cambridge University Press.

Wilson, J. W., Sylla, R. E., & Jones, C. P. (1990). Financial Market Panics and Volatility in the Long Run, 1830–1988. In E. N. White (Ed.), *Crashes and Panics: The Lessons from History*. Homewood: Dow-Jones-Irwin.

Winkleman, B. F. (1932). *Ten Years of Wall Street*. New York: John Winston Company.

Witter, L. (2006, August 21). The No-Money-Down Disaster. *Barron's*.

Wolf, A., Swift, J. B., Swinney, H. L., & Vastano, J. A. (1985). Determining Lyapunov Exponents from a Time Series. *Physica D, 16*, 285–317.

Woo, W. T. (1987). Some Evidence of Speculative Bubbles in the Foreign Exchange Markets. *Journal of Money, Credit and Banking, 19*(4), 499–514.

Wood, C. (2005). *The Bubble Economy: Japan's Extraordinary Speculative Boom of the '80s and the Dramatic Bust of the '90s*. San Luis Obispo: Solstice; London: Sidgwick & Jackson, 1992; and New York: Atlantic Monthly Press.

Wood, G. E. (2007). Stock Market Crashes. In M. J. Oliver, & D. H. Aldcroft (Eds.), *Economic Disasters of the Twentieth Century*. Cheltenham: Elgar.

Woodford, M. (2002). *Financial Market Efficiency and the Effectiveness of Monetary Policy*. Federal Reserve Bank of New York Symposium, April 2001.

World Economic Survey. (1999, September 25). *The Economist.*

Wu, Y. (1995). Are There Rational Bubbles in Foreign Exchange Markets? Evidence from An Alternative Test. *Journal of International Money and Finance, 14*(1), 27–46.

Wu, Y. (1997). Rational Bubbles in the Stock Market: Accounting for the U.S. Stock-Price Volatility. *Economic Inquiry, 35*(2), 309–319.

Xie, H., Qin, Q., & Wang, S. (2016, November). The Halloween Effect a New Puzzle? Evidence from Price Gap. *Review of Economics and Finance, 6.*

Yellen, J. (2009, April 16). *A Minsky Meltdown: Lessons for Central Bankers.* Presented at 18th Annual Hyman Minsky Conference.

Yergin, D. (2009). *The Prize: The Epic Quest for Oil, Money & Power* (rev ed.). New York: Free Press (Simon & Schuster).

Ying, C. C. (1966). Stock Market Prices and Volumes of Sales. *Econometrica, 34,* 676–685.

Youssefmir, M., Huberman, B. A., & Hogg, T. (1998). Bubbles and Market Crashes. *Computational Economics, 12,* 97–114.

Yuan, K., Zheng, L., & Zhu, Q. (2006). Are Investors Moonstruck? Lunar Phases and Stock Returns. *Journal of Empirical Finance, 13*(1), 1–23.

Zhang, F. X., Green, J., & Hand, J. (2016). Errors and Questionable Judgments in Analysts' DCF Models. *Review of Accounting Studies, 21*(2), 596–632.

Zhou, W. X., & Sornette, D. (2006). Is There a Real-Estate Bubble in the US? *Physica A, 361,* 297.

Zhou, W. X., & Sornette, D. (2007). Analysis of the Real Estate Market in Las Vegas: Bubble, Seasonal Patterns, and Prediction of the CSW Indexes. *Physica A, 387.*

Ziemba, W. T. (2005). The Symmetric Downside-Risk Sharpe Ratio. *Journal of Portfolio Management, 32*(1), 108–122.

Ziemba, W. T. (Ed.). (2012). *Calendar Anomalies and Arbitrage.* Hackensack/ Singapore: World Scientific.

Ziemba, W. T., & Schwartz, S. L. (1991). The Growth in the Japanese Stock Market, 1949–90 and Prospects for the Future. *Managerial and Decision Economics, 12*(2), 183–195.

Ziemba, R. E. S., & Ziemba, W. T. (2007). *Scenarios for Risk Management and Global Investment Strategies.* Chichester: Wiley.

Ziemba, W. T., Lleo, S., & Zhitlukhin, M. (2018). *Stock Market Crashes: Predictable and Unpredictable and What to Do About Them.* Singapore/Hackensack: World Scientific.

Zweig, J. (2008a, November 22). 1931 and 2008: Will Market History Repeat Itself? *Wall Street Journal.*

Zweig, J. (2008b, August 30). With Buybacks, Look Before You Leap. *Barron's.*

Zweig, J. (2009, July 11). Does Stock-Market Data Really Go Back 200 Years? *Wall Street Journal.*

Zweig, J. (2010, June 19). So That's Why Investors Can't Think for Themselves. *Wall Street Journal.*

Zweig, J. (2011, November 5). The Extraordinary Popular Delusion of Bubble Spotting. *Wall Street Journal.*

Zweig, J. (2015, November 14). Deciphering the Dialect: A Wall Street Glossary. *Wall Street Journal.*

Index[1]

---

[1] Note: Page numbers followed by 'n' refer to notes.

© The Author(s) 2018

H. L. Vogel, *Financial Market Bubbles and Crashes, Second Edition*, https://doi.org/10.1007/978-3-319-71528-5

Printed by Printforce, the Netherlands